STRATEGIC COMMUNICATION

STRATEGIC COMMUNICATION

IN BUSINESS AND THE PROFESSIONS

FIFTH EDITION

Dan O'Hair
University of Oklahoma

Gustav W. Friedrich
Rutgers University

Lynda Dee Dixon
Bowling Green State University

HOUGHTON MIFFLIN COMPANY
Boston New York

Senior Sponsoring Editor: Mary Finch
Developmental Editor: Julia Casson
Senior Project Editor: Fred Burns
Senior Manufacturing Coordinator: Priscilla Bailey
Senior Composition Buyer: Sarah Ambrose
Senior Art and Design Coordinator: Jill Haber
Marketing Manager: Elinor Gregory

Printed in the U.S.A.

Library of Congress Control Number: 2003110191

ISBN: 0-618-43249-3

4 5 6 7 8 9—DOW—08 07 06

Brief Contents

Contents

PART FOUR GROUP COMMUNICATION STRATEGIES 269

15 Persuasive and Special Presentations 427

Preface

The fifth edition of *Strategic Communication in Business and the Professions* represents the combined effort of many talented parties, not the least of whom are the students and instructors who have used the book in the past. We have taken special care to retain the content and features that users of the first four editions tell us work best—in particular, those features that bring business and professional communication to life for the reader. We have also listened to people who work in business and the professions in order to make *Strategic Communication* the most up-to-date and responsive text of its kind on the market. Without question, we continue to learn that communication is one of the most important skills, if not the centerpiece of how people become successful in their careers. Our goal was to make this text the most useful tool possible for someone entering the professional world in the near future.

Meeting the needs of college-level courses that *focus on oral communication* within an organizational context has always been the primary goal of this text. While crafting a well-written memo or proposal is also an important business communication skill, many students find that presentations, personal interviews, or group meetings represent their first—and sometimes their biggest—communication challenge. *Strategic Communication* also emphasizes the most essential skills in business and professional communication:

- Thinking critically
- Embracing cultural diversity
- Promoting ethical communication
- Listening
- Managerial and leadership communication
- Managing conflict
- Team and group communication
- Making public presentations

Students and instructors alike find that *Strategic Communication* offers thoroughly integrated communication theory and practice. Our goal is to help instructors teach students to recognize the basic similarities among all forms of communication. We focus on how people in business and the professions succeed by communicating effectively on the job.

The Model of Strategic Communication

The Model of Strategic Communication, unique to this textbook, provides students with an easy-to-use framework for mastering oral communication skills. Introduced in Chapter 2, the model emphasizes that effective communicators have mastered four basic skills. They all

- Set goals
- Understand the communication situation and their audience
- Demonstrate competence
- Manage anxiety effectively

As in previous editions, we integrate these four essential elements throughout the text within our strategic model of communication. By practicing the skills of effective communicators, students can approach any communication situation with confidence.

Our strategic approach helps students *understand, remember,* and—most importantly—*employ* the essential communication skills in any business and/or professional setting.

Features of the New Edition

Our text is designed for introductory business and organizational communication classes. We believe that the increasing demands of the workplace mean that the role of communications skills as the foundation of successful professional development is more important than ever before.

To help students master the basics, each chapter in *Strategic Communication* includes numerous in-text features that emphasize the following:

Relevant Real-world Examples

- *Practicing Business Communication* boxes describe how business and professional communication actually works. The real-life companies profiled range from small businesses to global corporations.
- *Strategic Scenarios* start out each chapter with a hypothetical case that students are asked to keep in mind as they read the chapter. At the end of each chapter, a *Strategic Scenario Wrap-Up* asks the student to consider the case again, this time using the knowledge and skills they've learned while reading the chapter.
- *Technology Tools* boxes enhance the text's integration of current communication technologies with practical advice on topics ranging from e-mail etiquette to the pros and cons of PowerPoint presentations.

Critical Thinking

- *What Do You Think?* and *What Would You Do?* boxes give students the opportunity to think through communication situations and problems that they eventually may encounter in business settings.
- A set of *Questions for Critical Thinking,* which concludes each Practicing Business Communication box, encourages students to examine the connections between concepts in the book and communication in actual companies and organizations.

Focus on Ethical and Unbiased Communication.

- *Ethical Issues* boxes, many updated in this edition, challenge students to think seriously and critically about the role of ethics in business communication.

- *Diversity coverage.* Although contemporary examples link text content to real-world cultural- and gender-related issues throughout the book, Chapter 3 is devoted entirely to the topic of managing diversity in the workplace. This material has been designed to help students see the value of a diverse workforce, as well as understand (and avoid) the potential pitfalls in communication that can result.

Effective In-Chapter Learning Aids

- *Learning Objectives* allow students to know what they are expected to master in each chapter.
- *Chapter Summaries* have been written in easy-to-understand sentence format to help readers identify and focus on important points within the chapter.
- *Key Terms* contain definitions for easier reference.
- *Activities* and *Discussion* questions, designed for students to complete on their own or in a group, further test understanding of concepts.

The Approach and Plan of the Fifth Edition

Each chapter emphasizes that successful communication depends on the commitment to shared meaning between communicators. To this end, each chapter provides readers with a basis for thinking about how cultural differences, gender-related issues, and ever-improving technology affect business communication. Beyond offering new examples and topics, we've worked to make this edition of *Strategic Communication* even more accessible to students.

Strategic Communication contains five three-chapter parts:

- Part One introduces the major issues in business and professional communication: organizational and communication theory and practice in Chapter 1; the strategic model of communication in Chapter 2; and workplace diversity in Chapter 3.
- Part Two focuses on developing basic communication skills with Chapter 4 on listening and Chapter 5 on verbal and nonverbal skills. Chapter 6 moves into the areas of leadership and management skills and theory.
- Part Three begins our exploration of communication contexts with three chapters on the basics of interpersonal, one-on-one communication. Chapter 7 concentrates on work relationships. Chapter 8 covers the basic principles of interviewing, and Chapter 9 provides insights into the unique aspects of interviews in business settings.
- Part Four reveals the changes and adaptations that occur in group communication contexts. Chapter 10 covers fundamentals of group communication. Chapter 11 addresses the specific opportunities and challenges for problem solving that meetings provide. Chapter 12 familiarizes students with proven methods of negotiation and conflict management.
- Part Five thoroughly examines presentational speaking: developing and delivering effective presentations—including media presentations—in Chapter 13; informative presentations in Chapter 14; and persuasive and special-occasion presentations in Chapter 15.

Supplementary Materials

The following items are available to users of *Strategic Communication:*

- The Instructor's Resource Manual is a useful tool and helpful resource for both experienced and beginning instructors.The manual provides a range of teaching aids and activities for instructors to use in their business communication courses. Test questions for each chapter are included in the manual.
- A computerized test bank contains the test questions in the Instructor's Resource Manual.
- The expanded textbook website contains useful material for both instructors and students. Address for instructors and students are: Instructors:http://college.hmco.com/communication/instructors/ Students: http://college.hmco.com/communication/students/
- PowerPoint slides, available on the website for the fifth edition, may be used to aid instructors in delivering their lectures. Students can test their comprehension of chapter-by-chapter content with quizzes, flashcards, and other study aids.

Acknowledgments

We would like to express our gratitude to the extremely helpful and supportive editorial, production, and marketing teams at Houghton Mifflin: Mary Finch, Laura Edwards, Julia Casson, Fred Burns, and Elinor Gregory.

We have benefited greatly from the participation and assistance of many people throughout our work on this edition. Peggy Beck, Kent State University—Stark Campus; Merry Buchanan, University of Central Oklahoma; Stanley R. Crane, Hartnell Community College; Rozell R. Duncan, Kent State University; Lisa M. Millhouse, West Chester University; J. Kanan Sawyer, University of Texas—Austin; David K. Scott, Northeastern State University; and Jennifer Strange, Centenary College of Louisiana.

D.O
G.W.F
L.D.D

PART ONE

AN INTRODUCTION TO COMMUNICATION IN ORGANIZATIONS

CHAPTER 1

Covers the basic communication process and major theories about organizational communication.

CHAPTER 2

Introduces the model of strategic communication—a four-part process of setting goals, gathering situational knowledge, building communication competence, and managing anxiety.

CHAPTER 3

Explores cultural diversity and the impact that different cultural groups have on communicating in the workplace.

Part I provides an overview of communication in business and professional settings. It explains the role of communication in achieving organizational goals and the challenges posed by the new communication technology, the diversification of the work force, and the globalization of the marketplace.

CHAPTER

1 Communication in Organizations

After completing this chapter, you will be able to:

1. Identify the major challenges the information age presents to business communication
2. Describe the components of the interactive communication process
3. Summarize four theories of organizational communication
4. Explain the differences between classical and humanistic theories of organizational communication

STRATEGIC SCENARIO

Kate Hullison and Jeremy Sandusky were relaxing after work one day during happy hour. Both worked for e-businesses, Jeremy as a software designer and Kate as a mid-level manager. They liked the type of work they did, but both really wanted to work for themselves. Although the era of dotcom riches had passed, they believed that good businesses could still be developed for the Internet. All they needed was a sound business plan, some guts, and a venture capitalist who believed in their ideas. After honing the details of their business strategy, they found a venture capitalist in Sonya Peterson, who wanted to invest in a start-up.

Their new business began as a consulting company for other Internet businesses and quickly grew to seven employees (Sonya, Kate, Jeremy, and four others). They managed themselves without much hierarchy or bureaucracy in part because they were small, but more so because that is the way they liked it—especially Jeremy.

Rapid growth caused the ranks of their employees to swell to fifty-five, forcing them to move out of their comfortable digs in a converted apartment complex into a high-rise office building. The way that Sonya, Kate, and Jeremy organized and managed their work and employees changed quickly as well. More structure, hierarchy, meetings, plans, and, as Jeremy puts it, "administrivia" have become the norm. Sonya and Kate seem to thrive on the excitement of success that the company is experiencing, but Jeremy feels differently. He now finds himself in the same type of organization he left for the start-up—except now he is one of the bosses. His communication with others has expanded 100-fold, and he doesn't feel prepared for the responsibility. It seems to him that his interactions with others are different, more formal—exactly why he left his old company in the first place.

As you read through the chapter, think about the issues involved with managing, organizing, and communicating in various types of organization.

OVERVIEW

The mere fact that you are reading this book suggests that you want to succeed in your professional career. Although it may not be entirely obvious how important communication is to your professional success, you can be sure that effective communication practices are vital to your career advancement. Recent surveys of businesses confirm what we have been hearing for years: employers are looking for people who possess competent communication skills.[1] Oral presentations and report briefings, interviews, small-group communication, listening, and leadership are just a few of the communication activities you will perform in the real world. Your career success depends on your ability to communicate effectively within an organization.

Over the years studies of Fortune 500 executives have uncovered the value, and continuing necessity, of effective communication to business success.[2] Without exception, these executives have reported that communication, especially oral skills, is a key component of success in the business world. Interestingly, these executives have indicated that college courses (rather than in-house training or input from outside consultants) provide the best oral communication training. Furthermore, executives who hire college graduates believe that the importance of oral communication skills for career success is going to increase. Thus, our goal is to integrate you into a successful career by providing you with the information necessary to become an effective organizational communicator.

The increasing importance of communication skills grows out of one feature of the present age: the amount of information that must be transmitted, consumed, analyzed, returned, or discarded. The information age of the present is considerably different from the industrial age of years past. Today's information age, played out on the global stage, has ushered in a New Organizational Style that emphasizes constant, interactive management of knowledge among organizations and individuals all over the world. Given that the amount of human knowledge *doubles* every year, new organizational styles focus on how to empower employees with information. One way to study this contrast further is to look at the distinctions between industrial age organizations and information age organizations summarized in Figure 1.1.

The shift in the value and volume of knowledge in the marketplace means a shift in the criteria that determine business success. The companies that succeed in the information age are those that integrate new technologies without alienating employees, handle information so efficiently that they are not swamped by data, and actively seek to enhance their communication through technology. None of this can be accomplished unless employees—from the president to the shipping clerk—know how to communicate effectively.

Indeed, communication skills are central to promoting excellence now and in the coming years.[3] These skills have five components:

1. *Creative insight* is the ability to ask the right questions. Asking tough questions is not the most pleasant task, but such inquiries are necessary if a business is to deal with a dynamic work force and economy.

1. Job Outlook 2002, a survey conducted by the National Association of Colleges and Employers. S. B. Parry, "The Quest for Competencies," *Training*, July 1996, pp. 48–57.
2. J. C. Bennet and R. J. Olney, "Executive Priorities for Effective Communication in an Information Age," *Journal of Business Communication* 23 (1986), 13–22; V. S. DiSalvo and J. K. Larsen, "A Contingency Approach to Communication Skill Importance: The Impact of Occupation, Direction, and Position," *Journal of Business Communication* 24 (1987), 3–22.
3. W. Bennis and R. Thomas, "Crucibles of Leadership," *Harvard Business Review* (September 2002), 39–45.

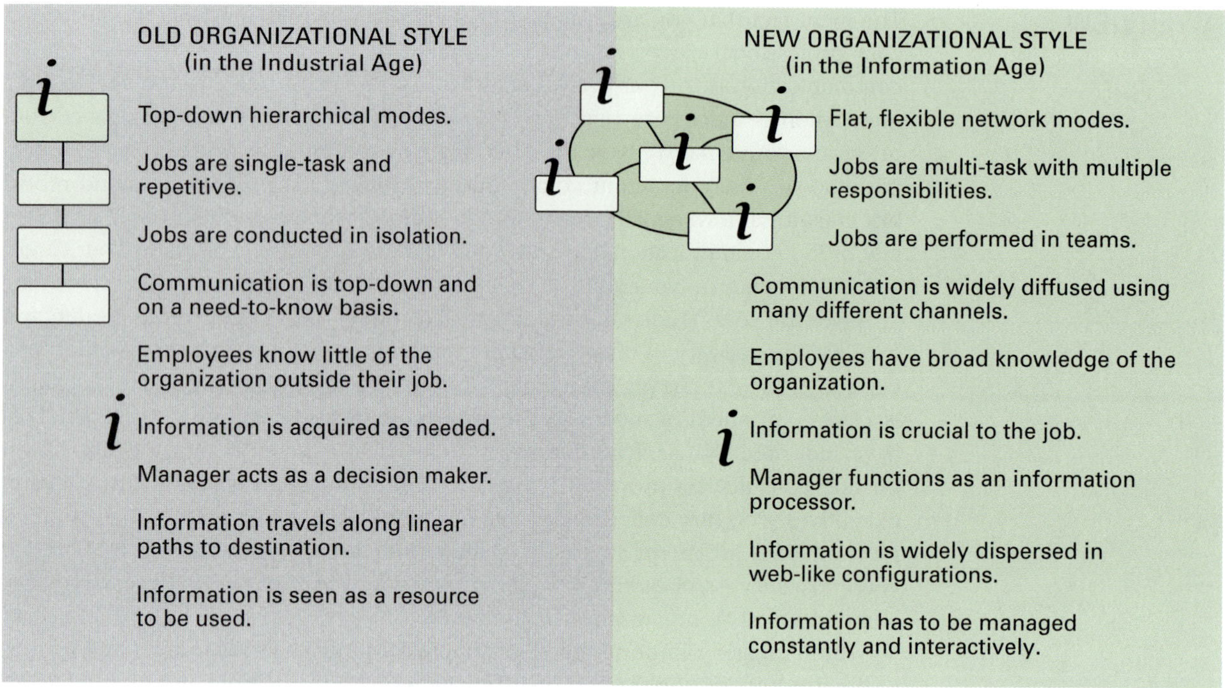

FIGURE 1.1 The Industrial Age Versus the Information Age

The nature of many jobs is changing due to shifts in information and organizational styles.

Source: "21st Century Skills for 21st Century Jobs," A Report of the U.S. Department of Commerce, U.S. Department of Education, U.S. Department of Labor, National Institute of Literacy, and the Small Business Administration (Washington, DC: U.S. Government Printing Office, 1999); D. O'Hair, J. O'Rourke, & M. O'Hair, *Business Communication* (Cincinnati: ITP, 2001); W. V. Ruck, *International Handbook of Corporate Communication* (Jefferson, NC: McFarland, 1989); M. Rothschild, "Mapping Your Web," *Forbes,* 154 (1994), 96.

2. *Sensitivity* means a business practices the Golden Rule with its workers: "Do unto others as you would have them do unto you." In communication, it means paying attention to the needs of others, listening empathetically, and monitoring their reactions when you speak.
3. *Vision* means being able to imagine the future. Leaders of organizations must have a clear picture of where their organizations are going in turbulent times. In a more everyday sense, business speech should have a point—such as an idea, response, or vision to convey—that the speaker focuses on making in the talk or presentation.
4. *Shared meaning* concerns how you engage others. Can you connect to your listeners on their level and they on yours? Do you understand their perspective? Do you have common language?
5. *Integrity* builds trust and confidence in relationships. If people trust you, they will believe what you say. If that trust has been damaged, and people don't believe what you say, it won't matter how well you communicate your point.

Globalization, the trend toward conducting business with and in foreign countries, is a fact of life. We live in an international marketplace, where the Internet places foreign businesses, services, and businesspeople at our fingertips. Globalization today means that every business, no matter how big or small, operates within a global community. International trade, immigration, and the Internet have created a diverse work force, requiring communication skills that can bridge cultural gaps and reach far-flung locations. Our technology has evolved, requiring businesses to adapt themselves to advanced communication media: e-mail, fax, Web pages, and so on. The modern "global" employee will not only have to be more skilled at using these new media, but also be flexible and adaptive to rapidly changing communication technologies.

THE INTERACTIVE COMMUNICATION PROCESS

Communication in a business or professional setting draws on the fundamental skills and concepts of communication used in social contexts, although the differences must be carefully considered. The essence of communication in all contexts is that people exchange messages to accomplish goals and objectives. Because people bring different goals, backgrounds, styles, habits, and preferences to the process, truly effective communication is **interactive:** each person taking part in the communication listens and responds to the others. Each element of the communication process contributes to making communication interactive. These elements, discussed briefly below, are diagrammed in Figure 1.2.

Messages are the content of communication with others—the ideas people wish to share. Messages may be expressed verbally—in spoken (oral) or written

FIGURE 1.2

The Interactive Communication Process

Shared meaning is the mutual understanding that results when the sender and all intended receivers interpret the message in the same way.

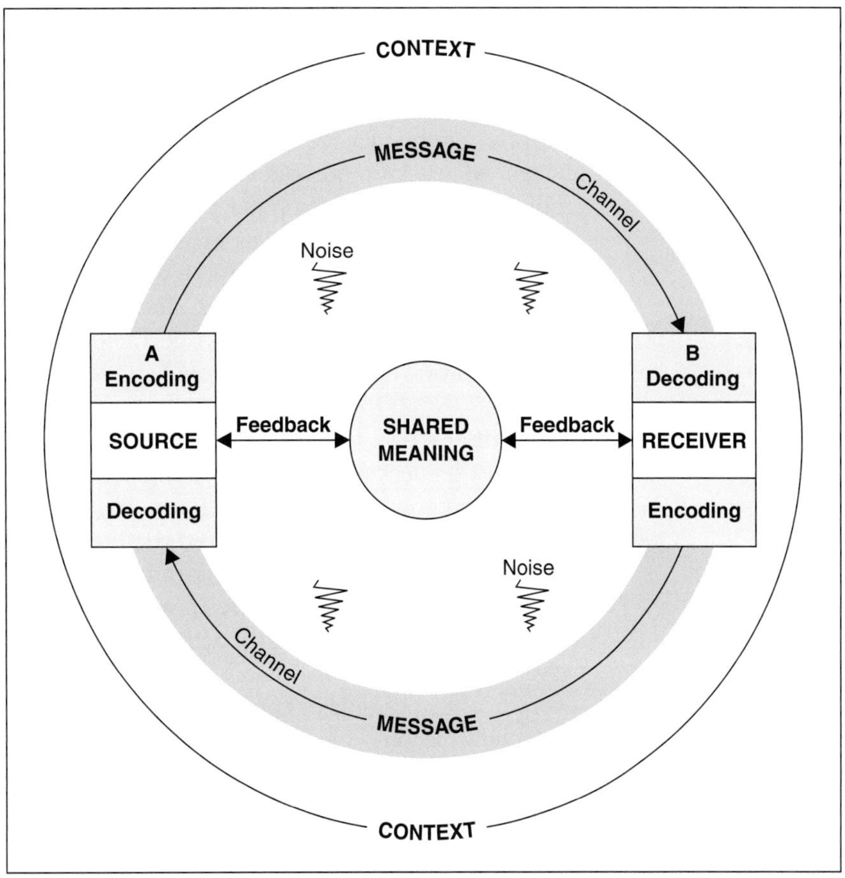

form—or nonverbally through gestures, posture, facial expressions, and even clothing. The **source** creates the message. Sometimes referred to as the sender, the source determines what type of message is to be sent and the best way to send it. When deciding how and what to send, a sender practicing interactive communication takes into account the needs of those who will be receiving the message.

Encoding is the physical process of organizing elements of the message for transmission to the receivers. In oral communication, encoding is the act of choosing and vocalizing words or sounds. In nonverbal communication, encoding means gesturing, smiling or nodding, and so on. Effective interactive communicators continually monitor the verbal and nonverbal cues from their audience to improve the accuracy and meaning of the messages they intend to send. For example, they may consider adding visual aids and friendly gestures to spoken messages to make them more understandable and accessible, or they may consider adding graphics to a computer-generated message. In some cases, the characters on your keyboard combine to form a "new electronic message." For example, you can "smile" at someone by typing **:-)** on your keyboard. The **channel** is the medium that carries a message once it is encoded by a source. Channels include "live" meetings that range from personal one-on-one interactions, group meetings, and even on-line chat sessions to telephone calls and video conferencing. In other communication channels, such as letters, memos, e-mails, faxes, and Web pages, the parties don't interact simultaneously. This can affect the communication process.

The destination of the message is the **receiver.** The receipt is the primary determinant of whether communication ever takes place. In other words, messages become communication only when a receiver picks up the message. Receivers include *all* persons who pick up the message, regardless of whether they were the sender's intended targets. "Sidestream listening"—where some receivers get messages inadvertently—can create problems, particularly in terms of breached confidentiality.

New communication technology increases the chance that unintended receivers will pick up messages. Just a few examples include leaving memos at the copy machine or at a computer printer, receiving e-mail meant for someone else, or even having computer files broken into by hackers. One must be especially careful with messages posted on the Web since these messages are public.

The counterpart of encoding, **decoding** is the process that receivers go through to make sense of the message. Decoding is influenced by many factors, including cultural background, listening abilities, and attitudes toward the source or channel.

Feedback is any response, verbal or nonverbal, that a receiver makes to a message. Most senders seek feedback during the communication process because it lets the sender know whether the message has been understood correctly. Feedback can take the form of a verbal or nonverbal response, a written memo, a phone call, a reply via e-mail, or an organized forum such as a status meeting or quality circle.

Noise is anything that interferes with communication. The common definition of noise is distracting sounds that prevent people from hearing or making themselves heard, but noise may take several forms. Have you ever met someone with an overpowering perfume or cologne at a party? The strong odor may be distracting to your conversation—a noise. But noise is a more encompassing phenomenon than this description suggests. It includes psychological distractions such as nervousness or tension, emotional distractions such as extreme happiness or sadness, and even physiological distractions such as fatigue or illness. Bias and prejudice are forms of psychological noise because bias against a speaker can interfere with a listener's reception of a message. All of these affect the quality of the message sent and received. Noise can occur at any point in the communication process.

Context is the situation or setting in which communication occurs. Whenever communication takes place, it does so within a context. Context can influence the content, the quality, and the effectiveness of a communication event. This may include the *physical context,* or the actual physical place (office, conference room, cafeteria) in which communication occurs; the *chronological context,* or the time/date at which an interaction takes place (after work hours, during a peak business cycle, first thing in the morning); the *cultural context,* or the ethnic/national and/or organizational backgrounds of the people communicating (New Englanders and Southwesterners, managers and staff, Native Americans and Asians); and the *social context,* or the social histories and relationships among communicators (age differences or similarities, out-of-the-office friendships, personality harmonies or conflicts). No matter what forms it takes, context is an important and ever-present component of the communication process.

Figure 1.2 illustrates the communication process just described. Notice the term **shared meaning** in the center of the illustration. Shared meaning is the mutual understanding that results when the sender and all intended receivers interpret the message in the same way. It is the primary desired outcome of any communication. Even though sources and receivers nearly always try to share meaning with one another, they do not necessarily succeed in doing so. There are degrees, or stages, of shared meaning attained through this process.

Point A represents the first opportunity for shared meaning. At this point, the source has just encoded a message intended for the receiver, and the receiver is aware that a message is being sent. This is shared meaning at its lowest level. The sender has simply caught the attention of the receiver.

Point B represents a potentially higher degree of shared meaning. At this point, the receiver is decoding the message and making sense of it. Notice we qualify Point B as a "potentially" higher degree of shared meaning. In an unsuccessful communication, the receiver may decode the message incorrectly—that is, in a manner inconsistent with the sender's original meaning. The receiver may assume a wave means "Hello" when in fact the sender means "Go away; I'm too busy to talk now!" The receiver responds by giving feedback to the sender. The feedback message indicates whether shared meaning was attained.

Imagine that you and your supervisor are in a crowded and noisy elevator. Your supervisor tells you the location, time, and agenda for an upcoming meeting, but because you can barely hear, you exit the elevator certain only of the location and time. You know enough to be able to get to the meeting, but your supervisor intended for you to know what was going to be discussed so that you could prepare some notes. Shared meaning was not fully achieved: even though the meeting was held, it did not accomplish all that the supervisor expected. Communication is not an either/or concept; rather, varying degrees of communication are possible, depending on how the message is treated at each point. A great deal of communication can occur without the benefit of fully shared meaning, but enough information must be exchanged between sources and receivers so they can function together in a minimal fashion.

Although business and professional communicators strive for shared meaning, there are many obstacles to achieving it.

TECHNOLOGY TOOLS

The Burden of E-mail

How much e-mail do you get at work? If you work full-time or even part-time, you already understand how taxing dozens of e-mails per day can be, especially when you're busy. In the next couple of years, you will likely spend more than four hours per day dealing with fifty or more work-related e-mail messages. However, of the 57 million American workers who use e-mail, most agree that e-mail is essential to their work and improves teamwork. E-mail has become an indispensable part of organizational communication. What is the answer to this "necessary burden"? Experts recommend that you use folders to organize your messages. You can set up folders that will hold messages that are "urgent," those e-mails that need immediate attention; "aging," those messages that are a few weeks old; "copies," those e-mails where you were not the primary recipient; and "misc.," a catchall category for messages that don't fit elsewhere but should not be deleted. Most communications software can be configured to organize your messages in this way and to filter out some junk e-mail. Other suggestions include using two e-mail accounts (one personal and one professional), avoiding mail distribution lists, and limiting how often you check incoming messages to two to three times a day.

Non-work-related e-mails are also an increasingly significant problem. In 2003, of the billions of e-mails sent every day, roughly half will have been junk e-mail or "spam." Ninety-six percent of all users have received some sort of spam. Most people receive between eleven to one hundred per day. Some estimate that spam will have cost U.S. organizations more than $10 billion in 2003. In 2002, the European Union adopted spam control legislation, and currently the United States is considering various methods of controlling unsolicited e-mail without violating constitutional freedom of speech.

Source: "Spam's Cost To Business Escalates": http://www.washingtonpost.com/ac2/wp-dyn/A17754-2003Mar12 (accessed July 30, 2003), "Spam: How much do we get?": http://www.silicon.com/news/165-500001/1/4618.html (accessed July 30, 2003), "U.S. Workers Spared Junk E-mails": http://news.bbc.co.uk/2/hi/technology/2558113.stm (accessed July 30, 2003), "Managing the E-mail Explosion": http://CNN.com/2000/TECH/computing/09/06/e-mail.management.idg/index.html (accessed September 7, 2000).

REASONS FOR COMMUNICATION FAILURE

In your everyday communication with others, you have probably noticed that some messages, despite the best intentions of the sender, are not decoded by the receiver as expected. Errors are so common that one expert has likened communication to Murphy's Law—"If communication can fail, it will." "If you are sure that communication cannot fail, it necessarily will fail." "There is always someone who knows better than you what you meant by your message."[4] Errors can occur at any step in the communication process (see Figure 1.2). Inadequate, poorly timed, or too much information can impact decoding; the feedback loop may fail; a channel may be inappropriate; cultural or psychological factors may create too much noise; or a sender may simply be ineffectual.

Inadequate Information

One manager, Sarah, intentionally withholds information from her subordinates because she feels that they will be confused by "too much information." In fact, managers and employees frequently complain that they do not receive enough information to do their jobs effectively. In some cases, upper management provides too little information when issuing orders. In other cases, information is provided, but it is not the right type. In our example, Sarah is actually working at cross-purposes

4. O. Wiio, *Wiio's Laws—And Some Others* (Espoo, Finland: Welin-Göös, 1978).

with her employees because they usually have to get needed information from other sources.

Information Overload

Sam owns and runs a successful used-car business. He believes it is "good business" to tell all his sales associates when new shipments of used cars arrive from various destinations. Sam, however, goes into great detail, even providing vital statistics about vehicles that are not yet on the lot! The technology of the information age has for the first time made it possible for employees at all levels of an organization to be overwhelmed by information. To ensure that people get enough information, managers often overcompensate and provide employees more information than necessary (especially in situations where they are not sure what is useful). To be safe, they, like Sam, send so much information that much of it winds up being ignored.

Poor-Quality Information

Information that is readily available to employees may be of little use because of its poor quality. When a builder asks a construction site manager for a quick report on the progress of the project and receives a lengthy, disorganized, jargon-filled description of bedrock at the site, neither person is benefiting from the communication. Other examples of poor-quality information include outdated, erroneous, misleading, overemphasized, and disorganized information.

Poor Timing

Having the right amount of information at the wrong time does little good. Sales reports, marketing figures, or consumer trends are of little value to decision makers if the information arrives too late to be used. For example, if you purchase a stereo on Saturday from one store and find out on Monday that the same stereo is on sale at another store, you have received information too late. Similarly, if information arrives too early, the receivers may set it aside for later use but then forget that they have it. Information timing is just as important as information quantity or quality.

Lack of Feedback or Follow-Up

Frequently, a sender forwards a message with the expectation that the receiver will respond with feedback or a follow-up message. If the receiver does not recognize that a response is requested or does not bother to reply to the message, the sender is forced to waste time waiting for a follow-up or sending a second message asking for feedback. In either case, time and effort are wasted. Even with e-mail, it is a good idea to reply to a sent message. This way the sender is assured that the message has been received. In one instance, Jill called Charlie to inform him about the next budget meeting. Charlie was not in, so his secretary took the message about the meeting. "Tell him to let me know" was the last thing Jill said to the secretary. Charlie did not respond, so Jill did not schedule Charlie's report for the meeting. When Charlie showed up expecting to make his report, both he and Jill were angry, blaming each other for the feedback error.

PRACTICING BUSINESS COMMUNICATION

IKEA

When a "build-up team" arrives on-site to open a new IKEA home furnishing outlet, it is fulfilling the management vision of the company's founder: "No method is more effective than a good example." Arriving at the store site anywhere from a year to a day prior to opening, experienced employees from IKEA's worldwide network of one hundred ten stores in twenty-seven countries assist new employees with operations and special events, speed up problem solving, and shorten the learning curve for their new coworkers.

IKEA's loose organizational structure and streamlined operations encourage employees to participate in decision making and to assume responsibility for the ideas they contribute to the business. Ingvar Kamprad was just seventeen years old when he founded IKEA as a mail-order business in 1943. (The name is an acronym composed of his initials and the name of the farm and the parish in Sweden where he grew up.) Early on, Kamprad distilled his philosophy into a business goal—"to create a better everyday life for the majority of people"—a goal that translates into "freedom with responsibility" for IKEA employees.

A NETWORKED COMPANY

IKEA began using e-mail soon after it was introduced as a workplace communication tool by MCI in the early 1980s. As a cost-cutting innovation, e-mail enables IKEA coworkers around the world to communicate effectively without paper waste and costly international telephone service.

On IKEA's network, coworkers also can keep up-to-date with worldwide operations by accessing electronic bulletin boards and company databases, which are available on-line, no matter where they work or travel. The ability to stay in constant communication with coworkers while traveling is vital because travel connects employees to corporate management in Sweden and Denmark.

Throughout the year, IKEA store managers from around the world gather to meet with top management and to learn what's going on in product development. Just as travel and face-to-face communication are important for educating store managers about new IKEA products, so it is also important that they share their expertise with coworkers when new stores open. Hence the concept of the "build-up team."

Problems with Channels

The communication channels that carry organizational messages include face-to-face conversation, telephones, e-mail, public speeches, memos, and letters. Problems can occur when senders use the wrong channels to convey information—for example, using a phone call to notify an employee that he is not going to get a promotion or has been fired. Issues that are very personal and sensitive require face-to-face contact; any other channel would be inappropriate. Likewise, contacting ten people separately about a new dress code is an inefficient use of time and resources because they can be informed collectively by e-mail or during a meeting.

Incompetent Communication

Some organizational members do not possess the communication skills necessary to be effective in today's professional world. For instance, a multimedia presentation will be ineffective if the presenter does not know how to use the equipment, experiences technical difficulties, or tries to liven up a dull topic merely by adding

COMMITMENT TO QUALITY AND ETHICS

By maximizing communication efficiency, IKEA minimizes costs and increases productivity. The company's philosophy is to produce low-priced, high-quality furniture for the widest possible range of incomes. All IKEA products are first developed in Sweden under strict quality standards and are then introduced to visiting managers at informational presentations that serve to link each manager to corporate production and procedural goals.

At the retail level, furniture shopping at IKEA is a bare-bones process: customers buy items ranging from tableware to wicker furniture after viewing them on display at the store's "marketplace" of shops or in the annual, full-color IKEA catalog. Shoppers then pick up their purchases—often unassembled—in an on-site, self-service warehouse. Employees are on hand to answer questions at storewide "Information Stations," but mostly they allow customers to shop or browse at their own pace, armed with "tools" (a catalog, tape measure, pencil, and shopping list) supplied by IKEA at each showroom entrance for making notes and taking measurements along the way. IKEA also provides free interior design assistance to customers.

As IKEA has grown to more than one hundred fifty stores in twenty-nine countries worldwide, with more than forty thousand employees (about 15 percent of them are in the United States), and as maintaining close communication among all coworkers has become more complex, Ingvar Kamprad's vision serves as a common resource for all IKEA coworkers. Managers act as "ambassadors," passing on the culture and the operations of the company to new employees, with everyone applying themselves to achieve the goal of satisfying customers.

QUESTIONS FOR CRITICAL THINKING

1. How does IKEA's communication network help to minimize costs?
2. Why is it important for IKEA managers to travel to corporate headquarters and to meet face-to-face with top management and with each other?
3. What advantages do IKEA's build-up teams offer to new employees? What benefits does team training provide to experienced employees who comprise the build-up team?
4. What does "freedom with responsibility" imply about IKEA's communication climate?
5. How might managers communicate IKEA's organizational culture to new employees?

flashy graphics rather than by improving the content of the presentation. People who attend meetings unprepared waste others' time. People with poor listening skills frustrate those who have to repeat information for them. Those who make inappropriate grammatical or vocabulary choices embarrass themselves and those around them. Incompetent communicators hurt the organization they represent.

Ineffective Goal Setting

One of the most important skills in effective communication is setting appropriate goals. When goals are too low, the communicator wastes the opportunity to influence, motivate, or inform the audience effectively. When goals are too high, the communicator becomes disappointed or disillusioned because the audience fails to grasp the message or simply dismisses what was said. For example, after you make a C on the first two tests, a final grade of A for the course might be an unrealistic goal. More realistic goals would be to turn in all remaining assignments on time and to begin studying for the remaining tests at least one week before they are scheduled. What other examples of ineffective goal setting have you encountered?

The need for communication may arise anywhere, and technology should help you to facilitate communication, not create communication anxiety. (© R. W. Jones/Corbis)

Communication Anxiety

When communication situations cause you to feel nervous, stressed, or apprehensive, the effectiveness of your efforts is at risk. Anxiety can hamper the ability to think, talk, gesture, or even listen. Not all communication situations cause anxiety, however; each person reacts differently. To minimize your own communication anxiety, recognize the situations in which you experience it and use the techniques described in this book to control your nervousness.

Some people may suffer communication anxiety about new technologies. For example, most people who have been exposed to e-mail embrace this form of communication as efficient and helpful. However, a small percent of the population suffers some form of anxiety when using a new technology. These people may choose to ignore e-mail and use more "traditional" methods of communicating even if they are less efficient.

When communication failures occur in social situations, at worst the communicators wind up confused, embarrassed, or annoyed. But when communication fails within a business organization, the results can be much worse—inefficiency, loss of morale, decreased productivity, or job termination. The specter of such negative results highlights the importance of studying organizational communication, particularly when it is possible to do so before you join an organization.

Cultural Barriers

Cultural barriers may also contribute to communication failure. Biases and prejudices against cultures other than your own can interfere with listening to and understanding a message. An accent may influence your perception of a coworker or manager. Sometimes individuals are afraid to ask a sender who is from a different culture to repeat a message that is not understood. Sensitivity to diverse cultures and culturally different ways of communicating is essential for effective business communication.

UNDERSTANDING ORGANIZATIONAL COMMUNICATION

Organizational communication is the exchange of oral, written, and nonverbal messages among people working to accomplish common tasks and goals. This definition encompasses much of the activity that occurs at work. It includes such tasks as alerting workers to production goals, scheduling meetings within and between departments, planning how the company will communicate with its customers and respond to their messages, and producing in-house informational material about policies and goals. A good understanding of organizational communication provides you with options when you face tasks that need to be accomplished efficiently and effectively. When you understand how an organizational context affects communication, you will be in a much better position to achieve the goals you have set for yourself.

Communicating in organizations is not an easy task. Obstacles to effective communication are always present. Assumptions about other people can be wrong ("I thought you were going to cover the *southeastern* sales territory this month!"), and closed communication channels can inhibit the exchange of messages ("I only want to hear good news about sales figures!"). Reluctance to receive new ideas and information—especially when they differ from your own ideas—can be detrimental to organizational goals ("I own this business, and I think I know best what it needs").

Many theories have been advanced to explain how organizations work, what relationship exists between management and labor, and what function, if any, communication performs in the working of an organization. The theories we address in this chapter examine the structure of an organization in relation to its communication techniques. These theories, which sometimes overlap, have had significant, and in some cases continuing, influences on organizational practices.

Classical Theory

The classical school of thought includes theories that emphasize structure, rules, and control. Included in this category are scientific management theory and bureaucracy theory. Although developed near the turn of the twentieth century, many of the principles of classical theory are still in use.

Scientific Management Frederick Taylor published *The Principles of Scientific Management* in 1911 and revolutionized the way managers thought about work in general and employees in particular.[5] Taylor had a great deal of respect for workers and was one of the first advocates of systematic training and development to improve workers' proficiency in their duties. He also encouraged organizations to match workers' abilities with the duties and responsibilities of their jobs. According to Taylor, four principles promote good management: (1) the development of a true science of work, (2) the scientific selection of the worker, (3) the scientific education and development of the worker, and (4) friendly cooperation between management and labor. From these principles grew a philosophy that advocates the following goals:

- Science, not rule of thumb, should be stressed.
- Harmony, not discord, should be encouraged.
- Cooperation, not individualism, should be advocated.
- Maximum output should be valued in place of restricted output.

5. F. Taylor, *The Principles of Scientific Management* (New York: Harper, 1911).

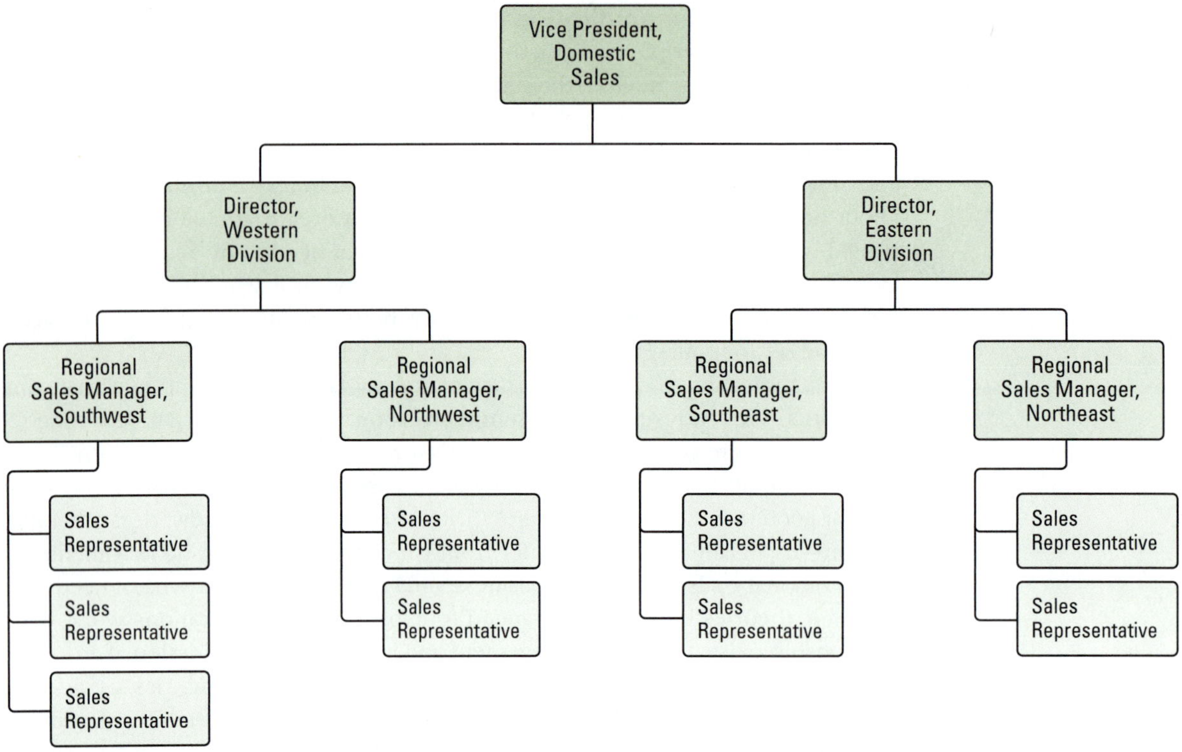

FIGURE 1.3 Typical Organizational Chart

This "org chart" shows the hierarchical nature of many businesses, in which each layer of workers is dependent on and subservient to a higher level.

- The development of workers and managers to their greatest efficiency and prosperity should be a priority.

Bureaucracy Max Weber, generally considered the father of the study of bureaucracy, worked to understand how authority and control were used in groups and organizations. His major contribution was a description of authority structures. He proposed three types: charismatic, traditional, and rational-legal.[6] **Charismatic authority** results from the personal qualities (expertise, knowledge, vision, values) of a leader. **Traditional authority** results from the recognition of and adherence to power produced by history, succession, or norms. **Rational-legal authority** grows out of rules, policies, procedures, laws, or other legalistic avenues of conferring power.

Rational-legal authority is the basis for bureaucracy (Weber is best known for this aspect of his theory). Government agencies, large corporations, and even the college or university you are now attending are good examples of bureaucracies. A bureaucratic structure enables organizations to define very clearly what behavior in employees is acceptable and expected. Bureaucratic authority structures concentrate a great deal of power at the top of a hierarchy. Successive, or lower, levels get their power from upper layers. The typical hierarchical chart shown in Figure 1.3 depicts how each succeeding layer is dependent on and subservient to the previous

6. M. Weber, *The Theory of Social and Economic Organizations* (New York: Free Press, 1947).

level of authority. Bureaucracies adhere to formalized rules and policies that they put in place for themselves, and communication within a bureaucracy goes by the book. Workers cannot skip levels of authority when sending messages to superiors or inferiors—the message must pass through each layer on its journey to the receiver. Communication in a bureaucracy is highly routine. Procedures, probably written ones, regulate oral and written communication.

Strengths and Weaknesses of Classical Theory **Classical theory** describes an organization that functions like a machine.[7] Machines perform repetitious tasks in specific and unchanging ways that are determined by their structures. The classical theory of management is appropriate in an organization when the same product is produced time and again, precision is at a premium, and the human "machine" parts are compliant and behave as they have been designed to do.

Think of organizations with which you are familiar. Do any of them have these characteristics? It would not be surprising if your response is "no." Changes in the American work force—larger numbers of college graduates and white-collar workers and larger business organizations—have lessened the popularity of classical theory, and few contemporary organizations rely strictly on its principles. Its views now seem overly mechanistic and impersonal, unsuited to the developing view of workers as human beings with needs rather than as faceless, impersonal "parts" of a business machine.

Humanistic Theory

A school of thought known as **humanistic theory** gained popularity in response to classical theory's mechanistic approach. It focused on the needs of labor rather than on the structure of management.

Human Relations Theory In the late 1920s and early 1930s, a number of studies on productivity were conducted at the Western Electric Hawthorne plant in Cicero, Illinois, under the leadership of Elton Mayo, a Harvard professor.[8] One of the first studies examined the effect of lighting in the workplace on workers' productivity.

As researchers increased the lighting of the experimental group in the Hawthorne plant, productivity increased, not just in the experimental group but also in the control group (which did not get increased lighting). Furthermore, when the experimenters *reduced* the illumination for the experimental group, productivity *continued* to increase. The engineers at the plant were delighted but puzzled.

The researchers concluded that increases in productivity were the result not of the changes in lighting but rather of the special attention being paid to the workers. Thus, the researchers proved that technical factors are not the only influences on work efficiency. Human factors, they discovered, also affect the work of employees.

According to Mayo, "Social study should begin with careful observation of what may be described as communication: that is, the capacity of an individual to communicate his feelings and ideas to another, the capacity of groups to communicate effectively and intimately with each other."[9] Mayo's most important finding, which stood in stark contrast to classical theory, was that informal groups and camaraderie

7. G. Morgan, *Images of Organizations* (Newbury Park, Calif.: Sage, 1986).
8. E. Mayo, *The Human Problems of an Industrial Civilization* (New York: Macmillan, 1933).
9. E. Mayo, *The Social Problems of an Industrial Civilization* (Andover, Mass.: Andover Press, 1945), p. 22.

ETHICAL ISSUES

Are You Being Watched?

Surfing the Web and sending e-mails are pretty routine activities in the workplace. Many jobs require these kinds of communication tasks as part of an employee's duties. But what about personal e-mails and browsing the Internet for personal reasons, such as buying concert tickets or checking to see if you are still the high-bidder on an auction? One estimate suggests that non-business-related Web surfing by employees costs U.S. firms $63 billion every year (that's $2,000 a second!). Many organizations have become so concerned about productivity losses from personal electronic communication at work that they have implemented surveillance processes to determine what employees are doing when they are on their computer. Employee Internet management (EIM) is a growing software industry. This software can monitor e-mail messages, Web-surfing, software usage, computer idle-time, and even individual keystrokes. Currently, employees have very few privacy rights at the workplace. The courts tend to support the employers' sovereignty over company-owned computers and networks. An employer can legally monitor nearly everything involving workers' computers, and they can do it with no notification to employees whatsoever.

Is it ethical for employers to snoop on workers? Is it ethical for employees to send messages to their friends and family on company time? If employees are putting in a certain amount of unpaid overtime, should they be allowed to use company electronic messaging to make up for it? Where should businesses and employees draw the line?

Source: "Employee Monitoring: Is There Privacy in the Workplace?": http://www.privacyrights.org/fs/fs7-work.htm (accessed July 30, 2003), "Trying to Measure Your Surfing at Work": http://www.cnn.com/2001/CAREER/trends/08/14/employee.net.use.idg/(accessed July 31, 2003).

among workers; supervisors' demonstrated interest, encouragement, praise, and recognition; and the ability to form relationships on the job were more effective than economic incentives in increasing workers' productivity and morale.

Human Resources Approach Human relations theory came under criticism for focusing too narrowly on workers' happiness and for not taking into account that happy workers might be unproductive. A reevaluation of human relations began, based on one of the most influential motivational theory books ever written: *The Human Side of Enterprise* by Douglas McGregor.[10] This book struck a compromise between classical theory and human relations theory: McGregor suggested that productivity will increase if workers not only are happy but also are given the proper working conditions.

McGregor proposed two theories of motivation that have become part of everyday language in business, government, and even academia: theory X and theory Y. According to theory X, workers are unproductive and unmotivated and must be coerced through constant supervision to perform their tasks. According to theory Y, workers are creative and motivated persons who do not require coercion (except in rare circumstances) and, when given the chance, can perform exceedingly well. These theories have generated a great deal of debate between supporters of their competing viewpoints (see Table 1.1).

McGregor's X/Y theory continues to influence organizational theory even though it is not fully understood. The contrasting characteristics seem to stem in part from human nature and consequently are difficult to dismiss. As a number

10. D. McGregor, *The Human Side of Enterprise* (New York: McGraw-Hill, 1960).

TABLE 1.1

Contrasting Viewpoints: Theory X and Theory Y

Theory X	Theory Y
1. Workers have an inherent dislike of work and will seek to avoid it if possible.	1. Activities and tasks at work are as natural as those at rest or play.
2. Most workers have to be coerced, forced, controlled, directed, and threatened to put out adequate effort on the job.	2. Control and coercion are not methods for obtaining adequate effort. Workers can and will exercise self-control to accomplish organizational objectives.
3. The average person prefers to be directed, likes to avoid responsibility, lacks motivation, and desires job security above all else.	3. The most significant reward for a worker is satisfying ego or self-actualization needs. The result of personal effort can be reward enough.
	4. Under the right conditions, the average worker may even seek responsibility.
	5. The ability to creatively and imaginatively solve organizational problems is widely distributed in the population. Creativity is not a managerial monopoly.
	6. The potential of the average worker is underdeveloped.

of managers told us, "Some people are theory Xers who have to be watched and supervised carefully; others are theory Yers whom you can leave alone." Of course, the same distinction can be applied to managers and supervisors. Think for a moment of organizations that fit a theory X profile. Were the employees lazy and unmotivated, causing management to constantly coerce and control them? Or were employees unmotivated because management did not trust them? What about theory Y organizations? Were the managers trusting, open-minded, and nurturing with workers, thereby causing them to be self-reliant and independent? Or did the workers demonstrate initiative, persistence, and reliability and thus lead management to think of employees more humanistically?

Systems Theory

The debate about organizations did not end with theories X and Y. Both classical and humanistic theories finally revealed a common shortcoming: neither considered the effect of the environment on organizational effectiveness. To fill this void, **systems theory** added a third element, the environment, to an equation that previously had contained only two: management and labor.

Concepts of Systems Theory Systems theory draws heavily from the work conducted in botany by Ludwig von Bertalanfy.[11] Bertalanfy's research suggested that organizations are comparable to living organisms and have needs, desires, faults, shortcomings, and other features characteristic of living creatures, and that the

11. L. von Bertalanfy, *General Systems Theory: Foundations, Development, and Applications* (New York: Braziller, 1960).

parts of an organization and the parts of an organism are related in a similar way. If one part of an organism breaks down (for example, if you catch a cold), the rest of the system is directly affected (through fatigue, achiness, fever). Similarly, if one person on an organizational team is absent or fails to do her or his share of the work, the entire team suffers.

In systems theory, this concept of relatedness is termed **interdependency.** If each member of a group is assigned a portion of a presentation, each member must participate for the presentation to succeed. If even one member fails to do her or his share of the work, then the overall quality of the presentation suffers. The notion of interdependency gives rise to the concept of **synergy.** This is the phenomenon whereby the combined and integrated talents, energies, abilities, and knowledge of organizational members are greater than the sum of the isolated efforts of individuals. In other words, people who work in systems can learn from one another and be more creative because of their interactions with one another.

From these two concepts comes a third: **environment.** It includes the political, economic, and social characteristics of society that affect the way an organization operates. Classical theory did not recognize environment as a factor in workers' effectiveness. Even humanistic theories did not emphasize the strong influence that the environment has on an organization. Figure 1.4 illustrates the relationship of these concepts in systems theory.

Consider the example of the fast-food industry. Several years ago few fast-food restaurants offered chicken sandwiches because customers apparently were satisfied with burgers and fries. Then along came the "health" movement, and people began

FIGURE 1.4

Systems Theory
Systems theory uses the concepts of interdependency, synergy, and environment to explain organizational behavior.

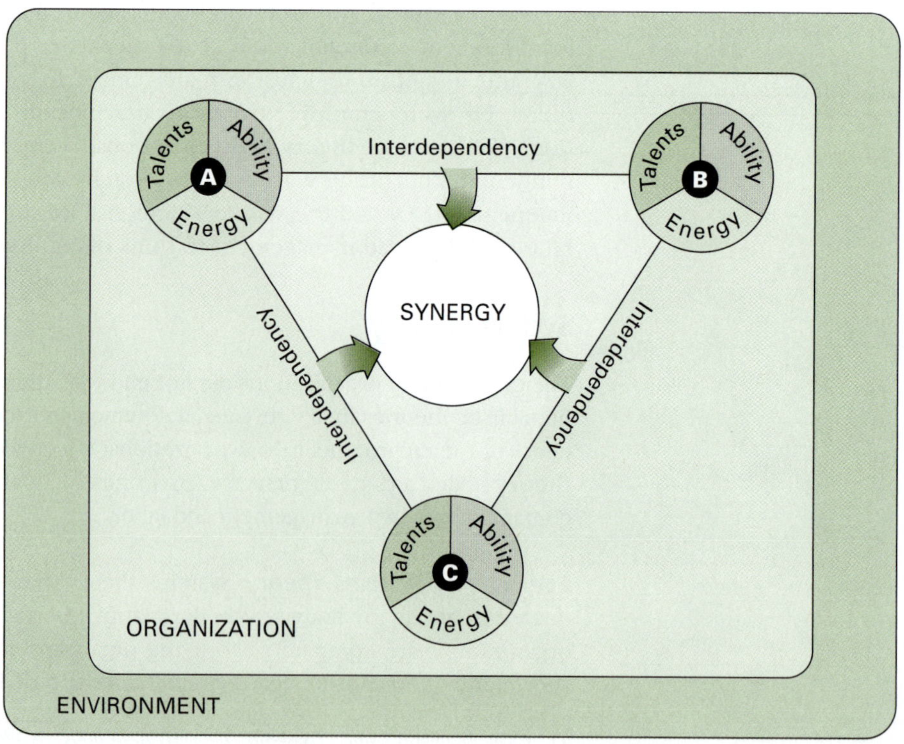

to demand healthier and less fattening choices at fast-food restaurants. Fast-food companies that ignored the demands of health-conscious customers stood to lose a lot of business. So it is hardly surprising that today nearly all fast-food outlets offer (and strongly promote the health benefits of) salads, low-fat foods, and all-natural ingredients.

Open and Closed Systems Organizations that attempt to respond to customer desires and needs are faced with a number of critical issues. What is the competition doing? What will suppliers be able to provide? What shape will the economy be in next year or the year after? Where can capital be raised? In terms of systems theory, responses to these issues are developed in either open systems or closed systems.

Open systems are systems that allow free movement of energy, information, ideas, data, people, and so on across organizational boundaries. **Closed systems** deliberately shut themselves off from the outside environment—sometimes with disastrous results, as markets expand and become more open, and as competition intensifies, leaving companies unable to keep up with the new business environment. The music industry offers a prime example.

In 1999, Shawn Fanning wrote a program he called Napster, which made it easier to swap mp3 music files over the Internet. At no cost to the user, hundreds of thousands of files were available at any time. One electronic copy of a song could be instantly shared with millions of people. Within a year, the RIAA (Recording Industry Association of America) sued Napster for copyright infringement. Nonetheless, 28 million people had already downloaded Napster by 2001. In February of 2001, Napster was shut down by a court order. However, this made little or no impact on Internet music sharing, since there were already many Napster imitators, including Grokster, Blubster, and Kazaa, where free music was still readily available. Today, despite hundreds of lawsuits against individuals swapping files on-line, music sharing continues to be extremely popular.

The point here is that the recording industry was too slow to take advantage of the file-sharing revolution in information technology, even in the face of an obvious, huge, untapped new market for downloadable music. Instead, executives clung stubbornly to their belief that the only way to do business was the way they always had done it: selling hard copies in music stores. Only in 2003, after a massive drop in CD sales, was there launched a Napster-like *legal* pay service, iTunes. As it turned out, despite industry fears to the contrary, people were willing to pay for easy access to a large selection of music files. In the first week, iTunes sold over 1 million songs at 99 cents each, and today sales of on-line songs exceed sales of CD singles. Even Napster has resurfaced: Napster 2.0—now a legitimate pay service—was launched in late 2003. But because the recording industry was a closed system—reluctant to allow new ideas, information, or changes in environment cross its boundaries—it lost billions of dollars over those five years.

Open systems can take a variety of forms. Organizations may develop work groups that invite expert outsiders to discuss cutting-edge technology or invite representatives of several different departments to discuss new ideas for cooperation. They may encourage outside speakers at their meetings, hold open houses, or sponsor joint fundraising activities with the community.

Open systems encourage employees to take college courses, obtain advanced degrees, participate in special workshops outside the organization, volunteer in the community, or even collaborate with persons outside the organization. Open

Where Do You Stand?

Which of the organizational theories describe some of the organizations you know? For example, are churches better described by certain theories compared with school organizations? What theories have your employers followed? Have you developed your own theory of organizations?

systems also embrace diversity among workers and learn from the cultural differences of their workers. The new knowledge generated by these activities not only helps the organization by providing additional expertise and ideas, but also improves morale among the work force.

Organizational Culture

Systems theory went far in explaining the dynamics of organizational communication and the reasons why some businesses are able to adapt to environmental change faster than others. But unanswered questions remained. One of the most significant was "Why would a communication system that is highly successful at one company be a failure at another?" The answer was provided in part by a relatively recent concept: organizational culture.

Organizational culture is "the social or normative glue that holds an organization together. It consists of values and beliefs that some groups or organizational members come to share."[12] Two best-selling books in the early 1980s—*Corporate Culture: The Rights and Rituals of Corporate Life* and *In Search of Excellence: Lessons from America's Best-Run Companies*—drew public attention to organizational or corporate culture.[13] Table 1.2 outlines the components of organizational cultures described in these two books.

Organizational culture provides a portrait of the actions, norms, motives, and philosophies that an organization values. In a sense, an analysis of organizational culture is an attempt to understand how organization members feel about themselves as a collective whole. *Shared meaning, shared understanding,* and *shared sense making* are all different ways of describing that culture. In talking about organizational culture, we are really talking about a process that allows people to see and understand particular events, actions, objects, or situations in distinctive ways. These patterns of understanding also provide a basis for making behavior sensible and meaningful.[14] For example, part of your school's organizational culture includes rules about the graduation ceremony, sports rituals such as bonfires and mascots, and norms such as an identifiable hand signal as a logo or activities at the student union building. These norms, rituals, and activities help create the shared understanding among the students about what it means to be a part of their campus. Knowledge of an organization's—in this case, your school's—culture provides members with a sense of purpose. They come to realize their importance within the organization.

Organizational theories were designed as rational ways of managing workers and activities. Organizational culture, however, provides a useful framework for understanding the structure of an organization and how messages flow within it. Communication skills are essential in the information-rich environment of the modern organization. While it may be natural to simply talk or write on a personal level, this book will introduce you to the valuable approach of *strategic* communication, which will help you develop the communication skills you will need to succeed in the world of business.

12. R. H. Kilmann, *Managing Beyond the Quick Fix* (San Francisco: Jossey-Bass, 1989).
13. T. Deal and A. Kennedy, *Corporate Culture: The Rights and Rituals of Corporate Life* (Reading, Mass.: Addison-Wesley, 1982); T. Peters and R. Waterman, *In Search of Excellence: Lessons from America's Best-Run Companies* (New York: Warner Books, 1982).
14. Morgan, *Images of Organizations.*

TABLE 1.2

Organizational Cultures

Component	Description	Example
Values	Goals, ideals, and philosophies that an organization holds important	A company's mission statement
Rites and rituals	The activities and performances that illuminate the important issues of the organization	Annual picnic; quarterly sales meetings
Heroes	The noteworthy organizational members who have achieved success in advocating the culture of the organization	Carli Fiorina (Hewlett-Packard); Bill Gates (Microsoft)
Communications	The networks that carry messages about work and social topics	Chain of command; grapevine
Norms	The task, social, and personal norms, standards, or ways of doing things in an organization	Allowing one casual-dress day per week; parking lot privileges
Stories, myths, and legends	The retold experiences that function as important events in the history of the organization	The frequently repeated story of how the first Compaq computer was designed: the original founders met one day in a coffee shop and drew the first design on the back of a placemat
Climate	The feeling or general attitude formed by the way members interact with one another and with persons outside the organization (customers, suppliers, vendors)	Feeling good about the way people are treated

STRATEGIC SCENARIO WRAP-UP

Based on what you read in this chapter, how should Jeremy find ways to feel more comfortable in his new organization? Are there things that Jeremy could do to improve his own and others' communication in the new organization?

SUMMARY

- Communication skills are becoming increasingly important. An organization's success depends on effective communication.
- The components of communication skills include creative insight, sensitivity, vision, shared meaning, and integrity. These elements are essential in facing the challenges posed by globalization and diversity.
- The desired outcome of communication is shared meaning between sender and receiver.
- Several factors prevent the achievement of shared meaning: inadequate information, information overload, poor-quality information, poor timing, lack of feedback or follow-up, problems with channels, incompetent communication, ineffective goal setting, and communication anxiety.
- Many theories have been advanced to explain how organizations work.
- Classical theory emphasizes structure, rules, and control.
- Classical theories include Taylor's scientific management theory and Weber's bureaucracy theory.
- Humanistic theory emphasizes camaraderie among workers, praise and recognition from supervisors, and relationship formation.
- The human resources approach suggests two theories of motivation for workers: theory X holds that workers must be coerced to be productive, and theory Y maintains that workers are motivated persons who do not require coercion.
- Classical and humanistic theories concentrate on management and labor.
- Systems theory adds the dimensions of interdependency, synergy, and environment.
- Systems theory distinguishes between two types of systems.
- Open systems allow free movement of information, ideas, and data across organizational boundaries.
- Closed systems shut themselves off from the outside environment.
- Organizational culture consists of the values and beliefs of an organization.
- An organization's culture tells how members feel about themselves as a collective whole. The components of this culture allow people to understand particular events, actions, or situations in distinctive ways, and they provide members with a sense of purpose.

KEY TERMS

Globalization: the trend toward increasing business transactions between foreign countries, which requires recognition of work force diversity and changing technologies

Interactive communication: communication in which each person taking part listens and responds to the others

Message: the content of communication with others—the ideas people wish to share

Source: the person who creates a message

Encoding: the physical process of organizing elements of the message for transmission to the receivers

Channel: the medium that carries a message once it is encoded by a source

Receiver: the destination of the message

Decoding: the process that recipients go through to make sense of the message they receive

Feedback: any response, verbal or nonverbal, that a receiver makes to a message

Noise: anything that interferes with communication

Context: the situation or setting in which communication ocurrs

Shared meaning: the mutual understanding that results when the sender and all intended receivers interpret the message in the same way

Organizational communication: the exchange of oral, written, and nonverbal messages among people working to accomplish common tasks and goals

Charismatic authority: authority structure that results from the personal qualities (expertise, knowledge, vision, values) of a leader

Traditional authority: authority structure that results from the recognition of and adherence to power produced by history, succession, or norms

Rational-legal authority: authority structure that grows out of rules, policies, procedures, laws, or other legalistic avenues of conferring power

Classical theory: describes an organization that functions like a machine and is management-oriented

Humanistic theory: focuses on the needs of labor rather than on the structure of management

Systems theory: acknowledges the interrelationship of an organization's environment, labor, and management

Interdependency: the concept of relatedness within systems theory

Synergy: the phenomenon whereby the combined and integrated talents, energies, abilities, and knowledge of organizational members are greater than the sum of the isolated efforts of individuals

Environment: includes the political, economic, and social characteristics of society that affect the way an organization operates

Open systems: systems that allow free movement of energy, information, ideas, data, people, and so on, across organizational boundaries

Closed systems: systems that deliberately shut themselves off from the outside environment

Organizational culture: the social or normative glue that holds an organization together, consisting of values and beliefs that are shared by some groups or organizational members

DISCUSSION

1. How can communication help an organization to achieve its goals?
2. What implications do the information age and globalization have for organizational communication?
3. How is the communication process affected by an organizational context?
4. What is shared meaning?
5. Which of the causes of communication failure discussed in the chapter have you experienced? What were the results, and how could you avoid repeating the situation?
6. What are the major differences among classical theory, humanistic theory, and systems theory?
7. What elements make up an organization's culture?

ACTIVITIES

1. This chapter discusses eight elements of the communication process. Select one element that was a particularly important problem in one of your recent communication transactions. Describe to the members of your class the role that the problem played during communication.
2. Examine these messages:
   a. "Need directions."
   b. "A. S. A. P." (As soon as possible)
   c. "Forward to appropriate personnel."

What different meanings might these messages have for a receiver? Explain how misinterpretation of these messages (lack of shared meaning) could create problems within an organization.

3. Choose a student organization—a fraternity, sorority, political or religious club, or student government body—and examine its structure in terms of the organizational theories presented in the chapter. Write a brief report describing the structure. Include specific examples from the organization to support your ideas.
4. Using your own school, work, or volunteer experience, explain how you believe effective communicators
   a. Obtain adequate information to do their jobs
   b. Avoid information overload
   c. Receive and send information in a timely manner
   d. Set goals effectively
   e. Manage communication anxiety
5. Many people believe that communication and culture are so closely linked that a change in one effects a change in the other. Write a brief essay in which you explain whether or not you believe this link exists. Be sure to give some supporting examples.

CHAPTER

2

The Model of Strategic Communication

After completing this chapter, you will be able to:

1. Recognize the importance of strategic organizational communication
2. Name the four elements of strategic communication
3. Use situational knowledge to enhance communication
4. Understand how values and ethics influence communication activity
5. Set goals that are appropriate and effective
6. Demonstrate communication competence by choosing the proper message, form of exchange, and channel
7. Understand the causes of communication anxiety and how to deal with it

STRATEGIC SCENARIO

Sam Klausner is one of four associate vice presidents for administration at Kempinik Industries in the Midwest. Sam was called into the executive suite to meet with the CEO/president, Joan Randall, and the vice president for administration (Sam's boss), Chase Montegro, to discuss a plan to reduce the work force. The company is in jeopardy of being bought by a fierce competitor if they do not quickly and substantially improve the bottom line. Since a large investment was made in automation earlier in the year, Ms. Randall and Mr. Montegro feel the time is right to reduce the enormous costs associated with manpower. This means that 1,000 employees (about 25 percent of the company) will be let go. They want Sam to develop a series of messages that clearly and accurately communicate their plans for the massive layoff and to devise the best ways for carrying these messages to the work force. They stressed to Sam they must not tell anyone about their plans because they do not want the best employees to be alarmed and quit, nor do they want the public (competitors, media) to know about their plans until the time is right. Sam is concerned about this responsibility, since he has a lot of friends in the company who will likely be laid off, many of whom have debts and families. Ms. Randall and Mr. Montegro want Sam to take a week to prepare his plan and report back to them on how he will implement this plan successfully.

As you read this chapter, think about the various tasks, and even dilemmas, that Sam faces with this new responsibility.

A MODEL FOR COMMUNICATION IN THE INFORMATION AGE

The information age demands that communication be planned carefully because there are so many new options to consider in the creation and transmission of messages. To succeed in this age, you need to know how to integrate technology with communication skills and how to communicate with people who have diverse backgrounds and a wide range of goals and expectations. To make the most of your business career, you need to present yourself as a competent communicator because your communication skills will be your best selling point in job interviews, sales meetings, and company presentations. To be effective, you will be wise to communicate *strategically*. This approach, developed and applied both in the classroom and in the real world, is designed to maximize the opportunities for communication you will encounter now and after graduation. Managers, employees, students, or friends can use the model of strategic communication as a guideline for effective communication. The model can be employed in any situation to maximize your competency—a job interview, a business proposal for a client, a class presentation.

Strategic communication means achieving your potential in four areas:

1. **Situational Knowledge:** Information that you have (or can collect) about the requirements for successful communication in a particular context is situational knowledge. You greatly improve your chances of successful communication if you know what is appropriate and expected of you.
2. **Goal Setting:** Each communication situation can be approached as a goal-setting activity. You will be more likely to succeed in your communication if you set clear and appropriate goals for yourself.
3. **Communication Competence:** When you plan communication strategically, you choose a number of factors—such as type of message, type of channel, style of delivery—that demonstrate your understanding of the organization's values and needs. Communication competence also entails adapting correctly to situational demands. You will learn to make these choices consistently and correctly.
4. **Anxiety Management:** Job interviews, meetings with superiors, and group problem-solving meetings are a few of the many situations that may cause anxiety on the job. Control of anxiety is a critical element in effective and strategic communication. You can learn to keep your nervousness at a level that energizes your communication without destroying its effectiveness.

These four components (Figure 2.1) provide a basis for developing communication skills within the context of the dynamic business environment.

FIGURE 2.1

Model of Strategic Communication

These four components provide a basis for developing solid communications skills within a business environment.

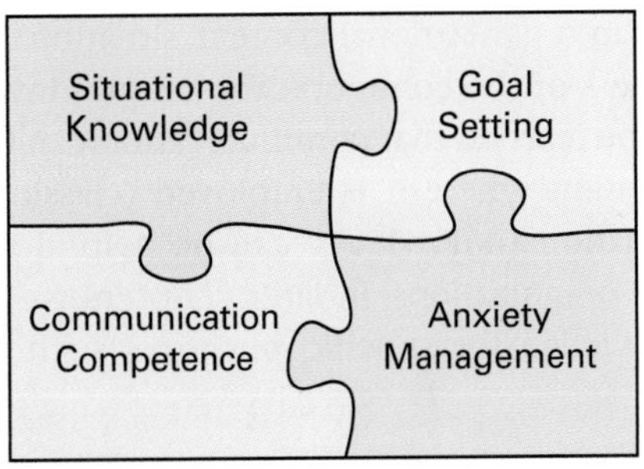

Over the years, many businesspeople, communications theorists, and teachers have advocated approaches to business communication similar to the model of strategic communication. Elements of this model are evident in the theories discussed in Chapter 1. For example, communicating competently allows a manager to provide the kind of special attention and feedback that, according to human relations theory, makes workers respond positively. These approaches are much talked about and even partially implemented in the workplace, yet they have not had the broad impact expected of them. The main reason for their limited success has to do with another concept mentioned in Chapter 1: environment. Up through the 1970s, the environment of American business was relatively stable and insulated. Companies were relatively homogeneous and tended to focus on domestic markets. There was no pressing need for American businesses to adopt the flexible and open communication systems described in Chapter 1. Such insularity is no longer possible. In the past two decades, radical changes have occurred. Among them are increasing competition, diversity, globalization, and increasing dependence on technology and access to information. As a result, there are new demands on managers' time as organizations try to become more competitive by holding down costs without cutting back on products and services. Work is being redefined as all types of job descriptions become increasingly complex and require knowledge of new technologies and information systems. In addition, the computerization of the workplace allows employees quick access to information that even a decade ago was not available to top management and planners.[1] This competitive environment demands a new approach to on-the-job communication that provides efficiency (communication opportunities are not wasted for lack of planning) and flexibility (people at all levels can be encouraged and included in communication).

Strategic communication is effective because it helps you pinpoint the areas in which you excel and those in which you need to improve. This chapter uses the model to illustrate strategic communication in organizations. The four components of strategic communication—goal setting, situational knowledge, communication competence, and anxiety management—are the basis for understanding and improving your skills for interpersonal, group, and public communication. As each component of the model is discussed, you will be introduced to practical and straightforward methods for setting and achieving communication goals in a number of contexts.

SITUATIONAL KNOWLEDGE: THE CONTEXT OF ORGANIZATIONAL COMMUNICATION

The first component of the model of strategic communication is **situational knowledge,** the information or facts you use in devising an effective communication strategy. In an organizational context, situational knowledge also refers to employees' awareness of the communication issues involved in their jobs. In the previous chapter, you learned that communication can be different, depending on the type of organization where it is employed (classical versus humanistic). Having this type of situational knowledge can be helpful in knowing how to deal with people in those organizations. In later chapters we will show you how to gather situational knowledge for specific purposes such as developing work relation-

1. J. Case, "The Open-Book Managers," *INC.*, September 1990, pp. 107–108.

ships, preparing for meetings, and giving presentations. The fundamental concept, however, is that you can increase your communication effectiveness by gathering a thorough knowledge of the person or people with whom you are communicating. In the following sections, you will learn how an organization's values and ethics, organizational structure, organizational learning, on-the-job training, politics, and communication climate build situational knowledge.

Values and Ethics

A key element in any communication activity is the values of the organization. **Values** are the principles and ideas that people or organizations strongly believe in and consider important. When people are in doubt about decisions, they frequently rely on deep-seated values to help them make the right choice. In organizations, reliance on shared values makes setting goals easier in the face of the competing ideas, desires, and objectives of individual employees.

Values How are shared values established in an organization? The process is difficult because values are fundamental and enduring and because each person has a particular personal value system. Despite these drawbacks, an organization has several choices when it comes to establishing values. Upper management can organize focus groups, small groups ranging from seven to twelve employees who meet to identify values they believe are vital to the organization. These lists of values are then circulated among all the focus groups for review and analysis. Next, a committee studies the values generated by the focus groups and arrives at a composite set that organizational members can vote on.

You can get a good idea about the values of an organization by examining its vision and mission statement. These statements are short descriptions of the purpose of organizations and the directions they try to take to achieve success. Many organizations post their vision and mission statements in several places so that employees know what the organization values. Take a look at the vision and mission statement of Anheuser-Busch Companies. Did you get a sense of what it values?

Values can also be derived through members' responses to questionnaires, which provide quantitative data about issues of importance to employees and about the values they uphold. Another way to establish values is through the work of organizational consultants. One of their tasks is to interview key employees to determine their value systems. As objective outsiders, consultants can play an important role in assessing which values are common among members as well as which values promote the mission of the organization.

Organizational values vary, depending on the nature of the business or profession. Values found in a large number of organizations include the following:

- Primacy of the customer
- Honesty and integrity
- Respect for other workers
- Importance of every person
- Maintenance of high professional standards
- Fair treatment
- Innovative thinking
- Quality service
- Creativity

Anheuser-Busch's Vision and Mission Statement

Our vision: Through all of our products, services, and relationships, we will add to life's enjoyment.

Our mission:

- Be the world's beer company
- Enrich and entertain a global audience
- Deliver superior returns to our shareholders

Our values:

- Quality in everything we do
- Exceeding customer expectations
- Trust, respect, and integrity in all of our relationships
- Continuous improvement, innovation, and embracing change
- Teamwork and open, honest communication
- Each employee's responsibility for contributing to the company's success
- Creating a safe, productive, and rewarding work environment
- Building a high-performing, diverse work force
- Promoting the responsible consumption of our products
- Preserving and protecting the environment and supporting communities where we do business

Courtesy of Anheuser-Busch Companies, Inc.

- Reliance on ethical standards
- Profitable returns to shareholders

Communication Ethics In the late 1990s a telecommunications firm called WorldCom had the world's largest Internet "backbone" network and was the second-largest long-distance provider in the United States. Between 1995 and 2000 WorldCom bought more than sixty other companies, including MCI for $37 billion. Despite all of this apparent success, in July 2002 WorldCom, facing $41 billion in debt, filed for bankruptcy, the largest bankruptcy in history.

During the investigation that followed, WorldCom was revealed as having a "culture of fraud." For several years profits fell below estimates. If investors knew about the decrease in earnings, the price of the stock would also decrease. Many of the people in positions of authority inside of WorldCom had huge amounts of money to lose if the stock price were to drop. To appear as though they were meeting earning estimates and to maintain high stock prices, WorldCom falsified over $2 billion of revenue and ignored over $7 billion of expenses in earning reports for 1999 through 2002. This fraudulent communication of profits was finally uncovered in 2002 and the senior executives involved went on to face criminal charges. Although WorldCom has emerged from[2] bankruptcy, this unethical behavior cost creditors and stockowners billions of dollars.

2. Information from http://www.washingtonpost.com/wp-dyn/articles/A51549-2003Sep9.html; http://www.usatoday.com/money/industries/telecom/2003-06-10-worldcom_x.htm; http://www.usatoday.com/news/opinioon/editorials/2003-06-09-vfickers_x.htm.

A general suggestion for ethical communicators is that they have a "well developed sense of social responsibility."[3] The following guidelines come in handy when uncertainty arises about ethical communication behavior.[4] Before you consider them, read this case as an example of ethical communication in businesses:

> Kent had been with his company for twenty-seven years and was disturbed to learn that he was being demoted, with a decrease in pay, because the company was merging with another company and his position was being eliminated. Kent was angry but could not resign because he was too old to get a similar job elsewhere. He began to take two-hour lunches, help himself to office supplies that he took home, and talk incessantly with coworkers about how unfairly the company was treating him. When he was asked to relay information to others, he always delayed until the information was virtually useless, and he actually changed the tone or intent of the message. Before the merger, Kent was one of the company's most trusted and loyal employees.

Consider these ethical guidelines, and apply them to Kent's case:

1. **Maintain Candor.** Candor refers to truthfulness, honesty, and frankness in your communication with other people. Although revealing everything you know about a situation may not always be appropriate—for instance, providing *all* your information to adversaries during intense and sensitive negotiations will only compromise your position—it is usually wise and ethical to be as open and frank about information as possible. Others will take note and mirror your behavior, creating openness throughout the organization.
2. **Keep Messages Accurate.** When you are relaying information from one source to another, communicate the original message as accurately as possible. Ethical communicators do not take liberties with the messages they pass on.
3. **Avoid Deception.** Ethical communicators are always vigilant in their quest to avoid deception—the fabrication, intentional distortion, or withholding of information—in their communication.
4. **Behave Consistently.** One of the most prevalent yet noticeable areas of unethical behavior is communicating one thing and doing another. You must always monitor your behavior to ensure that it matches what you say to others.
5. **Keep Confidences.** When someone tells you something and expects you not to divulge that information to others, a sacred trust has been placed on you. Even if you then tell someone else and make her or him promise not to tell others, you cannot really expect that person to take you seriously. More often than not, the original information gets back to the source and the confidence that person placed in you is undermined.
6. **Ensure Timeliness of Communication.** The timing of messages can be critical. When you delay sending messages so that others do not fully benefit, they can (rightly) assume that you have acted unethically.
7. **Confront Unethical Behavior.** To maintain a consistent ethical viewpoint, you must confront unethical behavior when you observe it. Public indictment

3. W. S. Howell, *The Empathic Communicator* (Belmont, Calif.: Wadsworth, 1982), p. 192.
4. S. P. Golen, C. Powers, and M. A. Titkemeyer, "Ethics," in S. P. Golen (ed.), *Methods of Teaching Selected Topics in Business Communication* (Urbana, Ill.: Association for Business Communication, 1986), pp. 3–8.

of unethical persons may not be necessary, but it is important that people understand that your own tolerance for unethical behavior is low.

8. **Cultivate Empathic Listening.** By lending a sensitive and empathic ear to those who are troubled by their own or others' unethical behavior, you can better understand and help to solve the problems associated with these acts. After all, many unethical acts are the result of circumstances that coworkers feel are beyond their control.

Although ethical behavior seems easy to recognize, ethics is a complex issue. It is often difficult to decide between conflicting guidelines. For example, if a coworker confides to you that she will be quitting in two weeks, and your supervisor asks you whether your soon-to-be-gone coworker would be capable of managing a long-term project, the guidelines of "keeping confidences" and "avoiding deception" are in direct conflict. Because of the complexity of human nature, situations such as this are not uncommon; therefore, maintaining ethical behavior can be difficult. In situations that require a choice, it may be wise to examine the outcomes and consequences of your actions, to maintain respect and empathy for others involved, and to maintain open communication. Openness in communication can help resolve ethical issues.

The Advantage of Ethics Many experts do not expect substantial progress in the area of business ethics given the present state of affairs, but we are not so pessimistic. For one thing, more and more students are thinking about the issues of ethical behavior in organizations. Once employees realize the advantages of ethical behavior, progress is likely to be made. But what are the advantages of ethics in the professional world?

One advantage of ethics in the workplace is long-term integrity. Surveys report that all employees want to work for organizations with high ethical standards.[5]

Competent people are likely to search for organizations that maintain high ethical standards. They know that ethical practices are the only sure way to succeed in life. When competent people migrate toward ethical firms, everyone benefits because both competence and ethics are perpetuated. Indeed, it is quite easy to make the argument that competence and ethics go hand in hand. Those who understand how to succeed know that unethical behavior leads only to covert and clandestine activities that are time-consuming and unprofitable. Ethical firms therefore enjoy the advantage of employing greater numbers of competent professionals.

Furthermore, employee commitment is likely to be higher in ethical businesses. Employee commitment yields a number of benefits, including higher employee morale, less turnover, greater productivity, and enhanced creativity. Although compromises on ethics may yield short-term benefits, over the long haul most unethical acts are eventually uncovered, contributing to a dishonorable, unscrupulous, and unprincipled professional atmosphere. Such an atmosphere perpetuates the myth that the only way to get ahead is by engaging in unethical behavior. But when leaders maintain high ethical standards, they can use their power for the good of the organization and its employees. (A detailed discussion of leadership ethics is in Chapter 6.)

Where Do You Stand?

Would you stop patronizing a business if you learned it engaged in unethical practices? Do you believe that, as a consumer, you should strive to make yourself aware of the ethical practices of the businesses whose products and services you consume?

5. C. M. Kelly, *The Destructive Achiever* (Reading, Mass.: Addison-Wesley, 1988), pp. 196–197.

Organizational Structure

Each organization's ability to respond to challenges depends on its structure. **Organizational structure** consists of the actual environment where the organization is located. Some organizations occupy several floors in one office building; others have branch offices, resulting in employees being physically spread out. Departments within an organization may be contained in one location or split among several locations. An organization's physical structure has a strong effect on its communication style. For example, college academic departments that concentrate faculty members on one floor create more frequent communication than do those that disperse faculty over several floors or several buildings. Organization members who are located away from their colleagues are likely to feel isolated and lonely.

One of the newest types of organizational structure is the **virtual organization.** It is called "virtual" because the physical structure of this organization doesn't really exist—the organization is structured through telecommunications connections. People in an organization can do their work from a remote place (home, hotel room, car, airplane) through a computer that is linked to other people's computers via telephone lines or satellite transmission. For example, this book was written and revised essentially through a virtual organization. The authors were located at universities in Oklahoma, New Jersey, and Ohio, the executive editor was in New York City, the developmental editor was in Colorado, the publishing company was in Boston, and the printing company was in Pennsylvania. Communication among these organizational members was conducted by telephone, e-mail, and surface mail. Some members of this virtual organization never even met each other, much less worked in the same building, yet the result was the publication of this book.

Sometimes organizations may be partially virtual if some of the employees work from home and communicate in the way previously described. These employees, called **telecommuters,** maintain regular communication with their organization through e-mail, phones, fax, pagers, and the Internet. In 2003 about 9.3 million people, 7 percent of the total U.S. work force, worked from home at least one day a week, and around 6 million people did all of their work from home. With telecommunication advances, the number of American workers who telecommute is expected to increase.[6] Another way to understand structure is to look at the hierarchy, or pyramid of authority, a business maintains. **Tall organizations** have a large number of hierarchical levels. Banks, for example, are notorious for tall structures. At the top of the hierarchy is the board of directors, followed by the chief executive officer, the president, executive vice presidents, senior vice presidents, vice presidents, associate vice presidents, assistant vice presidents, cashiers, assistant cashiers, tellers, and finally bookkeepers. The chain of command in tall organizations usually requires subordinates who want to suggest any change to top management to first communicate with their boss, who then talks to her or his boss, who then contacts someone at the next level, and so on. In extreme instances, a message can take weeks or even months to make its way up the chain of command.

In contrast, **flat organizations** have few hierarchical levels. They place a large number of employees at the same level and do not rank most jobs as being

6. Information taken from http://landview.census.gov/pubinfo/www/radio/pa303.htm.

FIGURE 2.2

Tall vs. Flat Organizations
A shorter chain of command, as in flatter hierarchies, allows for faster movement of messages throughout the organization.

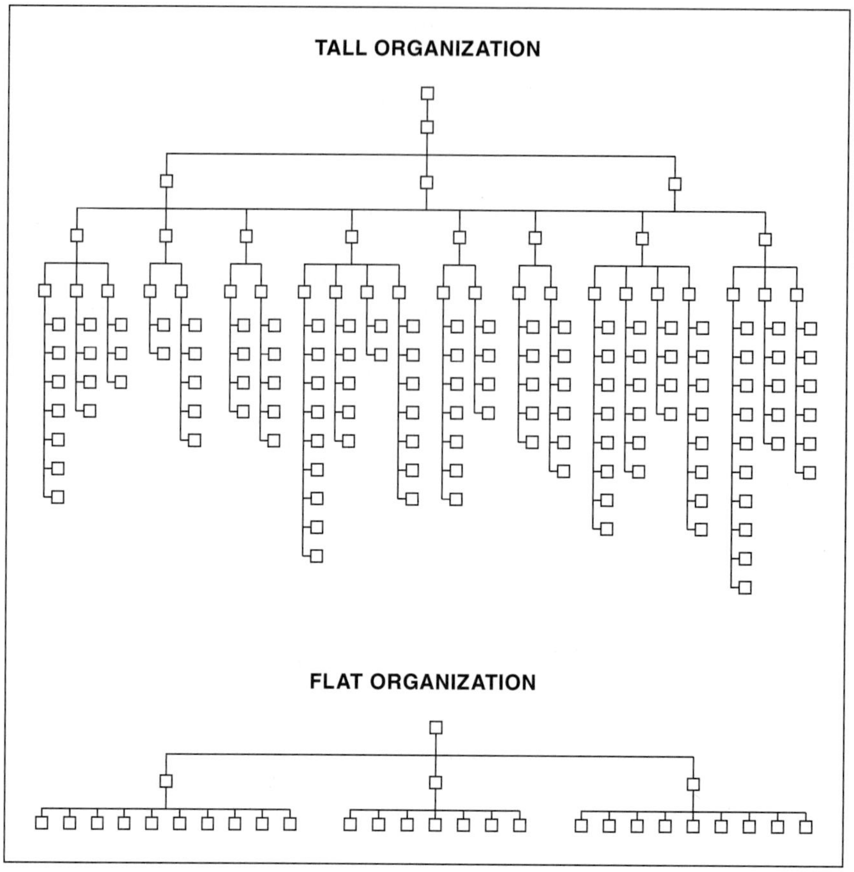

"above" or "below" other jobs in the organization. The short chain of command in flat organizations allows a relatively rapid movement of messages throughout the organization. The modern trend in business is toward reducing the middle-level hierarchy and "flattening" the organization. Figure 2.2 contrasts a tall organization with a flat organization. The bottom line is that knowing about structure gives you an important piece of the situational knowledge necessary for effective communication.

Organizational Learning

To communicate effectively, people in business have traditionally thought it best to know as much as possible about an organization and its environment. Employees who monitor the organization and environment for new information are in the best position to make informed decisions about communication, but the demands of the information age have altered how such monitoring takes place. There is much more information than can be analyzed piece by piece. Clearly, both new employees and workers dealing with large amounts of information for the first time need methods for learning about the organization without being overwhelmed. There are several ways to accomplish this goal:[7]

7. P. Shrivesta in R. L. Daft and G. P. Huber, "How Organizations Learn: A Communication Framework," *Research in the Sociology of Organizations* 5 (1987), 1–36.

1. You can engage in **adaptive learning** by seeking to understand how goals, policies, procedures, and other people's actions conform to the dynamics of the workplace. Adaptation is a survival skill in today's organizations.
2. You can learn about the organization by **understanding organizational values.** Knowing and embracing organizational values will clarify your awareness of how and why organizations make the decisions they do.
3. **Developing specific knowledge of the organization** is another way to learn. You can cultivate awareness of the norms, policies, procedures, politics, and accepted behaviors that govern the workplace. A communication strategy benefits from knowledge about what rules and boundaries are in place; otherwise, the strategy can result in errors or violations of policy.
4. You can learn by **observing successes and failures.** Essentially, you can learn a great deal about what works in an organization and what does not by assembling a track record of who succeeds and fails, and why.

On-the-Job Training

One of the first opportunities a new employee has to learn about an organization is likely to be an orientation program. The initial period of employment is referred to as "assimilation."[8] New workers coming into the organization are expected to assimilate the philosophies and operations of the workplace. Employee orientation programs provide important information about how the company operates, the chain of command, the relationships among departments, and so on. New employees can also gain knowledge through formal on-the-job training programs or through informal meetings with an immediate supervisor, handbooks, or conversations with coworkers. The "breaking in" period is crucial because during this time employees learn how to deal with the various relationships in the organization.

Once you have mastered the various bits of knowledge about the company and the job, a "metamorphosis" occurs: you become a functioning member of the organization. By this time, your situational knowledge has improved substantially.

You can continue to increase situational knowledge by finding out about and participating in performance appraisal interviews, career development activities such as seminars and workshops, and annual business meetings. Even the informal grapevine provides a forum through which you can gain knowledge of the organization. It is to your benefit to take advantage of ongoing training and educational opportunities, even when you are no longer new to the company.

Politics

Knowledge of an organization is incomplete without awareness of the organization as a political entity. All organizations are political systems because they organize and distribute power, resources, and rewards in pursuit of specific goals. When you collect situational knowledge about an organization, it is important to consider the political climate that the organization maintains. Organizational politics is usually described as the exercise or negotiation of power.[9]

8. F. Jablin, "Organizational Communication: An Assimilation Approach," in M. Rolof and C. Berger (eds.), *Social Cognition and Communication* (Newbury Park, Calif.: Sage, 1982), pp. 255–286.
9. P. Frost, "Power, Politics, and Influence," in F. Jablin, L. Putnam, K. Roberts, and L. Porter (eds.), *Handbook of Organizational Communication* (Newbury Park, Calif.: Sage, 1987), p. 518.

TECHNOLOGY TOOLS

Web Pages and the Intranet

Employees can learn a lot about where they work from the organization's Web page and/or intranet. The nice part of an organization's Web page is that employees can learn a great deal about what the organization says about itself to outsiders such as vendors and potential customers. Another way that one learns about the organization electronically is by communicating through the internal network of the company called an intranet. Employees are networked together just like participants on the Internet, but an intranet is limited only to people who work for the company. One can get e-mail addresses easily from an online director, become a member of special "chat" groups, and belong to listserves for people with specialized interests or needs. Intranets are protected by "firewalls" that prevent outsiders from getting into the company network but allow users to get outside to the Internet.

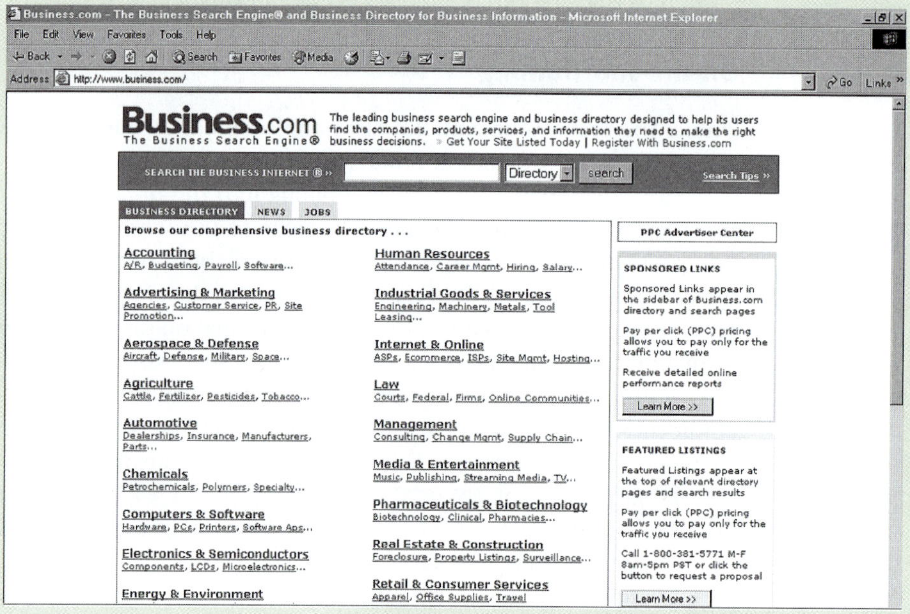

Business.com URL: www.business.com. Reprinted with permission.

Politics can be viewed from two perspectives: (1) as negative and destructive behaviors that should be avoided or (2) as important aspects of communication that must be accounted for in a strategic communication plan. Although frequently used in a negative sense, politics is not necessarily disastrous. For example, in your years in school, you may have found yourself in a situation in which you needed the support of faculty, alumni, parents, or administrators to achieve a goal you strongly believed in. Building cooperation among different groups and influencing people's opinions to support worthwhile goals or causes are political actions.

You may have little choice about whether to use politics, simply because business communication requires it. Even small details such as dressing appropriately

On-the-job training can be informal or highly structured—from the simple advice of an experienced employee giving a newcomer a lesson in transferring a phone call to a week-long orientation session, like the one shown here. (© Tom McCarthy/Corbis)

and treating coworkers politely can be considered politics. The following political strategies are frequently employed in the workplace:[10]

- Controlling the agenda of a meeting so that only items of interest to you appear
- Building coalitions of "friendly" people
- Trading favors
- Adhering to policies thought desirable by powerful people
- Being sensitive to dress

Other political strategies include

- Associating with the "right" people
- Appearing at official functions and meetings
- Assuming seating positions at group meetings that display power

If you decide to use any of these strategies, consider the ethical consequences of your communication. One way to do this is by posing questions such as the following about the potential results of the decision you intend to make:[11]

- Who may be affected by my decision/action?
- Will my decision/action violate any commitments to these parties?
- What may be the negative consequences of my action?
- Will people be better or worse off in the long run?
- Would I be comfortable if my decision became company policy for others to use?

It is wise to take stock of the political atmosphere in the organization and to determine how your own political communication style fits in. This type of situational

10. Ibid., pp. 504–548.
11. R. E. Reidenbach and D. P. Robin, *Ethics and Profits* (Englewood Cliffs, N.J.: Prentice Hall, 1989).

knowledge will be valuable as you try to influence others to accomplish your goals, as the following example indicates:

> Teresa, a recent graduate of Brugle College, has taken a job with a merchandising firm in a neighboring state. She is bright and generally perceptive when it comes to figuring out what other people are up to. Teresa was a bit shy at first but over time has made good friends of just about everyone. She prides herself on this accomplishment. She also has little trouble recognizing who has "real" power in the company and can therefore help to advance her career. She initially steered clear of the two political factions in the organization but managed to stay on amicable terms with members of both. Not until the two factions disagreed over whether to begin a paper-recycling program did Teresa decide to affiliate with the side supporting the program. She believed recycling to be an important project and felt that in the long run the company's interests would be best served by the prorecycling faction.

Communication Climate

Situational knowledge includes information on an organization's character. **Communication climate** is one aspect of character. Climate is a function of the interactions and social processes that occur in the workplace. Climate may change, depending on how communication changes in the organization.[12] Thus, although climate may be relatively stable, it is nevertheless subject to modification.

The ideal communication climate has five dimensions:[13]

Supportiveness: Superiors, subordinates, and coworkers provide psychological and physical support to one another.

Participative Decision Making: Workers have opportunities to formulate decisions that affect them directly.

Trust, Confidence, and Credibility: The workplace is characterized by integrity.

Openness and Candor: Free, honest, and open communication abounds.

High Performance Goals: Established goals reach beyond average performance.

The ability of an organization to achieve an "ideal" climate depends on the knowledge it has of its own shortcomings. Recognition of this gap between the actual and the ideal is the first step in establishing a desirable climate. Of the five dimensions, openness is a particularly critical influence on climate.

Openness **Openness** is a receiver-oriented concept: it focuses on being receptive and responsive to information from others. An open organization promotes communicative responsiveness among people at different levels of authority and responsibility. Being receptive and responsive to messages shows others that you are interested in what they have to say.

You can encourage openness in several ways. Ask questions that demonstrate a desire to communicate with other organizational members; they will probably

12. M. Poole and R. McPhee, "A Structural Theory of Organizational Climate," in L. Putnam and M. Pacanowsky (eds.), *Organizational Communication: An Interpretive Approach* (Newbury Park, Calif.: Sage, 1983), pp. 195–219.

13. C. Redding, *Communication Within the Organization: An Interpretive Review of Theory and Research* (New York: Industrial Communication Council, 1972). Reprinted with permission.

appreciate your efforts and respond positively to you. Show genuine interest in discussions with others (Chapter 4 discusses specific listening skills that can be used for this purpose). Respond to others' communication actively. Feedback is one of the most important indications of an open organizational climate. A measure of communication openness that reflects an open organization follows:[14]

1. Supervisors ask for suggestions.
2. Supervisors act on criticism.
3. Supervisors listen to complaints.
4. People ask for supervisors' opinions.
5. Supervisors follow up on people's opinions.
6. Supervisors suggest new ideas.
7. People ask coworkers for suggestions.
8. Supervisors listen to bad news.
9. People listen to new ideas from coworkers.
10. Supervisors listen to new ideas.

How many of the organizations that you have been associated with have had these characteristics? Often it is difficult to be receptive and responsive to people whom you do not like, trust, or respect. Nevertheless, openness, even if initially forced, can yield positive results.

Researchers studying organizational communication have described the potential advantages of open communication. Included among the advantages are improved organizational performance, enhanced job satisfaction, improved role clarity (understanding what your duties are), and increased information adequacy (having the right amount of information to do your job).[15] Open communication also encourages conscientious, open-minded, and innovative people to interact with and positively influence others. People respect those who are receptive and responsive to communication and can learn from their success in the organization. Recall from Chapter 1 classical and humanistic organizations. Which ones do you think embody the concept of openness?

Remember that tall and flat organizations have different communication styles. Because of the large number of hierarchical levels in a tall organization, openness can be difficult. The structure of tall organizations discourages feedback and immediate responsiveness. In contrast, flat organizations allow rapid movement of messages, a situation more conducive to openness.

Strategic Ambiguity A completely open communication climate may seem ideal, but it may turn out to be unrealistic given the complexity of communication in most organizations. Indeed, some types of information are best communicated in vague and nonspecific ways. Such "strategic ambiguity" is appropriate for topics that cannot be discussed in an open fashion.[16] For example, some employees may

14. D. Rogers, "The Development of a Measure of Perceived Communication Openness," *Journal of Business Communication* 24 (1987), 53–61. Reprinted by permission of the author.
15. Ibid.
16. E. Eisenberg and M. Witten, "Reconsidering Openness in Organizational Communication," *Academy of Management Review* 12 (1987), 418–426.

feel uncomfortable discussing organizational politics. Others may not feel comfortable talking about the personal problems of coworkers. Especially common is the use of strategic ambiguity to cushion a possibly offensive message.

You can identify specific situations that may require strategic ambiguity rather than communication openness. Bargaining and negotiation may not lend themselves to totally open communication. Negotiators who are too open may "give away the farm" if they reveal all their bargaining strategies. Crisis situations may also require that information traveling up or down the hierarchy be communicated with some ambiguity. Full disclosure of the details of a crisis may ignite an overload of counterproductive emotions that could hurt the organization's ability to take action.

> Reuben was the purchasing agent for a large design firm. He had requested a quote for top-of-the-line fabric to be used in a remodeling job for one of his company's clients. After receiving the quote from the manufacturer, he called Cynthia, the manufacturer's customer service representative. He wanted to know the absolute bottom-line dollar figure for the type of fabric he needed. When he heard her price, Reuben felt it was too high. He plans now to check with some other fabric manufacturers to compare prices. Rather than say this directly, however, Reuben replies, "Thanks for that information. I'll run those numbers by my client and get back to you." In this way, Reuben buys himself some time to get additional information without alienating Cynthia. Having more information gives Reuben a better negotiating position.

Think about your own work experiences. Can you think of times when information was withheld from you or others for similar reasons? Did you agree with the decision at the time? Such examples suggest that although communication openness should be highly valued as a general standard, situations may arise in which strategic ambiguity is a better option. If faced with such a choice, use your goals, organizational values, and situational knowledge to guide your decision.

The Benefits of Situational Knowledge

Situational knowledge is a significant component of our model of strategic communication for four reasons. First, knowledge about the organization helps you to accomplish your personal and organizational goals. Knowing with whom to communicate and how enhances the possibility that your idea will be accepted. Second, knowledge of an organization's reward system gives you an idea of what is valued and considered important. One of the biggest problems you will face as an employee is lack of information about the value of your contributions to the organization. This problem can be minimized when situational knowledge is high. Third, situational knowledge allows for better coordination between you and other members of the organization. Recognizing and understanding the relative relationships among various people and units can save you time and effort. Fourth, situational knowledge helps you grow as an employee. When you recognize the different paths to enhancing your career, you are in a good position to perform roles that could lead to promotions. When you know that you can grow, develop, and mature within an organization, you are likely to be loyal and remain with the company.

GOAL SETTING FOR ORGANIZATIONAL COMMUNICATION

Recall that goal setting is one of the four parts of the strategic model of communication. Once you feel knowledgeable about the organization's values, you will be able to work on appropriate goals for your communication. It is not enough simply to set positive-sounding goals ("I hope my department does better this quarter"). Research reveals that goals must be set with particular criteria in mind. In situations in which you must communicate to achieve objectives, it is usually best to set specific, rather than vague, goals. Specific goals enable communicators to map out the conditions that must be met for the goals to be reached.[17] In addition, organizations have found that performance is better when high goals, instead of low ones, are set. Therefore, setting specific and high goals is in your best interest when you anticipate a communication encounter. Consider the following example:

> Charlene Perkins, head of distribution at Popular Ice Company, made an appointment to discuss budget problems with her boss, Harold Danzak. Charlene planned to ask Harold for an increase in operating funds because the distribution department was having a tough time making ends meet. Charlene and Harold occasionally bowled on the same team and went to the same church, so Charlene felt pretty comfortable about the meeting. She did not plan out what she was going to say because she felt sure that Harold would see the situation her way.
>
> When Charlene arrived at Harold's office, she was kept waiting for almost thirty minutes. When Harold finally saw her, he told Charlene that he had to catch a plane for Detroit in twenty minutes. He looked at Charlene and said, "This is the worst year for budgets I have ever seen. Every department seems to need more funds to operate, and I don't have much to give. I can help only the departments that really show a need." Charlene swallowed hard because she had planned to use the hour-long meeting to secure money from Harold on the basis of their friendship.
>
> Charlene had come into the meeting with no data, hard facts, or specific goals. She did not even have a figure in mind for her budget increase request. She left the meeting with Harold encouraging her to keep up the hard work. Unfortunately, Charlene left without any increase in her operating budget.

Charlene's experience shows the importance of specific goals. Goals are valuable because they take set conditions into account and identify targets for communication. Specific goals allow you to plan your actions and behaviors in advance of the communication encounter. Charlene should have set specific goals such as these:

- "I will present four points each with supporting material."
- "I will prioritize my points so that if we run out of time, the most important ones will be covered."
- "I will show how our department is in genuine need of extra funds."
- "I will demonstrate how, with the increased funds, our department will be able to exceed its goals for next year and help the company achieve other goals."

By setting specific and high goals, Charlene would have been in a better position for handling such a difficult situation.

Nevertheless, sometimes flexible goals are a better alternative. The business and professional world is often uncertain, and setting highly specific goals may

17. E. A. Locke, D. Chah, S. Harrison, and N. Lustgarten, "Separating the Effects of Goal Specificity from Goal Level," *Organizational Behavior and Human Decision Making* 43 (1989), 270–287.

PRACTICING BUSINESS COMMUNICATION

FedEx Corporation

FedEx pioneered fast-track delivery of express packages in the mid-1970s. Founder, chairman, and chief executive officer Fred Smith sees communication competence as the foundation of his business, which is the world's largest express transportation company, handling roughly 2 million packages each day. At FedEx, communication is viewed as the single most important process managers use to accomplish their goals, and more than 200,000 FedEx employees worldwide subscribe to Smith's corporate philosophy of People—Service—Profit, or PSP.

STRATEGIC COMMUNICATION IN ACTION

The PSP credo is based on a simple, powerful idea: if the company treats employees with dignity and respect, they in turn will provide excellent service. Excellent service leads to satisfied customers, who will repeatedly choose FedEx delivery. Repeat business increases company revenues and helps to keep FedEx profitable. As a result, employees gain better benefits, ranging from profit sharing to a family-life resource and referral service.

Does PSP work? The U.S. Department of Commerce thinks so. FedEx was the first service company awarded the prestigious Malcolm Baldrige National Quality Award, in the early 1990s. But for PSP to thrive, both upward and downward lines of communication in the organizational structure at FedEx must remain open and direct.

The five components of Managerial Communication Competence (MCC), a program created by top management and employee communications personnel at FedEx, concentrate on developing the company's 7,000 supervisory managers' communication skills. By turning these employee leaders into effective communicators, FedEx enhances company-wide communication. These are the MCC components:

Awareness The goal for FedEx managers is to understand what the company expects from them as communicators. Every manager attends the FedEx Leadership Institute in Memphis, Tennessee, for management training in such areas as conveying job responsibilities to employees, listening and offering feedback on employees' needs and concerns and on their performance, and ensuring open information flow between higher-level managers and front-line workers.

Managers learn to communicate the "big picture" to their work groups—what and how FedEx is doing company-wide and how the work group's activities relate and contribute to overall company goals. Equally important, FedEx managers learn to communicate individual work-group goals, roles, and information about project progress.

Assessment In this diagnostic component of MCC, employees evaluate their managers' communication skills. Every spring FedEx conducts a company-wide survey, the SFA (for *S*urvey, *F*eedback, *A*ction), to gather employee feedback about individual managers and working conditions.

About one-third of the survey questions provide a "leadership index," which measures employees' perceptions of their managers' leadership skills. Most of the remaining survey questions evaluate managers' communication skills.

SFA is the main mechanism for improving working conditions throughout the company and for strengthening employee relations. This formal process is the main upward

lead you to an inflexible position or give you an unfavorable reputation as a rigid or difficult person. Communicators must plan for some flexibility when the environment is uncertain so that they have some room to maneuver. In general, however, set goals in as many instances as possible, even if the goals have to be less specific than you would like.

The Goal-Setting Process

Once you have recognized its importance, goal setting in business communication is not much different from setting goals for other aspects of performance. You can communication link between employees and management. Communication initiated by SFA builds trust and confidence between managers and employees.

Development and Training The employee communication department provides training workshops on such topics as communication skills and group dynamics, which are tailored to address the needs of particular groups of managers. As a back-up to their training, all managers also receive a *Manager's Guide,* which features an entire chapter on communication and has sections covering management theory and leadership theory.

Support Corporate policy reinforces managers' communication efforts, for example, by altering employee timecards to allow credit for official work-group meetings on company time.

Measurement and Reward Each manager receives a communication profile generated from employee SFA surveys during MCC's assessment phase. Top management uses annual SFA survey results to gather feedback from employees on the work environment and to review and, when needed, to change corporate policy. Supervisory managers use the information in their own profiles to work on skills that need improvement.

COMMUNICATION AND CORPORATE CULTURE

The effectiveness of FedEx's MCC program is apparent in the company's use of internal media ranging from weekly newsletters to *Worldwide UpDate* (the company magazine) to the FedEx television network. These media keep employees up-to-date on issues, policy changes, company activities, and benefit plans.

Managers act as opinion leaders, opening dialogues with employees, keeping communication lines between employees and upper management open, and generally helping their employees perform their jobs better. At FedEx communication has gained a cultural dimension that helps managers develop as aware, able, face-to-face communicators who reinforce the company's commitment to maintaining satisfied employees, satisfied customers, and financial corporate health: People—Service—Profit.

QUESTIONS FOR CRITICAL THINKING

1. What is "direct" communication, and how does FedEx demonstrate its commitment to this concept?
2. Why do you think FedEx focuses on the communication competence of its managers?
3. FedEx depends on managers to relay information upward and downward in its organizational structure. What does this arrangement tell you about its organizational culture?
4. What are the advantages of the *S*urvey, *F*eedback, *A*ction (SFA) survey?
5. What leadership/management style do you think works best at FedEx?

You can visit FedEx on-line at www.FEDEX.com
Reprinted by permission of FedEx.

achieve effective goal setting by using the following six steps, which are also shown in Figure 2.3:[18]

Step 1: **Identify the Problem.** Specify as exactly as possible what is to be accomplished from the communication event: the job, assignment, or responsibility to be completed. Whether you are giving a persuasive presentation, being interviewed for employment, or just talking with your boss, specific goals ensure that your performance will be effective.

18. E.A. Locke, K. N. Shaw, L. M. Saari, and G. P. Latham, "Goal Setting and Task Performance: 1969–1980," *Psychological Bulletin* 90 (1981), 125–152.

FIGURE 2.3

Goal-Setting Process
Effective goal setting is achieved by using these six steps.

Based on Locke et al., "Goal Setting and Task Performance: 1969–1980." *Psychological Bulletin* (90), 1981; pp. 125–152. Copyright © 1981 by The American Psychological Association. Adapted by permission.

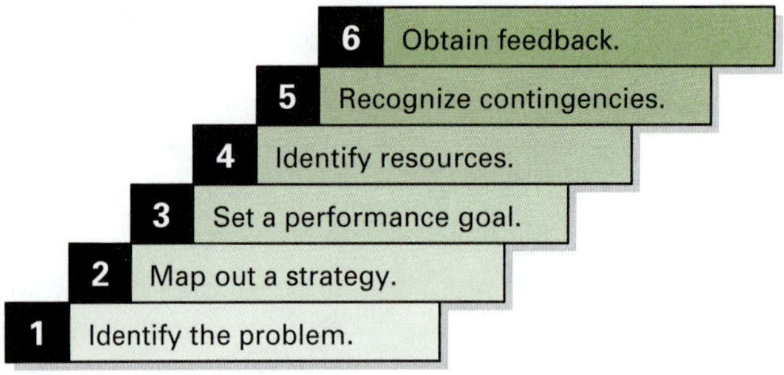

Step 2: **Map Out a Strategy.** Determine the level of performance necessary to achieve the desired goal, and create an evaluation measure that will tell you if you have reached that level. This measure may be as simple as an informal checklist that points out specific items necessary for success, or it may be a complex and sophisticated formal evaluation form that measures your level of performance in a variety of categories.

Step 3: **Set a Performance Goal.** High goals are preferable to low goals because low goals may keep you from realizing your full communication potential. But in setting your goals, you must realize your limitations. You may not be able to "give the best public speech in the world," so stating that as a goal is not productive. But it is a good idea to push yourself beyond what you honestly feel would be your best performance. You will reach that goal more often than you think!

Step 4: **Identify the Resources Necessary to Achieve the Goal.** Time, equipment, money, favors, encouragement, and moral support are just a few of the resources you may need to achieve your goals. Anticipating your resource needs will strengthen the plans and actions you take later, and planning how you will use resources can make your goals more real and concrete.

Step 5: **Recognize Contingencies That May Arise.** Contingencies are events, obstacles, or circumstances that may prevent you from reaching your goal. If you keep in mind the adage "If communication can fail, it will," you will anticipate potential problems such as equipment failure (for example, overhead and slide projector failures), hostile people, cramped spaces, time constraints, and even illness.

Step 6: **Obtain Feedback.** Recall from Chapter 1 that feedback clarifies messages and verifies shared meaning. Feedback also makes goal setting more effective because it indicates when and where you may need to adjust your direction or methods so that you are achieving your best. Feedback can also provide encouragement. If you receive feedback messages that support your goals and your progress toward them, you are more likely to reach those goals and set higher ones in the future.[19]

19. Locke et al., "Separating the Effects of Goal Specificity"; Locke et al., "Goal Setting and Task Performance."

What Would You Do?

Think of a situation where you had to persuade someone—perhaps getting a friend to go to a particular concert you want to see or convincing your professor to grant you an extension on your paper. How would the way you try to persuade your friend differ from the way you try to persuade your professor? Would you treat the two situations the same?

The following example illustrates the goal-setting process:

> Kevin Burd was elected chairperson of the program committee of the chapter of the Preprofessionals Club at the local junior college. His responsibility was lining up speakers for each month's meeting. He immediately identified his duties as getting speakers committed well in advance of the meeting (Step 1). He knew that he had to contact a variety of people to suit the varied interests of the club membership, that the speakers had to be well respected in their fields, and that they had to be willing to participate on an assigned date (Step 2). He set the following as performance goals (Step 3): speakers are to be known to the membership, and they must have ten years' relevant experience in their field, possess effective speaking skills, and be willing to answer questions and socialize with the members after the presentation. Kevin then developed a game plan for attracting the best speakers (Step 4).
>
> First, he listed all the people he personally knew who fit his speaker profile. Next, for names of qualified speakers, he contacted the local chamber of commerce, the speaker's bureau on campus, all the professional associations in town, and his relatives who were businesspeople in the community. Then he submitted the names to other committee members for their advice and feedback. Finally, he contracted with the campus media center to provide all the visual aids needed by the speakers.
>
> Kevin then listed all the things he thought might go wrong (Step 5). He made sure that he called the speakers one week before and then one day before the presentation to ensure that they were still committed. He made sure to contact in advance the proper person regarding audiovisual support and double-checked that all equipment was in working order on the day of the presentation. He also arrived early for each presentation to ensure that the room temperature was appropriate, that the refreshments had arrived, that the chairs were set up, and that ample lighting was available.
>
> Finally, Kevin devised an evaluation sheet that he submitted to each club member after the speaker left to determine how he or she felt about the speaker, topic, visual aids, and other details that were relevant to his job as program chair (Step 6). In this way, he was able to gauge his performance through feedback and improve on each month's meeting.

The Benefits of Goal Setting

The primary benefit of effective goal setting is higher performance level, but that is not the only benefit.[20] Goals help to direct attention and action during communication because they give you a target to shoot for. During communication you

20. Ibid.

can become easily confused or distracted if you do not have a specific goal toward which to direct yourself.

Goals are useful in mobilizing the effort you need to perform at peak levels. Setting goals makes you aware of the mental, emotional, and physical energy you will need for the communication task and encourages you to conserve and mobilize energy carefully.

Goals can help you persist in your efforts over time. Lacking desirable goals, you may feel the temptation to reduce your effort when you meet with an obstacle or other interference, and you may be easily distracted from your mission. Goals hold you to specific results within specific time periods. Goals also aid you in developing relevant and innovative strategies. When you have set important goals, you will be surprised at how ingenious and innovative you can be in devising communication strategies to reach those goals.

COMMUNICATION COMPETENCE

Communication competence, the third component of our model, is the ability to communicate both *appropriately* and *effectively* with other people. Communication strategies can be effective without being appropriate. Consider the following example:

> Trudy Berstein knew months in advance that her budget would be exhausted before the end of the fiscal year. She thought that if she asked the district manager, Joe Chang, for more money ahead of time, he would simply ask her to wait until she had run out of money. So she waited, calling Joe on the phone just before the end of the year with the message that she needed him to transfer funds

STRATEGIC SKILLS

Relaying Competent Messages

Follow these general suggestions to ensure that your messages are competent:

1. **Be Specific.** Include as many details and definite facts as necessary to prevent vagueness.
2. **Be Accurate.** Ensure that what you are communicating is as authentic and reliable as possible.
3. **Be Honest.** Don't give in to the temptation to use data, facts, and relationships in ways that are less than forthright just to strengthen your case.
4. **Be Logical.** Keep in mind that messages are most easily understood when they follow a logical, rational, and sequential path that others can readily follow.
5. **Be Complete.** Check your potential message to ensure that you have provided all the information the receiver requires.
6. **Be Succinct.** While being complete, be as brief or concise as possible. No one in the professional world has time for unnecessarily long messages.
7. **Include Time Frames.** All receivers need to know the time frames you have in mind for acting on your message. When you need action, give a specific indication in your message.
8. **Be Relevant.** Make sure that the only people getting your message are those who need or want it. Sending messages to just anyone wastes your time and theirs.
9. **Be Timely.** Be sure to send messages in a timely fashion. Messages should not arrive too early or too late.
10. **Ask for Feedback.** Ask receivers for feedback to elicit information about their feelings and reactions to your message.

to meet her budget obligations. Not happy with the request because he was virtually out of money himself, Joe told Trudy that he would go along with her request this time, but he stressed that he did not appreciate her phoning him at the last minute: "Next time, put your request in writing, well in advance of the end of the budget year!"

Trudy's communication may have been effective because she accomplished her goal, but it was inappropriate. Trudy did not handle the situation properly and may have hurt her chances to gain Joe's cooperation in the future. To ensure effective and appropriate communication, you must consider four factors: messages, internal communication, external communication, and channels.

Messages

As you learned in Chapter 1, **messages** are the ideas you wish to communicate. Whether instructive, informative, persuasive, humorous, complimentary, or critical, a message must be effective and appropriate to be competent. You will not be able to achieve communication competence if your message does not meet that standard.

Internal Communication

Messages that are sent and received within the organizational boundaries of the company are called **internal communication.** Formal types of internal communication include policy statements from the president, notices of changes in operating

Internal communication takes many forms. Upward, downward, and horizontal communication can take place in groups, teams, and informal meetings. In this photo, task force members from various parts of the organization discuss a project for costs reductions. (© Jose Luis Pelaez, Inc./ Corbis)

procedures, and instructions from superiors. Less formal types include conversations in the hallway and phone calls at home. The box on p. 34 discusses how employees can communicate electronically through the company's intranet. Of course, not every organization communicates in the same way. Think of the communication patterns that you have encountered in your work or school experience. Were they formal or informal?

Messages can be exchanged in three directions: downward, upward, and horizontally. In tall organizations, communication tends to be from the top down, and upward communication is likely to take weeks or months to reach the top of the hierarchy. In flat organizations, communication tends to be horizontal. Of course, communication in all three directions occurs in both tall and flat organizations. There are specific reasons for communicating in each direction, and how you use these strategies depends on your needs.

Downward Communication **Downward communication** consists of messages from superiors to subordinates. Examine the following five types of downward communication in organizations:[21]

1. **Job Instructions:** Messages that specify how to conduct tasks on the job: "Always submit budget requests two months in advance."
2. **Job Rationale:** Messages that explain why tasks must be performed and how these tasks relate to other activities of the organization: "We require advance notice so that we can plan ahead."
3. **Procedures and Practices:** Messages that inform organizational members about responsibilities, obligations, and privileges of the organization: "According to the procedures manual, we follow affirmative action guidelines to the letter."
4. **Feedback:** Messages that inform employees of their performance in the organization: "I am happy to note that your last project was a real success."
5. **Indoctrination of Goals:** Messages that teach employees the mission, goals, and objectives of the organization: "As you can see from our shared-values list, we feel that customer service is our number-one job."

Though very common and often necessary to ensure that employees can do their jobs, downward communication generates its share of trouble. One problem results from the chain of command. Typically, a message originates near or at the top of an organization (for example, in the president's office) and is sent down the chain person by person. This *serial communication* negatively affects the accuracy of the message.

Think of the "gossip" game, in which one person whispers a message to another, who in turn whispers it to the next person. By the time the message reaches the last person in the chain, it is usually quite different from the original message. The same effect can occur in a message that must travel down a long chain of command, especially if the message is circulated through more than one channel. Figure 2.4 shows the percentage of information lost in each transfer.

When practicing downward communication, imagine yourself as the receiver. Does the message make sense to you? Is it effective without being disrespectful? Asking these questions of all your messages can help prevent miscommunication.

21. D. Katz and R. Kahn, *The Social Psychology of Organizations* (New York: Wiley, 1966).

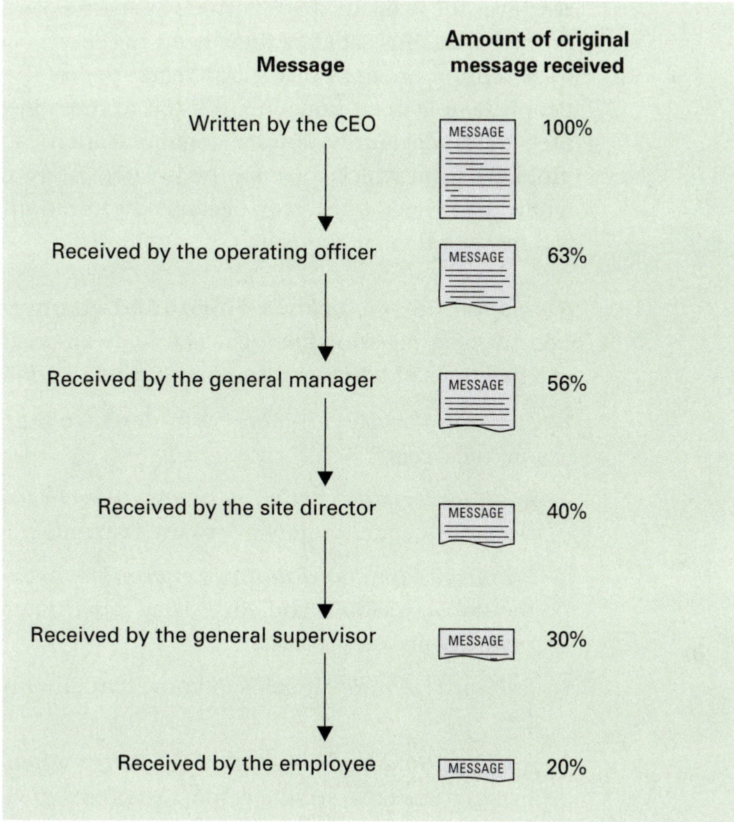

FIGURE 2.4

Effect of Serial Communication

Information is lost as a message travels down the organizational chain of command.

A carefully considered message can forestall many of the most common communication failures.

Upward Communication **Upward communication** consists of messages from subordinates to superiors. Four types of upward communication follow:

1. *Reflects employee performance and job-related problems:* "George, we continue to have trouble getting the proper notice for shipping dates."
2. *Reveals information about fellow employees:* "Freda and Elizabeth are unable to participate in the fundraising campaign."
3. *Communicates attitudes and understanding about organizational practices and policies:* "It is becoming obvious that most line employees do not appreciate the new work schedule."
4. *Reports on the activities and tasks associated with goal accomplishment:* "I am glad to report that the McKenrick project is now finished."

Upward communication offers several advantages.[22] It shows superiors whether subordinates are accepting their ideas, plans, and policies. Upward communication

22. J. Koehler and G. Huber, "Effects of Upward Communication on Managerial Decision Making" (paper presented at the annual meeting of the International Communication Association, New Orleans, 1974).

also gives subordinates an opportunity to participate actively in the decision-making process and thus satisfies their need to feel valued. Talking to superiors can release tension or stress that subordinates feel as they cope with their jobs. Often, people simply need someone to listen to them in order to feel good about what they are doing. Finally, upward communication can alert superiors to impending problems from which they may be isolated. Be aware, however, that upward communication tends to be rosy because organization members rarely want to send bad news to their supervisors.

Horizontal Communication **Horizontal communication** consists of messages exchanged at the same hierarchical level in an organization. Take a look at the several functions of horizontal communication that follow:[23]

1. *Facilitates problem solving:* "Why don't we get together over lunch to hammer out the details?"
2. *Allows information sharing across different work groups:* "Send that information over computer network to the Dayton office."
3. *Promotes task coordination between departments or teams:* "I am glad that the public relations and advertising departments are exchanging information on the Donavon project."
4. *Enhances morale:* "It helps to know that other units experience similar frustration."
5. *Affords a means for resolving conflicts:* "When we are able to get together, it makes it easier to see the respective points of view."

The frequency and effectiveness of horizontal communication depend on the structure of the organization. Some organizations, particularly tall ones or those in traditionally conservative fields such as banking, may rely primarily on vertical (especially downward) communication. Flat organizations frequently use horizontal communication because it is appropriate to their structures. Companies in highly innovative or creative fields—for example, software development companies or toy manufacturers—use horizontal communication because they need flexibility.

Despite its benefits, horizontal communication does have drawbacks. Consider the following three reasons for these problems:

1. *Territoriality:* Individuals or departments may feel that communicating with others will reveal ideas and plans prematurely and thus reduce their overall impact. In other cases, jealousy or envy may prevent effective horizontal communication.
2. *Specialization:* As members of departments work together on projects, they develop certain frames of reference, mind-sets, and jargon specific to their responsibilities. Lacking this knowledge, people outside the departments (even if they are at the same level in the organization) have a difficult time understanding or appreciating such specialized communication.
3. *Lack of Motivation:* Some employees may not understand the importance of horizontal communication and simply avoid it because it is too much trouble.

23. T. Daniels and B. Spiker, *Perspectives on Organizational Communication* (Dubuque, Iowa: Brown, 1987).

Attitudes such as "If you want something done right, do it yourself" and "Why cooperate with the other departments if they get all the credit?" demonstrate cynicism about horizontal communication.

Another way that companies are encouraging horizontal communication is through *work teams*. Management will take employees from different work areas and ask them to solve problems that affect the entire organization. Usually the team will manage itself without much oversight from upper management. Although each team decides its own decision-making rules and operating procedures, these small entrepreneurial units work best in an informal structure where horizontal communication is free-flowing and unrestricted. Companies such as Colgate-Palmolive, Hallmark Cards, and Johnson & Johnson are jumping on the "team approach" bandwagon in an effort to involve more workers in decisions that affect them. The Boeing Company, for example, designed work teams made up of engineers, pilots, mechanics, marketing specialists, and a customer (United Airlines) for developing the Boeing 777.[24]

Teams perform well for the following reasons. (1) The synergy created by bringing together complementary skills and experiences exceeds what any individual on the team can provide; (2) teams establish communication methods to support problem solving and provide initiative by jointly developing goals and methods; (3) teams provide a social communication dimension that enhances economic and administrative aspects of work; and (4) teams have more fun.[25] You will learn more about groups and teams in Chapters 10 and 11.

Informal Networks Informal networks frequently open up outside of official paths of communication. Often called the grapevine, informal networks are a substitute for formal downward, upward, or horizontal communication. Messages exchanged in the hallway, in the coffee room, at parties, or in restaurants are examples of informal communication. Informal networks develop more rapidly in flat organizations that emphasize team building than in formal, tall organizations. Figure 2.5 shows the path of informal communication along a grapevine.

Much of the research in the area suggests the following:[26]

- The grapevine is fast.
- The grapevine is generally accurate.
- The grapevine carries much information.
- The grapevine gives an indication of employee attitudes and sentiment.
- The grapevine is a common channel for rumors.
- The grapevine travels by clusters.

Experts sometimes argue that informal communication occurs because there are not enough opportunities for formal communication. Although some people believe that informal communication must be minimized or controlled, the grapevine is generally highly effective, especially if formal paths of communication are overburdened. For example, one manager in a paper-manufacturing firm became so frustrated with the delay in getting information to his fellow workers via formal paths that he used Friday afternoon socials to provide them with the needed information.

24. J. Main, "Betting on the 21st Century Jet," *Fortune*, April 20, 1992, pp. 102–117.
25. J. R. Katzenbach and D. K. Smith, *The Wisdom of Teams* (Boston: Harvard Business School Press, 1993).
26. G. Goldhaber, *Organizational Communication* (Dubuque, Iowa: Brown, 1990).

FIGURE 2.5

Path of Information Through the Grapevine

Communication in the grapevine tends to be informal yet efficient, diffuse yet effective.

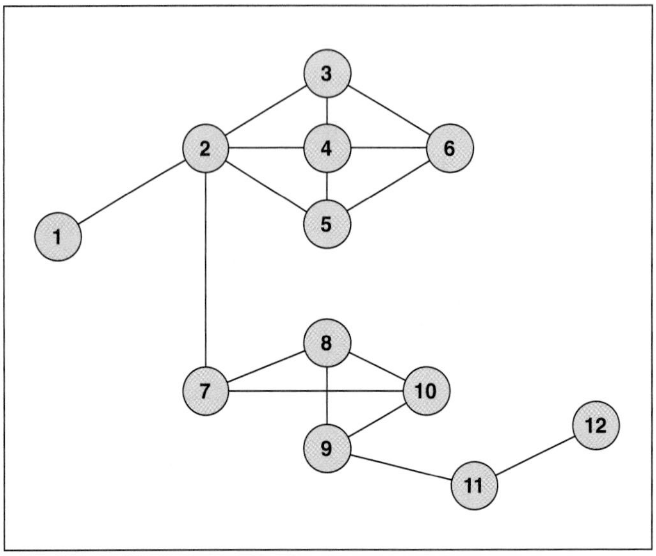

External Communication

Messages that are exchanged between the organization and its environment are called **external communication.** Although many of the messages that are sent to, and received from, the environment are perfunctory—for example, newsletters, annual reports, advertising, goodwill speeches, or notices of corporate sponsorship of nonprofit events—many of these messages are exchanged in an effort to improve communication. They can also enable workers to understand how the environment affects the internal efficiency of the organization.

An excellent method of learning about the external environment is through the Internet. Literally thousands of businesses now advertise their services and products on Web pages, and within these Internet sites you can learn about what organizations are doing. Browsing these resources can provide useful information about customers, competitors, and current conditions. Search engines—such as google.com, yahoo.com, or excite.com—will direct you to places on the Internet that interest you. One such place is brint.com, a search engine or index of Web sites that are specific to business. This resource can help you find the information you need when you type in keywords such as "economic trends," "profitable companies," or "business technology" as examples.

Listening carefully to customers' needs, being receptive to new ideas or to information from competitors, learning new techniques from new employees, employing expert consultants, and searching the Internet are some of the ways that organizations can "listen" to their environments in order to reduce uncertainty. To a large extent such activity is compatible with our discussion of situational knowledge: as you gain additional information about the environment, you build on your knowledge of the overall situation.

Channels

Choosing the appropriate channel for your messages is critical to communication competence. **Channels** are the media that carry messages to receivers. Channels include conversations, speeches, interviews, memos, letters, phone calls, and computer

FIGURE 2.6

Range of Channel Richness

Wide variations exist in channel richness. To identify the most appropriate channel, the sender considers the goal of the message and characteristics of the intended receiver. Where do you think the Web might fall on this chart?

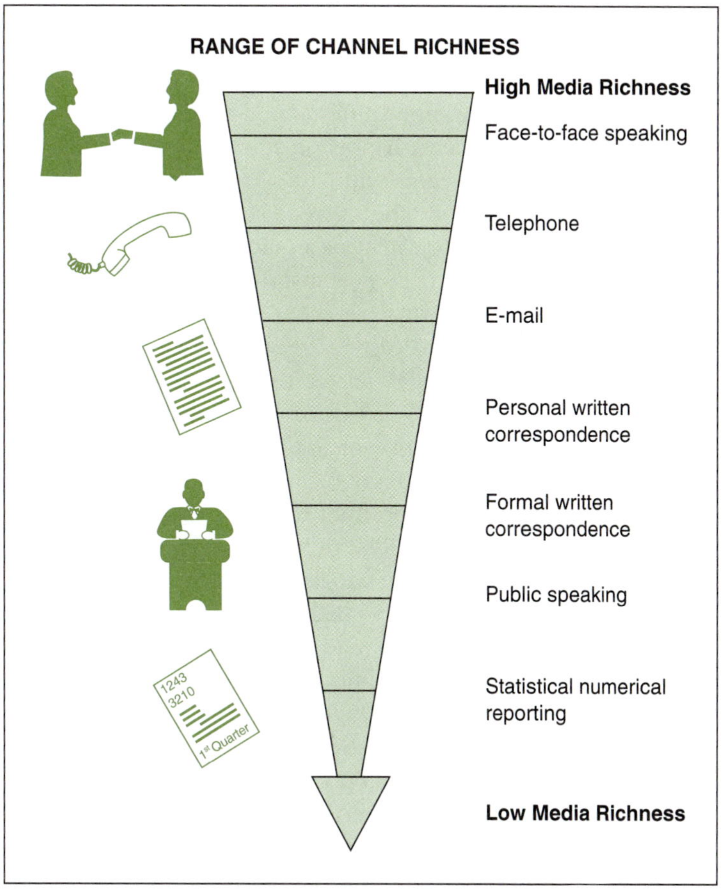

and satellite networks. A channel's characteristics, especially its richness, determine its usefulness.

Channel Richness **Channel richness** is the ability of a communication channel (such as a telephone call) to handle information or convey the meaning contained in a message.[27] Some channels are best for certain types of messages, whereas other channels may be inappropriate for those same messages. Whether a channel is high or low in richness depends on four conditions: (1) the capacity for obtaining immediate feedback from the receiver; (2) the ability to transmit multiple communication cues such as facial expressions, body language, appearance, and dress; (3) the shaping or tailoring of messages for the specific situation; (4) language variety, or the ability to use a wide range of word choices.

If you think about those criteria, it becomes clear that the richest channels are face-to-face meetings with few language restrictions. The least rich channels are undirected written memos (such as flyers addressed to "Occupant"). Figure 2.6

27. R. L. Daft and R. H. Lengel, "Organizational Information Requirements, Media Richness, and Structural Design," *Management Science* 32 (1986), 554–571; R. L. Daft and G. P. Huber, "How Organizations Learn: A Communication Framework," *Research in the Sociology of Organizations* 5 (1987), 1–36; G. P. Huber and R. L. Daft, "The Information Environments of Organizations," in F. Jablin, L. Putnam, K. Roberts, and L. Porter (eds.), *Handbook of Organizational Communication* (Newbury Park, Calif.: Sage, 1987), pp. 130–164.

illustrates the range of channel richness. As you move down from the top of the figure, where the richest channel is located, each successive channel is less able to satisfy the criteria we just listed.

Organizations differ about which channels are most effective for sending messages. In "memo happy" organizations, communication is defined as an $8\frac{1}{2}$-by-11-inch page that begins with "To." Other organizations emphasize videos that inform employees about the current state of affairs. The increasing use of e-mail demonstrates its popularity as a quick and moderately rich channel. In fact, e-mail and intranets have become substitutes for other channels of communication.

Selecting the Proper Channel Competent communication involves choosing the appropriate channel for the message. Think about the effort you have put into the message so far—setting a goal, collecting situational knowledge, and formulating an effective message. Your work will be wasted if you send the message through an ineffective channel—for example, if you send an important report on a competitor's product through interoffice mail rather than hand-delivering it to your supervisor. Research has shown that managers prefer the richest types of media or channel: face-to-face meetings and telephone calls.[28] Increasingly, however, they are choosing e-mail as a channel for conducting business because using e-mail at home or on the road can be convenient and time-saving.

The rule of thumb is that rich channels are best when messages are designed for specific people, when time is important, when immediate feedback is necessary, when the situation is stressful, when the message is vague or difficult to understand, and when personal information is to be conveyed. Less rich channels are most useful for communicating routine information, for giving orders or conveying policy, for communicating to large numbers of people at once, and when immediate feedback is unnecessary or formal communication is appropriate (such as public presentations at an awards banquet).[29]

Choosing the proper channel for communication is not easy, but consideration of these factors can help you evaluate your options:[30]

- **Speed:** Oral and electronic channels provide the fastest means of communicating.
- **Accuracy:** When accuracy is at a premium, written and, to a lesser extent, electronic means are the preferred channels.
- **Feedback:** Feedback can be obtained from any of the three channels. Oral communication, especially when conducted face-to-face, provides a great deal of immediate feedback, not only about the content of the message but also—from nonverbal behavior—about the state of mind of the communicator. Written channels are less likely to encourage spontaneous feedback. Even e-mail may not yield an immediate response.
- **Selectivity:** Some messages are not appropriate for or effective with everyone in an organization or even in a work group. Highly sensitive or confidential

28. Daft and Lengel, "Organizational Information Requirements."
29. Daft and Huber, "How Organizations Learn."
30. Adapted from D. A. Level and W. P. Galle, *Business Communication: Theory and Practice* (Dallas: Business Publications, 1980); A. J. Melcher and R. Beller, "Toward a Theory of Organization Communication: Considerations in Channel Selection," *Academy of Management Journal* 10 (1967), 39–52.

messages may need to be directed to only some people. Therefore, oral communication channels are often used for sensitive messages, although private memos may be used as well.

- **Appropriateness:** Some communication channels are not appropriate for some messages. Communicating company-wide policy changes through an oral channel exclusively is not appropriate, nor is communicating the termination of an employee on a bulletin board. Some issues are sticky and require a special channel.
- **Cost:** A number of cost issues may affect the selection of a communication channel. While it may be ideally effective to have a telephone conversation with someone, if that person is on another continent, the cost may be prohibitive. Low cost is one reason companies encourage employees to use e-mail. The ability to attach documents, photos, and other files to e-mail messages has greatly reduced the need for surface or interoffice mail. Fax machines, once the cutting edge in electronic communication, are now used primarily to fill in gaps, as when a document requires a signature or isn't available in electronic format. Employee expenses must also be kept in mind and that includes *time*. It could take someone an hour to craft a well-written memo. If the telephone were used instead, forty-five minutes of company time could be saved.
- **Accountability:** Accountability is the responsibility that a receiver has for responding to a message—not only providing feedback to the sender but also responding to the instruction, information, directive, request, or other purpose of the message. Message senders also have accountability for what they communicate. Consider, for example, the recent lawsuit against stockbrokers who made fraudulent buy/sell recommendations to clients over the Internet. Written channels are the most obvious form of message accountability since there is some form of documentation involved such as a memo, letter, or e-mail post.
- **Acceptability:** Some forms of communication are more acceptable to some people than to others. Some people despise memos; others believe oral channels are too informal. If you are concerned about the impact of your message, you should try to choose a communication channel that your receiver will find acceptable.

Surveys of businesspeople suggest that these are the most effective modes of communication (in descending order):[31] (1) presenting information through both oral and written channels, (2) presenting information to a group orally, (3) presenting information to each member of a group in written form, (4) posting information on a bulletin board, (5) making no presentation of information in either oral or written form but instead allowing informal channels to pick up the slack. Because humans tend to be attracted to multimedia stimuli, it stands to reason that information presented through oral and written channels will be most effective. Consider the following example:

> A small southwestern bank was acquired by a large northeastern bank. The president of the small bank sent a memo to the vice presidents informing them of a meeting to provide the details of the takeover. News of the takeover spread rapidly

31. P. Pace, *Organizational Communication: Foundations for Human Resource Development* (Englewood Cliffs, N.J.: Prentice Hall, 1983).

through the grapevine. Some key employees changed jobs, morale was low, and customers began to complain about ineffective treatment by bank employees. Many customers and employees changed banks after news of the takeover became generally known.

This outcome indicates that the channel to convey sensitive and confidential material needs to be carefully chosen.

Where Do You Stand?

How do you use communication media? On a piece of paper, write down your answers for the following questions. Are there some channels that you use more often? Are you a letter writer? A phone addict? An e-mailer? An instant-message user? Or is face-to-face the only way you like to communicate? For which situations do you prefer to use one channel over another? What do your answers say about your media preferences? What do your media preferences say about you?

ANXIETY MANAGEMENT

For our purposes in this book, **anxiety management** is the ability to control nervousness, fears, stress, and worries associated with a communication event. Some people are most anxious prior to the act of communicating. Some are most anxious while they are communicating. Others worry and fret about their communication performance after it is over. In any case, one thing is certain: each person handles the anxiety associated with communication episodes differently.

Because stress or anxiety can prevent you from doing your best, the ability to manage communication anxiety is an essential ingredient of an effective communication strategy. Such management requires knowing the causes and effects of your anxiety and knowing how to treat it.

Causes of Communication Anxiety

For many years, researchers have tried to identify the causes of communication anxiety. The best conclusion that can be drawn from their studies is that multiple factors are responsible for the fears and worries that people have about communicating. Common factors include the following:[32]

- **Novelty:** People are especially anxious in new communication situations.
- **Formality:** Communication situations that require prescribed actions and behaviors and allow little deviation from those norms frequently cause anxiety.
- **Subordinate Status:** Being in a subordinate position often causes people to feel intimidated and ill at ease.

32. A. H. Buss, *Self-Consciousness and Social Anxiety* (San Francisco: Freeman, 1980); J. Daly and J. L. Hailey, "Putting the Situation into Writing Research: Situational Parameters of Writing Apprehension as Disposition and State," in R. E. Beach and L. Bidwell (eds.), *New Directions in Composition Research* (New York: Guilford, 1983).

- **Conspicuousness:** Communication situations that put people at the center of others' attention (such as public speaking) can be uncomfortable.
- **Large groups:** Some people, while comfortable in small groups, struggle when speaking in front of large groups.
- **Lack of Skill:** A communicator who knows that he or she does not have the communication skills necessary to be effective in some situations is likely to feel anxious.
- **Past Experiences:** Failure in certain communication situations (such as job interviews) may cause anxiety about future encounters.
- **Evaluation:** Knowing that communication skills are being assessed can cause anxiety, especially if there is a lot at stake.

Another cause of anxiety stems from the channel preference of the sender. Sometimes communicators experience nervousness when using a highly rich channel. For example, someone delivering bad news may experience anxiety because of the likely uncomfortableness of a face-to-face encounter and so may try to reduce the anxiety by choosing a less rich channel, such as a memo.

Because the choice of a channel can create problems for both the sender and the receiver, anxiety management is a crucial component of strategic communication. Knowing the causes of communication anxiety is a first step toward managing the stress and fears associated with communication. Take out a piece of paper and rank-order the causes of communication anxiety that most affect you. Think about them as we continue our discussion.

Effects of Communication Anxiety

Communication anxiety takes a toll on the occupational, professional, and vocational interests of some individuals. Research has demonstrated a number of negative effects resulting from the uncontrolled anxiety associated with communication.[33] People who are afraid to communicate may be viewed negatively by others. Coworkers and bosses will see those who refuse to communicate as uncooperative and may not trust them with important tasks. In others cases, communication anxiety may cause people to pause, stutter, fail to maintain eye contact, and appear incompetent. People who suffer from a high degree of communication anxiety may be less assertive and more shy than people who do not experience such anxiety.

These negative perceptions result in many unfavorable outcomes for anxious communicators. They have fewer leadership opportunities, they are less likely to be chosen for leadership positions, and they take less initiative in attempting to gain leadership roles. Anxious communicators are also perceived as less attractive, for communication skills are considered socially important in occupational settings. Because of these factors, anxious communicators are granted fewer job interviews, receive lower pay and fewer promotions, enjoy less job satisfaction, and do not retain their jobs as long as communicators who are less anxious do. It is no wonder that people who experience high degrees of communication anxiety seek out occupations with relatively low communication demands (accountants, forest rangers, telecommuters, computer programmers, construction workers).

33. V. P. Richmond and J. C. McCroskey, *Communication: Apprehension, Avoidance, and Effectiveness* (Scottsdale, Ariz.: Gorusch, Scarisbrick, 1985).

STRATEGIC SKILLS

Identifying Stressful Situations

On a scale of 1 to 10 (with 10 being the highest level of stress and 1 being the lowest), rate your degree of stress for the following communication situations.

1. ——— Interviewing for a job
2. ——— Leading a group
3. ——— Arguing with your boss
4. ——— Asking friends for a charitable donation
5. ——— Disagreeing with a coworker
6. ——— Speaking up in a hostile group
7. ——— Telling jokes or funny stories at a bull session
8. ——— Making an excuse for a mistake
9. ——— Giving a media interview
10. ——— Challenging someone's point of view
11. ——— Presenting a report to your boss's boss
12. ——— Giving a brief report to coworkers
13. ——— Conversing with a new acquaintance
14. ——— Persuading a coworker
15. ——— Giving a formal presentation to strangers
16. ——— Answering questions
17. ——— Refusing to grant a request
18. ——— Explaining your actions
19. ——— Demonstrating leadership skills
20. ——— Denying responsibility for a misunderstanding

Managing Communication Anxiety

You may think that we have painted a very dreary picture for those who experience some degree of communication anxiety. Actually, most people are anxious in at least some situations. As you look back at the causes of communication anxiety, you may feel that only one or two of them apply to you, or you may identify with many of them. Controlling anxiety requires understanding where you stand and how you feel about the stressfulness of a communication situation. When you listed the causes of anxiety, you learned what may be producing nervousness in certain situations. Another way of identifying anxiety is by recognizing which specific communication situations are most stressful for you.

As you look over your ratings, you will probably notice that some situations elicit a greater degree of stress than do others. It is perfectly natural to be "situationally" anxious. In certain circumstances, each of us has to work especially hard to be an effective communicator. You can do so by learning to focus your nervous energy and thereby maximize your effectiveness. Keep your responses to this self-check in mind as we discuss communication anxiety in later chapters, where we will suggest methods to assess and control it in interviews, meetings, presentations, and other business contexts.

STRATEGIC SCENARIO WRAP-UP

Based on what you read in this chapter, how would you advise Sam to proceed with the responsibility that was given to him by his bosses? To what extent would goal setting be helpful as Sam crafts messages about the layoff? What are some of the ethics issues involved with how Sam is to carry out his task? What are some of the more important aspects of the situation that Sam must know about before developing his messages and choosing the channels for carrying them? Do you think Sam has any anxiety about his new task? What could he do to reduce his level of anxiety in this situation?

SUMMARY

- The model of strategic communication presents a practical perspective on communicating in organizations. It also offers tools for dealing with the effects on business of globalization and the dependence on information.
- Situational knowledge, the first element, allows for greater flexibility in assessing, selecting, and evaluating the messages that are exchanged within the organization and with the external environment. Such knowledge also reduces uncertainty and helps the communicator to know when strategic ambiguity is appropriate.
- Goal setting, the second element of the model, enables you to plan the most effective campaign or tactics.
- Communication competence, the third aspect, enhances your ability to achieve goals in the context of differing communication networks, allowing greater opportunity for improved productivity.
- Anxiety management, the fourth element, focuses on maintaining the elements of organizational communication that are essential for establishing and maintaining the highest level of performance.

KEY TERMS

Values: the principles and ideas that people or organizations strongly believe in and consider important

Situational knowledge: the information or facts you use in devising an effective communication strategy

Organizational structure: the actual environment where the organization is located

Virtual organization: an organization structured through telecommunications connections

Telecommuters: employees who maintain regular communication with their organizations through e-mail, phones, fax, pages, and the Internet

Tall organizations: organizations characterized by a large number of hierarchical levels

Flat organizations: organizations with few hierarchical levels

Adaptive learning: understanding how goals, policies, procedures, and other people's actions conform to the dynamics of the workplace

Communication climate: an aspect of an organization's character that is a function of the interactions and social processes that occur in the workplace

Openness: a receiver-oriented concept that focuses on being receptive and responsive to information from others

Communication competence: the ability to communicate both appropriately and effectively with other people

Internal communication: messages that are sent and received within the organizational boundaries of the company

Downward communication: messages from superiors to subordinates

Upward communication: messages from subordinates to superiors

Horizontal communication: messages exchanged at the same hierarchical level in an organization

External communication: messages that are exchanged between the organization and its environment

Channel richness: the ability of a communication channel to handle information or convey the meaning contained in a message

Anxiety management: the ability to control nervousness, fear, stress, and worries

DISCUSSION

1. How are shared values established in an organization? In your opinion, which techniques are most effective, and why?
2. What are some advantages of ethical behavior in organizations?

3. Why are specific communication goals more useful than general goals? How does goal setting improve organizational communication?
4. Discuss the methods for collecting situational knowledge. Which would be most effective for large organizations? For small organizations?
5. What is organizational politics? How can you evaluate the integrity of political actions and communications?
6. Why is downward communication in organizations sometimes problematic? What does the balance of downward, upward, and horizontal communication reveal about an organization's structure, climate, and culture?
7. Discuss the criteria for choosing an appropriate communication channel. In the following situations, which criteria would be most important?
   a. Scheduling a performance review
   b. Doing a performance review
   c. Demonstrating a new product to sales managers
   d. Announcing a new benefits policy
8. What are some causes of communication anxiety in organizations?

ACTIVITIES

1. Select a major organization that you wish to research. Through an examination of its advertising, pamphlets, shareholder statements, and recent media coverage, or through interviews with executives and other employees, explain what you believe the organization's values are.
2. Drawing on your own experience, explain how you think ethical communication strengthens businesses and organizations.
3. Imagine you are a department manager in a large electronics store. For each of the six steps in goal setting, design a proper goal for the communication behavior of a new salesperson. What changes or improvements might you expect in the salesperson's performance as a result of the six goals?
4. Some organizations are flattening their hierarchies by eliminating the jobs of middle managers. How do you think this restructuring has affected communication in those organizations?
5. Share with the class an example of when you communicated horizontally (with a coworker) instead of vertically (with your boss). Why did you choose to communicate in that direction?

CHAPTER

3

Diversity in Business and the Professions

After completing this chapter, you will be able to:

1. Set goals for positive communication between people who are different from you
2. Use situational knowledge to improve communication by defining diversity and understanding its impact on communication
3. Understand your own cultural perspectives and appreciate the cultural perspectives of others
4. Develop communication competencies that will improve your communication with all people
5. Manage anxiety by acting in a positive manner during cultural conflict

STRATEGIC SCENARIO

Haloke Jim is a Navajo student whose family has moved from a reservation near Gallup, New Mexico, to Mountain Grove, Missouri. She is in her second year at a local branch campus of the state university. Her family is the only American Indian family living in the small town in southern Missouri. Until this move, she had only limited contact with people outside of her culture, but she is bilingual. Her classes are small and require all students to participate orally. Most of the assignments require group work and formal, public presentations to the rest of the students. Haloke has become more and more reluctant to participate. She has begun to miss classes.

Think about Haloke's dilemma as you read this chapter. What should she do? What should her professors do? What should her group partners and class peers do?

OVERVIEW

Diversity is a positive factor in business and the professions. People who are different from one another can provide interesting and rich experiences for one another and for their respective organizations. When people are different, however, they sometimes communicate differently. Their verbal and nonverbal languages may be different, and their expectations are not the same. During interaction with diverse people, differences in communication and in expectations about communication can sometimes result in cultural conflict.

Diversity has been defined as the differences among people. These differences can be due to gender, age, ethnicity, physical abilities, religious affiliation, sexual orientation, and other factors.

Business and professional people face daily challenges in management and work relationships that result from diversity. In this chapter, we define and characterize diversity in the United States so that you will be able to:

1. Understand *your own perspectives* that make you unique.
2. Appreciate the *perspectives of others*.
3. Achieve *positive outcomes* from diversity conflict.

Insights into your own and others' cultural perspectives will give you tools to improve your working relationships with others. In this chapter we also look at legal guidelines for discrimination issues. Using the strategic communication model, we discuss the importance of goals, situational knowledge, communication competence, and anxiety management when we interact with culturally different people.

THE ISSUES OF DIVERSITY

News headlines and television stories are constant reminders that diversity is a major issue in business and the professions. Here are some headlines from recent U.S. newspapers:

"U.S. Must Counteract Image in Muslim World"
"Hospital Apologizes for Barring Black Workers"
"Accused [Rape] Graduate Remains in Military"
"When Racial Discrimination Is Not Just Black and White"
"Pope Cautions Anglican Heads on Gays"
"Job Hunts in Unstable Times"

Those headlines underscore the need for (1) positive communication in a rapidly changing workplace and (2) support for work environments that discourage discrimination. **Discrimination** is differences in treatment, either positive or negative, of individuals because of the attributes of diversity that set them apart from others.

The Definition of Diversity

The word **diversity** is one of many terms used to explain how people differ by gender, age, ethnicity, physical abilities, religious affiliation, and sexual orientation. Discrimination is often based on these differences. Terms such as *ethnicity* and *culture* are used by people in everyday language and by researchers to explain those elements of diversity. **Culture** is a broad term that explains why people from various nations and co-cultures (groups different from mainstream populations in those countries) act and speak as they do. While there are hundreds of

Where Do You Stand?

Your university newspaper has printed a letter to the editor that argues that words or phrases that are considered racist or sexist are really not important. The writer insists that such terms are not meant to be demeaning. For instance, the letter says that *chick* (referring to a woman) could be just humorous or that *chief* (referring to a Native American) could be used in fun. Do you agree or disagree?

academic researchers who have defined culture, we define culture in this book as the beliefs and values of a particular group of people that affect the way that they

Worship
Educate their children
Choose life partners
Build buildings
Define family
Treat their children or their elders
Judge what is beautiful or ugly
Dress as they do
Speak
Behave

Cultural ways-of-doing affect people's social and work worlds. Because U.S. society is heterogeneous, organizations that cultivate diverse cultural perspectives encourage the development of a positive, productive climate in business and the professions.

Diversity in the Workplace

Researchers, media, government initiatives and reports, and special-interest groups have documented the changing patterns of the U.S. population. The issue of diversity has spawned a consulting industry with day fees as high as $10,000 for training on cultural differences, harassment, and other issues.[1]

In the 1960s, demographers began making some startling predictions: that European American males soon would be the smallest population group in the work force and that more women would work outside the home than not. Researchers predicted that business and professional organizations would be transformed into transnational companies that would hire more part-time than full-time employees and would adopt an employment philosophy that would induce employees to work at many companies and change careers several times. Twenty years ago, some did not take these predictions seriously, but they have proved to be accurate. Hon and Brunner (2000), in their discussion about public relations, suggest *diversity* as *social responsibility*:[2] Ragins and Gonzalez note that researchers need to add to the information about diversity in the workplace for "the broader goals of promoting social justice and group equality in organizations."[3] Diversity in the workplace is a

1. K. Hein, "Making Diversity Work," *Incentive* 171(2) (February 1997), 18–21.
2. Linda Childers Hon and Brigitta Brunner, "Diversity Issues and Public Relations," *Journal of Public Relations Research* 12(4)(2000), 309–340.
3. B. Ragins and J.A. Gonzalez, "Understanding Diversity in Organizations: Getting a Grip on a Slippery Construct, in J. Greenberg (ed.), *Organizational Behavior: The State of the Science,* 2nd ed. (Mahwah, N.J.: Lawrence Erlbaum Associates, 2003), pp. 125–163.

TECHNOLOGY TOOLS

Diversity Resources On-Line

The waters of diversity can be tricky to navigate as both a citizen and a businessperson. Your ability to interact and communicate effectively with diverse people is vital to building relationships with employees, managers, coworkers, vendors, and customers. One Web site that is dedicated to helping people enhance their competencies in diversity and cross-cultural management is *Diversity Central*, which can be accessed at http://www.diversitycentral.com. The site offers information and programs for executives, managers, employees, educators, students, and consumers, providing a wide array of resources to help you gain a stronger understanding of diversity and its function within business and the professions.

worldwide issue: U.S. citizens work in countries around the globe, and citizens from many countries come to work in the United States.

Perceived differences between and among people in the workplace strongly affect management and work relationships.[4] Understanding diversity and its impact on the workplace will be helpful to you in your career.

How We Are Affected by Diversity

At work, we are all affected by our own culture as well as by the cultures of others. The elements that create diversity can become sources of conflict because of prejudices against unfamiliar language and behavior.

Ethnocentrism is belief in the superiority of one's own culture. Our levels of ethnocentrism can be on a continuum from low to high. Extremely high levels of ethnocentrism are likely to result in repeated and unproductive conflicts in diverse business and professional settings. Comparing and contrasting your culture with the culture of someone else is natural and can be enlightening. You can use this activity as a self-evaluation tool, rather than as an opportunity to disparage the cultural activities of others.

Most people rush to say "I'm not prejudiced." What is prejudice? **Prejudice** is a negative preconception about people, activities, or places. Prejudice is a negative stereotype that is based on personal experience, hearsay, or other incomplete data. Although prejudice is a negative judgment, *stereotypes* can be positive or negative. Stereotyping is essential to the way humans process information. We are usually overwhelmed by information overload. Stereotyping lets us make generalizations about people, language, behavior, and situations based on our experiences.

Diversity conflicts arise primarily from negative stereotyping. Here are some real-life examples of such conflict:

- **Gender:** A professor at a small community college objected to the inclusion of evaluations by students in her promotion dossier. The students wrote that she was not a good professor because women should not be as "pushy" and "bossy" as she was.

4. "The Dismantler of Discrimination," *Director* 49(22) (October 1995), 20–21.

- **Age:** A biochemist who was one of fifteen employees fired from his job of twenty-five years at an international corporation discovered that, like himself, the others fired were all over forty-five years of age.
- **Ethnicity:** In preparation for the Thanksgiving program at a local elementary school, the teacher of the third-grade class called the parents of an Osage child in her class and asked that the child and her parents come to the program in their "Indian" clothes.
- **Physical ability:** An employee requested that the annual picnic not be held at a park because the attractions at the site were not accessible to people with disabilities.
- **Religion:** A new employee complained because the only company-paid dinner was held during the Christmas holiday—a holiday that the employee's religion forbade him to observe.
- **Sexual orientation:** A man petitioned his employer to provide domestic partner benefits for his same-sex partner equal to those available for heterosexual spouses.

In these examples, the conflict occurs because one group's perspective differs from that of another's.

Our perspectives arise from cultural stereotypes. *Culture* is the "way things are" and the "taken-for-granted" in our lives. Because we take certain things for granted, we tend to assume that our work partner, supervisor, or employee lives in a house like ours, worships as we do, or has a family like our own. Often these assumptions are not accurate. The ultimate goal of a diverse society should not be to make everyone alike but to ensure that people have the knowledge and the skills to manage conflict arising from diverse cultural perspectives. Understanding that our assumptions about others are sometimes inaccurate is the beginning of a positive approach to cultural conflict.

Cultural Metaphors for the United States

The earliest metaphor for diversity in U.S. society was *melting pot*. Many of the early immigrants to the United States made great efforts to conform to the melting-pot image. In some cases, parents forbade their children to speak their native language or practice non-American cultural activities. The cultural assimilation of immigrant children often resulted in the loss of native cultures. This assimilation was often in response to expressions of bias made at places like Ellis Island or when Europeans made contact with Native Americans. While this metaphor is still commonly used, many cultural groups consider it to be a threat to their cultural identities. This metaphor offers a negative view of cultural differences because it suggests that to be accepted you must be just like everyone else. Today, knowledge of other languages and of your heritage is more highly valued than it was decades ago. Discrimination has continued in the workplace and in schools and resulted in social status differences.

Where Do You Stand?

Q Write the negative stereotypical generalization that resulted in the cultural conflict in each of the examples—gender, age, ethnicity, physical ability, religion, sexual orientation—listed on pages 62–63. In your opinion, which of these is the most damaging? Why?

One example of the efforts of some people to be in the melting pot is the experience of Madeleine Albright, who served in the Clinton administration as secretary of state. Ms. Albright discovered information about her family by accident after many years. During a hearing for her appointment, she found out that she was a member of a Jewish family who had many relatives who had died in the Holocaust during World War II, and in 1997, Albright visited the site of their deaths. While she and others may never know all the facts, some people have said that their families kept information from them to protect them from bias. People who are first- or second-generation immigrants from European countries, or who are Native American, may discover that their parents deliberately kept them from speaking their parents' native language.

Other metaphors for U.S. society have been suggested. *Societal stew* implies that each ingredient loses part of its identity to create the "gravy." *Tributaries* suggests many paths leading to one common goal. *Tapestry* is a more positive metaphor because the threads, textures, and complexities of a tapestry allude to the different elements of various cultures that define U.S. society. *Garden salad,* the most recent metaphor, also implies that each cultural group retains some aspects of its original identity. Some people may not believe that any of these comparisons truly describes U.S. diversity. The point is, they need to examine their own cultural beliefs and become aware of cultural differences between themselves and others.

COMMUNICATION BETWEEN DIVERSE PEOPLE

Cultural groups name and rename themselves to solidify their own group identity and to keep nonmembers at a distance. The words that cultural groups use to describe themselves and that outsiders use to describe them are important. Names can imply prejudicial meanings and can perpetuate negative stereotypes.[5] Sensitivity to currently accepted group names promotes positive communication and provides insights into others' perspectives.

Some people referred to as *American Indians* prefer the term *Native Americans* because it is a broader name that includes native people of Hawaii and Alaska. Others object to the use of the word *tribe* and prefer *nation,* while still others who are Native People prefer to be called by the name of their nation, such as Creek or Osage.

No single term can refer to people who are from Mexico, Spain, Latin America, or South America. Although most populations formerly called *Hispanic* are now known as *Latino* (male) and *Latina* (female), Hispanics in New Mexico, who trace their ancestry to the Spanish explorers of the 1500s and 1600s, do not call themselves *Latino* or *Mexican American* because their roots are neither in Latin America nor in Mexico, but in Spain. A large group of *Latinos/Latinas* in California is determined not to be called *Chicano* (male) or *Chicana* (female), although some Mexican Americans in the West use those terms. From time to time, Hispanics in the East have identified themselves as *Hispanic Euro-Americans.*

More recently researchers and the media are referring to diversity in more encompassing phrases, like *people of color. Black* took the place of *Negro* and *Colored* during the civil rights movement in the 1960s and was still common usage as recently as 1991. By the late spring of 1991, however, *African American* was being used more than *Black*. The word *Afro* had also fallen into disuse during the 1980s, but in 1994, CNN reported that young African American trendsetters were beginning to ask for *Afro* haircuts. On May 13, 1994, the *Chicago Tribune* reported that the poet Gwendolyn Brooks in a speech urged her fellow *Black* people not to use *African American*. She exhorted them to emphasize their blackness by using the word *Black*.

5. R. Brady, "Freedom of Speech Doesn't Cover Racial Slurs," *HR Focus* 73(9) (September 1996), 20.

You increase the likelihood of positive cultural communication when you display your awareness of the importance of names for groups and show sensitivity when you use them. Listen to others carefully to find the best term to use.

These terms are used to describe cultural communication: **international** (between representatives of different nations), **interracial** (between people with physical differences), **interethnic** (between people who identify themselves as members of different ethnic groups), and **cross-cultural** (between people from two cultures). The connotative meanings of some of these terms (the emotional ideas associated with them) can be negative, so you might wish to use the more positive terms *intercultural* or *multicultural communication* or *diversity*.

We use many criteria to identify ourselves or others as members of a cultural group—for example, gender, age, and ethnicity. What are the meanings of these labels, and what are some of the critical issues that they raise among group members?

Gender

Each society—indeed, individuals within every society—views and values the roles of men and women in different ways. Conflict occurs when these perspectives clash.

For centuries in Western European societies, women were considered to be chattel or property. Even after laws changed their roles, women were not permitted to own property. The woman's father, brother, husband, or nearest male relative became the *owner* of her possessions and had the right by law to beat the woman and physically restrain her to do his will. By contrast, in the 1600s and 1700s, Cherokee women had so great a voice in tribal matters that U.S. congressmen derisively referred to the Cherokee Nation as a "petticoat" government.

Students in one business communication class listed the attributes that a good manager with the fictitious name of George William might have. Some weeks later,

Each person at this conference table shares in organizational goals, but because of diversity, they will have different ways of presenting ideas, revealing their contributions, and working cooperatively. Difference can mean richer communication. (© Frank Herholdt/Getty Images)

they listed the attributes of a good manager with the fictitious name of Jane Payne. The two lists were not the same:

George's List	*Jane's List*
Decisive decision maker	Reasonable
Strong leader	Willing to compromise
Dependable	Dependable
Fair	Friendly
Assertive	Caring

The lists revealed that the students believed that male and female managers should behave differently.[6] As a result of such differences in role expectations, women are often perceived as poor managers if they do not display expected female role behavior, which includes smiling, friendliness, hospitality, and nurturing. An outcome of these perceptions is the phenomenon described as the **glass ceiling**—a barrier that is not visible but is real enough to keep women from top-management positions in many businesses and professions. In 2002, *Media Week* concluded that "women are still missing from the executive suites."[7]

Nonprejudicial language does not convey gender or ethnic assumptions about people. For example, the use of *humans* instead of *men* to encompass all people regardless of gender is more positive toward women. In contrast, name-calling is a prejudicial use of language. How many of the following words have you heard used either in jokes or in a matter-of-fact way?

Men	*Women*
Studs	Chicks
Dirty old men	Hags
Boys	Girls
Jocks	Tomboys
Old fogies	Old hens

Such terms maintain stereotypes that are hurtful to men and women. Sexual harassment is an issue that women and men face daily. A definition of **sexual harassment** in the workplace includes (1) inappropriate demands made on an employee by a fellow worker or supervisor and (2) the development of uncomfortable and unprofessional work environments. Behaviors that make a work environment uncomfortable include but are not limited to name-calling, touching, making rude remarks, joking, making overt sexual requests, and using innuendo. We discuss sexual harassment in detail in Chapter 7. Offices of the U.S. Equal Employment Opportunity Commission (EEOC) have federal guidelines that clarify issues that include topics ranging from inappropriate behavior to types of posters in the workplace.

Another issue is that of differences in communication styles between men and women. The two main arguments are that (1) women/men are socialized to communicate and behave differently and (2) women and men communicate and behave

6. This is a summary of unpublished class exercises directed by L. Dixon during four semesters (1992–1994) at a midwestern university. The students were asked to list good management attributes for female and male managers. Participating student demographics and details about the course: sophomores, juniors, and seniors enrolled; twenty students per class; 30 percent more females than males; nineteen to fifty-two years old; majors from all university divisions; sophomore-level class in business and professional communication; course required for business majors and elective for others.

7. "Women Still Missing from Executive Suites." *Media Week* 12(31), September 2, 2002, p. 21.

People can experience discrimination due to many factors (age, ethnicity, gender), but your success in business and professional communication depends on your being able to recognize each person for their individual capabilities and not for external differences. (Chabruken/Getty Images)

differently from one another not just because of socialization but because of hormonal and other physiological reasons. This debate will continue, but regardless of causation, many men and women believe that the other gender has problems in communicating.

Age

People of any age can experience age discrimination. Organizations may think that you are too old, too young, or unsuitable because you are middle-aged. Certain national accounting firms do not hire married middle-aged accountants for jobs that require travel. All branches of the military have maximum-age ceilings. The chances for middle-aged American males of any ethnic group to find new jobs decrease with every year of age. Although the age requirement has been changed to accommodate older students applying for medical school, many schools limit the number of older applicants who are allowed to enter. A chain of restaurants was challenged for its practice of hiring only people of a certain age, gender, and body type to work as wait staff.

What Would You Do?

Your boss has asked you to interview a prospective new hire for a job you know requires a lot of evening overtime. During the interview, the applicant reveals that she has five young children. You know your boss is not aware of this information. Do you tell your boss what you learned? Why or why not?

Ethnicity

Ethnic issues are broad and pervasive because they are dynamic, multilayered, and affected by social changes. Ethnicity arises from a variety of reasons that include but are not limited to the following:

- People were born in a country other than the one in which they are living (for example, political refugees from Cuba).
- They are living in another country temporarily (a Nigerian living in Sweden for two years while working as a consultant).
- They identify themselves with the region from which their ancestors originally came (African Americans).
- They have physical characteristics different from those of many of the people with whom they work (color of skin or body type).

In some states with large Native American populations, the history of conflict between European Americans and Indians is such that people who identify themselves as Native Americans are perceived as incompetent and unreliable. But in states without a recent history of such conflict, American Indians may be treated no differently than any other group.

Prejudice against certain ethnic groups also increases and decreases in response to public events. People of Arab heritage have been treated with considerable suspicion in the United States since the 9/11 attacks, in which nineteen terrorists—all Middle Eastern men—hijacked planes and crashed them into the World Trade Center, the Pentagon, and rural Pennsylvania. Despite the anti-Muslim backlash that followed, in which security measures were enacted that many fear violated basic civil liberties, many organizations have made efforts to curb racial profiling and treat all individuals fairly. As U.S. residents of German and Japanese heritage discovered during World War II, public prejudice against ethnic groups can occur quickly, be widespread, and have devastating, long-lasting effects.

Ethnicity is a fact of life in the workplace today because business is global. The U.S. company that has parts imported from China and production in the United States is part of an international market. The skills needed for success in the international setting are valued by employers. *Time* magazine started a new section called "Global Advisor" in the fall of 2003. Such expensive space allocation suggests there is a need within the general populace for current knowledge of international issues and intercultural skills.

Physical Abilities and Appearance

Humans have many different physical characteristics. Societies show their preferences for particular physical features by rewards and punishments (sanctions). Cultural groups decide (1) what an acceptable body type is for men and women, (2) what facial features are attractive or unattractive, and (3) what physical skills are essential for a person to be considered a productive member of society.

What Would You Do?

Your new employee is one of the underrepresented minorities in the United States. He is the first person from his ethnic group to be employed by your company in a town that has shown prejudice toward his ethnic group. What are your options if he comes to you with complaints of biased behavior by his peers?

ETHICAL ISSUES

Honoring Religious Practices

Many religions have holy days or practices that can conflict with a person's duties at his or her place of work. Many Christians celebrate Lent, a forty-day period that consists of fasting and other major penitential exercises that often come into conflict with the normal functions of daily life.

Among Muslims (or people who practice Islam), it is customary to recite the *salat* prayer five times a day while facing Mecca, the site of the sacred Ka'aba shrine. Prayers are said at dawn, noon, midafternoon, sunset, and nightfall, thus determining the rhythm of the entire day. Although it is preferable to worship together in a mosque, Muslims may pray almost anywhere, such as in fields, offices, factories, and universities.

Similarly, for many Jews, keeping the Sabbath (or *Shabbat*) holy is a central tenet of faith. The Sabbath is the seventh day of the week, beginning around sunset Friday night and ending around nightfall Saturday night. It is a time to rest the soul and spirit, a time to rejuvenate, and a time to study the Torah. Since activities such as cooking and driving a car are forbidden on the Sabbath, Jews must arrive home and finish preparations before sunset. In the winter sunset comes early, so Sabbath observers have to leave work early. They arrange with their management to make up the time by working extra hours other days or by coming in early on Friday to make up for leaving early. Now, consider the following scenario:

The Independent Student Senate (ISS) meets on Friday afternoons at Ocean State University. The campus has a history of uninterested students and of faculty who rarely meet with their students. After several months of negotiation, both students and faculty are determined to solve this problem. Because of busy schedules, the only time that both groups are willing and able to meet is after the senate meetings on Fridays. For four Fridays, they plan to meet from 5:00 P.M. to 9:00 P.M. With growing dismay, Joseph Stein, student president of the ISS, who has led the way toward this important breakthrough between students and faculty, has listened to the discussion of meeting times. His Sabbath begins at sunset on Fridays, and he is not permitted to work. What should he do?

Depending on the society and on their social status, people may be discriminated against if they are short or tall, light or heavy, sick or well. They may be considered less capable if they are born with legs of different lengths, have limited speech skills, or have an appearance that has been changed by an accident.

While some societies consider thinness to be a sign of low status and poverty, U.S. culture imposes the image of thinness as the ideal body type for women and men. The fitness craze of the 1980s and 1990s is a good example of the shifting perspectives of acceptable body types. As late as the 1980s, some airline companies would fire male and female flight attendants or suspend them when they gained weight. Asher cites a study that found that weight is much more often the basis for prejudice in hiring than is race or gender.[8]

What Would You Do?

In a doctor's office, the medical files from previous years are on the top shelf, which the former employee (who was six feet tall) could reach with ease. You are a new employee who is four feet eleven inches tall. What will you do if your first request for changing the location of the files is not answered?

Religious Affiliation

Although the Constitution guarantees the right of Americans to worship as they choose, workweeks and holidays in business, government, and educational organizations in the United States reflect the assumption that the mainstream population is Christian.

Muslims, whose religious practices require several times of prayer a day, often find that organizations are not sympathetic to their needs.

8. D. Asher, "Discrimination: A Weighty Matter," *Psychology Today* 33 (May/June 2000), 14.

What Would You Do?

Your new personal manager has petitioned for health benefits for her same-sex life partner. As the company owner, what do you do?

Only recently have concessions been made to accommodate people whose holy days, days of worship, and dietary requirements are different from those of Christians. Planners of a cultural seminar for new international teaching assistants at a major university provided food vouchers at the university cafeteria. The planners were chagrined to discover that neither vegetarian nor kosher diets could be obtained with the vouchers. Universities have begun to send reminders to faculty about the holy days of Muslims and Jews.

Sexual Orientation

A frequently debated topic in local, state, and federal governments is the right of individuals to act in accordance with their own sexual orientation. An outcome of this debate is a challenge to mainstream traditions and definitions of family, spouses, work benefits, and living styles. States and cities are considering the issues of same-sex marriage or life partners who choose not to marry. The implications for changes in health and retirement benefits are multiple. Since 1996, some states have presented bills for approval of same-sex marriage, and some discussed bills that condemned such marriages. Despite ongoing debates on the issue in courts and various legislatures, many companies now offer benefits to same-sex partners. During the spring of 2004, some politicians began to call for a constitutional amendment to ban same-sex marriage.

SITUATIONAL KNOWLEDGE: UNDERSTANDING YOUR PERSPECTIVES

The three steps mentioned at the beginning of this chapter to improve cultural communication are to understand your own perspectives, to appreciate the perspectives of others, and to act in ways to ensure that conflict stemming from diversity is positive. How can we reach the first goal of understanding our own cultural perspectives?

You are *who* you are because of where you were born, to whom you were born, and how you were raised. You are unique. You could find a person your age who practices the same religion, is of the same gender, and so on, who would be very much like you in many ways, but would still have different behaviors and attitudes.

Your perspectives about life are based on your culture, but those perspectives are affected by the thousands of experiences of daily life. Your **attitudes** (learned likes and dislikes), **beliefs** (judgments about right and wrong), and **values** (deep cultural assumptions that affect all areas of life) form your perspectives and patterns of language and behavior. These communication patterns constitute language culture and are both verbal and nonverbal.

Language culture is the means by which we represent ourselves and the means by which we interpret others. Language culture includes the spoken word, written word, body movements, architectural styles, furniture placement, signs on walls, and color schemes.[9] For instance, handwritten signs in the lobby of a free public health clinic for Native Americans warned that patients who miss their appointment times will not be allowed to receive health care. Through language culture, the

9. L. Dixon Shaver, "The Relationship Between Language Culture and Recidivism Among Women Offenders," in B. Fletcher, L. Dixon Shaver, and D. Moon (eds.), *Women Offenders: A Forgotten Population* (Westport, Conn.: Praeger, 1993), pp. 119–134.

signs created an adversarial climate that is not usually found in private health-care clinics.[10]

Your language culture and that of others are the means by which culture comes into being and changes. Language culture reveals what we think about ourselves and our world. Analysis of your language and the language of others can give you insight into your own perspectives and the perspectives of others.

Analysis reveals that certain issues between culturally different people become "sites of conflict."[11] These sites are cultural dilemmas that occur again and again. The reasons for continued, repeated, and negative conflict can often be related to the societal role that a person believes he or she plays in an organization. For instance, an African American woman who is a middle-level manager may see herself as a productive and professional member in the workplace, but another person may perceive her as an example of a successful placement through affirmative action efforts. The two perspectives can lead to conflict.

In business and professional settings, your work standards, expectations of timeliness, relationships, status, and verbal and nonverbal behaviors reflect your cultural training. Conflicts occur because your colleagues have different cultural expectations.

COMMUNICATION COMPETENCE: PERSONALITY TRAITS

When you experience cultural conflict because others do not share your perspectives, certain personality traits can help you be an effective intercultural communicator.[12] We all have traits such as flexibility and tolerance for ambiguity in varying degrees. These traits help us deal with cultural differences, and if we cultivate them, we can improve our communication competence.

Flexibility

The ability to tolerate change and the willingness to compromise are necessary when you are working with someone who is culturally different. Even if differences

10. C. Bantz, *Understanding Organizations: Interpreting Organizational Communication Cultures* (Columbia: University of South Carolina Press, 1993); U. Eco, *The Limits of Interpretation* (Bloomington: Indiana University Press, 1990); Y. Lotman, *Universe of the Mind: A Semiotic Theory of Culture* (Bloomington: Indiana University Press, 1990); J. Potter and M. Wetherell, *Discourse and Social Psychology: Beyond Attitudes and Beliefs* (Beverly Hills, Calif.: Sage, 1987); P. Shaver and L. Dixon, "'Icons' of Bureaucratic Therapy: An Application of Eco's Semiotic Methodology", *Intercultural Communication Studies* 8(2) (1998), 115–130; L. Dixon and P. Shaver, "The Cultural Perspective of a Public Health Facility for Oklahoma American Indians: Architectural Changes as Organizational Rhetoric," in A. Gonzalez & D. Tanno (eds.), *Rhetoric in Intercultural Contexts: International and Intercultural Communication Annual NCA 22* (Thousand Oaks, Calif.: Sage, 2000); L. Weisman, *Discrimination by Design: A Feminist Critique of the Man-Made Environment* (Chicago: University of Illinois Press, 1992).
11. P. Shaver and L. D. Shaver, "Applying Perspectival Rhetorical Analysis in Intercultural Consulting: The Chromosomal Bivalency Model," *Intercultural Communication Studies* 2(2) (1992), 1–22.
12. This discussion of personality traits incorporates ideas from these sources: L. Barna, "Stumbling Blocks in Intercultural Communication," in R. Samovar and L. Porter (eds.), *Intercultural Communication: A Reader,* 6th ed. (Belmont, Calif.: Wadsworth, 1991), pp. 345–352; C. Dodd, *Dynamics of Intercultural Communication,* 3d ed. (Dubuque, Iowa: Brown, 1991); M. Lustig and J. Koester, *Intercultural Competence: Interpersonal Communication Across Cultures* (New York: HarperCollins, 1993); B. Spitzberg, "Intercultural Communication Competence," in R. Samovar and L. Porter, *Intercultural Communication: A Reader*, 6th ed. (Belmont, Calif.: Waveland Press, 1991), pp. 353–365.

Working situations combined with informal behaviors, such as sharing meals, create discomfort for members of some cultures, distractions for other, and an enforced physical intimacy that can be uncomfortable. Understanding how differently people perceive these experiences can help you toward successful communication. (© Royalty-Free/Corbis)

outnumber similarities, your goal should be to find specific areas in which you can "give" without endangering your primary goals.

Ability to Tolerate Ambiguity

Most people feel more comfortable knowing what to expect from a supervisor, a parent, a friend, or a social situation. When you are not in your own social group—when you will be interacting with persons from Brazil, for example—you may not know how unfamiliar your companions' accents will be or how different their nonverbal communication will be from yours. Ambiguity in such instances makes some people uncomfortable

In traditional U.S. bureaucracies, employees are accustomed to having a list of job duties. If a new supervisor from another country uses ambiguity as a management strategy, what should employees do? They might give themselves time to get used to the new style of management. Or, if they find the new level of ambiguity

What Would You Do?

You have spent your working career in a for-profit manufacturing company. As a new employee in a state bureaucracy that is not-for-profit, you are to work with a group to change the organizational structure so that productivity and communication will improve. You know very little about what the organization is like or its history, and your peers and subordinates are resentful of the many changes that are threatening the status quo. Your supervisor has yet to tell you the timetable, the funding for the project, or the criteria for evaluating the final results. How do you handle this level of ambiguity?

intolerable, they might choose to discuss the issue with the supervisor. In either case, they will be handling intercultural conflict in a positive fashion.

Nonjudgmental Attitudes

One of the difficulties in communication is the tendency to pass judgment on the behavior of others. That which is familiar and taken for granted is perceived as "good," and the unfamiliar is deemed "bad." Withholding, delaying, and tempering judgmental responses are ways to deal with this often involuntary negative reflex. While it may not be possible to avoid having an emotional response to a given cultural conflict, in order to be professional in the workplace, you must be able to control your behavior.

Respect for Self and Others

At the foundation of any work environment and work relationship are the respect for individuals that the organizational culture fosters and the respect for others that you bring as part of your personal culture. Respect is embodied in the belief that others have the right (1) to opinions that differ from yours, (2) to behave in ways that you may find confusing or wrong, (3) not to be ridiculed, and (4) to feel confident that they will be treated fairly.

Analyzing Your Perspectives

Often your own ways of doing things and behaving are unconscious. Unless you take time to become self-reflective—that is, to examine deliberately your own behavior and language culture—you may find it difficult to be flexible during intercultural interactions.

The first of the three steps to succeed in a diverse workplace is to analyze your own cultural perspectives. Write brief descriptions of the items listed in the Cultural Analysis Inventory (CAI) in the Strategic Skills box on page 74.[13] This activity will give you insights into your "taken-for-granted" ways of thinking or "everyone-knows-to-do-this" ways of behaving.

The Social Perspectives Explanation Form (SPEF)[14] in the Strategic Skills box on page 75 may help you discuss the "why" for your interpretations of how people are, what they are, and who they should be. Most people tend to either find logical, reasonable justifications for individual behaviors, or blame someone for unreasonable, biased behavior. Your explanations for the events described in the SPEF can give you clues about your perspectives.

Your working environment and working relationships are both created and maintained by communication. Gaining insights into your cultural perspectives will help you to understand others and to communicate more effectively.

The second step to working successfully with different people or managing a diverse workplace is to know that the perspectives of others may be different from your own. The importance of knowing about other cultures cannot be overstated. Culture is not static but is an ever-changing, dynamic reflection of human interaction. Total knowledge and complete understanding of another culture are

13. The CAI was developed by L. Dixon.
14. The SPEF was developed by L. Dixon.

STRATEGIC SKILLS

Cultural Analysis Inventory

For each topic, there are two questions. Write brief responses to each. After you are finished, your instructor may wish to discuss your responses as a class; you may share them in small groups; or you may conduct a "culture hunt" by trying to find people in your class who answered the questions as you did.

1. Weddings
   a. What is the most important part of the wedding ceremony?
   b. What is the most important part of the reception?
2. Dinners
   a. Who serves as the "head" of the table and tells people to begin eating at large family dinners?
   b. Who cleans the kitchen at large family dinners?
3. Funerals
   a. What is the correct decision regarding "viewing" the remains?
   b. Where should a funeral be held?
4. Family
   a. What is the most important activity that your family does together?
   b. How far down the family tree does the obligation go to be responsible for a family member (for example, lend money, take care of children, pay for food, or let the person live with you temporarily)?
5. Ethnicity
   a. How does your family identify itself ethnically?
   b. What represents your family's cultural and ethnic identity? (For example, if you put "Hungarian," you might refer to a Hungarian lullaby or Hungarian food that your family eats.)

impossible, but you can begin by realizing that your colleagues may not see the world exactly as you do. Knowing facts about people who are different can also prepare you for some of their reactions to you or for their behavior toward you. (See the Strategic Skills box on page 76.)

Cultural facts can be helpful as long as you keep in mind that they increase your understanding but neither guarantee harmony nor prevent conflict. Many research studies and books provide specific information on various cultures. Research articles, intercultural communication texts, general-information books, and media reports on cultural facts are readily available at libraries, in bookstores, on television, on videocassettes, and in movies. Some of them focus on

What Would You Do?

You have never traveled more than two hundred miles from your midwestern home. You attended a local state university, and your work experience has been at one locally owned firm. Your excellent work came to the attention of a headhunter (a professional job-hunter who tries to match openings in organizations with the right employees). Within a month, you are living outside Madrid, Spain, making a large salary, battling traffic for two hours each day, working with people from all over the world, and learning how to live in a large urban setting. What role does ethnocentrism play in your transition to this new life?

STRATEGIC SKILLS

Social Perspectives Explanation Form

Each statement is followed by a question or an instruction. Write your response. There are no right or wrong answers, but you can interpret your answers when you are done.

1. The surgeon was not able to save the little boy. Make up a name—including first and last names—for the doctor.
2. Benjamin was waiting for a bus with several others in a large, unfriendly city. Two strangers spoke to Benjamin and offered to help him, and one person actually put hands on Benjamin and on his possessions without his permission. Why did this happen?
3. Lou Jane is a quiet person with long black hair and dark skin. She is an environmentalist; she respects the land and its people. She protested against the celebration of Columbus's supposed discovery of America. She protested with her whole family against the use of the word *Braves* for the Atlanta baseball team. Identify her ethnicity.
4. The Jones family has three teenage children—one girl (Mindy) and two boys (Joe and George). They are required to do the family chores. List the basic household chores, and assign them to each child.
5. Mary had a severe asthma attack. She took a public bus to the hospital—one that she had been to many times for the same problem. The attending physician was friendly and helpful. Mary was a partner in her health care because she was knowledgeable about her own health. The physician was eager to get Mary's medical file. When it came, the physician read it and immediately started speaking to Mary in a louder and higher-pitched voice, using simple words as if speaking to a child. The physician started overexplaining the decisions that were being made, refusing to continue treatment until Mary's husband or parents were in the hospital. What information in the file prompted the physician to change the way in which Mary was treated?

Interpretation: The key to processing the SPEF is that the answers are somewhat predictable. Discuss the predictable responses, and understand why they are predictable. Discuss different responses, and attempt to understand their implications: (1) The name given the surgeon reveals the gender of the physician. (2) Benjamin could have any type of physical difference that was visible to others. (3) Lou Jane is probably Native American, but she could belong to any ethnic group. (4) The assigning of tasks reveals expectations of gender behavior. (5) Mary (in real life) was legally blind, but the physician could have had the same response to any physical or mental difference that was noted in Mary's file.

specific business and professional settings, such as *Business in Mexico: Managerial Behavior, Protocol, and Etiquette*.[15] or *Big in Asia: 25 Strategies for Business*.[16]

Language Culture

Although many authors give detailed descriptions of cultural facts, even more can be learned by the analysis of language culture (perspectives revealed through verbal and nonverbal speech) to provide insight into the dynamic and ongoing relationship between people. Such research is important to you because you need to know both cultural facts and cultural perspectives about people from the United States and from other countries.

15. C. McKinnis, *Business in Mexico: Managerial Behavior, Protocol, and Etiquette* (New York: Haworth Press, 1994).
16. M. Backman and C. Butler, *Big in Asia: 25 Strategies for Business* (New York: Palgrave Macmillan, 2003).

STRATEGIC SKILLS

Cultural Facts

The following facts about various cultures suggest that knowledge of facts about others can help in international communication. First, discuss the impact on your communication if you *knew* this fact *before* you communicated with a member of that culture; second, discuss the impact if you *did not know* this fact before you communicated.

1. *Japanese:* Japanese businesspeople rarely invite foreign business colleagues to their home to meet their family. Business and private life remain separate in Japan.
2. *American Indians:* Some traditional Plains Indians, such as the Kiowas and Apaches, do not touch each other casually. They are offended if people, particularly non-Indians, touch them during conversation.
3. *Arabs:* Members of many Arab cultures have a different sense of personal space than do people in the United States. Arabs stand very close to the person to whom they are talking. Americans require a greater distance between themselves and others.
4. *Physically different:* People who are physically different do not wish to have people help them without asking. Although you might perceive that a person in a wheelchair needs help, do not touch that person or his or her chair or possessions. Ask whether your help is needed, and then do what is requested.
5. *Elders:* Age does not necessarily make people incompetent or out of touch. Automatically speaking louder, directing talk to a younger companion, and assuming that elders will be incompetent in a social gathering are inappropriate behaviors. Do not make assumptions about a person's abilities or interests based on their age.
6. *Religious affiliation:* Unsolicited inquiries about coworkers' religious practices ("Where do you eat after church on Sunday?") reveal ethnocentric perspectives. You risk making inaccurate assumptions that the person goes to church, goes to a religious service that is held on Sunday morning, and follows the custom of eating out afterward.
7. *Sexual orientation:* Assuming that all people have the same sexual orientation can result in embarrassing situations. Don't automatically ask a new male employee if his wife likes the new town. Don't assume that workers in a specific career field have a particular sexual orientation.

These are some types of language analysis:

1. **Semiotics:** The study of the social and political significance of verbal and nonverbal language as signs
2. **Sociolinguistics:** The study of different kinds of speech markers used by different ethnic groups who speak the same language
3. **Semantics:** The study of linguistic meanings of words

Knowledge of the customs of a specific group is helpful, but additional information is needed if you hope to anticipate responses and issues that are important to people. Language culture analysis can provide these data.

The formal and informal ways in which language is used, regional accents, and the use of specialized language identify individuals as group members. **Argot** is specialized language used by a particular group. Groups as different as inner-city gangs and intellectuals have their own argot.

Jargon is the language-shorthand used by people in a particular trade or profession. *A-OK* was once jargon used in the military and at the National Aeronautics and Space Administration (NASA), but it is now part of American English. When communication professors ask, "Have you seen the new study on CA?" most of

Organizations create a culture in which people are constrained to conform to certain norms. Employees whose ways-of-doing conflict with organizational language culture find ways to communicate in more comfortable ways, such as in dyads rather than with a group around a table. (© Royalty-Free/Corbis)

their peers know that *CA* stands for "communication apprehension." Computer users know that when they are asked to "download" some data, they will not be expected to physically move files.

Regional accents tend to classify people. During Jimmy Carter's and Bill Clinton's presidential campaigns, political pundits and stand-up comedians considered a southern accent funny, and jokes were made implying that people with southern accents were less intelligent than people from other regions of the United States. Conversely, some consider a British accent to be indicative of a higher intelligence regardless of an individual person's abilities. Many people believe that John F. Kennedy's distinctive Boston accent showed him to be from the influential Northeast and increased his credibility with some voters. In the 2003 California gubernatorial recall race, Arnold Schwartenegger's accent became the topic for comedians and political pundits who opposed his campaign. People evaluate others by the way they speak, by their grammar, and by their use of group talk.

Language culture is verbal, written, and nonverbal. Edward Hall and others have identified many categories of nonverbal communication.[17] You may agree

17. E. Hall, *The Silent Language* (Garden City, N.Y.: Anchor Books, 1973).

with Hall and others who say that nonverbal communication is more believable than verbal communication. Nonverbal communication includes but is not limited to appearance, clothing, kinesics (body movements), posture, facial expressions, oculesics (eye movement and contact), tactilics (touch), olfactics (smell), paralanguage (pitch, stress, tone, nonword sounds, sound fillers), proxemics (space), territoriality, chronemics (time), and silence, as discussed in Chapter 5.

If you were to videotape a highly educated, wealthy man from Iran having a moderately heated argument in a business context with another Iranian man of the same status and compare that video with one showing two European American men in a similar professional setting, you would probably see certain nonverbal differences. The following is a *generalization* of the likely differences but should not be interpreted to mean that all well-educated, wealthy Iranian or European American males would act in this fashion: The physical space separating the arguing Iranians is likely to be less than the distance between the arguing Americans. The Iranians, but not the Americans, are likely to raise their voices, gesticulate often, and express their emotions openly. American businessmen generally maintain a social distance of at least two feet, they keep their hands and bodies still to avoid sending signals, and they rarely let their emotions show.

Nonverbal elements result in countless differences in communication styles and meanings. When nonverbal messages are confusing to the receiver, misunderstandings are likely to occur. If the Iranians and the American males were in conflict, the Iranians would likely misinterpret the American males' composure to mean that they were not interested in or committed to their own side of the argument. The Americans possibly would assume that the Iranians were out of control.

ANXIETY MANAGEMENT: RESOLVING CULTURAL CONFLICT

The third step to working in or managing a diverse workplace is to realize that conflict resulting from diversity can be positive.

Positive Cultural Conflict

Just as it is not possible to understand everything about another culture, it is also not possible to eliminate all conflict—even with people who are very similar to you.

Negative effects from diversity occur because participants do not analyze their own language culture or the language culture of others to identify the source of conflict. People select sites of conflict as a result of cultural experiences, expectations, prioritized life decisions, and communication contexts. Certain topics or issues give rise to conflict because they revolve around differing values that are important to one or more communicators, who insist on discussing the controversial topic or retreat until it is discussed. Unaddressed sites of conflict create tension that can stop work or hinder relational activity. Furthermore, if both parties fail to identify and discuss the sites, the conflicts often increase in number and intensity.

As conflict continues or new incidents occur, we might mistakenly decide that all interactions with people who are different will be unproductive. We might also conclude that we must solve *all* cultural differences in order to work well with others. That, however, is not a realistic goal. Specific conflicts can be managed, even if many differences remain unresolved. To manage anxiety successfully, one should have an understanding of oneself and others while utilizing competent communication skills.

The first two steps, understanding your perspectives and appreciating the perspectives of others, are prerequisites for managing the third step, which is acting in ways that render cultural conflict positive. If you are informed about your own perspectives and sensitive to the perspectives of others, you may find these assumptions helpful:

1. Language and behavior may vary among different U.S. cultures; people from other countries may have different language and behavior.
2. Complete knowledge about diverse cultures is not possible.
3. Conflict is likely to result from interaction between unlike people.
4. Workers and managers are not willing to change their own behavior, language, attitudes, beliefs, and values just to avoid conflict.
5. Managing conflict is necessary for organizations to continue to function.

If there is agreement on those assumptions, the question is "Can conflict between culturally diverse people be productive rather than destructive in business and the professions?" The answer is "yes." However, passive communication and interaction will not result in positive communication. Sites of conflict must be identified. They are important because they reveal people's pressure points or high-priority agenda items. For conflict to be productive, participants must analyze themselves, events, context, and their language cultures in order to identify the sites and what they and others believe about the issues.

For example, when construction workers complained about Native Americans wanting their jobs at a project on a reservation, the site of conflict was revealed to be the workers' pride in their professional behavior, their safety record, and their camaraderie, which had developed over time. The men resented any group's erroneous assumption that untrained workers could do their job as well as they did it. The conflict was not with the Native Americans because they were Indians. The conflict was with the Indians' assumption that the workers were not professionals who did worthwhile work.[18]

Diversity training is used in many organizations. Some training is effective; other types are less so. In your workplace, you can serve as your own consultant. The following steps are suggestions to help you analyze conflict and potentially turn it into a productive discourse:

1. *Examine the topics* of the conflict. They are of great importance in understanding the perspectives of the other person or group. The topic may be the primary point of the conflict, or it may suggest another, more deep-seated problem.
2. *Analyze your own contributions.* Did you initiate the confrontation, enable (or encourage) others in their conflict, or react to someone else's agenda? Knowing who initiates certain types of encounters can help determine both the "whys" and the sites of conflict.
3. *Make notes* in a permanent file about the encounter so that over time you can identify patterns of behavior, timing, and relational activity. Use dates, names, and specific references. You may be able to compare this information with other activities, issues, or recurring topics. This file will help you to analyze conflict and language culture in cultural conflict. The analysis can help you to

18. P. Shaver and L. Dixon Shaver, "Applying Perspectival Rhetorical Analysis."

What Would You Do?

You are working with Italian members of your manufacturing plant who have moved to Alabama, where you have lived all of your life. You are a nondrinking, church-going person who is worried about the newcomers. To get to know them, you agree to attend a party at the home of the lowest-ranking Italian accountant and his wife. At the party, you are horrified to see that their ten-year-old son is given wine to drink by his father—highly diluted wine but wine nevertheless. At the next evaluation meeting, you have the final vote on whether this accountant will stay or be sent back to Italy. What do you do?

understand others' perspectives. You can adapt your behavior and language culture to mediate the most critical points of controversy. These notes are also invaluable if conflicts go from productive to destructive and lead to court cases or intraorganizational disciplinary hearings about issues such as firing with or without cause, sexual harassment, and unfair work conditions.

4. In some cases you may decide to *discuss the conflict* with a trusted supervisor, an affirmative action officer, or an employee advocate who attempts to handle conflict in a nonbiased way. Be careful about this step. Confidentiality about interactions is important to ethical behavior.

The Cultural Communication Conflict Triangle

One way to think of the process of conflict analysis is to compare it to a dynamic triangle in which communication is constantly in flux but reaches intersections of (1) cultural self-knowledge, (2) knowledge about the context, and (3) discourse from the conflict (see Figure 3.1). At one intersection of the triangle are your perspectives and, if you've analyzed your own perspective, some cultural self-knowledge.

FIGURE 3.1

The Cultural Communication Conflict Triangle

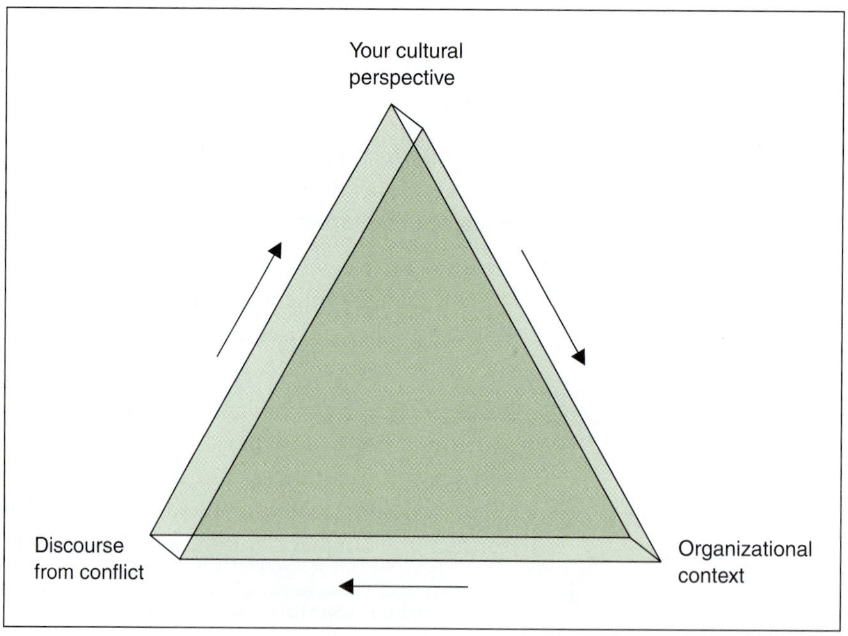

A valuable tool in productive cultural communication is what you know about your own culture and your assumptions about the ways things should be.

At another intersection of the triangle is the organizational context (for example, the school, the corporation, the accounting firm, the manufacturing plant) in which communication between culturally different people occurs. Types of clothing, modes of behavior, social rules, appropriate language style, nonverbal communication, and topics of conversation are all affected by where and under what circumstances they occur.

At the last intersection is the discourse from the conflict. Your language culture and that of the other person give clues to the perspectives of each. Your ability to communicate effectively is based on your ongoing analysis of yourself and the other person.

The discourse—the talk—that emerges during conflicts should be carefully examined. First, use the triangle by examining the elements in the conflict that are products of your own cultural perspectives. If the conflict is about the timeliness of meetings, consider your attitude toward punctuality. For example, being ten minutes late for the weekly sales meeting may be acceptable if people always just eat doughnuts and drink coffee during the first ten minutes of the meeting.

Second, analyze the organizational context to determine its effects on you, on the other person, and on the conflict. For example, conflict in an insurance company that prides itself on a formal, high-status climate results in low voices, euphemisms instead of plain talk, and an understated description of conflict.

Third, the discourse between people during conflict reveals cultural perspectives and points to the sites of conflict. As an example, a company's Japanese representatives say that they are offended by the lack of respect shown to their company by the joking manner of the U.S. representatives during business meetings. The site of conflict is respect. That the Japanese representatives feel that their organization has been dishonored by less-than-serious behavior provides deep cultural information. Unlike their Japanese counterparts, few U.S. workers would assume that disrespect to their company was more important than disrespect to them personally.

The dynamic qualities of the Cultural Communication Conflict Triangle show that the same conflict can occur over and over. With attention to the language culture, the U.S. representatives may discover that the Japanese are not without humor but are careful to segregate humor from business. Their personal agenda and need for relational activity may not be the foci in a business setting, as they often are for American workers. Japanese culture requires honor to be shown to the organization and attention to be given to the primary task.

In this model, each person is allowed to retain his or her own cultural identity and manage conflict positively by learning from the process. Representatives of the United States are not required to become Japanese, but their positive response to their Japanese counterparts will promote productive business interactions.

The following example of two women from different cultural backgrounds in the workplace further demonstrates the Cultural Communication Conflict Triangle:

> A woman from Japan—Yasuko—is a manager for a Japanese computer chip company in South Carolina. She has a female supervisor—Delta—from the South who believes in southern hospitality. Delta tells Yasuko that she will bring a welcome basket to Yasuko's home on Saturday so that she can see her employee's new apartment. It is obvious that Delta expects to be invited into Yasuko's home.
>
> Yasuko analyzes her cultural reaction—horror and dismay—at the rudeness of the American woman who expects to invade the privacy of her home. The

What Would You Do?

Your new employee at the Bradley Oil Company in Tulsa, Oklahoma, is Mousa from Saudi Arabia. At your first meeting, he shakes your hand but does not grip it tightly. He doesn't meet your eyes. He does not bring his wife to the first employee and spouse social event. What would you do if fellow workers complain about his behavior?

organizational context is a Japanese computer chip company that hires both Americans and Japanese, who must work as a team. Yasuko responds to Delta's offer in a noncommittal way that appears to Delta to be a rejection of her goodwill.

As Yasuko reflects overnight on the embarrassing encounter and recalls hearing other American employees discussing their social gatherings at one another's homes, she realizes that she has offended her supervisor. This example of American informal behavior is confusing to Yasuko, but as she reflects on it, she comes to understand that Delta is not trying to be offensive. Delta is simply applying her "taken-for-granted" cultural perspectives in an inappropriate manner.

Delta may or may not be alert to the reasons behind Yasuko's rejection. If she, too, is analyzing her perspectives, she will become aware that her manifestation of goodwill is not accepted by all cultural groups.

As both people analyze the discourse from the conflict, they realize that their individual expectations were based on their different definitions of *friendliness, courtesy,* and *hospitality.* When Yasuko examines Delta's language culture, she becomes aware that Delta equates friendliness with personal activity in individual homes. Delta may not understand fully that many Japanese people keep their homes isolated from business acquaintances, but she may conclude that Yasuko doesn't see friendliness in the same way that Delta does.

This conflict can help each understand that they have different perspectives. Coping and managing this one site of conflict does not mean that either Yasuko or Delta must give up her unique cultural identity. Rather, they may find a neutral way to define friendliness—to share the welcome basket in a park or have a meal together in a restaurant. Such a solution allows for southern hospitality and maintains Japanese standards of privacy.

The differences between Japanese and American ways are not solved by one positive conflict outcome. Rather, the continual interaction will provide other opportunities to utilize the Cultural Communication Conflict Triangle as a model to evoke positive outcomes from conflict.

LEGAL GUIDELINES AND DIVERSITY

Conflicts resulting from diversity can be productive when people strive to understand one another. Discrimination, however, is always harmful and is prohibited by various laws. In the United States, many of these laws are under the management of the Equal Employment Opportunity Commission (EEOC) and local affirmative action offices, which implement and process the legal guidelines and directives from the EEOC.

The laws have been enacted to ensure fairness in the hiring, firing, and management of people regardless of gender, age, ethnicity, physical abilities, or religious affiliation. Courts are continually redefining these laws in response to changes in U.S. society. As a result, affirmative action officers must stay current

with changes as they occur through laws and court decisions, such as the 2003 Supreme Court ruling that while diversity can be a part of university admissions criteria, the use of a point system is inappropriate.

In most organizations, one person is designated to be the affirmative action officer responsible for keeping up with the constantly changing guidelines. Affirmative action is a policy or a program that seeks to redress past discrimination through active measures to ensure equal opportunity, as in education and employment. Affirmative action officers may be full-time, or they may do the job in addition to their other responsibilities. The designated person handles the initial stages of any complaints and also makes sure that EEOC guidelines are followed in recruiting and hiring.

TABLE 3.1

Affirmative Action Laws

Law	Year	Provisions
Affirmative Action and Title VII	1964	Prohibits discrimination on the basis of race, color, religion, sex, and national origin; Title VII was enacted as a part of the Civil Rights Act of 1964, which established the Equal Employment Opportunity Commission.
	1968	Prohibits sex discrimination and requires affirmative action for women
Age Discrimination in Employment Act	1967	Protects employees from age discrimination in hiring, compensation, promotion, job classification, and termination
Rehabilitation Act	1973	(Sections 501 and 505) Prohibits discrimination against people with handicaps defined as physical or mental
Immigration Reform and Control Act	1986	Prohibits employers from knowingly recruiting, hiring, or referring to another person for hiring people who are not U.S. citizens, including part-time employees, and requires new employees to produce legal documentation before employment
Americans with Disabilities Act	1990	(Titles I and V) Prohibits discrimination for the disabled in employment, public service (including transportation), public accommodations, private services, and telecommunications
New Civil Rights Act	1991	Redefines issues on race and changes the responsibilities of burden-of-proof cases

Source: Based on S. Kahn, B. Brown, B. Zepke, and M. Lanzarone, *Personnel Director's Legal Guide*, 2d ed. (Boston: Warren, Gorham & Lamont, 1990), and *Personnel Director's Legal Guide: 1990 Supplement*, 2d ed. (Boston: Warren, Gorham & Lamont, 1991).

TECHNOLOGY TOOLS

Affirmative Action Resources On-Line

The anxiety that can come from communicating with culturally different people can be managed when you increase your diversity competencies and become your own consultant by understanding yourself, others, and your communication together in business and professional settings. As we've noted in this chapter, many large companies and nonprofit organizations offer formal cultural diversity training, but often these services are costly and difficult to launch. You can expand your knowledge about the legal guidelines of diversity via the Web, at sites that offer reliable and credible information in this area. The EEOC's Web site, at http://www.eeoc.gov, is an excellent resource for employment guidelines and policy guidance. The Americans United for Affirmative Action site, at http://www.aaua.org, offers legislative news and a cyber-primer guideline that follows the affirmative action movement from 1776 to the present day. At http://www.essential.org/ussa/foundati/aamyths.html, hosted by the United States Student Association, you can learn to distinguish between the myths and the facts associated with affirmative action programs. Visit these sites and compare their offerings with what you may already know about the legal guidelines of diversity.

Instead of just offering cultural diversity training that is focused on better working relationships and productivity, large organizations often provide special counseling, training, and mediation processes regarding discrimination to avoid legal ramifications of illegal and biased treatment of employees. These activities are designed to assist victims of unfair treatment, to educate employees on how their behavior can be interpreted, to explain hiring and firing rules, and to use mediation as an alternative to legal action.

The affirmative action office and the organizational culture are instrumental in developing a climate in which employees feel that they can make complaints and in which employees who are accused feel that they will have a fair hearing.

The laws listed in Table 3.1 protect and safeguard the civil liberties and rights of many people. Employers must follow these laws in recruiting, hiring, and managing employees to avoid discriminatory practices. Unaddressed wrongs have been the norm in many business and professional settings (both public and private). However, government bureaucracy associated with affirmative action laws creates much paperwork and loss of work time. The courts are filled with the legal consequences of organizations and individuals who allegedly did not obey the laws. As an employee, a manager, a business owner, or an affirmative action officer, you will appreciate the safeguards of affirmative action laws, but you will also wrestle with their intricacies and ambiguities.

STRATEGIC SCENARIO WRAP-UP

Haloke, her professors, and her classmates all have obligations in this situation. Haloke's reluctance to participate in the non-Navajo classroom activities is a dilemma that she may be able to handle by talking to her parents and getting their advice. She should, if possible, approach her professors and ask for an appointment to talk about this problem. She might be able to talk to an approachable peer who has some understanding of her perspective. Haloke can use the Cultural Communication Conflict Triangle as she attempts to survive in a very different educational context. Rather than seeing her professors' and classmates' demands as unreasonable, she may be able to see that they are the mainstream ways of conducting education.

Haloke's situation and the problem for her professors and classmates should be analyzed using the Cultural Communication Conflict Triangle. First, knowledge about Navajo life perspectives and experiences would be helpful. Many traditional Navajos prefer to maintain a greater amount of personal space between themselves and others. As such, mainstream U.S. group work, which is based on close physical proximity and interpersonal skills that aim for positive relational activity, would seem intrusive to many Navajos. For example, if a classmate asked a simple question about a deceased grandparent, a traditional Navajo might be hesitant to speak about the person or to say the person's name because of cultural taboos.

When Haloke's professors and classmates have knowledge about other cultures, and as they realize that their cultural, academic, and social needs are in conflict with the life habits and cultural training of others, they have the opportunity to discuss these issues with Haloke. Haloke's professors may have to create alternative assignments that foster a positive learning experience for her by being in harmony with her cultural norms.

SUMMARY

- Diversity is the differences among people.
- Differences can be due to gender, age, ethnicity, physical abilities, religious affiliation, and sexual orientation.
- Cultural perspectives are the result of the society in which people are reared and their differences from others.
- Business and the professions should be representative of the society in which they exist. As such, they should mirror that society and gain from the strengths that each cultural group brings to the "tapestry" or the "garden salad" known as the culture of the United States.

- We suggested that you have three goals:
  1. Understand *your own perspectives* that make you unique.
  2. Appreciate the *perspectives of others*.
  3. Achieve *positive outcomes* from diversity conflict.
- Personality traits that can help you be a successful communicator include (1) flexibility, (2) tolerance of ambiguity, (3) nonjudgmental attitudes, and (4) respect for yourself and others.
- You can analyze your own and others' cultural perspectives through facts about cultures and analysis of language culture.
- Steps to help you manage conflict include (1) examining the topics of conflict, (2) analyzing your own contributions to the conflict, (3) making notes, and (4) ethically choosing an unbiased person with whom you can discuss the conflict with guarantees of confidentiality.
- This process of analyzing conflict can be compared to a triangle. The intersections of the triangle are your perspectives, the organizational context in which the conflict occurs, and the discourse that emerges from the conflict.
- Discourse associated with the conflict can be analyzed to gain information about the culture of others and to reveal more about your own culture.
- Insights into the discourse of conflict will give you the tools to produce positive outcomes.
- No member of one culture has complete knowledge of another culture, but knowledge and analysis can inform people so that they can improve intercultural communication competencies.
- A successful conflict outcome, however, does not mean that all differences are understood.
- The sites of conflict are likely to recur as they are deemed important to each person.
- Your goals for more positive intercultural interactions can be achieved by utilizing situational knowledge about yourself and others, improving your communication competency, and managing anxiety by your knowledge of diversity and the realization that conflict can be productive.

KEY TERMS

Discrimination: favoritism or differences in treatment of individuals because of the attributes of diversity that set them apart from others

Diversity: one of the many terms used to explain how people differ by gender, age, ethnicity, physical abilities, religious affiliation, and sexual orientation

Culture: a broad term that explains why people from various nations and co-cultures (groups different from mainstream populations in those countries) act and speak as they do

Ethnocentrism: belief in the superiority of one's own culture

Prejudice: a negative preconception about people, activities, or places based upon personal experience, hearsay, or other incomplete data

International cultural communication: communication between representatives of different nations

Interracial cultural communication: communication between people with physical differences

Interethnic cultural communication: communication between people who identify themselves as members of different ethnic groups

Cross-cultural communication: communication between people from two cultures

Glass ceiling: a barrier that is not visible but is real enough to keep women from top-management positions in many businesses and professions

Sexual harassment: includes (1) inappropriate demands made on an employee by a fellow worker or supervisor, and (2) the development of uncomfortable and unprofessional work environments

Attitudes: a person's learned likes and dislikes

Beliefs: a person's judgments about right and wrong

Values: a person's deep cultural assumptions that affect all areas of life

Language culture: the means by which we represent ourselves and the means by which we interpret others

Semiotics: the study of the social and political significance of verbal and nonverbal language as signs

Sociolinguistics: the study of different kinds of speech markers used by different ethnic groups who speak the same language

Semantics: the study of linguistic meanings of words

Argot: specialized language used by a particular group

Jargon: the language-shorthand used by people in a particular trade or profession

DISCUSSION

1. What three steps can be helpful in communication with culturally diverse people?
2. Define and give examples of *diversity, culture,* and *language culture.*
3. Discuss some of the factors that are labeled as diversity among people.
4. Several terms were mentioned that show a negative perspective of cultural communication. Discuss some of these.
5. Discuss the Cultural Communication Conflict Triangle. How could this concept be helpful to you as (a) an employee, (b) a manager, (c) a coworker?

ACTIVITIES

1. It is 1955, and you are an engineer who has been sent to a country that is very different from your own to work as a consultant on a waste treatment plant. The people's diet and family activities bother you, and you suspect that they are not good for them or for their children. One weekday when you are not working, you walk by the local elementary school and see that all the children are lined up. Officials in special ceremonial outfits are doing something to each child. The children are screaming in pain and are in distress. You are told by others that the children will be disfigured for the rest of their lives. They are subjected to this pain and disfigurement twice before they are twenty years old. How do you, an outsider, judge this activity? What do you do when you believe that people who are culturally different from you are doing "bad" things?
2. What are the problems in analyzing your language culture? How would you start? Who could help you? What research or library sources could be informative?
3. What are the advantages and the disadvantages of learning about a specific culture—for instance, the culture of Japan—if you plan to live abroad for a year?
4. Share with the class an experience that you have had in intercultural communication. What cultures were involved? Was there conflict? If so, what was it about? Were there communication difficulties? Which of the personality traits identified in this chapter would have been or were most useful in your communication experience?

ANSWER FOR ACTIVITY 1

The engineer is from Nigeria. The country that he is visiting is the United States. The parents and the children eat something called "TV dinners," which are high in fat and salt. Family members drink soft drinks and eat candy. The children at the school are receiving smallpox vaccinations, which prevent the disease but leave a scar.

PART TWO

BASIC COMMUNICATION SKILLS

CHAPTER 4

Explains the role of perception in listening and teaches interactive listening skills.

CHAPTER 5

Discusses the relationship between verbal and nonverbal communication and suggests ways to create effective messages.

CHAPTER 6

Illustrates the importance of management and leadership in business settings and reveals methods of developing leadership skills.

Part II introduces the fundamentals of successful communication: listening, verbal and nonverbal skills, and management and leadership skills. These chapters discuss how each contributes to successful interaction and how to avoid communication breakdowns. Self-tests and evaluation activities help to identify areas for improvement.

CHAPTER

4

Listening Skills

After completing this chapter, you will be able to:

1. Understand the importance of listening in business and the professions
2. Differentiate between listening and hearing
3. Identify problems caused by ineffective listening
4. Recognize how perception shapes listening
5. Use interactive listening skills to enhance strategic communication
6. Gain control of your listening and eliminate receiver apprehension
7. Know how to evaluate the success of your listening

STRATEGIC SCENARIO

Chris Georgapoppio has been accepted as a summer intern to work at the corporate headquarters of a large financial holding company. The person to whom Chris reports is the vice president for human resources. Typically, student interns are assigned to a department and are given specific responsibilities for the summer. Chris's assignment, however, is different. Because of his outstanding grades, previous work experience in small branch banks, and strong recommendations from people who work in this holding company, Chris is actually being groomed to become an employee when he graduates next spring. As a result, his assignment is to spend the summer gathering as much information as he can about the inner workings of the corporate headquarters and make a report to the administrative committee at summer's end. The HR vice president wants Chris to put together a plan that details how he will go about getting the information he needs for his report. Chris is expected to "leave no stone unturned" in his quest for information about how people get along, stay motivated, and get the job done.

As you read this chapter, think about the many listening issues that will confront Chris as he anticipates his task and the plan he is supposed to submit to the HR vice president.

OVERVIEW

Listening is the most frequently used communication skill. Researchers have estimated that employees typically spend much of their workday communicating; a large portion of this time is spent listening. Communication consultant Germaine Knapp contends that "effective listening can be used to help persuade, motivate, improve productivity, boost morale, obtain cooperation, sell, teach, inform, or achieve other goals."[1] Yet most people take listening for granted.

The lack of attention to the significance of listening is heightened by the popular belief that technology will be able to solve most, if not all, problems in the workplace. According to one business professor, "Technology has led us to impose tighter time frames on ourselves, to reduce standards and fundamentals, to be information-obese, and to substitute technology for basic skills and problem solving. . . . Because information is available, we consume it indiscriminately without thinking through whether we need it."[2] Thus, while technology has increased worker productivity, we emphasize throughout this book that society's increasing dependence on technology makes basic communication skills—listening skills, verbal skills, and nonverbal skills—*more critical* in business than ever before.

Your listening ability is particularly susceptible to information overload because you are constantly exposed to sounds—from televisions, radios, peers, professors, supervisors, and others. It is more difficult to filter out and analyze important information than ever before and easier to get distracted and lose concentration.

In the first three chapters, the strategic communication model focused on generating effective communication from the sender's perspective. This chapter incorporates the strategic communication model from the receiver's perspective. Goal setting, situational knowledge, communication competence, and anxiety management are important elements of effective listening. Listening ability, as well as speaking ability, creates a competent communicator.

LISTENING IN YOUR CAREER

Many people assume that competence and excellence in a career must be demonstrated through speaking—showing others what the speaker knows and how well she or he can articulate it. In many cases, however, excellence can be demonstrated through effective listening as well. In organizational settings, the managers who are perceived as most competent are those who know their employees well and are sensitive to their ideas and concerns. These managers are also rated as the best listeners in the organization.

Recall from Chapter 1 the discussion of organizational communication theories. Many, such as the humanist motivational theory Y, are founded on effective listening. According to theory Y, workers respond to encouragement and are motivated when coworkers and managers carefully listen to their ideas and thoughts. As a future manager or employee, and as a student, developing the ability to listen well will be a vital part of your accomplishments.

Benefits of Good Listening

At this point in your life, your primary "career" is as a student, although you may be working as well. You may or may not know exactly what field you want to pursue after graduation, but you will find that effective listening is a critical skill in

1. Quoted in T. Harris, "Listen Carefully," *Nation's Business* 77 (June 1989), 78.
2. M. Buck-Lew, "Making Technology Work for Us," *Boston Globe,* December 4, 1990, p. 48.

becoming successful. As a student, listening is crucial during presentations such as a professor's lecture or a public speech. As a prospective employee, listening is critical during a job interview. It is also essential to develop listening skills in order to work in the teams that will be required in the workplace of the future. Research has shown that listening is the most important skill for entry-level professionals in business.[3] Furthermore, some researchers estimate that approximately 45 percent of a businessperson's salary is earned listening and that that percentage increases as a person rises in his or her career. Additional research concludes that effective listening is critically important to the success of upper-level managers' career advancement.[4]

Many people earn a great deal of their income by listening. Physicians, therapists, and attorneys must listen carefully to patients and clients to provide desired services effectively. In other jobs, listening can save lives. For example, police officers assigned to work on emergency 911 hotlines use their listening skills to identify and respond to emergencies as they occur. According to an officer in the division of training and education in the Boston Police Department, 911 officers are required to take a forty-hour training course that emphasizes skills such as listening for key information (for example, specific descriptions of people or locations), using silence to calm upset callers, and focusing listening concentration to make up for the lack of visual cues inherent in phone communication. This training yields more and better information—even from highly disturbed callers—and enables officers to use new technology, such as computerized response programs, to supplement their listening skills.[5]

The following example illustrates that, in some situations, listening can even be a matter of life and death:

> On June 1, 1990, in a southwestern city, a series of blunders resulted in the death of a seventy-four-year-old woman who called 911 because she was having chest pains. At the heart of these blunders was a breakdown in communication.
>
> Geraldine Jones was visiting the city and staying in Room 222 at the Days Inn on South Parkway Drive. At 8 P.M. on June 1, she telephoned 911 and requested an ambulance. A dispatcher immediately sent an ambulance to Room 22 at the Days Inn located at 1319 South Parkway Drive and filled out a response card, giving the address of the motel as 600 North Parkway Drive, which was actually the location of the Days End Motel. When the ambulance arrived at the Days Inn, motel employees told the emergency medical technicians (EMTs) that there was no Room 22 and, unaware of an emergency call from their motel, directed the ambulance to the Days End on North Parkway Drive.
>
> When the ambulance arrived at Days End, the EMTs were told that there was no Room 22. A check of rooms 122 and 222 disclosed no one needing medical assistance. The central dispatcher telephoned Days Inn, asked whether Geraldine Jones was registered there, and was erroneously told that no one with that name was registered. The dispatcher then requested the help of the telephone company, which traced the original

Where Do You Stand?

What situations have you experienced in which a breakdown in listening occurred? What were the consequences of poor listening? Bring to class two or three instances in which poor listening created major problems for you or someone else.

3. V. S. Di Salvo, "A Summary of Current Research Identifying Communication Skills in Various Organizational Contexts," *Communication Education* 29 (1980), 283–290.
4. J. Brownell, "Managerial Listening and Career Development in the Hospitality Industry," *International Journal of Listening* 8 (1994), 31–49.
5. Interview with Captain Robert Dunford, Boston Police Department, December 10, 1990.

Listening is the most frequent and possibly the most important type of on-the-job communication. When we listen effectively, we develop better workplace relationships, learn from the experiences of others, and begin to better understand the goals, needs, values, and expectations of our coworkers and clients. (© Bill Lai/Index Stock Imagery)

call to a laundromat on Water Street. It was finally decided that the call was a prank.

Mrs. Jones was found dead in Room 222 of the Days Inn the next morning by the housekeeping staff.[6]

After reviewing the 911 telephone recordings, the tragic communication breakdown was determined to be a result of poor listening, and the outcome was death. Strong listening skills are essential in many other fields as well. And yet poor listening occurs every day and results in the loss of jobs, profit, relationships, or even life.

Problems with Ineffective Listening

Trouble arises when you do not listen carefully to others. Comments such as "You need to pay closer attention to directions," "Concentrate on what you are doing," and "I don't think you understand what I'm saying" are good indications that your listening skills can use improvement. Failing to listen effectively can produce some embarrassing moments, like the time a business traveler sleepily boarded the red-eye flight to Oakland, California (she thought), and landed hours later in Auckland, New Zealand. Faking attention, or **pseudolistening,** can be just as harmful and embarrassing as failing to listen altogether! There are three areas in which poor listening can cause trouble in your career.

Poor Listeners Are Perceived as Less Intelligent When other people perceive that someone is not listening carefully, their first reaction is that this person is unable to handle what is being said. This is especially true when poor listening

6. Excerpted from the *Las Cruces (New Mexico) Sun News,* June 4, 1990.

becomes a habit. Others become wary of a poor listener's ability to handle even the simplest amount of information, and the results can be quite negative, as the following example illustrates.

FLORENCE: Why don't we get Zack to join our work group?

FERNANDO: Oh, I don't know. He doesn't seem all that bright. He has to have stuff repeated all the time, and sometimes he doesn't seem plugged in at all.

BUD: I know. He is either slow, or he is uninterested in what other people say. Either way, I would prefer to think of someone else for our team.

FLORENCE: I guess you're right.

Poor Listening Is Costly One of the greatest costs of ineffective listening is wasted time. Repeating information is time-consuming and causes problems if the task at hand requires a quick response. Repeating messages also consumes effort and energy that can be put to better use. If you are experiencing fatigue or are enduring stressful conditions, an ineffective listening partner compounds your problems.

Poor listening can cost money, too. Misinterpretation, failure to hear information correctly, and physical or mental distractions are listening problems that cost businesses money. For example, if you are traveling and fail to hear your flight number being called, you lose time and money if you have to take a later flight. When you book hotel rooms, if you are not listening carefully to the reservation clerk when she or he mentions that your company is eligible for a corporate rate, you cost your company money. Consider the magnitude of poor listening in dollars and cents. If each employee in the United States made a $10 listening mistake, it would cost us $1 billion. If you consider that all employees make two of these listening mistakes per week, the cost of poor listening on the job explodes to $100 billion per year![7]

Poor Listening Limits Your Chances for Success Most people's careers are characterized by steps toward a particular goal. Effective listening is necessary in the journey toward this goal. Promotions, recognition, salary increases, and awards are possible only after employees have demonstrated their competence in critical areas, and performance appraisals are often based on criteria directly related to effective listening abilities. Even now, while you are in school, you can achieve more success by improving your listening skills. Concentrating on what others are saying before you ask a question can prevent you from repeating a question that someone has already asked. Being open to new information allows you to make creative connections while learning.

Listening enables you to take advantage of opportunities and avoid potential problems. Professionals who maintain only average listening abilities will probably achieve only average success in their careers. People with exceptional career success will tell you that they consider listening to have been a critical element in their strategic climb up the career ladder. An example of corporate commitment to listening is Unisys, the information technology giant that has been a leader in promoting listening among its employees. This organization is so convinced of the importance of listening on the job that more than twenty thousand of its employees have received formal training in listening.[8]

7. J. M. Kouzes and B. Z. Posner, *The Leadership Challenge* (San Francisco: Jossey-Bass, 1987), p. 60.
8. M. Osborn and S. Osborn, *Public Speaking*, 4th ed. (Boston: Houghton Mifflin, 1997), p. 57.

HEARING VERSUS LISTENING

You have been using your sense of hearing longer than you are able to remember. Even before you were born, you heard sounds generated outside your mother's body. Of course, there is a critical difference between the sensory process of hearing and the skill of listening, which we will address in this chapter. **Hearing** is an automatic process in which sound waves stimulate nerve impulses to the brain. **Listening** is a voluntary process that goes beyond simply reacting to sounds and includes understanding, analyzing, evaluating, and responding.[9] Listening is also more than just part of "spoken communication." Messages are both verbal and nonverbal. An effective listener must use more than just her or his sense of hearing to understand, analyze, evaluate, and respond.

Listening requires concentration, which means holding a key idea in your mind while you consider alternative or conflicting concepts. Effective listening entails synthesizing new information with what you already know.[10] You may have heard people refer to others' "short attention span," "lack of consideration," or "weak concentration." All these remarks boil down to the same message: "that person does not listen well."

Both now and after graduation, you will need strong listening skills, and others will expect you to use them. By reading this chapter, you can learn why effective listening is indispensable in organizations. You can also understand how listening fits into the total human communication process—that is, you can comprehend the *interactive* nature of communication. You can acquire skills and techniques to help you become a more effective listener.

We cannot guarantee that this chapter will solve all your interpersonal problems, make the rest of your college years a smashing success, and get you the job of your dreams. We cannot even guarantee that it will make you a perfect listener. But we can assure you that skillful listening will improve your chances for personal and professional success.

THE ROLE OF PERCEPTION

You may have heard the adage "You have to know where you are before you can go anywhere." To improve listening skills, you need an idea of your listening framework—your perceptions. **Perception** is the process of creating meaning based on experience. In other words, your understanding of events depends on your accumulation of sensory knowledge about people, objects, and events.

Think about the Department of Homeland Security's "Terrorism Advisory System." Different people may perceive the various color levels differently. Which seems like a more threatening color to you: blue or green? Does a blue level of terrorism alert seem "safer"? Blue is generally a "cooler" color than green. Green, however, is often associated with "go," as in traffic lights. In the case of the Terrorism Advisory System, green is the lowest level of threat, while blue is a "Guarded" level of alert. But then what does that mean? Some might interpret "guarded" as meaning that we are guarded and protected. Others might see "guarded" as signifying the presence of threats of terrorism from which we need to be guarded. Because of this variation in perception, different people often interpret a given message in different ways. Such dissimilar perspectives often lead people to respond to messages in unpredicted ways. Take a moment to look at Figure 4.1. What do you see in

9. W. Pauk, *How to Study in College,* 4th ed. (Boston: Houghton Mifflin, 1990), p. 122.
10. J. Patterson, "Better Listening for Business and Personal Success." Accessed September 19, 2003.: www2.pvc.maricopa.edu/~patterson.listening.doc.

FIGURE 4.1

Perceptual Tricks

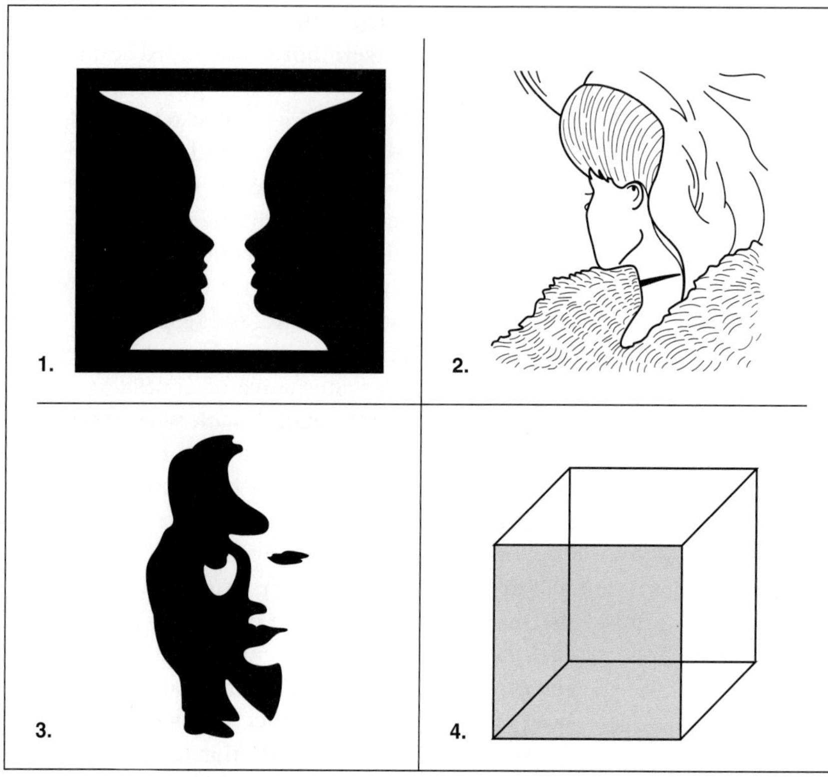

What do you see in the images labeled 1–4 above? Depending upon your own perceptions, your first impression of image 1 might be of a vase, image 2 may appear to be a young woman's profile, image 3 may look like a portrait of a girl, and the blue side of the box in image 4 may appear to be the front of the cube. However, look again, and image 1 becomes two faces staring at each other, image 2 becomes an old woman's profile, image 3 becomes a man playing the saxophone, and the blue side of the box in image 4 appears to shift to the back of the cube.

these four images? Your perceptual framework determines what you initially see in the figure.

If every person who receives a message perceives it somewhat differently, consider what happens when a message is sent in a business environment. The message is likely to be received by a large number of people from a wide range of backgrounds and with very different organizational experiences. A message such as "Because of a drop in business, some personnel cuts in some key areas may occur in the near future" can become a source of controversy and insecurity among employees because it is vague and thus likely to be interpreted in myriad ways. Therefore, it is extremely important to assess your perceptual framework and the possible perceptions of others when communicating. The first step is understanding the factors that influence perception.

Factors Influencing Perception

Reception and attention are important factors in perception. **Reception** is the physical process of hearing aural and seeing visual stimuli (including nonverbal cues). Although it may seem obvious, the condition of your hearing and sight determines to some degree the amount and type of information you receive. If your hearing is impaired or your prescription eyeglasses need updating, you are likely to miss information and thus have inaccurate perceptions of messages.

Even if reception is perfect, so much information reaches the brain that only some of it can actually be processed meaningfully. **Attention** is the cognitive ability that allows us to select certain types of information for processing and ignore others. Selective and focused attention to the message is crucial for accurate perception. Blaine Goss has suggested three principles that describe the listener's attention process:[11]

1. The number of stimuli to which a person can attend at one time is very limited.
2. Some stimuli go unnoticed or are attended to only in an unconscious way.
3. The amount of attention a person gives to a stimulus varies according to the difficulty of the task at hand.

Goss's three principles highlight what you probably already know from everyday experience: there's only so much you can do, or pay attention to, at one time. Being a good listener requires paying attention. The greater the number of distractions—from either external factors (such as an uncomfortable seat or a pressing time constraint) or internal ones (such as fatigue or emotional state)—the more difficult it will be to concentrate on what a speaker is saying, and the poorer a job of listening you will do. One of the most important of these factors is perceptual assessment.

Assessing Your Own Perceptions

Although perception is often blamed for communication problems, it is a necessary element in making sense of the world. Your perceptions act as a category system that helps you to understand messages. If you were unable to categorize messages according to your supply of knowledge and experience, *every* message would be difficult to understand. It would be like having to learn how to read every time you open a book.

Problems with perception occur when erroneous impressions or category systems distort your interpretation of people or events. Such impressions can distort perception in either a positive or negative way. Even a positive bias toward someone—imagine interviewing someone whom you happily discover went to the same school as you—can result in unfair treatment for someone *else* if that erroneous factor is weighted too heavily. In extreme cases, perception is replaced by prejudice—preconceived negative judgments or opinions formed without a basis in reality. For example, you may have difficulty communicating with a member of the legal profession because you have been raised to believe that lawyers are corrupt and untrustworthy. Recall from Chapter 3 that prejudice prevents the acceptance of individuals from other cultures. This same prejudice can affect the interpretation of their messages as well.

Prejudices and biases inhibit effective listening. These biases are not limited to cultural differences; they can also arise from differences in gender, age, sexual preference, religious affiliation, and ethnic background. Instead of facilitating communication, prejudice acts as a barrier

What Would You Do?

Imagine that you are with a group of people and several people are talking at once. Could you listen to more than one person at a time and make sense of what they are saying? Or would you have to concentrate on just one person? What would you do?

11. B. Goss, *Processing Communication* (Belmont, Calif.: Wadsworth, 1982).

STRATEGIC SKILLS

Personal Listening Profile

Rate each statement according to the following scale: (5) Always true for me; (4) Frequently true for me; (3) Sometimes true for me; (2) Rarely true for me; (1) Never true for me.

1. ______ Listening to public speeches is boring.
2. ______ Listening to someone talk on the radio is very entertaining.
3. ______ It is easy to concentrate when others talk about their problems.
4. ______ Listening to my supervisor over the telephone is more difficult than talking to him or her in person.
5. ______ Listening to several people talk at once in a group discussion is very distracting.
6. ______ Listening to small talk is an enjoyable activity.
7. ______ Listening to videotaped instructional or training materials bothers me.
8. ______ Listening to critically important information makes me nervous.
9. ______ Listening to people in authority is exciting.
10. ______ I avoid listening to people I do not like.
11. ______ I am often distracted if I must listen for a long time.
12. ______ It is easy to concentrate on what others are saying if they gesture with their hands.
13. ______ I enjoy listening to others talk about themselves.
14. ______ I feel uncomfortable when listening to technical information.
15. ______ I look forward to the opportunity to listen to people argue skillfully about a controversial topic.

Look back over the responses you gave. Add your score for numbers 1, 4, 5, 7, 8, 10, 11, and 14. Call the total "Score A." Add your score for numbers 2, 3, 6, 9, 12, 13, and 15. Call the total "Score B." Subtract Score A from Score B. If the resulting total is between twenty and twenty-seven, you see yourself as a very competent listener. If you scored between twelve and nineteen, you see yourself as an average listener. If you scored between eleven and negative fifteen, you see yourself as a below-average listener. If you scored negative sixteen or below, you perceive yourself as a poor listener.

to effective and open exchange. Separating the message from the speaker and concentrating on the message can aid in overcoming prejudice. In addition, good listeners take care to hear what is actually said, not merely what they wish to hear. One's own desires or expectations can bias the perception of a message, resulting in hearing nothing but confirmation of your existing beliefs. Therefore, it is essential to be aware of your expectations and try to separate those from the message itself.

The first skill necessary for interactive listening is the ability to diagnose your own listening behavior. The personal listening profile in the Strategic Skills box on page 98 shows you "where you are" and can help you to plan specific improvement strategies. Think carefully about each statement before responding. Only honest and well-considered answers will allow you to learn about yourself. The personal listening profile helps you to understand your own listening preferences in specific circumstances. For example, if you rated statements 4 and 7 with a five, you may be uncomfortable with nonpersonal communication—that is, communication mediated by technology. You can then cultivate awareness of this perception and make a conscious effort to overcome your hesitation so that you can benefit more from communication such as e-mail or videoconferencing.

Developing empathy or even sympathy for another person's position or perspective requires accurate perception. In this photo, these men are engaged in a lively discussion to better perceive and then sympathize with each other's perspective. Active listening will be the key to their success. (Index Stock Imagery)

Of course, the listening profile is not comprehensive. People often mistake their ability levels, and you may find that particular situations that influence your perceptions have not been included. But thinking about these issues is a good way to identify others and can be the first step toward improving your listening.

A second step in understanding your perceptions is discovering your listening priorities. Listening priorities can vary quite a bit among people and situations. Some people set their listening priorities highest for situations involving close interpersonal relationships (family, relatives, close friends, coworkers). Others reserve listening priorities for social situations (socializing at the office, talking to neighbors and acquaintances). Still others focus their listening priorities on occupational or professional matters (listening to reports, superiors, subordinates, peers, briefings). If you perceive a listening situation as important, you are likely to be open and willing to engage in interactive listening.

Finally, it's a good idea to consider how emotionally charged words affect your perceptions of people and ideas. You may hold very strong opinions about certain words or subjects, such as *conservative, liberal, AIDS, chemical weapons,* or *taxes.* Your opinions are likely to be accompanied by strong emotional energy that derives from your experiences or knowledge of those issues, the way you have been brought up, or the environment you are living in.

Emotion is a positive quality because it reflects the strength of your beliefs. However, it can also be a barrier to listening if you focus on the charged words, instead of on the message, and fail to process information objectively. You may stop listening to the speaker entirely to prepare a defense of your position on the issue. To listen effectively, you are wise to recognize others' points of view and actively control your emotions.

PRACTICING BUSINESS COMMUNICATION

United Psychiatric Group

Listening is the foundation of good psychiatric practice. When he founded United Psychiatric Group (UPG) in 1984, chair George Chopivsky, Jr., envisioned a network of mental health facilities distinguished by its responsiveness to community needs and its high-quality care. Since then, UPG has grown to nine hospitals countrywide, providing residential and outpatient treatment for psychiatric and chemical-dependency patients.

UPG facilities and the main administrative office in Washington, D.C., employ nearly one thousand people. The main office houses executive management and departmental staffs for finance, development, recruiting, and operations. The services of these departments are available to all facilities, and the vice presidents of each department travel often in order to keep in close touch with workers at each hospital.

AN INFORMAL COMMUNICATION APPROACH

Face-to-face communication with employees at different facilities and on-site listening and information gathering are critical to executive management's understanding of how the company is doing. An open, cooperative communication process linking UPG employees at all facilities is a key factor in the company's success.

Communication at the Washington office is casual, with few formal meetings. The vice presidents of each department visit each facility often, whether or not a problem exists. In this way, they avoid appearing as disciplinarians and can trust that the environment they are observing accurately represents the facility's day-to-day operations.

Each hospital is run by an administrator who meets with department heads formally once a week. Aside from this meeting, the administrator relies on informal communication with employees to get things done.

UPG employees do not follow rigid, hierarchical communication procedures. Instead, communication lines are kept open at all times. If a task needs performing or a question needs answering, an employee can go right to the source. For example, if the administrator of a facility is unavailable and the director of nursing has a pressing question, he or she can call the vice president of operations in Washington, D.C., for advice or help.

SHARED RESOURCES/INDEPENDENT ACTION

Forum groups are a unique UPG communication tool. These groups foster communication among people who hold the same position at different UPG hospitals, from controllers to directors of residential treatment care to ambulatory care providers.

The forum group consisting of the directors of residential treatment care at each facility, for example, regularly

Assessing Others' Perceptions

Sympathy is identification with others' feelings. **Empathy,** on the other hand, is the act of sharing the feelings of another person. For example, while a sympathetic friend could tell you what he would do in your situation, an empathetic friend would know what *you* would do. Sympathy and empathy are important elements of perception. By attempting to feel the same way as a speaker does (to empathize with her or him), you can better understand the message.

Nevertheless, it is important to remember that total empathy is impossible because individuals perceive things differently. No one can share the exact feelings of another. In fact, trouble often begins when you think, "I know just how you feel." You can, however, try to assimilate what you perceive another to be feeling. Furthermore, by demonstrating that you understand a speaker's feelings (sympathize with him or her), you can enhance the shared meaning of the communicated message.

schedules a teleconference among all group members. One member sets the agenda based on suggestions from the participants. During the call, the directors discuss each hospital's current activities and share information, ideas, and problem-solving techniques.

UPG also encourages communication among employees from different facilities by using its most effective workers as human resources. If employees at a facility need help with a particular problem, a UPG employee at another facility may be tapped as a resource to give advice or provide expertise. For example, the controller at UPG's Fox Run Hospital in Ohio helped personnel at the Mesilla Valley Hospital in New Mexico master a complex software package.

Common resources and interfacility contact among employees notwithstanding, each UPG hospital is a separate corporation that evolves according to the particular needs of the community it serves. The hospital administrator's job is not simply to report to the corporate office and to adhere strictly to established corporate policy. Rather, the administrator applies leadership and organizational skills to running the UPG facility as if it were his or her own business.

COMMUNICATION AND COMMUNITY INVOLVEMENT

An essential component of each facility's individuality is community involvement, which is guided at each hospital by the director of community relations. Community involvement can take many forms, from encouraging employees to become members of local professional groups—and giving them time to do so—to conducting educational programs to sharing faculty with local universities.

By communicating with professionals, patients and their families, and businesses and community groups in their region, UPG employees communicate their concern for their community's needs and learn how those needs might best be addressed by the hospital. Their success in working with the community is essential to the hospital's success and thus to UPG's success as a whole.

QUESTIONS FOR CRITICAL THINKING

1. How does UPG's organizational structure contribute to its success?
2. How do UPG managers and employees apply situational knowledge?
3. What advantages do UPG's forum groups offer to the organization?
4. What leadership skills do UPG hospital administrators need?
5. Why are community relations important to UPG?

Not all situations call for an obvious display of sympathy or empathy from the listener, but many situations do. Strategies for uncovering a speaker's feelings include questioning techniques ("Are you feeling all right?" "Is there anything you want to discuss with me?") that will be discussed later in the chapter.

Keep in mind, however, that it may not be appropriate in all situations to use these techniques, for some speakers do not wish to share their feelings. Lastly, be careful not to misinterpret cues, particularly an emotional display or tone. Don't assume that because you observe someone being happy, sad, angry, and so on, you know the reason. The boss who snaps at you when you knock on the door may be angry that your report is overdue, but may also simply be upset from something else he just read. Avoid taking such emotional cues personally. The most important part of empathy is true concern for others and respect for what they have to say.

GOAL SETTING FOR INTERACTIVE LISTENING

As with all important communication activities, such as speaking up in meetings, talking to coworkers, or interviewing, preparation for listening allows you to do the best job you can. You can prepare for listening situations by accomplishing several tasks. These include identifying objectives, knowing your listening style, building motivation, and generating energy. For example, attending a meeting or presentation can be more profitable if you identify specific objectives ("I will learn at least five new things at this meeting"), build motivation for the event ("I know that the things I learn will benefit me later"), and generate sufficient energy to be alert ("I will conserve my physical and mental energy for the meeting"). Let's examine each of these steps individually.

Identify Objectives

Three questions are worthy of consideration in goal setting: What must I get out of this listening situation? What would I like to get out of this situation? What should the other persons get out of my listening to them? As you answer these questions, keep in mind that goals should identify basic objectives, such as getting background information needed to perform at an adequate level.

Comprehensive goals also identify additional rewards that might be reaped from the listening situation, such as learning about how you and your actions affect larger processes in the organization or how the speaker feels about the subject of the conversation. Goals for listening situations, like all communication goals, must be specific, appropriate, and realistically obtainable given the resources and abilities available.

When identifying your objectives, it is also important to determine the setting in which the communication will occur. With certain technologies, you might need to modify your listening skills. For example, participating in your first videoconference changes the way you speak and listen. It can seem peculiar to speak to a television set or computer monitor and even stranger to realize the person you are listening to can watch you listening.

Consideration for the other person or people in the listening situation is another important goal. Remind yourself to keep an open mind, respond honestly, and concentrate fully on what is being said. It is a great advantage for those who are speaking or talking to know whether you are comprehending the communication.

Know Your Listening Style

Try to get a sense of what type of listening is called for. There are four types: for information, for enjoyment, for evaluation, and for feelings. Some people make more of an effort to listen in situations where information is exchanged than in situations

Where Do You Stand?

Think of a situation (school, work, or family) where it is important for you to listen well. On a sheet of paper jot down some goals that are important for you to achieve in this listening situation. Make sure that you address the three questions posed at the beginning of this section and identify rewards for yourself and the other people involved in the situation. After the event, look back at your goals and assess how well you accomplished them.

STRATEGIC SKILLS

Characteristics of a Good and Bad Listener

Good Listeners

- Maintain steady eye contact
- Devote full attention to the speaker
- Keep posture and demeanor alert
- Give verbal cues
- Paraphrase to clarify
- Demonstrate empathy
- Are patient
- Share the limelight
- Indicate an open mind
- Leave the answer for the speaker
- Listen for intent as well as content

Bad Listeners

- Interrupt
- Are inattentive and easily distracted
- Use negative body language
- Change the subject
- Give no short verbal prompts
- Are very critical
- Are impatient
- Take over the conversation
- Are discouraging
- Play "Mr. Fix-it"
- Think what they will say next

B. Lampton, "What Good Listeners Do: Becoming the Company Others Love to Keep!" *Expert Magazine* (2003) [on-line]. Available: http://www.expertmagazine.com/artman/publish/article 309.shtml.
C. Reid, "How to Promote OSH," *OSH Promotion in the Workplace* (1998) [on-line]. Available: http://www.safetyline.wa.gov.au/institute/level1/course7/lecture26/126 02.asp.

that speak to feelings. Others are more interested in being effective listeners when evaluation comes into play than when enjoyment is the point.

Knowing more about your listening style helps to improve your motivation. Several listening styles have been identified: appreciative, empathic, discriminative, analytical, passive, and negative. **Appreciative listening** is used to judge the aesthetic value of what is heard, such as a public speech, play, or comedian's routine, and is used mostly for enjoyment. **Empathic listening** concentrates on the feelings or attitudes of the speaker, rather than on the message, and is employed to discover the feelings of the speaker, such as during a therapy session or when listening to a friend's problem. **Discriminative listening** involves drawing inferences from auditory cues and evaluating reasons for the message. This is "reading between the lines" listening. **Analytical listening** encompasses a concentration on the content and includes understanding, interpreting, and analyzing a message. This style is useful in an exchange of information or ideas, such as at a staff meeting.

The appropriateness of appreciative, discriminative, empathic, and analytical listening styles depends on the situation. In any case, passive and negative listening are undesirable styles. **Passive listening** means that the receiver is not concentrating on the message and consequently loses much of its meaning. **Negative listening** is defensive in nature: the receiver is listening to find fault with the sender or is listening to attack what is being said. At times styles overlap. A business presentation, for example, can require both discriminative and analytical listening. Recognizing the listening situation will help you identify objectives, build motivation, and adopt an effective listening style.

Generate Energy

Some communication situations demand more energy than others. Consider the difference between listening to a fellow student talk about the success of a project that the two of you worked on together and listening to a group of people you do not know very well talk about their plans for the summer. You may be surprised to realize that the hidden benefits of the second situation far outweigh those of the first. Whereas you already know about the successful project (after all, you worked on it), you have the opportunity to learn quite a bit about the possibilities for summer jobs from listening to the group conversation. The key is to energize yourself and make the most of the situation.

Listening requires two types of energy: physical and mental. Physical energy is required to listen effectively. Did you ever play "telephone" as a child? By connecting two tin cans together with a string, you could speak into one can and be heard by your friend through the other. You may have noticed that as the connecting string got longer, the amount of physical energy you needed to hear your friend became greater. Similarly, under certain circumstances the physical energy you need to communicate effectively becomes greater. When videoconferencing first became available, the images were jerky and delayed for about twenty seconds between "image updates." Many argued that the images were more distracting than helpful. Certain new technologies may seem foreign and require high physical or mental energy, such as using the Internet for long-distance phone calling. But as time passes, the amount of energy you need to communicate effectively in these new contexts will decrease as technology improves and/or you become more comfortable with the context.

Fatigue, disappointment, and even frustration can take its toll on maintaining concentration. How effective do you think this employee's concentration will be when a coworker drops by to offer suggestions on a project they are working on? What can he do to generate enough energy to listen productively? (© Adrian Peacock/ImageState-Pictor/Picture Quest)

Fatigue can also have a surprisingly strong effect on listening ability, yet many people do not take this factor into account, particularly students for whom late nights and inadequate sleep are facts of life. Fatigue dulls the senses and can lower your ability to process information. If you are tired, sick, stressed, or otherwise incapacitated, the following advice can help you to make the most of the situation:

1. Indicate to the source of the message your physical condition and ask for consideration.
2. Muster stored energy for the listening situation (deep breathing, muscle tension/relaxation, avoidance of physically stressful activities ahead of time).
3. Avoid listening situations for which you simply cannot build any energy. Postponing such situations is preferable to not listening well.

The level of a person's mental energy also shapes the listening process. Many people put less mental energy into activities at the end of the day, either because they are tired or because they are beginning to think of other things—what to do after work or after class. Worries, anxiety, and apprehension over work-related or personal matters are other common causes of low mental energy.

Of course, putting such concerns aside to prepare for a listening situation is difficult (and sometimes impossible), but putting your worries in perspective nevertheless helps. If there is nothing you can do about a worrisome situation at the moment, accept that fact, resolve to tackle the matter at another time, and stop worrying about it.

SITUATIONAL KNOWLEDGE: PREPARING FOR INTERACTIVE LISTENING

As you recall from Chapter 2, situational knowledge is information that is useful for recognizing and understanding the variables operating in communication situations. Taking situational details into account as much as possible enables you as a listener to prepare effectively for the communication encounter. Such external factors include the speaker's communication style, various environmental distractions, emotions, and even the message itself. The communication style of a speaker is one of a number of situational factors that can affect your listening effectiveness.

Speaker's Communication Style

The speaker's communication style may call for the application of special listening considerations. Some people tend to talk rapidly, gesture broadly, or otherwise distract you from the message. Others show no expressiveness or talk slowly; this style may leave you second-guessing the meaning of the message because you have insufficient cues to guide your interpretation and a lot of time to question the meaning of the words.

Unusual dialects or accents may also cause listening difficulties. One of the best ways to overcome this obstacle is to familiarize yourself with new speech patterns. You can do this by listening especially carefully, talking little, and concentrating hard when communicating with someone who uses a dialect or has an accent that sounds strange to you. Do not focus on your own comprehension difficulties; listen instead for the speaker's ideas, the content of the message. Identify common speech patterns (for example, many native Spanish-speakers pronounce *bit* as "beet," and many people from the northern United States pronounce *hair* as "here") and become comfortable with them.

Do not hesitate to ask a speaker to repeat what she or he said or to slow down. You will both benefit from such requests, particularly if they are phrased in a polite, confident voice. The worst response is to decide that you simply cannot comprehend a speaker and to stop trying.

Environmental Distractions

The communication setting may contain a variety of distractions. Noise, the presence of others, or even listening on someone else's "turf" can lessen your capacity for listening. If possible, try to move the communication event to a setting with less noise or fewer distractions. If this is not possible, make the best of the setting. If you are in a crowded room, see whether you can find a relatively quiet corner. If you are in an unfamiliar office, visualize a more comfortable setting. Although setting is a situational parameter that is often difficult to adjust, both you and the speaker will benefit from making the setting as comfortable as possible.

The act of listening and communicating demands more attention than you might realize. Consider having a conversation on a cell phone while driving. We don't think about how much of our brain power is devoted to carrying on a conversation. However, research shows that driving while talking on a cell phone actually impairs your abilities more than being legally drunk.[12]

Is the weakening of your driving ability due simply to having too much of your finite attention drawn to the conversation or to trying to juggle the phone itself? Not really. After all, most people are easily able to both drive a car and have a conversation with someone else *in the car with them.* Rather, the problem arises with cell phone usage (even with headsets) because the other talker, who is not in the car, cannot view the driving environment and is unable to see the driver's nonverbal cues. Inside the car, however, most talkers recognize when the driver needs to give more attention to the road—and they will pause to allow him to do so. A prime example of interactivity in communication!

Emotional Distractions

The emotions of the communicators are a determining factor in any listening situation. Emotionally aroused people often react to communication situations differently from people who are calm. If you are negatively aroused, you may not listen effectively and thus compound the problems you already have. Speakers who are emotionally charged may mislead you into thinking that they are passionate about the topic when something else is actually bothering them.

When you listen to a highly emotional speaker, focus on the content of the message rather than on the delivery. Control your impulse to argue until you have heard the complete message. As you listen, evaluate the strengths and weaknesses of the speaker's position by summarizing the main points of the argument in your head. Doing so will help you to remain calm (much like forcing yourself to count to ten before losing your temper) and will also help you to respond effectively when the time comes.

12. D. L. Strayer, F. A. Drews, and W. A. Johnston, "Cell Phone-Induced Failures of Visual Attention During Simulated Driving," *Journal of Experimental Psychology: Applied* 9(23) (2003), 23–32. http://www.psych.utah.edu/AppliedCognitionLab/JEP_Applied.pdf.

Where Do You Stand?

Select a news or entertainment program that you *dislike* because it is emotional in its presentation. Watch the show and persons involved, and make mental notes of the main points being made. Consciously fight the distractions that you normally experience, and try to understand the meaning of the speaker as much as possible. Afterward, write down the speaker's position and her or his main points. Make some notes about how you were able to fight the emotional distractions that you usually have when listening to this type of speaker. Use these notes as a guide the next time you find yourself becoming distracted by your feelings about a speaker.

Message Content

The message itself plays an important role in listening. Most people are motivated to listen effectively if the consequences of the communication are important. Formal situations, such as presentations, lectures, or interviews, usually require systematic listening and precise comprehension of the speaker's language.[13] If the situation is informal, or if the topic is not particularly meaningful to you (for example, a colleague tells you about a report unrelated to your area), you may be tempted to minimize your listening effort. Keep in mind, however, that it is impossible to predict all the outcomes of a listening situation, so it is a good idea to make the most of every listening opportunity. That colleague's report may contain information you will find useful at a future date.

Small talk, social conversation, and personal self-disclosures usually do not require the same type of listening skills as does content that is highly technical, vague, controversial, or innovative. By considering the content of the message, listeners can anticipate the conditions of the listening situation.

COMMUNICATION COMPETENCE: INTERACTIVE LISTENING

Research from the workplace reports that listening is the number one reason given for believing that another person is a competent communicator.[14] Interactive listening is an ongoing, complex, and dynamic process. The maximum rewards from listening result from strategic planning, assessments of self and others, and feedback and verbal encouragement. Interactive listening is not only an auditory skill. You listen best if you listen with all your senses. Elements of verbal and nonverbal behavior can help you process maximum amounts of information in a listening context.

To become more interactive as a listener, reduce the amount of time you spend talking, use questions to become more aware as a listener and to help others, and use the strategic aspects of nonverbal behavior. These skills, along with the listening competence skills you learned earlier in the chapter, will be invaluable in improving your listening.

13. B. Goss and D. O'Hair, *Communicating in Interpersonal Relationships* (New York: Macmillan, 1988).
14. J. Haas and C. Arnold, "An Examination of the Role of Listening in Judgments of Communication Competence in Coworkers," *Journal of Business Communication* 32 (1995), 123ff. Accessed September 21, 2003: www.questia.com.

Talk Less

It is difficult to listen when you are talking. People who believe that what they have to say is the critical component of any conversation feel compelled to provide a play-by-play commentary on every event and idea that occurs to them. People with reputations as good listeners are admired—and their primary skill is the ability to keep quiet!

As a strategy, silence works in many communication situations. Speakers frequently elaborate or provide additional information if their conversational partner is silent. Consider the following situation:

> Clarissa knew that José recently had an important meeting with the district manager of the software division in which they both worked. She overheard two coworkers, Joan and Peter, pestering José with questions about the meeting. José's responses were evasive; he seemed uncomfortable with their aggressive questioning and gave them very little information. Clarissa and José were not particularly good friends, but she decided that if she approached him in a nonthreatening way and allowed him to talk, she might find out what had gone on at the meeting. When José referred to the meeting in a later conversation with Clarissa, she was strategically silent and did not prompt him for information. This behavior seemed to put him at ease, and soon they were discussing the goings-on of the meeting. José had wanted to talk to someone about the meeting, but he was uneasy and distrustful of people who seemed to care more about their questions than about his answers. He wanted to talk to someone who would really listen.

Ask Questions

Interactive listening entails more than simply receiving a message. It requires listeners to respond at critical points in the communication process. Questioning techniques are one type of response that can improve listening by making speakers more efficient. When listeners and speakers agree on the topic, consequences, and language use, listening effectiveness improves immensely.

Closed, open, probing, and leading questions improve the speaking/listening process. Each type is used for different purposes, depending on the listening situation. Table 4.1 summarizes the differences among these types of questions.

Questioning techniques are especially useful in guiding a speaker toward a conversational point that is necessary to accomplish a goal. Speakers can get off the track, mislead, provide aimless and useless information, or even deceive listeners. In the following situation, notice how one communicator uses questions to keep the discussion on-track:

VINCENT: I'm really glad that Phyllis joined the office staff.

TANYA: So am I. Aren't we going to finish our discussion about the new alarm system?

VINCENT: I guess. I think Joanne ought to replace the old copier. It's worn out.

TANYA: That's her choice. Vincent, should the new alarm system have both heat and smoke sensors? It would be more expensive if it does.

VINCENT: Both. I found a system that operates less expensively when both sensors work in tandem.

TABLE 4.1

Techniques for Questioning

Type of Question	Purpose	Example
Closed	Obtain a short, specific response	"Do you mean this fiscal year or last fiscal year?"
Open	Allow freedom and choice in the response	"What is your attitude toward cost accounting?"
Probing	Encourage the speaker to elaborate on the topic (by using *why*-type questions)	"Why do you feel that way?"
Leading	Imply expected response in question	"Are you saying that our computer system needs to be upgraded?"
Reflective	Show empathy with speaker	"Are you excited because we get more time off or because we get overtime pay?"

Use Nonverbal Behavior

To receive the optimum amount of information in the message, it is important to interpret a speaker's nonverbal cues correctly. It is just as important to give the speaker nonverbal cues to show that you are comprehending (or not comprehending) the message.

Effective listening requires more than simply concentrating on the words being spoken. Nonverbal signals such as gestures, pointing, frowning, and even chin stroking (as seen in this photo) reveal listening signals that help speakers adjust their messages. (© Paul Barton/Corbis)

TABLE 4.2

Nonverbal Behavior and Interactive Listening

Behavior	Function
Eye gaze, eye contact	Facilitates others' conversation
Gestures (open palm, motioning)	Encourages additional information
Paralanguage (increase volume, pitch)	Encourages clarification
Proxemics (giving people more space)	Makes people more comfortable
Tactile (pats on the back or shoulder)	Provides confidence builder
Body orientation (face person directly)	Provides sense of importance
Nodding, shaking head	Gives information about feelings

Of course, it is important to listen when someone speaks to you, but it is perhaps even more important for the other person to *perceive* that you are listening. Head nods, leaning forward, gestures, "uh-huhs," smiles, and so forth, are vital cues that let the speaker know that you are interested in what is being said.

Understanding, agreement, empathy, and emotional responses can be displayed effectively by means of nonverbal cues. For example, frowning generally indicates disagreement or misunderstanding. Nodding connotes agreement or comprehension. Shrugs communicate lack of interest or ambiguity. No response at all can convey a lack of awareness. To get a sense of how nonverbal behavior facilitates interactive involvement, take a look at Table 4.2.

Other behaviors—such as using time, taking turns, and avoiding racist and sexist language—also function to regulate the interactive nature of listening. We discuss these at length in Chapter 5. Because nonverbal communication is crucial to speakers, you are wise to recognize how your nonverbal behavior affects communication in particular situations.

Dismantle the Three D's

Competent listening involves dismantling the barriers to your own reception of the message. The most common listening problems are the three D's: distraction, disorientation, and defensiveness. Several strategies, such as listening for ideas, "planning to report," and taking notes, can help you both combat the three D's and make your listening pay great dividends.

Distraction, disorientation, and defensiveness severely inhibit listening. *Distractions* move the focus of attention away from the message. *Disorientation* is a breakdown in the mental and emotional processes that assign meaning to the message. *Defensiveness* produces biased judgment about messages because of overly emotional feelings about certain issues or people. Table 4.3 gives a more complete picture of the three D's.

One way to avoid the three D's is to listen for ideas by asking yourself questions while you listen. Ask yourself whether the speaker's points are logical,

TABLE 4.3

The Three D's

Problem	Components	Consequences	Actions
Distraction	Mental Environmental	Missing needed information Appearing uninterested	Place greater emphasis on the speaker. Withhold attention to distraction until you can deal with it. Take notes to stay on track.
Disorientation	Confusion Boredom Self-reflecting	Appearing dazed, flustered Seeming apathetic Appearing self-centered	Simplify information to its basic level. Focus on main points. Relate what speaker is saying to personal interests.
Defensiveness	Disliking the speaker Resenting the situation	Making biased judgments Reducing alternatives	Understand that it's not about "you" personally. Ask objective questions to self about content.

whether you agree or disagree, and whether what is being said corresponds with or contradicts your own experience. In this way, you can keep yourself focused on the content of the message and at the same time put the message in the context of what you already know.

Another method for dismantling the three D's is taking notes. You can take notes in two ways: writing down the highlights of what is being said or identifying the organizational pattern that the speaker is using. For example, many people organize their ideas into lists, arrange events in chronological order, identify a problem and then a solution, or present one point of view and then an opposing position.[15]

Listen for cues such as "The three causes of increased productivity are," "Since 1987, several important events have occurred," or "Absenteeism is increasing; we can survey the employees to find out why." If you hear a cue, get ready to take down that important information. Remember that other people are impressed by the care and effort demonstrated when a listener takes notes.[16]

Fight Boredom

Fighting boredom is another important skill for competent listening. You are able to process information at about 500 words per minute, but the average rate of speech is only 150 words per minute.[17] Inevitably, there are going to be instances when you are acutely aware of this difference—you are bored. In many other listening situations, without realizing it, you are tuning in and out of effective listening simply because the information is coming in much more slowly than you are processing it. In many business situations—particularly for managers and customer service environments—you may be required to listen to similar problems over and over again. These situations are probably the most dangerous kinds because

15. Pauk, *How to Study in College,* p. 127.
16. Harris, "Listen Carefully," p. 78.
17. A. Wolvin and C. Coakley, *Listening* (Dubuque, Iowa: Brown, 1988).

STRATEGIC SKILLS

Can You Tell When a Listener Is Bored?

While it may not always be possible to keep a listener closely attuned to your every word, good communicators remain aware of listener reaction—whether it is positive or negative—and take steps, if possible, to increase the interest level. How to tell if a listener is bored? Look for any of the following signs:

- Being easily distracted
- Needing to have information repeated
- Watching the clock
- Grooming or preening himself or herself
- Reducing eye contact
- Fiddling with objects or clothing

And remember, others can identify these signs of boredom if you display them, as well! So even if you are bored in a meeting, try not to show it.

what has become routine—and perhaps less interesting—for you is likely a matter of concern and urgency to the other party. To be a good listener in these situations, it is essential that you cultivate a genuine concern for the other person. To reduce your boredom, make the situation a contest in which you challenge yourself to retain the important information. Here are some suggestions for minimizing boredom in listening situations:

- Set goals for obtaining information in a listening situation.
- Remember the costs associated with missed information.
- Focus on the content of the message.
- Relate this information to your current knowledge base.
- Identify the main points of the message and memorize them.

Make the Most of Listening Opportunities

When we talk about making the most of a listening opportunity, we are referring to improving both the situation and your own skills. You can improve the setting of a communication by moving office furniture so you can listen better, ensuring that your seat at a luncheon faces the speaker, or getting a central seat in a group or committee meeting.

Controlling your listening is an important skill. If you hold strong opinions about a point that others are discussing, you may feel the urge to jump into the conversation prematurely, without invitation or planning. Patiently waiting until a speaker finishes allows you to know the other side of the issue better and gives you time to formulate just the right rebuttal. Table 4.4 gives you additional clues for maximizing the benefits of communication encounters.

ANXIETY MANAGEMENT

You may be wondering why anyone is anxious in listening situations. But if you think carefully about it, you will recognize that some situations evoke anxiety. Listening to a boss's reprimand, listening to highly technical information, listening to criticism, and listening to bad news are just a few of the circumstances that can cause anxiety. Other difficult situations can also evoke anxiety. Listening to jargon

TABLE 4.4

Making the Most of Listening Situations

Area of Improvement	Factors	Techniques
Situation control	Setting	Improve seating arrangements. Enhance privacy. Adjust room temperature to comfortable level. Reduce competing messages. Ensure ready access to necessary data.
	Time/timing	Do not overschedule appointments. Ensure enough time to avoid being rushed. Avoid situations that are poorly timed.
Personal control	Emotions	Avoid hasty generalizations. Control emotions by objectifying the situation (this is not about you).
	Patience	Wait until all the facts are on the table. While you wait to speak, analyze the speaker's points.

or other hard-to-understand material and listening to someone brag are also anxiety-producing situations. A small amount of anxiety or apprehension may actually stimulate and motivate your listening, but too much anxiety is harmful.

The problems associated with listening anxiety are numerous. Anxiety during the listening process can be distracting and can lead to forgetfulness, disorganization of information, distortions of data, and other cognitive shortcomings.

ETHICAL ISSUES

Ethical Listening Situations

When most people consider ethical issues, they usually think of situations in which a person is acting, speaking, or behaving in a way that is unethical. There are also many situations in which listening or receiving information can have ethical consequences. Consider the following listening/receiving situations and determine which you feel generate the least or most ethical implications.

- Not returning an e-mail message and saying that you never received it.
- Intentionally overhearing a conversation that is none of your business.
- Ignoring an urgent voice mail to which you do not want to respond.
- Failing to record information you gain in a job interview from a person you do not like personally.
- Telling a fellow employee that you "heard" information when in fact it is only your suspicion.
- Acting bored in a meeting in order to distract the speaker with a competing idea or proposal.
- Monopolizing conversations because you feel you are the only person worth hearing.

STRATEGIC SKILLS

Listener Anxiety Checklist

Use the following checklist to determine your level of listener anxiety. This scale is similar to the personal listening profile, but it focuses on listening anxieties rather than on listening preferences and habits. As a result, your score will have a different meaning from your personal listening profile score.

Answer the following questions according to whether you strongly agree (1), agree (2), are undecided (3), disagree (4), or strongly disagree (5).

1. ______ I have no fear of being a listener as a member of an audience.
2. ______ I feel relaxed listening to new ideas.
3. ______ I am generally overexcited and rattled when others are speaking to me.
4. ______ I often feel uncomfortable when listening to others.
5. ______ I often have difficulty concentrating on what is being said.
6. ______ I seek out the opportunity to listen to new ideas.
7. ______ Receiving new information makes me nervous.
8. ______ I have no difficulty concentrating on instructions given to me.
9. ______ People who attempt to change my mind make me anxious.
10. ______ I am generally relaxed when listening to others.

Add up your scores for items 1, 2, 6, 8, and 10 (set #1). Now add up your scores for items 3, 4, 5, 7, and 9 (set #2). Subtract set #2 from set #1 to get a composite score. If this score is positive (between fifteen and twenty), you have a strong tendency toward anxiety across a range of situations. If your score is between five and fifteen, you have an average level of anxiety. If your score is between negative twenty and five, you have a low base level of listener anxiety.

Understanding your own level of listener anxiety is the first step toward managing anxiety. Obviously, this test is limited; it does not ask about very many listening situations. Nevertheless, this test should give you a rough estimate of what your general feelings are toward the emotional component in the listening process.

Source: From P. Keaney, T Plax, V. Richmond, and J. McCroskey, "Power in the Classroom III: Teacher Communication Techniques and Messages," *Communication Education* 34, 19–28. Copyright 1985. Reprinted by permission of the Speech Communication Association and the authors.

Anxiety hampers your ability to process information and ideas in an efficient manner.[18] In addition, listening anxiety lowers your ability to pursue effective arguments.[19]

It is up to you to identify listening situations that may elicit anxiety. Then prepare for the situation—gather necessary information so that your background knowledge is at the level expected by the source. If you are not able to do this, tell the source of the message if possible. If you are able to control anxiety, you will be better prepared to move successfully through the subsequent stages of the interactive listening process.

18. M. Fitch-Hauser, D. Barker, and A. Hughes, "Receiver Apprehension and Listening Comprehension: A Linear or Curvilinear Relationship?" *Southern Communication Journal* 56 (1990), 62–71.
19. P. Schrodt and L. Wheeless, "Aggressive Communication and Informational Reception Apprehension: The Influence of Listening Anxiety and Intellectual Inflexibility on Trait Argumentativeness and Verbal Aggressiveness," *Communication Quarterly* 49 (2001), 53 ff. Accessed September 22, 2003: www.questia.com.

EVALUATING YOUR LISTENING

The final step in the strategic interactive listening process is evaluating your success. Although we discuss evaluation at the end of this chapter, you can use these skills to make evaluations at each stage of communication. It is important to conduct ongoing evaluations to determine how best to proceed as a listener even as the listening situation evolves. But it is critical for you to get into the habit of evaluating listening situations immediately after they occur.

The first step in evaluation is to assess whether you were able to achieve the goals you set for yourself. Assessing yourself can be difficult if you do not take an objective approach. You can achieve objectivity by answering these questions honestly:

1. To what extent did you fulfill your goal? If you had more than one goal, how many of them did you achieve?
2. Did you adapt your listening behavior during the course of the situation to better achieve your goals?
3. Were the goals that you set for this listening situation realistic?
4. What elements prevented you from achieving part or all of your goals?
5. What can you do in the future to achieve the same goals?

Answering these questions gives you a good picture of how to assess your current listening behavior and how to plan to become an even better listener.

TECHNOLOGY TOOLS

Internet Resources for Listening Skills

It is easy to understand the importance of listening skills in business and the professions when you become aware of the large number of vendors on the Internet and Web that offer services for developing listening skills. A search of Yahoo's Business site turned up a number of Web pages concerned with listening skills, and five of those are presented below.

We selected these five from many others for two reasons. First, these seemed highly relevant to listening skills in business and professional settings. Second, it was our feeling that these Web sites (and their respective organizations) would be in operation for some time to come. We invite you to visit these Web sites and others that emphasize the skill of listening!

http://www.toastmasters.org This is the most recognized organization for developing communications skills. It emphasizes listening skills as well as speaking skills. It is a nonprofit organization with local chapters in just about every major city.

http://www.listen.org This is another nonprofit, professional organization that promotes the "study, development, and teaching of listening." It offers a wide range of services for its members.

http://www.highgain.com This corporation offers individuals and companies a number of programs for developing listening skills.

http://www.esl-lab.com Focusing their services on Web-based instruction, this company can administer audio listening tests to determine your listening skills. A great deal of their focus is on people trying to master English As a Second Language.

http://www.thepargroup.com The Par Group is a comprehensive business consulting organization, although it has an extensive program for listening improvement.

STRATEGIC SCENARIO WRAP-UP

Remember Chris from the beginning of the chapter? Based on what you read in this chapter, how could Chris organize his planning report on how he will go about getting the information he needs for the final report at the end of summer? What aspects of listening will be more important to Chris as he obtains information from people in the company? What should be his listening priorities? What obstacles do you think he will encounter as he listens to people in the organization?

SUMMARY

- Interactive listening is a complex but invaluable method of communicating.
- Although many people take listening for granted, it is a crucial component of personal and professional activity.
- Much of people's financial compensation on the job is earned by listening, and as a person rises in her or his profession, the percentage of salary earned as a result of listening also rises.
- Skilled listening avoids such problems for the listener as being perceived by others as less intelligent, costing time and money, and limiting chances for success.
- Listening is difficult to conceptualize unless it is viewed as part of the whole communication picture, which includes the elements of perception and capacity to understand others' points of view.
- The communication process itself is interactive; it depends on at least two people exchanging verbal and nonverbal messages.
- Successful listening derives from setting appropriate goals for the communication, knowing your listening style, building motivation, and generating energy to make the most of the encounter.
- With specific goals as a basis, the masterful listener obtains the necessary situational knowledge about the speaker's communication style, environmental distractions, emotional distractions, and the physical condition of the communicators.
- Once engaged in communication, the listener cultivates silence, speaks to ask clarifying questions, and uses nonverbal behavior to communicate empathy and sympathy.
- Even the most accomplished listener encounters anxiety-producing situations.
- To manage them, the listener can use his or her analytical skills to identify and deal with causes of anxiety and then evaluate what is successful in the communication.

KEY TERMS

Hearing: an automatic process in which sound waves stimulate nerve impulses to the brain

Listening: a voluntary process that goes beyond simply reacting to sounds and includes understanding, analyzing, evaluating, and responding

Pseudolistening: faking attention; pretending to listen

Perception: the process of creating meaning based on experience

Attention: the cognitive ability that allows us to select certain types of information for processing and ignore others

Reception: the physical process of hearing aural and seeing visual stimuli

Sympathy: identification with others' feelings

Empathy: the act of sharing the feelings of another person

Appreciative listening: used to judge the aesthetic value of what is heard

Empathic listening: concentrates on the feelings or attitudes of the speaker, rather than on the message, and is employed to discover the feelings of the speaker

Discriminative listening: involves drawing inferences from auditory cues and evaluating reasons for the message

Analytical listening: encompasses a concentration on the content and includes understanding, interpreting, and analyzing a message

Passive listening: takes place when the receiver is not concentrating on the message and consequently loses much of its meaning

Negative listening: takes place when the receiver is listening to find fault with the sender or is listening to attack what is being said

DISCUSSION

1. How do hearing and listening differ?
2. What factors influence your listening perception and priorities? What are the implications of those factors for organizational communication?

3. How do mental and physical energy levels affect listening ability? With which listening styles are you most comfortable? What are some techniques for increasing your energy levels?
4. What are some of the common barriers to listening in an organizational setting?
5. How can questioning techniques and nonverbal feedback improve the interactive listening process for greater productivity?
6. What is listener anxiety? Why is it a particularly serious problem in business settings?
7. How can a listening evaluation help you to improve your confidence and productivity?

ACTIVITIES

1. Explain to other members of your discussion group why listening is important in these business situations:
   a. Conducting an employment interview
   b. Judging an employee's grievance
   c. Deciding whether two employees can trade vacation schedules
   d. Representing your company in a media interview
2. List three behaviors that you need to concentrate on to improve your own skills in listening. Next to each behavior, devise an action plan that you can implement to improve your skills.
3. List the listening styles that you see exhibited by other people when you believe that they are listening to you. Share your list with other class members.
4. Creating or tolerating distractions is detrimental to good listening. Select a recent situation in which you had particular trouble concentrating on listening because of distractions. Ask members of your discussion group for strategies that they would use in the same situation to improve listening.
5. Your instructor will divide the class into groups of four or five. Each group will be a project team for a soft-drink company, and the groups will be assigned to create a new slogan. After your group has developed a slogan, make an assessment. Compare and discuss your assessment with the assessments of other members of your group.

CHAPTER

5 Verbal and Nonverbal Skills

After completing this chapter, you will be able to:

1. Identify the importance of verbal and nonverbal communication to businesses
2. Understand the relationship among power, status, and nonverbal communication
3. Evaluate the messages sent through clothing choice and be aware of basic guidelines for business attire
4. Improve your use of language
5. Respect gender and cultural differences in communication
6. Employ and interpret nonverbal cues, including paralanguage, facial expressions, and kinesics
7. Manage anxiety in informal communication situations

STRATEGIC SCENARIO

You go to an interview for your first job. The office is very large. You have to walk across the entire room to get to the interviewer, whose desk is against the far back wall with just enough space for her desk chair. She remains seated and gestures with her hand toward two chairs that are at right angles to the oversized desk. If you sit in either one of the chairs, you will not be facing the interviewer. You begin to wonder if this is some kind of test devised by the interviewer.

As you read this chapter, think about these questions: What should you do? What have you learned about the interviewer? How would you have arranged your office furniture?

OVERVIEW

Think of a time when someone you were talking to did not believe what you were saying. Your words were probably clear and appropriate for the situation ("I'm sorry I was late for class yesterday; I had trouble finding a place to park my car"), but you may have avoided eye contact, spoken in a soft, hesitant voice, or used facial expressions that contradicted your words.

In that instance, you may have suffered only a reprimand from an instructor. In the business world, however, a contradiction between verbal and nonverbal messages can have severe effects: loss of trust between you and your manager, failure to close an important deal, lack of understanding with a coworker, or even conflict with others who are confused by your communication. Clearly, along with listening skills, verbal and nonverbal skills are the foundation of communication in business.

When you consider how much time a professional spends communicating with others during a normal workday, it is easy to understand the importance of this activity. The ability to send clear and coherent messages to supervisors, coworkers, outside vendors, and even the media and the public is critical to maintaining productivity and a positive image, regardless of the industry. Furthermore, as a person rises in the organization to higher levels of management, the need for communication increases.[1] Strong verbal and nonverbal skills are essential for personal success and for the health of the organization. A part of success as a communicator is understanding that all verbal and nonverbal messages are sent and received in cultural codes.

Verbal communication includes all messages composed of words, either spoken or written. Verbal communication is often taken for granted. Our lifelong familiarity with words and speaking makes it easy to neglect the importance of planning the oral messages we send to others. The result is communication failures that could have been avoided with some thought and preparation.

Nonverbal communication is any message—other than spoken or written words—that conveys meaning. How you use your voice, face, and body; how you dress; and even how you arrange your office or the seating configuration at a meeting—all these signal meaning to other people. Van Swol's (2003) research confirms the ongoing assumption: nonverbal messages are more persuasive than verbal messages.[2] Whereas verbal communication is, by and large, controllable and intentional, nonverbal behavior is often difficult to manage.

Successful verbal and nonverbal communication requires careful planning, analysis, execution, delivery, and appraisal. In this chapter we will apply the components of strategic communication to verbal and nonverbal interaction. Then we will cover verbal and nonverbal strategies that you are likely to encounter in business and professional contexts. You will undoubtedly recognize some of these strategies and may already know which ones you are good at and which you need to work on. We will start by discussing goal setting for effective messages.

1. J. C. Bennett and R. J. Olney, "Executive Priorities for Effective Communication in an Information Age," *Journal of Business Communication* 23 (1986), 13–22; V. S. DiSalvo and J. K. Larsen, "A Contingency Approach to Communication Skill Importance: The Impact of Occupation, Direction, and Position," *Journal of Business Communication* 24 (1987), 3–22; S. Tegmeyer, "Survey of College-Educated Managers in the Southwest" (Las Cruces, N. Mex.: New Mexico State Union, 1989).
2. Lyn M. Van Swol, "The Effects of Nonverbal Mirroring of Perceived Persuasiveness, Agreement with an Imitator, and Reciprocity in a Group Discussion," *Communication Research* 30, (2003), 461–480.

GOAL SETTING FOR EFFECTIVE MESSAGES

Successful verbal communication depends on identifying the purpose of a message—the idea you are trying to convey and the reaction you are hoping to elicit—and judging how likely the receiver is to respond appropriately. When you consider the goal or purpose of a message, you are anticipating the function that you want the receiver to perform in response to the message. Organizational messages serve three purposes or functions: task, maintenance, and human relations.[3]

Task messages are intended to make others accomplish specific goals. Task messages include orders, questions, and even confrontations (as long as they promote the primary goals of the organization). Task messages direct a specific project, activity, or behavior. They address performance of tasks. Here are some examples of task messages: "Do you have that order ready today?" "When will that shipment of microchips arrive next week?" "Put those graphs at the end of the report."

Maintenance messages keep the organization in working order so that tasks can be performed. Maintenance messages provide support for people who perform tasks. These messages indicate policy or procedure that directs the organization as a whole, rather than specific projects. For example, statements made about the organization's operations; about the roles of unions, salary, and benefits; and even about competitors serve maintenance functions. Here are some examples: "Be sure to fill out the departure form in triplicate." "Jim should contact Janice about safety procedures."

Human relations messages help employees fully realize their potential in the organization. Examples include statements such as "Sylvia, I appreciate the way that you always give us more than we ask for on special projects; you're a valuable employee" and "I really think you have potential in the area of accounting. Why not consider getting a degree?" Human relations messages promote workers' personal development and occur frequently in organizations that emphasize open communication.

When setting goals for oral communication, consider which of the foregoing categories the message fits into. For example, human relations messages generally do not promote extremely specific goals, so do not expect to get a concrete and definite response to such messages. A more appropriate goal for a human relations message might be "I will try to improve the attitude of my work group by making more positive comments." Task messages, in contrast, are used to make direct requests for specific results. When you set goals for task messages, make them definite and concrete, such as "Send three cartons of the new product to Elizabeth Martin in the Ohio office by 10:45 A.M. Wednesday, March 4."

SITUATIONAL KNOWLEDGE: PERSONAL AND ENVIRONMENTAL FACTORS

To set effective goals in communication, you must consider the person or people who will receive the message as well as the work environment in which the communication takes place. Characteristics that determine how receivers respond to the message include perceptual differences between you and the receiver and the number of people who will ultimately need to receive the message. If several people need the information that you plan to send, a group presentation may be the most appropriate means of communication. If large numbers of people need to hear your message, you may be most effective if you deliver a public speech. In addition, it is

3. W. C. Redding, "The Organizational Communicator," in W. C. Redding and G. A. Sanborn (eds.), *Business and Industrial Communication* (New York: Harper & Row, 1964), pp. 29–58.

prudent to consider the status of the person receiving the message and construct your message appropriately.

Status

Every message carries a great deal of information about how you perceive your relationship with the receiver. Many communication specialists have argued that messages have two parts: a **content element** (what you are trying to communicate) and a **relational element** (how you feel about the person with whom you are communicating). The relational element can be considered in terms of its **relational consequences**—that is, how the message will influence future communication with the receiver.

It is important to anticipate the relational consequences of your message. If you tell a coworker to "get that report in by 5 P.M.," you are not only asking for a task to be performed but also asserting that you have the power to make such a demand and expect others to acknowledge your power. You could have said, "Would it be possible for you to have that report to me by the end of the day?" The relational consequences of such a query would be quite different because you addressed the coworker as an equal engaged in a cooperative endeavor.

Nonverbal communication can influence perceptions of power and status, and it also can be influenced by status and power. Those who have power communicate nonverbally to reinforce their relative power position with others. Those who aspire to status and power may try to influence others by using high-status and high-power nonverbal communication. It is therefore important for you to know which nonverbal cues are generally associated with status and power so that you can use or respond to these forms of communication in appropriate ways. Table 5.1 summarizes much of the research on nonverbal indicators of status and power.[4]

You can use Table 5.1 as a guide to general nonverbal status and power indicators. You are probably familiar with some of these cues; others may be absent from your work or school environment. Recognizing such cues can be a useful starting point for evaluating the status of communicators, as long as you are careful to collect additional cues from the speaker and the communication situation. Please note that these are derived from U.S. cultural behavior. As suggested in Chapter 3, all verbal and nonverbal communications are the product of our own culture.

Although it is important to recognize the nonverbal cues that reveal status or power, you should be aware that the signs of power in organizations are changing. Many organizations are breaking down layers of power in favor of teams. Teamwork and the reduced status differential of flat organizations will characterize the work force of the future. Therefore, it is also important to remember that the display of nonverbal power cues may inhibit the quality of communication necessary for managers in the future. Today, many executives or superiors with large offices have developed furniture arrangements that include a small table and chairs. In order to create a less threatening, more egalitarian environment, a higher-status person with

4. For further reading on this subject, see P. Anderson and L. Bowman, "Positions of Power: Nonverbal Influence in Organizational Communication," in J. De Vito and M. Hecht (eds.), *The Nonverbal Communication Reader* (Prospect Heights, Ill.: Waveland Press, 1990), pp. 391–411; A. King, *Power and Communication* (Prospect Heights, Ill.: Waveland Press, 1987); J. T. Molloy, *Dress for Success* (New York: Warner Books, 1975); B. Linkemer, *Polishing Your Professional Image* (New York: American Management Association, 1987).

TABLE 5.1

Nonverbal Indicators of Power and Status

Power and High Status	Lack of Power and Low Status
Relaxed posture and body position	Erect and rigid posture and body position
Less attentive to others	More attentive to others
More expansiveness	More restrictiveness
Seated position	Standing position
Dark conservative clothes	Light or unusual clothing
More access to space	Less access to space
Finger pointing	Recipient of finger pointing
Less direct body orientation	More direct orientation toward superiors
Closed arm position (akimbo)	Open body orientation
Give less/receive more eye gaze	Receive less/give more eye gaze
Sarcastic smiling/laughing	Respectful smiling/laughing
Touch others more/touched less by others	Touch others less/touched more by others
Making others wait for you	Waiting for others (superiors)
Determine meeting time and length	Told of meeting time and length
More flexible time schedule	Rigorous and strict time schedule
Expensive office furniture	Economical office furniture
Larger office in nicest and most private location	Office location dependent on job duties

such an office will often rise and move to the table to have a conversation with a lower-status person.

Perceptions

Although perception is most commonly associated with the receiver of a message, it influences how messages are sent as well. **Perception** is the process of creating meaning based on experience. These meanings affect verbal communication in several ways.[5]

Your attitudes toward other communicators are influenced by your perceptions. When you speak to someone you like and respect, your verbal message is likely to reflect those positive attitudes; for example (smiling and using a friendly tone), "Jim, could you present a progress report on the XYZ project tomorrow?" If you have negative attitudes about the receiver—if you believe that he or she is lazy, untrustworthy, or careless—your message will probably reflect that perception; for example (frowning and using a stern tone), "Tom, regardless of your attitude about the XYZ project, I expect you to make a five-minute report on it tomorrow; make sure you have all the facts straight."

Another factor that influences perception is emotion. When you are highly aroused by emotions such as anger, surprise, joy, or even fear, you are less likely to perceive a situation accurately, and you may confuse others by using excessive or contradictory nonverbal cues. You are influenced by the emotion of the situation itself and by memories of emotions you previously experienced in similar instances. For example, if you have ever experienced an embarrassing lapse of

5. O. Hargie and P. Marshall, "Interpersonal Communication: A Theoretical Framework," in O. Hargie (ed.), *A Handbook of Communication Skills* (New York: New York University Press, 1986).

Where Do You Stand?

Which high- and low-status/power cues do you communicate to others? Are you a good judge of any of these cues—for instance, posture and expansiveness? Ask someone whom you trust and who knows you well (a friend or relative) to comment on each of these cues as they pertain to you (see Table 5.1). You might be surprised by the person's response.

memory in a group presentation, your perceptions during later presentations are likely to be tainted by that memory.

In all communication situations, but especially in those that involve strong emotions, attitudes, or the possibility of prejudice, ask yourself whether your message is based on accurate and objective perceptions or whether you are letting misperceptions limit your oral communication skills. These questions will help you to assess your perceptions:

1. Am I being influenced by my personal attitude toward this person?
2. Are my emotions clouding my objectivity in this situation?
3. Am I making judgments about this situation based on the facts as I know them?
4. Am I ensuring that my biases and personal prejudices are not affecting my verbal communication?
5. Am I being overly optimistic (or pessimistic) in my verbal communication because of previous experiences in these matters?

Proxemics

Proxemics is the study of personal space. Space plays an important role in communication. Personal space, or the distance between communicators, has two aspects: actual distance, which can be measured in feet and inches, and perceived distance, which varies among speakers. People differ in their need for personal space. Some prefer very close communicating distances; others require greater separation. Different cultures view the use of space differently. One researcher developed zones of space used by northeastern Americans.[6]

Intimate Zone The zone where people interact at the closest distance is the **intimate zone,** which ranges from skin contact to eighteen inches. Business associates rarely interact at this distance, except to give and receive congratulatory hugs, whisper during a presentation, and so on.

Personal Zone Ranging from eighteen inches to four feet, the **personal zone** is usually reserved for interactions that are personal or private, although some business interaction does occur in this zone. Talking semiprivately, illustrating something to someone on paper, and sharing a handout, chart, or other visual aid in a meeting all occur in the personal zone.

6. E.T. Hall, *The Hidden Dimension* (Garden City, N.Y.: Doubleday, 1966).

Our physical proximity to coworkers and clients influences the effectiveness of our communication. In a business setting, a greeting, like this handshake between a manager and his subordinate, should provide enough personal space so that each person feels comfortable. (Romilly Lockyer/The Image Bank–Getty Images)

Social Zone Ranging from four to twelve feet, the **social zone** is used a great deal in business settings. Interviews, small meetings, conversations among several people, and chance encounters usually occur in this zone. At this distance, people communicate in a normal voice and generally feel comfortable both verbally and nonverbally.

Public Zone The largest zone is the **public zone,** which ranges from twelve feet and beyond. It is used for events such as speeches and presentations, large-group meetings, and demonstrations. The public zone reduces the chance for immediate feedback among the participants and the ability to read facial expressions and eye movements. Vocal pitch and volume are usually at high levels, and gesturing may be exaggerated so that everyone within the zone can see.

It is important to recognize the social and cultural norms reflected by the four zones. When you violate the rules of personal space that are commonly observed in those zones, you may offend or repulse others. Crowding the intimate zone of a business acquaintance can result in tension or hostility. But if you choose to interact at distances that are greater than the situation calls for, you may be perceived as cold and aloof.

In addition, you need to be aware that people from various cultural backgrounds may have perceptions of these zones that differ from yours. In eastern European and Latin American countries, for example, hugging is equivalent to shaking hands. By gauging the proxemic patterns of people as they interact, you can get a good idea of the norms for each situation that you face.

Personal Bubbles Experts who study personal space have realized that each of us has a **personal bubble** that we live in and that marks our personal space.[7] The bubble expands or contracts somewhat, depending on the situation and the

7. Adapted from R. E. Axtell, *Gestures: The Do's and Taboos of the Body Language Around the World* (New York: Wiley, 1991).

people with whom we are communicating. When our bubble is invaded by someone, we become uncomfortable. The size of our bubble for business settings is pretty consistent, not varying much from one professional situation to another. The size of a personal bubble is influenced by cultural norms, as the following examples illustrate:

- Americans seem most comfortable with a personal bubble extending from twelve to fifteen inches. The distance between communicators is therefore between twenty-four and thirty inches.
- Asian communicators, particularly the Japanese, prefer even larger bubbles than Americans do.
- Communicators from Latino and Middle Eastern cultures have small bubbles; their interacting space is very small.

A culture clash occurs when American and Japanese communicators with large bubbles are confronted with the small bubbles of Bolivian or Mexican communicators. It is not unusual for a Latino to close in on the personal space of an American and for the American to step back in retreat from this "invasion." Some have called this process the "conversational tango" because one partner moves in and the other moves away as in a dance. An awareness of different cultural norms and personal bubble preferences can promote effective communication.

Territoriality

Another aspect of personal space is **territoriality,** or the behaviors or actions associated with the use, maintenance, or defense of physical space, so as to indicate ownership.[8] Territories are readily recognized in organizational settings, and many people go to great lengths to preserve and protect theirs.

Why is territoriality important? Territories provide a space that allows people to take comfort and refuge. Just as you may claim the same seat in a classroom lecture after lecture, members of organizations look for places that they can call their own. Offices are probably the best examples of territories. Some people strongly identify with their office, cubicle, or desk and may feel personally threatened or violated if others enter without asking or rifle through items on their desk. Some people are also extremely sensitive about their computers—it is usually best to first ask if you can use someone else's computer.

A recent territorial or privacy issue is technology based: some organizations feel the need to monitor employees' e-mail and voice-mail messages. Management tries to justify this type of surveillance in two ways. First, employees may be using e-mail or voice mail for personal reasons, and the management may want to cut down on such unauthorized activity. Second, employees may be sending communication that proves harmful to the organization (incorrect or inappropriate messages).

Employees feel that this type of "snooping" is an invasion of privacy, but generally the courts have allowed e-mail and voice-mail surveillance to continue based on the fact that these forms of communication are company property. The best advice is to use e-mail and voice mail for professional purposes only and to understand that your communications may be monitored.

8. M. Knapp, *Nonverbal Communication in Human Interaction* (New York: Holt, Rinehart & Winston, 1972).

Where Do You Stand?

Have you ever been in a cafeteria or restaurant standing, holding a tray, and looking for a seat only to discover that individuals or groups had used their possessions to block the only available seats? How did it make you feel? Did you think it was personal? If it happened at your university, would it make a difference if the offenders were faculty or administrators rather than fellow students?

Territory can also be a function of habit or routine. For example, a certain table in the cafeteria may be informally reserved by a group of people who sit there day after day and who may become annoyed or angry if another group "takes" the table. Seating positions in a conference room or training center may "belong" to certain people, and violation of their territory may be met with verbal and nonverbal opposition.

Informal observations by a professor and graduate teaching assistant in a large communication class at a university in the Southwest focused on how students indicated their territories. Two female students would sit side by side, while two male students usually kept an empty seat between them—but three or more males would sit side by side. People who chose to sit by themselves would place personal belongings on the two seats on either side of them, thereby signaling their preference to be alone. Although the room was very crowded, the last seats to be taken were, of course, the seats at the very front.

ETHICAL ISSUES

Touching in the Workplace

According to Allan Pease, a leading body language expert in Great Britain, companies that encourage staff to touch one another at work will improve their productivity more than those where workers keep colleagues at arm's length. The controversial advice flies in the face of the accepted wisdom on office behavior now enshrined in sexual harassment legislation, which has established that touching in the workplace can be both unwelcome and illegal.

According to Pease, a management consultant, such touching is essential in today's service-driven economy, where communication skills are valued more than macho aggressiveness. It is acknowledged that many men might react in the wrong way to being touched by a female colleague and that women who are touched may be very uncertain about the intention of the toucher. But it appears that some touches are acceptable (for example, to the elbow) while others (for example, to the hand) are unacceptable. Pease adds that the best way to respond to unwelcome physical contact is to confront the toucher about it and ask them what their intention is.

Pease offers some basic rules of tactile engagement that need to be understood by everyone before touching becomes more common in the workplace:

- Touch only the arm.
- Three seconds is the maximum time limit.
- A light touch to the point of the elbow, with a nod bringing the toucher's eyes below the touchee's, is the most effective contact.
- A gentle grip of the forearm—known as the parental grip—is a good way to comfort or show empathy.
- Touching the upper arm shows comradeship and support.
- Touching hands is an absolute no-no, apart from the handshake.

Adapted from A. Frean, "Soft Touch Is Master Stroke in the Office," *The London Times*, October 28, 1999, p. 10.

What Would You Do?

You are a work-study student in a department of communication. Your friend Sally Stuhlman has been looking for a job. You know that the office manager, Jim Gregory, needs another worker. However, Jim has a habit of physically touching people; you are not sure whether he does it as a friendly gesture, as a power move, or as a prelude to sexual harassment. Sally really needs a job, but you are conflicted about whether to suggest the job. What should you do?

Parking spaces, chairs, places to stand, and even coffee cups are considered territories. For example, at work or in organizations that you belong to, is the head of the table reserved for the boss or leader? What happens if someone invades this territory?

By being observant, you gain information about others' habits, territories, and preferences regarding personal space. You can then demonstrate your competence as a communicator by respecting these preferences.

Clothing and Style of Dress

Clothing and style of dress communicate a great deal about the wearer, especially in the workplace. You may have what you refer to as "interview clothes," clothes that you wear only to interviews or formal presentations. Special clothes show that you are aware of the importance of an event, whether professional, social, religious, or political.

In business and professional settings, dressing appropriately is a decision that may be conscious or unconscious. Strong impressions of others are formed in the opening moments of communication. Interpersonal relationships are established, reconfirmed, or denied within the first four minutes of contact.[9] The most important cues that can be picked up in that time frame are your appearance and manner.

A number of books instruct employees in the art of choosing the proper attire for work.[10] One of the authors of this text once overheard a superior remarking to a subordinate, "If you want to fit in around here, you need to buy a 'dress for success' book and live by it!" Most older business-dress etiquette books conveyed the same basic message: an understated, conservative style is preferred. For men, this has traditionally meant a dark suit, light shirt, and conservative tie. For women, it has meant a skirted suit or a jacket-and-skirt combination with a light blouse.

Of course, guidelines have changed and are specific for each company. In fact, the trend is toward a more casual look on the job. Some organizations offer a "casual Friday," when open collars and jeans are encouraged, while others have casual dress each day. During a recent televised interview with the CEOs of two of the largest companies in the United States, a reporter joked that only newscasters and politicians were wearing ties.

9. L. Zunin and N. Zunin, *Contact—The First Four Minutes* (New York: Ballantine Books, 1972).
10. Molloy, *Dress for Success;* J. T. Molloy, *The Women's Dress for Success Book* (New York: Warner Books, 1977).

When you are trying to decide what to wear to work, observe what others are wearing and consider the climate of the organization. Is it formal, friendly, or trendy? The organizational context may suggest that variations can be made in standard dress. The term *business casual* is not universally defined, but generally refers to less than a suit, sport coat, or tie for men, and unstructured suits or slacks for women. For example, many companies expect employees to wear suits, but as soon as people arrive at work, they hang their suit jackets on their doors and do not put them on again until they leave the office. In this case, because everyone does it, the context has allowed a modification in the dress code.

For an idea of how dress codes have changed over the years, look at old yearbooks or old family pictures for the casual shots of people on campus. Compare the styles in these candid shots to your own dress habits.

Some occupations do not set any standards for dress and simply rely on the context to determine what clothing is appropriate. Some of your professors, for example, probably dress more formally on the days when they teach than on the days when they work in the office or library. Nonetheless, the late-1990s dotcom boom days when an interviewee could show up for an interview in jeans and T-shirt are gone. Even for e-business jobs, career counselors advise a "back-to-basics" dress strategy emphasizing a more conservative appearance. Just remember what clothes can say—true or not—about you. "Birkenstock liberals"—a name given by the media to failed 2004 presidential candidate Howard Dean and his supporters—might be complimentary in some quarters but derogatory in others. Be aware of messages you might be sending and who might be interpreting or misinterpreting them.

Environmental Factors

Knowledge of individual receivers is necessary for you to set goals, but it does not provide enough information for you to design an effective message strategy. You must also take into account the influence of the business environment. Office

STRATEGIC SKILLS

Court-Upheld Dress-Code Regulations

Organizations have gone to court to uphold their right to enforce a dress code.* Here are a few examples of dress-code regulations that have been upheld in court:

- No tight-fitting clothes
- No excessive makeup
- No long hair (men and women)
- No facial hair (mustaches, beards)
- Jackets to be worn during meetings
- No braided hair
- Suits only
- Required neckties
- No earrings for men
- No long sideburns
- Clean-shaven faces
- Generally conservative dress

If dress codes and court rulings regulating appearance and attire seem harsh, unfair, or ridiculous to you, you would be wise to check into a prospective company's policy on dress before you accept a position. It is better to pass up a job that is not suited to you than to take a position that will make you unhappy and cause you to search for other employment in a short time.

*E. Matusewitch, "Tailor Your Dress Codes," *Personnel Journal*, February 1989, p. 86.

arrangements, reception areas, and even furniture, lighting, fixtures, color schemes, floor coverings, music, and live plants are carefully chosen in professional settings. Visitors cannot help but form impressions of an organization based on how the building or individual offices look.

Think of any visits you have made to a building for an interview, a tour, or a meeting. What impressions did you have of the company before you even entered the front door? Several factors probably colored your impression. Was the organization located downtown at the epicenter of business and financial affairs? Was the building's architecture traditional or contemporary? Was the building old or new? Did it look cold and foreboding or warm and inviting?

Office design also shapes impressions of an organization. Large, attractively decorated, and expensively furnished offices are usually occupied by people in the upper rungs of the organization. Those farther down in the pecking order usually have workstations that are very visible and accessible to large numbers of people, small areas that are more functional than attractive, or cubicles that are noisier and less private than the offices of superiors.

As a new employee, your workspace, furniture, and even the color of your office walls will probably not be within your control. On the other hand, you will have control of the semifixed space. You can decide where your furniture is placed. Do you want your visitors or clients faced with the front of your desk as a barrier between you and them? Do you want two chairs at a conversational angle with a small table between them so that your visitor can sit and talk with you on an equal basis? These decisions can make your space as inviting and comfortable or as forbidding as you wish.

You also control the messages that your office or cubicle sends by your inclusion or exclusion of personal possessions: your coffee cup that says "My family went to San Francisco and all I got was a lousy cup!"; a picture of your dog; your sign that says "I'd rather be fishing." Some companies encourage personal statement through possessions, and others strongly discourage such nonverbal communication.

In an era of declining office size resulting from the rising costs of office space, office design can increase efficiency by creating the proper atmosphere for both employees and visitors. Industry experts predict that flexibility will be the key word in the office design of the future, as modular designs become more and more commonplace.[11]

As we mentioned in Chapter 2, telecommuters do not use offices—they work at home. In other organizations, employees may do the majority of their work at home but may have need for temporary office space on an occasional basis. Instead of assigning these employees offices that might be used four or five days out of the month, companies assign them temporary office space that suits their needs. This concept is called "hoteling." Employees can reserve rooms according to their needs (with chairs, desk, computer), just as in a hotel. They can check into their rooms, use them, and check out as if they were guests at a hotel. In this way, employees have a place to conduct meetings, and the organization saves on office space costs.

Probably the most important environmental factor is whether you and the organizational environment fit together smoothly and project a capable and businesslike

11. W. Taubert, "Open and Closed Offices: Designing for Productivity," *The Office*, October 1989, p. 81; G. Mong, "Work Stations: Building Blocks in Office Design," *The Office*, December 1989, p. 14; P. Fernberg, "Modular Systems: Divide and Conquer Space," *Modern Office Technology*, September 1989, p. 84.

In both of these pictures, the participants are at a table, but the long table scene with a rug, and with the informality of movement and dress, gives a sense of individuals talking with each other in a comfortble and positive environment. In contrast, the two men in suits at a table with others appear to be involved in unshared communication in a more formal climate without the friendliness of the other group. (Photodisc Green/Getty Images) (© Royalty-Free/ Corbis)

image. When you enter an office, ask yourself the following questions: Does the place communicate pleasant feelings? Is the design highly functional? Do employees appear to enjoy privacy? Do they feel comfortable talking to you about their organization? Does the company seem to have the technology and equipment necessary to do an effective job? Does your personality seem to fit the office and building?

COMMUNICATION COMPETENCE: VERBAL AND NONVERBAL SKILLS

To develop skills in verbal and nonverbal communication, you must make decisions about the setting in which your message will be sent and received and the length of the message. You must also choose appropriate words and nonverbal gestures and avoid the use of jargon, euphemisms, tag questions, and language that is racist or sexist.

Choosing the Setting for Communication

Consider the following situation:

> Sam was anxious because his boss, Sandy, had not informed him of his raise for next year. Sam had spent a lot of time thinking about how much he needed and deserved a raise and how to phrase his request to Sandy. The issue was so important to him that when he saw Sandy talking to some other employees in the hallway, he immediately approached her and asked whether she had made a decision about his raise. He did not pause to think about the appropriate setting for the request. Sandy wheeled around and in a hostile tone said, "I can't talk about that right now!"

It is important to think about the setting in which your message will be sent and received. The reaction elicited by a message that is received in the privacy of an office is likely to be different from the reaction elicited by a message received in the company cafeteria or in the presence of casual bystanders. Messages sent and received in formal settings, such as a class or a meeting, sound different from messages communicated in informal settings, such as a hallway.

Three variables are worth considering when you are choosing a setting: (1) the likelihood that bystanders will receive the message unintentionally; (2) the physical characteristics of the setting—high ceilings, sources of noise, and so on; and (3) the formality of the situation as dictated by social or company norms. You can increase the effectiveness of spoken communication by thinking about these variables beforehand. If Sam had done so, he would have realized that the hallway was an inappropriate setting for a discussion of his raise for several reasons.

Where Do You Stand?

Have you given much thought to an ideal office or work space? Would it be functional, stylish, or both? Where would you sit? Would you have windows? Take out a sheet of paper and draw your ideal office. Bring your sketch to class, and share your ideas with your instructor and classmates. What inferences can your classmates make about you from your office design?

First, money and salary issues are generally sensitive and private and should not be discussed in front of others unless the organizational culture promotes such discussions. Second, the hallway is generally not an appropriate setting for lengthy discussions because such talk can distract others or interfere with their work. Third, most companies have specific procedures for giving raises. Sam should have familiarized himself with his company's formal procedures before confronting Sandy.

Chronemics

Chronemics is the use of time as each culture determines it to be appropriate. The use of time can affect verbal and nonverbal communication. At business meetings, U.S. businesspeople spend relatively little time on interpersonal relationships as they rush to the main purpose of the meeting. Such multitask activities and the intense pressure to use time to its best advantage are perceived as rude behavior in some other countries, such as Japan and Spain.

Just as the use of time is important, so is the timing of messages. The story about Sam's asking about a raise in the hallway shows not only that the place was inappropriate but also that the timing was poor. Additionally, the length of the message becomes an important factor. Even if Sam had chosen the right place and the right time, he still should consider the length of his message, as well as the likely length of the response.

Most people do not consider how long a specific message actually needs to be. You have undoubtedly suffered through long and wordy messages. To keep a message concise, you can write it out on a piece of paper and then circle the key words, crossing out all unnecessary words. Communicators in professional settings often provide extra details and elaboration to impress the receiver when in fact most receivers are busy and want the quickest and most efficient message possible.

Another way to check the length of a message is to see whether you can break it into two or more separate messages. Frequently, people try to communicate too many ideas at once. Your communication will be much more successful if you send several short, self-contained messages instead of one long message

TECHNOLOGY TOOLS

Technology Can Help with Timing Messages

With certain types of technology, you are able to send messages to others even if you do not expect them to be available. You may already do this on a personal basis by leaving someone who you know isn't home a message on his or her home answering machine. Likewise, you can use a client's or collegue's voice mail at just about any hour of the day so that a message is waiting when the person returns to the office. E-mail makes the timing of messages less of a problem as well. Your message can be sent anytime, and it will be waiting when the recipient checks his or her e-mail. Even pagers, cell phones, and personal digital assistants will store numbers and messages when it is not a convenient time for a recipient to respond. Faxing is another way to meet the challenge of message timing—you can fax when you want, and the message will be waiting for the receiver. Remember, it is better to send a message via one of these communication technologies and know that it will arrive eventually than to wait for the right moment (telephone call, visit) and find out that your receiver is not ready for you.

that wanders from point to point. Of course, your message must be long enough to contain the necessary information.

We mentioned in Chapter 2 the importance of messages arriving at their destinations at the appropriate time. The timing of messages is something of an art—it is often difficult to gauge when receivers can best handle the message you wish to send. In deciding when to send a message, consider these three elements of timing: when messages are likely to pile up, what the receiver's schedule is, and whether all aspects of your message are in sync:

- Know the organization well enough to understand when messages are likely to pile up all at once. In a university, for example, messages are most numerous at the beginning and end of the semester, and telephone calls are likely to be most numerous during midmorning and midafternoon.
- Know the schedule of the receiver. Find out if the receiver's duties and responsibilities are seasonal or cyclical. You can obtain some of this information from the receiver or from her or his assistant.
- Consider using e-mail or voice mail as an alternative to actually speaking to people. In that way, you can leave a message, and they can get back to you when it is convenient for them, especially if you leave a choice of times for them to call when you will be in your office.

Think of yourself, the receiver, and your message as a package or team. All three must be in sync before you send the message. The more receivers agree with the timing of the message, the more likely you are to get an appropriate response. Receivers, in other words, need to believe that now is the best time to receive your message.

Using Language Effectively

Using language effectively, particularly in business and professional settings, is not always easy. The relationship between a word and what it represents is not always based on real or concrete shared characteristics that can be analyzed or predicted. You can increase your skill in using language by continually learning new ways to say what you mean.

One way to familiarize yourself with appropriate language is by reading journals in the field you plan to enter. Another way is by writing down new words and their definitions when you come across them. The act of writing helps you to remember the word and how it was used. It is in your best interest to be familiar with as many words related to your field as you can.

Language varies in its preciseness. Legal, medical, and technical language is very specific and not open to a wide range of interpretation. Other types of language are vague, abstract, or open to multiple meanings. For example, *toast* can be used as both a noun and a verb. As a noun, it can mean a slice of heated and browned bread or a clinking of glasses in celebration. As a verb, it can mean the act of clinking glasses or a method of cooking (such as toasting marshmallows). As a slang noun, *toast* means that a person or idea is finished or has lost significance.

When you formulate a spoken message, choose words that are neither too specialized nor too general. Be accessible without being ambiguous. For example, "I will try to accommodate you" sounds cooperative and flexible, unlike "Well, I don't know if I will be able to help you." Also, be aware of the difficulties that you are likely to encounter if you use jargon, euphemisms, or tag questions.

Jargon **Jargon** is the specialized language that professionals use to communicate efficiently with one another. Jargon is also "nonsensical, incoherent, or meaningless talk."[12] The contrast between these two meanings vividly shows the potential and the limits of jargon. At its best, jargon makes communication among members of a group more efficient and precise and provides definite advantages for shared meaning. Medical care personnel, for example, cannot live without specialized vocabulary ("Myocardial infarction in the later stages of pulmonary edema suggests a code four procedure"). But the use of jargon in inappropriate situations, such as around people who are unfamiliar with it, tends to result in an undesirable image—silly, inconsiderate, out of touch—for the communicator and a failure to achieve shared meaning.

Euphemisms **Euphemisms** are agreeable, neutral, or indirect phrases used to describe unpleasant events. A vice president who says, "Because of declining sales, we have to implement a retrenchment program that might temporarily displace some people" is using euphemisms. What she or he really means is "The drop in sales means that we have to cut costs and fire people."

Some euphemisms become mainstream terminology and therefore require euphemisms of their own. An example of this is the succession of terms for the act of firing. In the 1970s people were not fired but *laid off.* The noun *layoff* was so widely adopted that it was no longer effective as a euphemism. New euphemisms were coined to replace it: *temporary displacement, voluntary retirement,* and *redundancy.* Even more recently, terms such as *right-sizing* or the military's *build-down* appear in popular managerial texts.

Euphemisms are often used to soften the blow of communicating bad news, but they are also used in less positive ways. Some speakers use euphemisms to build ambiguity or vagueness into their messages. Stressful or difficult circumstances promote whitewashing or distorting explanations that forestall confrontations or criticism. These motives call into question the communicator's integrity. Use euphemisms with care, and employ them only when you are making an honest effort to help or to spare the feelings of others.

Tag Questions "These cost overruns are killing us, don't you think?" "I'm really feeling the heat from the accounting department, know what I mean?" "It's disgraceful that we have to attend this meeting, isn't it?" "You'll finish the report, OK?" Tag questions tacked onto the end of a statement undercut the effectiveness of your message. Women who use tag questions are often perceived as less assertive or as lacking power.[13] They soften the original statement to the point of feebleness. The use of tag questions by women or men does nothing to advance important points and makes the speaker seem overly dependent on the opinions of the receiver.

Where Do You Stand?

Do you belong to any groups that use jargon? Are you careful to avoid jargon with people who are not members of your group? Do certain situations cause you to use tag questions? What about euphemisms? Can you think of circumstances in which you feel you need to soften your language?

Avoiding Racist and Sexist Language

As discussed in Chapter 3, over time, the use of some words and phrases in some contexts becomes unacceptable. For example, it is insulting to refer to a female employee as a "girl" or to a male African American as a

12. Copyright © 1992 by Houghton Mifflin Company. Reproduced by permission from *The American Heritage Dictionary of the English Language,* 3d ed.
13. C. Kramarae, *Women and Men Speaking* (Rowley, Mass.: Newbury House, 1981).

"boy." Such usages were once common but are unacceptable now. Many other words and phrases are equally objectionable. For example, the term *stewardess* has been replaced with *flight attendant,* and the use of *man* and masculine pronouns to refer to both women and men is avoided by savvy communicators.

Here are some examples of sexist language and language that is gender-free:

Sexist

A *human* seeks *his* physical comforts.
Man needs language to create reality.
The *chairman* is ready to begin.

Gender-Free

Humans seek *their* physical comforts.
People need language to create reality.
The *chair* is ready to begin.

Regardless of your position, you need to cultivate respect for the people with whom you work and communicate. You need to avoid sexist, insulting, and racist language. The guidelines for nondiscriminatory communication are easy to understand and remember: respect and be considerate of others, and commit yourself to thoughtful language choice. Do not immediately say the first words that come to mind; instead, consider the connotations of your words and the values and assumptions that they imply. A quick mental check before speaking will prevent you from promoting stereotypes and making damaging generalizations.

If you assume that the people with whom you are speaking don't care about such issues, and if you make no effort to avoid offensive language, you will not be prepared to communicate effectively with people who care very strongly about this issue. Racist, sexist, and insulting language is likely to cause many receivers to refuse your message and to perceive you as incompetent and insensitive.

Here is a list of possibly offensive terms (left column) and suggestions for neutral alternatives (right column):[14]

actress	actor (to refer to male or female)
airman	flier, pilot
anchorman	anchor
businessman	businessperson
chairman	chair, chairperson, moderator
cleaning girl	cleaner, maintenance worker
congressman	congressperson, congressional representative, member of Congress
fireman	firefighter
foreman	supervisor
gentleman's agreement	honorable agreement
maiden name	family name
maiden voyage	first voyage, premier voyage
mailman, postman	mail carrier, letter carrier, postal worker
male nurse	nurse
man and wife	husband and wife
manpower	staff, labor, personnel

14. B. D. Sorrels, *The Nonsexist Communicator* (Englewood Cliffs, N.J.: Prentice Hall, 1983), pp. 124–142.

poetess	poet
queer	homosexual, gay
salesman	salesperson, sales representative
secretary	assistant, associate
woman doctor	doctor

Paralanguage

Paralanguage refers to voice qualities, or characteristics of speech, such as pitch (how high or low the voice is), tempo (rate of speaking), volume (loudness of voice), rhythm (timing and emphasis on words), and articulation (how clearly words are pronounced).[15] You can get a good idea of the personality and mood of a speaker by paying attention to his or her voice qualities. Rapid, high-pitched speech often signals that the speaker is excited or distressed. Poor articulation may suggest fatigue, lack of interest in the topic, physical handicaps, or other problems.

Paralanguage has significant effects on communication. You often inadvertently communicate certain ideas to others through the sound of your voice rather than the words you use. It is important to monitor whether your vocal cues are signaling what you are thinking and feeling. Changes in vocal tone and rate, for example, can help you to manage a conversation. When you want to signal that you are ready to give up the floor of conversation, you can use a rising vocal inflection to indicate a question or a falling inflection to show the end of your message.

You can also use paralanguage to communicate your feelings. When you greet someone in a pleasant tone of voice, you reinforce the verbal message that you are glad to see that person. An expressionless greeting gives a person the impression that she or he is unwanted. Either way, paralanguage gives people an idea about your feelings toward them.

Interpreting Nonverbal Cues Accurately

Nonverbal communication accompanies verbal communication. Nonverbal behavior can reinforce what is said verbally (smiling while saying that you are satisfied with a business report). It can help to regulate verbal behavior (breaking eye contact to signal that a conversation is about over). It can complement oral communication (talking very slowly and deliberately to make an important point). It can take the place of words (nodding, winking, or gesturing your approval). It can even contradict what you say verbally (avoiding eye contact when you say that you are really glad to meet someone). Three types of nonverbal expression require accurate interpretation: paralanguage, facial and eye expressions, and kinesics.

Facial and Eye Expressions The face is the most expressive outlet for nonverbal communication; it can display more than a thousand different expressions.[16] That the face serves as a conspicuous mode of communication is both advantageous and problematic. Facial expression can be a powerful reinforcement of a verbal message, whether the message is positive or negative. But facial expressions and

15. G. Trager, "Paralanguage: A First Approximation," *Studies in Linguistics* 13 (1958), 1–12.
16. P. Ekman, W. Friesen, and P. Ellsworth, *Emotion in the Human Face: Guidelines for Research and an Integration of the Findings* (New York: Pergamon Press, 1972).

Because nonverbal communication is more believable than verbal, your understanding of others can improve if you are aware of their nonverbal behaviors as well as your own. Notice the eye gaze of the listener. His serious, intent expression gives the speaker strong clues that the listener is giving his attention; the listener has bent his body forward while leaning into the speaker's personal space. The listener's nonverbal clues (eye gaze, expression, body position, and proximity) should reassure the speaker that he has the listener's full attention. (Fischer–Thatcher/Getty Images)

phenomena such as blushing may be difficult to control—and many people often wish they had a better "poker face." For the message recipient, interpreting facial expressions is often challenging.

Our discussion here is about the facial and eye expressions of members of *mainstream* U.S. culture. It is impossible to generalize about all groups in the United States. Many Native Americans and some Asian cultures, for example, are taught that direct eye contact with elders is a sign of disrespect. Recall from Chapter 3 that an effective communicator appreciates cultural diversity. Understanding how the meanings of facial and eye expressions differ in various cultures may prevent misinterpretations and promote the acquisition of shared meaning. Our discussion, however, is only an overview of commonly practiced facial and eye expressions in the U.S. work force.

Understanding the facial expressions of coworkers can give you an opportunity to determine the real motivations and intentions behind their actions (for example, are smiles real? do frowns mean suspicion or contemplation?). But simply observing another person's face for emotional cues is probably not enough to establish a high degree of accuracy. Rather, you must act like a detective and put together a number of cues that help to paint a complete picture of the person's emotional state.

Eyes are an important source of information. Because humans are so visually oriented, **ocuselics,** or **eye behavior**—the movement of the eyes and how they are focused on other people and objects—reveals a great deal of information. It is only natural to search the eyes of others in an effort to understand their feelings, intentions, and motives.

The eyes are also an important tool for regulating the flow of communication. With a direct look, you can notify another person that you are ready to communicate. Eye contact is also useful when you wish to influence others. Why does a salesperson who is trying to convince a buyer to make a purchase seldom resort to letters or phone calls, especially to close a sale? The salesperson needs "to read" the buyer for signs of support, anxiety, or hesitancy. Lack of direct eye contact, a shifting gaze, or a fixed stare can signal that the buyer has doubts about the seller or the product or has lost interest. Some cultures do not value direct eye contact.

Whenever you are trying to influence someone, communicate in person so that you can use the other's eye behavior as a source of information to strengthen your case. The following factors relate to eye behavior and the regulation of communication:[17]

- People have a tendency to "match" the gaze duration of their conversational partners.
- Speech rate is higher when the speaker looks at the listener.
- Eye gaze increases when the information being communicated is positive and decreases when it is negative.
- Smiling causes a decrease in direct eye contact.
- People in groups tend to look more while speaking and less while listening (the opposite effect occurs when only two people are talking).
- People who gaze longer are better liked.
- Increased gazing causes favorable impressions when positive information is communicated and unfavorable impressions when negative information is revealed.
- People with lower status (less power) look more when listening than when speaking compared to high-status people.

Kinesics **Kinesics** is the study of gestures and body movement that can be intentional or unintentional. Although it is difficult to monitor what you are doing with your hands and body at all times, familiarizing yourself with a few nonverbal cues can enable you to be more aware of the nonverbal messages you are sending to others.[18]

Emblems are body movements that substitute for words. A thumbs-up signal indicates "Go ahead," "Good job," or "Keep up the good work." A thumbs-down signal indicates disapproval or disagreement. Making a circle with the thumb and index finger signals "OK" or "I understand." Emblems are intentional nonverbal acts and are usually reserved for people who know their meaning. If you try to use emblems with people who are unaware of their meanings—particularly with people from another culture—you risk miscommunicating with or even insulting them.

Illustrators are body movements that amplify, accent, or supplement what is being said orally. Illustrators generally are less intentional than emblems and are often used without conscious thought. For example, someone who has a habit of

17. R. Harper, A. Wiens, and J. Matazzaro, *Nonverbal Communication: The State of the Art* (New York: Wiley, 1978), p. 173.
18. P. Ekman and W. Friesen, "The Repertoire of Nonverbal Behavior: Categories, Origins, Usage, and Coding," *Semiotica* 1 (1969), 49–98.

waving his arms wildly when he is trying to make a point may have no idea how flamboyant he appears to others.

In business and professional settings, illustrators can help make verbal communication more meaningful as long as they clearly correspond to the message. Some illustrators, however, may contradict the verbal message. Consider the following situation:

> Priya always smiled when she presented material to her coworkers. Several years previously, at a company communication seminar, she had been encouraged to smile while speaking publicly. One afternoon, she was asked to tell her coworkers about an impending plant closing. As she spoke about the closing, her coworkers looked at each other, wondering why Priya was smiling.

Consider your own use of illustrators. How often do you illustrate with your hands, arms, and body without really thinking about it? Do people readily recognize and understand your illustrators? You can improve your illustrating behavior by observing others who are good at illustrating and modeling what they do. Some people use their fingers in a very detailed manner; others use their hands and arms to depict their thoughts. By copying the gestures of effective illustrators, you will enhance your overall communication ability.

Regulators are nonverbal, usually automatic acts that help to maintain the flow of a conversation. Communicators are often unaware of how these nonverbal behaviors control conversation. Regulators function in a number of ways. You can signal to others that you are ready to give up the floor of conversation, for example, by opening your palms, reducing your gestures, or even motioning toward another person to encourage him or her to take a turn. You can signal to others that you would like to keep talking by increasing your gesturing, holding up your hands, or leaning toward your conversational partner. You can request a turn by raising your index finger or hand or by rapidly nodding your head. You can even deny someone else the chance to speak by holding up your hand or shifting your posture away from that person.[19]

Adaptors are actions that reveal psychological or physical needs. Head-scratching, ear-pulling, or hair-fussing, as well as pointing, shrugging, or nodding, can be interpreted as positive or negative by the other person. You may have a new haircut and nervously keep trying to tuck the hair behind your ear. The listener, however, may misinterpret the action to mean that you are distracted and not really listening. Adaptors are not conscious behaviors, but they can be very distracting to the other person.

Affect displays are also unintentional movements that reflect the sender's true emotions. Slumping or showing a sad facial expression could reflect problems in your own life or could indicate empathic responses to the other person's words.

Monitoring gestures, body movements, and other nonverbal cues will help you to respond appropriately to the needs of friends and coworkers. If you work to become aware of the various nonverbal cues with which people communicate, you will develop skills that will improve your strategic communication.

ANXIETY MANAGEMENT

Do you associate anxiety primarily with formal speaking presentations and speaking in front of large groups? Or are you aware of how nervousness affects your everyday speech? For example, if you are speaking to someone who outranks you in an organization, or if you are discussing an important subject or a topic that

19. Knapp, *Nonverbal Communication.*

makes you uncomfortable, your voice may rise to a high pitch, you may stammer, or you may speak very softly.

Everyday situations such as meeting someone new, presenting ideas for a group project, or disagreeing with a friend may cause communication anxiety. This anxiety can give rise to verbal and nonverbal communication problems and cause the receiver to perceive you negatively. Verbal symptoms of nervousness include a shaky voice, dry mouth, mispronunciations, and incoherent sentences or phrases. Nonverbal symptoms include a change of voice pitch, fidgeting, and shaking. There are several skills that can help you manage these symptoms of nervousness.

One tactic for managing anxiety is to identify particular weaknesses in your spoken communication. The best way to do this is to record yourself by video or audio. Choose a topic that is important to you, such as asking for a raise. Record your reasons for requesting the raise; then play back the tape. Did your voice sound convincing? Were there mispronunciations or stammering? Did your phrases form complete thoughts? Even if your reasons are valid, you can undermine their effectiveness by speaking softly, stammering, or choosing inappropriate language (such as tag questions added to your statements). Although listening to yourself may be uncomfortable, it reveals the impact of anxiety on your speech.

An effective way to control anxiety is to breathe deeply and regularly. Indeed, if you breathe too shallowly and rapidly (hyperventilate), the build-up of carbon dioxide in your bloodstream may cause you to feel dizzy and disoriented in addition to feeling nervous. Hyperventilation can cause tingling in your arms and legs, a "lump" in your throat, or tightness in your chest. Breathing deeply and regularly will relieve these physical symptoms and help you relax.

Another way to relieve the anxiety is to take a brisk walk. Walking will help dissipate some of the adrenaline that your body produces in stressful situations. The decrease of adrenaline has a calming effect.

An additional tactic is to slow down your communication and consciously focus on one idea at a time. As you well know from your school experience, a workload sometimes seems so overwhelming that you do not want to begin tackling it. The same can be true in communicating—you have much to say but do not know where to begin. If you say nothing, your anxiety will only increase. Just as you prioritize your schoolwork and tackle one project at a time, you can sort out which ideas are most important and concentrate on communicating them first.

Finally, do not be too hard on yourself. If you create unrealistic scenarios ("I'll instantly win my coworkers' respect by telling them about my dedication to the organization") rather than appropriate goals ("I'll speak to others with respect and plan my messages so that they are clear and effective"), you are likely to be anxious when you communicate.

Be aware that others in the communication situation may be nervous as well. Most people have experienced communication anxiety, so you are not alone in feeling nervous.

MESSAGE STRATEGIES

Message strategies are combinations of skills designed to communicate specific ideas to achieve a goal. A vast array of message strategies are used in business and professional settings. In this section we analyze three: conversation, making requests, and giving directives.

Conversation

Many people believe that they are good conversationalists—that they have the ability to talk with ease about a wide range of topics. Even for such gifted individuals, in professional settings, conversation must be handled carefully. Conversation is an important message strategy because the business and professional environment provides so many opportunities for it to occur.

Conversational Turns Turn-taking is one of the most important elements of conversation. Turns may vary in length and intensity but are necessary to maintain a conversation. You come to understand the "rules" of conversational turn-taking by watching others engaged in conversation.

An *interruption* occurs when a challenging speaker is successful in taking an unsolicited turn. Interruptions are useful for correcting inaccurate information or verifying what has been said. Other reasons for interruptions include disagreement ("Wait a minute; I think that there are four, not three, departure points for that supply order"), agreement ("Yes, you're absolutely right in hiring her!"), and changing the subject ("Excuse me, but aren't we late for that meeting with Scott?").[20]

Although interruptions can serve important functions, most people do not appreciate being interrupted. If you have a tendency to interrupt without thinking, before you jump into a conversation, ask yourself whether the interruption is worth the risk it entails. Many times you will realize that it is best to wait for your turn in the conversation to get your point across. You can try to prevent yourself from being interrupted by using stronger and more active language and by leaning forward. You can also assert yourself in conversations simply by speaking up more often.

Conversations Between Women and Men Researchers have observed several differences in the ways women and men participate in conversation, as Chapter 3 explained. Men interrupt more often than women do; thus, men control conversations more often than women do. Men also talk more than women do, both by taking more conversational turns and by taking longer turns. Women are generally more informative, more receptive to ideas, and more concerned about others in their conversations than men are. Stop for a moment and consider what this means for communication between coworkers.

Another difference in men's and women's conversational patterns is in giving orders.[21] Women are often less comfortable with hierarchy than men are and generally prefer to achieve goals through consensus. Men are more likely to give orders without options. This difference causes confusion. Men may feel confused or manipulated if a woman does not give a direct order but nevertheless expects results. Women may be put off by a man's use of rank, authority, or power in giving orders.

Intercultural Conversations Culture influences communication and can therefore lead to communication differences.[22] In addition to the suggestions in

20. C. Kennedy and C. Camden, "A New Look at Interruptions," *Western Journal of Speech Communication* 47 (1982), 45–58.
21. D. Tannen, "Power Talk," interview by L. Lusardi, *Working Woman,* July 1990, pp. 92–94.
22. M. L. Hecht, S. Ribeau, and J. K. Alberts, "An Afro-American Perspective on Interethnic Communication," *Communication Monographs* 56 (December 1989), 386–399.

PRACTICING BUSINESS COMMUNICATION

Communication Media

Is it a contradiction for an information technology company to view old-fashioned, face-to-face communication as a potent part of its corporate culture? Hewlett-Packard Company (HP) employs over 140,000 people in 178 countries who speak in more than ten languages. HP's emphasis on one-on-one interaction between managers and employees stems from a tradition of openness established by the company's founders and from its strong belief that open communication leads to greater productivity and job satisfaction.

EMPOWERING EMPLOYEES

Both communication and work at Hewlett-Packard are based on one central value: employee empowerment. HP's founders believed that people want to do a good job and that given the proper tools and support, they will. Consider this example:

At HP's factory in San Jose, California, hundreds of employees manufacture computer chips. The company began to offer training in statistical methods, which enables workers to measure the quality of their own work, and in formal problem-solving techniques.

As a result of her training, one worker was able to determine that a layer of material that her team was adding to a batch of chips was too thick—a delicate measuring job since the layers are microscopic! Rather than calling in an inspector or supervisor, her team stopped its regular work, spent an hour tracking down the problem, fixed it, and got production moving again in record time. That's how empowerment benefits the company as well as the worker.

A GROWING DIALOGUE

HP's business growth has encouraged strong interpersonal communication. Originally, each division was responsible for an individual product, and each division manager was, in effect, the chief executive officer of a small, independent company.

Beginning in the mid-1970s, HP's move into computing systems altered that structure. Increasingly, divisions worked together, each producing one component of a system. Today managers lead multiple work teams, and work teams share multiple tasks. Coordinating schedules, taking advantage of ideas, clarifying responsibilities, and keeping productivity high make effective verbal—and nonverbal—communication vital.

Managers are highly visible in the HP workplace, and they talk to employees regularly, encouraging a free flow of ideas. This interaction, an example of "management by wandering around," helps managers collect the information they need to perform their jobs well. And it provides individual workers with managerial support.

COFFEE TALK

Communication takes other forms at HP, including frequent "coffee talks," informal presentations by managers about HP's earnings picture, product development, job concerns, and new responsibilities. Coffee talks may occur as often as once a week or as infrequently as once a month. They function as ongoing forums. Most important, coffee talks give managers a chance to solicit questions and suggestions from employees.

Chapter 3, here are several strategies for improving conversations among a diverse work force:

- **Open-mindedness:** Considering others' ideas rather than dismissing them too quickly
- **Treatment as an equal:** Not taking a superior or self-righteous attitude toward the conversation
- **Avoidance:** Acknowledging that certain conversations should not take place
- **Interaction management:** Regulating the amount and the rate of talk so that both partners are comfortable with the communication

One of the most important functions of the coffee talk occurs when HP makes its quarterly earnings announcement. Along with a standard press release, managers receive packages of support materials—slides and other visual aids, and "talking points"—for presentation to team members.

The manager's presentation includes an organizational overview and a discussion of how the local unit contributed to overall company performance, what the company's performance means for the unit, and what the results mean for employees. Managers try to schedule coffee talks as soon after the earnings announcement as possible—often on the same day.

COMMUNICATION MEDIA

HP's voice-mail system supplements coffee talk. Employees can access a voice-mail program, listen to a three- to five-minute message related to a current issue, then record a response. The manager can sign onto the system, collect employees' input, and issue a response or make notes on topics for future coffee talks.

Some concern exists that voice mail may eventually replace, rather than enhance, coffee talk. The challenge is to improve communication technology while supporting and maintaining the open, face-to-face culture at Hewlett-Packard.

In fact, voice mail can sometimes be more useful than face-to-face interaction. Voice mail allows managers to handle routine concerns and simple questions quickly and easily and to make information available constantly. Managers can monitor and update their voice mail from anywhere in the world and thus maintain that invaluable employee-manager link.

The goal of communication media at Hewlett-Packard is to reach the broadest range of employees possible and to support their joint efforts. HP also uses worldwide e-mail, an electronic newsletter, a fifteen-minute bimonthly video magazine, and teleconferencing.

Employees and managers choose the media that work best for them. Ultimately, communication media give people at Hewlett-Packard the information they need to interact effectively face-to-face.

QUESTIONS FOR CRITICAL THINKING

1. How does Hewlett-Packard maintain its people-oriented culture?
2. In what ways does one-on-one interaction differ from communication in work teams? Consider both verbal and nonverbal aspects of communication.
3. What are the advantages and disadvantages of HP's coffee talks?
4. Why do you think HP has standardized presentations for earnings announcements?
5. How do communication media support higher productivity and job satisfaction in a business setting?

You can visit Hewlett-Packard on-line at www.hp.com.

- **Other orientation:** Attempting to involve the other person, find common ground, and create identification

Participants in successful intercultural conversations show concern for others as individuals and do not expect an individual to speak for an entire group. They avoid lazy and thoughtless communication based on broad stereotypes—for example, not all British citizens are stuffy, not all Hispanics enjoy Mexican food, and many Italians are not overly expressive.[23] Treating others with respect and acknowledging their professional status can also help to bring about shared meaning.

23. M. J. Collier, "A Comparison of Conversations Among and Between Domestic Culture Groups," *Communication Quarterly* 36 (Spring 1988), 130–148.

Conversational Ethics Each time you speak, you should provide enough background information to give listeners a frame of reference. In most organizations, manipulating listeners by giving them only partial information is unacceptable. It is generally unproductive as well, for receivers who discover that they were treated unethically in conversation may refuse to work with the person who misled them or may tell coworkers that the person cannot be fully trusted.

Conversational messages should be truthful. Speakers should not provide false information to accomplish some goal or make claims for which they lack evidence. In both instances, the conversationalist is violating ethical principles. Unfortunately, deceiving others and lying are common in professional settings, even though they rarely produce the desired results over the long term. Most lies are discovered and do more harm than telling the truth would have done.

The final rule of conversational ethics involves clarity. When you converse with others, articulate your thoughts and ideas in ways that reduce the uncertainty the listeners may have about you and your messages. Avoid obscure language, make points logically, and eliminate extraneous information that may distract receivers from your primary message.

Understanding and Agreement Conversationalists do not always understand or agree with one another. Consider the following four combinations of understanding and agreement.[24]

1. **Mutual understanding with agreement:** Communicators understand each other's point of view and agree with it. This type of casual and nonconfrontational conversation is very common.
2. **Mutual understanding with disagreement:** Conversationalists understand each other's viewpoint but disagree with it. This is a case of honest disagreement between parties.
3. **Mutual misunderstanding with agreement:** As a polite way of carrying on conversation, participants may act as if they understand each other's viewpoint (agreement) even though they actually do not. Or each conversationalist may agree with what the other is saying but may not understand the purpose or deeper meaning of the topic. This is why it is often necessary to revisit a topic or phrase it in a different way in order to find out if the other person has understood the message.
4. **Mutual misunderstanding with disagreement:** Participants in a conversation have no understanding of each other's viewpoints and demonstrate no agreement about the issues. This is a stalemate situation until each party agrees to respect and sympathize with the other's position.

Keep those four possible outcomes in mind when you are speaking to others. Do not assume that a person who agrees with you necessarily understands what you have said or that someone who disagrees with you did not understand your point. Also, do not jump to the conclusion that people who disagree with you have nothing relevant to say. The best way to achieve shared meaning is to make sure you have answered the basic questions about the "what," "where," "who," "when," "why," and "how" of the subject and that you and the receiver agree on the answers to those questions.

24. E. M. Rogers and D. L. Kincaid, *Communication Networks: Toward a New Paradigm for Research* (New York: Free Press, 1981).

What Would You Do?

Assume that you are in a group working on a class project. One of the members says enough that you can interpret that he/she does not understand the assignment. How would you revisit the topic (see #3 in text, p. 144) in order to make sure all members understand the assignment?

Making Requests and Giving Directives

Making requests is a crucial activity on the job, particularly when you are a new employee. Consider your past working experiences. During your first few weeks at a job, you undoubtedly needed to ask a large number of questions to learn the basic requirements of your position.

Many people are reluctant to request information or help for fear of appearing unintelligent or helpless. But you can phrase requests so that they benefit you in two ways: by providing you with necessary information and resources and by fostering a positive image of you because of your curiosity and enthusiasm for your job.

How can you be sure your requests are effective? First, be specific. Second, be sure you are asking the right person for the information. If you're not sure, ask an exploratory question first, such as "Are you in charge of accounts?" If the answer is affirmative, make your request—for example, "How do I allocate the money for next month's regional meeting?" Third, be confident when making your requests. If you have tried without success to find the information or to complete the job yourself, you are justified in asking for help. Others are usually willing to cooperate, particularly if you know exactly what you are asking for and phrase your request in clear and friendly language.

Giving directives is another important message strategy, particularly when it complements a positive request-making style. Regardless of your position in the organization, you are likely to need both of these strategies to achieve your goals. The following list shows the difference between requests and directives:

Requests	***Directives***
"Can you help me solve this problem?"	"Be sure you finish this project today."
"Can we meet sometime today?"	"See me at 10:30."
"Which file should this go in?"	"File this."
"Is there any way we can finish this project today?"	"I am expecting the report today."
"Can you help me find the XYZ file?"	"Find the XYZ file now."

Making requests creates a supportive climate and gives people a sense of control in carrying out their responsibilities. Those who carry out requests are likely to have a better attitude and to perform their duties in a more effective manner than those who are expected to obey directives. Nevertheless, in situations that call for specific action, directives may be more appropriate than requests.

It is possible to give directives in a positive way that does not assume a power imbalance. You can do this by explaining the reason for the directive. Do not simply make a demand without telling coworkers why they should do what you say. Indeed, if you give a directive, you should have an important reason for doing so and be willing to explain it to others. They are much more likely to cooperate when they see the need for such action. The directives in the preceding list can be rephrased like this:

Original Version	***Rephrased Version***
"Be sure you finish this project today."	"Be sure you finish this project today. Lisa needs the results tomorrow morning."
"See me at 10:30."	"See me at 10:30. We need to discuss the plans for the sales meeting."

"File this."	"File this. I am expecting an important call."
"I am expecting the report today."	"I need the report today because it is important that we stay on schedule."
"Find the XYZ file now."	"Please find the XYZ file. I have my hands full looking for the Logan file."

STRATEGIC SCENARIO WRAP-UP

The interviewer may have chosen to place her office furniture near the far back wall so that interviewees and others would have to walk to her. This may give her a sense of power and give others a feeling of humility—the sense that they are on display and must do homage to her by walking to her power position. Or she may have chosen the position in order to feel secure by having a wall to her back.

If other clues indicate that she is insecure, your conscious nonverbal behavior should be nonthreatening. Men (1) should not cross their legs with the ankle on the knee; (2) should not slump in their chair; (3) should use moderate volume in speaking; and (4) should smile. Women (1) should maintain a good but not an inflexible posture; (2) might cross their ankles but should not cross their legs unless wearing slacks or long skirts; and (3) should smile but should not laugh loudly. Neither men nor women should offer to shake hands unless or until the interviewer does so.

The chairs placed at right angles to the desk could be a test for the interviewee. By just sitting at the odd angle, you might give the impression that you do not have initiative or that you do not want to look at your interviewer. This is problematic, however, because it is inappropriate to move someone else's furniture, especially when you are the lower-status interviewee. One alternative is to ask the interviewer if she minds if you move the chair. Her response should indicate whether this is a test or whether the chairs have just accidentally been left at the odd angle.

SUMMARY

- A great deal of care must be taken when anticipating, preparing for, delivering, and evaluating verbal messages.
- Problems with communication can usually be traced back to people who take this important process for granted.
- The oral communication skills you can develop to avoid these problems can be categorized by their relation to the model of strategic communication.
- Skills related to goal setting include identifying your purpose, analyzing your target, and understanding the influence of perception. Situational knowledge skills relate your communication to the organizational culture as a whole.
- Communication competence includes choosing the appropriate setting, deciding on the length and timing of the message, using language effectively, and avoiding racist, sexist, and insulting language.
- Anxiety management can, and should, be accomplished in your daily communication with others.

KEY TERMS

Verbal communication: all messages composed of words, either spoken or written

Nonverbal communication: any message—other than spoken or written words—that attempts to convey meaning

Task messages: messages intended to make others accomplish specific goals

Maintenance messages: messages that keep the organization in working order so that tasks can be performed

Human relations messages: messages that help employees fully realize their potential in the organization

Content element: what you are trying to communicate

Relational element: how you feel about the person with whom you are communicating

Relational consequences: the way in which a message will influence future communication with the receiver

Perception: the process of creating meaning based on experience

Proxemics: the study of personal space

Intimate zone: the zone where people interact at the closest distance, ranging from skin contact to eighteen inches

Personal zone: ranging from eighteen inches to four feet, this zone is usually reserved for interactions that are personal or private

Social zone: ranging from four to twelve feet, this zone is used a great deal in business settings

Public zone: the largest zone, ranging from twelve feet and beyond

Personal bubble: the space that we live in, and that marks our personal space

Territoriality: the behaviors or actions associated with the use, maintenance, or defense of physical space so as to indicate ownership

Chronemics: the use of time as each culture determines it to be appropriate

Jargon: the specialized language that professionals use to communicate efficiently with one another

Euphemisms: agreeable, neutral, or indirect phrases used to describe unpleasant events

Paralanguage: voice qualities or characteristics of speech, such as pitch, tempo, volume, rhythm, and articulation

Oculesics: the movement of the eyes and how they are focused on other people and objects

Kinesics: the study of gestures and body movement that can be intentional or unintentional

Emblems: body movements that substitute for words

Illustrators: body movements that amplify, accent, or supplement what is being said orally

Regulators: nonverbal, usually automatic acts that help to maintain the flow of a conversation

Adaptors: actions that reveal psychological or physical needs

Affect displays: unintentional movements that reflect the sender's true emotions

DISCUSSION

1. Which of the nonverbal status indicators listed in Table 5.1 do you believe are most prevalent in business communication? How might cultural differences result in misinterpretation of these cues?
2. How do office design and arrangement affect communication and perceptions of status? In your experience, is office design an accurate predictor of an organization's communication climate?
3. If you have worked in an environment where a dress code was enforced, what effect did the code have (either positive or negative) on morale, communication patterns, and organizational climate?
4. What specialized jargon do you use on the job or as a student? How might it cause problems for others who are not familiar with its meaning?
5. Describe a situation in which a coworker's nonverbal communication contradicted his or her words. Which message was stronger? How did the contradiction affect your trust in the other person?
6. Discuss the effect of gender and cultural differences on communication. How have you handled such differences (successfully or unsuccessfully) in your work experience?
7. Explain the complementary nature of requests and directives. When should each be used?

ACTIVITIES

1. Write an essay in which you react to the statement "One cannot not communicate."
2. Describe some typical settings in a business or organization in which the following would be an appropriate zone for communication:
   a. Intimate
   b. Personal
   c. Social
   d. Public
3. In a small-group discussion, explain to your classmates how important you believe "correct" business dress is to a professional and to an organization.
4. Think of some of the consequences for an employee who uses racist and sexist language in an organization.
5. List at least five circumstances in which a manager would be wise to use a request rather than a directive in organizing and planning employees' work.

CHAPTER 6

Leadership and Management Skills

After completing this chapter, you will be able to:

1. Identify the functions leaders perform and the skills they need
2. Understand the major theories of management
3. Explain the concept of strategic leadership
4. Develop goal-setting skills based on vision and values
5. Collect knowledge about yourself and the organization's leadership needs
6. Demonstrate leadership competence by empowering others
7. Manage leadership anxieties through optimism, persistence, passion, and acceptance of responsibility for failure

STRATEGIC SCENARIO

The Melanae Group is a B2B (business-to-business) company that delivers information and data management services to other businesses. It is a company constructed from four smaller businesses that have either been bought or merged into the larger business. The four groups comprising Melanae are (1) the information storage/encryption/security (ISES) division, (2) the data entry/management (DEM) division, (3) the Web page design (WEB) division, and (4) the management consulting (MC) division, specializing in entrepreneurship. The business plan of the Melanae Group is to offer a wide range of information and data services and thus to position itself as a "knowledge company" that helps other businesses—such as insurance companies, banks, financial institutions, and government agencies—with their information and data needs.

Jacquere Shubar has been made regional manager for Melanae, with responsibility for all four operations in his geographic region. Jacquere came from the management group (MC), which is open-minded, energetic, and optimistic about the merger. His employees, scattered in four offices within his region, include some telecommuters working from home. Employees from the ISES division are distrustful and disillusioned, unhappy that they must now report to anyone outside of their group. DEM employees are friendly but set in their ways. The WEB division employees are young and on-the-edge, stressing creativity over typical management practices. In essence, Jacquere is considered to be one of "the suits" who has been made boss. He much prefers to work with his own kind—consultants—but his performance as regional manager is based on his ability to get his region thinking and working like one organization, not four. Jacquere will have to draw upon his very best leadership and management skills to pull this off.

Think about the challenges facing Jacquere as you read through this chapter.

OVERVIEW

When you enter the work force, you will probably be expected to assume a variety of complex roles. If you are in management, you may be expected to act as a generalist who coordinates the technical, human resources, operational, and creative functions of your organization. If you are in research, design, or other production-related jobs, you may be expected to use new technologies and communicate effectively with a diverse set of coworkers. Added to these responsibilities may be a need to increase competitiveness of your products and efficiency of production. To meet challenges at work, you will want to apply the skills you are learning now in new and creative ways. The previous chapters have provided you with a means to acquire effective communication skills through the strategic communication model. In this chapter, we provide you with the means to incorporate that model and your communication skills into the development of leadership. Regardless of your position in the organization, this chapter will help you to know and apply leadership skills in the performance of your duties.

One way to develop leadership skills is to adopt an outside-in perspective on your organization. This means focusing on the technological forces outside the organization and assessing its strengths and weaknesses from the perspective of outside stakeholders, such as customers, suppliers, and even the government. It means adopting a wider view of your organization's role in the environment.

To do so requires vision. According to David Campbell of the Center for Creative Leadership, "The best visionaries aren't necessarily those who can predict the shape of the 21st century. Rather, they are people who can draw a conceptual road map from where the organization is now to some imagined future and say, 'This is how we get there.'"[1] This sort of leadership has few, if any, mystical qualities. It is a practical and strategic approach designed to meet the specific challenges of the information age.

Leadership can be learned, and it can be adapted to solve problems. That is what this chapter is all about: understanding and developing leadership skills. We review the skills and functions traditionally associated with management and leadership. We give a brief overview of management theory, which will help you understand and cope with different management styles. We introduce an approach to leadership based on the strategic communication model. Our approach includes skills, attitudes, and techniques to help you succeed professionally, academically, and personally.

WHAT DOES A LEADER DO?

The terms *leadership* and *management* are often used interchangeably. The result sometimes is confusion about the actual delegation of responsibilities in organizations. Leadership and management are complementary concepts that emphasize slightly different mind-sets and courses of action. **Managers** coordinate and organize activities. **Leaders** influence people and their behavior. For example, when you work on a classroom group project, your professor acts as a manager when he or she makes assignments and organizes the groups. Leaders, in contrast, are the individuals in each group who motivate other members to excel in the assignment. Management and leadership, despite their differences, are based on the same fundamental skills. We begin with some of the behaviors, skills, and functions generally associated with both management and leadership.

1. Quoted in W. Keichell, "A Hard Look at Executive Vision," *Fortune,* October 23, 1989, p. 207.

Managerial Functions and Leadership Skills

Management generally has four functions: planning, organizing, motivating, and controlling.[2] **Planning** comprises setting goals and outlining steps to achieve those goals. **Organizing** is the process of accumulating and coordinating the human and capital resources necessary to undertake a plan. **Motivating** is generating commitment and support for a plan. **Controlling** means using authority and power to ensure that a plan succeeds. All of these functions are important to organizational success, but the degree to which each is emphasized depends on the circumstances. The planning function may be most important in industries that experience a great deal of change or innovation. Controlling may be used least in businesses where creativity is at a premium. Organizing may not be particularly important in routine labor operations such as assembly lines, where motivating may be the most important function.

While management always seeks to accomplish planned goals, it rarely succeeds without solid leadership—whether that leadership comes from managers themselves or from someone else involved. Good leadership means that worthy, achievable goals are set in the first place. Leaders also excel at the motivation aspect of management. And while managers are often the ones who *have* control, leaders are the ones who effectively put control (theirs or someone else's) to its best use in achieving team goals. Good managers, on the other hand, typically excel at organizing. To some extent, these management functions and leadership skills are also important to you as a student. You are already developing the ability to plan your time, organize study or research materials, and motivate yourself to finish your work. You may or may not be in a position to control others. But consider your experiences on sports teams, in previous jobs, or at other activities in which you were in a position to direct a group of people toward a goal. You may be surprised at how many potential leadership situations you have already encountered. You can prepare yourself for leadership responsibilities now by identifying those opportunities and actively seeking to incorporate leadership functions in your daily routines.

Technical, human, and conceptual abilities are important to managers' work.[3] **Technical skills** include the ability to use data, information, innovations, and techniques. As a new employee, you may be given special training in technical areas, such as seminars in using the company's computer software. Often you may be expected to learn technical skills on your own. One of the best ways to do this is to observe an expert or someone with a lot of experience. Asking questions is another way to gain technical information and at the same time show your enthusiasm for learning.

Human skills include the ability to work with people to accomplish goals. Regardless of your position in an organization, you will be called on to understand your coworkers' needs and motivations and to recognize their strengths and weaknesses. In your past work experience, have you found yourself more, or less, productive when working with a person whose strengths and weaknesses differed from your own? With what types of people did you work best? Developing leadership ability starts with being able to figure out which people will work well together. To make these decisions, you must know how to gauge others' abilities objectively and to draw on your past experience.

2. P. Hersey and K. Blanchard, *Management of Organizational Behavior: Utilizing Human Resources* (Englewood Cliffs, N.J.: Prentice Hall, 1982).
3. Ibid.

Conceptual skills include the ability to see your job in its relationship to the entire organization and to recognize how the organization interacts with its environment. A good way to begin developing conceptual skills is to think critically about how organizations in which you are currently a member interact with the environment. For example, think about the relationship your school has with the town or city in which it is located. How could the relationship be improved? In particular, what could students do to encourage the improvement? Students at several college campuses hold a biannual "Neighborhood Day," when they help to clean up the campus and surrounding neighborhood, volunteer to make minor repairs to neighbors' houses, or run errands for neighbors who are elders or invalids. Such activities can promote leadership skills.

Future-Oriented Skills

The ability to handle information is a vital leadership skill and an important management function. Gareth Morgan suggested that as information becomes the most important product in the global and national economy, the ability to obtain, assimilate, analyze, and communicate information will be critical to organizational success. According to Morgan:

> New modes of electronic communication will increase the amount of data available in decision making, creating the problem of information overload. Managers will have to learn to overcome the paralysis, or clouding of issues, that can result from having too much information and develop "information management mind-sets" that allow them to sort the wheat from the chaff. Skills in the design of information systems, data management, and data analysis and interpretation will become increasingly important. Managers will also have to be more computer literate and learn to dialogue electronically—with both people and data—with a high degree of skill.[4]

As a new employee, you may be faced with unexpected technological demands. If you are a recent graduate, you may be expected to know more than long-time employees about new communication and information technology because your employers consider you a member of the "computer generation." If you have been out of school or the work force for some time, you may find that you are still expected to know about the latest in technology, regardless of your experience.

Be sure to do your best to prepare for the technological demands of the workplace. Learning word processing and computer programming and even getting familiar with presentation equipment through classes like this one are invaluable ways of making yourself effective. If, despite your best efforts to prepare, you find yourself in need of additional skills training, consider taking workshops or classes that will benefit you and others in the company as well. In this way, you can demonstrate forward-thinking leadership skills.

Listening Skills

In addition to future-oriented skills, managers must acquire excellent communication skills. While communication entails giving and acknowledging feedback about actions or decisions made in the workplace, probably the most important communication skill is listening. Listening skills are necessary for understanding

4. G. Morgan, *Riding the Waves of Change* (San Francisco: Jossey-Bass, 1988), p. 11.

and responding to employees, motivations, and intentions (see Chapter 4). And on a broader scale, upper-level managers must listen constantly to information in the environment, as well. To improve business, managers must keep an "ear to the ground" in terms of monitoring market conditions, managing relationships with suppliers and other business partners, and keeping abreast of government regulations.

Although most leaders and managers practice the skills and functions described here, the ways in which they do so vary widely. Just as organizations develop different structures and patterns of communication to achieve goals, leaders and managers use a variety of techniques to motivate and reward employees. In the next section, we will introduce you to some important theories of management that describe these techniques.

MANAGEMENT THEORY

A number of researchers have proposed theories about how management is accomplished in organizations. Recall from Chapter 1 that organizations are structured differently and that organizational structure indicates the flow of communication within an organization. Researchers have developed theories to account for the specific styles of communication within organizations. Rensis Likert and the team of Robert Blake and Jane Mouton based their work on the ideas of Douglas McGregor, whose theory X and theory Y explanations of what motivates workers we discussed in Chapter 1. In more recent years, other ideas have been suggested in response to changes in the structure and goals of business organizations and in employees. We will introduce you to some of them.

Likert's Systems of Management

Rensis Likert described management in terms of whether managers focused on tasks or on relationships with their employees; he assumed that more emphasis on one meant less emphasis on the other.[5] Likert's thinking can be illustrated by a continuum bounded by task orientation at one end and relationship orientation at the other (see Figure 6.1). He proposed four systems that characterize common management styles.

System 1. A system 1 style of management is task oriented and has a highly structured, authoritarian focus. Interpersonal relationships do not seem important. System 1 managers trust subordinates very little and do not involve them in decision making. Subordinates work in a climate of

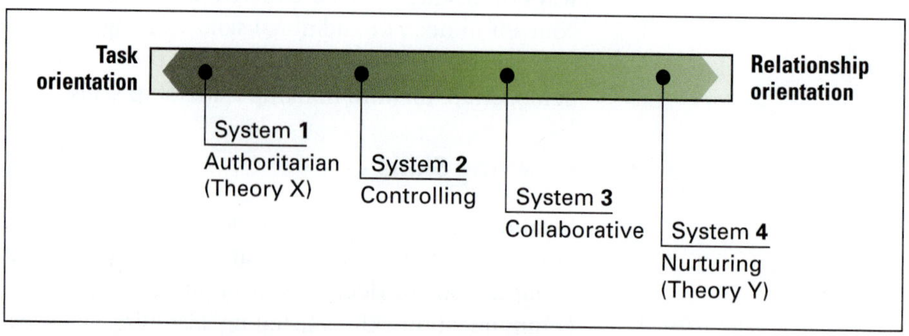

FIGURE 6.1

Likert's Management Continuum

In Likert's theory, as a management system becomes more nurturing, it becomes less authoritarian.

5. R. Likert, *New Patterns of Management* (New York: McGraw-Hill, 1961).

intimidation and fear. Communication takes place from the top down, following the chain of command.

System 2. A system 2 style of management is task oriented, but control of the organization or unit is less authoritarian. Managers are condescending to subordinates and, though not as strict, continue to demonstrate distrust of subordinates. Some decision making is allowed at lower levels, but organizational problems are resolved at the top of the organization. Although most of the communication from managers follows the chain of command, some interaction is carried out directly between upper management and lower-level subordinates.

System 3. System 3 managers openly place confidence and trust in subordinates. Managers control subordinates through negotiation and collaboration. Decision making is allowed at lower levels, especially in matters that directly affect workers. Communication flows relatively freely both up and down the organizational hierarchy.

System 4. System 4 managers concentrate on the relationships between superiors and subordinates. They nurture confidence and trust in workers and encourage decision making at all levels of the organization. System 4 managers do not use fear, threats, and intimidation. Workers' motivation results from their participation in goal setting. Free and open message exchange occurs among superiors, subordinates, and peers.

Notice that these systems are quite similar to the classical and humanistic schools of organizational theory that we examined in Chapter 1. Systems 1 and 2 correspond to the assumptions of Taylor's scientific management and Weber's theory of bureaucracy. Systems 3 and 4 reflect more concern for the worker's personal growth and satisfaction, a tenet of the human relations and human resources schools of thought.

Blake and Mouton's Managerial Grid®

In a theoretical model such as Likert's—that is, a single continuum with two opposite "ends"—an increase in (or movement toward) one end *requires* a decrease in (or movement away from) the other end. But what if the so-called opposites can actually exist together at the same time? In other words, what if they're *not* mutually exclusive opposites? In the case of management, is it possible for managers to focus on *both* relationships and tasks? Robert Blake and Jane Mouton thought so. They considered each potential focus—concern for people and concern for production—as having its own amount of variability. They pictured management as a grid composed of two interdependent aspects of concern present in any situation when people work together to reach an outcome. The degree of concern for outcomes ranges on a scale from 1 (low) to 9 (high) (see Figure 6.2).[6] The grid theory allows a leader to explore how two levels of concerns interact to form one of five distinct styles of relating to others in the workplace.

Concern for people can be seen in a manager's regard for her or his workers, particularly the concern that subordinates are being treated well by the organization. Concern for production refers to a manager's emphasis on achieving the goals and objectives of the organization. Although a very large number of combinations

6. R. Blake and J. Mouton, "Managerial Facades," *Advanced Management Journal* 31 (July 1966), 30–37.

FIGURE 6.2

A Leadership Grid

In Blake and Mouton's managerial model, concern for people and concern for production goals are separate variables, which combine to create a wide variety of management styles.

The Leadership Grid® figure, from *Leadership Dilemmas–Grid Solutions,* by Robert R. Blake and Anne Adams McCanse. Houston: Gulf Publishing Company. Copyright 1991 by Scientific Methods, Inc. Reproduced by permission of the owners.

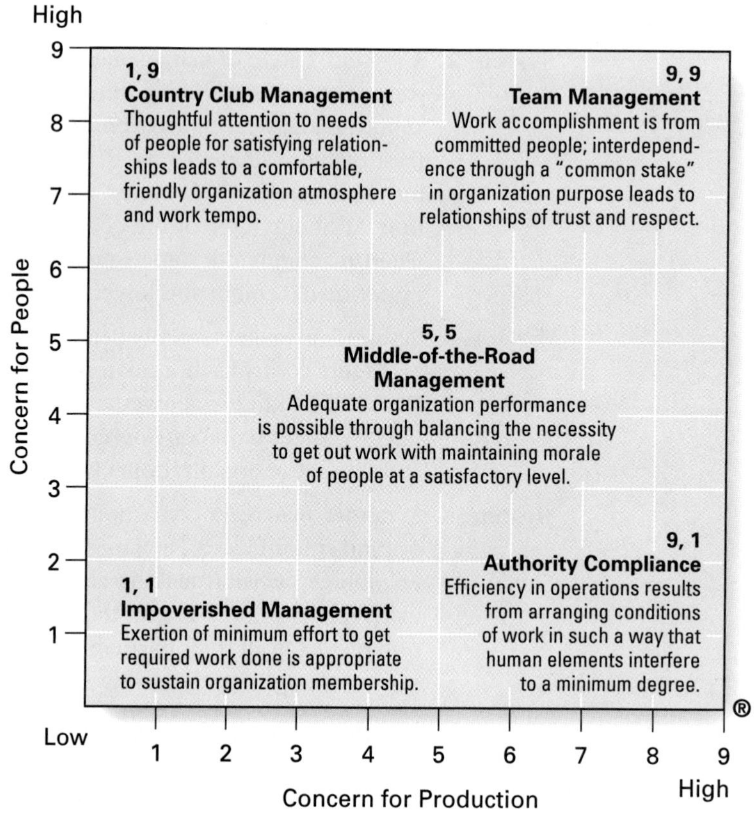

can be made from the two factors, Blake and Mouton proposed five major managerial styles. Figure 6.2 provides a brief explanation of each of them.

LEADERSHIP THEORIES

Vroom and Yetton's Leader-Participation Model

How difficult is it to get people to do things when they had no part to play in reaching the decision? Victor Vroom and Philip Yetton's research focused on followers' participation in decision making.[7] According to their model of leader participation, five options describe how subordinates can be involved in decision making. The options range from no participation at all to full participation. Table 6.1 indicates how the five levels of leader participation differ. As the table shows, decision making can range from authoritarian (levels 1 and 2) to democratic (levels 4 and 5). Level 3 represents moderate follower involvement.

The leader-participation model is important for two reasons. It can describe leaders who choose one level of participation consistently and whose subordinates have come to expect that level of participation in decision making. It also shows that flexibility exists among decision-making styles. Sometimes more participation by employees is appropriate; at other times less participation is needed. Some situations may not involve employees directly, so no participation is necessary.

7. V. Vroom and P. Yetton, *Leadership and Decision-Making* (Pittsburgh: University of Pittsburgh Press, 1973).

TABLE 6.1

Vroom-Yetton Leader-Participation Model

Level	Follower Participation	Decision Process
1	None	Leader only
2	Leader gathers information from followers	Leader only
3	Leader obtains ideas and suggestions from selected followers	Leader only
4	Leader shares problem with followers as a group and collectively obtains ideas and suggestions from them	Leader only
5	Leader shares problem with the group	Joint decision making of leader and group of followers

In emergency conditions, because of time constraints, decisions may be made without participation by employees. People are most likely to accept decisions when they have had a hand in making them.

Kuhnert and Lewis's Transactional Leadership Theory

Transactional leadership, a theory proposed by Karl Kuhnert and Philip Lewis, describes relationships between superiors and subordinates that are based on exchanges for mutual gain. According to this theory, leaders offer subordinates things they want—such as higher salaries, time off, or benefits—to obtain certain things in return—such as their extra work on special projects, working overtime, and loyalty. A **transaction** occurs when each party gives up something in exchange for something else.

Transactional leadership works only if each party has something the other wants. What happens, however, if leaders cannot offer anything that followers value? In times of financial hardship, for example, leaders may be unable to provide bonuses for extra work, yet the work still has to be done. In such a situation, a leader must find alternatives to offer workers, such as promises of raises when times improve or public approval or recognition. For this leadership style to be effective, both parties have to realize their mutual dependence.

Kuhnert and Lewis's Transformational Leadership Theory

Kuhnert and Lewis identified a type of leadership known as transformational leadership.[8] In contrast to transactional leadership, transformational leadership focuses on reaching goals through appeals to deep-seated values among organizational members.[9] The transformation begins when the manager communicates her or his values

8. K. Kuhnert and P. Lewis, "Transactional and Transformational Leadership: A Constructive/Development Analysis," *Academy of Management Review* 12 (1987), 648–657.
9. J. M. Burns, *Leadership* (New York: Harper & Row, 1978); J. Kouzes and B. Posner, *The Leadership Challenge* (San Francisco: Jossey-Bass, 1987).

to employees. As employees reach agreement on a set of organizational values, they elevate one another to new heights of inspiration, motivation, and morality.

Transformational leaders do more than just communicate their values to followers; their behavior reinforces the values they represent. According to Kuhnert and Lewis, successful transformational leaders possess self-confidence, a dynamic personality, strong convictions, the ability to communicate goals, a facility for image building, and a talent for motivating others. Notice that those qualities are not used in an exchange process—transformational leaders do not view the needs and desires of followers as bargaining chips, as is the case in some forms of transactional management. Transformational leaders communicate well and thus inspire others by their own example to achieve excellence in the workplace. Their goal is to emphasize workers' growth and development.

Transformational leadership is important because it is value based. As you recall from Chapter 2, the identification and promotion of values are keys to organizational success. Transformational leaders view workers as willing participants in a value-conversion process that strengthens the entire organization.

LEADERSHIP VERSUS MANAGEMENT

The famous leadership scholar Peter Drucker said that "Management is doing things right; leadership is doing the right things."[10] Knowing what is the right thing to do requires a different skill than getting it done. This kind of leadership skill may or may not be part of a person's management style. Many mid-level managers, in particular, can function very well without tremendous vision. Most management positions, however, offer the opportunity to demonstrate leadership. Consider the following example:

> Manuel and Ahmad are managers in a video production company. Manuel is in charge of accounts receivable, and Ahmad is a marketing manager. The company has recently created a new job, director of human resources, and plans to promote a current employee to the position soon. Manuel and Ahmad are top candidates. Upper management wants the chosen candidate to demonstrate exceptional leadership skills because the job is an important and highly visible component of the company's new program to recruit more women and minorities to management positions.
>
> Manuel is a superb technician. His department has a flawless record, and he has been very loyal to the company, even turning down competing job offers. But Manuel tends to do things the way they have always been done; his personal motto is "Why fix what isn't broken?" Ahmad, in contrast, is quite vocal in his recommendations for change in his unit and focuses more on "what should be instead of what is." He has an effective track record in his department, although he is not overly concerned about the day-to-day details of the job. Upper management selects Ahmad for the new position, and Manuel is outraged that someone like Ahmad has been chosen.

If you were upper management, what would you tell Manuel? In this situation, upper management chose Ahmad's creativity over Manuel's dependability. The high profile of the job, as well as the program's newness and forward-thinking focus, made Ahmad the better choice. Manuel's skills, though recognized and valued, were not as appropriate for the job.

10. This is an often-used quote of Peter Drucker.

Organizations are shaped by effective managers and leaders, but the terms *manager* and *leader* are not interchangeable. As a manager, the woman pictured here might oversee the workload and budget, among other tasks. As a leader, she will move her team and her company in new directions by taking measured risks and implementing plans for the organization to change and grow. (© Jeff Greenberg/ Photo Edit)

In your career, you will find that some promotions are made on the basis of creativity, personality, or other intangible qualities, and other promotions are based on demonstrated talent and dedication. The job, not the candidates themselves, often determines whether a leader or a manager is needed.

There is no shortage of definitions for leadership. Table 6.2 compares several views of leadership.[11] These definitions agree that leadership is a process and that leaders are influential in achieving important goals. After considering these definitions and our own leadership experiences, we define leadership as the process of influencing subordinates, superiors, and peers toward the attainment of goals by using strategic communication methods. Strategic communication methods encompass values, vision, goal identification, future-oriented thinking, and other important behaviors that enable adaptation to the challenges of the information age.

With determination and practice, you can develop the communication skills vital to becoming an effective leader. Keep in mind that leadership is not reserved for the wealthy or the well connected, nor are people necessarily born with leadership skills.

The model of strategic communication provides the direction for our discussion of leadership skills. The skills are divided into four major components: goal setting, situational knowledge, communication competence, and anxiety management. Attending to each of these areas can ensure that you cover all the bases necessary for developing leadership ability.

11. G. Terry, *Principles of Management,* 3d ed. (Homewood, Ill.: Irwin, 1960); R. Tannenbaum, I. Weschler, and F. Massarik, *Leadership and Organization: A Behavioral Science Approach* (New York: McGraw-Hill, 1959); H. Koontz and C. O'Donnell, *Principles of Management,* 2d ed. (New York: McGraw-Hill, 1959); J. Kotter, *The Leadership Factor* (New York: Free Press, 1988).

TABLE 6.2

Views of Leadership

Theorist	Leadership Definitions
Terry	Leadership is the activity of influencing people to strive willingly for group objectives.
Tannenbaum, Weschler, and Massarik	Leadership is the interpersonal influence exercised in a situation and directed, through the communication process, toward the attainment of a specialized goal.
Koontz and O'Donnell	Leadership is influencing people to follow in the achievement of a common goal.
Kotter	Leadership refers to the process of moving a group of people in some direction through noncoercive means; it also refers to people who are in roles where leadership is expected.

For a more thorough comparison of leadership theories from a communication perspective, we highly recommend Gail Fairhurst's chapter in *The New Handbook of Organizational Communication*. G. Fairhurst, "Dualisms in Leadership Research," in F. Jablin and L. Putnam (eds.), *The New Handbook of Organizational Communication* (Thousand Oaks, Calif.: Sage, 2001), pp. 379–439.

GOAL SETTING: MANAGING THE PRESENT AND THE FUTURE

Chapter 2 stressed the need for goal setting in any communication situation. Leadership is no different. Leaders must be forward thinkers and doers. To set goals for yourself, as well as for an organization, consider three factors: shared values, vision, and management of change.

Shared Values

A widely discussed aspect of leadership is the values that leaders hold. A leader's identification and promotion of values are critical to organizational success because values provide all members of the organization with a sense of guidance as they perform their daily tasks. Without shared values, a leader is unlikely to be successful. The following example is helpful in beginning our discussion of shared values:

> Chita, Ming, and Sallie are entry-level unit management trainees at HighTech, Inc. During their orientation sessions, the personnel director stressed the shared values of the organization. Chita was impressed with these values but was impressed even more by the fact that the company believed in them enough to actively promote them to new employees.
>
> Chita decided to follow the personnel director's example. She made up a laminated handout identifying the values to distribute to each of her subordinates. She held three meetings to discuss the values, and her subordinates were eager to embrace them as their own, especially after suggesting two more that were specific to their unit.
>
> Ming and Sallie were also impressed with the values of the company, but they made no obvious attempt to instill the values in the members of their units. Indeed, Sallie's and Ming's behavior sometimes contradicted those values. After a while, other managers began to notice that Chita's unit was showing impressive increases in customer satisfaction and operating efficiency and decreases in absenteeism.

At HighTech's annual awards luncheon, Chita was asked why her unit had been so successful. She distributed copies of the laminated handout of values to everyone in the room and stated, "The single best action I took last year was believing in this company's values and having my people believe in them, too. Once people know, understand, and believe in the company's values, you really don't have to do much more. They will know what to do." Chita's understanding of the importance of shared values paid off.

How do leaders ensure that values are shared by organizational members? Three approaches can help leaders promote shared values among their coworkers: clarity, consensus, and intensity.[12]

Clarity Good leaders try to ensure that values are clear to all. Asking people how they feel about the organization's stated values is one way to evaluate how clear they are. Workers' impressions of, and reactions to, stated values reveal the depth of their understanding of those values. As an effective leader, you will often act as a cheerleader for the organization's values, articulating them frequently in clear and concise language. Once values are clear to others, they can internalize them and even adapt them to specific work situations.

Consensus When there is consensus about values, people not only understand the stated values but also share them. Leaders and those who aspire to leadership can do a great deal to achieve consensus by setting an example. When followers see a leader acting on the stated values of an organization, they are assured that those values really are important to the organization.

Leaders can also use values to assess the work of others. If employees excel on a project, the leader can point out ways in which their work promotes the values of the organization. Consider work experiences you have had. Did managers consistently relate the importance of organizational values? Did they respond to suggestions from subordinates, but only after lengthy complaints? If you were in a management position, how would you treat your coworkers?

Intensity Employees in companies with high levels of intensity about shared values frequently discuss them in regular conversation.[13] Intensity means that employees connect emotionally with the company's values, live up to them, and demonstrate more than a passing interest in keeping them alive. Leaders can reinforce intensity by showing strong commitment themselves.

The Significance of Shared Values Barry Posner, James Kouzes, and W. H. Schmidt studied the merits of shared values.[14] They surveyed more than twenty-three hundred employees in a number of different organizations across the United States. They found that organizations with strong shared values enjoyed a number of benefits:

- High levels of company loyalty
- Strong norms about working hard and caring
- Strong feelings of personal effectiveness
- Consensus about key organizational goals
- Reduced levels of job stress and tension

12. Kouzes and Posner, *The Leadership Challenge*, p. 336.
13. Ibid., p. 196.
14. B. Posner, J. Kouzes, and W. H. Schmidt, "Shared Values Make a Difference: An Empirical Test of Corporate Culture," *Human Resource Management* 3 (1985), 293–310.

Shared values also promote ethical behavior at work. The ethical differences of a culturally diverse work force can be transcended by a coherent set of ethics for the organization as a whole. Indeed, the organization's ethical standards may be better suited to resolve differences than members' specific codes of ethics are.

Vision

The visions that leaders have for their departments, units, or organizations are based on shared values and play an important role in goal setting. According to Warren Bennis and Bert Nanus:

> A leader must first have developed a mental image of a possible and desirable future state of the organization. This image, which we call a vision, may be as vague as a dream or as precise as a goal or mission statement. The critical point is that the vision articulates a view of a realistic, credible, attractive future for the organization, a condition that is better in some important ways than what now exists.[15]

Developing Vision A key aspect of vision is originality—the ability to see new goals and new ways to reach those goals. Developing original ideas is not easy. It helps to be always looking for alternatives as well as getting inspiration from your own experiences.

Jeff Bezos had a rather ridiculous-sounding idea for a business. He wanted a bookstore; only he didn't want his bookstore to have a store at all. In fact, the bookstore he envisioned wouldn't even have any books! The idea was to have an automatically run Web site that could connect customers with book distributors. Customers could order books on-line. The order would then automatically be sent to publishers and distributors. In this way, he would need almost no real estate, capital, or workers. In 1994 Amazon.com "opened its doors." A year later the price of his stock had doubled, and within two years the price was seven times higher than its initial offering. Bezos's vision, Amazon.com, was one of the few "dotcom-boom" companies to survive the "dotcom-crash." This seemingly silly idea was a truly new, original, and very successful vision of how to do business.[16]

Managers practice creativity in a specific context and with a specific focus. For example, Joyce, a marketing manager, believed that her department could increase its profits by offering its market research service to outside clients for a subscription fee. She knew demand for the service existed because her department had received many requests from outsiders to use the marketing statistics it had gathered. Although Joyce was not sure how to approach potential subscribers or how to bill for the service, she knew that Randy, an administrative executive, would be able to give her some suggestions. His experience plus her own interest in developing new ideas helped Joyce to create a realistic and worthwhile vision for her department.

Clarifying Vision Just as values must have clarity, so too must visions be readily understood by those who are expected to act on them. According to Edwin H. Friedman, "Leadership can be thought of as a capacity to define oneself to others

15. W. Bennis and B. Nanus, *Leaders: The Strategies for Taking Charge* (New York: Harper & Row, 1985), p. 89.
16. Information from http://www.economist.com/displaystory.cfm?storyid=S%26%28XH%2FRA7%?=21%0A.

in a way that clarifies and expands a vision of the future." A vision must be presented so that others can see the potential benefits of acting on it. Followers of a vision know that they are contributing to its fulfillment in a large or small way. Employees often need to feel that the tangible results of a vision will benefit not only themselves but also the organization in which they work.

The most effective visions are described in language that others can understand. Choosing the right words may be one of the hardest things a leader has to do, not only because of the inherent difficulty of the task but also because articulating a vision makes it less of a personal dream.

Adjusting Vision Developing a vision can pose a major challenge, but leadership does not stop there. Leaders must make a conscious effort to behave in ways that consistently reflect the vision.

The vision may require occasional adjustment. When problems occur, workers and leaders are wise to remain flexible and strive to modify and improve the original vision. A vision need not be scrapped the moment an obstacle appears. Visions are general images of the future that can be achieved with the understanding that different approaches often lead to the same destination. A vision that produces a rigid pattern of behavior instead of presenting an inspirational challenge may do more harm than good.

The Benefits of Vision Many people face an ongoing problem of keeping up with the various maintenance activities their jobs require. Routine phone calls and visitors, meetings, and paperwork take time. So too do unexpected crises that must be taken care of immediately. One manager taped an eloquent summary of her company's goals to her desktop but then found that she usually could not read the list because she had so much paperwork on her desk.

The organization as a whole can benefit from a clearly articulated vision. Vision can be used to prioritize daily activities, guide decisions about what project to handle first, and remind managers to delegate some activities to others who are dedicated to the same vision.

Management of Change

Articulating a vision almost always entails changing the status quo for an as-yet-untested alternative. Consider Nintendo. Did you know that this videogame company was founded in 1889? One of Japan's most successful makers of playing cards, Nintendo had been profitably producing cards for close to a century when it produced its first piece of electronics (toy Beam Guns) in 1970. The success of this new direction for Nintendo was quickly apparent. Within twenty years, Nintendo went from a highly successful Japanese playing card manufacturer to the global giant in home videogames. In 1989, exactly one hundred years after Nintendo was founded, the "Nintendo Entertainment System" videogame console was the best-selling toy in the United States.

Think about how hard it must have been to initiate such a drastic change—from printing cards on paper to producing consoles, microchips, and programs. Nintendo had been producing cards for eighty years, and were very successful at it! Why change anything? Changing meant hiring new employees like electrical engineers and computer programmers. It was a huge and very risky investment.

Many people within the Nintendo company must have felt uneasy about the change in corporate direction.[17]

To set goals, astute leaders anticipate and manage change effectively. There is always resistance to change. Some people like the status quo. Others fear that change will affect them adversely. Still others resist change because the effects of change are unpredictable. For example, an update of technology within an organization, such as a new computer system, might cause employees to become apprehensive about learning new procedures, become resistant to the time required to install the new system, or become defensive about the old system because the new computer is unfamiliar to them. Leaders become agents of change by making and publicizing decisions that support the plan for change.

Managing change in an organization requires a four-step strategy:

1. Anticipate the problems that are likely to occur when a vision is implemented. A back-up plan can help avoid potential problems. For example, confusion can result when people perceive a vision differently. This difficulty can be avoided when employees have written details for reference.
2. Focus the organization on the vision. Day-to-day obstacles frequently discourage dedication to the original vision. After evaluating the obstacles, the leader can either modify the vision or solve the problems.
3. Leaders and employees alike look at results rather than at processes. This step enables everyone to consider alternative approaches to tasks.
4. Build a strong, supportive network of people committed to change. Several members of this network must be in key positions of power, maintain strong working relationships with one another, and be highly motivated to accomplish tasks related to the change.[18]

Once leaders have made change agents out of influential people in the organization, they can motivate others to recognize the value of change and embrace it with enthusiasm. Leaders cannot manage change alone. They must empower others to advocate productive change at all levels of the organization. Grassroots participation is a very effective means of implementing change.

SITUATIONAL KNOWLEDGE: THE FOUNDATION OF STRATEGIC LEADERSHIP

John F. Kennedy once observed that "leadership and learning are indispensable to each other." Within our model of strategic communication, learning involves gaining as much situational knowledge as possible. The ability of leaders to set goals is enhanced by situational knowledge—the information a leader needs to manage a situation effectively. This knowledge includes information about the organization and its employees as well as knowledge about one's self. The more leaders discover about their own abilities, weaknesses, and personal style, the better prepared they are to take charge.

Knowledge About Self

How well defined is your self-concept? Most people think they have very accurate self-awareness. We are not so sure. We have met a number of people who believed they had skills in certain areas when they did not. Like everyone else, leaders are

17. Information from http://www.nintendo.com/corp/history.html.
18. Kotter, *The Leadership Factor*.

STRATEGIC SKILLS

Leadership Self-Concept Evaluation

Complete the following self-evaluation to check your awareness of your own characteristics. Add the numbers that you listed beside all the descriptions. If you scored between 26 and 87, you have a low opinion of your leadership ability. If you scored between 88 and 173, you think you have average leadership skills. If your score was 174 or above, your opinion of your leadership ability is high. How many 3's, 4's, and 5's do you have? These are areas that can use improvement. Look for areas where you wrote 7's, 8's, 9's, and 10's. Are these areas where you have been told you excel or you have been recognized for your talents? These are areas worth promoting and emphasizing.

Rate yourself on a scale of 1 to 10 in each of the listed areas, with 1 being weakest and 10 being strongest.

______ Adaptability
______ Ambition
______ Challengeability
______ Cleverness
______ Confidence
______ Creativity
______ Dedication
______ Education
______ Empathy
______ Experience
______ High self-esteem
______ Imagination
______ Intelligence
______ Interpersonal skills
______ Intuition
______ Likeableness
______ Loyalty
______ Motivation
______ Open-mindedness
______ Persistence
______ Physical attractiveness
______ Resourcefulness
______ Sense of humor
______ Strong values
______ Tolerance for ambiguity
______ Trustworthiness

not perfect. They have shortcomings and weaknesses that challenge their ability to lead. Effective leaders inventory their imperfections and minimize them to gain others' support.

Your opinion of yourself—your self-concept—is important to the development of leadership skills. Leaders need to have a healthy view of themselves. This does not mean that leaders should be self-righteous, self-promoting egotists. It does mean that they should know their own strengths and weaknesses. As you think about your own strengths and weaknesses, recall from Chapter 3 that your perception of yourself is culturally specific. This perception is further complicated by organizational culture, which has its own perception of what a leader should be.

Another method of self-evaluation is to assess your views on current issues that affect you. Your views have been formed in part by your culture, and people from different cultures are likely to have different attitudes and beliefs about the same issues. However, it is important for you to assess your own personal views. You may think that you have opinions on certain issues, but until you actually write them down or articulate them, they may be surprisingly vague.

Try this exercise. Select an issue with which you are familiar, and review your knowledge of and opinions about it. It can be a personal issue such as your feelings about a relationship, a political issue such as gun control or environmental protection, or a social issue such as welfare or health insurance. Draw a line down the middle of a piece of paper. On the left side write the heading "Things I Feel Very Strongly About." On the right side write the heading "Things I Am Unsure About." Honestly assess the strength of your personal opinion and knowledge of the issue as you write statements on each side of the page. You may be surprised at the number of items you list on the right side.

It is always a good idea to take stock of yourself and gauge your point of view. Doing so is not always easy, but knowing yourself can help you to perform better in all areas of your work as well as to develop leadership ability.

It is crucial to avoid hubris. Hubris is excessive pride—a belief in personal invincibility and omnipotence. Successful leaders sometimes develop hubris and tend to believe that they are able (and permitted) to do anything, including illegal or unethical actions. Success does build self-confidence. But when you are successful, you are smart to consider the organization, its vision, and others' contributions to your success so as to avoid developing hubris.

In school and in your career, consider keeping a journal of your achievements, and in that journal mention others who also received or deserved credit for these accomplishments. You can refer back to these cooperative accomplishments when you are tempted to give yourself all the credit for whatever success you achieve. Chances are that if you give others the credit they deserve, they will do the same for you.

Organizational Knowledge

Astute leaders recognize all the tasks involved in the organization's operation, although they are unlikely to know the specifics of every single job description. Only by recognizing both the big picture and the fine print are leaders able to coordinate all the factors required for achieving goals.

Thomas Peters and Robert Waterman suggested that managers learn about the business by "wandering around."[19] Others have talked about "hands-on management." Such phrases suggest that effective leadership is both active and interactive and depends in part on leaders taking an interest in others' contributions to the organization. Such phrases also suggest that the best leaders may be people who began modestly and worked their way up from the lowest levels of the organization. Such people bring years of real and practical experience to leadership decisions.

Organizational knowledge extends beyond the internal structure and functions of the company. Leaders and workers must also be receptive to the environment in order to know what the competition is doing, what the customers want, what the national economy is doing, and how the global market is performing. This type of knowledge is acquired only by continual learning.

Leaders master the skill of continual learning. They analyze and learn from the past and present. Continual learning can be practiced regardless of a person's position in the organization.

An important source of continual learning is failure. Most people view failure as something to avoid. Leadership experts, however, stress the importance of taking risks and learning from failure. Effective leaders experience failure but are able

19. T. Peters and R. Waterman, *In Search of Excellence: Lessons from America's Best-Run Companies* (New York: Warner Books, 1982).

to learn from it and use what they learn to strengthen their leadership. It is often said that employees who do not fail every now and then are not trying hard enough. Leaders may feel that employees who never make mistakes are not taking risks or being creative enough.

You can become more comfortable with risk (and demonstrate your leadership potential) by developing a response plan to turn failures into learning experiences. Formulating such a plan entails performing four tasks in response to failure:

Review ⟶ **Assess** ⟶ **Predict** ⟶ **Resolve**

Immediately after a failure has occurred, either by yourself or with those involved, *review* the chain of events leading to the failure. Determine the point at which reality deviated from the ideal. Next, *assess* the deviation. Was the problem minor or major? Were there several problems? Did the problem result from lack of preparation, incorrect information, conflicts between workers, or some other factor? Use the assessment to *predict* the likelihood of such a problem occurring again. Was it a one-in-a-million situation? Or is the problem likely to recur next week? Finally, using your analysis of the first three factors, *resolve* how to handle such a situation in the future. Consider the following example:

> David Wildon is responsible for supplying data charts to an account manager whose projects are generally behind schedule. David noticed that the spreadsheet program for preparing the charts had recently caused some errors in the account figures but assumed that taking care of the problem was not his responsibility. One month, the data provided by the manager did not match the results produced by the spreadsheet, so David decided to use estimates to save time and get the project finished. The manager, running late as usual, did not check the finished chart before sending it to his boss for the annual planning meeting. The next day, the manager stormed into David's office demanding to know how the mistakes got into the chart and warning that David would get both of them fired.

In this situation, David and his boss can make several resolutions to avoid the recurrence of such a failure. The boss can resolve to keep his projects on schedule. David can resolve to alert those responsible for maintaining the software if he notices a problem with it. David and his boss can resolve to go over the completed charts together to make sure that they are free of error. Such resolutions can reduce the likelihood of failure as well as the stress resulting from fear of failure. Implementing plans for learning from failure can be an important step in developing leadership ability.

COMMUNICATION COMPETENCE: DEMONSTRATING LEADERSHIP SKILLS

What communication skills are necessary for leadership, and how can you begin to develop them now? In addition to effective listening (discussed in Chapter 4) and verbal and nonverbal skills (Chapter 5), the critical elements of communication are building trust, promoting understanding, and empowering others. **Trust** results from a strong commitment to ethical behavior within the organization's system of values. **Understanding** comes from listening to others, using clear and respectful language, and relying on appropriate techniques for behavior control. **Empowerment** means giving people the opportunity to think and act for themselves within the guidelines of the shared values and vision of the organization.

PRACTICING BUSINESS COMMUNICATION

United Negro College Fund

Strong leadership, progressive business strategies, and dynamic communication are at the heart of the United Negro College Fund's history of successful fundraising. Founded in 1944, this not-for-profit partnership among college presidents, corporate leaders, volunteers, and donors has grown to more than 250 paid staffers and over 30,000 volunteers.

In its first fifty years, UNCF raised nearly $1 billion. A hefty portion of these contributions resulted from the efforts of Christopher Edley, the College Fund's president from 1972 until 1990, and of former congressman William H. Gray III, who became president in 1991.

STABLE MANAGEMENT, STRONG LEADERSHIP

The College Fund demonstrates its strong leadership in many ways. UNCF nurtures and retains bright, creative people who move up through the organization and provide continuity of leadership and vision. The chief operating officer, for example, moved from middle management into the position as second in command more than a decade ago.

Individual leaders like the College Fund's prominent board members and Gray, who has a vast network of business and political contacts, generate major contributions during annual and capital fund drives. An outstanding example is the success of its Technology Enhancement Capital Campaign, which is aimed at reversing the disparity in access to computer technology between students at UNCF member institutions and college students nationally. Microsoft, IBM, and AT&T have signed up as partners in the campaign, and Gray estimates that the total value over the next three years at approximately $130 million.

Two governing bodies at UNCF, the board of directors and the institutional members, carry out the complementary leadership functions of setting and implementing policy. The board of directors includes committed leaders from business and industry. The board is responsible for business functions such as staffing executive management, managing property, distributing funds, and making policy.

The institutional members, who are presidents of member institutions, have authority in matters relating to education. They track new government legislation, identify programs that should receive special funding, and determine the formula by which the board of directors distributes funds. The member presidents also make all nominations to the board. Together, these governors and their staffs nurture UNCF's many ties to the business, academic, and legislative communities.

STRATEGIC PLANNING

Member college presidents and corporate board members provide another source of leadership through their participation on committees, which focus on major issues ranging from strategic planning and budget and investment to policy review. A public information task force monitors the messages conveyed to the public by advising ad agencies and

The benefits yielded by trust, understanding, and empowerment include enhanced creativity and increased productivity as workers take initiative to succeed without the direct control or coercion of managers or leaders.

Trust

Trust, the first of the critical leadership skills, is the faith and confidence that workers place in the organization's leaders. Leaders do not receive trust automatically; they must earn and re-earn it.

Trust is a two-way street. Followers will not trust leaders who do not trust them, and vice versa. Mutual trust is important. Managers or supervisors who trust employees with additional or important responsibilities often win respect for other outside suppliers about maintaining continuity in presenting UNCF's image, by ensuring that all affiliated institutions are treated equally, and by suggesting strategies for future College Fund campaigns.

High-profile alumni of UNCF colleges and scores of celebrities from the media, entertainment, and sports industries contribute their time, talent, and dollars to UNCF initiatives. Special-event fundraisers include the annual Lou Rawls Parade of Stars telethon, the Bryant Gumbel/Walt Disney World golf tournament, and the Magic Johnson all-star basketball game.

The ongoing success of the award-winning campaign "A mind is a terrible thing to waste," which is sponsored by the Ad Council, has increased public awareness of UNCF and its goals. This slogan is one of the most widely recognized in America.

The leadership structure and style at UNCF reflect an efficient organizational culture. Under Gray's leadership, a well-defined management style and long-term fundraising strategies ensure the organization's continued success. UNCF attracts young, creative, ambitious people who stay with the College Fund because it gives them the opportunity to develop a wide variety of skills and to tackle multiple responsibilities—and rewards those who do.

COMMUNICATION MEDIA

Leaders and employees at all levels emphasize face-to-face communication in both identifying challenges and deciding how to resolve them. Informal and formal discussions and meetings are the source of many solutions and ideas.

Field staff employees and volunteers located in thirty area offices receive additional support from the UNCF magazine, *A Mind Is,* which highlights the achievements of UNCF member colleges and alumni. In addition, headquarters keeps staff apprised of issues and activities affecting UNCF around the nation through memos and press clippings. UNCF uses computers for communicating, desktop publishing, and accounting.

The people at UNCF work to provide the best educational and leadership opportunities for African Americans. The talent and resources mobilized by UNCF make those opportunities a reality.

QUESTIONS FOR CRITICAL THINKING

1. What communication obstacles do you think UNCF has had to overcome?
2. What is the organizational structure of UNCF?
3. What leadership qualities are necessary for UNCF to succeed in its fundraising efforts?
4. How does UNCF display communication competence to the public?
5. How might UNCF improve its internal communication?

You can visit the United Negro College Fund on-line at www.uncf.org.

their insight into the employees' abilities. Followers then begin to trust managers in other areas ("Well, if she trusted me with the ABC project, she must know what she's doing; I trust her judgment"). Over time, leaders and workers can build a mutual store of trust that can be tapped to achieve important goals.

Another characteristic of trust is its fragility. Building trust can be a long and slow process, but often only one or two betrayals are all it takes for many followers to lose faith in a leader they have trusted for years. Trust is one of the most important ingredients in leadership, yet it is one of the most fragile.

The Relationship Between Trust and Ethical Behavior In Chapter 2 we discussed the importance of communication ethics. Trust in organizations begins with leaders serving as role models of ethical behavior. Employees may refrain from ethical behavior if they see their leaders performing unethical acts.

ETHICAL ISSUES

Leadership Using Fear

Management has always used fear to some degree. Although most leadership books ignore this tool altogether in favor of more accommodating techniques, many highly successful executives use terror to lead their employees.

Scott Snook, a Harvard Business School professor of organizational behavior, suggests that fear can become a barrier to taking risks, but at the same time can "provide the essential emotional kick" needed to meet a challenge. The use of fear to lead can cause many problems because no one will question the leadership or suggest changes. For example, Enron would have its employees rank one another's performance every year—and would then fire the lowest 10 percent. This practice could not have made questioning authority easy, and such questioning could have helped to avoid Enron's scandal and collapse.

Workers who have more credentials and experience are less reliant on a single employer, and for them, fear-inspiring bosses are less of a factor. In strong economic times, workers are more difficult to come by, and so bosses must be careful. However, in times of downturn such as the last few years, management has more power over employees and "cracking the whip" becomes more common.

Most successful companies are made up of people who are "productively neurotic." That is, their neuroses makes them more productive workers because they have "a strong self-imposed fear of failure." Firms with such workers don't use fear directly to encourage employees; rather, they simply reinforce people's own natural tendency to strive for success.

Do you think it is ethical for an organization to allow their leaders to use fear as a communication tactic? What have been your own experiences with fear as a leadership tool?

Information from http://www.economist.com/PrinterFriendly.cfm?Story ID=1595341.

Ethical behavior reflects the values espoused by the organization. Values can be directly stated. A code may state: "We value honesty and integrity as a way of doing business." Ethical standards can also be communicated indirectly. Leaders may choose to uphold standards of honesty and equality instead of pursuing questionable courses of action that may be more profitable.

Defining Ethical Behavior Employees constantly watch managers and executives for cues to guide their actions. It is imperative that managers demonstrate ethical behavior for employees to emulate. According to Kenneth Andrews, "The personal values and ethical aspirations of the company's leaders, though probably not specifically stated, are implicit in all strategic decisions. They show through the choices management makes and reveal themselves as the company goes about its business. That is why this communication should be deliberate and purposeful rather than random."[20]

Defining a code of ethics is one of the most difficult aspects of leadership. All employees have personal systems of ethics that they have cultivated over the years, and these codes are their first reference in a questionable situation. Although a grand set of rules by which to communicate in the business world would be helpful, such a code would ultimately fall short in specific circumstances.

Managers may ask, "If ethical behavior means different things in different situations, how do I know for sure that my own actions are proper?" This question is

20. K. R. Andrews, "Ethics in Practice," *Harvard Business Review,* September-October 1989, p. 103.

best answered by consulting experts in business ethics.[21] Their experience and research have generated a number of guidelines that can help individuals determine whether their behaviors are in line with ethical principles.

Sustaining Trust Once leaders and employees have achieved a state of mutual trust, they have to work at maintaining that trust. You should be aware of four keys for sustaining trust: constancy, congruity, reliability, and integrity.[22]

Constancy is the ability to stay on course, to remain focused on the vision and goals regardless of setbacks. Followers respect and trust leaders who stay calm and undistracted in the face of adversity. **Congruity** is the parallel between what a leader says and what a leader does. Leaders' actions and behavior should match their statements, goals, and views. **Reliability** means that leaders support employees and coworkers in times of need, whether personal, organizational, or professional. **Integrity** is the keeping of promises and commitments, coupled with the refusal to make promises that compromise the well-being of coworkers and the organization. Employees may not like all of a leader's decisions, but they will trust a leader who clearly upholds their interests and keeps her or his word.

Problems with Mistrust As you can imagine, a number of complications are associated with mistrust. People generally do not give their best effort to someone they do not trust. Furthermore, when leaders are mistrusted, the whole organizational climate may deteriorate. The outcome may be the withholding of information, the distortion of facts, rampant suspiciousness, low levels of information exchange, deception, closed-mindedness, low morale, and poor interpersonal relations.[23]

Trust is an essential component of leadership. Without it, leaders fail. With it, leaders have a chance to make a real impact on how the organization prospers. Most of the characteristics, elements, and qualities of strategic leadership discussed in this chapter can only be actualized if trust is established between leaders and followers.

Understanding

Understanding, the second critical leadership skill, begins with attending to what employees are saying. Listening promotes understanding because it shows that leaders think highly of employees' input and take their comments seriously. Asking for advice, gathering opinions, and soliciting suggestions from followers are ways in which leaders can demonstrate their openness to listening. Consider these helpful suggestions to leaders for asking advice from followers:[24]

- Include coworkers in discussions of problems and issues.
- Encourage individual thinking.
- Make it easy for subordinates to communicate their ideas to you.

21. S. Kerr, "Integrity in Effective Leadership," and R. Harrison, "Quality of Service: A New Frontier for Integrity in Organizations," in S. Shrivastva (ed.), *Executive Integrity: The Search for High Human Values in Organizational Life* (San Francisco: Jossey-Bass, 1988), pp. 122–139, 45–67; C. C. Walton, *The Moral Manager* (Cambridge, Mass.: Ballinger, 1988).
22. W. Bennis, *On Becoming a Leader* (Reading, Mass: Addison-Wesley, 1989).
23. Kouzes and Posner, *The Leadership Challenge*.
24. J. K. Van Fleet, *The 22 Biggest Mistakes Managers Make and How to Correct Them* (West Nyack, N.Y.: Parker, 1982), p. 147.

- Follow through on these ideas.
- Reward those who give advice.

When employees see that their advice is valued, they are more likely to give it. This is just one example of how effective listening helps to accomplish the goals of the organization.

Understanding also requires that leaders sidestep the trap of "framing." Framing refers to the tendency to frame problems in ways that are familiar, comfortable, or easy to deal with instead of identifying and developing problems as they are actually presented.[24] If a leader is prone or biased to seeing problems, say, from a sales perspective, he or she is framing problems in a narrow way. The problem may very well be in marketing, finance, or public relations.[25]

Language The capacity for understanding includes a conscious and respectful relationship with language. The language of effective leaders has been studied, and the conclusions are quite interesting. In his study of U.S. presidents' language, Rod Hart identified four categories of commonly used words or phrases:[26]

1. *Realistic words* are tangible and concrete words that reflect reality: *budget, profit,* and *overhead* are realistic terms that have specific and practical meanings in business.
2. *Optimistic words* give employees positive projections about their organization. Such words express hope, promise, and encouragement and can increase feelings of job satisfaction and security. Examples include *rosy, bright,* and *reassuring*.
3. *Activity words* describe specific actions that must be taken to realize goals: *expand, mobilize,* and *support* are examples. Activity words provide motivation for achieving the organization's vision.
4. *Certainty words* express belief in the organization's vision and values. Words that convey certainty include *assurance, conviction,* and *confidence*.

The use of words from these four categories produces successful communication. Think about the language choices of your professors, elected officials, fellow students, or coworkers. What types of words do they use most?

Communication Styles Like language choices, communication styles vary according to the form of leadership and its intention. Several styles are described below:[27]

Tell: The leader makes decisions and tells followers how to carry them out.

Persuade: The leader unilaterally makes decisions but attempts to persuade followers to accept them.

Consult: The leader asks for input on decisions, followers provide different options, and the leader chooses from among these alternatives when making the decisions.

Join: The leader brings employees together and participates in the decision-making process as an equal group member.

25. D. Gouran, "Communication Skills for Group Decision Making," in J. Greene and B. Burleson (eds.), *Handbook of Communication and Social Interaction Skills* (Mahwah, N.J.: Erlbaum, 2003), pp. 835–870.
26. R. Hart, *Verbal Style and the Presidency* (Orlando, Fla.: Academic Press, 1984).
27. G. Hines, "Management of Leadership Styles," in A. Dale Timpe (ed.), *Leadership* (New York: Kend, 1987), pp. 105–111.

Give: The leader provides group members with all necessary information and asks them to make the decision on their own; the leader agrees to abide by any decision reached.

Which of those styles are you most comfortable with? Does your answer depend on the situation? Once you have identified your natural or usual style(s) of communication, make a conscious effort to adopt an alternative style for a set period of time, such as a day. Observe how others treat you. Does the alternative style seem to work for you?

Empowerment

Empowerment, the third critical leadership skill, means entrusting people with the authority to act independently. Empowerment can promote creativity, cooperation, and inspiration among employees. Warren Bennis writes, "Good leaders make people feel that they're at the very heart of things, not at the periphery. Everyone feels that he or she makes a difference to the success of the organization. When that happens people feel centered and that gives their work meaning." Although managers may resist the idea because they fear losing control of their employees, allowing employees to be independent increases managers' effectiveness. Employee empowerment can be realized only through effective leadership skills, such as reduction of status differences and team building.

Reduction of Status Differences Effective leaders are generally perceived to be of higher status than followers. Their status allows them to assume responsibility for making important decisions. Large status differences between leaders and followers, however, can have a debilitating effect on morale, efficiency, and productivity. Leaders who concentrate on creating status differences are likely to encounter those problems. A workable balance occurs when employees view leaders as senior partners working with employees to achieve goals.

Leaders can reduce status differences by being considerate. Consideration for employees includes showing warmth, asking for opinions, showing concern for employees' welfare, giving credit where credit is due, and being open to suggestions. An example of considerate leadership can be found at RLI Insurance in Peoria, Illinois. RLI avoids giving away big prizes for suggestions and instead rewards every idea, whether it is used or not, with a \$2 bill. When an idea is used, the responsible employee is entered into a quarterly drawing for prizes ranging from \$50 to \$100. RLI reports a dramatic increase in the total number of suggestions made as well as an increase in the quality of suggestions received.[28]

Peak Electronics in Orange, California, has moved to an even more innovative method of soliciting employee suggestions: Employees are encouraged to suggest one idea per month. Two employees with the best suggestions are named "Thinkers of the Month" and given prestigious and convenient parking spaces. Managers have the authority to implement the idea on the spot or pass it on to someone with the authority to do so. Suggestion boxes are located in restroom stalls to guarantee confidentiality.[29]

Leaders can also reduce status differences by being less directive in their communication. Getting cooperation and productivity through positive communication

28. Example from *INC. Magazine,* August 1993, p. 28.
29. Examples from *INC. Magazine,* October 1992, p. 36.

reduces the perception of a leader "cracking the whip" over employees and results in a more enthusiastic climate. Cultural difficulties, however, can be related to status differences. Leaders who are less directive and ask for employees' opinions may find that a response is not forthcoming or comes slowly or tentatively from employees whose culture views such inaction as inappropriate. These cultural differences must be considered in the empowerment strategies of a leader.

Team Building Team building empowers people because it enables work to be accomplished with less direction from management. Team building contains two related elements: involvement and integration.

Involvement, or getting people working on activities other than their daily tasks, gives employees a sense of importance in the organization. Participating in special activities such as self-directed teams (see Chapter 10), goal-setting sessions, professional development workshops, and organizational surveys can give employees a sense of involvement and enhance their feelings of empowerment.[30]

Integration, or bringing people together so that their varied talents and skills can be complementary and mutually supportive, gives employees a sense of cooperation. Just as sports teams integrate members' talents to win contests, employees can appreciate one another's skills when they successfully complete a project together. Teamwork can be especially gratifying because working with others can make each employee perform better than she or he would perform alone.

ANXIETY MANAGEMENT

Managing anxiety is an important part of leadership. You may have heard people make remarks such as "He could really be a successful person, but he is afraid of failing" or "She has all the skills, but she is afraid of success." Leaders experience anxiety just as everyone else does. The nature of the fear may be different for each person, but it is present for all leaders at some time or other. Effective managers and leaders control their anxieties and do not let them become overwhelming. Optimism, persistence, passion, and accepting responsibility for failure enable leaders to overcome the anxieties of their jobs.

Optimism

Effective leaders remain optimistic even in the face of adversity. Those with an optimistic attitude consider setbacks a challenge. They try to justify their optimism by overcoming setbacks and proving pessimists wrong. Strong self-confidence and self-awareness form the basis for an optimistic attitude. Notice the different outlooks revealed in this dialogue:

NEW ATHLETIC DIRECTOR: This program has potential because of dedicated team members, strong alumni support, and a new leader who is willing to do what it takes to produce a winning attitude and a winning season.

BOARD MEMBER: I wish I could say the same. Our head coach was caught paying players, and we were put on probation for a year. The following year we were unable to recruit top players and ended the season with one win and eleven losses. Team morale is low, and the stands are empty.

30. D. Seibold and B. Shea, "Participation and Decision Making," in F. Jablin and L. Putnam (eds.), *The New Handbook of Organizational Communication* (Thousand Oaks, Calif.: Sage, 2001), pp. 664–703.

NEW ATHLETIC DIRECTOR: Once the program's reputation is restored [trust is reestablished] the team will realize that only by coming together as a team [empowering others] can we all earn the right to enjoy a winning season.

Persistence

Leaders overcome anxieties by being persistent in their actions and behavior in spite of the pessimism of others and short-term setbacks. Persistence reflects dedication to the vision of the organization in spite of tense situations, ominous events, or failures. All these have the potential to cause great anxiety among employees and managers alike, but persistence can diminish fear of them. Where would Sam Walton's family be today if he had given up on his small local drugstore in Arkansas in the 1960s? Persistence, or "hardiness," helps people to "take the stress of life in stride. When they encounter a stressful event—whether positive or negative—(1) they consider it interesting, (2) they feel that they can influence the outcome, and (3) they see it as an opportunity for development."[31]

Passion

Passion reduces the anxiety that leaders face. Enthusiastic commitment helps managers to set aside their doubts and worries and concentrate on the important issues. Employees have confidence in managers who demonstrate commitment to the shared values of the organization, and their support helps to lessen the anxieties that leaders may have. Do you know of people with the passion that will make them successful leaders?

> Ana Olivarez is a well-known and respected interior designer in her community, and she has recently expanded her designing business. Because her business is growing, Ana has been interviewing creative and innovative designers who have the same intensity and desire she has for aesthetics. Ana breathes, feels, talks, and walks artistic ability, and she is very successful at what she does.

Accepting Responsibility for Failure

To accomplish goals, leaders must take risks. Some risks result in mistakes and failure. Leaders have an obligation to own up to their mistakes and accept blame for failure. People under supervision know that management is fallible, and their trust in the organization's leadership will waver if they observe managers blaming subordinates for their own mistakes.[32] Consider this example:

> Ms. LeFann, a junior high school band director, loved to challenge her symphonic band students. A spring concert was coming up, and Ms. LeFann decided at the last moment to include a difficult but popular piece of music as the last number on the program. Her students rose to the challenge and practiced the piece to perfection. But when the selection was performed at the concert, the timing was off. The woodwinds lagged behind, and the brass section rushed ahead. After the concert, Ms. LeFann apologized to the audience and to her students and took full responsibility for the poor performance of the last number.

31. Kouzes and Posner, *The Leadership Challenge,* p. 67.
32. Van Fleet, *The 22 Biggest Mistakes.*

Where Do You Stand?

Of the four components of strategic leadership (goal setting, situational knowledge, communication competence, and anxiety management) and related behaviors, will any of these activities be more difficult for you? Which skills will be the most important to your career plans? Should you try to develop these skills now, or will they evolve naturally on their own? Consider activities you engage in now—like giving advice to a friend, working on a group project for a class, or even trying to organize a party. What strategic leadership skills and behaviors are the most important in those cases?

Once you have decided that you will admit your mistakes, you will be less anxious about what you do. Think about it. One of the most stressful activities is speculating on the possible outcomes of your actions. You can decrease your anxiety, if only a little, by resolving to accept whatever happens and to be honest about it. You can believe in your integrity no matter what else happens. You will have more respect for yourself if you admit mistakes instead of trying to blame them on someone or something else.

Figure 6.3 illustrates the major aspects of personal leadership development.

FIGURE 6.3

Strategic Model of Leadership

STRATEGIC SCENARIO: WRAP-UP

Based on what you read in the chapter, what should Jacquere's first steps be in demonstrating strategic leadership in his region? Which elements of strategic leadership will be most difficult? Can you relate this scenario to similar experiences of your own?

SUMMARY

- Management and leadership, though not the same conceptually, do share several functions—planning, organizing, motivating, and controlling—and do require similar technical, human, cognitive, and future-oriented skills. These functions and skills are made more effective by astute and practiced communication.
- How management is conducted and what makes for good management are subjects of research and debate. Likert's systems of management, Blake and Mouton's managerial grid, Vroom and Yetton's leader-participation model, and Kuhnert and Lewis's transactional and transformational leadership theories provide a broad perspective on the varieties of management found in organizations.
- Strategic leadership skills can benefit anyone who needs to communicate with a group or win support for an idea. These skills are not the exclusive property of executives; they can benefit everyday communications.
- The four components of the model of strategic communication can show any communicator how to address the major aspects of personal leadership development.
- Goal setting includes developing and promoting shared values and visions and managing change. Situational knowledge encompasses obtaining information about the organization and oneself.
- Communication competence means demonstrating organizational ethics, promoting understanding in decision making, and learning effective communication strategies for the purpose of empowering others.
- Anxiety often accompanies the risks of leadership communication, but it can be counteracted by optimism, persistence, passion, and acceptance of responsibility for mistakes.

KEY TERMS

Manager: coordinates and organizes activities

Leader: influences people and their behavior

Planning: setting goals and outlining steps to achieve those goals

Organizing: the process of accumulating and coordinating the human and capital resources necessary to undertake a plan

Motivating: generating commitment and support for a plan

Controlling: using authority and power to ensure that a plan succeeds

Technical skills: the ability to use data, information, innovations, and techniques

Human skills: the ability to work with people to accomplish goals

Conceptual skills: the ability to see your job in its relationship to the entire organization and to recognize how the organization interacts with its environment

Transaction: occurs when each party gives up something in exchange for something else

Trust: a characteristic resulting from a strong commitment to ethical behavior within the organization's system of values

Understanding: a characteristic resulting from listening to others, using clear and respectful language, and relying on appropriate techniques for behavior control

Empowerment: giving people the opportunity to think and act for themselves within the guidelines of the shared values and vision of the organization

Constancy: the ability to stay on course, to remain focused on the vision and goals regardless of setbacks

Congruity: the parallel between what a leader says and what a leader does

Reliability: a leader's support of employees and coworkers in times of need, whether personal, organizational, or professional

Integrity: keeping promises and commitments and refusing to make promises that compromise the well-being of coworkers and the organization

Involvement: getting people working on activities other than their daily tasks, giving employees a sense of importance in the organization

Integration: bringing people together so that their varied talents and skills can be complementary and mutually supportive, giving employees a sense of cooperation

DISCUSSION

1. What are the major skills and functions of managers? How are managers affected by the contemporary business environment?
2. Compare the management theories of Likert, Blake and Mouton, Vroom and Yetton, and Kuhnert and Lewis. Identify some basic similarities in these approaches. Which would you prefer as an employee? As a manager?
3. What is the relationship between leadership and management?
4. How can a strong value system improve leadership in an organization?
5. What can managers and employees do to learn from communication failure? Discuss the four-step process of continual learning, and explain its role in the development of organizational knowledge.
6. What is empowerment? How can effective communication result in the empowerment of employees?
7. What are some methods for handling leadership anxiety?

ACTIVITIES

1. For each of the five management styles identified by Blake and Mouton, explain the communication behavior you believe would be exhibited in a business or professional organization.
2. Use the leadership/management styles and descriptions from this chapter to classify each of the following well-known leaders. Give reasons for your classification.
   a. Bill Gates
   b. George W. Bush
   c. Oprah Winfrey
3. Watch a television news program such as *20/20* or *60 Minutes*. As you watch, write down examples of words that Rod Hart has characterized as realistic, optimistic, activity, and certainty.

PART THREE

INTERPERSONAL COMMUNICATION STRATEGIES

CHAPTER 7

Explains the skills needed to maintain constructive relationships with superiors, coworkers, customers, and others.

CHAPTER 8

Focuses on basic principles of interviewing, including types and sequencing of questions and responses.

CHAPTER 9

Covers key interviews common in a business environment, giving special attention to the responsibilities and regulations of employment interviews.

Part III applies the theory and skills discussed in Parts I and II to one-to-one communication in a variety of settings. Although often taken for granted, one-to-one communication can be one of the most difficult aspects of communication, both for employees and for those who strive to join an organization through employment interviews.

CHAPTER

7

Work Relationships

After completing this chapter, you will be able to:

1. Understand the importance of work relationships
2. Describe the characteristics of strong manager-employee relationships
3. Resolve relational difficulties with coworkers
4. Develop productive relationships with customers
5. Initiate a mentoring relationship with an experienced employee
6. Understand the positive and negative aspects of romantic relationships at work
7. Recognize sexual harassment

STRATEGIC SCENARIO

Tomas Chavez was hired recently by Vangard Equipment Corporation as their director of training. Vangard manufactures heavy earth-moving equipment. Although it is one of the youngest and smallest companies in its industry, Vangard has a solid track record for earnings and profits. Tomas found out on the first day of his job that his position had gone unfilled for almost a year. During that time, training had been conducted by the various departments in the corporation. He knew he had a lot of catching up to do. His first task was to conduct a needs assessment to determine where the corporation had the greatest training needs. He sent out surveys, conducted interviews, reviewed policy manuals, read memos exchanged among employees, and even conducted some focus groups. He rapidly learned that several training needs were apparent. First, customers of Vangard were having a great deal of difficulty getting their questions answered about new equipment purchases. Some customers became so disgusted that they switched their business to a competitor. Second, dozens of employees expressed a great deal of resentment toward upper-middle and upper management for its lack of sensitivity to their needs. Salary wasn't so much the issue as was respect and recognition for their performance on the job. Third, many younger employees were leaving Vangard after only a year or two. Although a lot of reasons were given for their exodus, Tomas got the distinct impression that these less-experienced employees were not given enough guidance, direction, and encouragement for their efforts. Fourth, Tomas learned that Vangard, much like the industry itself, was male-dominated and somewhat chauvinistic. Two recent sexual harassment suits (settled out of court) were testament to the fact that many employees lacked the knowledge and/or sensitivity to deal with gender and sexual issues in the workplace. Finally, Tomas learned that a general lack of respect and civility was the norm among coworkers in the organization. He couldn't put his finger on it, but it was apparent that few of the employees or managers enjoyed positive professional relationships.

As you read this chapter, think about the issues that Tomas uncovered during his needs assessment. At the end of the chapter, we will revisit Tomas's situation and get your impression of what he should do next.

OVERVIEW

Interpersonal relationships are critical to achieving organizational goals. In your work experience you have probably encountered many of the relationships we discuss in this chapter, but you may have been unaware of their importance to you and to the organization itself. The following cases are just two examples of how relationships can promote organizational goals and values:

> Paul, an employee at Delen Corp., was strongly committed to Delen's mission statement, which emphasized providing service to customers and promoting good relations with the local community. He frequently thought about how business practices and community relationships might be improved. Nevertheless, he usually felt a little nervous about suggesting changes. Angela, Paul's supervisor, was an experienced employee who knew the organization well. Her opinions and decisions were generally well respected, and she had achieved a reputation for supportiveness and honesty. Paul approached her with some ideas, and the two of them worked out a plan for starting an educational partnership with the local high school and providing internships for college students. In doing so, they increased Delen's visibility in the community and ensured that young, well-educated people would be interested in working for the organization.
>
> Amy, a sales manager in a large department store, noticed that customers frequently became annoyed when approached by clerks. She knew the clerks were trying to provide prompt and courteous service, yet she also understood the customers' desire to be undisturbed. She resolved the situation by suggesting that the clerks remain alert, attentive, and visible to customers but refrain from approaching unless invited by a customer. She emphasized that when clerks did interact with customers, they should strive to be friendly and responsive at all times. In the weeks after her suggestions were implemented, several customers commented to Amy on the wonderful service in her department. Amy had succeeded in identifying and providing the level of service that customers wanted and needed.

Strong, positive work relationships can be difficult to achieve, despite their importance. Developing positive relationships is an area frequently neglected among coworkers in the quest for increased productivity. Increasing dependence on technology-mediated communication creates an environment that may discourage relational development. Office politics and striving to get ahead may create friction among coworkers. The organizational culture may discourage dynamic relationships, or it simply may not suit individuals' communication styles. Strong interpersonal skills can help you to overcome these obstacles and develop relationships that benefit both you and the organization in which you work.

Most work relationships, such as the relationship between a salesperson and a customer, follow norms, standards, and rules. All work relationships, in addition, rely on ethical communication:

- Refraining from comments intended as personal attacks, from gossip, and from careless communication that reveals sensitive information
- Being straightforward and honest with coworkers, customers, and supervisors
- Avoiding delays and distortions, not hiding information, and not manipulating a relationship for personal gain
- Recognizing that work relationships exist for the primary purpose of achieving organizational goals and acting on this principle when and if a conflict of interest arises

These guidelines are applicable regardless of the type of relationship in which you are involved.

In this chapter, we examine the basic elements of several relationships common in business and the professions: relationships between managers and employees and between coworkers, mentoring relationships, romantic relationships, and relationships between employees and customers.

MANAGER-EMPLOYEE RELATIONSHIPS

One of the most important of all work relationships is the one between managers and employees. These relationships are so important for the simple reason that everyone (except perhaps the chief executive officer in some cases!) has a boss.

Research continues to confirm the high importance of the manager-employee relationship. In a survey of over 2 million people at seven hundred organizations, the top reason employees reported for either staying with the organization or leaving was the relationship they had with their immediate supervisor.[1] The following activity[2] will help you identify the characteristics of your "ideal boss."

Who Is Your Ideal Boss?

Rate the importance of the following characteristics that make up an ideal boss (5 = most important; 1 = least important).

Allows you to show initiative and responsibility	1	2	3	4	5
Communicates clear goals and objectives	1	2	3	4	5
Listens well	1	2	3	4	5
Is reliable	1	2	3	4	5
Gives credit and praise where it is due	1	2	3	4	5
Is not moody	1	2	3	4	5
Is fair and understanding	1	2	3	4	5
Is not afraid to reprimand employees for improper behavior	1	2	3	4	5
Is talented	1	2	3	4	5
Is persuasive with her/his boss	1	2	3	4	5

Goal Setting

In this section we examine the manner in which communication is used by managers and employers to establish and maintain effective interpersonal relationships.

1. C. Warren, "Monster Managers," *American Way Magazine*, June 1, 2003, 62–63.
2. Adapted from www.humanresourcemanagement.co.uk/idealboss (retrieved October 13, 2003). Also adapted from www.staff.pl/en/publications_more.php?idart=42&idkat=57 (retrieved October 16, 2003).

FIGURE 7.1

Manager-Employee Relationships

Characteristics of strong manager-employee relationships include good communication, mutual influence, and power sharing.

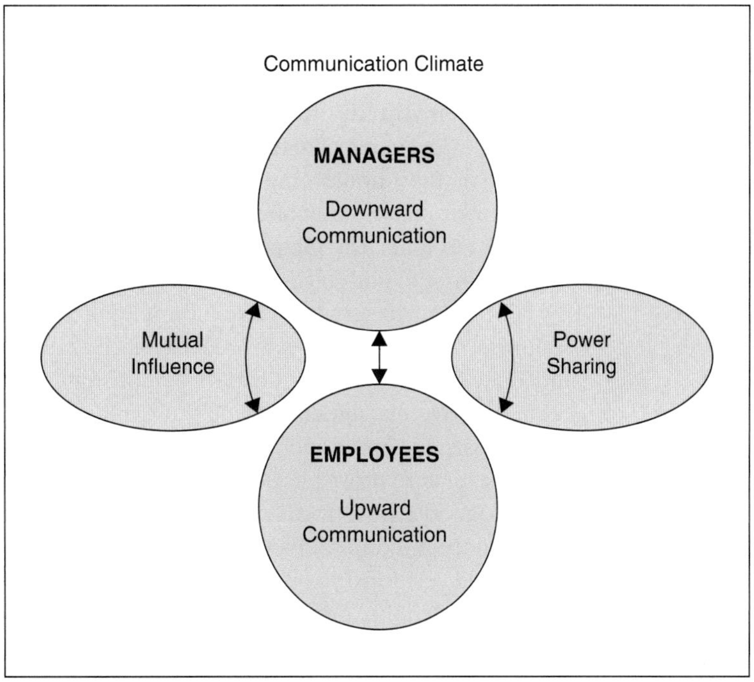

Goal setting is an important feature of manager-employee relationships in ensuring coordination. Situational knowledge is also a key element in this type of communication relationship, especially in determining the climate in which managers and employees work. Communicating competently is most effectively accomplished between managers and employees when power is shared and diversity is carefully managed. Since the manager-employee relationship is one of the most important relationships you will form on the job, it is essential that you learn how to communicate effectively with both managers and employees.

Managers and employees have not only personal and organizational goals but also goals for the manager-employee relationship. Setting goals for a work relationship requires an analysis of the organization, its communication flow, and its political atmosphere. The goals set for a manager-employee relationship should be consistent with the values of the organization. Typical goals are openness, cooperation, honesty, and friendliness.

Situational Knowledge: Communication Climate

As Figure 7.1 shows, the manager-employee relationship develops within a communication climate that is produced by the behaviors and attitudes of all managers and employees. Important contributors to the climate are patterns of communication (upward and downward) and the personal characteristics of managers and employees. The outcomes of the relationship are mutual influence and power sharing.[3]

3. For further reference, see F. M. Jablin, "Superior-Subordinate Communication: The State of the Art," *Psychological Bulletin* 86 (1979), 1201-1222; G. Goldhaber, *Organizational Communication* (Dubuque, Iowa: Brown, 1990); F. Dansereau and S. E. Markham, "Superior-Subordinate Communication: Multiple Levels of Analysis," in F. Jablin et al. (eds.), *Handbook of Communication Science* (Beverly Hills, Calif.: Sage, 1987), pp. 343-388; R. Klauss and R. Bass, *Interpersonal Communication in Organizations* (New York: Academic Press, 1982).

As we discussed in Chapter 2, the organizational climate is affected by how decision-making power is shared and how supportive supervisors and workers are toward each other. Climate is changeable because organizational members' behaviors and their attitudes toward the organization can change.

What effect does climate have on manager-employee relationships? It may encourage or discourage employees' communicating in the organization, exerting control over matters that affect them, and obtaining satisfaction from their responsibilities.[4] In a healthy climate, managers and employees communicate effectively and support each other.

Effective managers have a number of characteristics that make their communication successful. They are approachable, sensitive, credible, supportive, confident, and honest. Their communication demonstrates frankness, respect, empathy, and calm. Effective managers are quick to explain decisions, are articulate and clear in their messages, and encourage information and input from employees.

Managers are most pleased with employees who display the following characteristics: good job performance, ability to handle pressure, help in promoting the boss's success, cooperativeness, honesty, and supportiveness. Subordinates who enjoy good relationships with their bosses provide feedback about how superiors perform their jobs, demonstrate appropriate forms of persuasion, disagree in a constructive manner, and confirm the messages that are sent downward.

In an effective climate, employees are encouraged to give their opinions about a new advertising slogan, and employees willingly provide constructive feedback about improvements or changes for the ads. Managers then consider the feedback and explain why the decisions to incorporate or ignore suggestions were made. In an ineffective climate, managers would not welcome suggestions or comments about the new ad campaign, employees would not give suggestions or constructive criticism, and managers would not offer any explanations for decisions made about the campaign.

Managers and employees rely on each other to get their jobs done. When they possess the characteristics that we mentioned earlier, and when they display open and appropriate communication styles, they do more than simply work together: frequently they positively influence one another.[5] Thus, it is not enough to consider the manager-employee relationship only from the manager's point of view. Employees have a significant effect on their bosses. Employees' actions, attitudes, performance, and communication styles play a very large role in how managers conduct their own business. Managers cannot do the job of their unit or department without the cooperation of employees.

A popular approach to understanding how managers and employees mutually influence one another is through Leader-Member Exchange Theory, or LMX. Employees get a sense of trust and respect with their boss when she or he offers or exchanges resources, support, and influence. This can be particularly effective when these

4. W. C. Redding, *Communicating Within the Organization: An Interpretive Review of Theory and Research* (New York: Industrial Communication Council, 1972); T. L. Albrecht, "The Role of Communication in Perceptions of Organizational Climate," in D. Nimmo (ed.), *Communication Yearbook 3* (New Brunswick, N.J.: Transaction Books, 1979), pp. 343–357; Dansereau and Markham, "Superior-Subordinate Communication."
5. H. P. Sims and C. C. Manz, "Observing Leader Verbal Behavior: Toward Reciprocal Determinism in Leadership Theory," *Journal of Applied Psychology* 69 (1984), 222–232.

exchanges occur outside normal business hours or the business context. Likewise, members or employees reciprocate with support, resources, effort, and influence.[6]

Mutual influence is an informal negotiation process between managers and employees. Each party affects the attitudes and work performance of the other. When managers are approachable, sensitive to employees' needs, and supportive, employees are responsive with feedback about their concerns, dedicated to improving on-the-job performance, and cooperative. In a healthy communication climate, the two parties can recognize and understand each other's needs and work to accomplish mutual goals.

Communication Competence: Managing Power and Diversity

Communicating effectively in a manager-employee relationship means understanding the power structure and diversity of a work force. Understanding power sharing will enable you to adapt your communication in a manner that demonstrates a sensitivity to the power structure of an organization. Recognizing diversity will enable you to communicate effectively and appropriately with all sorts of people.

Power Sharing At first glance, an organizational chart may imply that people in management hold all the power and those they supervise possess none. Signs of power in an organization include decision-making ability and the authority to distribute rewards (such as pay raises) and punishments (such as firing people). Power, however, can be distributed in four ways: (1) managers hold all the power, and workers hold none; (2) neither supervisors nor workers have much power; (3) workers hold most of the power, and supervisors hold little; and (4) managers and workers share power.[7] Let us briefly consider each arrangement.

Organizations in which *management holds all the power* are rare now, but they were common in the early part of the twentieth century and were described by Frederick Taylor, Max Weber, and Henri Fayol (see Chapter 1 for a review of classical organizational theory), among others. Such organizations are characterized by rigidity, strict adherence to process, and communication from the top down.

When *neither managers nor employees have much power,* organizations suffer numerous problems. Small or family-owned businesses often have figurehead managers who possess little power. According to James Kouzes and Barry Posner, "People who feel powerless, be they managers or subordinates, tend to hoard whatever shreds of power they have. Powerless managers also tend to adopt petty dictatorial management styles. Powerlessness creates organizational systems where political skills become essential and 'covering' yourself and 'passing the buck' become the preferred style for handling interdepartmental differences."[8]

Organizations in which *subordinates hold most of the power* are also rare, but they are becoming somewhat more common as the demands on business for innovation and competitiveness increase. For example, companies such as Ben & Jerry's Homemade Ice Cream and Honda put most of the power in the hands of the

6. G. Fairhurst, "Dualisms in Leadership Research," in F. Jablin and L. Putnam (eds.), *The New Handbook of Organizational Communication* (Thousand Oaks, Calif.: Sage, 2001), pp. 379–439.
7. J. Kouzes and B. Z. Posner, *The Leadership Challenge* (San Francisco: Jossey-Bass, 1987).
8. Ibid., p. 162.

What Would You Do?

Cherie is an accountant for a large advertising agency. After receiving notice of a prospective large account, she thinks of a creative advertising campaign and tells her idea to Charles, her manager. Charles shoots down her idea and reminds her that her job is accounting. Several days later, the design team visits Charles and asks him for more details on his "brilliant" campaign idea. Cherie realizes that the campaign being discussed is her idea. What does this outcome indicate about the communication climate and power holding in the ad agency? If you were Cherie, would you approach Charles about stealing your idea, or would you show support for your manager? Why?

employees. These companies de-emphasize differences in status between managers and employees and encourage employee input through lateral communication. However, such a structure may be too loose or decentralized for some companies.

When *managers and subordinates share power,* workers enjoy satisfaction and commitment without losing direction. When people feel they have some control and influence over the ways decisions are made and actions are carried out, they are more energetic in accomplishing the goals of the unit and the organization. Managers, in turn, have enough power to effectively manage the unit.

Like mutual influence, power sharing between supervisor and worker has to be negotiated. Management expert Rosabeth Moss Kanter identified four methods for sharing power:[9]

1. Give people important work to do on critical issues.
2. Give people discretion and autonomy over their tasks and resources.
3. Give visibility to others, and provide recognition for their efforts.
4. Build relationships for others, connecting them with powerful people and finding them sponsors and mentors.

In return, employees actually increase their productivity and strengthen their relationships with managers.

Remember that power and power sharing occur on a unit or department level as well. Power that is earned or bestowed on any member of a unit, whether manager or subordinate, is essentially the unit's power. Conversely, when a worker is denied power, the entire unit will suffer.

Managing Diversity Manager-employee relationships are affected by issues of gender and ethnicity. Since 1972, the number of female managers in the United States has nearly doubled. According to the U.S. Bureau of Labor Statistics, women, members of minority groups, and older workers are expected to increase as a percentage of the work force by the year 2008.[10] The prospect of a great influx of managers and workers from a wide variety of backgrounds has focused attention on the relationships between male and female managers, on the relationships

9. Ibid., p. 175.
10. Howard N. Fullerton, "Labor Force Projections to 2008: Steady Growth and Changing Composition," *Monthly Labor Review*, November 1999, pp. 19–32.

As the work force matures through increased diversity, more opportunities emerge for women and minorities to take leadership roles in the organization. Meetings such as the one depicted in this photo are commonplace in organizations and demonstrate the power of communication for managing power and diversity. (Jose Luis Pelaez/Corbis)

between male and female subordinates, and on how people of different cultural backgrounds can make the most of their work relationships—a concept known as managing diversity or valuing diversity.

Diversity of gender, culture, and managerial preference focuses on two issues: stereotypes and competence. Different experiences, opportunities, and educational preparation may account for varying levels of managerial skills in people, but these differences are not specific either to gender or to culture.

What are specific to groups are the stereotypes associated with them. Stereotypes associated with male and female managers are fueled by societal stereotypes about males and females in general, which may exist because of misunderstanding or failure to question their validity.[11] Men have traditionally been stereotyped as competitive, ambitious, assertive, risk taking, and power seeking. Women have traditionally been stereotyped as soft-spoken, passive, emotional, understanding, and sensitive. Whether or not typically masculine or feminine behavior is most effective for a given task, problems can arise when women and men do not behave as traditional gender stereotypes suggest they will. Consider the following example:

> Amber and Kelly were recently hired as manager trainees for a fast-food company. Most of the employees they supervise have never had a female manager before. Amber decided that the best way to advance in the company would be to emulate the management style of her two bosses, Fred and Juan. Fred and

11. V. Wheeless and C. Berryman-Fink, "Perception of Women Managers and Their Communicator Competencies," *Communication Quarterly* 33 (1985), 137–147.

Juan are very task oriented; they rarely socialize or show their emotions when on the job.

Modeling the behavior of these men, Amber maintained her distance from her line employees. She answered their questions but never volunteered additional information, and she tried not to get involved in her workers' personal problems. She figured that her efficient demeanor would ensure that her shift performed professionally.

Kelly, however, treated her line workers in a warm and informal manner. She asked about their personal lives and attempted to establish close relationships. She figured that her obvious care for her workers would ensure their doing a good job for her.

At their semiannual evaluations, both Amber and Kelly were informed by upper management that their relationships with employees needed improvement. Line workers had complained about how they were treated. Amber and Kelly were stunned by these comments. What were the causes of the line workers' complaints?

Although feminine stereotypes are not necessarily negative in the workplace, they can cause problems for women in management, especially if the organization has only recently moved women into management positions, because traditionally many traits associated with being a good manager (such as being task oriented or good at problem solving) have been considered masculine traits. Thus, on the one hand, if a female manager possesses stereotypic traits, some people may assume that she is too "feminine" to be effective. On the other hand, if a female manager does not conform to stereotypes and possesses "masculine" traits, some may be suspicious because she does not appear to "act like a woman." The term **gender role congruency** refers to the extent to which a person—through his or her behavior, interests, dress, communication style, and so on—conforms to gender stereotypes.[12] Although society's view of what is feminine or masculine continually changes over time, individuals often struggle with accepting any behavior that they believe is not gender role congruent. In the case of women managers, others' desire for gender role congruency may conflict with the behaviors required of the managerial role. Behavior that deviates from others' expectations can arouse mistrust or even hostility.

It is difficult for members of the majority to recognize subconscious stereotyping, yet it is nearly always present. The most destructive approach to managing diversity is to claim lack of prejudice. That claim usually masks a failure to acknowledge biases that are apparent to others or a tendency to dismiss others' perceptions of bias as misguided.

The double bind that minority and female managers experience is diminishing. As more minorities and women enter the work force and become managers, stereotypic behaviors will become more widespread and are likely to be perceived as positive. As you recall from Chapter 6, the most effective managers and leaders are sensitive to employees' needs, take a personal interest in their subordinates and nurture them, and are passionate about the goals and values of the organization. Most subordinates appreciate such positive traits. Moreover, research has revealed that women increasingly prefer female managers.[13] As women make

12. P. Johnson, "Women and Power: Toward a Theory of Effectiveness," *Journal of Social Issues* 32 (1976), 99–110; B. Ragins, "Power and Gender Congruency Effects in Evaluations of Male and Female Managers," *Journal of Management* 15 (1989), 65–76.
13. Wheeless and Berryman-Fink, "Perception of Women Managers."

up a larger percentage of the work force, support from subordinates will make a big difference in the overall success of female managers.

The best approach for managing people effectively is to capitalize on their individual strengths to get the most from them. Most managerial jobs require a certain level of competitiveness, risk taking, and power seeking as well as sensitivity, empathy, and emotional involvement. Good managers have always recognized this fact. Women and men who follow the leadership principles outlined in Chapter 6 are a step ahead of their managerial cohorts. An approach that stresses goals, situational knowledge, communication competence, and anxiety management will yield a high level of excellence for any manager.

COWORKER RELATIONSHIPS

Coworker relationships are the glue that holds an organization together. Positive and constructive coworker relationships enhance productivity, creativity, and teamwork as well as make work an agreeable place to be. Of course, coworker relationships can be voluntary or involuntary. You will do yourself a considerable service if you understand how coworker relationships develop so that you can devise a method for dealing with involuntary relationships that could undermine your productivity. Coworker relationships are based on proximity, shared interests, common tasks, and satisfaction of needs.

Proximity

The closer you are to people physically, the more likely you are to develop relationships with them. Officemates form friendships and alliances simply because of their **proximity,** or physical closeness, to one another. (Of course, common lounges, meeting areas, restrooms, and hallways are places where you can meet people who do not work in your area.) Think about the classes you are taking. You have probably become friends with the people who usually sit near you in the classroom.

Shared Interests and Common Tasks

People like to be with others who share their interests. Working in an organization automatically provides a number of common interests on which to build work relationships. Coworkers share a corporate identity, a work location, and possibly even the same bosses at times. Relationships often develop naturally around these common interests. The grapevine is one expression of shared-interest relationships among coworkers.

More and more jobs require the joint effort of two or more people. Work groups, task forces, and team projects show that cooperation is an increasingly popular way to solve problems and address complex issues. People are usually assigned to particular work groups because of their talents and expertise and regardless of whether they like the other group members.

Working with people on common tasks can provide both a great deal of satisfaction with the resulting relationship and professional enrichment. The more often you communicate with coworkers, the more likely you are to understand them on a personal level and form friendships with them. Unfortunately, the opposite is also sometimes true: the more you work with someone, the more you may dislike that individual's personal qualities.

Regardless of your personal feelings about your coworkers, several guidelines can help you to form positive shared-task relationships:

- Ignore personal idiosyncrasies as much as possible.
- Stay focused on mutual goals—the organization's success depends on employees working well together.
- Know your responsibilities, and be accountable for your performance.
- Share credit for success with coworkers, and take your share of the blame for failure.

These guidelines will help you to establish strong organizational relationships and overcome difficult or uncooperative coworkers. You may discover that it is actually very rewarding to work with someone you initially disliked for personality reasons.

Satisfaction of Needs

One of the most common reasons why relationships develop at work is to satisfy basic needs. In addition to basic subsistence needs such as food, clothing, and shelter, you have emotional and intellectual needs at every point in your life. As a student, for example, you are fulfilling your need for knowledge and skills.

Needs do not go away when you join an organization. Your needs for affiliation, social exchange, and the sharing of ideas with others are just as strong at work as they are in your personal life. Many people spend half or more of their waking hours at work, so it is only natural to satisfy these needs through their jobs. Most of the needs that can be fulfilled at work can be grouped into four areas: *support, power, expertise,* and *social exchange*.

Support The need for support can take various forms. People need professional support to ensure that they are performing correctly at work. They need friends at work who can provide professional support by serving as a sounding board for new ideas, giving suggestions, and acting as cheerleaders. On-the-job friends can also provide personal support. A friend can give you a lift after you have had a disagreement with your boss or have found out that you did not get the promotion or raise you were counting on.

Power When people leave their jobs, it is often because they feel powerless. To accomplish professional goals, workers need power, and sometimes relationships are the best source of power and control. Although power relationships can be abused, there is nothing inherently wrong with them.

Coworkers who have attained a certain level of power can serve as resources for learning how the organization's power structure operates. You can learn from those who have power by observing their actions and deciding whether their methods are acceptable to you. Some powerful people may use unethical means, and we encourage you to avoid mirroring them. You may want to observe unethical behavior, however, if only to protect yourself from it.

Expertise You have probably found that you sometimes need the expertise of others to achieve a goal. It is worthwhile to keep track of your coworkers' areas of expertise so that you know whom to call when you need help. For example, some

Where Do You Stand?

Assume that you are assigned to a team project with three other employees. One of the team members, Jay, has become a personal friend of your supervisor's wife. All members of the team work equally hard on the project. After the completion of the successful project, Jay receives a commendation and pay raise. You have heard the other two team members talk about meeting with your supervisor's boss to complain about his action. Was the behavior of your supervisor ethical? Did Jay use his friendship with the supervisor's wife as an unethical means for advancement, or was his strategic use of power ethical? Is the planned action of the other team members ethical? What strategies would you use to remedy the situation?

people may be mathematical or statistical whizzes who can help you interpret quantitative trends, others may be experts in budgeting matters, and still others may possess computer skills.

Remember that asking for expert advice is a reciprocal process, a two-way street. Some people are eager to share their expertise without any strings attached. Others may agree to help but are interested in getting something tangible in return. When asking someone for expert advice, think of some way you can offer some specialized help in return. A commitment to helping others increases your chances of receiving their expertise when you need it.

Social Exchange Humans have a basic need for social interaction; the need does not go away when they enter the work environment. Some socializing occurs at coffee breaks, at lunch, or in the lounges of the organization. Socializing also occurs during work, often to the chagrin of corporate leaders.

Socializing reflects the desire for self-expression and for knowledge of coworkers. Many people feel comfortable telling coworkers their thoughts, feelings, and opinions on any number of topics—politics, company policies, marriage, children, economics, finances, and even religion. Socializing helps people to handle the stress of a hectic, fast-paced work environment.

Technology and Work Relationships

It is easy to underestimate the importance of your work relationships. Technology has become so integrated that "a third of chief information officers and information-technology managers said a week without a working corporate e-mail system would be *more traumatic than a car accident or getting a divorce*." Because of this influx of technology into the modern workplace, face-to-face communication has been giving way to a strictly electronic communication network. In some organizations, nearly all communication takes place digitally. While productivity and efficiency have been increased by technology, it also has its downside. Tim Sanders, the chief solutions officer at Yahoo!, has described a problem that is caused by the information overload: constant interruption by technology and increasing personal isolation. He calls this state of work-related stress "New Economy Depression Syndrome." Some of his coworkers would instant-message him when they were only a few feet away. Sanders himself began to suffer from emotional detachment and problems with work relationships because of his almost exclusive use of technology to communicate.

According to one study, spending over five hours a day staring at a computer screen increases the risk of depression, insomnia, and other mental health problems. Sanders suggests making personal communication more important. When someone enters his office, he will turn off his computer monitor to concentrate on the person. As Sanders puts it, "I realized the relationships were my resiliency—that the friends and the colleagues that I had during the day made all the difference because the weekends and evenings weren't cutting it. It wasn't enough to recharge me. That evaporated in traffic the next morning."[14]

Relationships with Difficult Coworkers

Just about every organization has employees who are difficult to deal with. Some people cannot get along with anyone, others get along with only a few people, and still others have good relations with everyone but you. The chances are very good that at some time you will have to work and associate with someone whom you consider difficult.

Some interesting research investigating difficult (or troublesome) coworkers revealed some very definite ideas workers hold about their colleagues. Eight different types of troublesome coworkers were identified (Table 7.1). Which of these have you experienced?

TABLE 7.1

Troublesome Coworkers

Type	Description
The Independent Other	Basically harmless, has a tendency to reject legitimate authority and is perceived differently from others
The Soap Opera Star	Focused on personal problems, distracting, relatively incompetent, self-centered, busybody
The Bully	A hustling, controlling, rebellious peer determined to get the job done his or her way and to take credit for it
The Adolescent	Fearful someone will take his or her job, unprofessional (yelling, screaming), distracting, demanding, controlling, lacking in professional maturity, more concerned about self than the community
The Self-Protector	Job-protecting self-promoter primarily concerned with own self-interest and advancement
The Mild Annoyance	Low levels of most characteristics
The Rebellious Playboy/Playgirl	Sexually harassing, ignores orders of coworkers who have authority over him or her, unprofessional focus of attention
The Abrasive, Incompetent Harasser	Sexually harassing, incompetent, unprofessional peer who is fearful of his or her job, distracting, and bossy

Source: J. M. H. Fritz, "How Do I Dislike Thee? Let Me Count the Ways: Constructing Impressions of Troublesome Others at Work," *Management Communication Quarterly* 15 (2002), 410–438.

14. http://seattletimes.nwsource.com/html/businesstechnology/2001436284 neds08.html.

STRATEGIC SKILLS

Steps for Improving Relationships with Others

1. Make sure you are not the difficult person.
   a. Listen open-mindedly to others' suggestions.
   b. Don't be dogmatic.
   c. Be open, friendly, and approachable.
2. Ensure that you are doing your job.
3. Ascertain the goals of the "difficult" person.
4. Assess perception levels.
   a. Consider the different backgrounds of yourself and the other person.
   b. Ask the other person to explain the situation as he or she views it.
5. Accept the difficult person for what he or she is, not for what you want that person to be.
   a. Forget the past, and focus on the future.
   b. Do not sweat the little things.
6. Confront the person.
   a. Take the initiative toward establishing good relations.
   b. Ask questions.
   c. Ask for input/suggestions.
   d. Listen carefully.
   e. Focus on job-related issues as much as possible.
7. State how you feel.
   a. Express your goals.
   b. Do not apologize if you are certain you are right.
   c. Demonstrate political sensitivity. (Recognize the power dimensions of the organization.)
8. Give recognition when the other person deserves it.
9. Maintain a professional demeanor during interactions.
10. Seek mediation if all else fails.

You may find yourself in situations that require all of the preceding steps; less complicated situations might require only two or three steps for resolution. In the following scenario, Della is able to use steps 1 through 8 to resolve a conflict with Victor:

> Della and Victor are coworkers who share a large office suite with four other employees. Although they usually work on different projects, their work often overlaps, and they depend on each other's commitment to doing a good job. Lately, Della has perceived Victor's behavior to be increasingly unfriendly and aloof. Della has also heard rumors (apparently spread by Victor) that she is not doing her share of the work on their joint projects. Even Della's boss remarked that Della and Victor should work things out.
>
> Della did not see that she had done anything to upset Victor, and after evaluating her performance on their joint projects, she decided she was certainly pulling her weight. She thought about her goals and wondered whether she and Victor were striving for different results. She also suspected that they did not perceive the value of their work projects in the same way. Although Della had other independent projects that concerned her, she knew that Victor placed the highest priority on their joint projects.
>
> Della decided to approach Victor with an open mind and to listen sincerely to his complaints. At first Victor refused even to talk about the matter, but after a while he told Della that he was upset because she appeared to give their projects low priority and sometimes was not available when he wanted to work with her on them. Della acknowledged Victor's complaints. Although she did not feel that an apology was required, she did agree to be more cooperative with Victor.
>
> Later, when one of their joint projects enjoyed great success, Della openly and generously credited Victor for his role in the achievement. Although Victor and Della never became personal friends, their professional relationship grew stronger as they understood each other better.

The maintenance of appropriate work relationships with difficult people can be accomplished in several ways if at least one of the parties is willing to work out the problems. The outline in the Strategic Skills box above summarizes helpful steps to take when you deal with difficult people.[15]

15. This outline was partially developed from material in A. J. Di Brin, *Effective Business Psychology*, 2d ed. (Reston, Va.: Reston Publishing, 1985); Kouzes and Posner, *The Leadership Challenge*.

Of course, not all difficult relationships can be untangled in a productive manner. When you are dealing with people who are simply impossible and who refuse to work at resolving the difficulties, maintain a professional demeanor. Be patient, and do not lose your temper. Remain task oriented: focus on the goals you are trying to achieve. And seek third-party mediation from a boss, coworker, or counselor. There is no reason to allow others to affect your performance when they are unwilling to reason things out. You have a right to be productive without the distraction of an unfriendly coworker.

MENTORING RELATIONSHIPS

One of the most valuable relationships that you can establish early in your career is with a mentor. **Mentors** are experienced, mature, and successful employees who give help and guidance to newer employees (**protégés**) in many areas, including knowledge, skills, and appropriate attitudes and behavior.[16] The mentor acts as a role model who demonstrates how the new employee can develop and become successful.

In the places where you have worked, you may have already experienced the benefits of having a mentor. If so, you can compare this information to your experience and learn more about the workings of mentor relationships. For those of you who have not enjoyed a mentoring relationship, we provide suggestions for becoming involved with a mentor when you take a job after graduation.

The Importance of Mentoring Relationships

Successful mentoring relationships usually benefit everyone involved—the protégé, the mentor, and the organization. An organization that wants to be more successful should encourage mentor-protégé relationships.[17] Young employees can develop faster when they have the help of a mentor. John Kotter, the noted author and management consultant, championed these relationships when he stated, "Virtually all of the successful and effective executives I have known have had two or more of these kinds of relationships early in their careers. Some have had upwards of a dozen people they were able to rely on for different needs—some provided important contacts, others gave key information in specific areas, and still others taught them certain valued skills."[18]

Benefits to the Protégé Once a mentoring relationship has been established, the protégé has access to opportunities that may otherwise be unavailable. Benefits from mentoring relationships include the following:[19]

- Receiving support from the mentor
- Having the mentor influence others on behalf of the protégé

16. R. A. Noe, "Women and Mentoring: A Review and Research Agenda," *Academy of Management Review* 13 (1988), 65–78; K. E. Kram, *Mentoring at Work: Development Relationships in Organizational Life* (Glenview, Ill.: Scott, Foresman, 1985); R. J. Burke and C. A. McKeen, "Developing Formal Mentoring Programs in Organizations," *Business Quarterly* 53 (1989), 76–79.
17. R. M. Kanter, *The Change Masters* (New York: Simon & Schuster, 1984).
18. J. Kotter, *Power and Influence* (New York: Free Press, 1985).
19. Noe, "Women and Mentoring"; T. Daniels and B. Spiker, *Perspectives on Organizational Communication* (Dubuque, Iowa: Brown, 1987); E. A. Fagenson, "The Mentor Advantage Perceived Career/Job Experiences of Protégés vs. Nonprotégés," *Journal of Organizational Behavior* 10 (1989), 309–320.

- Getting public recognition from the mentor
- Having the mentor as a friend and role model
- Obtaining greater knowledge of the politics of the organization
- Being promoted by the mentor

The results of these benefits include rapid promotions, salary increases, challenging work assignments, career mobility, and work satisfaction. Although mentoring relationships usually require extra dedication to a job and possibly longer work hours, if you are serious about the "fast track," they can be extremely valuable.

Benefits to the Mentor and Organization Mentors can obtain a great deal of satisfaction from helping a less experienced employee. They may learn from the protégé. They may also increase their own value to the organization by demonstrating an ability to help new employees to develop.

The organization benefits from mentoring because protégés tend to develop faster than employees without mentors, have stronger leadership skills, demonstrate teamwork and shared values, and be less likely to leave the organization for other opportunities.[20] The following example shows how mentoring can benefit everyone involved:

> Connie worked part-time as an inventory clerk at Brooks, Inc., while attending City College. Brooks had a good reputation, and Connie hoped that if she proved herself as a part-time employee, she might land a job with the company after graduation.
>
> She noticed that Roger, an inventory manager, was competent, well liked by others, and friendly. Connie took on some paid overtime tasks in inventory control (a new area for her) and asked Roger for some advice on how best to do the work. Roger really appreciated having help from an enthusiastic worker and took time to teach Connie what she needed to know to handle inventory control. Soon, they were taking their breaks together to discuss various company and professional issues.
>
> Connie learned a lot about Brooks from Roger, and after graduation she started work full-time, bringing to the job the experience, knowledge, and contacts that made her a valuable employee from the start.

Characteristics of the Mentor and Protégé Roles

The mentor is usually older (eight to fifteen years) than the protégé and enjoys a secure, often prestigious position with the organization. The protégé is usually new to the organization or unit and is interested in career advancement.[21] Although assigned mentoring relationships exist in some organizations, prevailing opinion suggests that voluntary relationships are best, for required relationships may be viewed as a burden by one person or the other.[22]

Mentoring relationships require both partners to agree on their relative roles and understand each other well. Mentors must possess the knowledge and skills

20. J. Lawrie, "How to Establish a Mentoring Program," *Training and Development Journal* 41 (1987), 25–27.
21. Noe, "Women and Mentoring."
22. Ibid.; Burke and McKeen, "Developing Formal Mentoring Programs."

PRACTICING BUSINESS COMMUNICATION

Tom's of Maine

Decision making centers on relationships—relationships with customers, business partners, and the community; and relationships among coworkers. The company is Tom's of Maine. Tom's develops, produces, and manufactures personal-care products made from natural ingredients.

Cofounder Tom Chappell wrote a book, *Soul of a Business,* based on the mission statement he developed in 1989. The concluding point in the statement distills Chappell's approach to doing business: "to be a profitable and successful company while acting in a socially and environmentally responsible manner." This combination of capitalism and altruism may seem unlikely, but it works quite well for Tom's of Maine.

Chappell wrote a second book in 1999, *Managing Upside Down,* which details the steps managers can take to "lead with their hearts and their heads."

Originally, Tom's was a soap business, cofounded in 1970 by Tom and Kate Chappell. As the partners recognized that growing numbers of Americans were demanding products that are safe for both the body and the environment, the Chappells expanded their business into an entire range of personal-care products. Between 1981 and 1985, Tom's grew, on average, 25 percent each year, reaching $5 million in sales. By 2000, Tom's of Maine listed assets in excess of $40 million.

BUILDING RELATIONSHIPS WITHIN TOM'S

Tom's of Maine employs fewer than one hundred people and operates within a traditional, top-down business hierarchy. At the same time, flexible communication policies complement the formal structure. The combination of structure and flexibility fosters open communication among coworkers, promotes equality, and encourages a creative approach to work.

Two distinct all-staff meetings at Tom's, "company updates" and "company gatherings," illustrate the contrast. At formal quarterly updates, top management reports to staff on current business opportunities and problems, rewards notable work efforts, and discusses recent media coverage of the company.

Company gatherings are less structured. Every two or three months Tom's shuts down the phones for a few hours. Everyone gathers for coffee and bagels to spend a morning away from the "business" of the business. Company-supported, relaxed employee interaction translates into better employee relationships on the job.

Chappell sees two reasons for encouraging such relationships within his company. One is employees' need for meaning. "They are saying, 'In order for me to come to work in this culture day in and day out, I need more than just working by fear. I need to be connecting my life to something greater, and in that connection making meaning of my life,'" he explains. "We're in an age where a lot of

necessary to benefit protégés, and protégés must be willing and skillful learners. For a relationship to be successful and productive, mentors must also be confident, approachable, successful, skillful in communication, able to make decisions, secure, and possessed of strong interpersonal skills; protégés must be ambitious, eager to learn, open-minded, loyal, talented, energetic, and communicative.[23]

Mentoring Phases

Mentoring relationships go through phases. Changes in a person's knowledge, status, abilities, or work experiences can alter a mentoring relationship. Most mentoring

23. Reprinted with permission of *Business Quarterly.*

people are looking for more meaning out of not just their personal lives, but their work lives." The other reason is the ever-present bottom line. "The corporate leadership is looking for new ways to motivate employees and create innovative solutions," Chappell says.

BUILDING RELATIONSHIPS OUTSIDE TOM'S

To build relationships with customers, Tom's established a consumer dialogue program. When Tom's gets a call, fax, or letter with questions or comments about a product, an employee responds personally. Three workers staff the consumer dialogue program, and fifteen others from all over the company volunteer a few hours each week to answer calls and letters.

Employees answer questions about products, address problems, and even accept compliments on a one-to-one basis. By connecting personally with customers who have taken the time to contact the company, every Tom's employee has a chance to interact with the people who use the products they develop, produce, market, or sell. And customers see how important they are to Tom's.

Through "common good" partnerships, Tom's maintains a strong presence in local communities and in social and environmental issues. Tom's might team up with a business partner—a retail chain that stocks Tom's products, for example—to cosponsor a community project. Both partners strengthen their business relationship, and they also gain from the positive public relations generated by supporting a worthwhile event.

BUILDING EQUALITY

Tom's of Maine uses nonverbal cues as a way of promoting equality in relationships among coworkers. At meetings, chairs are set up in an open circle rather than around conference tables, where seating arrangements easily can appear hierarchical. When coworkers of differing status meet, they sit down together without a desk or table between them.

Tom's uses all aspects of effective communication to enhance its internal and external business relationships and to promote its values. By building relationships, Tom's strikes a balance between structure and flexibility, consumerism and environmentalism, commerce and community.

QUESTIONS FOR CRITICAL THINKING

1. Why do you think Tom's of Maine provides two distinct types of all-staff meetings?
2. How do you think Tom's of Maine should train employees who volunteer for the consumer dialogue program?
3. What are community relationships? Why are they important to Tom's of Maine?
4. How do physical surroundings affect communication at Tom's?
5. How does Tom's create a balance between structure and flexibility?

You can visit Tom's of Maine on-line at www.toms-of-maine.com.

relationships pass through four phases, although the amount of time spent in each stage may vary quite a bit.[24]

Initiation The protégé learns to appreciate the talents and expertise of the mentor. The mentor demonstrates support and interest by coaching, teaching, and listening to the protégé. The protégé exhibits loyalty, intelligence, and energy as she or he responds to the direction and advice of the mentor.

Cultivation Interpersonal bonding occurs between mentor and protégé. As the mentor coaches, protects, and promotes the protégé, their mutual admiration increases.

24. K. E. Kram, "Phases of the Mentor Relationship," *Academy of Management Journal* 12 (1983), 608–625.

What Would You Do?

Suppose you have worked for three months in an organization. As a beginner in public relations, you are eager to learn as much as possible as quickly as possible. You have often volunteered to work nights and weekends to help the vice president in charge of public relations meet important deadlines. During this time, the two of you have established a mutual appreciation, and he has agreed to be your mentor. As his protégé, you are often included in important projects. Lately your coworkers are cool and aloof when you approach them. What situational knowledge can help you assess your coworkers' attitudes? What communication is necessary to maintain both your mentor-protégé relationship and your positive relationships with your coworkers?

Separation The mentor and protégé drift apart because of physical separation (for example, one may travel more than the other), promotions, or greater independence on the part of the protégé.

Redefinition The (former) mentor and protégé reestablish a relationship based on different criteria. The mentor may still fulfill some of the old responsibilities, such as providing advice and expertise, but more likely the two now see each other as peers. By this time, they may hold similar positions in the organization. Not all mentoring relationships experience this phase because protégés may be reassigned through promotion or leave the organization for a different job.

ETHICAL ISSUES

Nicole's Protégé

Accuum Enterprises, a wholesale and distributing company, started a new mentoring program. All senior employees were expected to develop mentoring relationships with a younger, inexperienced employee. Nicole looked through the company directory and spotted Brian Fitzgerald's name. She knew him from when she was on the interview team that hired him, and she had seen him at several social functions sponsored by the company. He seemed bright and eager to learn. When asked, Brian jumped at the chance to be mentored by Nicole, given her strong reputation in the company. They began to meet frequently, and things were going very well. In fact, they began to see each other outside of work, and eventually they began a romantic relationship. They agreed that the relationship should be kept private, since the company was not keen on such relationships among its employees. The relationship deteriorated after a while, when Brian insisted on seeing other people. Nicole was very unhappy with this turn of events. Brian asked that the mentoring part of the relationship continue, but Nicole refused. She told Brian that continuing a mentoring relationship would be very awkward. After a couple of weeks, Brian told Nicole that if she would continue the mentoring arrangement, he would be willing to conform to her romantic relationship requirements.

Was it unethical for Nicole to terminate the mentoring relationship? If Nicole goes along with Brian's new plan, does this constitute sexual harassment on her part? What other ethical issues do you see in this situation?

STRATEGIC SKILLS

Finding a Mentor

If you are new to an organization and want to benefit from a mentor, what do you do? The following steps may be useful for securing an appropriate mentor in your first job:*

1. Ask the personnel or human resources department about formal mentoring programs in the organization.
2. Identify people who have the same specialization and interests as you do. Try to determine whether they possess the "mentor characteristics" listed earlier in the text.
3. Approach some of the people whom you have identified, and take an interest in what they do. Ask questions that reveal your enthusiasm for their jobs. If appropriate, volunteer for tasks that would facilitate their jobs and careers.
4. Let them know that you are upwardly mobile and interested in learning as much as you can about the profession and the organization.
5. Ask for advice on matters where their expertise would improve your productivity.
6. Ask them whether they would be interested in sponsoring you. Explain why you might be a good choice. Indicate your confidence in yourself, your admiration for their work, and the appeal their career track has for you.

* R. A. Noe, "Women and Mentoring: A Review and Research Agenda," *Academy of Management Review* 13 (1988), 65–78.

Gender and Cultural Issues

Minorities and women can particularly benefit from mentoring relationships. Even if an organization's corporate culture is geared toward white male norms and attitudes, a personal relationship with a successful person of the same gender or ethnic group can help you to adapt successfully. Unfortunately, it may be difficult for women and minorities to find such mentors because of the relatively low numbers of women and minorities in middle and upper management.

Although there is nothing inherently problematic about male-female or cross-cultural mentoring relationships, the potential for controversy can restrict opportunities for the protégé. Suggestions of romantic involvement, fraternization, and sexual intimacy may scare off male mentors. In mentoring relationships between white mentors and black protégés, whites are sometimes afraid to correct their protégés out of fear of appearing racist. Members of minority groups may also resent special attention if it appears to be presented as remedial help.[25]

The lack of mentors for female and minority employees is especially unfortunate because the absence of such relationships may significantly reduce job effectiveness.[26] Research on cross-gender mentoring relationships suggests that a large share of successful female executives benefited from mentoring by male role models.[27] Professional organizations such as the National Consortium for Black Professional Development, the American Society of Professional and Executive Women, the Hispanic Organization of Professionals and Executives, and the National Association of Asian-American Professionals can provide mentorlike support and networking opportunities for women and members of minority groups.

25. G. Haight, "Managing Diversity," *Across the Board* (March 1990), 22–29.
26. Noe, "Women and Mentoring."
27. Burke and McKeen, "Developing Formal Mentoring Programs."

TECHNOLOGY TOOLS

Virtual Mentoring

For several reasons, finding the right mentor can be a difficult task. The Internet and the Web can help. Numerous Internet sites offer professional guidance, coaching, and mentoring. Some are free services; others charge a fee or membership dues. Regardless of their approach, visiting Internet sites for mentoring opportunities can offer a number of possibilities that would otherwise be unavailable. Listed below are a few of the more prominent sites that specialize in mentoring services. Visit these sights and see for yourself how important mentoring relationships can be.

- International Telementor Center—http://www.telementor.org This is a nonprofit organization (Colorado State University) that connects mentors and protégés electronically.
- Center for Coaching & Mentoring—http://www.coachingandmentoring.com This site provides services for those interested in being a mentor or protégé.
- The Mentoring Group—http://www.mentoringgroup.com This site offers several services and products for mentors and "mentees."
- Women's Global Business Alliance—http://www.wgba-business.com This organization focuses on the tools, skills, and strategies that facilitate the success of businesswomen. Mentoring services and peer advice are part of their available services.
- Mentoring and Coaching Program Design Resources from Yellowbrick—http://www.mentoring-programs.com This site specializes in products and services for setting up and enhancing mentoring programs for various types of organizations.

ROMANTIC RELATIONSHIPS IN THE WORKPLACE

Have you ever been romantically attracted to someone you worked with? Have you ever dated someone from work? If you answered "yes" to either of these questions, you are not alone. The number of romantic relationships in the workplace is increasing each year as more women enter a once predominantly male work force.[28] Although only limited research has been done in this area, it is clear that romantic relationships in the workplace have the potential for creating widespread controversy if handled in inappropriate ways. Romantic relationships between superiors and subordinates might result in resentment from other coworkers, charges of discrimination or sexual harassment, or job termination. Romantic relationships with coworkers might result in diminished work performance or a hostile work environment. It is therefore important for you to be aware of the issues involved in organizational romance—whether or not you are a participant.

Pervasiveness of Organizational Romance

You may be wondering whether organizational romances are really all that prevalent. Organizational romance has been defined as an intimate interpersonal relationship between employees of the same organization—a relationship that is characterized by a substantial degree of mutual sexual attraction.[29] According to research, two-thirds of the workers surveyed observed romantic relationships

28. H. Witteman, "Organizational Romance: Whose Problem Is It?" (paper presented at the annual meeting of the Western States Communication Association, Salt Lake City, February 1987).
29. J. P. Dillard and K. I. Miller, "Intimate Relationships in Task Environments," in S. Duck (ed.), *Handbook of Personal Relationships* (Sussex, England: Wiley, 1988), pp. 449–465.

Organizational romance occurs because people naturally develop relationships after frequent interactions. Many challenges face organizations and their members when organizational romances spring forth, including office gossip, charges of sexual harassment, and even termination of employment. (Colin Hawkins/ Getty Images)

where they worked, and one-third of those surveyed claimed to have been involved in such a relationship.[30]

If you think about the workplace as a dynamic environment where people are interacting with one another for extended amounts of time, it is little wonder that close personal relationships form. As we mentioned earlier, work may offer the best opportunity for meeting and socializing with people. Romance often springs from close interaction.

Consequences of Organizational Romance

Negative and positive consequences can result from romantic work relationships.[31] Problems resulting from organizational romance can appear in task and relational areas and can include tardiness, absenteeism, poor work quality, and absent-mindedness. In addition, when people become involved in romance, their goals and emphasis in the workplace may become personal instead of organizational. According to an extensive survey conducted by the Society for Human Resource Management, many employees see the dangers in workplace romance and claim that they personally avoid such relationships. However, they also report that they do not completely agree that these romances always end in disaster.[32]

30. Ibid.
31. Dillard and Miller, "Intimate Relationships"; R. E. Quinn, "Coping with Cupid: The Formation, Impact, and Management of Romantic Relationships in Organizations," *Administration Science Quarterly* 22 (1977), 30–45; Witteman, "Organizational Romance."
32. http://eastbay.bizjournals.com/eastbay/stories/2003/02/17/ Smallb3;html?t=printable.

Relational problems may also emerge. If the romance hits a snag, relational partners may become distracted by their personal problems and neglect their other responsibilities. If the relationship is severed, the former romantic partners may be reluctant to work together.

Coworkers may also have problems with the romantically involved couple. Coworkers may feel envy, jealousy, or even disgust toward the romance. In extreme cases, disapproving coworkers may shun or ignore the couple.

Nevertheless, several positive consequences are associated with organizational romance. In a number of studies, organizational romance either did not affect the work performance or attitudes of participants or actually improved their behavior at work.[33] Participants in these relationships were easier to get along with, worked better in teams, improved their work flow, and were generally more productive. From the best available evidence, it appears that the nature of the consequences stemming from romantic relationships depends on the particular couple.

SEXUAL HARASSMENT

In 1991, the world looked on as Clarence Thomas's Supreme Court confirmation by the Senate became a public forum for the discussion of sexual harassment. Although the Equal Employment Opportunity Commission had set forth definitions and guidelines regulating sexual harassment in the workplace a decade earlier, it was the Thomas hearings that brought this issue into the living rooms, break rooms, and offices of everyone in America. Since then, numerous scandals involving high-ranking officials, corporations, the military, and various colleges and universities have made and continue to make headlines. Over 90 percent of Fortune 500 companies have reported cases of sexual harassment, and many instances go unreported.[34]

The Equal Employment Opportunity Commission describes sexual harassment as unwelcome sexual advances, requests for sexual favors, and other verbal or physical conduct of a sexual nature if (1) submission to the conduct is made a condition of employment, (2) submission to or rejection of the conduct is made the basis for an employment decision, or (3) the conduct seriously affects an employee's work performance or creates an intimidating, hostile, or offensive working environment.[35] Simply put, sexual harassment is unwelcome, unsolicited, repeated behavior of a sexual nature.

Two different, although sometimes overlapping, types of sexual harassment have been identified. The first type, termed **quid pro quo,** involves a situation in which an employee is offered a reward or is threatened with punishment based upon his or her participation in sexual activity. For example, a supervisor might tell his employee, "I will give you Friday off if you will meet me at my place

33. Quinn, "Coping with Cupid"; C. Anderson and P. Hunsaker, "Why There's Romance in the Office and Why It's Everyone's Problem," *Personnel* 62 (1985), 57–63; J. P. Dillard and S. M. Broetzman, "Romantic Relationships at Work: Perceived Changes in Job-Related Behaviors as a Function of Participant's Motive, Partner's Motive, and Gender" (paper presented at the annual meeting of the Western Speech Communication Association, San Diego, February 1988).
34. J. Keyton, P. Ferguson, and S.C. Rhodes, "Cultural Indicators of Sexual Harassment," *Southern Communication Journal* 67 (2001), 33–50.
35. H. Witteman, "The Interface Between Sexual Harassment and Organizational Romance," in G. Kreps (ed.), *Sexual Harassment: Communication Implications* (Cresskill, N.J.: Hampton Press, 1994).

TECHNOLOGY TOOLS

Preventing Sexual Harassment

Businesses are always in need of advice that can help them prevent instances of sexual harassment in the workplace. Although a large number of profit and nonprofit organizations offer such services, they can be costly and a bit awkward to put in place. The World Wide Web is a place that can respond to the need of business for rapid, reliable, and credible information on sexual harassment. The Richardson Company–Training Media Group provides a comprehensive on-line program called "Preventing Sexual Harassment" at http://www.rctm.com. Visit the site and compare their offerings with other types that you are familiar with.

tonight." The second type of sexual harassment creates a **hostile environment**—conditions in the workplace that are sexually offensive, intimidating, or hostile and that affect an individual's ability to perform his or her job. For example, if two males talk explicitly about the physical features of a fellow female employee in her presence, she asks them to stop, and they repeat the offense, sexual harassment has occurred.

Why does sexual harassment occur with such frequency in the workplace? The most obvious answer is *attraction.* One person can become so attracted to another that status and authority are used to convey sexual requests and suggestions. A second reason for harassment is *power.* The harasser attempts to exert power and authority by controlling the behavior of the victim. The perpetrator believes that obtaining sexual favors from another conveys ultimate power. A harasser may think that he or she can wield power over another until sexual favors are delivered. Whether real or not, it is a perception of an *imbalance* of power that allows sexual harassment to occur. When that perception is changed to one of balanced power, sexual harassment is harder to perpetrate.[36] A third reason for harassment is *communication styles.* Women are more likely than men to disclose personal issues to men. Some men perceive this communication as flirting or sexual interest. In fact, most women have no thoughts of sexual intimacy when mentioning personal matters. In addition, many women have been conditioned to act less assertively and aggressively than men. Consequently, when a man signals sexual interest in a woman, her unassertive behavior may be interpreted as game playing or as an invitation to express more sexual interest. Even nonverbal communication plays an important role in how men and women interpret their counterparts' communication. Women often use smiles and eye contact and touch innocently to indicate interest in a topic or person, whereas men may use these signals as openings for sexual intimacy.[37]

Reports summarized by Hal Witteman indicate that most targets for harassment are females under the age of thirty-five who have some college education

36. L. L. Jansma, "Sexual Harassment Research: Integration, Reformulation, and Implications for Mitigation Efforts," in M. Roloff (ed.), *Communication Yearbook 23* (Thousand Oaks, Calif.: Sage, 2000), pp. 163–225.
37. This section is influenced by C. Berryman-Fink, "Preventing Sexual Harassment Through Male-Female Communication Training," in Kreps, *Sexual Harassment.*

STRATEGIC SKILLS

Addressing Sexual Harassment

Sexual harassment is a degrading and dehumanizing act. *It is wrong!* A number of local, state, and federal agencies protect employees against sexual harassment, and these powers should be used whenever possible. If you believe that you are being subjected to sexual harassment in the workplace, you do not have to tolerate it. There are several things you can do to address the problem:

1. If you believe that certain conduct is wrong, say so. Tell the perpetrator in very clear terms that his or her conduct is not appreciated or welcome.
2. Immediately report the incident to your boss or to someone in the personnel office.
3. Document each incident in written form.
4. If witnesses were present, have them verify the details of the incident.

If you are a supervisor who hears of sexual harassment in your area, you must take the following steps:

1. Take the complaint seriously. Listen carefully to the complainant.
2. Conduct your own investigation. Gather as much information as possible about the situation. Find out who was involved, who could serve as witnesses, how often this has happened, where the incident occurred, what the accused perpetrator did, and so on.
3. Maintain objectivity throughout the investigation. Do not become caught up in the emotions of the situation. Remember, making a sexual harassment complaint is a difficult act, and complainants will need your professional support.
4. Suspend judgment. Not all sexual harassment complaints are valid. The alleged perpetrator has rights, too. Your job is to gather facts. A professional group such as the personnel department has expertise in evaluating the situation.*

* Summarized by H. Witteman, "The Interface Between Sexual Harassment and Organizational Romance," in G. Kreps (ed.), *Sexual Harassment: Communication Implications* (Cresskill, N.J.: Hampton Press, 1994).

and work in areas that are predominantly male. The woman is usually younger than the man and is either single or divorced. Men can also be targets of sexual harassment. Any unwanted sexual activity directed at either males or females is sexual harassment.

A major obstacle to ending sexual harassment is the tendency of the target to avoid confronting the harasser. Most instances of sexual harassment are not confronted, exposed, or reported. Instead, the victim usually avoids the situation by taking time off, transferring to another area, or changing jobs. One of the primary reasons for avoidance is that the perpetrator is usually someone in the organization with authority and status, and the victim feels that exposure or confrontation will backfire.

What are the signals of sexual harassment? Most come in the form of verbal and nonverbal communication. Verbal forms of sexual harassment include the following:

- Unwelcome remarks
- Embarrassing jokes
- Taunting
- Sexist remarks
- Displays of pornographic or offensive materials and photographs

Victims of sexual harassment report that perpetrators use pinching, patting, hugging, leering, touching, and kissing as means of nonverbal harassment.

STRATEGIC SKILLS

Is This Sexual Harassment?

Read each description. If this happened to you, would you consider it sexual harassment?

Yes Maybe No 1. Your supervisor often uses a suggestive and domineering tone of voice when speaking to you.

Yes Maybe No 2. Your coworker grasps your hand or arm to the point that you notice it lingering too long.

Yes Maybe No 3. Your coworker engages you in a conversation with implicit or explicit sexual tones.

Yes Maybe No 4. Your supervisor requests sexual favors.

Yes Maybe No 5. Your supervisor stands close to you, invading your personal space and making you feel uncomfortable.

Yes Maybe No 6. Your coworker speaks indirectly about things of a sexual nature.

Yes Maybe No 7. Your supervisor offers to help you with a project or promotion in exchange for "something in return." You perceive this to be a sexual favor.

Yes Maybe No 8. Your supervisor discusses his or her sexual activity with you.

Yes Maybe No 9. Conversations between you and a coworker frequently turn to personal, usually sexual, topics.

Yes Maybe No 10. Your coworker seeks or offers advice of a sexual nature.

Yes Maybe No 11. Your supervisor gazes at your body while you talk to him or her and there is little or no eye contact.

Yes Maybe No 12. Your coworker's sexually suggestive conduct has made you uncomfortable.

Yes Maybe No 13. Your supervisor constantly and unnecessarily brushes up against you.

Yes Maybe No 14. Your coworker makes private sexual remarks in a common gathering area, such as a break room.

Yes Maybe No 15. Your supervisor suggests changing your appearance to make you look more attractive in the workplace.

Source: Joann Keyton, University of Kansas, 2004.

EMPLOYEE-CUSTOMER RELATIONSHIPS

> The twenty-first century will offer the greatest opportunity for planned success ever seen. It won't be necessary to discover oil, . . . develop the telephone, or create the electric light bulb in order to gain wealth and influence. The only absolutely essential management characteristic will be to acquire the ability to run an organization that deliberately gives its customers what they have been led to expect and does it with pleasant efficiency.[38]

Those words by Phil Crosby illustrate the importance of customer relationships. Knowing who the customers are, what they want, and how they will react to products or services is a basic goal of businesses, especially now, when the economy has shifted from a manufacturing to a service orientation. More than three-quarters of

38. From *Completeness: Quality for the 21st Century* by P. B. Crosby. Copyright © 1992 by P. B. Crosby. Used by permission of Dutton Signet, a division of Penguin Books USA, Inc.

all jobs created in the United States in the last ten years are in service industries; thus, customer relations are a high priority for organizations and are likely to be part of your work experience.[39] Customers often base their opinion about a business and its ability to meet their needs on their communication with a business representative. Interpersonal communication is at the heart of customer relations. Customers must feel that the people they give their business to can listen carefully to and understand their needs. Five basic rules of conduct can ensure successful customer relationships, each corresponding to elements of the strategic model: know the customer; take responsibility for customer satisfaction; avoid unresponsive behavior; employ effective communication skills; and treat difficult customers with respect.

Goal Setting: Know the Customer

It is difficult to please customers if you are ignorant of their needs. All too often, excellent products fail because customers are not convinced that they need them. Successful organizations work to find out what customers want and to provide it.[40] You can work toward the same goal in your relationships with customers. Open and honest communication can aid you in achieving that goal. Successful communication helps you to discover customers' characteristics and idiosyncrasies so that you can respond to their desires.

Customer service can include solving problems to help customers obtain goods and services that are right for them. Often, this problem-solving process means planning for the customer's future needs and desires (changes in taste, technology, and economic outlook are constants in the business environment). Customer relations can also include mutual goal setting by employees and clients. Employees and clients together can set business goals for the client. If you understand customers' present and future needs, you will be able to plan for the services you will have to deliver. Knowing the customer well enough to set effective goals requires understanding and cooperation.

Communication Competence

Communicating effectively with customers means taking responsibility for customers' needs, addressing those needs enthusiastically, employing appropriate communication skills, and dealing sensitively with customer complaints.

Take Responsibility for Customer Satisfaction Customers enjoy doing business with organizations that personalize their service. Personalized service at its best means ongoing attention from a specific person. When customers call to place an order, make a complaint, specify a correction, or even give a compliment, they want to deal with someone who they know takes a personal interest in them.

Customer satisfaction can be monitored in a variety of ways. Many organizations provide comment cards as a means of gauging customer satisfaction. Surveys, studies by market research firms, and analyses of sales data can also give

39. K. Albrecht, *At America's Service: How Corporations Can Revolutionize the Way They Treat Their Customers* (Homewood, Ill.: Dow Jones- Irwin, 1988).
40. T. Peters and R. Waterman, *In Search of Excellence: Lessons from America's Best-Run Companies* (New York: Warner Books, 1982).

clues. The most effective way to learn about customers' level of satisfaction is to ask them in phone calls, face-to-face, or through your website. Questions such as "How do you like our new product line compared to the last?" "What would work better for you?" and "What are your most important concerns about the services that you use?" show the customer that you care about his or her satisfaction.

Taking responsibility for customer satisfaction also means taking follow-up actions. Attention to details, such as keeping customers notified about work-in-progress (even misplaced orders or other setbacks), sending holiday greetings, giving advance notice of specials, and taking interest in their personal lives, gives customers a feeling that someone is looking out for them. Customer loyalty is usually the result.

Avoid Unresponsive Behavior Customer relations can be enhanced significantly if you make the effort to avoid unresponsive behavior.[41] You may have seen problems caused by apathy, coldness, and inflexibility in the organizations with which you do business.

Apathy—lack of emotional involvement in the job—usually results in employees failing to treat customers with care and concern. The best way to avoid customer neglect caused by apathy is to learn about each customer. By remembering customers' names and expressing interest in their jobs or families, you can show that you view customers as more than simply a source of income for the organization.

Coldness also damages customer relations. Coldness is displayed in several ways. Condescending answers to legitimate questions or concerns, negative facial expressions, or demeaning comments indicate to customers that their satisfaction is not your highest priority. Sometimes you may give an impression of coldness unintentionally, especially if you are tired, under stress, or nervous about the customer relationship. Although keeping personal frustrations and concerns hidden is difficult, revealing them to customers is likely to hurt relations with them.

Robotism—rigid and inflexible behavior—is another form of unresponsive behavior. An organization's rules and procedures may encourage robotism among employees, but customers are likely to hold you personally accountable for any rigidity they encounter in their dealings with you. You may have experienced robotism if you have been systematically put on hold or transferred from department to department when calling a firm with a question, or if you continued to receive junk mail or solicitations long after you canceled a subscription to a publication. Another example of robotism is to be given the same answer at a service desk that everyone else gets.

Avoiding robotism means keeping an open mind about how to handle customer desires within the context of your organization's current policies and regulations. Some flexibility is nearly always possible, and recognizing occasions when customers deserve special consideration will keep them satisfied.

Employ Effective Communication Skills Customers prefer to deal with company representatives who display effective communication skills. Successful employee-customer relationships are based on assertive, open, and friendly communication. Customers expect to be treated well by someone who knows what he or she is talking about, can explain problems, and does not make the customer feel ignorant or pushy for asking questions. You can communicate effectively by smiling, making eye contact, asking pertinent questions, answering questions promptly and accurately, and using encouraging nonverbal communication.

41. Albrecht, *At America's Service.*

STRATEGIC SKILLS

Working with Difficult Customers

These guidelines can help you work through difficult situations with customers:*

1. Let customers talk. Listen carefully and with an open mind to their complaints, making note of instances in which your company may be at fault.
2. Reassure customers that their concerns will be heard and addressed.
3. Do not personalize the issue. Recognize that customer anger is not directed personally at you. People who go to the trouble of making a complaint are usually concerned with getting satisfaction rather than with making employees feel bad.
4. Acknowledge instances in which the customer is correct. Customers like to be told that they are right when they are.
5. Apologize and provide immediate satisfaction if you determine that the company was wrong. If blame cannot be determined immediately, promise the customer you will respond at a specific time, and be sure you follow up.
6. Ask the customer to suggest how problems could be avoided in the future.

* This list is adapted from D. Finkelman and T. Goland, "The Case of the Complaining Customer," *Harvard Business Review,* May–June 1990, pp. 9–21.

Treat Difficult Customers with Respect Handling difficult or hostile customers is often a thankless job. Nevertheless, few job duties are more satisfying than turning an angry customer into a happy one. Handling difficult customers is vital to maintaining successful customer relationships in general, for even the best customer relationships sometimes hit snags, and you are wise to be prepared for them.

You may think that appeasing difficult customers is not worth your time and energy. Statistics show, however, that hostile customers, through word of mouth, can reduce a company's business by 2 percent—certainly an amount worth considering.[42] The key to improving your relationship with a troublesome customer is maintaining a conscientious communication style. By giving an unhappy customer the attention he or she is seeking, you may be able to turn an enemy into a friend. In the following situation, the clerk successfully resolves a customer's anger about a damaged product:

CLERK: Can I help you?

CUSTOMER: I want a refund. The radio I bought here is defective.

CLERK: I'm sorry you're not happy. What exactly is the problem?

CUSTOMER: Quite a few things. The left speaker is giving off a lot of static, and I can't get my favorite station clearly enough. I want my money back!

CLERK: Sometimes static can be easily eliminated by tightening the wires inside the speaker, but just in case it's a more serious problem, I'll be happy to get you a new radio and send this one back to the manufacturer to be checked out.

CUSTOMER: Well, OK. Thanks. I need a few other items while I'm here, too.

CLERK: I'm sorry about this inconvenience. Always let us know when you're not completely satisfied.

CUSTOMER: Yes, I will.

42. D. Finkelman and T. Goland, "The Case of the Complaining Customer," *Harvard Business Review,* May-June 1990, pp. 9-21.

Learning to communicate effectively with hostile customers can bring success to your organization through repeat business and can help you to achieve your career goals.

Anxiety Management

Building relationships with customers, setting goals for customers, and communicating with difficult customers can produce anxiety. Nervousness may prevent you from effectively communicating with a new customer, or tension may limit your ability to deal with a difficult customer.

To reduce anxiety, concentrate on your goals. Remember that you are the representative for your organization and that your goal is to provide satisfaction for customer needs. Listen open-mindedly to the customer's suggestion or complaint. Rephrase the statement or problem so that you are sure you understand it. If you have questions, don't be afraid to ask. The customer will appreciate your desire to fully understand his or her needs.

Do not interpret complaints or hostility from a customer as a personal attack. When people become frustrated or angry, they often blurt out verbal attacks. Remain calm, and try to empathize with the customer's situation. Take a few deep breaths, and address the complaint without resorting to verbal attack. The calmer you appear, the more likely it is that the customer will soon run out of steam.

To control nervousness when establishing relationships with new customers, begin a conversation with small talk, and let the customer talk as much as he or she wants. Ask specific questions. Be enthusiastic and energetic. Once you realize that customers are ordinary people, your nervousness will disappear.

STRATEGIC SCENARIO: WRAP-UP

Based on what you read in this chapter, what should Tomas's first priority be for training? Are some of the problems uncovered by Tomas related to one another? Which ones? How could he design a training program that would address these related needs? How could Tomas get his superiors and fellow workers to buy into his plans to address these training needs?

SUMMARY

- Developing and maintaining relationships in the workplace is no simple task. Relationships require planning and effort to be desirable and productive. Ethical communication is vital to all forms of work relationships.
- The workplace promotes a variety of relationships, including those between managers and employees, coworkers, mentors and protégés, friends and lovers, and employees and customers.
- Manager-employee relationships are affected by the communication climate of the organization, the communication patterns and personal characteristics of the two parties involved, and the degree of mutual influence and power sharing in the relationship.
- Coworker relationships develop through proximity, shared tasks, shared interests, and satisfaction of needs.
- Some coworker relationships are involuntary and may involve working with difficult people. Getting along with these people requires that you keep focused on the job at hand and maintain a professional demeanor.
- Mentoring relationships provide valuable benefits for new employees, such as support, influence, recognition, friendship, role models, organizational knowledge, and even promotions.
- The drawback to mentoring relationships is the difficulty of finding a willing mentor, especially in organizations that do not have structured mentoring programs in place.
- Romantic relationships are a potential source of controversy in the workplace. Occurrences of romantic relationships between employees are reportedly increasing. Positive and negative

consequences of romantic relationships in the workplace have been noted.
- Sexual harassment is unwelcome sexual advances or comments by someone. It is a degrading and dehumanizing act that should be confronted when it occurs.
- Action can be taken by the complainant and the supervisor to prevent sexual harassment in the workplace and ensure a safe environment in which to work.
- Employee-customer relationships benefit from the employee's knowing the customer as well as possible, taking responsibility for customer satisfaction, avoiding unresponsive behavior, using effective communication skills, and treating difficult customers with respect.

KEY TERMS

Goal setting: an important feature of manager-employee relationships in ensuring coordination

Gender role congruency: refers to the extent to which a person—through his or her behavior, interests, dress, communication style, and so on—conforms to gender stereotypes

Proximity: a measure of physical closeness among officemates

Mentor: experienced, mature, and successful employees who give help and guidance to protégés in many areas, including knowledge, skills, and appropriate attitudes and behavior

Protégé: a newer employee who is guided by a mentor

Quid pro quo: a sexual harassment situation in which an employee is offered a reward or is threatened with punishment based upon his or her participation in sexual activity

Hostile environment: a sexual harassment situation in which workplace conditions are sexually offensive, intimidating, or hostile and affect an individual's ability to perform his or her job

Apathy: lack of emotional involvement in the job

Robotism: rigid and inflexible behavior

DISCUSSION

1. Why are strong interpersonal relationships important to businesses? What are some obstacles to such relationships? Discuss these questions in relation to each type of relationship covered in this chapter.
2. What are the implications of power sharing for manager-employee relationships?
3. What is meant by managing diversity? In your experience, in what ways has this concept been translated into practice?
4. Discuss ways to improve relations with difficult coworkers. What factors (personal or organizational) may stand in the way of improvement?
5. Who benefits from a mentoring relationship? How do the work and communication styles of managers and trainees affect the development of mentoring relationships?
6. What are some of the potentially positive and negative consequences of romantic relationships in the workplace?
7. What are the two types of sexual harassment? What steps should you take if you are sexually harassed on the job?
8. What are some of the problems caused by employee unresponsiveness toward customers? If you have experienced any of them, how did they affect your opinion of the organization?

ACTIVITIES

1. Assume that you supervise five employees who range from five years younger to seven years older than you. What kinds of personal and work relationships do you believe you would develop with this group?
2. What do you usually do when you encounter a difficult person? Would you react any differently in a work setting?
3. What challenges does each of the following classes of diversity present to workers in modern organizations? Share your opinions with your classmates in a small discussion group.
   a. Older citizens as coworkers
   b. Women as managers
   c. Japanese philosophies stemming from foreign ownership
   d. Mixed-ethnic work teams
4. Many employees become frustrated with fellow coworkers in nonwork settings because of the others' tendency to talk shop. How can you build positive work relationships without discussing work? What negative consequences may result from discussing only work issues in a nonwork setting?

CHAPTER

8 Principles of Interviewing

After completing this chapter, you will be able to:

1. Describe the nature and importance of the interview in business and the professions
2. Identify appropriate interviewing goals
3. Specify effective strategies for preparing for an interview
4. Structure an interview to enhance the achievement of your goals
5. Develop appropriate questions for an interview
6. Identify effective reactions to the responses of an interviewee
7. Manage communication anxiety in a dyadic (two-party) setting

STRATEGIC SCENARIO

Marci Cohen is a junior in college who is majoring in public relations. As a graded assignment for her business communication class, Marci has to set up an interview with a person who (1) does a considerable amount of interviewing and (2) is engaged in professional work related to her major. Marci has made an appointment by telephone to interview William (Bill) Walker, executive director of university relations at her university. Her task is to learn about Mr. Walker's interviewing practices (the techniques and methods he uses when interviewing) and interviewing training (things he has done to help him become a better interviewer).

As you read through this chapter, think about the skills that Marci will need to conduct a successful interview with Mr. Walker. At the end of the chapter, we will revisit this scenario to get your advice to Marci.

OVERVIEW

In the world of business, "as soon as you move one step up from the bottom, your effectiveness depends on your ability to reach others through the spoken word."[1] So said management consultant Peter F. Drucker. Although Drucker was not talking specifically about the communication skills involved in interviewing, he might well have been. Indeed, John Galassi and Merna Galassi, summarizing sixty years of research on the most important factors in employment interviews, conclude, "Researchers consider communication and interpersonal skills as the single most important set of factors in the interview."[2]

Not only are interviewing skills crucial for obtaining a job; they are equally important for success and promotion once you have a position. In a research report, Dan Curtis, Jerry Winsor, and Ronald Stephens identified more than thirty studies of employers' needs that agreed that the skills most valued in today's job market are the ability to communicate and to work effectively with other people.[3] Leaders in business and industry not only voice this view but also support their beliefs financially. Anthony Carnevale, Leila Gainer, and Janice Villet report that "employers spend $30 billion on formal training and approximately $180 billion on informal on-the-job training each year"—about the same amount spent for education at the primary, secondary, and college levels.[4] By far the most common type of business training is focused on interpersonal communication skills: more than 90 percent of business organizations provide communication training for their employees.[5] Many of these efforts and much of the money spent by business and industry are to improve employees' interviewing skills.

THE INTERVIEW

To get a feel for what makes up interviewing skills, let's look at a few definitions:

- The interview is a form of oral communication involving two parties, at least one of whom has a preconceived and serious purpose, and both of whom speak and listen from time to time.[6]
- We define interviewing as a process of dyadic, relational communication, with a predetermined and serious purpose designed to interchange behavior and involving the asking and answering of questions.[7]
- An interview occurs when there is planned conversation (give-and-take) between two (and, at times, more) people.[8]

1. P. F. Drucker, "How to Be an Employee," *Fortune,* May 1952, reprinted in N. B. Sighand and D. N. Bateman, *Communicating in Business* (Glenview, Ill.: Scott, Foresman, 1981), p. 454.
2. J. P. Galassi and M. Galassi, "Preparing Individuals for Job Interviews: Suggestions from More Than 60 Years of Research," *Personnel and Guidance Journal* 57 (1978), 188–192.
3. D. B. Curtis, J. L. Winsor, and R. D. Stephens, "National Preferences in Business and Communication Education," *Communication Education* 38 (1989), 6–14.
4. A. P. Carnevale, L. J. Gainer, and J. Villet, *Training in America: The Organization and Strategic Role of Training* (San Francisco: Jossey-Bass, 1990).
5. P. Page and S. Perelman, *Basic Skills and Employment: An Employer Survey* (Madison: University of Wisconsin System, Interagency Basic Skills Project, 1980).
6. R. S. Goyer et al., *Interviewing Principles and Techniques: A Project Text,* rev. ed. (Dubuque, Iowa: Kendall/Hunt Publishing, 1986), p. 6. Reprinted with permission.
7. The definition of interviewing is based on ones in W. V. D. Hingham et al., *How to Interview* (New York: Harper & Row, 1959); H. Kahn et al., *The Dynamics of Interviewing* (New York: John Wiley & Sons, 1964); and R. S. Goyer et al., *Interviewing Principles and Techniques: A Project Text* (Dubuque, Iowa: Wm. C. Brown Co. Publishers, 1968).
8. G. Hunt/W. Eadie: *Interviewing: A Communication Approach,* p. 4, © 1987. Reprinted with permission of Holt, Rinehart & Winston.

- We define an interview as a specialized form of oral, face-to-face communication between people in an interpersonal relationship that is entered into for a specific task-related purpose associated with a particular subject matter.[9]
- Here are ten general characteristics of interviews: (1) a serious purpose, (2) planned interaction, (3) oral interaction, (4) face-to-face interaction, (5) dyadic interaction, (6) inquiry and response, (7) objective and subjective information, (8) role differentiation, (9) alternating roles, and (10) multiple measures of success.[10]
- Interview: a form of goal-oriented, dyadic human interaction involving primarily oral/aural communicative behavior.[11]

Though emphasizing different features, these definitions share a common emphasis on three defining characteristics of an interview. They agree that an **interview** is planned, dyadic, interactive discourse. Let's explore each of these features briefly.

Planned Discourse

The interview has a purpose beyond initiating and developing a relationship between the two parties involved. Even though the interpersonal relationship is important to the interview, at least one of the two parties (sometimes both) has a predetermined goal—for example, to share information, to persuade, or to solve problems. That goal exists before the start of the interview, so you can plan in advance how best to initiate and conduct the interview.

Dyadic Discourse

A dyad is two units that are considered to be a pair. In an interview there are two parties; there is no third party to act as a mediator or arbiter if the two parties do not agree. Although each party in **dyadic discourse** is typically one person, there can be more than one person in each party. Thus, for example, in an employment interview, a number of representatives of a firm may interview a job applicant in a group interview; or, less commonly, one or more representatives of a firm may interview a number of applicants at the same time.

Interactive Discourse

An interview is a dialogue rather than a monologue. It involves the two-way interaction of two parties—both speak and listen. As a result, an interview requires that both parties adapt to the verbal and nonverbal messages being exchanged. Although an interview normally occurs face-to-face, it also can and does take place over the phone or by means of a computer.

Since we know that an interview is planned, two-party, interactive discourse, it should be easy to see why it is important to use strategic communication when participating in an interview. To illustrate, let's look in on Communication Design,

9. C. Downs et al., *Professional Interviewing,* p. 5 (New York: Harper & Row, 1980). Reprinted by permission of HarperCollins Publishers.
10. W. C. Donaghy, *The Interview: Skills and Applications,* p. 2, Copyright © 1984 by Scott, Foresman & Company. Reprinted by permission of W. C. Donaghy.
11. R. Goyer/M. Sincoff: *Interviewing Methods* (Dubuque, Iowa: Kendall/Hunt Publishing, 1977) p. 2. Reprinted with permission.

a small advertising studio with multiple clients, and identify a small number of interview possibilities. As we look around the office, we see:

A recent college graduate participating in a job interview with the owner (*employment interview*)
The personnel manager explaining insurance benefits to a new employee (*orientation interview*)
An account executive gathering information from a potential client (*research interview*)
The office manager conducting an evaluation interview with a graphic artist (*appraisal interview*)
The art director talking with a client who is very unhappy with the design of a brochure (*grievance interview*)
Two copywriters meeting to discuss potential copy for a new advertisement (*problem-solving interview*)
An account executive attempting to convince a client that it is time to redo the company's full-page advertisement (*persuasive interview*)

In each of these examples, the two parties in the interview are striving to achieve goals. They bring information to the interview and increase their knowledge as the interview progresses. They must employ appropriate questioning, responding, and listening skills, and they must regulate their levels of anxiety. These are general principles that apply across all types of interviews, as we illustrate in the next chapter. We begin our discussion of these basic principles with the first component of the model of strategic communication: setting goals.

GOAL SETTING: DYADIC COMMUNICATION

Since there are many kinds of interviews, there are no universally recognized labels to identify the two parties involved. The most common or general terms we use are *interviewer* and *interviewee,* but in certain situations the parties are more accurately and specifically described as *persuader/persuadee, counselor/client,* or *employer/applicant*. In most interviews, we can say that the interviewer carries the major responsibility for the success of the interview (the therapist in a counseling interview, the pollster in a public opinion survey, the persuader in a sales pitch). In some situations, however, we can't assign this responsibility as easily. To illustrate, in a problem-solving interview, the responsibilities for the interview's success may be equally shared. Even in an employment interview, it may not always be clear who should have the major responsibility: the employer, the applicant, or either one—depending on who has a greater stake in the outcome.

Whoever is primarily responsible for the interview's success (the interviewer, the interviewee, or both) is also primarily responsible for clarifying the goal of the interview. Is the goal, for example, to gather information, give information, counsel, or persuade? Goal setting brings the purpose into focus, and the purpose then shapes the relationship between the interviewer and interviewee.

If you decide that the goal of a particular interview is to gather information, you must then consider what type of relationship between the interviewer and interviewee will make that goal easier to reach. Without goal setting, you are likely to focus too much attention on interpersonal

Where Do You Stand?

In today's computer-driven business world, interviews may likely occur on-line in a series of e-mail exchanges. Compared to a traditional face-to-face interview, how do you believe you would perform in an on-line interview? Can you imagine that you might feel at an advantage or a disadvantage?

When professionals meet to "do business" there are at least three salient issues to be addressed: (1) What kind of person will I be dealing with (credibility)? (2) What will be the purpose of our interaction (orientation)? and (3) What is at stake in this interaction (motivation)? For the people in this photo, which of these issues is likely to be important? If asked this question, do you think all three individuals would give the same answer? (Ian Shaw/Getty Images)

concerns. For example, because you want to be friends with the other person, you may hesitate to ask provocative but necessary questions. Or, without goal setting, you might not focus enough attention on interpersonal concerns. For example, you might ignore nonverbal feedback telling you that the other person doesn't understand your questions. In either case, your decision of whether or not to emphasize the interpersonal relationship can interfere with achieving your goal: gathering information.

Once you determine your reasons for engaging in an interview, you can move on to the next task: identifying potential barriers to achieving the goals of the interview. Such obstacles can include an interviewer who isn't well prepared or who may have biases, misperceptions, and preconceived notions about the interviewee that can interfere with the interview. On the interviewee's side, obstacles can include his or her inability or unwillingness to help achieve the interviewer's goals; demographic, social, or psychological factors that detract from the interview; or a negative response to the interviewer.

The setting can also be a problem. The time of day or week, location of the interview, and seating arrangement can affect the success of an interview. Of course, careful preparation by the interviewer (and often by the interviewee as well) usually pinpoints these potential problems and remedies them. The following list shows possible barriers to effective communication in interviews. One goal common to both the interviewer and the interviewee is to expect and minimize these obstacles as much as possible:

- Competing demands
- Ego threats

- Lack of courtesy
- Trauma
- Forgetfulness
- Confusion
- Jumping to conclusions
- Distracting subconscious behaviors

SITUATIONAL KNOWLEDGE: STRUCTURING THE INTERVIEW

Because an interview involves two parties—each of whom will have an idea of how he or she wants it to proceed—its structure is seldom known ahead of time. Although each party may prepare in advance, each must be ready to use the second component of strategic communication—situational knowledge—to make the exchange of messages as smooth as possible during the interview. Nevertheless, it is useful to think of an interview in terms of three identifiable parts: the opening moments, the body of the interview, and the closing moments. Each part gives the interviewer and the interviewee a chance to get to know more about each other, the purpose of the interview, and the direction it takes. Although there are no hard-and-fast rules—or time limits—for any of these parts, consider the functions they potentially serve.

The Opening

The **opening** moments of an interview are useful for addressing three issues that may concern the interviewee: credibility (Will I like and can I trust this person?), orientation (What will this interview be about?), and motivation (What will I gain from participating in this interview?). The context of the interview may provide answers to these questions, but that is not always the case. Thus, the interviewee can use these three questions to determine if it is necessary to address one or more of the issues specifically.

If, for example, the interviewer and interviewee are getting together for the first time, issues of credibility will be important. When this is the case, the interviewer and interviewee are wise to consider and adapt to what Judee Burgoon and her colleagues describe as the key principles of impression formation:[12]

1. People develop evaluations of one another from limited external information.
2. First impressions are partly based on the stereotypes held by the perceiver.
3. First impressions are often initially based on outward appearance cues.
4. Initial impressions form a baseline of comparison for subsequent impressions and judgments.
5. Impressions consist of judgments on at least three different levels: physical (for example, age, gender, race), sociocultural (socioeconomic status, education level, occupation), and psychological (psychological makeup, temperament, moods).

Given these principles, and considering the importance of situational knowledge, when an interviewer meets an interviewee for the first time, both must be sensitive to anything they learn about each other that is based on nonverbal assets

12. J. K. Burgoon, D. B. Buller, and W. G. Woodall, *Nonverbal Communication: The Unspoken Dialogue*.

and liabilities. The astute interviewee asks herself or himself these types of questions: What is an interviewer likely to conclude from my physical appearance, body motion, vocal cues, use of space, and so on? Can I modify any of these characteristics? Do I want to do so? Is there anything I can do to tone down the effect of possibly unfavorable characteristics that I can't change?

An interviewer is smart to ask herself or himself similar questions about orientation and motivation. Will the interviewee know what the interview is about? If not, how can I provide orientation to the interview? Will the interviewee want to participate in the interview? If he or she doesn't really want to participate, what sources of motivation (for example, humanitarian appeals, promises of rewards, fulfillment of expectations, recognition, sympathy, or understanding) can I use to get him or her more involved?

Credibility, orientation, and motivation are, of course, not independent; ways to achieve one may work to achieve the others as well. As you consider the unique requirements of your situation, you may find that one or more common opening techniques apply. Table 8.1 outlines ten of the most common interview opening techniques.

The Body

While the opening sets the stage for the interview by establishing credibility, orientation, and motivation, it is in the body of the interview that the participants' goals are (or are not) achieved. When developing the body of an interview, the interviewer can choose from a spectrum between two contrasting approaches: directive and nondirective.

In a **directive interview,** the interviewer controls the purpose, structure, and pacing of the interview. Interviews that lend themselves to a directive approach include public opinion polls, employment interviews, and sales interviews. As an interviewer plans for a directive interview, the choices range from "nonscheduled" to "highly scheduled, standardized."

In a *nonscheduled interview,* the interviewer prepares an interview guide that lists potential topics and subtopics. These topics may or may not be covered in the actual interview and may or may not be covered in the listed order. What actually happens in the interview depends more on the interviewee's responses than on the interviewer's guide.

In a *moderately scheduled interview,* the interviewer prepares an interview guide that includes all major questions, with possible probe questions under each major question. The questions are asked in the order in which they are listed, but the probes may or may not be used.

In a *highly scheduled interview,* the interviewer prepares an interview schedule that contains all the questions that will be asked (including all probe questions) and the exact wording that will be used with each interviewee. Every interviewee receives exactly the same questions in exactly the same order.

In a *highly scheduled, standardized interview,* the interviewer prepares an interview schedule that includes not only all questions but also all answer options. The answer options normally ask the interviewee to select one of a number of alternatives (for example, "Do you intend to vote in the student government election?"—"Yes," "No," "Undecided").

In contrast to a directive interview, in a **nondirective interview** the interviewer chooses to cede control of the purpose, structure, and pacing of the interview to the

TABLE 8.1

Common Opening Techniques for Interviewing

Technique	Comments
Make a brief statement or rapid summary of the problem, issue, or need.	This strategy is appropriate when the interviewee is vaguely aware of a problem but not well informed on details.
Explain briefly how you happened to learn about the problem and suggest that the interviewee might want to discuss it.	This strategy avoids the appearance of lecturing or talking down to the interviewee and encourages a spirit of cooperative, objective discussion of a mutual problem.
State an incentive (goal or outcome) that the interviewee wants that he or she may reasonably expect if the proposal is accepted.	This is potentially the most powerful opening of all but is easily abused—it is frequently too obvious or exaggerated. Avoid sounding like someone giving a high-pressure sales pitch, and instead emphasize honesty and sincerity.
Request the interviewee's advice or help with a problem.	This approach is good when the request is sincere. Do not use this technique as a slick gimmick.
State a striking, dramatic fact.	This too is a potentially powerful opening, but it can be corny. This opening must be sincere, logically justified, and related to the interviewee's motivations; it can easily be tied in with incentives. This technique is particularly appropriate when a real emergency exists and when the interviewee is apathetic and must be aroused.
Refer to the interviewee's known position on a given problem situation.	This is the "common-ground" approach. It is excellent to use when the interviewee has taken a public position or the interviewer has already asked the interviewee to bring in proposals.
Refer to the background (causes, origins, and so on) leading up to the problem without stating the problem itself.	When the interviewee is fairly familiar with this background, the application of the common-ground approach may be useful when you expect the interviewee to react in a hostile manner when you reveal the purpose of your proposal.
Identify the person who sent you to see the interviewee.	This approach is appropriate when the interviewee is a stranger and when the interviewee respects the third party.
State the name of the company, organization, or group you represent.	This strategy is appropriate when added prestige is needed or when you have to explain why you are there.
Request a specified, brief period of time.	This opening can be too apologetic; use it only when necessary—for example, when dealing with an impatient, irritable, or very busy interviewee.

Adapted from R. S. Goyer, W. C. Redding, and J. T. Rickey, *Interviewing Principles & Techniques*, p. 10.

What Would You Do?

Take a few minutes to explore your options for a job or for graduate school after graduation. Identify a potential use for each of these interview structures in your immediate future:

- Directive interview
  - Nonscheduled
  - Moderately scheduled
  - Highly scheduled
  - Highly scheduled, standardized
- Nondirective interview

interviewee. This option is typically chosen for problem-solving interviews and counseling. In such situations, the interviewer either does not have enough knowledge to structure the interview or feels that more reliable and valid responses will be gained by allowing the interviewee more of a chance to participate in structuring the interview. In a counseling interview, for example, the interviewee may be asked to describe the problem to be confronted and possible solutions to be considered. The interviewer, instead of planning a structure before the interview, may instead react to the needs and thoughts developed by the interviewee during the interview, incorporating situational knowledge gained by interacting with the interviewee.

The choice of a directive or nondirective approach depends in large part on the interviewer's situational knowledge (which has increased during the opening of the interview). Once the decision has been made, it greatly affects the amount and kind of situational knowledge that may be discovered and employed during the rest of the interview.

The Closing

Effectively **closing** an interview requires as much careful thought as does opening an interview. Even though it may be tempting to move the process quickly to a close once you have achieved the purpose of the interview, an abrupt, awkward ending can do long-term damage to the relationship between the two parties. Thus, it is important to think through the functions of a closing and the nonverbal and verbal strategies that can fulfill these functions.

Mark Knapp, Roderick Hart, Gustav Friedrich, and Gary Shulman studied the functions and norms involved when people take leave of each other.[13] Within the interviewing context, these functions can be described as *concluding* (signaling the end of the interview), *summarizing* (reviewing the main portion of the interaction), and *supporting* (expressing pleasure with the interaction and projecting what will happen next). These functions can be accomplished nonverbally as well as verbally—for example, by breaking eye contact, straightening up in your seat,

13. From M. L. Knapp, R. P. Hart, G. W. Friedrich, and G. Shulman, "The Rhetoric of Goodbye: Verbal and Non-Verbal Correlates of Human Leave-Taking," *Speech Monographs* 40 (1973), 182–198.

An interview allows two people to discuss a job opening utilizing face-to-face communication. Keep in mind—whether you are the interviewer or the interviewee—that the first few minutes of your interview will set the stage for the entire interview process. (Benelux Press/Index Stock Imagery)

leaning toward the exit, smiling, rapidly nodding, or looking at the clock. The following closing techniques capitalize on both verbal and nonverbal strategies:

1. *Offer to answer questions.* Be sincere in the desire to answer questions, and give the interviewee adequate time to ask. Do not give a quick answer to one question and then end the interview.
2. *Use a clearing-house question,* such as "Does that cover everything?" The clearing-house question allows you to determine whether you have covered all topics or answered all the interviewee's questions. It can be an effective closing if your request is not perceived as a formality or an attempt to be sociable but rather as an honest effort to ferret out questions, information, or areas of concern not thoroughly discussed.
3. *Declare the purpose or task completed.* The word *well* brings more interviews to a close than any other. When people hear it, they automatically assume the end is near and prepare to leave.
4. *Make personal inquiries* (such as "By the way, how is Jane's father doing these days?"). Personal inquiries are pleasant ways to end interviews, but they must be sincere and show genuine interest in the interviewee. Interviewees judge sincerity by the way interviewers listen and react verbally and nonverbally.
5. *Signal that time is up.* This closing is most effective when a time limit has been announced or agreed on in the opening. Be tactful in calling time, and try not to give the impression that you are moving the interviewee along an assembly line.
6. *Explain the reason for the close.* Tell why you must close the interview, and be sure the justifications are real. If an interviewee thinks you are making phony excuses, any future interactions will be strained.

7. *Express appreciation or satisfaction.* A note of thanks or pleasure is a common closing because interviewers usually have received something—information, help, a sale, a story, and so on.
8. *Exhibit concern.* Expressions of concern for the interviewee's health, welfare, or future are effective if they are sincere, not merely habitual.
9. *Plan for the next meeting.* It is often appropriate to arrange the next interview or reveal what will happen next, including date, time, place, topic, content, and purpose.
10. *Summarize the interview.* A summary is a common closing for informational, appraisal, counseling, and sales interviews. Summaries may repeat important information, stages, and agreements or verify accuracy or agreement.[14]

COMMUNICATION COMPETENCE: ASKING EFFECTIVE QUESTIONS

In addition to setting interview goals and gathering situational knowledge before and during the interview, both the interviewer and the interviewee need to be able to think of effective and appropriate questions and responses. The ability to do so—and to use verbal, nonverbal, and listening skills to make the information flow smoothly—is the third part of the model of strategic communication.

In *The Art of Asking Questions,* Stanley Payne makes the important point that asking the right question in the right way is central to the success of the interview process.[15] Doing so requires that everyone participating in the interview masters three important characteristics of questioning: the question's meaning, form, and sequence.

Question Meaning

A favorite saying of computer junkies is "Garbage in, garbage out"—that is, what you get out of the computer can be no better than what you put in. Because this principle applies just as strongly to questions and answers in an interview, consider the clarity, relevance, and bias of each question you will ask.

Clarity The questioner's first concern should be whether the respondent will understand the words used in the question. To get the most valid response to a question, Payne suggests a number of strategies:[16]

1. Start by making sure you clearly understand the issue yourself. This means defining the issue precisely even if your words are hard to understand. To achieve this goal, ask yourself the stock journalistic questions: who, what, when, where, and how?
2. Once you have stated the issue precisely, turn to the dictionary to determine whether you can restate the question more directly or more simply. Look up each word, asking four questions about it: Does it mean what you intend? Does

14. C. Stewart and W. Cash, *Interviewing: Principles and Practices,* 9th ed., p.103. Copyright © 2000. Reprinted by permission of the McGraw-Hill Companies, Inc.
15. S. L. Payne, *The Art of Asking Questions* (Princeton, N.J.: Princeton University Press, 1951).
16. S. L. Payne, "Thoughts About Meaningless Questions," *Public Opinion Quarterly* 14 (1950), 687–696.

it have other meanings? If so, does the context make the intended meaning clear? Is a simpler word or phrase suggested (either in the dictionary or in a thesaurus)?

3. Try to keep questions somewhere in the neighborhood of twenty words or fewer. A study that compared "tight" questions with "loose" questions found that, on average, loose questions were one and one-half times as long as tight ones—thirty-one words to twenty-two words.[17]
4. Phrase questions positively. For example, "Do you agree with the statement 'School should be mandatory until age 16'?" is better than something like "Do you disagree with the statement 'School should not be mandatory until age 16'?" Research indicates that questions that are understood when stated in a clear, positive manner can be highly confusing when stated negatively.

Relevance Writing in *Time* magazine, March 14, 1947, Sam Gill reported the results of a public opinion poll in which he asked respondents, "Which of the following statements most closely coincides with your opinion of the Metallic Metals Act? (a) It would be a good move on the part of the United States. (b) It would be a good thing but should be left to individual states. (c) It is all right for foreign countries but should not be required here. (d) It is of no value at all." Seventy percent of the respondents chose one of the alternatives; 30 percent said they had no opinion.[18] The surprising feature of this poll was that the Metallic Metals Act was a fictitious issue—a creation of Sam Gill's imagination.

The urge many respondents have to answer questions that have no meaning for them has been demonstrated many times since 1947. George F. Bishop and three colleagues asked 467 people age eighteen and older in Hamilton County, which includes Cincinnati, Ohio, the following question: "Some people say that the Public Affairs Act should be repealed. Do you agree or disagree with this idea?" Even though the Public Affairs Act was fictitious, a full one-third of the group firmly gave an opinion. The people who were most likely to volunteer opinions were those with the least education.[19]

Given this tendency of respondents to answer meaningless questions, it is not enough to develop questions that are clear and understandable for the respondents; it is equally necessary to ensure that the questions are relevant for these respondents. Two strategies for accomplishing these goals are using pretests and using filter questions. In *pretesting,* a small number of people who are typical of the group who will be the eventual respondents are asked the target questions that will be included in the interview and are also asked what they think the questions mean. Proper pretesting is an excellent way to expose meaningless questions before the interview. The second strategy, *filter questioning,* recommended by George Gallup in his "quintamensional" plan (which we discuss shortly), asks respondents to define terms or give examples before answering the question as a means of sorting out people for whom the target question would be meaningless (for example, if an interviewer were about to question an interviewee about Barbara Boxer, an appropriate filtering question would be "What, if anything, do you know about Senator Barbara Boxer?").

17. S. L. Payne, "Case Study in Question Complexity," *Public Opinion Quarterly* 13 (1949), 653–658.
18. Cited in Payne, *The Art of Asking Questions,* pp. 17–18.
19. G. F. Bishop in C. T. Cory, "Newsline," *Psychology Today,* November 1979, p. 21.

Bias Once you have phrased a clear and relevant question, the last task is to locate unintended potential bias. The issue here is whether the wording of a question will lead some respondents to give different answers than they would give to a different wording of the same question. When a question doesn't give the respondent hints about the expected response, it is labeled *neutral*. When a question either subtly or blatantly clues the respondent to the expected response, it is labeled *directed*. **Directed questions** can be either leading or loaded. When the cue is subtle ("You like ice cream, don't you?"), the question is labeled *leading*. When the cue is blatant ("Are you a women's libber?" or "When was the last time you got drunk?"), the question is called *loaded*. Loaded questions usually involve the use of emotionally charged words or name-calling ("women's libber") or the asking of one question that is really two questions ("Have you ever been drunk?" "When was the last time you were drunk?").

There are many ways in which questions can produce unintended bias. One of the most commonly recognized forms of bias is that which appeals to the very human desire for prestige. Probably the strongest and most common prestige influence in interviews is something we have already discussed—respondents who feel that they *should* have an opinion on an issue. The prestige influence often operates in a subtle fashion, and its effects are sometimes unexpected. A most straightforward question such as "Do you own a laptop computer?" can, for example, be loaded with prestige.

As another form of influence, the words used to state alternatives affect the proportion of middle-ground and undecided replies. The less extreme the choices are, the more willing people are to report a commitment. For example, people who are asked whether they prefer/do not prefer an idea are more likely to express a commitment than are people who are asked whether they would vote for or vote against the same idea.

Given a list of numbers, respondents usually choose those near the middle of the list. Therefore, when you use a list of numbers as a test of knowledge, it may be wise to put the correct figure first or last.

Given a list of ideas or statements, respondents tend to select the statements at the extreme position rather than those near the middle, and they favor the top of the list more than the bottom. When you ask respondents to select from a list of ideas, therefore, rotate the order of the ideas for different respondents.

Questions that emphasize the existing situation take advantage of people's strong tendency to accept things as they are. Thus, when people read or hear such phrases as "as it is now," "or should it be changed," and "as you know" with a question, they are likely to give it higher approval than they would if the idea were presented without the leading phrase.

When there are two alternatives, it is safer to state both choices rather than just one. For example, the following versions of the "same" question are likely to produce different results:

- Do you think the United States should allow instant press coverage of wars?
- Do you think the United States should forbid instant press coverage of wars?
- Do you think the United States should allow or forbid instant press coverage of wars?

Additionally, the list of alternatives should be exhaustive if you intend to cover the range of possibilities. Otherwise, an idea may be underplayed not because it ranks low in the respondent's thinking but because the questioner either overlooked it or considered it insignificant.

It is normally best to avoid all-inclusive or all-exhaustive words such as *all, always, never,* and *none.* Such words usually produce an overstatement. Many people will go along with the general idea, accepting the overstatement as a form of literary license, but purists may refuse to give an opinion or choose the other side in protest when they see words that imply an absolute position.

Our discussion of bias in question wording up to this point could easily be taken as a blanket prohibition against directed questions (either leading or loaded). This is not the case. Although they should never be used unintentionally, there are circumstances in which directed questions can be put to good use. The interviewer may, for example, be dealing with an ego-threatening topic and may wish to let the respondent know that her or his response will not shock the interviewer. A direct question may, under certain circumstances, produce a more truthful answer than a neutral stating of the same question. This is why Alfred Kinsey used directed questions in his well-known study of sexual practices (e.g., "When was the last time you did X?"). He felt he would get more honest answers this way. There are also circumstances in which the interviewer may wish to use directed questions to see how the respondent reacts to stress. The key point, then, is to recognize the difference between neutral and directed questions and to use directed questions only when they help you get an unbiased answer from the respondent.

Question Form

In addition to considering the meaning of a question, the questioner must also consider the form. It is possible to identify many characteristics of questions, but we will examine only two dimensions: open/closed and primary/secondary.[20] Each and every question in an interview can be characterized in terms of both dimensions.

Open/Closed Questions The distinction between **open** and **closed questions** can be drawn by the *form of response*. Open questions ask respondents to answer in their own words from alternatives that they construct—for example, "If you could create your ideal job, what would it be?" Closed questions ask respondents to select from a list of offered alternatives—for example, "Answer 'yes,' 'no,' or 'no opinion' to the following question: 'Do you believe that women should be in combat roles in the military?'"

There are advantages and disadvantages to questions that fall at each end of the open/closed continuum. Open questions allow respondents the greatest amount of freedom and are thus useful when the questioner is initiating a topic, knows less than the respondents do about the topic, or wants to get an uninfluenced view of the respondents' thinking. Because there are normally no incorrect responses to an open question, respondents are also less likely to be threatened by it. Such advantages are, of course, gained at the cost of increased time per interview and answers that are difficult to summarize and compare. Thus, when the situation requires greater control by the questioner or when the questioner plans to compare the responses of numerous respondents, closed questions are normally the better choice.

20. Stewart and Cash, *Interviewing*.

Primary/Secondary Questions **Primary questions** introduce new topics or areas of questioning. **Secondary questions** develop topics or areas that have already been introduced by primary questions. You can start an area of questioning by asking, for example, "If you could create the ideal job for yourself, what would it be?" and then follow up or probe with a number of secondary questions (such as "Where would the job be located?" "Do you think, then, that it is important to work with like-minded individuals?" "Can you tell me more?"). While there are many different secondary questions, these are among the most useful:

- **Clarification:** Directly requesting more information about a response: "Could you tell me a little more about the kind of person you would like to work for?"
- **Elaboration:** Directly requesting an extension of a response: "Are there any other features of the location that you would consider important?"
- **Paraphrase:** Putting the response in the questioner's wording in an attempt to establish understanding: "Let's see whether I've understood what you're saying: you consider the type of people you work with more important than salary and benefits?"
- **Silence:** Not speaking while waiting for the respondent to begin or to resume speaking.
- **Encouragement:** Using brief sounds and phrases to indicate your attention to and interest in what the respondent is saying: "Uh-huh," "I see," "That's interesting," "Good," and "Yes, I understand."
- **Mirror:** Repeating the response while using the respondent's language: "You say, then, that it is important to you to be located near a university."
- **Summary:** Summarizing several previous responses and asking the respondent if your summary of his/her responses is correct: "Let's see whether I've got it: your ideal job involves a boss who appreciates you, supportive colleagues, interesting work, and a chance to live in a large metropolitan area."
- **Clearing-house:** Asking if you have received all the important or available information: "Have I asked everything that I should have asked?"

Question Sequence

Once the interviewer is sure that the questions are clear, relevant, and unbiased for the respondent (*meaning*) and that the issues related to choices between open/closed and primary/secondary questions (*form*) have been resolved, he or she then considers the order in which questions can be best asked to develop the topics of an interview (*sequence*). A common way of thinking about the sequencing of questions looks at three organizational patterns: funnel, inverted funnel, and tunnel.

Funnel In a **funnel sequence,** depicted in Figure 8.1, the questioner starts with broad, open questions and moves toward narrower, closed questions—hence the label *funnel* (an object that is broad at the top and narrow at the bottom). In Figure 8.1, the interviewer in interested in exploring a personnel manager's view of how best to conduct a job interview.

As this example illustrates, the funnel sequence is an excellent choice for situations in which the interviewee knows more about a topic than the interviewer

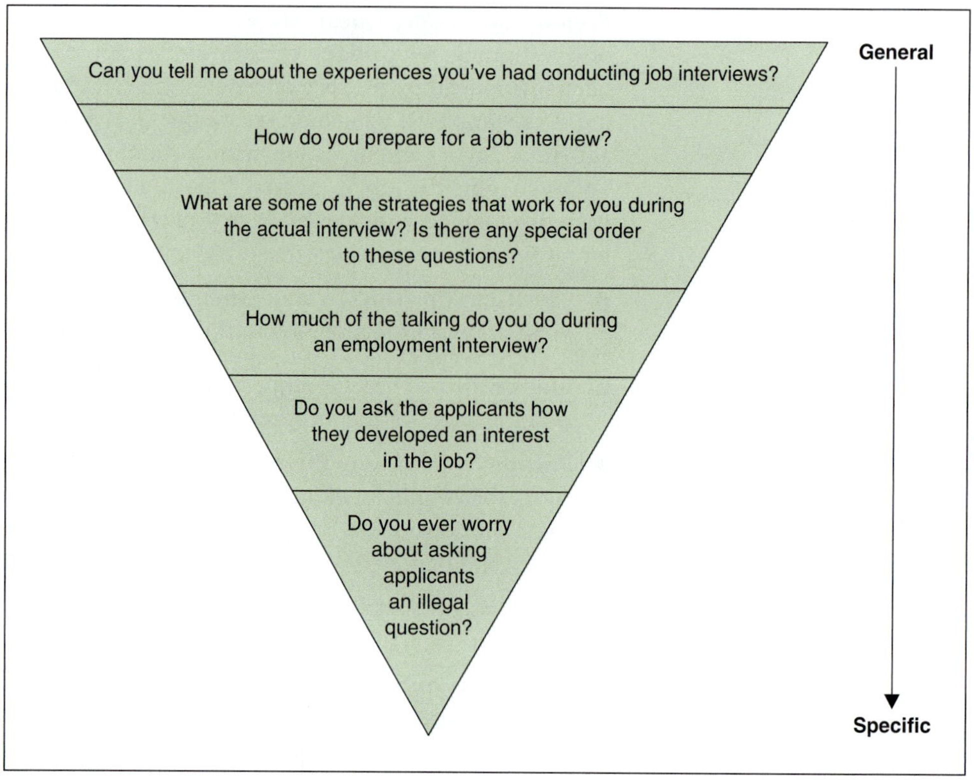

FIGURE 8.1

Funnel Sequence
In this technique, the questioner starts with broad, open questions and moves toward narrower, closed questions.

does. In such situations, a funnel sequence lets the interviewee begin talking about a subject in an unbiased, nonthreatening way—thus opening up areas that the interviewer can explore later with narrower secondary questions that require clarification and elaboration.

Inverted Funnel The **inverted-funnel sequence,** depicted in Figure 8.2, turns the funnel sequence upside down. It begins the questioning process with a closed question that seems to require a "yes" or "no" answer and gradually moves toward broad, open questions. The example in the figure assumes that you are exploring the use of videoconferencing in a small business organization with the owner.

The inverted-funnel sequence assumes that the interviewer has enough information about the topic and about the interviewee to frame specific, narrow questions. It is useful when the interviewee's memory requires focusing. A series of closed questions can jog the interviewee's memory on the topic and motivate her or him to respond to more open questions. This can be especially true when the topic involves an unpleasant event or when the interviewee may otherwise feel threatened or inadequate to comment on the topic.

Tunnel The **tunnel sequence** consists of a series of questions at a similar level of openness or closedness. Most frequently, the questions are closed, and the form of response is restricted: the interviewer asks a number of people a series of yes/no and multiple-choice questions. Because responses to open questions are difficult to replicate, code, tabulate, and analyze, interviewers who ask questions of more than one person and then summarize the results typically ask closed rather than open questions. Here is an example of a tunnel sequence:

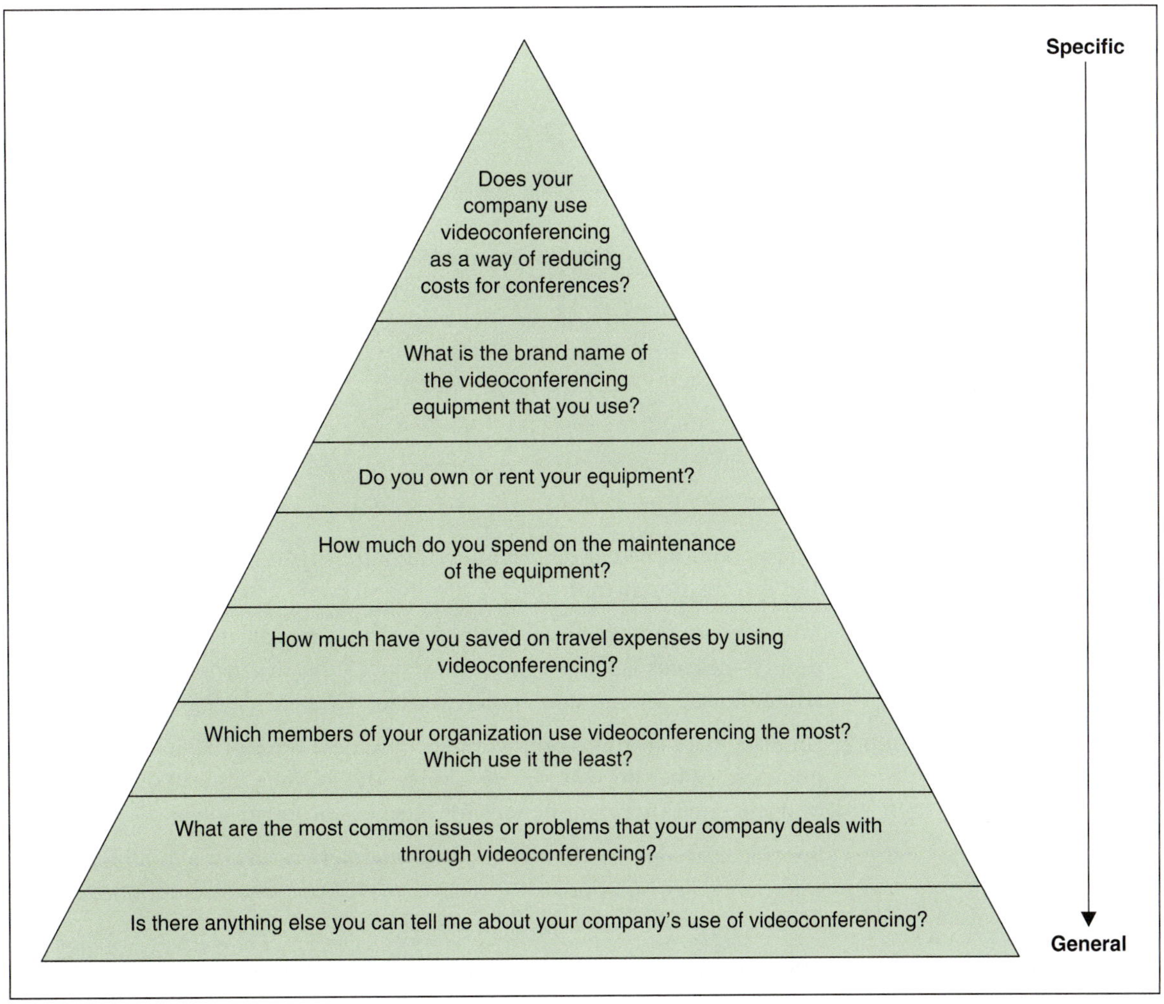

FIGURE 8.2 Inverted-Funnel Sequence

This questioning technique begins with a closed question and gradually moves toward broad, open questions.

Use the following scale (VF = very frequently, F = frequently, O = occasionally, R = rarely, and N = never) to indicate how often you have participated in the following types of interviews:

Employment	VF	F	O	R	N
Information giving	VF	F	O	R	N
Information gathering	VF	F	O	R	N
Disciplinary	VF	F	O	R	N
Appraisal	VF	F	O	R	N
Problem solving	VF	F	O	R	N
Persuasive	VF	F	O	R	N

Special Purpose The three sequences (funnel, inverted funnel, and tunnel) can be put together in various combinations within a single interview. Thus, an interviewer may start with a funnel sequence, develop the next two topics with a tunnel, and conclude with an inverted funnel.

There are also sequences that cannot be described by any of the three labels. Perhaps the best known of these is one that George Gallup developed for use in

TECHNOLOGY TOOLS

Consult Interviewing Experts on the Web

You can learn a great deal about the nature of questions and their sequencing by examining a professional public opinion poll. Use one of the search service sites on the World Wide Web (Yahoo!, Infoseek, Excite) to locate a current public opinion poll. Enter either a simple query (public opinion polling) to identify or link to specific sites or organizations or try the URL for Princeton University's Survey Research Center:

http://www.princeton.edu/%7eabelson/

Use the terminology of this chapter (e.g., open/closed questions, primary/secondary questions, funnel/inverted-funnel/tunnel sequence) to label the questions and their sequence. See if you can discover helpful devices that will aid Marci Cohen in her preparation for the interview with Bill Walker (p. 209).

public opinion polls aimed at determining the intensity of opinions and attitudes. Labeled the **quintamensional plan,** it has five steps:[21]

Step 1. Awareness of the topic is first gained through a free-answer, knowledge question (sometimes labeled a filter question): "What, if anything, do you know about the use of computer conferences for problem solving in business?"

Step 2. Uninfluenced attitudes on the subject are next developed in a free-answer question: "What do you perceive to be the advantages and disadvantages of using computer conferences for business problem solving?"

Step 3. Specific attitudes are then elicited through a two-way or a multiple-choice question: "Do you approve or disapprove of the use of computer conferences for problem solving in business?"

Step 4. The reasoning behind the attitudes is elicited in a free-answer question about the reasoning: "Why do you feel this way?"

Step 5. Intensity of feeling comes last in the form of an intensity question: "How strongly do you feel about this: strongly, very strongly, or 100 percent committed?"

RESPONDING AND PROVIDING FEEDBACK

In the reaction phases of the interview, the interviewer can benefit from the information gleaned by Carl Rogers in a series of research studies examining how people communicate with each other in face-to-face situations.[22] Rogers found that when one person reacts to what another has said, 80 percent of all responses can be classified into five categories:

1. **Evaluative responses** indicate that the interviewer has judged the relative goodness, appropriateness, effectiveness, or rightness of the interviewee's response. The interviewer in some way implies what the interviewee might or ought to do.

21. G. Gallup, "The Quintamensional Plan of Question Design," *Public Opinion Quarterly* 11 (1947), 385.
22. Carl Rogers's research is discussed in D. W. Johnson, *Reaching Out: Interpersonal Effectiveness and Self-Actualization* (Englewood Cliffs, N.J.: Prentice Hall, 1972), pp. 117–140.

ETHICAL ISSUES

Handling Tricky Questions

Malore Brown, a single mother of an eight-year-old son, is interviewing for a position as a pharmaceutical sales representative. During her interview, she is asked, "Do you have children? If so, who will take care of them while you are at work?" Malore knows these and other such questions are illegal according to the guidelines set forth by the Equal Employment Opportunity Commission. How should Malore respond? If you found yourself in a similar position, how would you respond?

Such questions are asked—sometimes out of malice, but more often out of ignorance on the part of the interviewer. One strategy for handling tricky interview questions is to identify and consider the concern behind the interviewer's question. Ask yourself, "What concerns this interviewer such that he or she would ask me this question? How can I address that concern ethically? In Malore's case, the interviewer is concerned that her status as a single mother will interfere with her abilities to perform her job competently. By addressing and responding to the concern behind the question rather than to the substance of the question, an interviewee can successfully manage a tricky or outright illegal interview question while still maintaining his or her own code of ethics.

Malore might respond to her interviewer by saying, "My son is a very important part of my life, but so is my career. I've had eight successful years of practice managing both at the same time. My previous employers can tell you that I am punctual, responsible, and well focused.

If you've ever been in a situation such as this one, in which you are asked a shocking or even offensive question but still must maintain your composure and continue the conversation, you know how difficult it can be to think on your feet and come up with a response that is at the same time polite, ethical, and personally advantageous. You can avoid this dilemma by thinking about these issues long before you arrive at the interview site. Spend some time thinking about how you might ethically and respectfully respond to the concerns behind any illegal, embarrassing, or otherwise tricky questions that may be asked of you without looking foolish or destroying the interview.

2. **Interpretative responses** indicate that the interviewer's intent is to teach or tell the interviewee what the response means, how the interviewee really feels. The interviewer either obviously or subtly implies what the interviewee might or ought to think.
3. **Supportive responses** indicate that the interviewer's intent is to reassure, pacify, or reduce the interviewee's intensity of feeling. The interviewer implies that it is either appropriate or not necessary for the interviewee to feel as she or he does.
4. **Probing responses** indicate that the interviewer's intent is to seek further information or to provoke further discussion.
5. **Understanding responses** indicate that the interviewer's intent is only to find out whether he or she correctly understands what the interviewee is saying.[23]

To illustrate Rogers's categories, consider the following situation, and compare the five responses that the interviewer might offer:

INTERVIEWER: How do you go about motivating employees?

INTERVIEWEE: Well, that varies with the employee. For some, rewards are intrinsic to the job itself—things like the satisfaction of knowing they are doing a good job. For others, motivators are more extrinsic—things like pay, benefits, and vacation.

23. This is paraphrased from Johnson, ibid., p. 125.

STRATEGIC SKILLS

Magazine Interview

Below is the opening portion of a *Syllabus* magazine interview with Graham Spanier, president of Penn State, on his view of technology integration at his university. Use the terminology of this chapter (e.g., open or closed questions, question sequence, response styles) to describe interviewer and interviewee behavior.

SYLLABUS: As president of Penn State University, you have a very high-level view of technology integration on campus. How do you see technology today, in 2003, impacting and supporting institutional goals, and how does this figure into top-level strategic planning?

SPANIER: I think higher education has been transformed by the deployment of new information technologies. We see it in almost every corner of the university—in our administrative systems, in our Web sites, in our on-line applications, in distance education, and in resident instruction classrooms. As far as strategic planning is concerned, we consider information technology as an integral part of campus planning activities.

SYLLABUS: Does technology impact your planning across the entire enterprise?

SPANIER: Technology is no longer isolated in discrete areas, and part of what we're able to do with more advanced technologies is to connect areas that weren't previously connected. I think a very good example is in university libraries.

SYLLABUS: So would you say that technology is changing the institution as a whole?

SPANIER: I think so, but it's not as clear as saying that the technology is causing the changes. A lot of this change has been bubbling, and technology is a response to the needs of faculty and staff out there, so it's a two-way street.

SYLLABUS: You mentioned the library. Where at Penn State are you seeing the most technology changes—in the realm of academics, or research, or student life, or operations and administration?

SPANIER: I think we're seeing it in all of those areas. It would be hard to rank-order them.

SYLLABUS: Are the lines blurring between administrative and academic systems? And if so, what are some of the key technologies at the intersection of the two?

SPANIER: Yes, the lines are blurring. Library systems, assistive technologies, e-commerce, Web services, and the course management systems are all areas in which we are very active here at Penn State.

Source: Adapted from "Transforming the Academic Enterprise: A Conversation with Graham Spanier," *Syllabus: Technology for Higher Education* 17, no.1 (August 2003), 11–12. © Syllabus Magazine. All rights reserved, 101COMMUNICATIONS, LLC.

- **Evaluative response:** "That doesn't seem like a very practical way of thinking to me. How can you get any work out of employees if you spoil them?"
- **Interpretative response:** "I guess that means that you think you need to be fair but firm with your employees. You find out what motivates them but make sure they understand your expectations for job performance."
- **Supportive response:** "I've noticed the same things where I work. Some people are intrinsically motivated; others, extrinsically."
- **Probing response:** "What are some of the best ways to motivate employees who are motivated extrinsically?"
- **Understanding response:** "So the first step is to find out whether the employee is intrinsically or extrinsically motivated."

Carl Rogers discovered that people in a wide variety of settings use the five alternatives in the following order of frequency (from most frequent to least): evaluative, interpretative, supportive, probing, and understanding. He also discovered

Where Do You Stand?

Recall any recent conversation in which you've participated. Think of a statement that was part of that conversation and respond to it using each of Rogers's five response styles: evaluative, interpretative, supportive, probing, and understanding.

that if a person uses one category of response as much as 40 percent of the time, others will see that person as always responding in that way. The message of Rogers's research is not that a person should prefer (or avoid) one type of response more than another. All five types of response are useful to an interviewer. Overuse or underuse of a category, however, or a failure to think about the importance of a category for a specific situation may well be dysfunctional. Thus, an interviewer should know how to produce all five types of responses and know when each is appropriate. In many situations it may be best to start with probing and understanding responses before moving to evaluative and interpretative responses.

ANXIETY MANAGEMENT: INTERVIEWER AND INTERVIEWEE

Interviewing is a source of communication anxiety for many reasons. As you recall from Chapter 2, anxiety is situational for many people. In other words, some people may be more anxious in some settings than in others or may find that their normal levels of communication apprehension are heightened by such factors as being in a new setting, speaking to an unfamiliar person, being the focus of attention, or having important decisions or outcomes rest on the success of their communication.

Interviewing can be a source of anxiety for both the interviewer and the interviewee. A competent interviewer can take steps to ensure that neither party's apprehension undermines the goals of the interview or damages the interaction between interviewer and interviewee. These guidelines for interviewers can help defuse tension that is a basic part of interview situations and put the interviewee at ease:

1. *Be prepared.* Know the specific purpose and goal of the interview, and review it for the interviewee at the very beginning of the time period. Plan questions in advance, and ensure that the interview is long enough to accommodate all questions without rushing the interviewee.
2. *Listen well.* Give appropriate and direct responses, and use the question forms and sequences discussed earlier in this chapter to gather additional information. Show sincere attention by nodding or leaning forward. Suppress distracting gestures such as tapping, crossing or uncrossing legs, or shifting in the chair, which may make the interviewee nervous.
3. *Treat the interviewee as an equal.* Set up the interview so that both parties have equal access to each other. Do not slouch behind an imposing desk or have the interviewee stand while you remain seated.
4. *Be personable, not personal.* Maintain a friendly demeanor, but do not become distracted by or comment on the interviewee's appearance, speech patterns, or gestures (such comments may make the interviewee extremely self-conscious). Apart from warm-up small talk, keep all questions and responses targeted to the interview goal.
5. *Respond to nonverbal as well as verbal cues.* Explain things if the interviewee appears worried or confused. Use supportive questions to offset the interviewee's anxiety. Ask if the interviewee has more to say if nonverbal gestures such as a furrowed brow or a shrug indicate that she or he has more to add but is too nervous or unsure to do so.

6. *Show respect for the interviewee.* Do not ask demeaning or belittling questions, lose your temper, use threatening or offensive language, listen halfheartedly, or attempt to intimidate the interviewee.

Nervousness is natural and often productive: the tension of an interview can charge a performance and make the experience dynamic. Nevertheless, an interviewee's uncontrolled tension can make the interviewer's job especially difficult and can negatively influence the interviewee's responses. If you are the interviewee, paying attention to the following points can help you manage your anxiety so that it improves, rather than undermines, your performance:

1. *Practice possible responses before the interview.* If you know what the interviewer is likely to ask, work in advance on giving competent responses to those questions. For example, if you are preparing for an orientation interview, make a list of the major points you would like to know about the organization. If you are participating in a research interview, be sure that you have gathered and reviewed the appropriate data. (These are just two examples; in the next chapter, we discuss specific questions to expect in employment, appraisal, disciplinary, and media interviews.)
2. *Concentrate on what you have to say.* Focus on both the question at hand and the big picture—that is, how the interview furthers organizational goals. Keep the interview in perspective. It is unlikely to make or break your career.
3. *Listen carefully to questions.* Do not respond until you have heard the complete question and thought about it carefully. Is it a funneled question, narrowing in on a particular area? Is it closed or open? Primary or secondary? The questions themselves can reveal much about the interviewer's goals and the direction the interview is taking. This knowledge can help to put you at ease.
4. *Mentally review and summarize your responses before beginning to speak.* Do not blurt out the first thing that comes to mind. Take time to pause, collect your thoughts, and then reply.

Remember, the interviewer requested a meeting with you because she or he believed you were worthy of her or his time—and you are! Anxiety is not a devastating problem; it is just one more factor that can be anticipated and prepared for to ensure that the interview is successful. Both interviewers and interviewees can benefit from taking steps to relieve the tension of an interview.

STRATEGIC SCENARIO WRAP-UP

At the beginning of this chapter you met Marci Cohen, a college junior who was preparing to interview Bill Walker, executive director of university relations, concerning his interviewing practices and training. What have you learned in this chapter that might help her prepare for this task?

- What characteristics of Marci and Bill's anticipated interaction would allow you to label it an interview? What kind of interview is it?
- What should Marci consider as she thinks about the goals of her interview?
- How should Marci begin the interview?
- Where on the directive–nondirective continuum should this interview be conducted? Why?
- What type of closing would work best for the interview?
- What can Marci do to be sure her questions are clear, relevant, and unbiased? What mixture of open/closed and

primary/secondary questions should she plan? What combinations of funnel, inverted-funnel, and tunnel sequences should she anticipate? Is the quintamensional plan relevant for this interview?

- As Marci anticipates reacting to the responding moves of Bill Walker, what combination of evaluative, interpretative, supportive, probing, and understanding responses is likely to be most appropriate?

SUMMARY

- This chapter covered basic principles of interviewing that apply generally to all dyadic (two-party) communication.
- The interview is a process of planned, dyadic, interactive discourse. Goals for interviewers may include gathering information, solving problems, persuading, counseling, or giving information. Preparation and cooperation by the interviewer as well as by the interviewee are essential to the achievement of any of these goals.
- Most interviews consist of three parts: the opening, the body, and the closing. In each part, the interviewer and the interviewee use verbal cues and nonverbal impressions to increase their knowledge of the situation and to respond to each other.
- Communication competence in interviews consists of the ability to ask meaningful questions phrased appropriately and in an effective sequence. Questions should be clear, relevant, and unbiased. They may take either an open form (respondents answer in their own words) or a closed form (respondents choose from a set of offered alternatives), and they may be classified as primary or secondary.
- Primary questions introduce new topics; secondary questions develop topics introduced by primary questions.
- Questions can be sequenced in funnel, inverted-funnel, or tunnel patterns.
- A funnel sequence moves from broad questions to specific, closed questions.
- An inverted-funnel sequence begins with a closed question and moves toward open questions.
- A tunnel sequence consists of a set of questions at the same level of openness or closedness.
- The interviewer's responses can indicate a range of intentions and implications. People tend to use evaluative and interpretative responses most frequently. Overuse or underuse of one type of response can skew the interviewee's perception of the interviewer in a negative direction.
- Anxiety is a common element in interview situations. It can affect the interviewer, the interviewee, and the success of the interaction.
- Anxiety can be controlled through conscious effort by both the interviewer and the interviewee to be prepared, to listen well, and to communicate clearly and considerately.

KEY TERMS

Interview: planned, dyadic, interactive discourse

Dyadic discourse: two parties engaged in a conversation; each party may consist of more than one person

Opening: initial moments of an interview in which issues of credibility, orientation, and motivation may be addressed

Directive interview: a situation in which the interviewer controls the purpose, structure, and pacing of the interview

Nondirective interview: a situation in which the interviewer cedes control of the purpose, structure, and pacing of the interview to the interviewee

Closing: ending an interview by performing functions such as concluding, summarizing, and supporting

Directed question: a question that either subtly (*leading*) or blatantly (*loaded*) clues the respondent to the expected answer

Open question: a question that allows the interviewee great choice in terms of form of response

Closed question: a question that gives the interviewee minimal choice in terms of form of response

Primary question: a question that introduces a new topic or area of questioning

Secondary question: a question that develops a topic or area that has already been introduced by a primary question

Funnel sequence: a sequence in which the interviewer starts with broad, open questions and moves toward narrower, closed questions

Inverted-funnel sequence: a sequence in which the interviewer begins the questioning with a closed question and gradually moves toward broad, open questions

Tunnel sequence: a sequence in which the interviewer uses a series of questions at a similar level of openness or closedness

Quintamensional plan: a special sequence of questions designed by George Gallup, it consists of five steps: awareness of the topic, uninfluenced attitudes, specific attitudes, reasoning behind the attitudes, and intensity of feelings

Evaluative response: a response indicating that the interviewer has judged the relative goodness, appropriateness, effectiveness, or rightness of the interviewee's response

Interpretative response: a response indicating that the interviewer's intent is to teach or tell the interviewee what the response means

Supportive response: a response indicating that the interviewer's intent is to reassure, pacify, or reduce the interviewee's intensity of feeling

Probing response: a response indicating that the interviewer's intent is to seek further information or to provoke further discussion

Understanding response: a response indicating that the interviewer's intent is to find out whether he or she correctly understands what the interviewee is saying

DISCUSSION

1. What are the three distinguishing features of an interview? How does each affect the nature of communication during an interview?
2. What are some things the interviewer should consider when setting goals for an interview? How might the time and setting affect the outcome of the interview?
3. How is situational knowledge (including credibility of the interviewer, first impressions of both interviewer and interviewee, knowledge level of the interviewee, and sources of motivation for the interviewee) developed during the opening portion of the interview?
4. Describe the differences among nonscheduled; moderately scheduled; highly scheduled; and highly scheduled, standardized interviews. In which situations would an interviewer most likely use a directive interview? A nondirective interview?
5. What makes a question effective? Be sure to discuss the importance of relevance, clarity, and avoiding potential bias when creating meaningful questions.
6. What are some ways that bias can unintentionally be introduced in a question? How can bias be avoided? When is it acceptable to use a biased question?
7. What are the differences between open and closed questions and between primary and secondary questions?
8. Describe the funnel, inverted-funnel, and tunnel sequences for questioning. Which sequence would be most appropriate in the following situations?:
   a. An interviewer interested in finding out the daily routine of a communications manager
   b. A market researcher exploring many customers' reactions to a new product
   c. A supervisor interviewing an employee to determine the success of a computer-training seminar
9. Discuss the five categories of response identified by Carl Rogers. Why is it important to be able to employ all five types of response?

ACTIVITIES

1. Construct a series of questions that you would ask in the opening portion of the following types of interviews:
   a. To obtain information from a county official about building permits for a report you have been assigned to deliver to senior management
   b. To write a biography of a long-time employee for a special presentation at her retirement party
   c. To counsel a subordinate about a problem he or she is having keeping his or her business expenses within budget guidelines
2. How does the nature of directive versus nondirective interviewing seem to match your own communication tendencies? Share your answer with your classmates.
3. With a partner, attempt to conduct an interview using only open or closed questions. How successful were you in gathering appropriate, useful, and detailed information? Was the experience frustrating? Why?
4. Select an important social topic that is worthy of a public opinion poll. Use the quintamensional plan, and devise appropriate interview questions for the poll.

CHAPTER

9

Interviews in Business Settings

After completing this chapter, you will be able to:

1. Understand the roles and responsibilities of the interviewer and interviewee during an employment interview
2. Prepare for and participate in an employment interview
3. Understand the importance of appraisal interviews
4. Conduct an effective appraisal interview
5. Describe the elements of a disciplinary interview
6. Describe the purposes and types of media interviews

STRATEGIC SCENARIO

As a graduating senior from Trimbell University, Sam Biltmore has recently completed on-campus interviews with three companies that want to invite him to their headquarters for day-long "finalists" interviews. The interviews at the university's placement center were informative, and Sam is interested in each company. The company representatives were knowledgeable and friendly, but Sam still does not have enough information about them to know whether he would be interested in working for one of them. He is also a bit concerned about his interviewing experiences in the placement center. One recruiter was very complimentary about his GPA, major, and work experience but seemed concerned that his résumé was incomplete. Another recruiter hinted that Sam seemed a bit bashful, maybe even complacent about the interviewing process. This made Sam nervous because the recruiter misinterpreted what Sam was feeling—apprehension about getting a good job. Plus, Sam knew that his past interviewing experiences were not all that successful. Sam lacked confidence and never seemed able to reveal what he knew about the company or to ask questions that seemed directly pertinent. All three recruiters wanted Sam to send in his résumé along with a cover letter explaining why he was the best person for the job. Sam hated writing letters and really dreaded going through this process.

As you read this chapter, think about Sam's concerns and determine whether they are real or imagined.

OVERVIEW

Chapter 8 introduced you to the principles and procedures of interviewing. In this chapter we apply the techniques and skills discussed there to interviews in a variety of business and professional situations. Our first focus is on employment interviews. They are likely to be of immediate importance to you, whether you are actively job hunting, considering the possibilities for summer or part-time employment, or anticipating your next move after graduation. And once you are established in your career, you will probably conduct such interviews to hire employees for your own organization. We also cover appraisal interviews, which are vital to maintaining strong and positive manager-employee relations, and disciplinary interviews, which prevent work problems from getting out of hand. Last, we discuss an increasingly important and frequent setting: media interviews.

EMPLOYMENT INTERVIEWS: INTRODUCTION

According to an old saying, "Your education, experience, and preparation will get you the interview, but it is your performance in the interview that will get you the job." Dozens of candidates with similar experience and education will get a chance to interview with the companies that interest you. It is the interview itself that will separate you from the pack.

Employment interviewing is probably the one work experience that everyone in the work force has in common. If you have gone through a job interview and have felt it was the most stressful event of your life, you are not alone. Most people are particularly anxious in this communication setting because the stakes are so high. Your future and career may seem to hinge on a successful job interview. Even interviewers are likely to be nervous. The success of their organization or department depends on their choosing correctly from among a number of candidates, many of whom appear to be equally qualified. Strategic communication in an interview situation, however, can reduce anxiety. Goal setting, situational knowledge, communication competence, and anxiety management can aid you in making an interview successful.

EMPLOYMENT INTERVIEWS: THE INTERVIEWER

As you move up in an organization, you may find yourself having to interview many people. As a job candidate, you will be on the receiving end. In either situation, you need to understand the role, responsibilities, and strategies of an interviewer.

Goal Setting

Although employment interviews vary in their sophistication, comprehensiveness, and formality, interviewers all have at least one goal in common: to select the best person from the pool of applicants. Also important is the interviewee's ability to sell the interviewer on his or her potential value to the organization.

Situational Knowledge

Conducting an interview means knowing your responsibilities as an interviewer and understanding how to acquire information about the person you are interviewing. Your situational knowledge as an interviewer will prove to be a valuable asset.

Businesses always face the challenge of attracting, recruiting, and hiring the best people. On the one hand, tight labor markets contain fewer qualified workers with highly developed job skills.[1] On the other hand, selecting from among dozens of solid applications per available position in a softer economy is not the simplest matter, either—although most personnel departments would rather have the latter problem. Whatever the economy, the challenge of getting the right person into the right job can be made much easier through effective preparation and interviewing techniques.

Developing Job Specifications When a position is to be filled, the person (interviewer) responsible for filling it must first develop job specifications, which are commonly referred to as bona fide occupational qualifications, or **BFOQs.** These include the necessary experience, educational background, and skills—the *concrete* requirements—for performing the job. Some BFOQs are highly specific because of the technical nature of the position—for example, an auditing accountant position that requires applicants to be certified and have from three to five years of experience in tax law in the state of Illinois, or a quantitative marketing position that requires applicants to possess strong communication skills, two years of experience in computer systems sales, a degree in applied mathematics, and superior analytic ability.

It is helpful for the interviewer to define the *minimum* qualifications necessary for the job as well—for example, a sales representative position that requires a B.A. in business or communications and one year of sales experience in any industry. Candidates with additional experience and demonstrated management ability might be welcome to apply, but it is important that the hiree be able to grow in the job. Interviewers who select overqualified candidates are likely to end up with bored and frustrated employees. When describing a position for a specialized area, the interviewer is wise to review past and current job descriptions similar to the one in question. Such a review is also an opportunity to redefine positions that have become outdated.

Regardless of the industry, organizations want to hire people who are honest, self-motivated, conscientious, and intelligent. In a survey, respondents reported that the personal characteristics most important for supervisory positions are general competence, leadership abilities, oral communication skills, and human relations skills.[2] It is important to think of the job qualifications in terms of these personal qualities, which will make the difference between a successful employee and another turnover statistic. For example, if one duty of a position is "to review sales reports and make regular presentations to management on profits and losses," the best candidates will have strong analytic and oral presentation skills.

Advertising the Position Most midsize and large organizations have full-time personnel departments whose main concern is to advertise job openings, hold recruitment sessions on college campuses, screen and interview applicants, and make formal offers of employment. In countless other organizations, especially small businesses and highly specialized firms, employee recruiting and hiring are more problematic. Interviewers in small or specialized organizations may not be well trained in employment interviewing techniques, or they may be distracted by

1. J. Beilinson, "Workforce 2000: Already Here," *Personnel* 67 (1990), 3–4.
2. H. Z. Levin, "Supervisory Selection Systems," *Personnel* 63 (1986), 61–65.

Completing a standard evaluation form after each candidate's interview allows the interviewer to compare and rank more fairly a number of candidates. (Jack Dempsey/ ©AP-Wide World Photos)

numerous other responsibilities in addition to interviewing. To attract candidates, they may rely on standard newspaper advertisements, which pull in an enormous number of responses that they have to sift through.

Although advertising in newspapers, magazines, and professional journals is an acceptable approach to finding employees, professional recruiters generally agree that it is not the best way. How can organizations avoid the expense and hassle of overresponse while still reaching a good number of qualified people? Several popular methods include networking, providing internships, and using employee referrals.

The prevalence of networking, or finding a job through personal contacts, highlights the fact that many, possibly most, people get their jobs because they "know someone." It is estimated that blue-collar workers find out about jobs through friends, family, and coworkers about 80 percent of the time. About 60 percent of white-collar workers initially use networks for job finding, and the number increases as they advance in their careers.[3] Employers can build their own networks by cooperating with college career centers, attending job fairs or community career days, or working with government employment agencies.

Reviewing Résumés Once applicants have responded to the job opening, you as the interviewer must review the materials that these applicants provide. Your primary goal is to reduce the applicant pool to a manageable size and to invite only top candidates in for interviews. Many companies interview only eight to ten candidates from a pool of two hundred, and of those perhaps three to five may be offered the

3. L. Bowes, *No One Need Apply* (Boston: Harvard Business School Press, 1990).

callback interview on which the selection will be based. Résumés actually screen out 90 percent of all job candidates.[4]

What should a well-prepared interviewer look for on an applicant's résumé? First, consider the applicant's work experience. Does the progression of positions show increasing levels of skill and responsibility? If not, what might be the reason? Are there any periods when the applicant did not work? What were the reasons? Has the applicant switched careers? Why?

Next, look at educational background. Is the level of education adequate? For example, does the applicant possess a B.A. or B.S. degree if it is required? Is the applicant certified to practice in a particular field if required to do so? Does the candidate's educational background indicate that the person has the knowledge and skills necessary for the job? Look for instances in which the candidate had to demonstrate mastery of basic skills.

For an entry-level marketing position, for example, look beyond each candidate's college major and consider the basic skills that anyone occupying the position will need to succeed. Someone with a major in English literature might possess valuable skills in analysis, writing, and organization. Automatically considering only applicants who majored in marketing could deprive your organization of the opportunity to hire a person with unusual insights. It is best to assess educational background in light of the demonstrated skills and abilities that are implied by the applicant's description of her or his work experience.

References provide a second opinion for the interviewer. Are any of the names familiar to you? What are the professional backgrounds of the references? What is each reference's relationship to the applicant? If you are seriously considering a candidate, it is a good idea to contact several of the references to get additional information on the candidate's skills, experience, and career goals. Be aware, however, that it is standard policy at many companies to refuse to give any information other than dates of employment, and this should not be viewed negatively.

If applicants complete a standard application form provided by the company, information from this form (which will most likely mirror the content of the résumé) can also be used to identify the most qualified candidates and to eliminate those who do not meet the minimum requirements. Once a manageable list of candidates is compiled, it is time to invite them in for interviews.

Communication Competence

After you have acquired situational knowledge, you must be prepared to communicate appropriately with the interviewees. Contact the interviewees in writing, and follow up with a phone call. Be sure the candidates know the exact location of your office and the times of their interviews. When scheduling interviews, keep in mind the nature of the position. For example, if the job requires alertness early in the morning, try to schedule the interviews for early in the morning so that you can assess the candidates' energy levels at that time of day.

Preparing a List of Questions Before the candidates arrive for their interviews, prepare a list of questions to guide and to organize the interview. The list will help you maintain control of the interview, and it will ensure that you question candidates consistently and focus on areas that you have identified as important to the job.

4. B. E. Bostwick, *Résumé Writing: A Comprehensive How-to-Do-It*, 4th ed. (New York: Wiley, 1990).

ETHICAL ISSUES

The Dilemma of Knowing Too Much

Assume that the personnel director has given you the responsibility for interviewing job applicants to eliminate all but the top three candidates. Several times during casual conversation, the personnel director has commented that the worst candidates are young, newly married women, because they are the most likely to become pregnant and take maternity leave. Although you do not ask candidates if they are married or if they have or intend to have children (because you know that the question is illegal), you establish a good rapport with a highly qualified candidate, who voluntarily tells you that her new husband is very eager to "start their family." Laughingly, she says that she has given too much personal information about herself and returns to her qualifications for the job. After conducting all the interviews, you decide that she is one of the top three candidates. Are you going to include her in your recommendations to the personnel director? Why or why not? Are you going to tell the personnel director what you learned about this woman's personal life? How can you handle this situation legally without betraying the trust of the personnel director?

First, develop preliminary questions that elicit information about the candidate's job qualifications, interest in the company, and personal characteristics. Keep in mind that you want to pose questions that obtain information that is not available from the application form, cover letter, and résumé. Otherwise, you will merely collect duplicate information and will learn little that is new about the applicant. The interview is the opportunity to round out the knowledge that you have already gained from the résumé, cover letter, and any phone contacts with the candidate.

After writing the preliminary questions, compose specific questions that are direct yet conversational and that conform to all legal requirements. Avoid questions that can be answered simply with "yes" or "no." For example, the question "Do you think you'd like to work for our organization?" is ineffective, for 99 percent of applicants will simply say, "Yes!"

Avoid skewing a candidate's answers or carelessly soliciting deceptive responses by hinting at the "correct" answer—which the interviewee may be only too happy to give. Also, avoid leading questions. Leading questions such as "We certainly encourage good relations between managers and employees—would you be likely to criticize your supervisor or coworkers?" may make a candidate hesitate to answer affirmatively even if he or she feels that constructive criticism and the expression of opinions are valuable on the job.

It is generally best to begin with open questions to warm up the interviewee and then move to more focused questions that require thought and analysis. The interview is your chance to assess the candidate's ability to think on his or her feet.

Legal Issues The process of obtaining information from job candidates is regulated by laws, and it is critical that these regulations be followed in both letter and spirit. The responsibility for conducting an interview legally rests with the employer, not the interviewee.

Title VII of the 1964 Civil Rights Act prohibits discrimination in employment on the basis of color, race, religion, sex, or national origin. This law has been supplemented by the Americans with Disabilities Act, which bans discrimination against

STRATEGIC SKILLS

Legal and Discriminatory Questions

The following lists give examples of legal and discriminatory questions:

Legal Questions

Have you been convicted of a felony?

Would you mind working overtime?

What three adjectives best describe you?

Where do you see yourself in five years?

Are you a U.S. citizen?

Do you speak any languages fluently?

Are you willing to relocate?

Why do you feel qualified for this position?

What do you like and dislike about your current (or previous) job?

Why should we hire you?

Can you give me some indication of your communication skills?

Discriminatory Questions

Have you ever been arrested?

Would your husband mind if you worked late?

Do you consider yourself to be happily married?

Will you need to arrange for child care?

Where were you born?

Where did you learn to speak Spanish?

Could your family relocate with you?

How old are you?

Do you get along well with members of the opposite sex?

Do you qualify for minority status?

Will you continue to dress like that once you are hired?

the nation's disabled citizens.[5] In addition, an Employee Non-Discrimination Act (ENDA), which would prohibit employment discrimination on the basis of sexual orientation, has been proposed. Although a federal ENDA has not been passed, a number of state and city governments have enacted this legislation—adding to the large number of corporations that now include sexual orientation in their employee nondiscrimination policies. When asking questions of a candidate, interviewers have to be particularly careful to maintain a legal profile conforming to the spirit of the law.

The official source for legal guidance in hiring is the Equal Employment Opportunity Commission's *Uniform Guidelines on Employee Selection Procedures.*[6] This guide provides prescriptive advice for avoiding potentially discriminatory practices during the interview process. It is a good idea to become familiar with its guidelines and to be aware of changes (which occur frequently).

As an interviewer, you must adhere to two general legal requirements: the same basic questions must be posed to all candidates, and all questions (even those touching on personal qualities, goals, hobbies, affiliations) must be job related. Technically, questions that touch on personal or non-work-related issues are not illegal in themselves; it is the interviewer's action on the information that constitutes discriminatory hiring practice.

5. E. P. Kelly and R. J. Alberts, "Americans with Disabilities Act: Undue Hardship for Private Sector Employers?" *Labor Law Journal* 41 (1990), 675–684.
6. K. E. Buckner, H. S. Field, and W. H. Holley, "The Relationship of Legal Case Characteristics with the Outcomes of Personnel Selection Court Cases," *Labor Law Journal* 41 (1990), 31–40.

An additional aspect of employment interviewing and of the law has significant implications for anyone responsible for conducting employment interviews. A flurry of lawsuits by customers, clients, and coworkers accusing companies of negligent hiring practices have been introduced in court. A plaintiff in Texas, for example, won a $4.5 million suit against a taxi company when she was abducted and raped by one of the company's drivers.[7] The court found that the company was negligent in hiring this driver because he had a criminal record prior to his employment with the company. In other words, the company should have known about his past and should not have hired him in the first place.

A situation like that is difficult for employers, especially if they are committed to protecting the rights of interviewees. But employers who base a hiring decision on incomplete information are leaving themselves open to litigation. Again, the best course of action is to be an effective interviewer: ask legal questions that elicit valuable information from a job candidate, and check references.

Anxiety Management

Although the interviewee feels most of the anxiety in an interview situation, the interviewer is also anxious. Finding the best candidate for a job is an enormous responsibility. The candidate hired will reflect the decision-making ability of the interviewer. Being prepared with a list of questions and researching the interviewee can relieve anxiety for the interviewer. Providing a comfortable environment to relax the prospective employee can also reduce the interviewer's nervousness.

Creating a Comfortable Atmosphere Nervous candidates are less likely to open up and fully disclose the information you need to accurately assess them for a job. An atmosphere in which candidates feel comfortable talking about themselves and their career goals is therefore essential. How do you establish one?

Begin by looking at the setting where the interview will take place. Is the office drab, sterile, or uninviting? If so, you may get responses to match. One interviewer we know has a very small, poorly lit, and crowded office, so when he interviews someone for a job, he reserves a conference room that is wood paneled, well lit, and comfortable.

Positive communication can also decrease a candidate's nervousness and put him or her at ease. When a candidate first comes in, smile, introduce yourself by name and title, engage in direct eye contact, shake hands, and express sincere interest and attention. Once seated, provide a succinct orientation to the interview. Include a brief recap of the job description and expected responsibilities, an overview of the questions that you will be asking, and some indication of approximately how long the interview will last. This information puts candidates at ease by letting them know what is ahead.

Sequencing Questions Within the general boundaries of your list of questions, plan questions in a sequence that accomplishes a specific goal. For example, asking opening questions about topics that seem particularly outstanding on a candidate's résumé is an effective way to help the candidate get over any anxiety and focus on relevant matters. Difficult and thought-provoking questions are usually best posed after a candidate has warmed up. Table 9.1 lists a variety of questions that might be used during an employment interview.

7. C. S. Atwood and J. M. Neel, "New Lawsuits Expand Employer Liability," *HRMagazine* 35 (1990), 74–75.

TABLE 9.1

Employment Interview Questions

Closed questions	Would you describe yourself as a people person or an individualist? Are you more interested in a career in marketing or in corporate communications? Did you know the salary for this job is $40,000?
Open questions	Why did you major in ________ ? How did college prepare you for the real world? What are your immediate and long-term career goals?
Hypothetical questions	How would you handle a hostile coworker? What would you do if a customer demanded a refund and you were not authorized to give one? How would you resolve conflicting demands on your time by department managers?
Probing questions	Why? Could you elaborate on your decision? What happened next? Who else was involved in the project?
Mirror questions	So, you're saying that salary is less important than flexible work arrangements? Did I hear you correctly in that you would be willing to travel four to five times a month? Let me be sure I understand you; you can't begin work until January?

Select an interview style that is best for the situation. A nondirective style allows a great deal of flexibility in the choice and order of questions; as a result, you may not ask all questions of all interviewees. A nondirective approach can decrease an interviewee's defensiveness or anxiety but increase an interviewer's tendency to talk and instances of inconsistency from one interview to the next.

A directive approach (which, as we discussed in Chapter 8, can range from nonscheduled to highly scheduled, standardized) provides the interviewer with more control. A moderately scheduled approach, which allows the interviewee some discretion in responding, lets the interviewer maintain control over the interview but helps the interviewee to feel comfortable about the process.

In a highly scheduled, standardized approach, all questions are asked of all candidates in exactly the same way and in the same order. This approach allows complete control by the interviewer, and consistency of responses is maintained for all interviewees. But it can produce the most nervousness for the interviewee and does not allow much room for improvisation by the interviewer.

It is occasionally helpful to invite interviewees to ask questions about the position as they understand it. In rare instances, after hearing your orientation, a candidate may realize that the job is not really what she or he had in mind, and you can end the interview and save yourself quite a bit of time. Asking questions allows candidates to clear up ambiguities about the position and makes them more relaxed and confident for the remainder of the interview. The key to effective interviewing is to have interviewees reveal direct and honest information about themselves.

Closing the Interview An effective closing has three parts. The first part consists of any final questions that the candidate may have. Asking questions gives the candidate a chance to clear up any remaining uncertainties about the position. It also gives you a chance to see how interested the candidate is in the position. Candidates without any questions may be using the interview as a warm-up for other interviews, or they may have decided during the course of the interview that the job is not for them.

The second part of the closing is a summary of the main issues discussed in the interview. Recap the main points about skills, responsibilities, scheduling, or other technical details, and give the candidate some indication of how the decision to fill the position will be made and when—for example, "I will report my findings to the personnel committee, and the final three candidates will be asked to come in for a second interview, which will be held the week of March 20." Keep in mind that summarizing gives the candidate a sense of closure and accomplishment.

The third part is the reestablishing of rapport. Thank the candidate for his or her time, shake hands, and make sure the candidate knows the way out of the office. Reestablishing rapport at the end of the interview creates a positive impression of you and your company.

Evaluating Candidates

As an interviewer, you are required by law to keep an accurate record of each interview. One way to do this is to complete a standardized evaluation of each interviewee.

Once the interviews are over, list areas of expertise and personal characteristics that are most important for the position. Although your review of the job in an earlier step accomplished this, the interviewing process may have modified your expectations. Rank each candidate either quantitatively (on a scale of one to ten) or qualitatively (poor to excellent) in each area. Complete the evaluation immediately after concluding the interview—your memory is subject to unintentional distortions or revisions over time. Figure 9.1 shows a typical employment interview evaluation form.

Check to see that information gained in the interview supports information on the résumé or cover letter. For example, a candidate may have listed programming skills on her résumé but when asked about them in the interview was vague and displayed only rudimentary knowledge.

Evaluation is a difficult task. If several candidates demonstrate excellent potential as future employees, hard decisions and choices must be made during this stage. Base your final ranking of the candidates on an objective comparison of the job's priorities with the strengths and weaknesses of the interviewees.

EMPLOYMENT INTERVIEWS: THE INTERVIEWEE

Early in your career, especially during your initial pursuit of a job after graduation, your role in an interview will be that of the interviewee. Knowing the elements of the strategic communication model will help you to establish effective interviewing skills.

Just about every survey of personnel directors and potential employers reveals their preference for job candidates who possess strong communication skills. For example, the National Association of Colleges and Universities released some recent findings indicating the top five qualities employers are seeking:

1. Communication skills (verbal and written)
2. Honesty/integrity

FIGURE 9.1

Standard Employment Interviewee Evaluation Form

Completing a standard evaluation form after each candidate's interview allows the interviewer to more fairly compare and rank a number of candidates.

Poor (P), Fair (F), Average (A), Good (G), Outstanding (O)

INTERVIEW WORK SHEET

Applicant's name ____________________ Interviewer ____________________
Last name

Internal _____ External _____ Other _____
Identify

Position(s) best qualified for: 1. ____________________ 2. ____________________

Type of Interview
❑ Screening
❑ For a specific job
❑ Other

Salary discussed? Yes ___ No ___ If so, range quoted: ____________
Earliest starting date ________ Interview availability ____________
Special instructions for contacting applicant (if any) ____________
Was the employment application completed? Yes ___ No ___

	P	F	A	G	O	*Interviewer's specific comments* (use back if necessary)
Communication skills						
Motivation						
Analytical skills						
Personal qualities						
Experience						
Reference and/or performance evaluation						
Other skills or impressions						

Overall evaluation of applicant: ___ Outstanding (we should make extra effort to remember and place)
___ Above average (probably able to do a good job)
___ Below average

Referrals: (Use back if necessary)
Unit *Supervisor* *Date*

3. Teamwork skills
4. Interpersonal skills
5. Motivation/initiative

Notice that three of these are direct communication skills you are learning in this course, and the other two are revealed through communication skills. The key to impressing prospective employers is communicating that you are skilled in each of the communication qualities. The way to accomplish this goal is by writing a competent résumé and cover letter and then by demonstrating your competence in the interview process.

Goal Setting

Although you may have secondary goals in an interview, such as acquiring a decent salary, your primary goal is to be offered a position with the organization. Achieving this goal requires situational knowledge of what to do before the interview and how to communicate effectively during the interview.

Situational Knowledge

Understanding your responsibilities as an interviewee is the first step to a successful interview. The work you do prior to an interview can be as important as the interview itself. This type of preparation requires your obtaining situational knowledge about yourself and the organization and written documentation.

A number of steps, procedures, rules, and behaviors are associated with the interviewee role. Indeed, much of your work in performing this role occurs before you ever shake hands with an interviewer. If you want to impress wary, experienced, and professional interviewers, you have to do your homework.

Developing a Personal Biography The first responsibility of an interviewee is to develop a personal biography containing information that may be relevant or interesting to a potential employer. Working on a personal biography may simplify the task of preparing your résumé later on.

Educational experience is a major section in any personal biography. Most employers are interested only in your most recent educational experiences—that is, college or graduate school as opposed to high school or junior high. Another essential section of any personal biography is work experience. List your jobs in reverse chronological order, starting with the most recent one. For each job, write down the following information: the employer's name, address, and phone number; position held; job description; salary history; supervisor's name; reason for leaving; and inclusive dates of employment.

Employers are always interested in the organizational activities in which you participate. Similar to extracurricular activities in school, organizational activities are those involving civic, religious, fraternal, philanthropic, or social organizations.

In a separate section include your hobbies, interests, and special skills. Employers know how important they can be to job success and usually ask about them in an interview. Try to make definite connections between your hobbies, interests, and skills and the job you seek. For example, musical skill or participation in musical events often indicates creativity, persistent practice, and even teamwork. One interviewer was particularly impressed when he learned that a job candidate traced family ancestries as a hobby because the company was about to launch new products for people older than sixty, who are generally interested in family histories.

Having comprehensive information about yourself will be a great help when you have to write a résumé and cover letter for a job you are interested in. Creating a personal biography may seem like a lot of work with little payoff, but we can assure you that the time you spend is worthwhile. This information can be used not only for your résumé but also to help you remember personal characteristics that are likely to be probed in an interview.

Researching the Company Once you have identified the organizations that interest you, learn as much about them as possible so that you have a sense of whether

Where Do You Stand?

Lying to Get a Job

How far, if at all, would you be willing to stretch the truth to get a job? How would you react if you hired someone and later found out the individual had misled you in the interview?

Research has demonstrated that as many as two-thirds of all job candidates lie on their job applications. Others engage in deception during the interview with an employer. Beyond the ethical problems of lying to others, what happens when you are asked to follow up on the information you lied about once you are in the job? Will you tell additional lies to cover up the first lie?

Lying to coworkers or even potential coworkers carries severe potential ramifications. If you are found out, many companies will terminate you and refuse to give you a positive recommendation for other positions.

Avoid deception during the interview process.

---

your values are compatible with theirs and can tailor your résumé to the positions available. In addition, researching a company will give you detailed knowledge that you can demonstrate in the employment interview. A job seeker who wanted to land a job at a major fundraising organization checked through business journals to find out which organizations had made large contributions recently and complimented his interviewer on those successes. There is nothing so impressive as a job candidate who cares enough about the job or organization to become familiar with it before the interview. And knowing about the company can increase your self-confidence about your ability to fit its needs.

Getting information about companies is not difficult. Much can be learned from the following sources:

School placement offices
On-campus recruiter presentations
Brokerage offices
The company's public relations department
Present or past employees
Macmillan's Directory of Leading Private Companies
Career Guide to Professional Organizations
American Society of Training and Development Directory
Dun & Bradstreet's Million Dollar Directory
Standard & Poor's Directory
Issues of *Forbes, Fortune, Business Week, Money, Inc.*, and the *Wall Street Journal*
Various on-line sources, such as the Step-by-Step Guide to Researching Companies (www.quintcareers.com/researching_companies_guide.html) or Business Week On-Line's Company Research (http://bwnt.businessweek.com/company/search.asp)

Preparing a Résumé and Cover Letter It is best to prepare the résumé and cover letter after you have done your research on a company. In this way, you can design these documents to reveal relevant personal strengths and genuine interest in the company. All too often, job candidates prepare only one résumé and cover letter, save them on a computer, find some jobs to apply for, change the company name and address on the cover letter, and send the same documents to every company to which they apply. This type of generic job search deprives you of the opportunity to demonstrate your uniqueness. Base your résumé and cover letter on your personal biography and on specific information about each company that you have researched.

Résumés should generally be one page long and never longer than two pages. For individuals with more money than time, there are literally hundreds of résumé services that can provide advice about preparing résumés, but we want to discourage you from using them. Doing your résumé yourself can give you the self-knowledge and self-confidence necessary to make a difference in an interview.

Most résumés include basic and essential information such as your career objectives, educational background, and work experience. Although this information will not change from one job application to the next, the manner in which it is presented may vary. For example, if an organization emphasizes teamwork, you will want to relate your experiences to team efforts; if a company values creativity, you will want to present your information as creative innovations or ideas. Often, information can be worded in such a way as to highlight its relevance to a specific organization.

Although the information is likely to be presented differently to different organizations, the résumé must be readable at a glance. Cluttered, confusing, and disorganized résumés probably will not make it past the first reader. Résumés should be concise, well organized, neat, and error free. Some organizations will not consider a candidate whose résumé has even one typographical, grammatical, or printing error. Here are some résumé basics based on research from hiring professionals:[8]

- *Identify your job objective.* At the top of the résumé, state your goal and the skills that directly demonstrate your qualifications for the job. In short, energetic phrases, spell out the area in which you wish to work.
- *Specify education.* Give names of institutions, major fields of study, and dates of attendance. Begin with your most recent educational experiences. Include continuing education classes or training classes if they are relevant. Mention academic awards or honors, such as membership in an honor society.
- *State work experience.* Along with your educational background, employers find work experience to be the most valuable piece of information about you. Most employers want to see your previous jobs listed in reverse chronological order (most recent first). They will be most interested in full-time positions, especially those with supervisory or leadership roles.
- *Include school projects or volunteer achievements, especially if they include leadership positions.* Especially for new graduates, the skills and responsibilities used in these contexts can substitute for a lack of formal work experience.
- *Do not cite personal characteristics.* Your experience and achievements will imply relevant personal qualities such as leadership, ability to work with others, and resourcefulness. There is no need to repeat them in a separate section. Listing other personal characteristics such as your age, race, height, weight, or marital status is also unnecessary.

8. K. Hutchinson and D. Brefka, "Personnel Administrators' Preferences for Résumé Content: Ten Years After," *Business Communication Quarterly* 60 (1997), 67+. Retrieved from Questia, October 15, 2003.

FIGURE 9.2

Basic Résumé Format
This format organizes "experience" using a chronological listing of jobs and responsibilities.

Barbara Dominco

Present Address	Permanent Address
1100 Woodbury Road	35 Marshall Avenue
Philadelphia, PA 19235	Eau Claire, WI 12345
Phone: (215) 936-1744	Phone: (423) 671-5783

OBJECTIVE	Public relations or marketing position requiring strong communication skills, creativity, and computer experience
EDUCATION	Temple University, Philadelphia, Pennsylvania Bachelor of Arts degree 2001 Major in business with emphasis on marketing, public relations, and organizational communication GPA: 3.5 cumulative; 3.7 in major Elected to Alpha Chi student honor society
EXPERIENCE	
September 2003 to present	**Public Relations Assistant,** Temple University, Philadelphia, Pennsylvania Assisted director of Public Relations in development campaign. Researched potential donors and wrote direct-mail correspondence. Participated in annual fundraising telethon.
May 1999 to August 2003	**Customer Service Representative,** Mellon Bank, Philadelphia, Pennsylvania Wrote a series of 15 "Answers to Common Questions" brochures for customers' questions about banking services. Used computer database to analyze customer needs and concerns.
Oct. 1997 to May 1999	**Manager/Sales Clerk,** Strawbridge's, Philadelphia, Pennsylvania Scheduled cashiers and other personnel and worked on merchandise inventories. Provided customer service and set up displays.
ACTIVITIES	
1998 to 2001	**Classified Editor,** *The Temple Times,* Temple University Layout staff 1998–2001 Used desktop publishing techniques to design and produce classified pages. Supervised five staff members.
2000 to 2001	**Chair,** United Way Student Volunteer Committee Member, 2000–2001. Organized campus-wide Volunteer Day. Participated in community rehabilitation projects.
SKILLS	WordPerfect and Microsoft Excel on PC and Macintosh computers Desktop publishing Typing (approximately 60 wpm) Fluent in Spanish
REFERENCES	Available on request

FIGURE 9.3

Functional Résumé Format

This format contains a chronological listing of jobs/responsibilities, but also highlights general skills and areas of strength.

Gervase Jackson
34 Waverly Street
Houston, Texas 77592
(806) 862-9913

CAREER GOAL	To obtain a sales position leading to management that utilizes strong communication and marketing skills.
SALES AND MARKETING	Managed over twenty accounts for large music club. Developed promotional campaigns for new product lines. Increased sales by $240,000 in nine-month period.
ADMINISTRATION	Implemented and supervised office records. Coordinated purchase orders and prepared contracts. Handled customer service training program for telemarketing employees.
WORK HISTORY	
2000–2004	Account Manager, SuperDisc Compact Disc Club, Houston, Texas
1999–2000	Telemarketing Coordinator, SuperDisc Compact Disc Club, Houston, Texas
1997–1999	Telemarketer, SuperDisc Compact Disc Club, Houston, Texas
EDUCATION	
2000	Certified by International Association of Business Communications
1997	Colorado State University, Fort Collins, Colorado, B.A. in English
REFERENCES	Available on request

- *References.* Simply state, "Available on request." An employer who is interested will be sure to ask for names. Applicants should be able to produce a list of references—including name, company and position, contact information, relationship, and years known—immediately when asked. Therefore, one should bring this list, prepared in presentable format, to the interview. Lastly, be sure to contact each person beforehand to ask if he or she is comfortable giving you a positive reference.

Figures 9.2 and 9.3 show two résumé formats attractive to organizations.[9] Figure 9.2 shows a résumé organized according to specific jobs and activities. Figure 9.3 shows a functional résumé, which highlights general skills and areas of strength. Functional résumés are generally used by people who have extensive experience in numerous jobs or by people who are applying for a job in a new field and need to call attention to their relevant skills.

9. Résumé formats based on J.T. Bostwick, *The Perfect Résumé* (New York: Doubleday, 1990).

Cover letters should begin with a specific, impressive paragraph. It is essential to grab the reader's attention, get him or her excited about looking at your résumé, and create the impression that you will be a valuable asset to his or her organization without actually using those words. Here is an example of a successful opening paragraph: "My experience in volunteer community work has provided me with the communication, management, and organizational skills required for the position of assistant to the public relations manager. During the past four years, I have designed and organized three fundraising campaigns for local hospitals that have brought in more than $450,000."

The body of the letter should specifically tell the reader what position you are applying for and briefly mention one or two accomplishments that demonstrate your qualifications. Indicate how you learned about the position and whom you know as a contact at the company. Close with specific language, such as "I will be in Houston on November 8 and would like to arrange an appointment" or "I will call on Thursday, May 22, to set up a time for an interview." Figure 9.4 shows an effective cover letter for the résumé presented in Figure 9.2.

Résumés and cover letters must be neat and printed or typed on high-quality paper (usually white, gray, or ivory bond paper with 25 or 40 percent cotton content). Make sure the print is dark and clear with no smudges. Give your current address and phone number on the cover letter just in case the résumé is lost.

STRATEGIC SKILLS

*Do's and Don'ts of Résumé Preparation**

Do's	***Don'ts***
Be honest.	Avoid using personal pronouns.
Prepare a flawless résumé.	Avoid unusual type styles or fonts.
Be concise. Use an abbreviated style of writing.	Don't use italics, underlining, or shadows.
Be positive in presenting information.	Avoid unusually colored paper.
Limit résumé to 1–2 pages.	Limit abbreviations and acronyms.
Use common headings (e.g., Education, Work History, References).	Don't include personal information except phone number and address.
Use action verbs (e.g., *managed, analyzed, sold, improved*).	Avoid reference to specific religious or political organizations unless they are job related.
Have multiple people read it for style, accuracy, and form.	Don't submit résumé without a cover letter.
Tailor the résumé for specific jobs.	Do not use borders.

* Partially based on material from the following sources: W. Baker, K. DeTienne, & K. Smart, "How Fortune 500 Companies Are Using Electronic Résumé Management Systems," *Business Communication Quarterly* 61 (1998), 8+, retrieved from Questia October 16, 2003; "Résumé Checklist," Champlain College, http://campus.champlain.edu/careerplan/current_students/handbook/resume_check.php; "Résumé Turnons and Turnoffs: What Readers Do and Don't Like," http://www.rcjobs.com/seeker-resources/resume _turnons.html. (Accessed October 13, 2003).

TECHNOLOGY TOOLS

On-Line Job Banks, On-Line Résumé Banks

The Internet has made it easier for employers and job seekers to find one another. A large number of on-line businesses offer services including job postings, helpful hints, résumé databases, and application tracking services. Never before has the employment process been so widespread and diverse. Instead of buying a newspaper and looking for positions in your local area, you can go on-line and search for positions in any city in the United States—or in the world for that matter. Although there are a large number of job sites to choose from, we have listed three of the more popular ones to get you started. Go on-line and investigate the opportunities offered by these services.

- Monster.com—http://www.monster.com Perhaps the most famous of job sites, due in no small part to its advertising campaigns, monster.com is a commercial Web site that offers a database where you can post and update your résumé, converse with others in chat rooms, read relevant articles in its newsletter, and click on pages offering career advice.

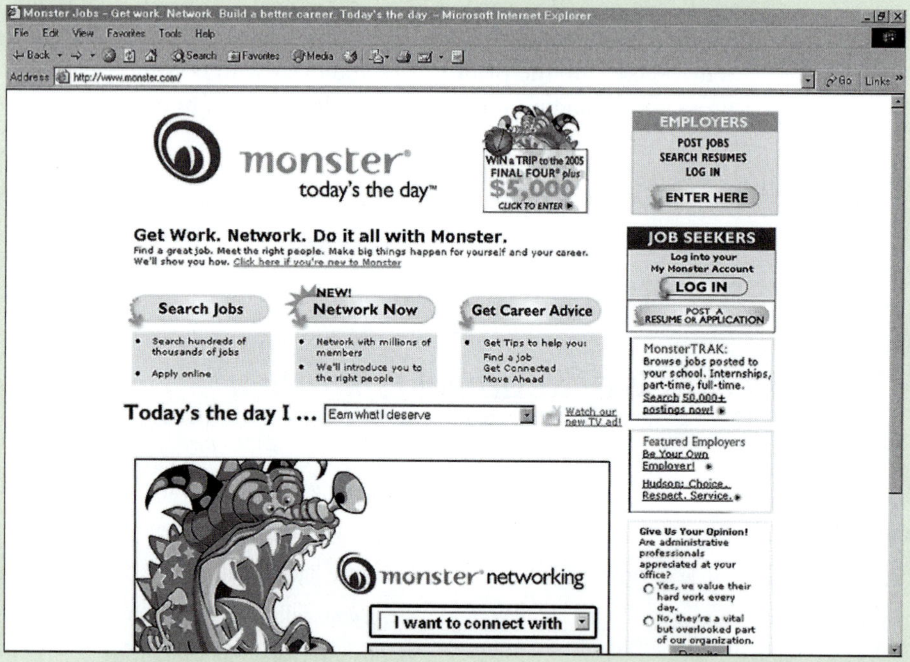

Reprinted with permission.

- American Jobs—http://www.americanjobs.com As you will quickly determine from visiting this site, American Jobs is more streamlined than other sites, but it offers an enormous database of jobs. It is reported to record more than 6 million hits per month by job seekers and employers. It is probably worth the time to access this popular Web site for jobs.
- America's Job Bank—http://www.ajb.dni.us This job site is a public service partnership of the U.S. Department of Labor and each of the states' employment service. As part of a comprehensive job-search service, this site allows you to post your résumé and cover letter, track job searches, and develop an individualized career account. The site also offers on-line training and education programs for the job seeker. Over a million jobs are normally posted at this site.

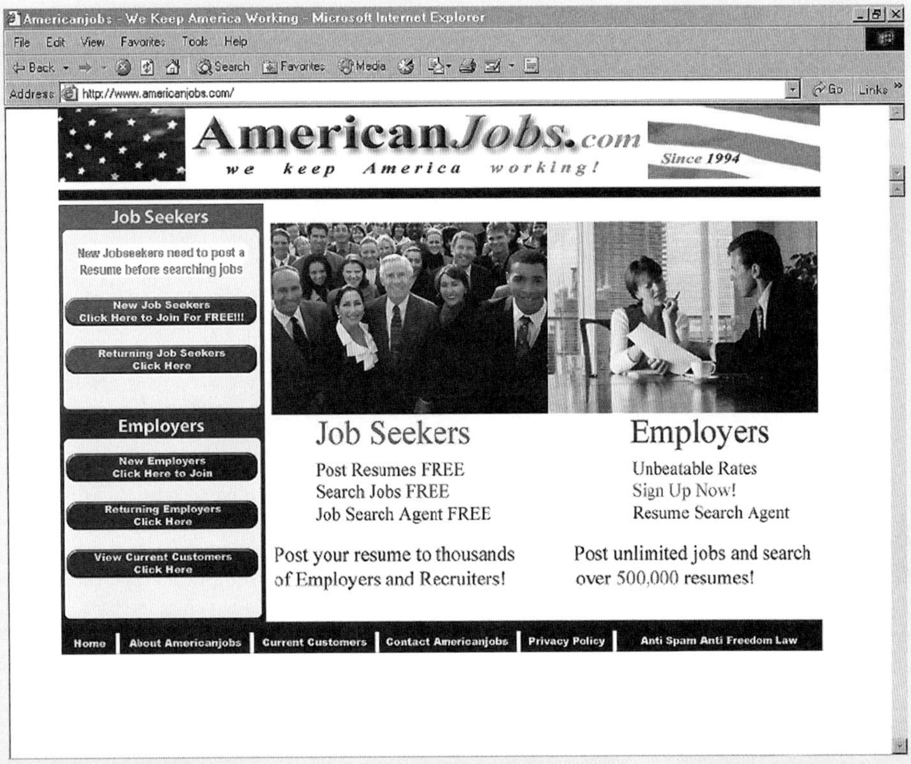

Reprinted with permission.

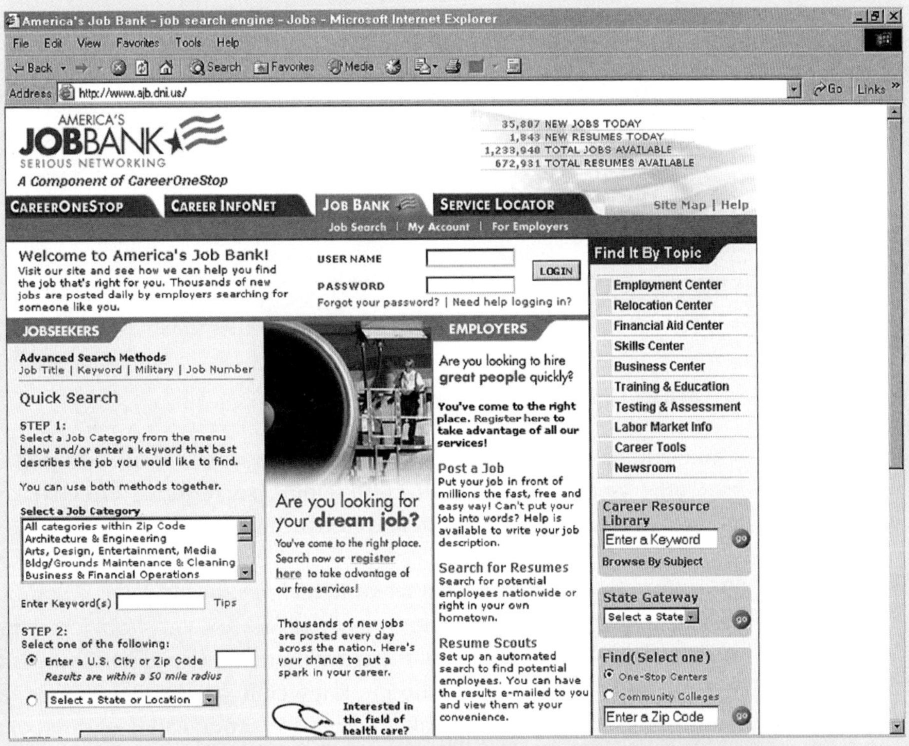

FIGURE 9.4

Sample Cover Letter

A strong cover letter is an important complement to the résumé.

1100 Woodbury Road
Philadelphia, PA 19235
March 24, 2002

Mr. Harold Britten
Personnel Manager
195 Hennepin Ave.
Phillips-Margolis Company
Minneapolis, MN 55213

Dear Mr. Britten:

Please accept this letter and the enclosed résumé as application for the position of assistant marketing manager at Phillips-Margolis. The Director of Public Relations at Temple University, George Holton, suggested that I contact you about the position as it is appropriate for someone with my background, experience, and interest in the area.

While at Temple University, I have balanced academic success in marketing and communication with real world experience. As a public relations assistant, I produced a direct mail campaign that raised over $238,000 with a response rate of 7 percent—compared with the previous year's 3 percent. As a customer service representative, I used computers for writing and producing brochures, news releases, and promotional materials as well as for research. As a sales clerk in a major department store, I shared rotating management and scheduling duties with a staff of three in my department.

My immediate goal is to apply this experience to the needs of Phillips-Margolis upon my graduation this May. I would like to meet with you to discuss my qualifications for the position. I will call you the week of April 2 to arrange an appointment. If you wish to contact me before that time, please call me at (215) 936-1744.

Thank you for your consideration.

Sincerely,

Barbara Dominco

Barbara Dominco

enc: résumé

Communication Competence

Once you have been invited for an interview, you will need to present yourself as a potential asset to the organization. Doing so requires effective and appropriate communication—both verbal and nonverbal.

Dressing Appropriately Just as your résumé should have a competent, neat, professional image, so should you. One of the first and most obvious ways in which you will make an impression is by the way you dress. The general rule is that you should match the style of dress of the interviewer. If you have a chance to visit the company before your interview, take note of the general style of dress of the employees. If you cannot visit before your interview but know someone who works for the

STRATEGIC SKILLS

Preparing for Your Interview

Preparing to answer questions requires thought. You can safely assume that some of the following boilerplate questions will be asked. How might you respond to these sorts of questions?

1. Describe a typical day in your current (or last) job. What are (were) your major responsibilities?
2. What are some of the things in your job that you have done particularly well?
3. What are some of the problems that you encounter in your job? What frustrates you the most? What do you do about it?
4. How has your present job prepared you to take on greater responsibilities?
5. What interests you about this position? To what kind of position would you expect to progress?
6. What are some of your reasons for leaving your current (last) job?
7. How would your last employer rate your job performance? What would he or she say you did well? What would be criticized?
8. How would you define an ideal work environment?
9. What are some of the things you would like to avoid in a job? Why?
10. What are your long-range goals?
11. What would you look for in an ideal supervisor?
12. How do you define success in your work?
13. What motivates you on the job?
14. Why do you want to work for us?
15. What did you think of your old boss?
16. What kind of salary are you looking for?
17. Do you like to work overtime?
18. Are you satisfied with your career at this point?
19. What has been the single most important professional experience of your life?
20. Why should we hire you?

This list could go on indefinitely but essentially covers four major categories: (1) Why are you here? (2) What can you do for us? (3) What kind of person are you? (4) How much will you cost us?

company, ask what the standard attire is. If visiting or making inquiries is impossible, use these general guidelines (see Chapter 5 for more specific information): for professional positions, dress conservatively (dark suits, white shirts/blouses, standard ties/ribbon ties, dark socks/neutral hose, dark shoes). You really cannot go wrong with that attire. Wear clothes that fit and are comfortable but not casual.

Preparing to Ask and Answer Questions Once you have been invited for an interview, prepare for your performance. The first step is devising questions that elicit information about the company that you were unable to obtain through your research. Arrange your questions so that the most important ones come first because you may not get a chance to ask all your questions during the interview. If some questions are answered spontaneously during the course of the interview, mentally move down your list to a question that has not yet been answered. Preparing and asking questions provides you with insight into the company, shows your interest in the job, and demonstrates communication skills. Inquisitive interviewees seem competent to interviewers.

Although interviewers may find hundreds of ways to phrase questions, the four critical areas listed in the Strategic Skills box on page 253 are of most interest to them. Your responses during the interview (regardless of how the specific questions are phrased) should be candid, well organized, incisive, relevant, to the point, and positive. It is fine to volunteer some negatives, especially in the context of challenges you have met or problems you have resolved. When responding, avoid making disorganized or irrelevant statements, evading or rationalizing, being overly critical of others, changing the subject or giving many unimportant details, talking only of favorable points, or making bad jokes. The following dialogues show weak and strong responses to basic questions, beginning with weak responses:

QUESTION: Describe a typical day in your current job. What are your major responsibilities?

ANSWER: Well, every day is different, so it sort of depends on the whim of my supervisor. You know, I really think that my skill in word processing would fit your company's needs. That's something I do a lot. Most of the time, I hardly make any errors, except for spelling, but I can always use a spell-checker. In fact, I think people who can't take advantage of computer technology are out of place in today's business environment.

QUESTION: I see. What other computer skills do you use in your job?

ANSWER: We use a database and spreadsheet to prepare budget reports, and the publications department produces a newsletter through desktop publishing.

QUESTION: How often do you prepare budget reports?

ANSWER: Ummm . . . That isn't exactly part of my job, although I am responsible for requesting funds for my department. It's a very important responsibility.

The interviewee has (intentionally or unintentionally) changed the subject, given a disorganized response, implied criticism of her or his current supervisor, given irrelevant details, and implied possession of skills not actually acquired.

Starting from the same question, the following exchange illustrates strong interviewee responses:

QUESTION: Describe a typical day in your current job. What are your major responsibilities?

ANSWER: Well, I am responsible for scheduling meetings in my department, so the first thing I do every morning is check the schedule to review upcoming meetings. I then prepare and distribute agendas for the meetings.

QUESTION: How do you do that?

ANSWER: These agendas are based on notes given to me by the department supervisor, who generally does a good job of getting me the necessary information early enough so that I can contact everyone who will attend the meeting. Recently, I have been doing a lot of the background research and preparation myself.

QUESTION: What do you find most challenging about this responsibility?

ANSWER: It is difficult to get people together, and I am sometimes frustrated when others don't seem to care about meetings that I have spent a lot of time trying to organize. Overall, though, I feel that this responsibility has taught me a lot about communicating with a variety of people, following up on messages, and working out conflicting interests and goals in order to find convenient times for people to meet.

The interviewee answers the questions asked, giving relevant, detailed responses. She or he volunteers some negative information in a candid way but in general speaks well of coworkers. The responses are well organized, describing a task and the skills necessary to accomplish it.

Listening and Utilizing Nonverbal Communication Skills Although you may be tempted to focus on responding to questions as the central interviewing skill, listening and nonverbal behavior can strengthen and improve your responses. During the interview, listen carefully to the entire question before responding. Pause briefly before answering questions. Doing so gives you a chance to formulate your response and indicates to the interviewer that you are developing a considered response. Focus on the content of the response, and speak with confidence. Always look the interviewer in the eye when responding. If you are asked a question that you cannot answer, simply say so and do not act embarrassed. An interviewer has more respect for an interviewee who admits to ignorance than for one who tries to fake an answer.

Handling Discriminatory Questions An interviewer may ask a question such as "What would your spouse think about relocating to the Southwest?" In an attempt to get a "complete" profile of a candidate, interviewers may purposely or unknowingly pose questions that are illegal. What do you do when asked an illegal question? You have several choices. You can answer it and hope to get the job. You can refuse to answer it on the grounds that it is illegal and risk losing out on a job offer. You can respond, "I'm sorry, but my spouse's opinion about relocating is not a bona

ETHICAL ISSUES

Equal Employment Opportunity Laws Protect Against Discrimination

The federal government has gone to great lengths to ensure that the hiring process is handled in nondiscriminatory ways. Three laws have been enacted to protect certain groups from employment discrimination:

- Title VII of the Civil Rights Act of 1964
- Americans with Disabilities Act (ADA) of 1990
- Age Discrimination in Employment Act of 1967 (ADEA)

For the most part, employers can remain in compliance with these laws if they ask questions of applicants/interviewees that are related to bona fide occupation qualifications (BFOQs). Below is a list of questions that are sometimes asked (legally and illegally) in job interviews.* Test your knowledge of questions that are and are not BFOQs.

1. Are you currently married? Legal Illegal
2. What is your current compensation? Legal Illegal
3. What is your birth date? Legal Illegal
4. How well did you get along with your previous employer? Legal Illegal
5. Do you have any physical limitations? Legal Illegal
6. What kinds of things do you do when you are not at work? Legal Illegal
7. Do you currently have trouble with drug or alcohol abuse? Legal Illegal
8. Why did you leave your previous employer? Legal Illegal
9. Who lives in your household? Legal Illegal
10. Where do you see yourself in the next five years? Legal Illegal

Answers: 1. Illegal—violates Title VII of the Civil Rights Act. 2. Legal. 3. Illegal—violates the Age Discrimination Act. 4. Legal. 5. Illegal—violates Title I of the Americans with Disabilities Act. 6. Illegal—not BFOQ. 7. Illegal—violates Title VII of the Civil Rights Act. 8. Legal. 9. Illegal—violates Title VII of the Civil Rights Act. 10. Legal

* R. D. Clarke, "None of your business," *Black Enterprise* [on-line] 30:(2), (September 1999): http://web7/infotract.galegroup.com (accessed on July 19, 2000).

fide occupation qualification, so I'm not going to answer that question." Such a reply, however, is not likely to promote good relations between you and the interviewer, especially if she or he was merely trying to be friendly.

The best way to handle marginal or illegal questions is to politely put the ball back in the interviewer's court. For example, if you are asked, "Do you have any small children at home?" you can respond, "I understand your concern about identifying possible obstacles to my commitment to the job, but be assured that I am fully prepared and qualified for the tasks and responsibilities involved and have the ability to manage my time effectively." In this case, you are answering an unasked question that reflects the interviewer's real concern.

If a job applicant thinks she or he has been discriminated against during the hiring process and can provide evidence of such discrimination, the law requires the employer to prove that no discrimination took place.[10] It is often difficult for the employer to do this. If you feel that you have legitimate cause for complaint and were unsuccessful in alerting the employer to illegal interviewing or hiring practices, the courts provide a last resort.

Judging the Success of the Interview Process You might be tempted to think that getting hired is the ultimate test of your interviewing skills. Getting a job is obviously an important goal of this process. However, getting a position that is an appropriate "match" for you and the organization is the *ultimate* objective. Many people are offered positions below their education, experience, and talent level and then find themselves miserable from day 1. Others get in over their heads and experience job stress and burnout. In still other situations, the match is perfect but the employee quickly learns that the organization does not offer the type of climate and culture desired. Therefore, it is essential that you and the prospective employer learn as much about each other as possible.

Can you still be successful if you are not hired or decide to turn down an offer? Of course. Every interviewing situation is going to give you more knowledge, background, and experience in handling these challenging opportunities. You will grow and mature as an interviewee as a result of your experience.

Following Up the Interview The employment interview does not end when the candidate walks out of the interviewer's office. If you are sincerely interested in the company and the job, take the time to follow up the interview with a letter of thanks to the interviewer. Such a letter accomplishes several purposes. It demonstrates your enthusiasm for the job and the company. It also reflects excellent communication skills, provides the interviewer with additional feedback about you and your interview, and can serve as a reminder of your interview and set you apart from the crowd. Figure 9.5 shows a thank-you letter. Although the letter is short, it is important because it creates a favorable impression of you and demonstrates communication competence.

Anxiety Management

Anxiety is produced primarily by the interview. Anxiety or nervousness is normal during an interview. After all, the result of the interview will affect your future. However, there are some things you can do to manage your anxiety.

10. M. S. Weisel, "Employer's Burden of Proof in 'Mixed Motive' Title VII Litigation and Available Remedies: *Hopkins v. Price Waterhouse* One Year Later," *Labor Law Journal* 42 (1991), 45–51.

FIGURE 9.5

Sample Follow-Up Letter Interviewees should always promptly follow up an interview with a thank-you letter.

1100 Woodbury Road
Philadelphia, PA 19235
April 15, 2002

Mr. Harold Britten
Personnel Manager
195 Hennepin Ave.
Phillips-Margolis Company
Minneapolis, MN 55213

Dear Mr. Britten:

Thank you for taking the time to talk to me on Wednesday about the open sales position in your company. After learning more about your organization in our interview, I realize the great opportunity and satisfaction I would have working for your company. I feel that my skills are well coordinated with your company's values and expectations. I appreciate the time and consideration you have given me.

Sincerely,

Barbara Dominco

One of the best ways to reduce anxiety is to be prepared. Although you cannot be prepared for all possible questions, you can be prepared with answers for questions that are likely to be asked. Rehearse your answers to probable questions, but remember to be flexible during the interview and adapt to the interviewer's questions. You can also prepare a set of questions to ask about the company. Doing so can relieve the tension associated with fear of the unknown.

Another way to manage anxiety is to practice self-confidence. Reread your résumé, and concentrate on the positive qualities you possess. Think of your background and experiences as assets that you can bring to the company. Be confident about your ability to do the job for which you are applying.

During the interview, concentrate on putting the interviewer at ease. Once you see the interviewer becoming comfortable with talking, your nervousness will diminish. Managing anxiety is also easier if you appear friendly and open. Nonverbal cues, such as smiling and head nods, will help relax the tension you may feel.

APPRAISAL INTERVIEWS

The purpose of **appraisal interviews** is to evaluate employees' performances over a certain period of time, generally specified by company policy. Some companies schedule an appraisal interview once a year to determine pay raises. Others hold appraisal interviews to address complaints or evaluate the work of new employees. Well-conducted appraisal interviews provide feedback to employees about their performance. Supervisors who conduct such interviews also obtain feedback from employees who prefer a confidential atmosphere in which to discuss their concerns. In some organizations, the appraisal interview may be the only time that managers and employees sit down face-to-face to talk about job performance and responsibilities.

Goal Setting: Purposes of Appraisal Interviews

Appraisal interviews are often used to motivate workers. By reviewing performance standards and comparing standards to the employee's performance, managers can motivate employees to increase the quantity and improve the quality of their work. Appraisal interviews can also build morale. Workers who know how they are doing and who are encouraged to continue their progress are likely to feel good about the organization and develop positive attitudes about the workplace.

Situational Knowledge: Reviewing Performance

As a first step in the appraisal process, the manager reviews the performance of each employee. In many organizations, frequent appraisal interviews allow managers and employees to work consistently toward mutually understood goals. Files should document every noteworthy incident or behavior.

Before the evaluation, a thorough analysis of all pertinent information for each employee is conducted, and the employee is given a chance to provide personal input about the job objectives and his or her success at achieving them. During the evaluation, superiors may use preestablished criteria presented in a standardized format to judge the performance of each employee. Most evaluators rate performance factors that are elements of an employee's job description and that can be evaluated objectively according to some baseline measure. In advance of the evaluation period, the employee should be told on what factors she or he will be rated. Performance factors likely to be rated include the following:[11]

Punctuality	Responsibility
Initiative	Dependability
Job knowledge	Neatness
Creativity	Communication skills
Planning	Versatility
Cost control	Cooperation
Accuracy	Delegation skills
Leadership skills	Productivity
Organizational skills	Consistency

When managers use a qualitative rating system, they simply discuss each performance factor in a descriptive and evaluative manner. They may write paragraphs using adjectives to describe how they judge the employee's performance on each factor. More frequently, rating systems are quantitative, and the manager rates performance according to some numerical system. Some organizations use scales that range from one to five or one to ten. Other companies rank-order employees according to each relevant performance factor. Quantitative and qualitative ratings can be combined, and this approach is quite common in organizations. Employees receive a quantitative rating for each performance factor and a written explanation of the evaluation. Figure 9.6 shows an appraisal interview form.

11. C. W. Downs, G. P. Smeyak, and E. Martin, *Professional Interviewing* (New York: Harper & Row, 1980).

FIGURE 9.6

Sample Appraisal Interview Form

Merryhill Enterprises, Inc.

Performance Evaluation Form

This form is to be used to evaluate all employees biannually. The immediate supervisor will consider all relevant factors associated with an employee's job description and render an objective evaluation along two dimensions. A quantitative score will be given for each area covered as well as a written description stating particular details. Employees will have an opportunity to discuss their evaluations with the evaluating supervisor before the evaluation is forwarded to the personnel office for disposition.

Scoring: 1 = very poor performance; 5 = average performance; 10 = perfect performance.

Motivation Comments:	1 2 3 4 5 6 7 8 9 10
Job knowledge Comments:	1 2 3 4 5 6 7 8 9 10
Executive potential Comments:	1 2 3 4 5 6 7 8 9 10
Communication skills Comments:	1 2 3 4 5 6 7 8 9 10
Leadership skills Comments:	1 2 3 4 5 6 7 8 9 10
Delegation skills Comments:	1 2 3 4 5 6 7 8 9 10
Overall evaluation Comments:	1 2 3 4 5 6 7 8 9 10

What Would You Do?

Assume you are the branch manager of a national retail chain. Company policy dictates that appraisal interviews be conducted every six months. As you schedule appointments with employees, you notice that one employee seems exceptionally reluctant to establish a meeting time. When he arrives for the interview, he is anxious and hesitant. What nonverbal cues alert you to his nervousness? How can you build rapport with this employee without minimizing corrective feedback?

Communication Competence: Conducting the Interview

When the interviewee arrives, quickly establish rapport, and then move directly into the interview.[12] Briefly discuss the purpose of the performance appraisal and give an overview of what will be covered. After this orientation, present your evaluation. Go over each major area of performance, explaining how you arrived at your rating and detailing the evidence used in the evaluation. As you discuss each issue, use specific language and provide examples, such as "One of your job responsibilities is to schedule quarterly meetings of the accounting staff and to distribute each meeting's minutes to the branch offices, ensuring that the data are accurate, readable, and timely. You have provided comprehensive minutes with clarity and speed, and it is my opinion that you are ready to take on some additional responsibilities in analyzing the data. I understand that the data are complex, and we have to discuss methods for setting new goals in this area."

During the interview, be sure to encourage participation, feedback, and explanation. Some interviewees may not provide verbal input because of the anxiety or stress associated with evaluation, yet it is important for you to know how they feel about your evaluations. Ask for their self-evaluation for each performance factor. Ask them to rate themselves objectively but from their own points of view. You will be surprised at how often employees overrate and underrate themselves. Such information can serve as a discussion starter for communicating about how they view their jobs.

Feedback is a critical element in an appraisal interview, and the responsibility for giving and receiving it rests with both the supervisor and the employee. The aim of feedback is not to pass judgment but to report specific events or behavior, their effects, and what to do about them. Subjective interpretations by the supervisor or the employee should be minimized during the interview.

Two types of feedback are given during an appraisal interview. **Corrective feedback** attempts to alter negative or inappropriate behavior. To be effective, corrective feedback should be expressed in specific terms as much as possible. For example, "You did not prepare charts for the presentation yesterday as you were supposed to do" highlights a specific problem that must be addressed.

Supportive feedback encourages desirable behavior. Supportive feedback lets the employee know what he or she is doing right, and such knowledge is as

12. C. J. Stewart and W. B. Cash, *Interviewing: Principles and Practices,* 5th ed. (Dubuque, Iowa: Brown, 1988); Downs, Smeyak, and Martin, *Professional Interviewing;* J. P. Zima, *Interviewing: Key to Effective Management* (Chicago: Science Research Associates, 1983).

important to performance as being told about areas that need improvement. When an appraisal interviewer concentrates not only on correcting problems or identifying new responsibilities but also on good work—especially behavior that goes beyond the employee's personal and work goals and contributes to overall organizational goals—the employee is likely to strive for outstanding rather than merely acceptable performance. For example, "I'm pleased that you have learned to work on the new computer system and have helped other people to use it too" shows the employee that the supervisor noticed and appreciates his or her willingness to go beyond what is expected. Providing supportive feedback is an opportunity for the supervisor to thank the employee for good work. Supervisors are wise to use both supportive and corrective feedback to achieve maximum benefits from a performance review.[13]

The appraisal interview is an opportunity for employees to learn about what is expected and valued in their work and to let their supervisors know how the employees are doing as well. The employee listens carefully as the supervisor discusses and gives feedback on each performance factor, noting areas of strength (supportive feedback), weakness (a combination of supportive and corrective feedback), or special problems (corrective feedback).

Anxiety Management: Receiving Bad News

If you are being evaluated and you disagree with the supervisor's assessment, discuss your reaction in a calm and objective manner and offer to provide evidence to support your position if necessary. If the supervisor has made general statements about your performance, ask for specifics—both of you may learn from them. Be familiar with your organization's policies on appraisal interviews. Knowing these guidelines ensures responsible communication by both parties.

Setting Revised Goals

Once both parties have discussed each performance factor, set mutually derived goals for the next evaluation. Both interviewer and interviewee should identify elements of the job that are critical to employee and organizational productivity and should specify realistic goals. Mutual goal setting during the appraisal interview encourages employee participation in a significant decision-making process.

Finally, end the interview on a positive note. Summarize the interview and ask for additional comments, questions, and explanations from the interviewee. Reemphasize the importance of the performance appraisal process and encourage the employee to think positively about the next evaluation period. Appraisal interviews are meant to help employees and supervisors work well together.

When receiving an evaluation, make a sincere effort to understand the supervisor's viewpoint and plan to act on the mutually agreed-to goals. When employees and managers seriously and conscientiously participate in the appraisal process, it provides a valuable source of feedback that can lead to improvements in their work relationship.

13. H. Karp, "The Lost Art of Feedback," in J. W. Pfeiffer (ed.), *1987 Annual: Developing Human Resources* (San Diego, Calif.: University Associates, 1987), pp. 14–24; A. Gabor, "Catch a Falling Star System," *U.S. News & World Report*, June 5, 1984, pp. 43–45.

PRACTICING BUSINESS COMMUNICATION

Aegir Systems

Powerhouse entrepreneur Ella D. Williams used her one-on-one communication expertise and her intricate network of business contacts to create Aegir Systems, a full-service engineering and consulting firm, in 1980. AT&T has named Williams "Entrepreneur of the Year," *Working Woman* magazine has named her among "The Nation's Ten Most Admired Women Managers," and *Business Digest* has named her "Businessperson of the Year."

Based in Oxnard, California, Aegir has more than seventy employees and branch offices in Los Angeles and Virginia. Williams's skilled interviewing helps her hire capable people, inspire them to perform their best, and encourage them to take an active role in selling Aegir's expertise. That means polishing their own interpersonal skills. "It's been an introvert's nightmare for some of us," engineer Jim Cahill, Aegir's Los Angeles director of operations, told *Working Woman,* "but it's working."

ONE-ON-ONE SKILLS CREATE OPPORTUNITY

The idea for Aegir Systems crystallized in 1980. Five engineers at Hughes Aircraft, where Williams had worked for twelve years before she quit in 1976 to earn her college degree, signed on right away. But it took Williams three more years of interviewing and making presentations to potential clients to win Aegir's first multi-million-dollar defense contract.

Over the next ten years, government spending on defense dropped sharply. Williams knew that her client base was shrinking, so she steered Aegir toward private-sector, commercial clients. Today, Aegir works with clients in the transportation, environmental, facilities, information systems, and multimedia industries.

ONE-ON-ONE SKILLS BUILD BUSINESS

Contacts are as vital to Aegir's success today as they were to its founding. Organizations with which Aegir consistently works—consulting companies, state and city agencies, and the federal Departments of Defense and Transportation—are essential sources of new contracts. That makes effective communication with clients a strategic necessity.

When a larger consulting firm awarded Aegir a contract to address an engineering problem in a major city's mass transit system, a team of Aegir engineers held on-site interviews with transit staff, then worked with them and the larger consultant to develop and implement an effective solution.

DISCIPLINARY INTERVIEWS

One of the most sensitive areas of business and professional communication is discipline. Given the more than a million terminations that take place each year, it is unlikely that the need for disciplinary action is going to disappear anytime soon, so it is in your best interests to learn how to handle the need for discipline effectively.[14] Most people do not relish the idea of disciplining others. Punishing those who are rebellious, unproductive, or lazy is not a pleasant activity.

When problems with employees occur, the skillful manager or supervisor must be ready to administer a disciplinary response that will improve the problematic condition. The administering of discipline can lead to productive outcomes if it is handled properly. Other employees take note and recognize the goals, boundaries, protocol, and procedures that are appropriate in that particular organization. Effective discipline can prevent problems from occurring in the future.

Disciplinary interviews must be handled with care. The federal government and labor unions have spelled out procedures for conducting such interviews, and ignoring those procedures can get a manager into a lot of legal trouble. In addition,

14. L.V. Imundo, *Employee Discipline: How to Do It Right* (Belmont, Calif.: Wadsworth, 1985).

Throughout the project, Aegir team members from the engineering, multimedia, and computer services departments held weekly progress meetings with both clients and sent each monthly status reports. The high levels of professionalism and interaction with clients are two ways Aegir employees help to ensure that their company is at the top of clients' lists when new projects arise.

ONE-ON-ONE SKILLS KEEP BUSINESS GROWING

Unlike the technically complicated projects that make up its workload, Aegir's internal communication policy is simple. Loosely structured, open interaction maintains effective working relationships and facilitates teamwork. Every engineering project, for example, requires a core staff of engineers who team up with multimedia and computer services staffs for support.

Multimedia staff format engineering reports and presentations in the clearest and most interesting media, and guarantee that information prepared for government projects fits established guidelines. Computer services staff maintain and upgrade Aegir's systems and network.

Over the years, both support departments have developed their own expertise. Today, multimedia and computer services coworkers tackle independent projects with company-wide support. This internal flexibility further expands Aegir's business expertise and its client base. The success of Ella Williams's business approach, fostering open communication and teamwork, allows her company to remain flexible as it continues to grow, both in size and in esteem within its industry.

QUESTIONS FOR CRITICAL THINKING

1. What communication skills has Ella Williams honed as an entrepreneur? As a business manager?
2. Why is consistently timed communication with clients essential for effective problem solving?
3. What internal communication needs do Aegir's projects require?
4. What are the advantages and disadvantages of teamwork at Aegir Systems?
5. How do Aegir's organization and culture contribute to an open communication climate?

You can visit Aegir Systems on-line at www.aegir.com.

clumsy or mishandled disciplinary interviews can provoke controversy in the workplace and stir employee resentment of supervisors. The most critical aspects of disciplinary interviews include notifying the employee of the problem, interviewing the employee, and instituting disciplinary action.[15]

Notifying the Employee

Once misconduct has been noticed, the next step is to notify the employee so that corrective action can be taken. Some offenses result from problems associated with the system, structure, or technology of a job rather than from misjudgment, bad faith, or carelessness on the employee's part. If you decide that the

15. G. H. Morris, S. C. Gaveras, W. L. Baker, and M. L. Coursey, "Aligning Actions at Work: How Managers Confront Problems of Employee Performance," *Management Communication Quarterly* 3 (1990), 303–333; M. L. McLaughlin, M. J. Cody, and H. D. O'Hair, "The Management of Failure Events: Some Contextual Determinants of Accounting Behavior," *Human Communication Research* 9 (1983), 208–224.

cause of an offense is technical difficulties, you can simply inform the employee that you are aware of the problem and will work with him or her to correct it. Technical difficulties include lapses in mail service, computer problems, and equipment failure.

If the employee is at fault, however, it is best to inform her or him of the problem calmly, directly, and quickly. Do not wait for a few weeks for the situation to cool down. Smooth and decisive disciplinary action will deter other employees from similar behavior. Schedule a disciplinary interview for a time when you will not be disturbed and when the office is relatively uncrowded.

Reviewing the Employee's Side of the Story

Interview the employee before conducting other investigations. If the particular situation requires you to interview others who may be involved in the misconduct or who know about the facts of the incident, be extremely careful to maintain the confidentiality of all employees.

Immediately get down to business, but maintain a nonhostile attitude. Ask for the employee's explanation of his or her behavior. Facts and explanations do not always coincide, so be sure to clarify any apparent contradictions between the employee's account and your understanding of the occurrence. Appropriate questioning techniques include open, mirror, and reflective questions, such as "Why do you think the equipment malfunctioned?" or "When James noticed the malfunction, you told him everything was under control. Were you distrustful of James's involvement in your project?" Such questions are appropriate because they allow the employee latitude to respond and facilitate understanding between interview parties.

An accused employee may concede or accept responsibility for an act of misconduct, make an excuse, or justify his or her actions. It is your responsibility to listen carefully to the employee.

Instituting Disciplinary Action

Base all decisions on company policy, and provide written documentation to the employee if necessary. Be specific in your evaluation, and apply disciplinary measures consistently.

If, for example, you have recorded several occurrences of tardiness and absenteeism, you will give a stricter punishment to this employee than to a first-time offender. Your organization is likely to have a standard policy for warnings and repeated transgressions. Be sure that your employees are aware of the rules. If an employee has given a reasonable explanation of what occurred during the offense, that explanation may lessen the punishment as well.

Explain the Purpose of the Discipline Base discipline on objective facts and common goals. Stress the productive aspects of discipline. Discuss the disciplinary action in terms of the employee's past record and future with the organization. Once you have informed the employee of the disciplinary action to be taken, discuss ways in which the situation can be improved. For example, if an employee is being disciplined for alcohol-related absenteeism, the supervisor might suggest counseling or referral to an employee assistance program to give the person the best chance of returning to full productivity. Be reasonable in your judgment of employee behavior, and ensure appropriate disciplinary action in the case of misconduct.

Document the Incident and the Interview Write an objective and detailed report of the incident, and file it with the appropriate offices (such as personnel and administration). Include in the report the steps that were taken with the employee, and note all aspects of the employee's defense. Doing so ensures that the case will be reviewed accurately if disagreements or additional problems arise later.

MEDIA INTERVIEWS

Have you ever wondered how the evening news finds out what's going on within companies? In some cases, investigative reporting may turn up newsworthy items, but more often than not companies release information through media interviews. As the following scenario illustrates, media interviews are a powerful communication tool:

> Isabel, a public relations assistant at a finance company, arrived at her office building one morning and was approached by a woman who asked her name and company affiliation. As Isabel responded, she noticed that the woman had a small notebook in hand and was ready to take notes. The woman introduced herself as a reporter with the local newspaper and informed Isabel that she wanted information for a story about a company employee who was suspected of illegal business activity. Isabel refused to comment to the reporter, but later in the day a local television station called to request an on-camera interview about the firm and its business practices. After consulting with her supervisor, Isabel agreed to a limited interview in which she would lay out the company's mission statement and its policy for dealing with ethical business behavior and make a statement about the situation. During the interview, using strong communication skills to present examples of company policy, she successfully demonstrated that her company's ongoing commitment to correct business practices was in no way diminished by the employee's behavior. She prevented an isolated incident from becoming a media event.

Media interviews are a frequent event for organizations. Sometimes organizations and individuals use the media for publicity such as Arnold Schwarzenegger did in announcing his gubernatorial candidacy on the Jay Leno show. In other cases, organizations would just as soon avoid media interviews when the subject matter is controversial. (© Reuters NewMedia Inc./Corbis)

More frequently than you may realize, businesspeople receive interview requests from the media. If the businessperson is a public figure, refusing the requests is news in itself. Entire public relations and external communications departments work with the media daily to promote favorable images of their organizations, limit the damage done by events or competitors' rumors, and advertise new products and services. Given that the chances to be seen and heard through media coverage are more numerous today than ever before, it is worthwhile to learn how to handle media interviews.

Types of Media Interviews

A common type of media interview is the **in-person press interview,** in which representatives from a press organization make personal contact, request an interview, and pose questions about a topic of interest.[16] These interviews can occur in the studio or newsroom or in the field. If the subject matter is controversial, reporters and photographers or camerapersons are likely to arrive on the scene to capture the story in a natural setting.

Mediated press interviews are conducted through mass communications devices such as cameras and microphones linked by satellite or teleconferencing. Although such interviews lessen the stress of face-to-face contact with a reporter, the equipment and technology involved may be very distracting.

You are probably familiar with another type of media interview: **talk shows.** With this format, topics are discussed among informed experts. *Wall Street Week* is an example of this type of interview. Talk shows are planned well in advance, and the program is sometimes broadcast several days after it is taped. In most cases, the level of questioning is less intense than it is in the first two interview formats.

Regardless of the type of media interview in which you participate, you will need to understand the factors you must master to be successful: preparation, format, practice, and performance.

Preparation

To prepare for a media interview, conduct as much research as time allows. Collect your information, including statistics, evidence, statements by employees, and a general statement of the organization's position. You may be the only voice to give your organization's side of the story, so have facts in order and clarified. Also be aware of the big picture—that is, how the interview can influence the situation and your organization's image in the long run.

Become familiar with the location, participants, and medium of the interview. Will the interview take place on location (at your place of work) or in a studio? How long will it last? What types of questions will be posed? Getting answers to these questions will help you to anticipate the interview's direction and focus.

If possible, collect information about the media organization and the person conducting the interview. How has he or she treated interviewees before? Should you be prepared for leading, biased, or loaded questions?

16. E. Blythin and L. A. Samovar, *Communicating Effectively on Television* (Belmont, Calif.: Wadsworth, 1985).

Practice

Practice reduces anxiety and smoothes out the wrinkles in an actual interview. If possible, memorize your responses and say them out loud. Practice in front of a mirror so that you can observe your nonverbal style as you respond. Have someone else role-play the interviewer so that you can get into the rhythm of the anticipated interview. Tape- or video-record yourself if possible so that you can hear and perhaps see your actual responses.

Performance

The key to an effective performance is listening. Concentrate on the interviewer's message, and reduce environmental distractions (such as bystanders or equipment) to a minimum. Before the start of the interview, mentally review your research and goals, and consider them as you listen to the interviewer's questions.

When you answer, pause to collect your thoughts whenever necessary. Communicate your response briefly and confidently. Saying too much is usually more risky than saying too little. Keep your emotions in check. Remaining calm and confident increases the credibility and effectiveness of your message.

STRATEGIC SCENARIO WRAP-UP

Think back to the beginning of the chapter and the situation with Sam. Answer the following questions based on what you read in the chapter.

1. How can Sam improve his interviewing skills so that he can be successful?
2. What can Sam do about developing an effective résumé and cover letter?
3. What tips could you give Sam about convincing his interviewers that he knows about their companies and really would like to work for them?
4. Are there certain kinds of steps that Sam could take to make himself feel more at ease during the interview process?

SUMMARY

- You are likely to encounter various interview situations in your career. The most prevalent type is the employment interview. You can be most effective as an interviewee by writing a personal biography in advance of the interview, researching the company, preparing a résumé and a cover letter tailored to the specific job for which you are applying, dressing appropriately, and preparing to ask and answer questions.
- You must also know how to respond to illegal questions diplomatically but precisely.
- As you move up in your career, you will probably assume the role of interviewer at some time. The skills required in this role include developing job specifications, reviewing applicant materials, scheduling and conducting interviews, and choosing the best candidate for the job.
- Another type of interview, the appraisal interview, is a common method of evaluating employee performance.
- Appraisal interviews can help to motivate workers, build morale, and allow an exchange of feedback between supervisors and workers. The appraisal is usually an evaluation of specific performance factors. The rating system can be quantitative, qualitative, or both.
- The appraisal that yields the greatest benefit is straightforward but considerate, nonhostile, encouraging, and specific.
- Disciplinary interviews, the hardest type of interview to conduct, must be handled with care. The interviewer identifies the problem, notifies the employee, reviews the employee's story, evaluates all the evidence, and institutes appropriate disciplinary action. The process must be documented carefully, and the interviewer must maintain objectivity.

- Media interviews, the last category, are an increasing fact of daily work life. To use this interview to best advantage, conduct as much research as time allows, know the format of the interview, practice answering questions aloud, listen carefully to the interviewer's questions, and respond confidently and succinctly.

KEY TERMS

BFOQs: short for bona fide occupational qualifications, these are the concrete requirements—including necessary experience, educational background, and skills—for performing a job

Appraisal interviews: interviews to evaluate employees' performances over a certain period of time, generally specified by company policy

Corrective feedback: feedback that attempts to alter negative or inappropriate behavior

Supportive feedback: feedback that encourages desirable behavior

In-person press interview: type of media interview in which representatives from a press organization make personal contact, request an interview, and pose questions about a topic of interest

Mediated press interview: type of media interview that is conducted through mass communication devices such as cameras and microphones and linked by satellite or teleconferencing

Talk shows: type of media interview that is planned well in advance and sometimes broadcast several days after it is taped

DISCUSSION

1. What are bona fide occupational qualifications (BFOQs)? What were the BFOQs for jobs you have held?
2. What are some ways for employers to locate job candidates? Which are most effective, and why?
3. What are the two basic requirements for a legal interview question? Give some examples of legal and illegal questions, and explain their status. How should an interviewee respond to illegal questions?
4. What information should be included in a personal biography? When this information is adapted for a résumé, what are the most important items that affect the content and appearance of the résumé?
5. Why are appraisal interviews critical to healthy supervisor-employee relations? What are the major steps in conducting an appraisal interview?
6. Discuss the role of disciplinary interviews in business. How should a supervisor determine what disciplinary action to take?
7. What are the different types of media interviews? What are the important elements in preparing for and participating in a media interview?

ACTIVITIES

1. Consider the employment interview. Rank-order ten factors that you feel can make or break the opportunity to produce favorable outcomes. Share your list with your classmates.
2. Write five illegally worded interview questions. Then make the necessary corrections to make each question legal.
3. In a small-group discussion, explain how much time you believe should be spent in opening small talk between interviewer and interviewee. What are the advantages and disadvantages of such chitchat? Would this time vary depending on the type of interview under consideration?
4. Select five performance factors that are important topics in an appraisal interview. For each factor, construct sample questions that are appropriate in the following business contexts:
   a. A principal appraising a teacher
   b. A production supervisor appraising a line worker
   c. A baseball manager appraising a player
   d. A music coordinator appraising the church organist

PART FOUR

GROUP COMMUNICATION STRATEGIES

CHAPTER 10

Explores the effects of factors such as size, norms, and participation on group functioning and introduces some special group formats.

CHAPTER 11

Describes the process of preparing for and participating in a meeting, using a variety of critical thinking skills and problem-solving techniques.

CHAPTER 12

Presents practical and value-based approaches to handling negotiation and conflict.

Groups are increasingly important to businesses because of their role in task sharing and problem solving. Part IV covers the principal influences in group dynamics and introduces a variety of techniques for problem solving, negotiating, and handling potentially destructive conflicts within an organization.

CHAPTER

10

Fundamentals of Group Communication

After completing this chapter, you will be able to:

1. Understand why groups are important in business
2. Identify the characteristics of an effective group
3. Recognize the factors that contribute to or hinder group communication
4. Improve your participation in groups
5. Understand the function and types of group leadership
6. Evaluate the role of special groups in business

STRATEGIC SCENARIO

Felipe Papageorgio arrived home from his first day of work sick at heart. His new employer, Stylist, Inc., is a firm believer in making work more productive by emphasizing teamwork, frequent group meetings, and team-based projects. Felipe was elated when he landed this job, since it paid 30 percent more than any other offer, Stylist is a rapidly rising company, and he was able to remain in his hometown. However, his consternation stems from the negative experiences he has had with groups in the past. In high school, the fundraising group he was assigned to in the Junior Achievement Club was a disaster. The group never set any realistic goals, they never gelled as a team, and everyone seemed to want to go their separate ways. As a result, the group never raised much money and was considered a failure by other club members. In college, Felipe joined a mock investment group that was suggested by his academic adviser. In no time, Felipe knew he was in the wrong group. The group elected a leader whom Felipe detested. This leader was arrogant, condescending, and wouldn't listen to other people's ideas—especially, it seemed, to Felipe's ideas. Secretly, Felipe knew he was a much better leader. The group quickly became embroiled in constant bickering, with several factions fighting for control. More recently, Felipe was assigned to a quality-control team during his senior-year internship at a large, local nonprofit organization. This group was especially frustrating because its members, employees and interns alike, all seemed to be more interested in generating ideas that they thought the bosses wanted than in taking risks and being creative. No one wanted to rock the boat. Felipe shook his head as he reflected on his memories of group work. He was convinced that he was in for more of the same with his new organization.

Think about Felipe's concerns as you read this chapter.

OVERVIEW

Take just a moment to think about all the groups in which you participate. If you are a fraternity or sorority member, belong to an athletic team, or attend meetings of some student society on campus, you are involved in a formal group. Indeed, your enrollment in this course makes you a member of the group that meets in this classroom! You probably also participate in a good number of informal groups. You have regular friends with whom you eat daily, others with whom you study, others with whom you go to movies or games, and still others with whom you interact as you travel to campus.

In the 1950s, social psychologist Kurt Lewin suggested that group dynamics are pervasive.[1] He argued that all people exist in a life space in which groups are an important part. Lewin based his theory on the notion that a person cannot be separated from the groups with which he or she identifies. This theory has several premises: people are members of many groups at one time; groups are an important part of a person's life space; groups create tensions in the life space; and groups therefore influence the movement of the person within the life space.

Groups are as prevalent in business and professional organizations as Lewin described them in humans' personal lives. As you enter the work force, you will be asked to become a member of work groups, and your participation will increase as you move up in the organization. (Researchers have estimated that executives spend as much as ten hours a week in various group meetings.[2]) You will become a member of formal departments—such as accounting, personnel, production, or computer services—which are likely to be subdivided into work groups. The human resources department, for example, may include groups that focus on employee benefits, training, recruitment, building maintenance, salary administration, and security. You will also serve as a member of formal committees within the organization, such as safety, credit union review, or security. In addition, you will participate in lunch groups, after-work "happy hour" groups, car pools, or break-room groups.

The communication between and within groups is vital to the organization. We cannot stress too much how differently businesses and professional organizations would operate without group communication. We offer the following propositions about communication in groups, all of which have a substantial research base:[3]

- Organizations that employ groups effectively have enjoyed substantial improvements in productivity, cost savings, and profits and have observed critical enhancements to employee commitment and satisfaction.
- Decisions made by groups are of higher quality than decisions made by individuals working alone.
- People who participate in group decision making are more committed to the group's decisions than to decisions given them by a manager or supervisor.
- Pitfalls and hazards that a person working alone may ignore are regularly uncovered by groups through debate and questioning.
- Employee morale is higher when people are teamed with coworkers on projects and tasks.

1. K. Lewin, *Field Theory in Social Science* (New York: Harper & Row, 1951).
2. R. Y. Hirokawa and D. S. Gouran, "Facilitation of Group Communication: A Critique of Prior Research and an Agenda for Future Research," *Management Communication Quarterly* 3 (1989), 71–92.
3. G. A. Yukl, *Leadership in Organizations*, 2d ed. (Englewood Cliffs, N.J.: Prentice Hall, 1989).

- People who regularly communicate with others in the organization are more satisfied on the job than are employees who are isolated from others.
- Employees who network with others in organizational groups are more committed to the goals and missions of their organizations than are those who do not so participate.
- People who are teamed together in work groups take greater responsibility for the task, and the fixing of blame for errors is shared by all.

Can there be any wonder, then, why organizations devote a great amount of time and energy to the maintenance and perpetuation of groups? The positive outcomes can make the difference between a profitable company and a loser. People who develop strong communication skills and use them effectively in group situations regularly exhibit the best performance.

In this chapter, we introduce you to the basics of groups—what they are, how they function, and what types there are. We start with questions: What do all groups have in common? What makes a group different from a collection of people?

WHAT IS A GROUP?

Most of our communication in groups takes place in five types of groups: the family; adolescent friendship groups; work groups; committees, problem-solving groups, and creative groups; and therapy groups.[4] We concentrate on work groups and problem-solving groups in the organizational context.

For years, one of the great debates among scholars of group communication centered on what constitutes a "group" and, specifically, in what circumstances a "small" group is no longer small. Definitions of small groups ranged from three persons all the way to fifteen or twenty.

Clearly, the interaction that takes place between two persons—a dyad—is different from what takes place among three or more—a group. As the size of a group increases, the interaction among the members becomes more formal, there is less chance for each member to participate, topics become less intimate, and tasks take longer to accomplish. Unlike a dyad, which has one relationship, groups have many relationships. The larger a group is, the more relationships there are to maintain (see Figure 10.1).

The best way to define a group is to look at the behavior of the people within the group. When a group is functioning, you can observe several important behaviors:

1. *The participants know each other by name or role.* In public speaking situations, the speaker knows the audience en masse—for example, the Los Angeles Lions Club, the University of Michigan Business School faculty, the Dallas Masonic Lodge, the 11 A.M. M-W-F general accounting class. In group situations, however, the members know each other as individuals. In each group to which you belong, you know the participants' personal names, their roles (for example, boss, vice president, discussion leader), or both.
2. *There is a considerable amount of interaction among the participants.* Communication plays an important role in every productive group. During group

4. M. Argyle, "Five Kinds of Small Social Groups," in R. S. Cathcart and L. A. Samovar (eds.), *Small Group Communication: A Reader,* 5th ed. (Dubuque, Iowa: Brown, 1988), pp. 33–41.

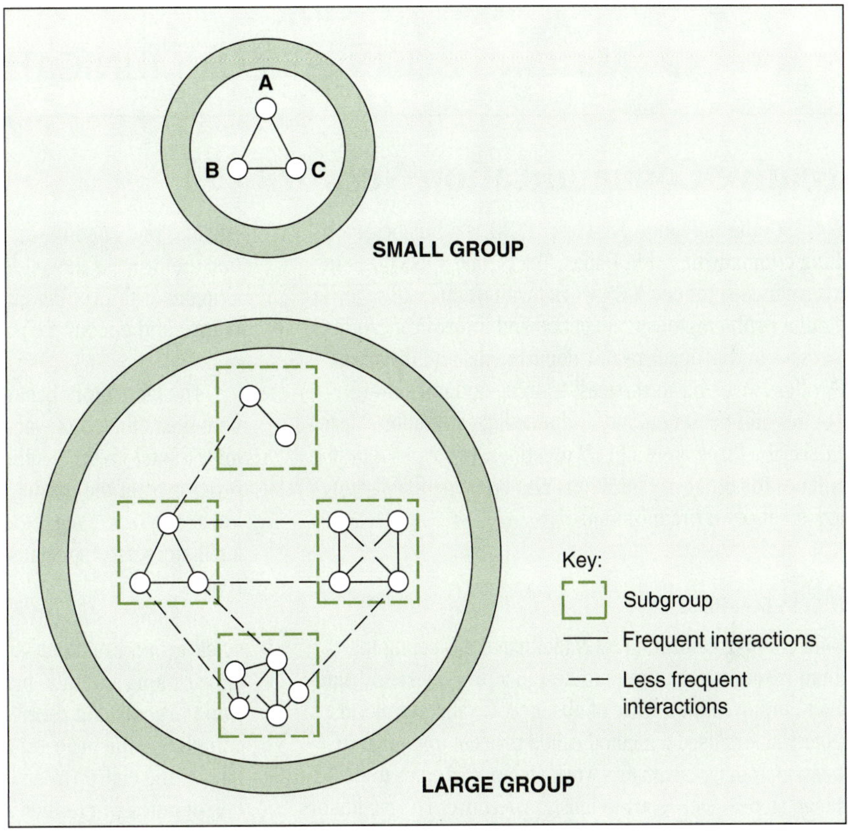

FIGURE 10.1

Communication in Small Groups Versus Large Groups

Size, location, and frequency of interaction are important factors in group communication. Members of small groups have more consistent interactions than do members of large groups.

Source: G. Moorhead and R. W. Griffin. *Organizational Behavior,* 2d ed. Copyright © 1989 by Houghton Mifflin Company. Used with permission.

meetings, some members request information, and others provide it; there are disagreements among members; and members clarify their positions and statements. Communication seldom occurs in a uniform or consistent pattern. In some groups, dominant participants "hog the floor" while isolated members contribute little, if anything. Sometimes participants are encouraged to interact with each of the other members. Sometimes the group leader controls who speaks, when, and for how long.

3. *Each participant has some degree of influence on each of the other members.* When group members get together, each person influences and is influenced by the others to some degree. Participants who express forceful arguments that are backed by powerful documentation may strongly influence others in the group. Influence can be nonverbal as well as verbal. A group member who scowls at another may influence the way that person reacts, speaks, or even votes.

4. *Each participant defines himself or herself as a member of the group and is also defined by outsiders as a member.* Over a period of time, as a group continues to meet and its members interact, the participants bond together. They take pride in their work. They are proud to be members of the group and express these feelings to people who are not members. Outsiders identify them as members of the group. A sense of membership is a key characteristic of an effective group.

PRACTICING BUSINESS COMMUNICATION

Creative Communication Network

Creative Communication Network (CCN) is a business consulting company based in Dallas, Texas, that specializes in performance solutions. CCN works with organizations by facilitating problem-solving meetings and improving group processes and procedures for departments and divisions. CCN offers three basic services: training and consulting, speeches and presentations, and meeting facilitation. Here we describe three types of CCN meetings: two types that it facilitates for other organizations and one type that it conducts for its own organization.

PROCESS MAPPING

In one client organization, CCN facilitated a meeting for human resources managers to design a procedure for placing an employee on a leave of absence. On that occasion, CCN facilitators used a method called process mapping. In process mapping, facilitators work with participants to design a linear, step-by-step, start-to-finish procedure. The facilitators draw the design on flip charts posted around the walls of the room, and the end result is a printed flowchart-type chart.

The facilitators' role in the meeting was to establish ground rules for the meeting, obtain agreement on the agenda, regulate interaction among the participants, ensure that the process moved forward on schedule, challenge participants with probing questions, provide summaries at key points, and encourage participants to explore differences of opinion.

The facilitators began by obtaining agreement on the final box: "the employee is on leave of absence." They then moved back to the beginning, drawing out each step in the process from the participants. Not all the steps followed a linear sequence; some occurred simultaneously, and the facilitators used special symbols to indicate these occurrences.

In some cases, the facilitators divided participants into small-group breakouts so they could work in depth on certain sections and then had them return to the general session to report and receive feedback from everyone. Before completing the process, all participants moved to the beginning of the chart. On an individual basis they: (1) placed Post-it notes where they had questions; (2) played devil's advocate to test the process by asking "why would this work?" and "what are we missing?"; and (3) worked through a recent actual case to see if the designed procedure worked.

5. *The participants share some common goal, interest, or benefit by holding membership in the group.* In almost all cases, common goals are the glue that holds a group together. They may be the reason why a person chooses to be part of a group. A person who does not see that working with others is a means to achieve a common goal, advance a common interest, or help facilitate a common benefit should withdraw and complete the task individually.
6. *There is leadership.* Within every functioning group, leadership is evident. External sources formally designate the leader of some groups. The manager at a restaurant, for example, was likely assigned that position by the restaurant owner. A leader can also emerge from the interaction of group members. Sometimes group members formally vote and select a person to lead. At other times, a person is simply considered the group leader because of the quality of her or his contributions to the group. In many groups, it is difficult to pinpoint any one person as group leader. Nevertheless, leadership is certainly present as group members interact. In these cases, we say that the group has *shared leadership*—all of the functions of leadership are present, but they are provided by several members, not just one.

VISIONING

CNN also facilitates strategic planning organizations. In these situations, it leads meeting participants through the process of establishing their mission, vision, goals, and objectives. In one session for the officials of a suburban city council, CCN facilitated a "rocks-in-the-road" session to explore barriers to the objectives and to design preventive action and contingency plans.

CORPORATE STRATEGY

The officers of CCN hold an annual meeting to plan their own business for the upcoming year. At that meeting, they discuss issues such as budgets, marketing plans to attract clients, maintenance plans for existing clients, attendance at professional development conferences, capital expenditures, and plans to develop and revise new training and development materials for the business. During the meeting, the participants brainstorm ideas, explore options, and resolve differences in viewpoints about how to allocate resources. They conduct this meeting at an off-site location in a retreat format and then print the finished product in a booklet.

These types of meetings are integral to the business of Creative Communication Network. These meetings not only offer CCN's clients attractive performance solutions but also provide a means to enhance business for CCN itself.

QUESTIONS FOR CRITICAL THINKING

1. What part does process mapping play in Creative Communication Network's success in designing new procedures for its clients?
2. For what purpose do CCN facilitators break participants into small groups? Why might this practice be useful?
3. What kinds of characteristics might a CCN facilitator need to possess to successfully consult with a client and to bring about positive results?
4. Why does CCN hold its own annual meeting as a part of its corporate strategy?
5. What kinds of discussions and meetings do you think would be most helpful for CCN to conduct during its own annual meetings? How might CCN best use its time and assets at these meetings? Why?

You can visit Creative Communication Network online at www.creativecommnet.com.

FACTORS INFLUENCING GROUP COMMUNICATION

We have pointed out in previous chapters that achieving effective communication is not easy. Group communication, because of the variety of people who participate, requires special effort. Among the several factors that affect the quality and quantity of group communication are cohesiveness, norms, roles, conformity, groupthink, advocacy, and conflict. Some have a positive effect on group communication; others are barriers that must be overcome. We examine each of these, highlighting methods for achieving successful group communication. However, before launching into a discussion of each of these factors, it is important to stress the interlocking relationships among all of them. Each factor affects and is affected by all of the other factors, constituting what you have learned before as a systems effect. Keep this in mind as you examine each of these factors separately in the following sections.

Cohesiveness

One major goal for any group is to remain intact no matter how difficult the situation or challenging the environment. **Cohesiveness** is the degree to which a group hangs together. There are two ways to talk about cohesiveness. A group is cohesive when each of its participants retains her or his membership. Reasons why group membership is desirable include attraction to other members, perceived benefits that an individual alone cannot obtain, and financial and social investments that cannot be abandoned. A group is also cohesive if members strongly identify with the group. The more participants identify with the group's purposes and goals, tell outsiders about the group's activities, and take pride in their membership, the more cohesive that group is. Rosabeth Moss Kanter suggests, in her most recent book, *Evolve!,* that effective teams distinguish themselves from ineffectual ones through a feeling and commitment to the greater good.[5] Effective teams are those that take on a sense of ownership for the things they do, the decisions they make, and the ways that they feel.

Highly cohesive groups are much more likely to meet challenges successfully and overcome obstacles than are groups that have low cohesiveness. Consider the following propositions:[6]

- The quantity and quality of communication in highly cohesive groups are much more extensive than in less cohesive groups.
- Highly cohesive groups exert greater influence over their members than do less cohesive groups.
- Highly cohesive groups achieve their goals more effectively than do less cohesive groups.
- Member satisfaction is greater in highly cohesive groups than in less cohesive groups.

Maintaining cohesiveness in a group is a challenge, but strong and effective communication can help. Taking time to encourage participants to take pride in their membership, to reinforce accomplishments both inside and outside of formal meetings, and to allow others to express themselves freely are ways that you can promote cohesiveness in your group interactions. The following case illustrates these principles.

> Akeme and Carol are members of a professional group that meets once a week to decide on fundraising activities for local charities. Because so many different types of people are members, the group lacks cohesiveness. Akeme and Carol realized that nothing substantive would be accomplished unless they helped to build a sense of belonging among participants. During group meetings they began to make comments such as these: "Jim, you know this area of town—what is your opinion of our efforts there?" "Elena, you always know where the big donors are in your own business—whom do you think we should target for donations to our group?" "I'm so proud of how we have pulled together in the last two meetings!" "People around town are saying so many nice things about our group's accomplishments." "It is wonderful that anyone here can freely give his or her opinion without criticism." After three meetings, group members were making similar statements, and cohesiveness rose to a productive level.

5. R. K. Kanter, *Evolve!* (Boston: Harvard Business School Press, 2001).
6. M. E. Shaw, *Group Dynamics: The Psychology of Small Group Behavior*, 2d ed. (New York: McGraw-Hill, 1976).

Norms

Group **norms** are "recurring patterns of behavior or thinking that come to be accepted in a group as the 'usual' way of doing things."[7] Norms are determined by the group and are used to regulate communication within the group. Norms can range from the mundane ("no private conversations while someone is speaking") to serious rules ("voting is required on every issue"). It is usually during the first few sessions of a group's life that norms are developed and refined. When new members join a group, they learn about existing norms through observations and trial and error. Norms help to facilitate the behavior of the group and affect the conduct of individual members. Consider the following norms:

Negative criticism of another person is unacceptable.
Meetings are "strictly business."
First names are allowed during meetings.
The discussion of a single topic should be limited to ten minutes.

As you can see, norms reflect group members' preferences and can influence the operation of the group. A member who fails to follow group norms may be isolated from other members, ignored, and, in some cases, not notified of group meetings. In other cases, norms protect group members and lead them to greater levels of productivity. This is especially true when the norms are directed toward creativity and the self-esteem of group members and the group itself. Consider the following:

There is no such thing as a stupid comment.
Taking risks with ideas is encouraged.
We take up for our group members.
It's all right to have fun while we work.
Electronic meetings are an acceptable form of participation from time to time.

Groups must carefully monitor their norms to prevent members from becoming disenchanted with petty rules or policies and to facilitate interaction among different members. That is why it is always a good idea to periodically review norms to ensure that they are serving the purposes of the group.

Roles

Every member of a group has a **role.** In many groups, members play several roles. Taking on a role leads others to have certain expectations about your behavior in the group. You have certain expectations about your teacher, for example. You expect your teacher to prepare for class, take attendance, lecture, facilitate discussion, meet with students outside of class, prepare examinations, and turn in final grades. You expect a work-group supervisor to regulate the work of employees, call staff meetings when necessary, give performance appraisal interviews, review complaints or grievances, and so on.

Group members can have clearly identifiable roles. A person's role is the function that the member performs in the group. Words like *leader, dominator, gatekeeper,*

7. D. Scheerhorn and P. Geist, "Social Dynamics in Groups," in L. R. Frey and J. K. Barge (eds.), *Managing Group Life: Communicating in Decision-Making Groups* (Boston: Houghton Mifflin, 1997), p. 92.

joker, and *analyzer* express some of the roles in a group.[8] Many roles are possible, but we will confine our discussion to three types: task roles, personal roles, and problem roles.

Task Roles Task roles are performed to achieve the goals of the group and to facilitate participation and decision making. They almost always focus on what the group is trying to accomplish. Here are some examples:

- *Information agent:* Offers facts, beliefs, personal experience, or other input; also asks for additional input or clarification of ideas or opinions that have been presented
- *Elaborator:* Offers further clarification of points, often providing information about what others have said
- *Initiator:* Helps the group get moving by proposing a solution, giving new ideas, or providing new definitions of an issue
- *Administrator:* Keeps people on track and aware of the time

Personal Roles Personal roles are enacted for the purpose of initiating, developing, or managing interpersonal relationships among group members. Sometimes these roles are described as socioemotional because they focus on the feelings, emotions, and personal needs of members. People filling these roles help the group operate during slack or difficult times. The following are a few examples of this type of role:

- *Harmonizer:* Seeks to smooth over tension in the group by settling differences among members
- *Gatekeeper:* Works to keep each member involved in a discussion by keeping communication channels open; may restrict information during periods of overload
- *Sensor:* Expresses group feelings, moods, or relationships in an effort to recognize the climate and capitalize on it

Problem Roles Sometimes roles are dysfunctional or distracting for the group. These roles consist of behaviors that attempt to satisfy individual rather than group needs, which are often irrelevant to the task at hand. Sometimes they are played by individuals who do not have enough commitment to the group or are simply not competent. How many times have you seen evidence of these roles in the groups you belong to?

- *Blocker:* Indulges in negative and stubbornly resistant behavior, including disagreements and groundless opposition to ideas; reintroduces an issue after the group has rejected or bypassed it
- *Avoider:* Displays noninvolvement in the group's proceedings by such behaviors as pouting, cynicism, nonchalance, or "horseplay"
- *Recognition seeker:* Calls attention to himself or herself by boasting, providing information about his or her qualifications, or reporting personal achievements

8. L. B. Rosenfeld, *Human Interaction in the Small Group Setting* (Columbus, Ohio: Merrill, 1973). This section is based on many works including K. D. Benne and P. Sheats, "Functioning Roles in Group Members," *Journal of Social Issues*, 4, 41–49; C. M. Anderson, B. L. Riddle, and M. M. Martin, "Socialization in Groups," in L. Frey, D. Gouran, and M. Poole (eds.), *Handbook of Group Communication Theory and Research* (1999), pp. 139–163; A. J. Salazar, "An Analysis of the Development and Evolution of Roles in the Small Group," *Small Group Research*. 27 (1996) 475–503.

What Would You Do?

Imagine you are in a group in which someone is playing a problem role—and doing so in a stubborn, obnoxious way. You know that this person's behavior is making the group less productive, yet you also know that controlling the problem would require a forceful intervention that is likely to be embarrassing to the individual. What would you do?

- *Isolator:* Sits and fails to participate
- *Dominator:* Speaks too often and too long
- *Free rider:* Does not do her or his share of the work
- *Detractor:* Constantly criticizes and gripes
- *Digressor:* Takes the group on wild-goose chases
- *Socializer:* Is a member of the group only for social and personal reasons

Do you excel at any of these roles? Which of them really irritate you? Which are incompatible with one another? Do you think that digressors and free riders get along well? What about isolators and socializers? Recognition of these roles provides the group with a means of maximizing the positive ones and minimizing the others.

Conformity

Conformity is agreement with or correspondence to a set of ideas, rules, or principles. In a group, the ideas are often the opinion of one or more dominant members. Participants who value conformity give in, compromise, or abandon their individual positions to align with others in the group.

Reasons for Conformity People conform to group ideas and opinions for many reasons, not the least of which is that no one can act with complete independence of all other group members. Inevitably, simply interacting with others will influence how you think about the issues being discussed.

Another force for conformity is time. If a group is about to conclude its work, you may receive hostile or uncooperative treatment if you bring up another idea or try to spark debate on an issue that has already been resolved ("C'mon, Bob, we agreed a week ago that we would hire the new candidate"). Highly directive or authoritarian leadership, which suppresses individual contributions to a group, also encourages conformity. Social pressure or the need to "belong" may also discourage disagreement with other group members. In highly cohesive groups, the desire to maintain the group as a unified body can limit a person's freedom to disagree with others.

Conformity and Group Functioning Conformity may be necessary for group effectiveness. Groups eventually must reach decisions, and conformity among group members provides a basis for consensus. Conformity to various rules, to standards, and especially to group goals is necessary under all conditions of group decision making. Members may be encouraged to disagree about the definition of the problem, the alternatives generated, and the criteria by which to evaluate alternatives. But certain fundamental issues—such as why the group exists and how it should operate—must be agreed on by everyone.

FIGURE 10.2

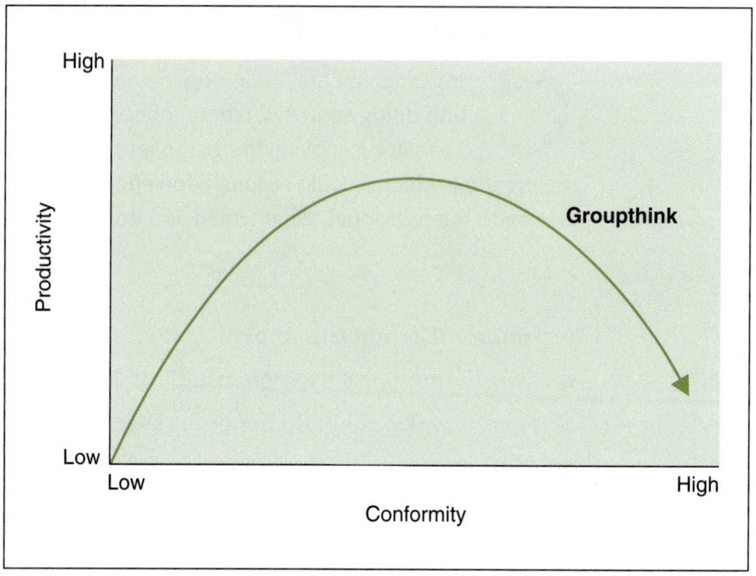

The Relationship Between Conformity and Groupthink

Although some amount of conformity is positive for group interaction, after a certain point, conformity becomes a disadvantage rather than an advantage to the group's communication and productivity.

Emergency situations, which require quick decisions, seldom offer the luxury of conflict or disagreement. Even in less tense situations, there are moments in group discussion when any additional advocacy or dissension among group members deteriorates into useless discussion. At that point, the group should strive for conformity to avoid wasting time.[9]

Groups that are naturally contentious and argumentative may benefit from promoting conformity. Getting group members to view a problem from others' perspective and to consent to a mutually agreed-on decision is a monumental task for some groups. In situations in which group conflict is common, failure to promote conformity can lower morale and undermine working relationships.[10]

Groupthink

Conformity, carried to its extreme, leads to groupthink. Figure 10.2 illustrates the relationship between conformity and groupthink. **Groupthink** is the tendency of group members to seek agreement solely for agreement's sake. A group gripped by groupthink fails to explore alternative solutions, problems, or concerns in an effort to present a united or cohesive front to outsiders. Four conditions give rise to groupthink:[11]

- *Being out of touch:* When a group meets for long periods of time away from its regular routines, members forget the big picture and do whatever is necessary to make the group succeed, regardless of how those actions may harm others.
- *Being out of order:* Informal and nonstandardized decision-making procedures let a group venture into unproductive areas with no way to get back on course.

9. J. Longley and D. G. Pruitt, "Groupthink: A Critique of Janis's Theory," in L. Wheeler (ed.), *Review of Personality and Social Psychology,* vol. 1 (Beverly Hills, Calif.: Sage, 1980), pp. 74–93.
10. I. L. Janis, *Victims of Groupthink: A Psychological Study of Foreign-Policy Decisions and Fiascoes* (Boston: Houghton Mifflin, 1972); D. M. Schweiger, W. R. Sandberg, and R. J. Ragan, "Group Approaches for Improving Strategic Decision Making: A Comparative Analysis of Dialectical Inquiry, Devil's Advocacy, and Consensus," *Academy of Management Journal* 29 (1986), 51–71.
11. From Irving L. Janis, *Groupthink*, 2d ed. Copyright © 1982 by Houghton Mifflin Company. Reprinted by permission.

- *Being overruled:* When group members feel that criteria and decision-making procedures are thrust on them by a leader, they are likely to follow along without much advocacy or dissension.
- *Being out of resources:* When faced with a critical problem, a short time frame for deciding, and no reasonable alternative other than the one favored by the leader, the group falls back on groupthink.

A tragic example of the effects of groupthink was the space shuttle *Columbia* disaster in February 2003. During its launch, a piece of insulating foam about the size of a suitcase fell off the shuttle's heat-resistant underbelly and collided with the left wing of the space vehicle. NASA flight managers knew about the impact within a day of the launch but decided not to pursue repair options or even to use satellite images to evaluate the damage. Pieces of foam had dislodged from the space shuttle in the past without causing any problems. Higher-level NASA officials decided that the missing foam presented little danger, but lower-level engineers were concerned that the falling piece of foam might have punctured *Columbia*. In actuality, the foam had indeed torn a fatal hole in the heat shielding of the left wing. Upon reentry, the damage let superheated gases inside the wing, where it melted the wing's frame. The shuttle broke up fifteen minutes before it was scheduled to land, forty miles over Texas, killing all seven astronauts.

In retrospect, a fundamental breakdown in communication contributed significantly to the disaster. "NASA's organizational culture had as much to do with this accident as foam did," described the Columbia Accident Investigation Board. Plans for rescue and repair missions had been considered, and with better communication they might have been implemented. However, we will never know if the tragedy could have been prevented because no attempts were ever made. In its review and recommendations the board concluded that the space agency suffered from all four of the conditions just mentioned: *being out of touch*—"organizational barriers that prevented effective communication of critical safety information and stifled professional differences of opinion"; *being out of order*—"the evolution of an informal chain of command of decision-making processes that operated outside the organization's rules"; *being overruled*—"engineers initially presented concerns as well as possible solutions," but "management did not listen to what their engineers were telling them"; and *being out of resources*—"NASA's budget was inadequate for all the programs the agency was executing."[12]

Symptoms of Groupthink How can groups determine whether they are victims of groupthink? Three major symptoms can be observed:[13]

- *The group's tendency to view itself as omnipotent:* Prior success, self-indulgence, and feelings of superiority can produce this attitude. Group members may share illusions of invulnerability that encourage excessive risk taking. Furthermore, the group may feel that its behavior is beyond scrutiny and may therefore enact decisions without regard to moral consequences.
- *Closed-mindedness:* A group experiencing groupthink tends to shut out information that does not conform to prevailing group opinion. Group members rationalize this avoidance by claiming that the contradictory information is

12. http://www.cnn.com/2003/TECH/space/08/26/sprj.colu.shuttle.report/index.html; http://www.cnn.com/2003/TECH/space/02/03/sprj.colu.shuttle.investigation/index.html.
13. Janis, *Groupthink*.

The elements of group communication processes influence one another interdependently and work together to make groups function more effectively, productively, and synergistically. (© Farmhouse Productions/Getty Images)

insignificant or irrelevant to the group task or that the source of the information is ill advised or inconsequential.

- *Pressure toward uniformity:* Uniformity in members' opinions, values, and ideas usually leads to one-sided decisions. Pressure toward uniformity comes from two sources: self and group. Self-imposed uniformity minimizes personal doubts or counterarguments about prevailing group opinion. It may occur because individuals value the opinion of the group more than their own opinion ("We know they must be right; they always are"). Groups press for uniformity by exerting direct pressure on deviant members to compel them to conform to group desires. Such pressure may range from subtle tactics, such as expressing disapproval nonverbally (frowning) and ignoring nonconforming members, to attacking deviant members verbally and questioning their motives and loyalty ("So, Betsy, you want to make us look as if we don't get along just because you're nervous about the decision?").

Minimizing Groupthink There are several ways to lessen the tendency toward groupthink.[14] Group members must question themselves and their actions to ensure high-quality decision making. One technique that encourages open discussion is to have the group leader ask each member to assume the role of critical evaluator. It should be stressed that the role is that of constructive rather than destructive questioner. Another technique is to have the group from time to time divide into subgroups with similar tasks to determine whether group composition and size

14. Ibid.

affect the ability of group members to remain adversarial and objective. Sometimes splitting a group into subgroups leads to fresh perspectives.

A third technique conducive to warding off groupthink is to have each group member discuss the group's communications and actions with trusted outsiders to obtain an untainted and objective viewpoint. Even friends or spouses can serve in this role. A fourth way to avoid groupthink is to have the group hold a special meeting where all misgivings, second-guessing, and objections are aired. At such a meeting, each member is encouraged to express any doubts she or he may have about any phase of the group's deliberation.

A very special method of minimizing groupthink is to have a measure of cultural diversity within a group. When groups are composed of males and females, whites, blacks, Hispanics, and Asians, as well as young and old group members, the opportunity for diverse thinking increases, and the emergence of diverse ideas, opinions, and arguments can counteract the effects of groupthink. When group members from various cultural backgrounds feel free to express their feelings and thoughts on all of the issues being discussed, one-track thinking is likely to be avoided and groupthink minimized.

Advocacy

Another factor that can help minimize groupthink is advocacy. **Advocacy,** or presenting competing views on a controversial issue, greatly increases a group's insight into that issue. Advocacy improves group problem solving by identifying alternative positions and promoting awareness of the important issues that must be resolved. Advocacy also forces group members to consider the strengths and weaknesses, pros and cons, and advantages and disadvantages of various viewpoints.

Without advocacy, groups tend to become closed-minded, likely to choose solutions that are personal favorites or are easy to implement or sell to upper management. Advocacy in group problem solving can take two forms: devil's advocacy or dialectical inquiry. Both are attempts to encourage groups to compare the relative values of competing viewpoints.

Devil's Advocacy You are probably familiar with the term *devil's advocate*. You may even have been accused of playing this role. Devil's advocacy is described as "structured conflict in business decisions. . . . The **devil's advocate** role should involve the formal introduction of dissent into decision-making processes in which premature consensus inhibits the challenging of assumptions and the consideration of a range of alternatives."[15] In other words, devil's advocacy is a good way to fight groupthink or excessive conformity.

Some group members may enjoy playing devil's advocate and challenging the assumptions and ideas of other group members. Although sometimes called detractors because of their apparently negative attitude, "volunteer" devil's advocates provide the group with a valuable service if their arguments are constructive. You may recall the scene in the film *Big* in which twelve-year-old Josh (in adult form) responds to a slickly packaged, jargon-filled marketing report about a less-than-exciting new toy with "I don't get it." His remark broke the group's conformist attitude and sparked inquiry and brainstorming.

15. C. R. Schwenk, *The Essence of Strategic Decision Making* (Lexington, Mass.: Lexington Books, 1988), p. 87.

Devil's advocacy is a sequential process beginning with formal or informal commitment from the group.[16] Group members must recognize the value of devil's advocacy during problem solving and commit themselves to an objective and open-minded attitude toward the arguments presented against prevailing opinion.

If a devil's advocate does not emerge naturally from a group, the role may be assigned to a group member. Assuming the role can be both fun and challenging if the advocate is prepared. By playing this role properly, you can command the attention of important decision makers and enhance your stature within the group and the organization.

Selection of the devil's advocate (in the absence of volunteers) must involve group members who are competent and credible. Group members must feel that the advocate knows what she or he is talking about and has a track record of effectiveness. In other words, the advocate must be credible enough to be taken seriously.

The devil's advocate has to decide which part of the problem-solving process to focus on. Advocacy can be advanced in the problem identification stage through challenges to the assumptions on which the problem is based. It can also be employed in the problem definition and analysis phase through questioning of the evidence or data presented in support of particular arguments. And it is often used during the phase of problem solving when group members are evaluating and promoting possible solutions. The devil's advocate may even decide to engage in all these phases, although strategic selection is advised to avoid being labeled a detractor.

The next step is preparation. The devil's advocate must do her or his homework so that the case presented against differing viewpoints is solid and persuasive. Although other group members may focus their attention on information and ideas that lead to solutions, the job of the devil's advocate is to present information and opinions that contradict these viewpoints. When you as devil's advocate conduct research in preparation for group meetings, concentrate on information that weakens, denies, or threatens positions that are likely to be taken by group members.

The final step in this process is issuing the challenge. Challenging others' viewpoints, opinions, ideas, or information can be accomplished in different ways. A devil's advocate can point out inconsistencies, irrelevancies, or inaccuracies in the data or the logic being used to present arguments. In addition, a devil's advocate can use previously established criteria to undermine positions being taken by group members. Of course, the most competent method of refutation or advocacy relies on critical thinking skills and effective techniques of argument. By way of example, consider the following group meeting, in which John has decided to assume a devil's advocate role during the problem identification phase.

The group was formed to determine what could be done about poor customer service. The group has concluded that the fault lies with customers' not being informed about services that the company offers. It thinks that customers' expectations about what the company can deliver are too high. John remarks, "It seems that if we want to increase our share of the market, we should not be blaming customers for their lack of knowledge of our services. Rather, we should be responding to their needs by providing new services that they want. Let me give some evidence that proves my point. Research and development has mentioned on several occasions that they can develop new products if they know the market is there." Notice how John moves the discussion into a new light by playing devil's advocate.

16. Ibid.

Dialectical Inquiry **Dialectical inquiry** is similar to devil's advocacy in that the advocate opposes prevailing opinion but then goes one step further by proposing another opinion or plan of action.[17] Consider the four stages to this process:[18]

1. A prevailing or recommended strategic plan and the data used to derive it are identified.
2. An attempt is made to identify the assumptions underlying the plan.
3. A counterplan is identified that is feasible, politically viable, and generally credible but that rests on assumptions opposite those supporting the first plan.
4. A structured debate is conducted. Those responsible for formulating strategy hear arguments in support of both the plan and the counterplan. The debate, in contrast to a traditional management briefing, is a forceful presentation of two opposing plans that rest on different interpretations of the same data.

   The following example illustrates key elements of this process:

> During the testing of a new hypertension drug, a pharmaceutical company learns that the drug induces hair to grow in places where none existed before. A meeting of researchers and marketers is held to discuss the problem. One team of researchers is concerned that this side effect may prevent the introduction of the drug into the hypertension market ("People will search for something else that doesn't grow hair on their necks and backs. We should just shelve the product until we can eliminate this side effect"). Marketing people argue that the drug should be refined to capture the market of people going bald who are trying to grow their hair back. The research team retorts that the idea is impossible—there is no way to stop unwanted hair growth on other parts of the body. After a pause, one person responds, "Why can't you formulate the drug as a topical treatment that grows hair only where it is applied?" Research members look at one another and agree that that may just be possible.

This new interpretation of the problem and its potential solution opened the way for a different product to be developed and marketed—and it prevented the loss of time, effort, and resources that had gone into developing the original drug.

Advocacy in the form of dialectical inquiry must attack and defend, whereas a devil's advocate only has to attack. Some researchers rate dialectical inquiry as superior to devil's advocacy because advancing a counterplan leads to the generation of constructive alternative positions.[19] In addition, some people may not appreciate someone who attacks their position without offering one of her or his own ("If you're so sure this won't work, what can you suggest that's better?").

When group members are faced with competing plans, however, they may tend to focus myopically on the relative advantages and ignore the underlying assumptions supporting their positions.[20] Devil's advocacy can prevent this myopia. Groups may decide to employ both techniques, enacting them strategically. Regardless of which approach is taken, advocacy is an essential part of the problem-solving process.

17. Ibid.
18. C. R. Schwenk and R. A. Cosier, "Effects of the Expert, Devil's Advocate, and Dialectical Inquiry Methods on Prediction Performance," *Organizational Behavior and Human Performance* 26 (1980), pp. 409–424.
19. R. A. Mason, "A Dialectical Approach to Strategic Planning," *Management Science* 15 (1969), 403–414; Schwenk, *Essence;* Schwenk and Cosier, "Effects."
20. Schwenk and Cosier, "Effects."

Conflict

Conflict is a greatly misunderstood facet of group communication. Many group leaders avoid conflict because they think it detracts from a group's purpose and goals. Their attitude is that a group experiencing conflict is not running smoothly. We believe, however, that conflict is what group meetings are all about. Leaders can use conflict productively to test group-generated ideas or propositions before they are implemented.

Conflict does not signal that a meeting is disorderly, raucous, or rude. It is a sign that people are actively discussing issues. We believe that if a group does not exhibit conflict by debating ideas or questioning others, there is very little reason for it to exist. The members may as well be working by themselves. Conflict, then, is part of the essence of group interaction. Leaders can use conflict as a means to determine what is and what is not an acceptable idea, solution, or problem. In a very real sense, conflict and advocacy are kindred spirits.

There is one word of caution, however. The conflict we are talking about is debate about issues, not about personalities. A group will not be productive if arguments are centered on the participants rather than on what the participants are talking about. A contribution such as "You've never known what you're talking about before, and you don't know what you're talking about now" is not the type of conflict we advocate. When conflicts arise, group members and especially leaders must be diligent in refocusing members' attention on the issues, not on personalities. We discuss conflict management and other challenges to communication in depth in Chapter 12.

Groups as Systems

As we mentioned at the beginning of this section, the various components of group communication processes can be thought of in an integrated manner as producing a *systems effect*.[21] Recall from Chapter 1 that systems theory refers to interdependency, or how various parts are related to each other; if one part changes, the other parts are also affected. Likewise, synergy describes how the various parts of a system work together to produce something greater than the sum of the individual parts.

Both interdependence and synergy characterize group communication. Take, for example, the relationships among norms, roles, and conflict. Because of a certain norm ("do not interrupt someone who is speaking"), a frustrated group member assumes the role of "distractor," which inflames other group members, leading to conflict. Or, the same norm may allow members to instill greater cohesiveness in the group. For example, groups with an overemphasis on conformity tend to slide into a groupthink mentality. Effective leaders avoid this pitfall by utilizing certain norms and roles to manage productive conflict. In this case, a "don't interrupt" norm helps group members air their doubts, frustrations, or new ideas. As you consider the dynamics of group communication, keep these issues in mind.

21. E. Mabry, "The Systems Metaphor in Group Communication," in L. Frey (ed.), *The Handbook of Group Communication Theory and Research* (Thousand Oaks, Calif.: Sage, 1999), pp. 71–91; B. Haslett and J. Ruebush, "What Differences Do Individual Differences in Groups Make? The Effects of Iindividuals, Culture, and Group Composition," in Frey, *Handbook*, pp. 115–138.

Group Leadership

Participation and leadership in groups are likely to be interrelated. The degree to which group members make their own decisions affects the leadership style with which they will be most comfortable. There are many different descriptions of leadership, as you recall from Chapter 6. Some emphasize that a **leader** is a person who influences the actions of others. A communication-specific definition is that a leader is the member of a group who speaks the most, speaks the most to the group as a whole, is spoken to the most, and directs communication in the group to productive levels.

A manager or supervisor is not necessarily a group leader. A person can be in charge of a group without exhibiting any leadership qualities. A member who leads a group may be its *least* experienced, *lowest*-ranking participant. If you have played organized team sports, you probably remember teams in which the captain did not exhibit true leadership and the person who fired up the team, gave it direction, and assisted others when needed was just one of the gang, not the designated leader. Many training and development programs today attempt to teach managers or supervisors how to be leaders. The focus of these programs is on transforming managers from people with titles into people who exhibit true influence, direction, and motivation.

Leaders in business organizations and the professions can be viewed in four ways.[22] Each defines leadership differently and provides insight into how a person can become a leader. These four approaches are traits, style, situational leadership, and functional leadership.

Traits Think of some people you believe are leaders. Now contrast them with some people you definitely know are not leaders. In what ways do the personalities, physical appearances, or behaviors of people in these two groups differ?

The **trait** approach is the oldest method by which people have attempted to measure leadership. In general, leaders seem to be higher than nonleaders in intelligence, scholarship, dependability and responsibility, activity and social participation, and socioeconomic status.[23] Leaders also outdo nonleaders in presenting a compelling vision, exhibiting power, exemplifying organizational values, taking risks, and displaying entrepreneurial imagination and transformation.[24] Negative traits that prevent a person from assuming a leadership role include uninformativeness, nonparticipation, extreme rigidity, authoritarian behavior, and offensive verbalization.[25]

Style One way to conceptualize leadership is to focus on **leadership style**—the behaviors that leaders use when interacting with group members. A discussion of leadership style assumes that there is one style that works best in most situations.

The most popular classification of leadership styles divides them into authoritarian, participative, and laissez-faire styles. Notice that when you classify a leader

22. K. Barge and R. Hirokawa, "Toward a Communication Competency Model of Group Leadership," *Small Group Behavior* 20 (1989), 167–189.
23. R. M. Stogdill, "Personal Factors Associated with Leadership: A Survey of the Literature," *Journal of Psychology* 25 (1948), 35–71.
24. J. Jaworkski, "The Attitude and Capacities Required of the Successful Leader," *Vital Speeches of the Day,* August 1982, pp. 68–70.
25. J. G. Geier, "A Trait Approach to the Study of Leadership in Small Groups," *Journal of Communication* 17 (1967), 316–323.

FIGURE 10.3

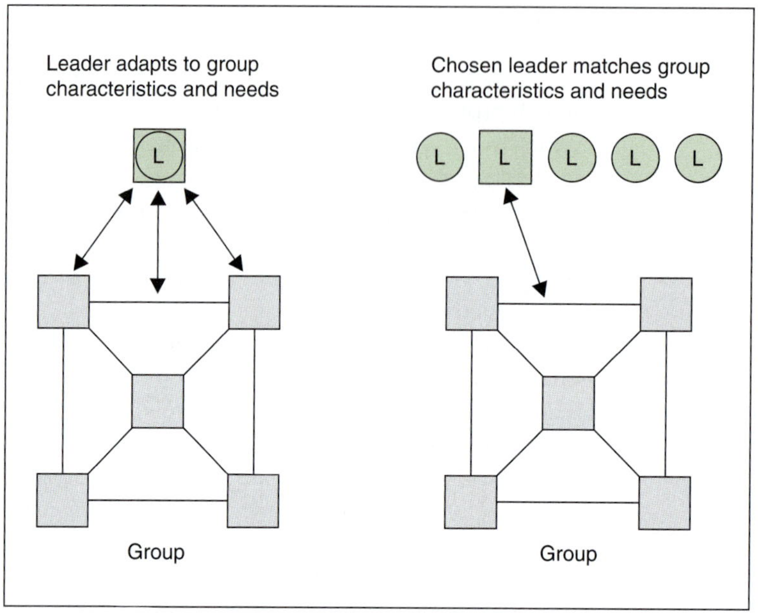

Situational Versus Functional Leadership Styles
Situational leadership theory suggests that the best style of leadership is adapted to the situation at hand. (A.) If a group's ability to handle problems on its own increases, the situational leader is flexible and decreases his or her direct involvement appropriately. (B.) If a leader's style is inflexible, the best situation is one whose style matches the needs of the project. (C.) With functional leadership, a group's members take turns leading the group to meet various needs, such as task orientation or social relations.

into one of these three categories, you necessarily focus on behavior. Actions—what leaders say or do—determine whether a leader exhibits one style or another.

Another way to conceptualize leadership style is by determining how a leader emphasizes tasks (the problem at hand) and relationships in the group through communication with the participants. According to Robert Blake and Jane Mouton, an emphasis on both people and production (tasks and relationships) yields the best results in most situations.[26]

Situational Leadership Another view of leadership suggests that there is no one best style, but rather that the best style is the one adapted to the situation at hand. **Situational leadership** can manifest itself in two ways (see Figure 10.3). In one, the leader is flexible and adapts his or her behavior to the demands of the situation. The leader reads a situation and selects behaviors appropriate for that circumstance. An effective situational leader of this type does not always place equal emphasis on tasks and relationships because a given situation might call for the emphasizing of one over the other.

One of the best examples of this view of situational leadership is the work of Paul Hersey and Ken Blanchard, whose situational leadership theory is based on a leader's ability to *adapt* to a group's maturity level.[27] According to the theory, **maturity** is a combination of a group's willingness and ability to perform a task. The more willing and able a group is, the more mature it is. As a group progresses in maturity, it requires less direction and less socioemotional support.

26. R. Blake and J. S. Mouton, *The Managerial Grid* (Houston: Gulf, 1964).
27. P. Hersey and K. H. Blanchard, *Management of Organizational Behavior: Utilizing Human Resources,* 5th ed. (Englewood Cliffs, N.J.: Prentice Hall, 1988).

ETHICAL ISSUES

Ethical Qualities of Leaders

Recall the ethical leadership principles from Chapter 6. Leaders who adhere to these principles are open and honest, selfless, fair, consistent, and willing to give credit where it is due. How could unethical leadership affect the following?

- Norms
- Cohesiveness
- Roles
- Conformity
- Groupthink
- Conflict

What can you do now during college to ensure that you always promote ethical leadership principles?

Hersey and Blanchard suggested that a group begins in a **directing phase;** here the leader must provide a great deal of guidance. As the group matures, it moves to a **coaching phase,** which allows the leader to instruct, act as a role model, and nurture group members. In the **supporting phase,** the leader is in the role of peer and gives compliments, reassures, minimizes doubts, and encourages productivity. In the most mature phase, the **delegating phase,** the leader directly or indirectly moves responsibility for group tasks, creativity, solutions, and decisions to group members. In this phase, members shoulder much of the group's work.

In the second type of situational leadership, the leader's style is inflexible, and the goal is to match the leader to situations that are appropriate for his or her style. It is assumed that leaders cannot with any degree of effectiveness act one way with some groups and another way with other groups.[28] This approach calls for leaders who are competent in particular tasks and with particular types of people to be placed with groups that are similar in their task and relational orientations. For example, a communication department composed of young faculty members who were bright and energetic and demanded complete participation in the decision-making process chafed under the leadership of a department head who was very experienced and somewhat dogmatic and preferred to make decisions first and then inform the faculty. She was replaced by a person who was young, energetic, less experienced, and certainly less set in her ways. The new department head sought input from department members to assure herself that decisions were correct. This appropriate match between group and leader was very successful.

Functional Leadership Sometimes groups contain several members who can perform many of the duties and responsibilities of a leader. When various group members rise to an occasion and perform needed leadership functions, the group is demonstrating **functional leadership.** Some group members may be very task oriented and push the group toward solving the problem. These members supply the group with a task function. Other members may be adept at maintaining harmony and social relations within the group.

Think about the last time you were in a group situation. Did you notice that several people were fulfilling the roles and functions of leadership? Perhaps you were successful at persuading group members to adopt a particular viewpoint or

28. F. E. Fiedler, "The Leadership Game: Matching the Man to the Situation," *Organizational Dynamics* 4 (1976), 6–16.

In groups, conflict avoidance often leads to groupthink. Poor decisions are often the result of "too much agreement" among group members. Whenever you take part in a group discussion or group decision, be sensitive to the symptoms of groupthink. (Steven Peters/Stone–Getty Images)

were able to reduce conflict. If so, you were providing the group with functional leadership.

FACTORS AFFECTING GROUP PARTICIPATION

Now that we have covered the basic factors (size, norms, cohesiveness, and so on) that influence group dynamics, we turn to factors that affect members' participation in a group. In the workplace, you may be assigned to formal task groups, or you may choose to volunteer for special project groups. In any case, your level of involvement affects the group process and your attitudes toward the group.

Approachability

Approachability gives group members the impression that you are open and accessible to their ideas and opinions. Effective listening is one way to demonstrate approachability, as in an accessible nonverbal demeanor (smiling, eye contact, open body orientation, and so on).[29] Approachability can also be established by asking for opinions, commenting on ideas, and expressing positive regard for the groups or team members.

Commitment

Commitment to the group and its mission must also be present. Commitment reflects group members' willingness to care personally for the group and its members and to maintain a dogged determination to help the group succeed. This type of commitment is developed primarily through explicit clarification of the goals entrusted to the group. Facilitation skills must also include convincing members of

29. D. A. Romig, *Breakthrough Teamwork: Outstanding Results Using Structured Teamwork* (Chicago: Irwin, 1996).

the importance of the group's mission and providing feedback about how their efforts are making a difference within the larger organization. *Commitment* can be demonstrated by the following:[30]

- Caring personally about the group and its success
- Being loyal to the group, its members, and its mission
- Remaining focused on the group's mission and goals
- Maintaining high-intensity levels for the group's work
- Demonstrating to others your positive attitude about the group's mission and vision
- Asking for commitment from others
- Taking pride in being part of the group effort

Participation Styles

An important factor affecting group involvement is the style of participation possible in the groups. Authoritarian, laissez-faire, and participative styles of decision making allow varying degrees of participation by members, with very different results.

An **authoritarian** style of decision making is one in which a leader hands down a decision to the group. The participants are not involved in making the decision; they simply do what the leader tells them to do. Two situations call for authoritarian decision making: crises and lack of knowledge. When a group faces a crisis, decisions must be made swiftly, and there is little time for discussion. When members are asked to give opinions, provide evidence, or supply details on material about which they have no knowledge or information, valuable time and effort are wasted, and other participants may be embarrassed or offended.

Apart from those circumstances, authoritative decision making has major disadvantages. It lowers morale among participants who want to contribute but cannot. It reduces the members' confidence in their leader and stirs feelings of suspicion about the leader's intentions. The chance for a poor decision is high because some valuable input may never surface and ideas may remain untested.

A **laissez-faire** style of decision making is one in which there is minimal involvement by the group leader. Members of a group operating with this type of decision making in essence make decisions without guidance or direction from a leader. The group is on its own. This type of group is difficult to deal with because some people may see themselves as fulfilling the leadership function without actually demonstrating the necessary skills. Laissez-faire groups are likely to grope around for ways to identify problems or establish decision criteria unless various group members make a concerted effort to do so. Some people probably enjoy group work without a directive leader, but research indicates that valuable time and resources can be wasted in a directionless group.

According to Gary Yukl, participation "usually refers to a management style or type of decision procedure through which subordinates are allowed to influence some of the manager's decisions."[31] When decision making is authoritarian, the leader makes decisions for the group. When decision making is laissez-faire, the leader turns decisions over to the group. But when decision making is **participative,** the leader makes decisions with the group.

30. D. C. Kinlaw, *Developing Superior Work Teams* (San Diego: Lexington Books, 1991).
31. G. A. Yukl, *Leadership in Organizations* (Englewood Cliffs, N.J.: Prentice Hall, 1981), p. 203.

STRATEGIC SKILLS

Managing Participation Styles

Some group members have problem styles that interfere with group functioning. These styles can be managed through effective facilitation skills.*

Style	*Description*	*Facilitation*
Rambling	Much discussion except on the subject. Gets lost.	Raise hand slightly, get floor, refocus attention on the issue. Glance at watch.
Verbose	Excessive talkativeness, anxious to show off; very wordy.	Ask difficult questions to slow them down. Ask others to interpret their meaning. Ask for additional input.
Inarticulate	Can't put thoughts into a coherent form. Can't express themselves.	Paraphrase their comments. Ask others if they feel the same way.
Prone to sidebar conversations	Two people talk privately during group discussion.	Call one by name and ask for his or her feelings on the discussion.
Avoiding	Noninvolvement; little participation.	Call on them by name. Ask for opinions.
Blocking	Indulge in negative or disagreeable comments.	Ask *why* they feel that way. Have them compare their view to others'.

*D. O'Hair, G. Friedrich, J. Wiemann, and M. Wiemann, *Competent Communication*, 2nd ed. (New York: Bedford St. Martin's Press, 1997); "Dealing with Different Types of Participants," http://www.wi-scd.org (Accessed June 19, 2001).

Research indicates that participative decision making offers a number of benefits. Group members who participate in decision making are more committed to the outcome or result than are group members who have no say about what happens. Participation also yields an interesting and satisfying experience for group members. In addition, the quality of decisions improves when group members who have skills or knowledge not possessed by the leader are willing to cooperate with the leader.

For participative decision making to work, several conditions must be met. A leader must have sufficient authority to delegate and share decision making with the group. Within the group there must be members who are knowledgeable about the subject matter and willing to participate in discussions about it. There must also be enough time for the group to complete discussion and reach consensus. And the leader must be competent in such participative methods as questioning, delegating, defining, gatekeeping, and agenda setting.

However, there is a downside to participative decision making. Participative decision making not only takes more time than other forms of leadership but also can create expectations among members that they will be influential in all group affairs. Some participants may perceive their leader as deficient in confidence and expertise. Furthermore, when a decision belongs to a group as a unit rather than to individuals, assigning responsibility for failures and shortcomings is difficult. On balance, however, participative decision making seems to be highly valued in organizations that practice it.

TECHNOLOGY TOOLS

Networked Group Meetings

You will find that within a few years conducting conferences or group meetings will increasingly be accomplished via computer. You will sit at your desk, connect to a network with your coworkers (some in the same building, some in different locations), and conduct a group meeting. Depending on the type of system your company has, you may conduct this meeting with just text (such as interactive e-mail), or you may use video, allowing you to see who is communicating. This kind of meeting is possible when everyone in the network has a camera installed on her or his computer screen. When one either types or speaks into a microphone, others connected to the group network can see the person. In this way, meetings can be planned and conducted among remote people in a short period of time—and at a fraction of the cost of having everyone come to a central location.

TELECONFERENCES AND VIDEO-CONFERENCES

Because of increased time and financial pressures, modern business practice is depending more and more on electronic means of conducting group meetings. More than other types of meetings, discussions that are conducted electronically require precise and well-defined rules of interaction because nonverbal communication is restricted or unavailable. In teleconferencing, participants are limited to the voice. There is no way to judge the reactions that can usually be discerned from facial expressions. These reactions—confusion, anger, hesitancy, surprise, dismay, displeasure, pain—are evident to participants in face-to-face meetings.

In videoconferencing, nonverbal reactions are available to participants but on a limited basis. Members do not feel that the group is "in a meeting." And there is a great loss of control over who takes the floor when. As a result, there is no naturally identified way of deciding "who speaks when on what."

In an ordinary meeting, a change of speakers is signaled by behavior such as pointing, leaning forward, and sitting back. These signals are not available in teleconferencing or videoconferencing. Thus, the group must establish rules and procedures for changing speakers. Without them, there will be offensive interruptions, "floor hogging," several people speaking at once, and shouting, among other possibilities.

The group leader can control the flow of communication by stating, "To obtain the floor, you must be recognized by me." Another may say, "No one may speak longer than three minutes at a time." Controlling the flow of communication through these or other means is a major challenge in teleconferencing and videoconferencing. Despite these challenges, electronic conferencing is becoming more and more popular. Even as corporate travel budgets tighten, the time and money (and hassle) saved by *not* traveling have increased.

After the terrorist attacks of September 11, 2001, business air travel declined, since it was seen as either too risky or too frustrating because of the long security waits at airports. Videoconferencing, which had been growing before the attacks, began to grow even faster. Since then international health concerns such as the SARS epidemic of 2002, as well as continued terrorist threats against American interests overseas, have made videoconferencing even more attractive.

Contributing to this trend, videoconferencing technology has become better and cheaper. Equipment that went for $40,000 to $100,000

Where Do You Stand?

For what type of group would your leadership style be most suited? Could you adapt your leadership style for the group? For what types of groups would you be unable to provide leadership?

a few years ago now costs as little as $10,000. Thus, videoconferencing is not only easier in many ways than traveling, but it is also more economical. With the latest hookups, video and audio streaming has television-like quality, a big improvement from a few years ago, when the audio was garbled and the video was one frame every ten seconds. Given these changes, many firms have said that even when the economic climate brightens, they will not increase their travel budgets, preferring instead to invest in videoconferencing equipment.

SPECIAL GROUPS

While video- and teleconferencing represent forums that increase efficiency in group meetings, other efforts to increase productivity have resulted in new kinds of groups altogether. Quality circles, self-managing teams, and affinity groups are a few examples of groups that bring together people with different experiences and perspectives to encourage mutual learning. All these special group formats have significant impacts on group communication.

Quality Circles

Quality circles are groups of employees who meet on a regular basis during work time to improve quality control and job methods. These groups have increased in prominence in many kinds of organizations and saved countless numbers of businesses thousands of dollars. Quality circles were extremely popular in the 1970s and 1980s, and their impact and presence are still felt today.[32]

The benefits of quality circles have been reported by a number of organizations, and we will only summarize their findings here.[33] Quality circles produce high-quality solutions to work-related problems. Enhanced work productivity results from the implementation of these solutions. Substantial improvement in horizontal and vertical communication within the organization occurs after quality-circle work. This benefit seems to derive from the increased diversity of communication among participants who would otherwise not interact. Participants in quality circles demonstrate an increased commitment to the organization and its goals. A related advantage is enhanced job satisfaction and lower absenteeism among employees involved with quality circles. Finally, members of quality circles claim that their participation in these groups provides both information and emotional support for dealing with the complexities and uncertainties of the organization. Although considered by some as a passing fad, quality circles as a form of group communication yield benefits that are difficult to deny. Perhaps that is why many organizations continue to enjoy their advantages.

Quality circles are based on the belief that the people who know the work the best are those who do it. In today's exceedingly specialized working world, many managers or supervisors are not as skilled or as knowledgeable about tasks as subordinates are. Quality circles invite these workers to attend meetings and actively participate in making their work better and more productive. They are commonly employed throughout the company. A quality circle whose focus is improved customer relations may include a vice president, a receptionist, a public

32. F. G. Elias, M. E. Johnson, and J. B. Fortman, "Task-Focused Self-Disclosure: Effects on Group Cohesiveness, Commitment to Task, and Productivity," *Small Group Behavior* 20 (1986), 87–96.
33. M. L. Marks, P. H. Mirvis, E. J. Hackett, and J. F. Grady, "Employee Participation in a Quality Circle Program: Impact on Quality of Work Life, Productivity, and Absenteeism," *Journal of Applied Psychology* 71 (1986), 61–69; Elias, Johnson, and Fortman, "Task-Focused Self-Disclosure."

TABLE 10.1

Benefits of Self-Managing Teams

Employee Benefits	Organization Benefits
• Higher job satisfaction • Increased self-esteem • Greater employee development • Increased job security	• Increased flexibility • Increased productivity • Leaner staffs • Less bureaucracy • Lower turnover • Decreased absenteeism

relations manager, an accountant, and a dock worker. The diversity of the group creates a climate of uniqueness and unfamiliarity that leads to creative solutions.

Self-Managing Teams

Self-managing teams, which are similar to quality circles, are small groups of employees who share the responsibility for a significant task. These employees work together to solve day-to-day problems and are involved in planning and coordinating activities. Because these teams manage themselves, they do not need to report directly to a supervisor. This is the primary difference between quality circles and self-managing teams, as quality circles still have an authority figure (manager or supervisor), whereas self-managing teams have autonomy. Self-managing teams also speak to a trend in the marketplace to lower the vertical hierarchy by eliminating or thinning the ranks of middle management and chunking the system into small, lateral units. In addition, organizations are increasingly relying on employees to be heavily involved in decision making and problem solving. Table 10.1 provides an overview of the benefits of self-managing teams.

Major companies in the United States—such as Xerox, Procter & Gamble, Volvo, and General Electric—have introduced self-managing teams and have reported a 25 to 40 percent gain in productivity and a lowering of production costs by as much as 25 percent.[34] At Federal Express, for example, a team of clerks spotted and solved a billing problem and thereby saved the company more than $2.1 million a year. Self-managing teams at Federal Express reduced billing problems and lost packages by as much as 13 percent.[35]

Self-managing teams have demonstrated that it can be a major mistake to underestimate the value of involving lower-level workers. When given the opportunity, these workers manage themselves quite well and accept high levels of responsibility. Workers who have participated in self-managing teams have discovered a sense of ownership in their jobs that they otherwise would not have experienced.

Teams perform four major activities. They uncover and analyze problems, complete tasks, establish and maintain personal relationships, and facilitate group and organizational processes. In accomplishing these tasks, each member of the group is considered a credible resource, and the team is committed to making maximum use of individual contributions. Thus, team members tend to be committed and motivated to implement team decisions. Team building entails attention to both

34. B. Dumaine, "Who Needs a Boss?" *Fortune,* May 7, 1990, pp. 52–60.
35. Ibid., p. 52.

tasks and relationships. When a team is charged with the responsibility of performing tasks, it must identify and diagnose problems, implement action to provide a workable solution, and follow up with a strong and thorough evaluation of any action that has been taken.

The relationship dimension shapes the climate in which the team operates. Teams operating in a favorable climate exhibit a strong degree of participation in group decision making, demonstrate productive and managed conflict, and use feedback effectively. There are substantial advantages for a group that can work as a team. Participants are motivated to pull together, decisions are made with high levels of commitment and motivation, and a spirit of camaraderie develops within the group.

Texas Instruments (TI) provides a good example of the team concept working well. In the past, at a TI factory in Dallas, workers put in their forty hours and went home. They had little commitment to the job or to the product they were helping to produce. Pressured by defense contract cutbacks and intense competition, TI developed self-managing teams. The teams operate according to their own schedules and responsibilities and monitor their own attendance and productivity. Communication within the team is much more frequent than in the old assembly-line style of production, and as a result, team members discover potential problems before they ever happen. TI was pleased with the results—productivity increased between 20 and 50 percent.[36]

Affinity Groups

What Is an Affinity Group? An **affinity group** consists of eight to twelve members in a sponsoring organization that meet on a regular basis to exchange information, ideas, opinions, and experiences on a variety of issues in a safe and supportive atmosphere, resulting in personal and professional growth.

What Is the Purpose of Affinity Groups in Organizations? Participants in affinity groups do not hold membership in the same or in any single business unit or division within an organization. Indeed, one of the landmark characteristics of an affinity group is that it meets in a safe, confidential atmosphere, where members may freely and openly share information, opinions, and recommendations in order to discuss issues, solve problems, and harness emerging opportunities.

Participation in affinity groups has a positive impact for the individual and the sponsoring organization. For example, it provides the following:

- A sounding board of peers to discuss personal and professional issues and to solve problems
- A nonthreatening environment in which to explore options; to receive impartial and objective, yet caring, feedback; and to contribute to the success of others
- Knowledge that there are others who share similar experiences and a source to find new ways to approach life and work opportunities and challenges
- The opportunity to associate with peers who are committed to personal and professional growth

36. L. Moran and E. Musselwhite, "Self-Directed Workteams: A Lot More Than Just Teamwork" (paper presented to the national conference of the American Society for Training and Development, Dallas, 1988); H. P. Sims and J. W. Dean, Jr., "Beyond Quality Circles: Self-Managing Teams," *Personnel* 62 (1985), 25–32. Data courtesy of Zenger-Miller, Inc. © 1990.

- Development of friendships and an experience of community within the organization

Organizations, whether businesses or associations, have reported the following benefits after implementing affinity groups:

- Increased relevance to their employees and members, brought about by providing a uniquely differentiated benefit of high value
- Closer relationships with their employees and members, resulting in their serving the organization more effectively
- Heightened loyalty and increased employee or member retention

Table 10.2 compares and contrasts affinity groups with other types of groups employees participate in, and the Practicing Business Communication feature about Nokia in the following chapter explains how affinity groups have impacted that organization.

TABLE 10.2

Affinity Groups Compared with Other Types of Groups

Characteristic	Therapy Group	Recovery Group	Religious Study Group	Professional Group	Networking Group	Affinity Group
Membership makeup	Emotional issues, history	Addiction history	Shared theological belief	Similar work focus	Entrepreneurial	Diverse peer group
Objective	Improved mental health	Addiction cessation	Expertise, insight	Idea exchange or development	Personal advancement	Personal and professional growth
Meeting length	1 hour	1 hour	1–2 hours	1–2 hours	1–2 hours	3–4 hours
Meeting frequency	Varies	Varies	Varies	Varies	Varies	Varies
Retreats	No	No	Sometimes	Sometimes	No	Yes
Leadership	Certified professional	Member	Professional clergy or certified volunteer	Member	Professional	Member
Confidentiality	Yes	Yes	No	No	No	Yes
Conflicts of interest	N/A	N/A	N/A	Yes	Yes	Non-competitive
Member behavior protocol	No	No	No	No	No	Yes
Specific attendance requirements	No	No	No	No	No	Yes

STRATEGIC SCENARIO WRAP-UP

Based on your reading of this chapter, do you think the fear and disgust that Felipe felt toward the group-oriented climate of his new organization were justified? Why do you think the groups that Felipe was in before seemed so unsuccessful? What could Felipe specifically do to avoid the problems he faced before? How much of effective group functioning is a matter of attitude? How do you feel about group work? Think about how you can use the material from this chapter to become a more positive and successful group member.

SUMMARY

- The focus in this chapter is on fundamental issues associated with group communication in business and professional settings.
- Groups are necessary because decisions reached by groups are usually superior to decisions generated by individuals.
- The nature of group communication grows out of what groups do, what purposes they serve, and what constitutes a group.
- The various elements of group behavior include roles, interaction, influence, membership, common goals, and leadership.
- A number of factors influence group communication.
- Cohesiveness refers to how connected group members are with one another; research demonstrates that cohesive groups are more successful than noncohesive groups.
- Norms, the standards or limits for defining acceptable behavior, also shape groups in obvious and not-so-obvious ways.
- Group members who do not conform to norms may be sanctioned by others.
- Another factor influencing groups is the roles that group members play.
- Roles can be positive or negative, and recognizing the differences among them is important.
- Conformity and groupthink are critical factors in group work.
- Groups must be able to conform to various procedures and methods of discussion to reach consensus on issues, but at the same time they must be wary of groupthink, or failing to discuss critical issues so as to maintain agreement and positive relations within the group.
- Groupthink can lead to poor decision making.
- Advocacy, including use of the devil's advocate role and dialectical inquiry, also reduces groupthink.
- Conflict, the most problematic aspect of group communication, can be the essence of group vitality and creativity.
- Another important dimension of group communication is leadership. Leaders can be classified according to the traits they exhibit, their behavioral styles, their adaptability to the situation at hand, or their ability to perform the duties and responsibilities of a leader.
- The extent of a group member's involvement depends on the nature of the group's participation style—is it authoritarian, laissez-faire, or participative?—and on how much team building occurs.
- Teleconferencing and videoconferencing, which are used more and more to reduce costs and avoid the dangers of flying, can rob participants of the benefits of face-to-face interaction, so appropriate adjustments have to be made to keep communication flowing.
- Quality circles, self-managing teams, and affinity groups can enhance productivity and increase communicative effectiveness.

KEY TERMS

Cohesiveness: the degree to which a group hangs together

Norms: recurring patterns that define accepted behavior

Role: behavior or expectations for behavior within a group

Conformity: agreement with or correspondence to a set of ideas, rules, or principles

Groupthink: the tendency of group members to seek agreement solely for agreement's sake

Advocacy: presentation of competing views on a controversial issue

Devil's advocate: the group member who introduces dissent into decision-making processes

Leader: the member of a group who speaks the most, speaks the most to the group as a whole, is spoken to the most, and directs communication in the group to productive levels

Traits: the personalities, physical appearances, or behaviors of people in a group

Leadership style: the behaviors that leaders use when interacting with group members

Situational leadership: leadership style that involves adapting behaviors to the situation at hand rather than relying on one "best" style in all situations

Maturity: a combination of a group's willingness and ability to perform a task

Directing phase: phase of situational leadership in which a leader must provide a great deal of guidance to the group

Coaching phase: phase of situational leadership in which the leader can instruct, act as a role model, and nurture group members

Supporting phase: phase of situational leadership in which the leader is in the role of peer and gives compliments, reassures, minimizes doubts, and encourages productivity

Delegating phase: phase of situational leadership in which the leader directly or indirectly moves responsibility for group tasks, creativity, solutions, and decisions to group members

Functional leadership: style of leadership in which groups rise to an occasion and perform needed leadership functions

Authoritarian decision making: style of decision making in which a leader hands down a decision to the group

Laissez-faire decision making: style of decision making in which there is minimal involvement by the group leader

Participative decision making: style of decision making in which the leader makes decisions with the group

Quality circles: groups of employees who meet on a regular basis during work time to improve quality control and job methods

Self-managing teams: small groups of employees who share the responsibility for a significant task

Affinity group: a group consisting of eight to twelve members in a sponsoring organization that meet on a regular basis to exchange information, ideas, opinions, and experiences on a variety of issues in a safe and supportive atmosphere, resulting in personal and professional growth

DISCUSSION

1. What are some of the organizational benefits of working in small groups? What characteristics distinguish a small group from a collection of unrelated people?
2. What is the relationship among cohesiveness, conformity, and groupthink? How does each affect the quantity and quality of small-group communication?
3. Why is group conflict important?
4. How does the group's participation level and decision-making style affect its results?
5. Discuss the four approaches to group leadership. How do group members and the group's task affect which approach is most appropriate?
6. What special communications issues are raised by teleconferencing and videoconferencing?
7. Discuss some of the advantages and disadvantages of quality circles, self-managing teams, and affinity groups.

ACTIVITIES

1. What types of tasks do you believe are best suited for groups? For dyads? For individuals? Compare your lists with those of others in the class.
2. Think of groups of which you have been a member that had the following characteristics. Explain how effective and efficient each group was.
   a. High degree of cohesion
   b. Participative group leader
   c. One dominant member
   d. Interpersonal conflict during discussion
   e. Unprepared, uninformed members
3. Do you believe that there is a single leadership style that is effective in most situations? If you do, explain in an essay what that style is and why. If you don't, use your essay to explain your position.

CHAPTER

11

Meetings: Forums for Problem Solving

After completing this chapter, you will be able to:

1. Evaluate how individual, group, and organizational goals influence a meeting
2. Create an agenda and adapt it to a variety of meeting formats
3. Use situational knowledge to prepare for a meeting
4. Develop and employ critical thinking skills to improve communication during a meeting
5. Choose appropriate problem-solving methods to achieve goals
6. Engage in effective decision making
7. Recognize what triggers anxiety in group situations and improve your handling of it
8. Evaluate group performance objectively

STRATEGIC SCENARIO

Phebe Hollis is a regional sales manager for Inspirion Corporation, an organization that sells and distributes seasonal gift items such as decorative artificial plants, caps, T-shirts, blankets, jewelry, and some perishable items. Traditionally, Inspirion has advertised and marketed its products to the public through catalog sales and to organizations through direct-sales representatives who call on business managers in need of gifts for their clients.

Phebe has been assigned to organize a meeting for all district and regional sales managers in a mountain resort in Colorado. The purpose of the meeting is to develop a strategic plan for implementing a new Web-based strategy for on-line sales—something they know very little about. Phebe knows that many of the "old guard" sales managers are resistant to the idea of e-business and on-line sales. She also knows that she has been selected for this task because she has been actively supporting the idea of on-line sales and that her chances of being promoted to vice president depend on the success of the venture.

Phebe has many tasks facing her. How will she organize the meeting? How can she keep the group sharp and focused on the mission of developing an on-line sales strategy? How can she promote the exchange of well-reasoned ideas? How will the groups eventually make a decision? It is imperative that the group members buy into the decision before they leave for their own regions and districts. How will Phebe know if she has been successful?

Think about the issues facing Phebe as you read this chapter.

OVERVIEW

In Chapter 10, we introduced you to the basic characteristics of groups, group leaders, and special group formats. Now we focus on the group process—the meeting—to show how groups use meetings to identify and achieve goals, share information, make decisions, and solve problems. As a functioning member of a business or professional organization, sooner or later you will have thc opportunity to plan, participate in, or lead a meeting. An understanding of the basic process of communication in this context can improve your ability to contribute to meetings.

Several types of meetings are common to most organizations. Planning meetings, staff meetings, and annual meetings bring together groups of employees or stakeholders to share information and update them on the direction the group and the organization as a whole are taking. Typically, these meetings are scheduled regularly and have set agendas—that is, the same basic issues are discussed in every meeting. For example, production schedules and budget control might be discussed at every weekly editorial staff meeting at a publishing company, but each week the group will have new developments and information to share and learn. Annual meetings present a similar situation. The basic activities—election of officers, a state-of-the-company address, voting on various referenda, and so on—take place every year, but each year the nominees are different, the company's performance varies to some degree, and new referenda are proposed.

Because information-sharing meetings are relatively planned and routine, we choose not to cover them in great detail in this chapter. Instead, we focus on problem-solving meetings, which add to the basic function of information sharing the tasks of finding solutions and making decisions about events or situations that have the potential to affect the organization's performance. Whether problem-solving groups are called task forces, troubleshooting teams, or strategic communication committees, their basic function is to identify and resolve specific problems by applying strong communication skills and problem-solving techniques. We structure our discussion of this process around the four components of strategic communication to show you how to maximize your effectiveness in problem-solving meetings.

GOAL SETTING: THE AGENDA

An agenda is like a road map. Have you ever decided to go on a vacation and just taken off with no prior planning? If you did, you probably missed seeing a lot along the way because you did not think in advance about what you wanted to experience. You also probably wasted a lot of time. The same principle applies to meetings. A meeting that is not well planned can neglect issues that need to be resolved, waste time, and produce frustration among members. An **agenda** is a guide that specifies what is to be discussed, when, in what order, and for how long. The degree to which each of those considerations is detailed and the format in which they are presented vary widely because of differences in organizational policy and the nature of the meeting itself.

We begin by presenting a formal agenda that contains the basic components that can be adapted to suit other types of meetings. Figures 11.1A and 11.1B show two formats for agendas. A formal agenda for a meeting may contain these items:

Roll call of participants
Reading and approval of minutes from previous meetings
Presentation of topics
Requests for additional topics

Communications to be read
Reports of special committees
Reports of standing committees
Unfinished business
New business
Closing concerns
Adjournment

FIGURE 11.1 Variations on the Formal Agenda

Managers' Meeting Agenda
March 25-29
25th Floor—Auditorium

Monday, March 25

Time	Item	Presenters
8:15-8:30	Overview of marketing	
8:30-12:00	Feedback/estimates on 2005 products	*Sales Managers* Paul McAllister Sam Kaplan Karen Friedman Ray Daley Bill Russell Joan Webster
12:00-1:30	Working lunch; marketing plans	
1:30-4:30	Introduction of new sales training plan for 2005	*Sales Managers* Paul McAllister Sam Kaplan Bill Russell Joan Webster
4:30-5:00	Wrap-up	*Sales Managers* Ray Daley Susan Ellis

A.

AGENDA FOR TRAINING SESSION

Thursday, January 5, 2004

7:30 AM	Buffet breakfast		Conference Room
	REGIONAL OFFICE	TRAINING GROUP LEADER	
8:30 AM-4:30 PM	Chicago	Thomas Ryderson	Room 120
	Miami	Margaret Brown	Suite 3
	Detroit	George Owens	Suite 4
	San Francisco	Jim Robertson	Room 110
	New York	Susan DeKooning	Suite 2
	Seattle	Cathy Atwater	Suite 1
10:00 AM	Break		
3:00 PM	Break		

B.

You may be familiar with this format, but let us take a moment to clarify the purpose of each item. **Roll call** is simply an attendance check—is everyone present and ready to begin? For many groups, a certain percentage of members must be present and without this **quorum** (such as 50 percent, two-thirds, or three-fourths of the members), the meeting cannot proceed. **Reading the minutes** summarizes what took place in previous meetings of the group. If this is the first (or only) meeting, this step is omitted. Often, the leader of a group will dispense with a reading of the minutes and simply ask if anyone has additions or corrections. In cases where formal approval of minutes is required, some member must "move" that the minutes be accepted and someone else must "second the motion." After the minutes, the leader reviews the topics to be discussed. If a group member wishes to add a topic to the list, it is done at this point, not later. Communications to be read include messages from people not present at the meeting that have to be considered during discussions. Many agendas present this information as an "overview" given at the start of a meeting.

Committee reports often form the bulk of formal meetings. **Special committees** are temporary subgroups created to look into short-term or specific problems. **Standing committees** are permanent subgroups that concentrate on long-term developments in broad areas such as budgeting, personnel, and purchasing. These committees meet on their own time and regularly report back to the complete group. In less formal meetings, individual members may report on findings or update the group on developments in a particular area.

Unfinished business and **new business** include topics that were not agreed on at earlier meetings and new issues that have to be addressed. Committees may be formed to look into these areas. In problem-solving meetings, addressing such issues takes the bulk of the meeting time. The agenda may include a "working lunch," periods of time set aside for small-group work on subparts of a problem, for training sessions, or for brainstorming possible solutions.

Closing concerns and adjournment round out the meeting, giving a summation of what has been accomplished and where the group may go next. Informal agendas may simply include a "wrap-up" or "summary" to provide closure to the meeting.

The Managers' Meeting Agenda (Figure 11.1A) shows an excerpt from a multi-day conference held to plan the sales campaign of a small regional company. The Agenda for Training Session (Figure 11.1B) shows the framework for a meeting in which employees from branch offices of a large national organization meet at company headquarters to participate in training activities.

The group leader takes the agenda and fills in any details about the business that are known in advance. One section of an agenda might look like this:

> ***Reports of Standing Committees***
>
> Finance (M. Jackson—5 minutes)
>
> Suspensions and reinstatements (D. Holloway—10 minutes)
>
> *Unfinished Business*
>
> Permanent meeting location (10 minutes)

Why are time limits included on the agenda? Time limits are not rigid boundaries that cut off discussion. Rather, they provide the group with a guide to the importance and depth of the discussion intended for specific topics.

If possible, all participants should receive a copy of the agenda before the meeting. The agenda can be mailed or hand-delivered, or participants can pick up a copy. In this way, everyone has an opportunity to prepare for the meeting and bring whatever materials may be necessary to have a productive discussion.

The agenda serves as the framework within which the group leader organizes time and topics. But leaders are not the only contributors to a group's direction. Effective group members must consider organizational, group, and individual goals.

Organizational Goals

Organizational goals are set at upper levels of the organization's hierarchy and describe pathways to excellence. Recall our discussion in Chapter 2 about how organizational goals are set, monitored, and evaluated. Groups are directly and indirectly affected by organizational goals because the ultimate purpose of groups is to solve problems that may prevent the attainment of organizational goals. To work effectively, serve the purpose of the organization, and avoid conflicts between group agendas and organizational goals, groups are wise to keep in mind the overarching goals of the organization.

Group Goals

Group goals serve the mission and purpose of the group itself. Often a higher authority forms a group and specifies a "charge." The charge serves as the fundamental goal of the group. For example, a chief executive officer may appoint a group to recommend a change in the distribution of wholesale products. The group's fundamental charge may be "to develop a new and more effective wholesale distribution system." Specific subgoals can then be established, such as "to develop a computerized tracking system for wholesale customers" or "to establish a new method for routing trucks to final destinations." Each of these goals may require a series of meetings in which strategies for achieving it are devised.

Groups that meet periodically without a specific charge from a higher authority develop their own goals. These goals depend on the nature of the group's tasks and the reason for its existence. For instance, ongoing groups devoted to improving on-the-job productivity may designate the general goal of "determining methods of increasing productivity." Specific subgoals such as "monitoring productivity in the tool shop" and "evaluating quality-control techniques" can then be set for individual meetings.

Groups may also set process goals. **Process goals** attempt to improve the working of the group itself. If, after a series of meetings, group members feel they are not working together as well as they could, they may set goals to improve their internal harmony, research skills, decision-making methods, or ability to deal with time pressures.

Because group goals may change as groups mature or as new information becomes available that affects original plans, a group must continually monitor its goals to ensure that its actions are serving the best interests of both the group and the organization.

Individual Goals or Needs

Individual goals are goals or needs that group members have in addition to the group's stated goals. Your motives for joining a group may reflect an individual goal such as to meet new people at work. Some people join groups to satisfy their need

Where Do You Stand?

Think about a group project that you worked on in one of your classes. Visualize the group members, the group meetings, and the finished project. Did your group establish goals? What process goals should have been established to improve group harmony? What goals should have been defined to improve creativity? How could you have persuaded the other group members that process goals were necessary?

for achievement. Others set goals to gain recognition, knowledge, power, information, or skills.[1] You probably belong to some groups now for personal reasons, and it is very likely that you will be involved in some work groups for personal reasons.

The setting and maintaining of individual goals are key ingredients in group effectiveness. Group members who are unable to accomplish their personal goals are likely to be unhappy and therefore less effective. All three types of goals—organizational, group, and individual—should be considered by participants in a meeting. As Figure 11.2 shows, they can reinforce one another. Groups function most effectively when members set effective and appropriate goals of each type.

SITUATIONAL KNOWLEDGE: PREPARING FOR THE MEETING

Proper advance planning is important for the success of a meeting. Location, participants, scheduling, and other environmental issues can affect the outcome of a meeting. Think about a meeting that took place in a very cold room. Were you eager to participate or pay attention to the discussion? No! Your mind was on the temperature of the room, the sweater you left at your apartment, or the weather forecast for the next day. Or consider a meeting in an auditorium-style arrangement in which the leader wants full group participation. How frequently will people need to turn around to see who behind them is talking? Finally, consider meetings in which you were thirsty but there were no refreshments. All you could think about was the soft drink you were going to get afterward. Knowing the conditions of the meeting beforehand will allow you to be a much more effective planner and participant.

Meeting Facilities

There are several issues to consider when you are deciding where to hold a meeting. The primary concern is that the physical characteristics of the room meet the needs of the people planning to attend. Visit the facility before scheduling your first meeting there. Does the room you are considering have enough space for everyone in your group? Are there large picture windows that may be distracting? Does the room have plenty of electrical outlets, proper storage space, adjustable lighting switches, and adjustable temperature controls? Are other meetings booked into the facility at the same time that yours is planned? If so, is the room soundproof so that noise from an adjacent room does not "bleed" through the walls? How far away from the room are restrooms, soft-drink machines, water

1. C. S. Palazzolo, "The Social Group: Definitions," in R. S. Cathcart and L. A. Samovar (eds.), *Small Group Communication: A Reader*, 4th ed. (Dubuque, Iowa: Brown, 1984), pp. 1–23.

FIGURE 11.2 Individual, Group, and Organizational Goals

The relationship among individual, group, and organizational goals affects group performance.

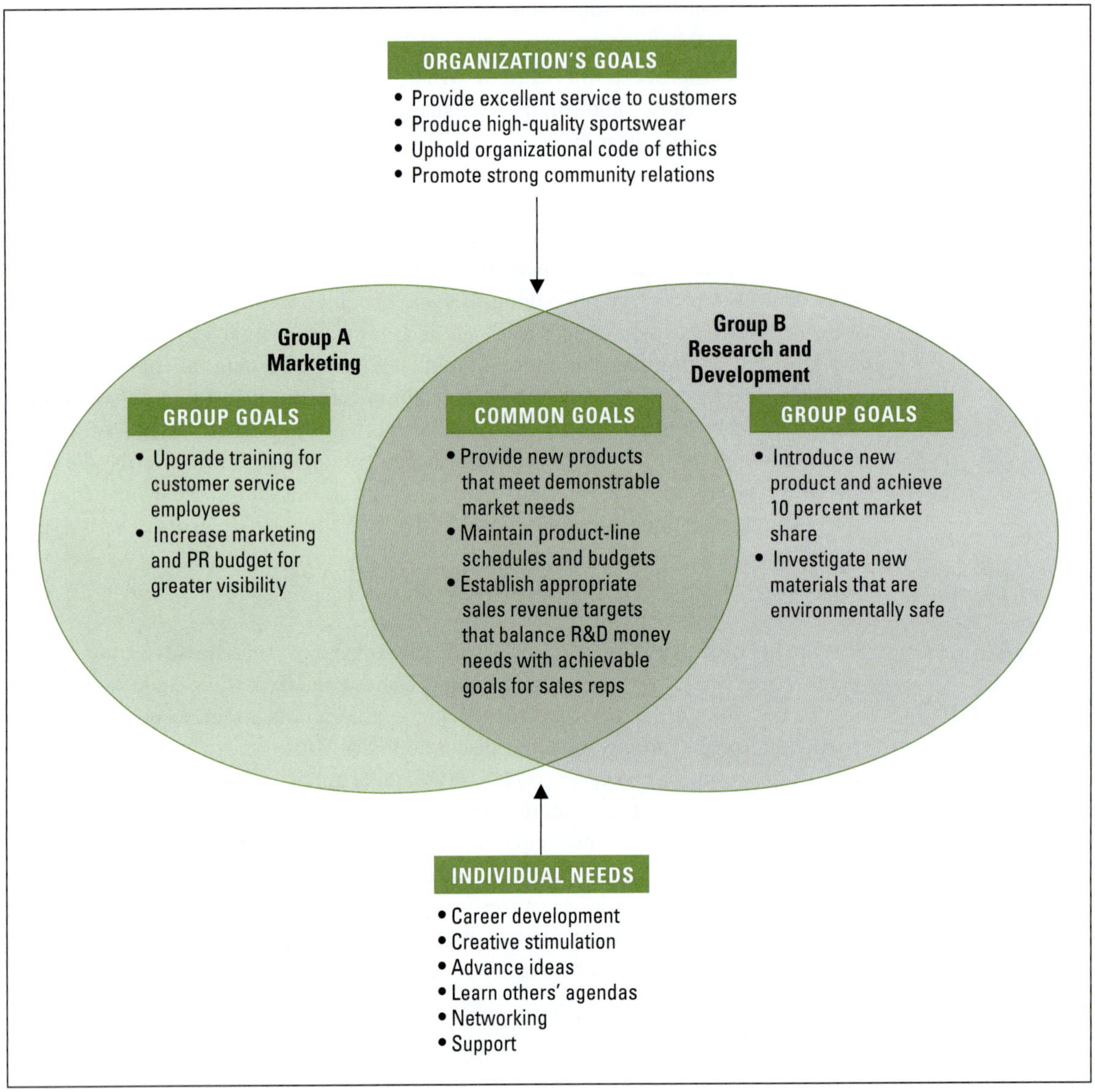

fountains, and telephones? Is the room large enough to provide for whatever seating arrangement you think is best?

There are several ways to arrange a room for a meeting, and it is important that the arrangement you choose be appropriate for the type of meeting to be held (see Figure 11.3). For example, an auditorium-style arrangement is not conducive to full-room participation, and a conference setup can isolate participants from the leader.

An **auditorium setup** includes chairs but no tables. The chairs are lined up in straight rows with a center aisle between them. All eyes are to the front, where the leader conducts the meeting. A **classroom arrangement** uses tables and chairs. Tables are typically lined up in straight rows with a center aisle separating them.

FIGURE 11.3

Typical Meeting Setups

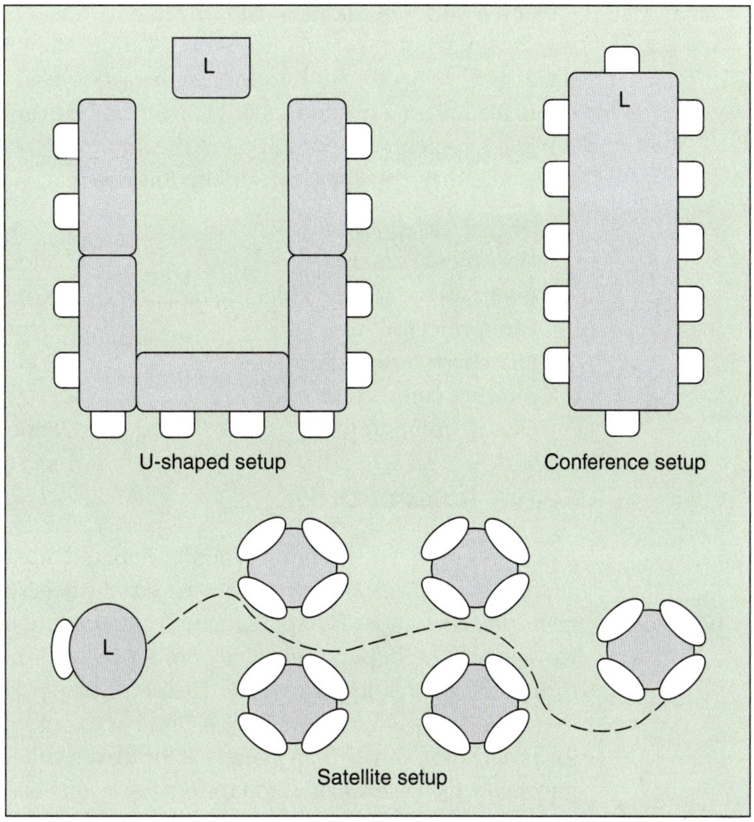

Two or three participants sit at a table. As in the auditorium setup, everyone looks straight ahead. The **U-shaped setup** is designed for full-room interaction. Tables and chairs are arranged so that participants sit adjacent to or directly across from one another. This arrangement is good for meetings that require discussion as well as presentation. The **conference arrangement** seats all members around the same table. The leader typically occupies the seat at the end. **Satellite tables** are an innovative arrangement that gives considerable room for the leader to roam around the room while conducting a discussion. Participants sit around individual tables, and each table occupies its own independent space in the room. This setup is excellent for subgroup meetings or breakouts when participants separate into teams to work on specific problems.

If you are responsible for renting a meeting area outside your company, do not overlook the need for a clear, signed contract specifying exactly what you expect to be furnished and how much you expect to pay for meeting items. Do not assume that a slide projector is always available or that pitchers of water are furnished free of charge. Find out in advance, and save yourself much grief later.

Audiovisual Requirements If you are meeting on-site or are bringing portable equipment to an off-site meeting, your primary concern is to ensure that the audiovisual equipment you plan to use works. Testing light bulbs in slide projectors, checking for adequate paper in a flip chart, and making sure that marking pens have not dried up are routine activities.

Often you will find it most convenient to use or rent equipment provided by the facility where you will hold the meeting. Many hotels and convention centers have slide projectors, microphones, projection screens, and lighting that can be controlled from a podium. Ask yourself, "Given the requirements of this meeting, what equipment is necessary for the meeting to be effective and productive?" Items you may consider include the following:

Display easels	LCD projector
Document camera	Microphone and speakers
Extension cords and electrical adapters	Notepads and pencils
Film projector	Overhead projector
Flip charts and marking pens	Podium
Internet connection	Projection screen
Laptop computer	Slide projector

Setting Rules of Order

Meetings run most smoothly when conducted according to an orderly procedure and established rules. The best-known set of rules is *Robert's Rules of Order,* which gives precise standards of parliamentary procedure to follow in specific situations.[2] How much you depend on rules of order for your meetings is determined by how formal the interaction is and the nature of past participation. If you have a group that is boisterous and disorderly, falling back on formal rules can be very effective for proceeding through an agenda. If, however, your group has always worked well informally, using strict rules for voting and points of order can have a chilling effect.

One major advantage of using established rules of order is that the group leader is less likely to be accused of personal bias in decision making. The leader's credibility increases when she or he states that "according to the rules, we must have a two-thirds majority to pass the amendment; because we do not, the motion fails." It is essential that rules be developed and communicated before the group begins deliberating. Everyone should know from the start what the rules are.

Knowing the Group

Recall our discussion in Chapter 10 of group roles, norms, and tendencies toward conformity, cohesiveness, or conflict. When preparing for a meeting or group activity, find out who the other members of the group are and how they are likely to interact. For example, you may find that the group consists of several dominators but also includes a person known as an excellent facilitator. You can thus hope that any problems of groupthink caused by the dominators will be lessened. Collect as much information as possible about how the meeting will be conducted, what topics will be discussed, and who will be present. The more prepared you are, the greater your opportunity will be to contribute to the group.

Nonverbal Communication

The importance of nonverbal communication in business and professional settings, discussed in Chapter 5, also holds true for the group context. Nonverbal communication—including such concepts as proxemics, territoriality, and chronemics—plays

2. H. M. Robert, *Robert's Rules of Order* (Glenview, Ill.: Scott, Foresman, 1990).

a key role in members' levels of participation, decision-making procedures, and ability to get along. You perhaps can imagine the effects of status in the group situation ("Oh well, since she has been a member longer than me and is older and more experienced, I'd better agree with her"). Territoriality certainly affects how groups operate ("Hey, he is sitting in my spot; I really resent that and now I won't even acknowledge his comments"). Chronemics are important in group functioning as well ("At least this group always ends on time. That's one reason why I always attend").

Research has demonstrated other critical aspects of nonverbal communication during group interaction.[3] Proxemics, or more specifically, seating positions, play a powerful role in group communication. The more central the seating position in a group, the more likely the potential for influence, dominance, and participation. So, if you are looking to be more involved and to exert more influence on the group's outcome, try finding a place to sit that is in the center of things. If the table is long or rectangular, you will be perceived more as a leader if you choose one of the end seats. If you know where certain people are going to sit or notice this as you walk into the room, and you want them to have a better chance of directing their comments to you, sit across from them. Termed the "Steinzor effect," this is the tendency of people to talk more to people directly across from them instead of to the people adjacent or beside them.

Group size has an effect on group communication as well. Larger groups have a tendency to disrupt equal participation rates among members. This "large-group" effect produces participation among only one or a few members, who are often thought of as leaders. Groups that communicate via technology (computer-mediated communication systems) are more likely to produce higher-quality ideas when they are large (nine to eighteen members) than when they are small (fewer than nine members).

SITUATIONAL KNOWLEDGE: DEVELOPING CRITICAL THINKING SKILLS

Many skills are necessary for effective communication, participation, and problem solving in meetings. The foundation of these skills is the ability to think critically about the subject or issue under discussion. Doing so allows group members to formulate and express ideas that move the group toward achieving its goals. In this section, we discuss the basic skills of critical thinking—analysis, reasoning, interpretation, and evaluation—and how to incorporate them into your communication.

Analysis

Analysis is the process of tearing apart an issue and examining its component parts to see how they relate to the whole. This skill is particularly important when group members are exploring the characteristics of a problem. To develop strong analytic skills for use in a group meeting, participants must exhibit the following:

- Patience with alternative viewpoints and methods
- Ability to define terms clearly and willingness to demand that other participants do the same

3. This section is based on a review of research by S. Ketrow, "Nonverbal Aspects of Group Communication," in L. Frey (ed.), *The Handbook of Group Communication Theory and Research* (Thousand Oaks, Calif.: Sage, 1999), pp. 251–287.

- A broad, open-minded approach to the problem
- A search for commonalities and differences
- A comparison and contrast of the problem under discussion with other problems that have been previously discussed
- A summary of what the group has discussed up to a certain point

As you can see from this list, group members must demonstrate a wide range of competencies for effective group communication, including the ability to hear a number of competing viewpoints. This is healthy for decision making. Furthermore, it is essential that group members stay on track with a focused purpose so as to reduce inefficiency. Comparing and contrasting viewpoints are two of the most important communication behaviors in a group context. And when group members summarize previous statements, they have an easier time recognizing where they have been and where they hope to go.

Reasoning

Reasoning is the ability to pull various data together and draw sound conclusions from them. There are two broad categories of reasoning: deductive and inductive. **Deductive reasoning** moves from general truths to specific conclusions. The most popular form of deductive reasoning is the **syllogism,** a three-part argument containing a general truth, a related claim, and a conclusion. A famous example is "All men are mortal; Socrates is a man; therefore, Socrates is mortal."

You can use deductive reasoning when others make general statements in a meeting. By relating general truths to specific experiences, you can draw valid conclusions. For instance, consider the following dialogue in a meeting of corporate managers:

DAVE: Our company reputation is built on keeping our regular customers happy.

AMANDA: The last reports showed customer complaints are rising. They're displeased with our service, from what I hear.

CHRIS: (drawing conclusion) I think we should put new product development on the back burner until we address current customer complaints with better service.

Chris listened to two general premises, then drew a convincing conclusion based on what had been presented in the first two premises.

Inductive reasoning moves from specific statements to general conclusions. There are four forms of inductive reasoning that you can use in a group meeting: example, sign, comparative, and causal.

Example Reasoning Reasoning by example is the most popular form of inductive reasoning. You will probably notice instances of it during most people's communication, whether in group, interpersonal, or public speaking situations. **Example reasoning** involves collecting specific cases and then making a generalization based on them. For example, if a staff member concludes that a temporary employee is needed because several employees are home sick with the flu, the conclusion is based on example. Effective group communication frequently depends on the ability to persuade group members to adopt a common point of view. Because it is based on true, observable situations, the conclusion is very persuasive.

The best way to argue *against* this kind of reasoning (if you *disagree* with the conclusion being expressed) is to show that the examples cited are not typical, representative, or timely. If a flaw can be found in the examples, the resulting generalization will also be flawed. For example, in response to the conclusion that a temporary employee is needed because of excessive employee absenccs, you could point out that the flu epidemic is an unusual circumstance and that no temporary employee has been needed in similar circumstances in the past. As this response shows, reasoning from examples is not the only way of looking at a problem.

Sign Reasoning **Sign reasoning** involves drawing conclusions from simple observations. Consider how often you use sign reasoning. You wake up in the morning, pull up the window shades, see heavy clouds, and assume that it will rain. You hear the bell clanging from the fire station and suppose that there is a fire somewhere. You pass a government building with the flag at half-mast and conclude that an important person has died. These are "signs" that lead to conclusions.

Those examples point out the drawback of sign reasoning: it encourages **hasty generalizations**—conclusions based on small or nonrepresentative samples of data. Basing your conclusions on a single observation, you have no way of knowing whether the bell is a false alarm or the worker who raises and lowers the flag was called inside to take a telephone call in midjob. You cannot safely assume that a sign has only one meaning (the one you are thinking of) that applies in all cases. Your perceptions have a strong influence on how you use sign reasoning in communication. It is important to remember that your view of the world may be different from the views of others and that the assumptions underlying sign reasoning can easily communicate misunderstanding, bias, or stereotypes detrimental to effective group interaction.

Comparative Reasoning **Comparative reasoning** occurs when a participant in a meeting pulls together two examples and reasons that what is true in the first case must be true in the second. Consider the following example. Rosa, a plant safety supervisor at Delmore Co., remarks, "Over at Bennzoil, a six-week course in new safety techniques cut work accidents more than 17 percent in just one year. We really need a program like that here. We could probably cut our accident rate 25 percent."

Rosa is reasoning by comparison. After comparing safety measures at Bennzoil and Delmore, she concludes that what worked at Bennzoil can work at her firm as well. She assumes that the two firms are similar enough to make the comparison valid. If, however, the two firms are not similar, or if Rosa's conclusion is based on inaccurate information, the comparison is *fallacious,* or unsound.

If you think that fallacious reasoning is being introduced in a group discussion, you will have to disconnect the two cases being compared and demonstrate the major differences that invalidate the comparison. For example, in response to Rosa's position, Loretta, an engineer, says, "I know someone at Bennzoil. He told me their original accident rate was so high that even with a 17 percent reduction, they still have more accidents than we do. We don't need a program like that because we don't have a problem like theirs."

Comparative reasoning is important to communication because it works to clarify the issue under discussion. Clear understanding by all group members is essential for sound decision making.

Causal Reasoning **Causal reasoning** tries to answer the question "Why did that happen?" When using causal reasoning, you assert that one factor is strong enough to produce an effect in another factor. If you have had several unsuccessful job interviews, for example, you may purchase a conservative or professional-looking outfit to improve your appearance when you interview for jobs.

During group meetings in businesses and professional organizations, the search for causes takes up a considerable amount of time and communication effort. Consider the following meeting in which several military officers are discussing low levels of morale in their division:

LT. COFFEY: The enlistees hardly ever get a chance to get out of here. They need some time away from the same old routine.

CAPT. JOHNSON: Maybe. But I think that what's really bothering them is the poor quality of food they get here.

Both Johnson and Coffey assert causes for low morale. But because the officers are engaged in a discussion, their ideas are open for rebuttal, which comes quickly from two others.

LT. BETTS: That's rubbish. You spend the money to make elaborate meals for them, and they might feel better for about five minutes. They won't work one bit harder, and you know it.

CAPT. GONZALEZ: Yeah, and we're really talking about the wrong stuff here anyway. Lack of off-base activity and bad food may hurt morale, but the real cause of the problem includes lack of recognition, lack of pride, and lack of motivation.

The example shows two ways to counter causal reasoning. Lieutenant Betts claims that Captain Johnson has identified the wrong cause of low morale—food could not possibly have that much effect. Captain Gonzalez argues that there are multiple causes, not just one cause, of the problem. Strong communicators can evaluate and discuss multiple causes without losing sight of the need for a solution. A group that becomes enmeshed in a search for causes may lose sight of its original goals. For this reason, group members need the ability to interpret causes.

Interpretation

Interpretation is an extension of causal reasoning in which you ask not only "Why did that happen?" but also "What does it mean?" Simply listening to facts, arguments, data, or opinions in a group meeting will not improve your decision-making ability. You must be able to take all this information, interpret it, and use it to draw valid conclusions.

What do you do when you interpret information? In essence, you are saying, "What this means is . . ." When you interpret, you apply your own knowledge and experience to the data to figure out what they mean, especially for other group members. Persuasive and effective interpretations typically stress the relevance, importance, or impact of data on the group and clarify information for the group. The key to interpreting information for others is to have a clear understanding of *why* the data look as they do. This understanding allows you to communicate a strategy for change.

In a group sales meeting, Mary, a manager, wants to make sure that all the sales representatives understand what three consecutive months of downward numbers mean to them and to the business:

MARY: Bill, please put the graph of our three-month sales plan and results up on the board. [He does.] As you see, we were down 3 percent in June, 4 percent in July, and 6 percent in August.

TIM: Doesn't look too good.

MARY: No, it doesn't. These figures mean that we have fallen short of our goals for three consecutive months. I believe the shortfalls result from slow sales in our new mall outlets. We need to improve our relationships with the mall vendors.

How many of the salespeople would have been able to draw that conclusion without Mary's interpretation? Furthermore, would the numbers have meant much to them without this input? Probably not. Interpretations are very important because they tie information and ideas together, helping to create shared meaning for group members.

Evaluation

Evaluation means making judgments about information or data. In most cases, judgments are made in categories such as positive/negative, favorable/unfavorable, valuable/worthless, workable/unworkable, expensive/cheap, or good/bad. Of course, evaluations are rarely clear-cut. People usually make evaluations in degrees, using qualifiers such as *fairly, moderately, basically, ordinarily,* and *partially*.

Some scholars advocate avoiding evaluation in group situations whenever possible. They believe that placing a value label on another person's contribution to a group produces hurt feelings and disharmony in the group and undermines the group's ability to communicate freely and openly. We believe, however, that before casting a vote or conforming to a group consensus, a group member must evaluate the information that has been presented.

Even if you try to avoid evaluation, you are likely to be asked for your opinions on ideas or proposals during meetings. Participants in a group expect you to assess information you have heard. If evaluation is an inevitable part of individual involvement in group decision making, then why not share your evaluation with all the participants? Evaluations are an important part of feedback in meetings, and feedback is essential to the group's success.

COMMUNICATION COMPETENCE: PROBLEM SOLVING

In addition to improving communication, critical thinking allows problem-solving and decision-making meetings to succeed. **Problem solving** involves defining a problem and generating solutions. Problem-solving groups are very common in organizations; they exist in more than 90 percent of the Fortune 500 companies.[4] Entire volumes have discussed the advantages and disadvantages of various problem-solving techniques. These techniques have much to offer groups that meet to make decisions in response to organizational and group goals. Decision-making meetings allow group members to decide on a course of action to incorporate the proposed solution.

4. R. Y. Hirokawa and D. S. Gouran, "Facilitation of Group Communication: A Critique of Prior Research and an Agenda for Future Research," *Management Communication Quarterly* 3 (1989), 71–92.

Three qualities are necessary for competent problem solving:[5]

Variety: When group members' perspectives differ, many aspects of the problem can be suggested and discussed.

Simplicity: Ideas generated during group deliberations should be arranged logically and checked for repetition and relevance.

Usefulness: Because ideas have varying degrees of usefulness to the group, members must be able to focus their energies on ideas that are most likely to result in the right decision.

Communication competence is vital to ensure that group members are able to understand the problem and share their ideas with one another appropriately and effectively.

Selecting the most appropriate problem-solving technique and then adhering to its format enable groups to recommend effective decisions. Popular and proven problem-solving methods include reflective thinking, the nominal group technique, and the Delphi technique. After surveying each of them, we present options for decision making.

Reflective Thinking

Reflective thinking is a five-step process whose success depends on each group member's willingness to participate. A major advantage of the reflective thinking technique is its efficiency. Reflective thinking provides a clear and concise road map that can save both time and energy; it prevents a group from rambling and floundering about with a problem.

Step 1: Introduce the Problem Group members state their perceptions of the problem and list the general goals the group is striving to achieve. The statements should be brief. At this point, no discussion, questions, or debate should be allowed. At the conclusion of step 1, the group knows the dimensions of the problem as perceived by the members. A variety of perspectives are essential in this stage.

Step 2: Define and Analyze the Problem Members try to agree on the problem and objectives. In this step, the group discusses qualities, characteristics, and elements of the problem. The leader quashes any attempt to talk about solutions. Members may present personal philosophies, evidence, opinions, statistics, or other relevant information, and they may compare and contrast the present problem with any related problems. Group members probe and challenge one another's perceptions of the problem.

The following substeps can increase the group's ability to define the problem:[6]

1. *Problem recognition* involves clarifying the extent of the problem, presenting evidence supporting the claims, and even challenging the problem's existence.
2. *Development of the problem statement* identifies those who have a stake in the problem, specifies values or goals associated with the problem, elicits various

5. B. J. Broome and D. B. Deever, "Next Generation Group Facilitation," *Management Communication Quarterly* 3 (1989), 107–127.
6. F. G. Smith, "Defining Managerial Problems: A Framework for Prescriptive Theorizing," *Management Science* 35 (1989), 963–981.

viewpoints on and attitudes toward the problem, and proposes a workable definition of the problem.

3. *Exploration* illuminates possible directions for the solution phase by breaking the problem into small parts for subsequent analysis, identifying related or associated problems, and suggesting possible causes for the problem's existence.
4. *Internal summary* builds consensus before moving to the next step. The leader may say, "We have decided that the problem is ________ and that ________ are related issues and probable causes."

As you can see, critical thinking skills play a vital role in defining the problem. When the problem has been identified, defined, and analyzed, it is time to move to step 3.

Step 3: Establish Criteria The group decides what elements the solution to the problem should achieve or include. These criteria will be used later in the discussion to evaluate potential solutions. For example, if you and your friends are deciding how to spend a Saturday night, and there are several activities to choose from, establishing criteria can help you to decide which activity is best for the group. One person may suggest that money is a factor, thereby establishing the criterion "Whatever we do, it can't cost more than $10 per person." Another may have to get up early the next morning, thereby establishing the criterion "We have to be back at my place by 12:30 A.M. at the latest." Still another may request that the activity be something new—for example, "Let's not go to a movie; we always do that." These criteria can help your group narrow the options and make the best decision for all concerned.

The criteria must be relevant to the problem at hand. The following guidelines can ensure the choice of relevant criteria:

Overall Strength: The criteria address the effectiveness and efficiency of proposed solutions, including the extent of the solution, possible future consequences, and realistic chances of carrying out the plan.

Resources: The criteria assess the time, money, effort, or employee morale necessary to implement each possible solution.

Ethics: Ethical criteria prevent possible infringements on the rights of other people or organizations. These criteria should address the legality, morality, honesty, and decency of each possible solution. Ethical criteria may focus on the employees of the organization ("Eliminating all vacation time for employees is simply not acceptable"), on other organizations ("We can't tell our competition we are going out of business when we are not"), on the environment ("Dumping waste into the river is cheap but will have serious consequences for the river ecosystem"), or on the community ("Building an adjacent plant would displace a lot of residents"). Ethical criteria should address each of the groups affected by the solution.

The best solutions are those that suit the criteria established in step 3. Keep in mind that criteria must be established *before* the group tries to come up with solutions. Doing so keeps group members from changing their minds about what they are trying to accomplish during the course of the meeting.

Establishing and adhering to criteria are essential for effective decision making and save the group countless hours of directionless deliberation. In sum, group members should probe and challenge one another to ensure they have worthy criteria against which to judge a solution. Selecting a solution will then be much easier.

STRATEGIC SKILLS

Problem Solving on the Job

The scene is a meeting to discuss how restaurant owners can be persuaded to increase the size of the soft drinks they offer in their restaurants. The group includes some of the top sales managers in the division, and the meeting is led by a vice president (VP). To understand this example, you need to know that the term *cup* refers to the size of the soft drinks sold in fast-food restaurants. The profits for a restaurant increase when large cup sizes are sold.

GOAL: *To convince food-service operators to increase the size of their fountain drinks.*

PROBLEM: *Operators do not want to sell large drinks.*

I. Introduce the Problem

VP: Let's start off by having each of you give a brief summary of the problem as you see it. Why are restaurants reluctant to increase their drink sizes?

LINDA: Operators don't understand that larger sizes are more profitable.

ROBERT: Operators are afraid consumers won't buy the larger drinks.

INGRID: Large drinks jeopardize our other promotions.

JACK: We just don't have the marketing materials we need to sell large drinks.

II. Define and Analyze the Problem

VP: Now that we've seen everyone's perception of the problem, let's dig into these ideas and find out exactly what we're trying to solve here. I want you to elaborate on what you've just said. Everyone should feel free to disagree, ask questions, add comments or experiences, or say whatever. I want to make sure we really know what we're dealing with, so let's analyze it in detail. Just as a springboard for discussion, Linda, let's start with your observation that the operators don't understand our strategy very well.

LINDA: Operators don't really understand why selling large sizes helps their business. We need to educate them about what kind of a gold mine they're sitting on.

ROBERT: I think they're just scared to put a large cup in front of the consumer. They're afraid it won't sell.

INGRID: I think we've made our free refill promotion so successful that we can't sell the big cup idea. No one will want to offer refills on forty-four-ounce cups. If they can't offer the large-size cup and the refill, they're going to stick with what's worked in the past—the refill.

JACK: Our promotional materials are really good on the forty-four-ounce cup, but they don't show the benefits of increasing the other drink sizes as well. Our salespeople don't have prepackaged information that they can use to push the larger drink sizes.

VP: So, if I could try to summarize what we've said here the last few minutes, it seems that although our sales force has been very effective in selling the forty-four-ounce cup, we have not been pushing the complete set of large cup sizes. We do not have promotional brochures outlining the advantages of the larger cup sizes, and restaurant owners need to be told about them. We've also said that many operators see refill promotions and large cup sizes as a contradiction.

III. Establish Criteria

VP: OK, we've got a handle on the problem! Before we start to look for specific solutions, let's try to figure out what we want the solution to do. Remember, we will

Step 4: Generate Possible Solutions In this step, often referred to as brainstorming, group members present logical and workable solutions to the problem. The goal is to generate a list of creative solutions but not to evaluate their worth. No solution is dismissed or even criticized at this stage. Although some ideas may seem bizarre when first presented, they can be modified to be effective and ingenious. Before moving to the next step, the leader reviews the list of possible solutions to make sure that all have been recorded correctly and to ensure that they do not repeat each other.

judge our suggested solutions by these criteria, so make sure you consider effectiveness, resources, and ethical questions when devising them! I'll be listing them on a flip chart as we go.

LINDA: I think the solution has to include a written explanation of why the large sizes are better. Operators will trust us if we put it in writing.

ROBERT: We need to have the solution ready as soon as possible.

INGRID: The solution must consider the customers. We can't expect operators to sell large drinks if customers end up getting less for their money.

JACK: The solution has to include some kind of financial bonus that equals the selling power of free refills.

VP: So, we've decided on criteria that our solution has to meet: the solution has to include written material that the field sales force can use with the trade; it has to be efficiently implemented; it has to include some sort of financial incentive for the food-service operator; and it has to be acceptable to the consumers.

IV. Generate Possible Solutions

VP: Now, let's think of as many possible solutions as we can. We are not going to evaluate any of these right now; I'll just make a list as you call them out. Now, it's OK to ask a question for clarification or to get more information, but we won't challenge or debate any of these solutions while they are being given. I'll list these for us.

LINDA: Let's talk to marketing about making a glossy brochure for our field sales force that begins with information about the profitability of soft drinks, moves to our brand, and then shows the value of increasing the cup sizes for the operator.

JACK: I think we should offer a free tank of syrup to any operator who goes to the large cup sizes and stays with them for three months.

ROBERT: We could just work with our bottlers in phasing out small cups. If the small cups weren't made, the restaurants couldn't sell them!

INGRID: We can use a coupon incentive to get operators to try the large cup sizes.

VP: So, these are the solutions we've come up with. Anything else? OK, let's move on to evaluating these solutions.

V. Evaluate Possible Solutions

VP: Now we'll take the solutions in this chart one by one and match them against our criteria. We'll rule out or modify any solution that doesn't match up and see what happens. OK, our first solution was to have a brochure made focused on upgraded cup sizes. Now, does this satisfy our requirement for written material? Yes! Does it touch on some kind of financial incentive for the operator? No, but we might be able to modify it. . . .

[Matching of solutions to criteria continues.]

VP: So, as a result of this discussion, we've decided to produce a marketing brochure that our sales force can use to show operators why they should increase their cup sizes. The brochure will include an incentive coupon for a free tank of syrup if operators increase their cup sizes for a minimum of three months. The solution meets our criteria of providing written information and financial incentive to operators, and because consumers can still purchase a twenty-four-ounce drink at the same price they have always paid for it, we are not proposing anything unacceptable to them.

Step 5: Evaluate Possible Solutions Using the criteria established in step 3, group members discuss the worth of each of the solutions generated in step 4. The leader introduces each proposed solution and asks the group to evaluate it by the criteria agreed on in step 3. The goal of this step is for the group to make a final decision by selecting the most viable solution—the one that best satisfies the criteria.

What if more than one proposed solution meets all the criteria, or what if no solution can meet all the criteria? In the first instance, the group must decide whether the two solutions are mutually exclusive. If they are not, then the group may implement both. In the second instance, the group selects the solution that fulfills the most criteria. Before adjourning the meeting, moving on to another problem, or continuing to another point on the agenda, the leader restates the problem and the solution so that all group members understand them.

The example in the Strategic Skills box on pages 316–317 shows how reflective thinking works. The dialogue presented there is typical of the discussion in problem-solving meetings. Although real-world discussions don't always progress to a mutually agreeable conclusion so easily, the example shows how reflective thinking can be effective.

Reflective thinking is a powerful tool for finding solutions to particular problems. After working through the example, you can understand the importance of taking each step in its proper order and systematically working through all five steps.

Nominal Group Technique

The **nominal group technique (NGT)** allows groups to discuss problems and solutions in a relatively structured setting. This technique is especially useful in newly formed groups and in groups with large differences in status and communication dominance among members. NGT has five steps: preparation, silent generation of ideas, round-robin recording of ideas, discussion, and voting.

Preparation The group leader or facilitator prepares a question for discussion. The question must be succinct and simple to understand and cover only one topic. Here is an example of a poor question: "What are our safety problems and objectives, and what specific projects and programs can we undertake to ensure greater safety and efficiency in our plant?" The question is vague and wordy and contains at least three different topics. A far better question clearly addresses one issue: "What objectives must our plant safety program accomplish?"

Before the meeting starts, the facilitator gathers flip charts on which to record members' responses, tape to attach the charts to the wall, and index cards on which participants can write ideas. At the outset of the meeting, the facilitator explains the subsequent four-step process and emphasizes the meeting's importance for the group and organization.

Silent Generation of Ideas After the question is posed and understood by all participants, the leader announces a specific period of time in which the group members may write down ideas related to the question. These ideas are best stated as phrases or brief sentences. The time period should be restricted to four to eight minutes.[7] A short time period limits the number of items that the participants produce so that the group will be able to manage all or most of them. During this time, participants work independently and silently.

Round-Robin Recording The leader calls on each participant and asks for one idea. The leader writes each contribution on a flip chart as it is given. No discussion or elaboration is allowed. The leader then moves to another member and

7. C. H. Moore, *Group Techniques for Idea Building* (Newbury Park, Calif.: Sage, 1987).

takes an idea, moves to another, moves to another, and so on until all ideas written by the participants have been recorded. As a page of the flip chart is filled, the leader tapes it to the wall, where it is visible to all participants. To save time, the leader asks participants not to contribute any ideas that have already been recorded. Each idea is numbered to simplify voting on the ideas.

Discussion This step clarifies any confusion among group members about ideas. The leader reads each idea and invites comments and questions. The leader encourages members to discuss any items they wish, not simply those they contributed to the group. No voting, expression of opinion, or other type of debate takes place at this point.

Voting In the final step, group members make decisions about the ideas that have been generated. The leader distributes five index cards to each participant, and each participant reviews the list, selects what he or she thinks are the five best ideas, and writes the number of one idea in the center of each card. The participant then ranks the five ideas by placing a number from one to five in the upper-right-hand corner of the card, with five being the highest rating and one the lowest. When the participants have finished, the leader collects the cards and assembles a tally in front of the group. Figure 11.4 shows the results of applying the nominal group technique to the fountain-drink problem presented in the Strategic Skills box on pages 316–317.

In many cases, a clear winning idea emerges. In others, a dead heat between ideas requires the group to rank the tied alternatives.

FIGURE 11.4

NGT in Progress

A flip chart shows the nominal group technique in progress. Each group member has considered the list of ideas on the left and ranked each one on a separate card. The completed tally for each idea is shown on the right. Idea 2 emerges as the highest-ranked idea.

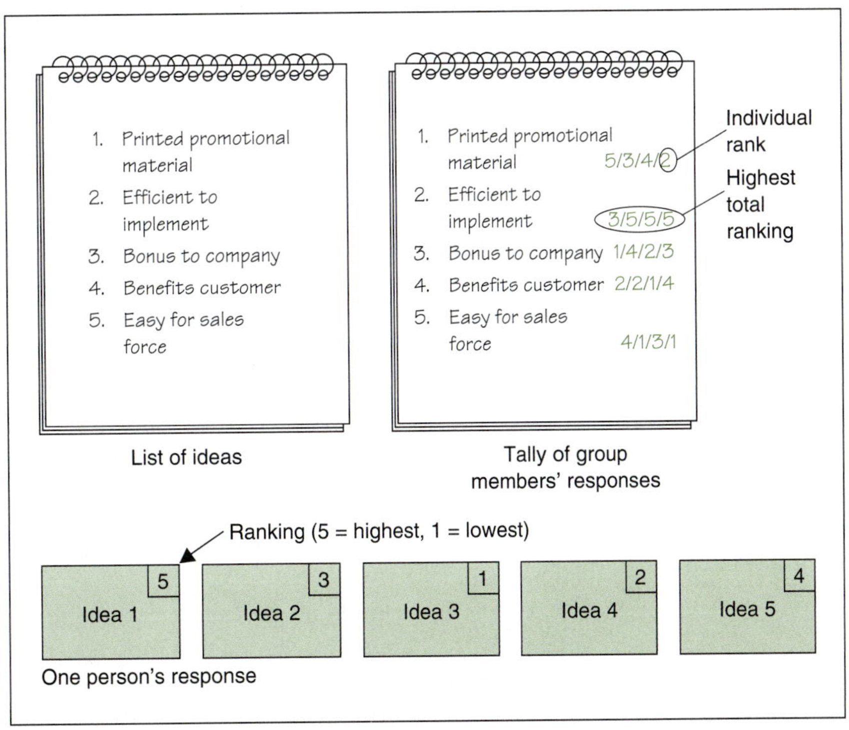

TECHNOLOGY TOOLS

Problem Solving On-Line

Computer technology makes it possible to conduct problem solving on-line. Several software programs exist that allow you to connect anonymously into a central "server" much like a chat room or electronic bulletin board and suggest ideas and solutions to problems without anyone knowing who you are. In this electronic version of NGT, you can contribute to this on-line group and be as risky and creative as you want without having to "own" your ideas. Many businesses see this technique as an opportunity to increase the effectiveness of their employees. Not only are many creative ideas generated, but employees don't even have to leave their offices to participate in the group. In fact, with computer groups, employees don't even have to be on-line at the same time. You can log in when you have the time, see what has happened while you were away, make a contribution, and log off.

The Delphi Technique

The **Delphi technique** uses questionnaires to collect opinions and judgments from experts, who usually remain anonymous. Typically, questionnaires are sent by mail, although they can be distributed via the Internet by means of teleconferences. The Delphi technique is not a survey or a one-time poll. The questionnaire is repeated over several rounds to collect progressively more specific information. The results from one round of questions dictate the questions for the next round. You would select this method of decision making in circumstances in which subjective judgments are desirable, face-to-face exchange is not possible because of time or cost restraints, or participants disagree to the extent that anonymity must be ensured to achieve results.

The Delphi technique includes four steps: (1) deciding to administer a questionnaire and selecting a group to respond, (2) formulating the questions and producing the questionnaire, (3) noting a deadline date for return of the questionnaires, and (4) receiving and analyzing the questionnaires. When using this technique, you must take into consideration several matters. The people to whom you address the questionnaire must be experts. To maximize response rates, you should include a personalized cover letter (or, in the case of a teleconference, personalized instructions), guarantee anonymity, and promise to provide all respondents with a copy of the results.

Keep the questionnaire brief and to the point. It is far better to increase the number of Delphi rounds than to complicate the questionnaire. The questionnaire will be easier to respond to if it includes closed questions (such as true/false and multiple choice) rather than open questions that require the respondents to write answers. Anticipate approximately a ten-week time frame for the process to be completed.

Here is an example of the Delphi technique in action. The personnel department of a large company wanted to improve its minority recruiting, so it surveyed personnel directors from similar-sized corporations throughout a three-state region for ideas. The first-round question posed by the Delphi technique was "What problems inhibit recruitment in large corporations?" Based on the results of the first questionnaire, the second-round questionnaire asked respondents to rank the top five problems and invited them to list others. Finally, based on those results, the third round solicited solutions for the problems. The outcome of the study allowed the firm to see which problems it had in common with other firms and to devise means to correct those problems. The results of the study were sent to all personnel directors who participated.

Each of the different problem-solving methods discussed here has its own merits, depending on the situation. Table 11.1 summarizes the techniques and suggests when to use them.

What Would You Do?

Assume you work for the bursar's office at your school. You are a member of a group that was formed to address complaints made by students who were billed twice for the same semester. What are the organizational goals and the group goals? Which problem-solving technique would you suggest? Why?

Decision-Making Options

There are many ways in which groups can engage in decision making. The entire reason they engage in that process, however, is to produce a result or a final decision. Two techniques that leaders can use to bring about effective decisions are consensus and voting.

Consensus **Consensus** is unanimous agreement among group members concerning a particular decision. Reaching consensus is the goal of many decision-making groups. Most reach consensus through the correct application of issue-specific conflict. Proper conflict management permits participants to debate, test ideas, question evidence, and so on. In groups in which conflict is used properly,

TABLE 11.1

Choosing a Problem-Solving Method

Problem-Solving Method	Essential Characteristics	Reasons to Use
Reflective thinking	• Groups members not necessarily experts • Face-to-face interaction valued and encouraged • Opportunity to clarify issues in person	• Straightforward process for complex problems • Develops cohesion and productive advocacy • Gives members a sense of ownership of solution
Nominal group technique	• Ideas generated silently • Repetitive, round-robin development of ideas • Potential solutions rank-ordered	• Effective with new groups • Useful if members have ample time to prepare for group problem • Useful if members perceive excessive risk or feel threatened
Delphi technique	• Progressive, repetitive process • Anonymous respondents/members • Participants experts in subject matter	• Opinionated, subjective judgments desired • Face-to-face interaction not possible (distance) • Useful if participants hold strong, disagreeable viewpoints that may lead to unproductive conflict

consensus can be reached because all participants are testing ideas in a systematic manner. Conflict as a means for discussion allows members to resolve their differences by identifying the single best solution to a given problem.

The major advantage of achieving consensus is that all group members leave the meeting committed to the same outcome. This is not true of decision-making methods that rely primarily on voting. In many cases in which voting is employed, members remain committed to the positions that they supported in the discussion but that the group voted down. As a result, they are uncommitted to the decision that was made, and they are resentful toward the group and the solution.

How do you achieve consensus in a group discussion? Several rules are useful:

1. Drop your personal position when it is shown to be unworkable or illogical.
2. Maintain an open mind concerning conflict and differences of opinion. Remember that conflict is a means by which the group can achieve its goals. If the group does not argue and exhibit conflict, why does it need to meet in the first place?
3. Unless pressed for time, do not substitute majority votes, trading, compromising, or averaging for reaching a consensus decision. Continue to work through the problem until all members agree with and are committed to a solution.
4. When discussion reaches a stalemate, try to identify issues that are agreeable to all members present so as to isolate issues about which there is disagreement. This is the *most-common-denominator rule*. Participants have to know on what issues opinions are divided; otherwise, arguments occur on several different issues at once.

Voting One of the most frequently used methods of resolving problems is voting. In most cases, voting imposes the will of the majority. Unlike consensus, voting forces a decision on some of the participants. The risk of having group members

A voting process often provides a useful method for arriving at final decisions. However, keep in mind that many group members would rather agree to a compromise than discover that "their solution" has been voted out of consideration. (© Howard Grey/Stone—Getty Images)

ETHICAL ISSUES

Maintaining Ethics When Working Alone

It can be difficult to maintain ethical behavior in businesses and the professions when individuals work alone on projects. At times their thinking can become focused on issues such as getting results or solving problems. Sometimes this single-minded purpose can lead to less-than-ethical decisions. When people work together in teams, there is a greater opportunity to challenge assumptions that are formed by individuals. Issues that border on unethical thinking and behavior can be brought out into the open through reflective thinking, reasoning, and devil's advocacy. Individuals working alone should strive to get feedback from others. Meetings provide excellent opportunities to ensure ethical communication during the problem-solving process.

uncommitted to a decision and holding a negative attitude toward the group and the decision is, in our opinion, not desirable, and we urge that this method be avoided if at all possible. Nevertheless, there are two circumstances in which voting is useful: (1) if the group is under time constraints that do not allow the group to proceed through a normal discussion and reach consensus and (2) if the group is too large to hold a consensus discussion.

If at all possible, use voting to narrow options on which a consensus decision can be reached. For example, suppose that a group has five mutually exclusive solutions that all seem reasonable and workable and that the size of the group and time constraints prevent the group from working through the proposed solution in a consensus-building fashion. The group can take a vote on each option and determine which two of the five the majority of the members seems to favor. Having narrowed the solutions down to two, the group can then hold a consensus discussion and work through to a single desired option. Notice that when the members finish this type of discussion, they have actively participated in the decision-making process and will be committed to the decision reached.

ANXIETY MANAGEMENT

There are several causes of anxiety in meeting situations. In some instances, the meeting is not an opportunity for open discussion but rather a closed forum in which powerful members monopolize communication or coerce others into agreement on issues. If you have low status in the group or simply are uncomfortable with an authoritarian style, such a meeting may upset you and result in communication anxiety. To address your nervousness, you can suggest that the group take a break from the discussion and allow everyone a turn to summarize the group's progress up to that point. In this way, others who may also be apprehensive will gain mutual support.

Another cause of anxiety is not knowing the other participants. If you are a newcomer and all the other participants know one another, you may feel shy, anxious, and nervous about speaking up or stating a position, and it may be difficult to become friendly with group members before the initial meeting of the group. Once you know people's names and positions in the organization, however, you will have some basic information with which to work. By approaching the relationship with the goal of improving group communication as well as lessening your own anxiety, you will be able to shift the focus from yourself and your nervousness and concentrate on becoming comfortable with group members.

In companies that have diverse work forces—people of many different educational or cultural backgrounds or varied ages—differences in communication styles may cause apprehension in a group meeting. Many companies, for example, cite instances in which men ignored a woman's input but accepted the same suggestion for discussion when it was made by a man. Conflicting cultural norms pertaining to boastfulness, dominance, or even use of nonverbal gestures such as touching, eye contact, or facial expressions may make group meetings anxiety-producing events if you fail to prepare for such differences by becoming familiar with different norms and styles.

Finally, meetings held to resolve a group conflict or to mediate serious arguments can cause apprehension because of the sensitivity of issues involved. Ways to contain anxiety that stems from conflict are discussed in Chapter 12.

EVALUATING GROUP EFFECTIVENESS

No matter how successful, productive, or effective modern business and professional organizations are, they are rarely satisfied. Unless there is a strong and clearly articulated vision for the future, today's successes are tomorrow's busts. One key method that organizations use to prepare for the future is evaluating the present. To define what we mean by evaluation, we must contrast it with description. Description focuses on what a group or person is doing; evaluation focuses on how well the group or person is performing the task. Evaluation requires a judgment or an assessment.

As John Brilhart noted, "Unless practice is constantly evaluated, it may result in bad habits. The means to learning is practice with analysis and evaluation leading to change in future discussions."[8] Therefore, you must monitor and evaluate the effectiveness of the groups in which you participate if you intend to join the future.

Many students of group communication have devised categories, rating forms, evaluation instruments, and questionnaires to assess the strengths of different units. In this section, we discuss the dimensions of group evaluations and techniques for conducting them successfully.

Dimensions of Group Evaluation

Albert Kowitz and Thomas Knutson divided group evaluation into three dimensions: informational, procedural, and interpersonal.[9]

Informational According to Kowitz and Knutson, the **informational** dimension is concerned with the task that the group is working on. Evaluation of that task can be broken down into several components. One is whether the task before the group lends itself to discussion. If it does not, the group may have to expand the scope and nature of its topic. If the task is suitable for discussion, a second component presents itself: How prepared is the group for discussion? Was needed research or necessary

8. J. K. Brilhart, "Observing and Evaluating Discussion," in Cathcart and Samovar, *Small Group Communication*, p. 559.
9. A. C. Kowitz and T. J. Knutson, *Decision Making in Small Groups: The Search for Alternatives* (Boston: Allyn & Bacon, 1980).

advance planning done by the members before the meeting? Is there a need to get more information before the group can make an adequate decision?

A third component is how well the group "tears apart" the problem. Analysis depends on successfully reducing an issue to its component parts. Is there evidence of high-quality information giving, opinion giving, evaluation and criticism, elaboration and integration? Note that evaluation and criticism are extremely important to the success of the group. The group meets to test ideas. If there is early agreement and signs that certain participants are reluctant to express reservations, the meeting is headed toward groupthink. Does anyone say, "Let me play devil's advocate for a moment"? In evaluating a group, you should see evidence of productive conflict—debate, questioning, and exploration of alternatives.

Procedural Evaluation of **procedural** functions looks at how well the group's activities and communication are coordinated. We said earlier in this chapter that the leader performs most of these functions. Yet in groups where leadership is a shared function, each participant has a responsibility to exhibit some essential leadership behaviors.

The key functions to be evaluated include eliciting communication, delegating and directing action, summarizing group activity, managing conflict, evaluating process, and releasing tension. Let us highlight a few problems that you may see in these areas.

One behavior that occurs with regularity in groups is some members talking too much and others talking too little. To counteract this behavior, an astute leader and others attempt to keep the lines of communication open among all group members. This function is known as *gatekeeping*. A remark such as "Tim, I think you've covered that issue pretty well. Bob, do you have anything to add?" is a tactful way to suppress and elicit contributions simultaneously.

Another recurring behavior is a return to issues that have seemingly been resolved or worked through. When this happens, many members get frustrated and tense. You will hear, "We never get anything done in here" or "We're just spinning our wheels." There are two possibilities for corrective action. One is the use of summaries. Does the leader or do other members continually keep the group posted on its progress with remarks such as "What we've been talking about is . . ." or "So, what we seem to be saying is . . ."? A second possibility is to determine whether the group has lost sight of its objectives. What is the group trying to accomplish, and how well does the present discussion help to accomplish these objectives?

Finally, there is a need for members to release tension at certain points of interaction. This can be done through a joke, a sharing of feelings, and so on. Kowitz and Knutson stressed that participants may need to be reminded of their individual responsibilities and importance in the overall group function. Once members are aware of what is expected of them, tension can decrease and the group can resume making progress.

Interpersonal In the **interpersonal** portion of the evaluation, the emphasis is on how well the members of the group work with each other. Of interest is the climate or atmosphere in which the task is accomplished. There can be little doubt that when the circumstances under which a group operates are uncomfortable or unpleasant, productivity and results are affected in negative ways. Interpersonal assessment can focus on four areas: positive reinforcement, solidarity, cooperativeness, and respect toward others.

PRACTICING BUSINESS COMMUNICATION

Nokia Corporation

Nokia is one of the most influential and powerful telecommunications providers in the world. The company is Finnish-based but has a strong presence in the United States, South America, Hong Kong, and many other countries. In 1999, Nokia surpassed Motorola to become the world's leading maker of mobile phones. According to the May 1, 2000, edition of *Fortune* magazine, Nokia lays claim to the world's eleventh most valuable brand and has the highest stock market value of any European company.

In the preceding chapter, you read about a special kind of small group, entitled affinity groups. You may be interested to learn that The Evans Group, a learning and development firm of consultants based in Dallas, Texas, originated the concept and methodology for affinity groups. Over the years, The Evans Group has established these groups in numerous corporations and professional associations, including Club Corporation of America and the Young Presidents Organization. Nokia is one of the companies that embraced affinity groups with great enthusiasm.

In 1999, The Evans Group worked with Nokia to evaluate the effectiveness of affinity groups with a representative group of managers who served as participants. What you will read here is based on The Evans Group's administration of affinity groups for eleven different collections of managers at Nokia.

AFFINITY GROUPS AT NOKIA

The Affinity Groups at Nokia are comprised of a cross section of managers who participate in a three-part series of management development training programs, called MAP. These managers participate in affinity group meetings for one full day in session 1 and one-half day in sessions 2 and 3.

Between sessions, Nokia invites participants to post updates and to continue to interact following the conclusion of the program through a confidential Web site sponsored by The Evans Group that is password protected for members of the group.

REACTIONS TO AFFINITY GROUPS

After the completion of the MAP programs, participants were asked to rate their perceptions of their experience in affinity groups on a questionnaire. The questions asked participants to react to the value of these groups, the quality of their own participation, and their adherence to the principles and spirit of the process. The results were very encouraging, with most participants very pleased with the process.

IMPACT ON PERCEPTIONS OF NOKIA

Following their third meeting, MAP participants completed a twenty-item questionnaire asking them about their attitudes and reactions toward their work in their current position at Nokia (see below).

Like any other support group, affinity groups are not for everyone. They are not panaceas for every individual and organizational problem. They are not "try it, you'll like it" propositions. However, those participants who "like it," or who have affinity toward their groups and the process, also perceive that they are doing some good for themselves, their fellow group members, and the organization.

The Evans Group and Nokia tested this premise. In a study, they divided respondents from the post–affinity group

One of the most dangerous things that can happen in a meeting is conflict shifting from tasks to individuals. Personality conflicts can distract the group from its primary task and responsibility. Whenever an outburst occurs—such as "You've never known anything about this before, and who are you to talk about it now?"—the group leader and the other members should attempt to reiterate that the group should "stick to the facts" or "get back to the problem."

If the atmosphere is negative or unpleasant, the leader or any other group member can use rewards to emphasize the positive aspects of the meeting. There may, however, be underlying reasons for the negative statements being made, such as an objection to the person's proposed solution or resentment questionnaire discussed in the preceding section into high-affinity and low-affinity groups at the fiftieth percentile. They then tested the differences between these two groups on the twenty Nokia items. In every case, the results indicate that participants in the high-affinity group felt more positive about their job, the company, and their interactions with others in the organization. Even more interesting, participants with high affinity toward affinity groups claimed that they found higher quality in their work meetings than did those with low affinity toward these groups.

INTERPRETATIONS ABOUT AFFINITY GROUPS AT NOKIA

These studies indicate that mangers' participation in affinity groups during MAP training has produced favorable reactions toward personal and professional relationships with others. One of the reasons that Nokia, as well as other organizations, endorses participation in affinity groups is to build a strong support network through which these managers may find reliable outlets to discuss work and personal issues. These data reveal highly favorable reactions toward the experience.

The studies also demonstrate that these mangers complete the MAP program with highly favorable attitudes about the company. Clearly, participation in affinity groups, as a benefit from the MAP program, has contributed to feelings of pride, connection, and congruence with corporate ideals and values. Additionally, the results indicate that providing participants from various divisions at Nokia with the opportunity to share perspectives is extremely valuable in establishing the value of cross-functional teamwork.

The affinity group experience in the MAP training program at Nokia provides transferable skills that managers can use to improve their performance on the job with their own managers, coworkers, and direct reports. These skills include coaching, counseling, listening, fact finding, analysis, synthesis, facilitating, presenting, and organizing. Due to the confidentiality norm that operates in affinity groups to prevent conflicts of interest, the purpose of the managers' participation is not to establish these groups in the workplace but rather to prompt skills that, on a daily basis, contribute to successful interaction. The management at Nokia is extremely excited about continuing and expanding the role of affinity groups throughout the corporation.

QUESTIONS FOR CRITICAL THINKING

1. Why do you think that Nokia decided to begin its affinity group participation with managers only, and then hold those meetings within the context of a training session?
2. What value do you believe participants would find in obtaining input, suggestions, and experiences about issues from others in an affinity group who do not do the same work they do, have the same type of family they do, or experience the same personal challenges they do?
3. Do any of the results or responses to the questions in the two surveys surprise you? How?
4. At Nokia, participation in affinity groups is a required part of the training program for these managers. What do you suspect would occur if participation were voluntary?

You can visit Nokia on-line at http://www.nokia.com.

over a stolen idea. If this is the case, the reason for the derogatory comments should be explored because it may provide information helpful for achieving the group's goals.

Individual Evaluation

Apart from the group as a whole, each individual participant can be assessed. The focus of such an evaluation is how well members helped the group accomplish its task and how well they performed functions during the process.

What Would You Do?

Suppose you are working in a group with three other members. Two of the members are adversaries, and you have heard each gossiping about the other to employees outside the group. The group facilitator has asked for suggestions for advertising budget reductions. One of the members begins his suggestion but is interrupted by his adversary, who snaps, "I don't like that idea!" The first member retorts, "That's because you don't like me!" A verbal brawl begins between the two. As a member of this group, what would you do? Is it your place to intervene and attempt to reestablish a more rational, critical thinking type of atmosphere?

Larry Samovar and Steven King created two excellent instruments for evaluating individual participants and leaders.[10] Eleven factors make up the individual member evaluation form shown in Figure 11.5. The form may be completed by the group leader or by another group member. There are also eleven factors on the leadership evaluation form (see Figure 11.6). This form operates best when the group has an assigned or designated leader. The evaluator can focus on one individual and how well he or she performs the leadership role.

10. L. A. Samovar and S. W. King, *Communication and Discussion in Small Groups* (Scottsdale, Ariz.: Gorsuch-Scarisbrick, 1981).

FIGURE 11.5

Participant Evaluation Form

Source: From L. A. Samovar and S. W. King, *Communication and Discussion in Small Groups* (Scottsdale, Ariz.: Gorsuch-Scarisbrick, 1981). Reprinted with permission of the authors.

NAME OF GROUP MEMBER: ____________________
NAME OF RATER: ____________________
DATE: ____________________

For each characteristic, fill in a rating from 1 (excellent) to 7 (poor). Write any comments in the space below the rating list.

Participant Characteristics

1. ______ Preparation
2. ______ Speaking
3. ______ Listening
4. ______ Open-mindedness
5. ______ Sensitivity to others
6. ______ Worth of information
7. ______ Critical thinking skills
8. ______ Group orientation
9. ______ Procedural contribution
10. ______ Assistance in leadership
11. ______ Overall evaluation

Comments:

FIGURE 11.6

Leader Evaluation Form

Source: From L. A. Samovar and S. W. King, *Communication and Discussion in Small Groups* (Scottsdale, Ariz.: Gorsuch-Scarisbrick, 1981). Reprinted with permission of the authors.

NAME OF LEADER: ____________________
NAME OF RATER: ____________________
DATE: ____________________

For each characteristic, fill in a rating from 1 (excellent) to 7 (poor). Write any comments in the space below the rating list.

Leadership Functions

1. ______ Opened discussion
2. ______ Asked appropriate questions
3. ______ Offered reviews
4. ______ Clarified ideas
5. ______ Encouraged critical thinking
6. ______ Limited irrelevancies
7. ______ Protected minority viewpoints
8. ______ Remained impartial
9. ______ Kept accurate records
10. ______ Concluded discussion
11. ______ Overall leadership

Comments:

Assessments can be made about the relative strengths and weaknesses of each group member. Evaluating these areas contributes to improvement in group work.

The Group Behavior Inventory

One of the most reliable methods of group evaluation is the Group Behavior Inventory (GBI).[11] It is a long instrument consisting of seventy-one items. Figure 11.7 includes items from the GBI that conform to the dimensions discussed in this and the previous chapter. This evaluation measure can come in handy after you meet with a group several times to identify areas of strength and weakness. All group members should score the measure and discuss their individual results with the group. In this way, everyone will understand the relative perceptions of their counterparts, weaknesses can be healed, and strengths can be maintained. Look for specific areas that need improvement, and work together to strengthen them.

11. The complete Group Behavior Inventory can be obtained from the Library of Congress, Photoduplication Service, Washington, DC 20540 (request document ADI-8787). For further information on the use of group evaluations, see F. Friedlander, "Performance and Interactional Dimensions of Organizational Work Groups," *Journal of Applied Psychology* 50 (1969), 257–265, and I. T. Kaplan and H. H. Greenbaum, "Measuring Work Group Effectiveness: A Comparison of Three Instruments," *Management Communication Quarterly* 2 (1989), 424–448.

FIGURE 11.7

Group Evaluation Form

Source: From L. A. Samovar and S. W. King, *Communication and Discussion in Small Groups* (Scottsdale, Ariz.: Gorsuch-Scarisbrick, 1981). Reprinted with permission of the authors.

Rate the following items according to how you feel about the group or its members: 1 = strongly agree, 2 = agree, 3 = neither agree nor disagree, 4 = disagree, and 5 = strongly disagree.

1. _____ The group is an effective problem-solving team.
2. _____ Divergent ideas are encouraged at group meetings.
3. _____ Members are more intent on satisfying the leader than on optimizing the potential output of the group.
4. _____ The goals of the group are clear-cut.
5. _____ It is important to be on friendly terms with other group members.
6. _____ Conflict within the group is submerged rather than used constructively.
7. _____ There is an open examination of relationships among group members.
8. _____ The group should be achieving more than it is.
9. _____ There is a destructive competitiveness among members of the group.
10. _____ Group meetings result in creative solutions to problems.
11. _____ There is no point in raising critical problems at group meetings.
12. _____ There is open examination of issues and problems at group meetings.
13. _____ Group members are willing to listen to and to understand me.
14. _____ Group meetings should be continued.
15. _____ The policies under which the group works are clear-cut.
16. _____ Meetings are not effective for discussing mutual problems.
17. _____ The chair should give the members guidance.
18. _____ Meetings are trival.
19. _____ The criterion for evaluating ideas in the group is "who said it" rather than "what was said."
20. _____ The chair is oriented toward production and efficiency.

To score this measure, reverse scoring for items 3, 6, 8, 9, 11, 16, 17, 18, 19 (that is, if you scored an item with a five, replace it with a one; replace a four with a two; keep a three the same; replace a two with a four; and replace a one with a five). Add up all twenty items using the replaced scores for the above items. A low score (20–50) suggests a very effective group. A high score (70–100) reveals group problems. A midrange score (51–69) indicates a group that could rapidly improve with a few changes in how it operates.

STRATEGIC SCENARIO WRAP-UP

Think back to the challenges facing Phebe Hollis from the beginning of the chapter.

- How important would goal setting be in Phebe's quest to have a successful meeting?
- In a meeting where there is no complete buy-in by all of the participants, such as in Phebe's case, what role does critical thinking play in making the meeting successful?
- What can Phebe do about detractors who may try to divert the meeting's purpose?
- Is reflective thinking the only way to generate solutions for this meeting, or would nominal group techniques work better?
- How can Phebe evaluate the meeting's success as she redevelops a report for the senior managers of Inspirion Corporation?

SUMMARY

- This chapter discussed how to conduct effective meetings—how to set the agenda, keep the focus on goals, and evaluate meeting effectiveness.
- To solve problems effectively, groups must develop strong and realistic organizational, group, and individual goals.
- The situational aspects of meetings include obtaining proper meeting facilities, setting up audiovisual equipment, maintaining rules of order, and getting to know the other participants in the group.
- The communication competencies for strategic problem solving in groups rest on the ability to think critically.
- This skill is made up of analysis, reasoning, interpretation, and evaluation.
- Groups must select the problem-solving technique that best suits their needs.
- Three techniques available to them are reflective thinking, the nominal group technique, and the Delphi technique.
- To make effective decisions, groups can either vote or reach a consensus (the preferred method).
- Decision making is not difficult if the previous steps have been completed properly.
- Meetings are not without anxiety-provoking circumstances, particularly when meetings are closed forums, when they are composed of people with diverse backgrounds, or when they are called to mediate serious arguments.
- Managing anxiety takes skill and inventiveness but is neither complicated nor impossible.
- No matter how successful a group's communication is, it cannot be maintained without evaluations.
- Group evaluations can be informational, procedural, or interpersonal.
- Evaluation can also be made of the specific individuals involved in the group.
- The Group Behavior Inventory (portions of which are shown in Figure 11.7) can be adapted and used for the group to which you belong.

KEY TERMS

Agenda: a guide that specifies what is to be discussed, when, in what order, and for how long

Roll call: an attendance check

Quorum: number of members required to be present for a group to conduct business officially

Reading the minutes: summarization of what took place in previous meetings of the group

Special committees: temporary subgroups created to look into short-term or specific problems

Standing committees: permanent subgroups that concentrate on long-term developments in broad areas

Unfinished business: topics that were not agreed on at earlier meetings

New business: new issues that have to be addressed

Organizational goals: goals that are set at upper levels of an organization's hierarchy and describe pathways to excellence

Group goals: goals that serve the mission and purpose of the group itself

Process goals: goals that attempt to improve the working of the group itself

Individual goals: goals that group members have in addition to the group's stated goals

Auditorium setup: setup with chairs, but no tables; chairs are lined up in straight rows with a center aisle between them

Classroom arrangement: setup that uses tables and chairs; tables are lined up in straight rows with a center aisle separating them

U-shaped setup: tables and chairs are arranged so that participants sit adjacent to or directly across from one another; designed for full-room interaction

Conference arrangement: all members are seated around the same table

Satellite tables: an innovative arrangement that gives considerable room for the leader to roam around the room while conducting the session; participants sit around individual tables that occupy independent spaces in the room

Analysis: the process of tearing apart an issue and examining its component parts to see how they relate to the whole

Reasoning: the ability to pull various data together and draw sound conclusions from them

Deductive reasoning: type of reasoning that moves from general truths to specific conclusions

Syllogism: a three-part argument containing a general truth, a related claim, and a conclusion

Inductive reasoning: type of reasoning that moves from specific statements to general conclusions

Example reasoning: type of reasoning based on collecting specific cases and then making a generalization based on them

Sign reasoning: type of reasoning that draws conclusions from simple observations

Hasty generalizations: conclusions based on small or nonrepresentative samples of data

Comparative reasoning: type of reasoning that pulls together two examples and assumes that what is true in the first case must be true in the second case

Causal reasoning: type of reasoning that asserts that one factor is strong enough to produce an effect in another factor; asks the question, "Why did that happen?"

Interpretation: an extension of causal reasoning in which you ask not only "Why did that happen?" but also "What does it mean?"

Evaluation: the process of making judgments about information or data

Problem solving: the process of defining a problem and generating solutions

Reflective thinking: a five-step process whose success depends on each group member's willingness to participate

Nominal group technique (NGT): technique that allows groups to discuss problems and solutions in a relatively structured setting

Delphi technique: technique that uses questionnaires to collect opinions and judgments from experts, who usually remain anonymous

Consensus: unanimous agreement among group members concerning a particular decision

Informational: dimension of group evaluation concerned with the task that the group is working on

Procedural: dimension of group evaluation that looks at how well the group's activities and communication are coordinated

Interpersonal: dimension of group evaluation in which the emphasis is on how well the members of the group work with one another

DISCUSSION

1. Why is an agenda a useful starting point for a meeting? How might a standard formal agenda be adapted for the following meetings: coworkers meeting with a human resources representative to discuss benefits; an ongoing employee support group; a self-managing team assessing its progress?
2. Discuss the various seating arrangements for meetings. In what circumstances would a particular setup be most appropriate?
3. Why are critical thinking skills vital to communication? In what ways are you now using critical thinking skills in school or on the job?
4. Discuss reflective thinking, the nominal group technique, and the Delphi technique. What seem to be the strengths and weaknesses of each method?
5. What are some advantages and disadvantages of consensus and voting as decision-making processes?
6. What are some causes of communication anxiety in a meeting? Which of these have you experienced, and how did you manage them?
7. Discuss a variety of approaches to group evaluation. How does evaluation provide direction and suggest areas for improvement?

ACTIVITIES

1. Construct sample agendas for each of the following group meetings:
   a. Disciplinary committee meeting
   b. Corporate safety board meeting
   c. Company credit union committee meeting to approve loan requests
   d. Fraternity's annual election of officers
2. When is interpreting information appropriate or inappropriate for a leader or for a group? In your answer, consider the difference between "telling" and "discussing."
3. If you were group leader of a decision-making body and consensus was difficult to achieve, what steps would you take to reach a decision? Compare your list with the lists of other members of your small discussion group.

CHAPTER

12

Negotiation and Conflict Management

After completing this chapter, you will be able to:

1. Explain how argumentativeness and verbal aggressiveness differ and evaluate yourself in each area
2. Identify the three dimensions of every negotiation
3. Employ bargaining strategies appropriate to the situation
4. Define conflict and differentiate it from other competitive situations
5. Recognize conflicting goals and know how to deal with them
6. Take steps to manage conflict productively

STRATEGIC SCENARIO

Justin McLeroy, director of operations, has just returned from an emergency meeting in the senior vice president's office. He learned that he is to leave in two days to negotiate a contract with one of the local unions over health benefits, maternity/paternity leave, and on-site day-care centers. The person who was going to handle the negotiation, the local general manager of the manufacturing plant, suddenly died and Justin seemed like the ideal choice since he is somewhat familiar with the local situation. This plant was in his territory when he was a sales representative four years ago. Union support for the contract is very important to the company, although it will not be easy since the company is losing money and must find ways to reduce costs. The biggest sticking points will be maternity/paternity leave and the day-care centers. Justin's company knows that giving in on these benefits to this local union will set a precedent and create the same demands among all the union's locals in the company. The people that Justin will be negotiating with run the gamut of older, traditional workers, young workers wanting to start families, and workers with established families. Justin has heard from the grapevine that even his negotiating counterparts cannot completely agree on their highest priorities. They are simply saying that the company must produce a contract granting all their demands, in spite of how unrealistic this would be. Justin also knows that the negotiating sessions could become very heated, even volatile.

As you read this chapter, think about the situation that Justin faces. We will return to his challenge at the end of the chapter.

OVERVIEW

In addition to their function as forums for problem solving and decision making, groups are a source of competitive communication in organizations. Competitive communication is characterized by interdependent yet conflicting goals, and it can occur at all levels of an organization. Commitment to organizational values and ethical standards, strong verbal and listening skills, interpersonal communication ability, and understanding of group roles, norms, and dynamics are all essential to the successful handling of competitive communication.

People may choose to avoid negotiation and conflict because of their difficulty and the stress they produce. People may also choose to avoid negotiation and conflict because they dislike arguing or have been the targets of attacks by verbally aggressive communicators. Certainly, failing to reach a resolution in either situation can produce negative results for individuals and for the organization. Nevertheless, negotiation and conflict are vital to the long-term growth and health of a company and its employees. Tension resulting from unredressed needs or conflicts can undermine employees' morale, motivation, and trust in the organization. By learning productive methods of negotiation and conflict management, you can contribute a great deal to the groups, organizations, and people with whom you work.

And that is the true focus of this chapter—helping you apply the skills necessary to communicate successfully and effectively in difficult, even competitive, circumstances. We begin with a brief summary of the difference between argumentativeness and verbal aggressiveness. Then we address the unique skills and demands of negotiation and conclude with one of the most complex situations in communication: conflict management.

ARGUMENTATIVENESS AND VERBAL AGGRESSIVENESS

What makes one person more likely than another to engage in argument? What happens when people who are arguing about issues refocus their attention on each other? We touched on the subject of group conflict in Chapter 10. Here we show you how to evaluate your own tendencies toward verbal aggressiveness, and we explore the implications of verbal aggressiveness for communication in your career.

An inclination to argue or a fondness for arguing is called **argumentativeness.** "Argumentativeness includes the ability to recognize controversial issues in communication situations, to present and defend positions on the issues, and to attack the positions which other people take."[1] Generally speaking, argumentativeness in the workplace is a positive and constructive strategy. Arguing for causes, positions, and ideas within organizations is often viewed favorably because people who are effective arguers are likely to achieve their goals. Research has shown that subordinates prefer superiors who are high in argumentativeness because they feel that their bosses will be more successful with their superiors and therefore the entire unit or department will benefit from effective argumentation skills.[2] The review of critical thinking skills in Chapter 11 is designed to improve your ability to argue constructively.

The tendency to attack other people instead of other points of view is termed **verbal aggressiveness.** "Verbal aggressiveness . . . denotes attacking the

1. D. A. Infante, *Arguing Constructively* (Prospect Heights, Ill.: Waveland Press, 1988), p. 7.
2. D. A. Infante and W. I. Gorden, "Superiors' Argumentativeness and Verbal Aggressiveness as Predictors of Subordinates' Satisfaction," *Human Communication Research* 12 (1985), 117–125.

self-concept of another person instead of, or in addition to, the person's position on a topic of communication."[3] The difference between verbal aggressiveness and argumentativeness is the focus of the attack. Argumentative people concentrate on positions, issues, reasoning, and evidence. Verbally aggressive people attack others personally. The difference affects others' view of the arguer/aggressor, career relationships, productivity in groups, and ability to achieve organizational goals. People can possess both traits, but people with a high degree of argumentativeness are less likely to use verbally aggressive strategies.[4]

Controlling Verbal Aggressiveness

Are you inclined to be argumentative or verbally aggressive? One way to find out is to score yourself on scales designed to measure argumentativeness and verbal aggressiveness.[5] The Strategic Skills box on page 336 measures argumentativeness. It identifies your reactions to controversy. The Strategic Skills box on page 337 measures verbal aggressiveness. It reveals how you usually try to get people to comply with your wishes. To ensure honest and accurate results, when responding to each statement, think of specific examples that confirm your assessment.

Whether or not you yourself feel prone to such behavior, verbal aggressiveness exists in the workplace, which means you will likely encounter it at some point in your career. Uncontrolled verbal aggressiveness can lead to interpersonal difficulties. Attacking the personalities or self-concepts of others demonstrates lack of sensitivity to feelings and usually hurts those who are targets of this aggression. Controlling verbal aggressiveness is a multistage process that begins with identification of the various forms of such aggressiveness. Types of verbal aggressiveness include:[6]

character attacks	nonverbal signs
threats	ridicule
teasing	insults
physical appearance attacks	ethnic or gender slurs
competence attacks	profanity

When you notice yourself using any of these tactics, change your strategy to focus on the issues instead.

The next step in reducing verbal aggressiveness is to understand how and why it occurs. There are at least four reasons for this behavior.[7] *Psychopathy,* or mental disorder, can stimulate attacks on people (clinical counseling is recommended in this case). *Dislike of others* can cause verbal aggressiveness, especially if you are put off by the appearance or personality of the person with whom you are communicating. *Social learning*—or observing and imitating parents, siblings, peers,

3. D. A. Infante and C. J. Wigley, "Verbal Aggressiveness: An Interpersonal Mode and Measure," *Communication Monographs* 53 (1986), 61. Used by permission of the Speech Communication Association.
4. Infante, *Arguing Constructively*.
5. These scales were developed by D. A. Infante and A. S. Rancer, "A Conceptualization and Measure of Argumentativeness," *Journal of Personality Assessment* 46 (1982), 72–80. This version was reported in D. De Wine, A. M. Nicotera, and D. Parry, "Argumentativeness and Aggressiveness: The Flip Side of Gentle Persuasion," *Management Communication Quarterly* 4 (1991), 386–411.
6. Infante, *Arguing Constructively*, p. 21.
7. Ibid.

STRATEGIC SKILLS

Argumentativeness Scale

This scale contains statements about arguing controversial issues. Indicate how often each statement is true for you by placing the appropriate number in the blank to the left of the statement. If the statement is almost never true for you, place a 1 in the blank. If the statement is rarely true for you, place a 2 in the blank. If the statement is occasionally true for you, place a 3 in the blank. If the statement is often true for you, place a 4 in the blank. If the statement is almost always true for you, place a 5 in the blank.

1. ______ While in an argument, I worry that the person I am arguing with will form a negative opinion of me.
2. ______ Arguing over controversial issues improves my intelligence.
3. ______ I enjoy avoiding arguments.
4. ______ I am energetic and enthusiastic when I argue.
5. ______ Once I finish an argument, I promise myself that I will not get into another.
6. ______ Arguing with a person creates more problems than it solves.
7. ______ I have a pleasant, good feeling when I win a point in an argument.
8. ______ When I finish arguing with someone, I feel nervous and upset.
9. ______ I enjoy a good argument over a controversial issue.
10. ______ I get an unpleasant feeling when I realize I am about to get into an argument.
11. ______ I enjoy defending my point of view on an issue.
12. ______ I am happy when I keep an argument from happening.
13. ______ I do not like to miss the opportunity to argue a controversial issue.
14. ______ I prefer being with people who rarely disagree with me.
15. ______ I consider an argument an exciting intellectual challenge.
16. ______ I find myself unable to think of effective points during an argument.
17. ______ I feel refreshed and satisfied after an argument on a controversial issue.
18. ______ I have the ability to do well in an argument.
19. ______ I try to avoid getting into arguments.
20. ______ I feel excitement when I expect that a conversation I am in is leading to an argument.

Tendency to approach argumentative situations: add scores on items 2, 4, 7, 9, 11, 13, 15, 17, 18, and 20.

Tendency to avoid argumentative situations: add scores on items 1, 3, 5, 6, 8, 10, 12 ,14, 16, and 19.

Argumentativeness trait: subtract the total of the ten tendency-to-avoid items from the total of the ten tendency-to-approach items. A higher positive score indicates high argumentativeness (twenty to forty). A higher negative score reflects low argumentativeness.

Source: From Infante and Rancer, "A Conceptualization and Measure of Argumentativeness," from *Journal of Personality Assessment*, copyright 1982 by Lawrence Erlbaum Publishers. Reprinted by permission of Lawrence Erlbaum Publishers.

and significant others who use verbal aggressiveness with you or in your presence—can encourage verbal aggressiveness. *Desperation* can lead to verbal aggressiveness in a final effort to win an argument. Desperation as a motive is particularly common if the aggressor possesses deficient critical thinking skills. She or he may be unable to express clear and objective dissenting opinions and may feel there is no alternative to attacking the self-concept of others. Understanding and being aware of these causes of verbal aggressiveness can help you to control the urge to attack people personally, as well as be more understanding of those who attack you.

STRATEGIC SKILLS

Verbal Aggressiveness Scale

If the statement is almost never true for you, place a 1 in the blank. If the statement is rarely true for you, place a 2 in the blank. If the statement is occasionally true for you, place a 3 in the blank. If the statement is often true for you, place a 4 in the blank. If the statement is almost always true for you, place a 5 in the blank.

1. ______ I am extremely careful to avoid attacking a person's intelligence when I attack her or his ideas.
2. ______ I use insults to "soften" stubborn people.
3. ______ I try very hard to avoid influencing people by making them feel bad about themselves.
4. ______ If someone refuses to do a task I know is important for a reason that does not seem valid to me, I accuse him or her of being unreasonable.
5. ______ When others do things I think are misguided, I try to be extremely gentle with them.
6. ______ If someone I am trying to influence really deserves it, I attack her or his character.
7. ______ When people demonstrate poor taste, I insult them to shock them into proper behavior.
8. ______ I try to make people feel good about themselves even when I think their ideas are useless.
9. ______ When people simply will not budge on a matter of great importance, I lose my temper and make strong emotional outbursts.
10. ______ When people criticize my shortcomings, I take it in good humor and do not try to get back at them.
11. ______ When people insult me, I get a lot of pleasure out of overreacting.
12. ______ When I dislike someone strongly, I try not to show it in what I say or how I say it.
13. ______ I like poking fun at people who do or say careless things to "wake them up."
14. ______ When I attack a person's ideas, I try not to damage his or her self-concept.
15. ______ When I try to influence people, I make an effort not to offend them.
16. ______ If I see someone act cruelly, I tell everyone else how terrible he or she is in hopes of changing his or her behavior.
17. ______ I refuse to participate in arguments when they involve personal attacks.
18. ______ When I am unable to influence others through conventional tactics, I resort to yelling or screaming at them.
19. ______ When I am not able to refute others' positions, I try to make them feel defensive to weaken their positions.
20. ______ When an argument shifts to personal attacks, I try very hard to change the subject.

Add your scores on numbers 1, 3, 5, 8, 10, 12, 14, 15, 17, and 20. Call this Total A. Add your scores on numbers 2, 4, 6, 7, 9, 11, 13, 16, 18, and 19. Call this Total B. Subtract Total B from Total A. If the result is between twenty and forty, you have a low tendency toward verbal aggressiveness. If your score is between zero and nineteen, you have a moderate tendency toward verbal aggressiveness. If your score is a negative number, you probably use verbal aggression frequently.

Source: "Verbal Aggressiveness: An Interpersonal Model and Measure," by D. A. Infante and C. J. Wigley, *Communication Monographs* 53 (1986), page 61. Used by permission of the Speech Communication Association.

The best way to control verbal aggressiveness is to become a better communicator. The critical thinking skills discussed in Chapter 11 will make you more proficient at formulating and expressing your ideas. Remember:

- Conduct a thorough *analysis* of the situation.
- Provide logical *reasoning* for your position.
- Develop a careful *interpretation* of the conflict issues, both yours and theirs.
- *Evaluate* your position and that of your partner.

Learn and practice these skills on a regular basis. You will find that engaging in constructive argumentation decreases the urge to attack others personally.

NEGOTIATION

Negotiation, or bargaining, frequently involves argumentation and verbal aggressiveness.[8] It generally occurs when communicators—for example, buyer and seller, union leader and company representative, supervisor and employee—are not in agreement. Since managers spend more than one-fifth of their time dealing with conflict, they need to learn how to negotiate effectively.[9]

Goal Setting

Because of differences in affiliation, the goals, needs, and communication styles of negotiators are likely to be very different from those of problem-solving groups that work toward one goal. Or participants in a negotiation session may have a common goal but disagree on the means and methods to achieve it.

Negotiation is usually a planned and structured process of communication. Although arguments may arise spontaneously from something said in the course of discussion, negotiators frequently plan tactics to be used and topics to be covered before an encounter. In a negotiating session, two or more people with different goals exchange communication to produce a mutually desirable outcome.[10] The parties involved must recognize that they are mutually dependent—seldom can an acceptable outcome occur unless all parties to negotiation recognize this fact.[11] Most bargaining scenarios require give-and-take in the form of concessions or acknowledgments of an opponent's truth, right, or privilege in a specific instance. Communicators must bargain forcefully and strategically, using effective argumentation skills while at the same time remaining aware that some concessions must be made so that all parties feel satisfied with the outcome. It is vital to remember that there are two sides to any negotiation, and keeping multiple perspectives in mind during this process will lead to greater satisfaction and more long-term benefits.

8. The distinction between bargaining and negotiation is not enough to quibble over. See L. L. Putnam and M. S. Poole, "Conflict and Negotiation," in F. Jablin, L. Putnam, K. Roberts, and L. Porter (eds.), *Handbook of Organizational Communication* (Beverly Hills, Calif.: Sage, 1987), pp. 549–599; D. F. Womack, "Assessing the Thomas-Kilmann Conflict MODE Survey," *Management Communication Quarterly* 1 (1988), 321–349.
9. M. A. Rahim, *Managing Conflict in Organizations*, 3rd ed. (Westport, Conn.: Greenwood Publishing Group, 2001).
10. L. L. Putnam and T. S. Jones, "Reciprocity in Negotiations: An Analysis of Bargaining Interaction," *Communication Monographs* 49 (1982), 171–191.
11. Putnam and Poole, "Conflict and Negotiation."

Situational Knowledge: Formal Versus Informal Bargaining

The bargaining process can be observed in both formal and informal situations. **Formal bargaining** situations develop when recurring issues require deliberation and confrontation over time. One of the most important examples of formal bargaining is labor-management negotiations. Labor contracts usually run for a specified length of time, so bargaining sessions are needed when the contract expires. Other examples of formal bargaining include negotiation between representatives of government and industry over laws or policies, bargaining with subcontractors or law firms over services to be rendered, bargaining with financial institutions over credit or credit ratings, and negotiation with suppliers over prices. Formal bargaining is recurring, anticipated, planned, and structured.

Informal bargaining, also quite prevalent in the workplace, usually involves spontaneous situations that are seldom repeated. Informal bargaining may occur any time two or more parties must depend on one another to resolve divergent goals. For example, managers and employees often bargain over job descriptions, salary, roles, and performance standards. Each is interested in having the other accommodate her or his goals. Peers bargain with each other to resolve issues such as turf or territory disputes, recognition for accomplishments, work schedules, and even personality differences. Informal bargaining may even occur across organizational boundaries. Asking for discounts from vendors, negotiating with airlines about how frequent-flier miles are counted, and bargaining with hotels about corporate rates constitute informal bargaining situations. Regardless of whether a situation is informal or formal, similar negotiation strategies are used.

Communication Competence: Basic Skills for Presenting a Position

The first step in negotiation is advancing an offer within limits acceptable to the other bargaining party—making sure, of course, that the offer is also within limits acceptable to your own organization! Many bargaining positions are first expressed as broad statements that lay out a general goal. An offer that appears to be unreasonable on first hearing may in fact become persuasive as the negotiator takes it through the subsequent steps in the bargaining process.

Of course, it is better for the negotiator to begin with an offer that is obviously reasonable. Reasonable offers, which seem to make sense and correspond to known facts and standard beliefs, show that the negotiator is bargaining in good faith. Regardless of the quality of your initial offer, you will usually need to persuade others that your position is worthy of their support. Strong use of evidence gives credibility to your position more effectively than does any other tactic. Evidence usually consists of some form of information—published documentation, statistics, expert opinion, examples and illustrations, or testimony. Summarizing is another persuasive element because it demonstrates consistency and steadfastness during negotiation. Summarizing your argument may clear up confusion about the position you have taken and your reasons for taking it. Negotiation is most effective when all participants understand one another's positions on the issue and when there is no equivocation or inconsistency.

Finally, look at the position taken by the other side. In what ways is the position realistic or unrealistic? If any elements of the opposing position are weak or irrelevant, identify them as such and try to avoid having them become the focus of the negotiation. In the long run, it is best for you to address the major strengths

PRACTICING BUSINESS COMMUNICATION

Tootsie Roll Industries, Inc.

America's original penny candy, the Tootsie Roll, celebrated its one hundredth birthday in 1996. Management at Tootsie Roll Industries (TRI) encourages an open organization where employees confront and resolve conflicts, and a culture where business thrives on skilled negotiating with business partners, competitors, and even with the government.

In the 1990s, TRI President Ellen Gordon negotiated with city officials in Chicago to secure an urban enterprise zone around the company's headquarters on the city's South Side. The agreement offers area businesses tax incentives. Chicago also offered TRI a low-interest loan to buy the plant it was leasing and $200,000 in job-training funds.

Since TRI employs union workers, its hundreds of middle-income jobs are valuable to Chicago's economy. For its part, Tootsie Roll Industries agreed to open a loan fund for employees who wanted to buy homes in Chicago and to add about two hundred more jobs by the end of the decade.

COMMUNICATION TOP-DOWN AND ACROSS THE ORGANIZATION

With annual sales approaching $400 million, Tootsie Roll Industries employs fewer than two thousand workers. The basic corporate structure is traditional. Departmental staff report to department directors who report to TRI vice presidents. Corporate VPs report to Ellen Gordon and to Chairman and CEO Melvin Gordon.

TRI complements its top-down structure by encouraging accessibility and teamwork as keys to successful communication. Employees are invited to learn more about how other departments work by sitting in on their meetings, offering their viewpoints, or simply observing. Employees initiate frequent, impromptu meetings in the workplace, extending TRI's "open-door policy."

Employees from different departments work in cross-functional teams to solve problems and to come up with business ideas. For example, employees from research and development, finance, marketing, manufacturing, and purchasing team up to analyze the feasibility of introducing a new product.

By "cross-training," TRI workers learn different aspects of the business, broaden the range of creative solutions to business problems, and increase team members' sensitivity to the implications a proposed action might have on other business functions. The go/no-go decisions on a new product or business venture at TRI are thoroughly informed and well reasoned.

BUILDING NEGOTIATING SKILL

The flexibility reflected in Tootsie Roll's internal communication is equally important—but more strategic—in its negotiations with suppliers. The company requests bids from suppliers, carefully indicating exact specifications for ingredients and for quality.

of the opposing position, mindful of opportunities to use such arguments to support your own position. Throughout the negotiation, use critical thinking skills to analyze, evaluate, and interpret the opposing position. Doing so allows you to formulate effective counterarguments.

Dimensions of Negotiating According to the experts, there are three dimensions to negotiation: information management, concessions, and positioning.[12] Each of them represents a category of strategies, tactics, and behaviors that are used by negotiators to advance their goals.

12. W. A. Donahue, M. E. Deiz, and M. Hamilton, "Coding Naturalistic Interaction," *Human Communication Research* 10 (1984), 403–426.

TRI negotiates with potential suppliers to obtain the best balance between high quality and low price within specifications. Even after suppliers are chosen, negotiation continues as part of the business relationship.

More than forty years ago, Tootsie Roll Industries began to explore foreign markets, opening a subsidiary in Mexico late in the 1960s. Encouraged by its warm reception in Mexico, where Tootsie Roll is "Tutsi," TRI opened a branch in Canada in the early 1970s. Today the company licenses production and distribution in the Philippines and has added a sales office in Hong Kong.

Negotiating skills proved pivotal to the growth of Tootsie Roll Industries. TRI has expanded its sales revenue by acquiring established candy companies as well as by expanding its own product line.

Established brand names are attractive to TRI, whose founder, Leo Hirschfield, named the candy after his baby daughter Tootsie and advertised to popularize the brand early in the 1900s. In 1972, TRI purchased the Mason Division of Candy Corporation of America, adding well-known brands such as Mason Mints to the product line. In 1985, TRI bought Cella's Confections, makers of chocolate-covered cherries. In 1988, TRI acquired the Charms Company, making it the largest lollipop producer in the world. TRI's purchase of the chocolate and caramel brands of Warner-Lambert Company in 1993 increased Tootsie Roll Industries business by 20 percent and added such well-known brands as Junior Mints, Sugar Daddy, Sugar Babies, and Charleston Chew to the product line.

When looking at an acquisition, TRI management meets over time with the company's management or parent company. At successive meetings, opportunities and risks for both parties are debated and discussed. The ability of Tootsie Roll Industries and the representatives of the potential acquisition to resolve their conflicts and to negotiate to their mutual satisfaction will make or break the deal.

QUESTIONS FOR CRITICAL THINKING

1. How does Tootsie Roll Industries communicate its values to suppliers and employees?
2. What communication techniques demonstrate the company's flexibility?
3. How do cross-functional teams benefit Tootsie Roll Industries?
4. Why are effective negotiating skills vital to TRI's expansion?
5. Why does Tootsie Roll Industries discuss the benefits and problems entailed by the deal during acquisition negotiations?

You can visit Tootsie Roll Industries, Inc., on-line at www.tootsie.com.

Information Management When engaging in bargaining with others, have at hand as much research and information as possible, but manage the information effectively. Use it to promote your goals for the negotiation session. Information can be managed in a number of ways that strengthen a bargaining position. You can seek explanations from your opponents in an effort to clarify the issues, realign their position according to prevailing evidence, or reduce ambiguity that can be used against you. Sometimes bargainers enter a negotiation session with a grocery list of objectives they hope to achieve, knowing they will have to compromise on some. You can manage information in a bargaining session by requesting that your adversaries assign priorities to their goals and objectives. Ask the opposing party to rank its objectives in order of importance.

You can also refocus the discussion on your own agenda. In bargaining sessions, abundant information favoring the opposition's position may be introduced.

If one negotiating party has access to greater resources—time, money, special research, legal services—than the other, that party may attempt to overwhelm the negotiation with excess data. Such information, however, does not decrease the importance of your evidence and your group's position. If you feel you are being overwhelmed by the quantity of your opponents' information (regardless of its relevance), redirect the focus of the discussion toward your own objectives so that you can move the negotiation toward a settlement that supports your position. For example, saying, "I can see your point, but if you look at our data, you will see that the statistical trends point to a strategy more in line with what we are offering" can prevent sheer quantity of information from overriding a fair negotiation.

Positioning **Positioning** is moving the focus of the negotiation to issues that are important to you. You must use this technique carefully to remain ethical. Ask yourself whether the issues that interest you are the central issues in the discussion. If they are not, refrain from emphasizing them at the expense of more important organizational goals. Many negotiators use positioning to show their side in its most favorable light. Be careful that when you highlight the positive aspects of your group's agenda, you do not distort or misrepresent your actual position.

Positioning can result from preestablished rules and procedures. Many formal bargaining situations prescribe certain methods of discussion, procedures for decision making, or an agenda of topics to be discussed. Here is a list of preestablished rules:

Each side must allow the other to take a turn talking.
All parties must agree on each major issue.
We will determine relevant topics before beginning the negotiation.

If during a negotiation session the other group's representatives prevent your side from having a turn to speak, you can remind them that the negotiation is to follow a pattern of alternating turns, and you can request an opportunity to speak. In this way, you will be able to bring up your side's concerns within the agreed-on rules. You can then go on to discuss your side of the issues under negotiation.

Positioning can also be accomplished by asserting your side's right to a balanced negotiation. If you sense that the discussion has concentrated on the other side's goals and objectives, call the imbalance to the attention of the entire group in an effort to bring the discussion back into balance. Negotiators have ethical obligations to bargain in good faith, respect the rights of other negotiators, and encourage fair and open discussion of issues.

Concessions Negotiators come to the bargaining table expecting to give up, or concede, some of their goals to obtain something in return. **Concession** is useful in several ways. Making concessions demonstrates cooperativeness, which usually makes a positive impression on others and may encourage them to reciprocate.

Making concessions is also a good way to maintain interest in the negotiation. Lags or lapses in the bargaining process can occur as participants become bogged down by old issues and stale ideas. Providing a minor concession from time to time can open new windows of opportunity, stimulate fresh approaches to the negotiation, and revitalize communication among the bargaining parties. Concessions early in the bargaining process communicate a conciliatory tone. You can avoid accusations of rigidity and closed-mindedness by making concessions that demonstrate a belief in cooperative discussion.

When you decide to make a concession, objectively evaluate the opposing argument's strengths to identify a concession that will be appropriate. Concessions can take the form of time, money, resources, responsibilities, autonomy, and even changes in job descriptions. After you make a concession, show how it serves both your own and your opponent's needs and goals, and clearly redefine your position so the negotiation can continue.

Strategic Bargaining The bulk of research literature on negotiation points to two types of communication strategy: cooperative and competitive. **Cooperative strategies** are open, honest, and upfront attempts at objective and productive problem solving.[13] They are often termed integrative because they frame the bargaining session with the potential for mutual gain and multiple goals. Bargainers using cooperative strategies are interested in fully understanding the respective positions of all parties. Information is exchanged in a frank and open manner so that everyone has a clear picture of all the issues. Effective listening and responding skills aid in minimizing misunderstandings. The primary objective of cooperative strategies is to use communication in a way that maximizes the goals of the bargaining participants. Cooperative tactics include the following:

- Expressing agreement with or approval of the opponent's position
- Offering information or assistance
- Offering concessions
- Offering promises/commitments
- Summarizing arguments
- Indicating conciliation
- Providing clarification
- Seeking a problem-solving approach
- Facilitating discussion through adherence to proper procedure

Cooperative strategies can be used to achieve a win-win outcome, in which both sides benefit from the bargaining session.

Competitive strategies, often referred to as distributive, seek to maximize one's own position at the expense of the adversary. The term **distributive** refers to the bargainer's assumption that a gain for her or his side equals a loss for the other side—that is, limited benefits are redistributed through bargaining. Competitive bargaining strategies do not consider problem solving and cooperation to be valid tactics. Rather, the goal of these strategies is to win at all costs. In fact, these strategies tend to result in a lose-lose outcome—neither party leaves the negotiation satisfied.

Competitive strategies use information in self-serving ways, giving only enough information to create the impression of disclosure while eliciting maximum information from the opponent. Competitive bargainers see each other as combatants whose side must either prevail or perish. These tactics may even involve deception or diversionary maneuvers to gain a competitive edge. Competitive tactics such as the following rarely involve concessions or compromise:

- Challenging, disagreeing with, or rejecting the opponent's position
- Changing the topic to refocus the discussion to one's advantage
- Asking for concessions
- Accusing an opponent of incompetence, negligence, or bad faith

13. R. E. Walton and R. E. McKersie, *A Behavior Theory of Labor Negotiations: An Analysis of a Social Interaction System* (New York: McGraw-Hill, 1965); Putnam and Jones, "Reciprocity in Negotiations"; Putnam and Poole, "Conflict and Negotiation."

Bargaining and negotiating sessions are often used to settle disputes and to resolve conflicts. When negotiation is handled poorly, it can leave a problem unresolved and possibly worse than it was before negotiations began. When negotiation is handled effectively, however, it can improve the positions and outlooks of all parties involved. (© José L. Pelaez/Corbis)

- Requesting information
- Making threats or demands
- Issuing ultimatums
- Making personal attacks against an opponent
- Advancing arguments against an opponent (rather than the opponent's position)

Notice that none of these tactics would occur if critical thinking were used.

You should be aware of one caveat at this point. In professional situations, it is seldom a good idea to become involved in bargaining and negotiation at the level of personal values and beliefs. Multiple reasons exist for this cautionary note, but we will discuss the two most salient ones. First, values and beliefs stir up emotions like no other bargaining topic. When emotions come into play, negotiation processes take on a different form and can easily lead to verbal aggressiveness. Second, many people are not equipped for a discussion focusing on values.

For example, imagine a situation in which your job requires you to negotiate for the best parts deal among prospective suppliers on a project. Imagine further that the supplier who ultimately offers the best deal recently laid off your best friend. Would that affect your decision?

Understanding the deep-seated thoughts and feelings of another person's values takes time, sensitivity, and commitment. These are not elements that come naturally to negotiation contexts. When values come into play (as they naturally can), you are better off acknowledging that these issues are important but are best left for discussion at another time, while at the same time asking that the discussion focus as much as possible on the issues, facts, and merits of the opposing sides.

What Would You Do?

Consider the last time you received a grade on a term paper or essay exam that you thought should have been higher. Assume you are going to approach your professor about raising your grade to a level that you think is fair. What positioning will you use? What data will you need to support your position?

Using Bargaining Tactics Effectively As you look at the lists of competitive and cooperative bargaining tactics, you will quickly notice that the cooperative tactics appear positive and the competitive tactics seem negative.

This is true in a general sense, but remember that bargaining situations are demanding, complex, and argumentative and that a combination of tactics is usually required for effective negotiation. Cooperative tactics promote rationality and reasonableness; only in extreme cases should competitive tactics be used to ensure that your side is not taken advantage of.

How are bargaining tactics to be used? That depends on the situation, although there are some general guidelines to follow:[14]

1. Initial strategies should include firm but cooperative messages. Adversaries should get the idea that you are serious about the negotiation but are not so inflexible that you will refuse to yield on any issues. ("I don't think my salary compensates me fully for the work I do.")
2. Opening bids (such as offers or proposals) should be high because you value your proposals. By asking for more than you really expect to get, you allow concessions to be made later while at the same time communicating your desire to obtain your highest goals. ("I would like a salary increase of 25 percent.")
3. Cooperative tactics (such as promises and concessions) can be used to clear roadblocks in negotiations. When you sense that the discussion is going nowhere, it is often helpful to give in a little to get the bargaining back on track. ("A 25 percent increase may be too much. How about 20 percent?")
4. Competitive tactics may be introduced (although they are not encouraged) if you perceive that the opposition is taking advantage of the situation. ("That offer is not acceptable.")
5. A high level of enthusiasm should be maintained during bargaining. An upbeat and energetic attitude communicates commitment and perseverance to achieve goals. ("I'm sure we can work this out.")
6. A variety of information should be relied on in order to maintain a strong position. Remembering what has been said and approved in previous sessions as well as keeping track of information during the current session ensures a high degree of bargaining competence. ("In my appraisal interview, you said I was doing an 'excellent' job.")
7. Issuing threats, ultimatums, or demands against adversaries is rarely useful. Negative tactics such as these usually lead to resentment and conflict. ("If I don't get that raise immediately, I'll quit today.")
8. A professional demeanor should be maintained throughout the bargaining sessions. Avoid resorting to underhanded or unethical tactics during bargaining. Be sure your conduct is beyond reproach. ("You just don't like me, do you?")
9. The equality of bargaining parties should be acknowledged. ("What is your counteroffer?")
10. Effective critical thinking skills should be used. Strong use of evidence, reasoning, and analysis can improve your position in the bargaining situation. ("I've been a productive employee, I have good rapport with customers, and others in my career field have higher salaries.")

14. W. A. Donahue, "An Empirical Framework for Examining Negotiation Processes and Outcomes," *Communication Monographs* 45 (1978), 247–257; L. L. Putnam and T. S. Jones, "The Role of Communication in Bargaining," *Human Communication Research* 8 (1982), 262–280.

Anxiety Management

Negotiations can often produce anxiety, but there are some strategies you can use to reduce nervousness. First, remember that bargaining is a normal, accepted business practice; you are not a troublemaker for entering into a bargaining situation. Second, set a specific date and time for the bargaining session. Although negotiations can take place informally, scheduling a bargaining session will give you time to gather the evidence and data needed to support your position. This will build your confidence and reduce anxiety. It may also be helpful to practice your negotiating skills with a friend. Ask a friend to listen to your position and to help you practice the bargaining session. Third, keep in mind that bargaining is not a do-or-die situation. Be open and flexible during negotiations. Sometimes making the first concession to demonstrate your willingness to bargain cooperatively will create a nonhostile bargaining environment.

Negotiation is a common communication strategy in business and professional settings. The more effectively you can bargain, the more likely you are to attain positions of enhanced responsibility and authority because you can be trusted to get the best deal for your group. In the first scenario in the Strategic Skills box on pages 348–349, identify the positive and negative actions taken by each group.

CONFLICT MANAGEMENT

When bargainers come to the table with serious purposes, strong negotiation skills, and mutual dependency, they can attain productive outcomes. But there are many examples of bargaining sessions that lead to serious conflict among parties. The second scenario in the Strategic Skills box just mentioned shows a breakdown in the bargaining process. The bargaining session escalated into a full-blown conflict that was unproductive and out of control. How did this happen? How does conflict differ from negotiation?

What Is Conflict?

Conflict can take many shapes in the workplace. It can occur between people representing different organizational units, it can occur between organizational levels such as labor and management, and it can occur between people who work together. Conflict is a dynamic process that is precipitated, developed, and governed by the joint communication strategies of the parties involved.

Conflict is "an expressed struggle between at least two interdependent parties who perceive incompatible goals, scarce rewards, and interference from the other party in achieving their goals."[15] The parties must be interdependent. Conflict results when people view other people—people on whom they depend—as the reason they cannot attain their goals. Interdependency forces the conflict: if a person could accomplish goals without the interference of others, conflict would not arise. The same dynamic properties that make group and organizational communication valuable are also the spark for potential conflict.

The ability to recognize, engage in, and manage conflict is an important skill for everyone but especially for those who aspire to succeed in organizations. Conflict is widespread in organizational life. It is not overstating the case to say

15. J. L. Hocker and W. W. Wilmot, *Interpersonal Conflict,* 3d ed. (Dubuque, Iowa: Brown, 1991), p. 12.

that dealing with conflict is one of the most troublesome communication activities in organizations. Conflict in organizations may range from disputes over territorial encroachment to personal disharmony. A major source of conflict is misunderstanding and communication failure. Conflict may also erupt from differences in goals or values, diverse economic or financial interests, role conflict, environmental changes, or even contradictory group loyalties.[16] Even technology can be blamed, since increasing use of computer-mediated communication (e.g., e-mail, Web-based communication) has created a more desocialized work atmosphere, with a resulting decrease in interpersonal skills. Anytime people perceive that a person, group, or difficult situation is preventing them from accomplishing a goal, conflict is possible.

Causes of Conflict: Competing Goals

The primary cause of conflict is competing goals. Even though people usually enter into a conflict situation with established goals, the goals may change as the situation develops and understanding of the opponent increases.[17] As goals shift, so does the communication of the conflict. Essentially, there are two types of goals in most conflict situations: content and relational.

Content Goals **Content goals** involve the apparent issues or obvious reasons for a dispute. They are characterized by such issues as competition for finite resources (computers versus offices), decision making (participation in decisions), and rights (maintaining fairness). Here are three examples of competing content goals:

JIM: If Joe gets the new service vehicle, I'll have to wait.

JOE: Jim's new service route lets him get home earlier.

MARY: Tanika is taking over this project without much input from me.

TANIKA: Mary hasn't shown much initiative with special projects in the last six months.

ROBERTO: Cicely never consults me on the important decisions made around here.

CICELY: Roberto always seems too busy to ask about the new emerging issues in the company.

In each example, the conflicting parties believe they understand the real content goals in the situation, yet each has a perspective that is different and unknown to the other. Each party understands his or her own goals but has few ideas about the goals of his or her conflict partner.

Failure to communicate differing goals usually leads to conflict. Understanding the respective goals of conflict partners is one of the keys to conflict management.

Relational Goals In every conflict situation, the conflicting parties pursue goals that are likely to be less obvious than the content goals. **Relational goals** "define each party's importance to the other, the emotional distance they wish to maintain, the influence each is willing to grant the other, the degree to which the parties are seen as a unit, or the rights each party is willing to grant to the others."[18]

16. M. L. Knapp, L. L. Putnam, and L. J. Davis, "Measuring Interpersonal Conflict in Organizations: Where Do We Go from Here?" *Management Communication Quarterly* 1 (1988), 414–429.
17. Hocker and Wilmot, *Interpersonal Conflict.*
18. Ibid., p. 48.

STRATEGIC SKILLS

Successful and Unsuccessful Bargaining

Treecorp, a paper-manufacturing company in the Northwest, is expanding its corporate headquarters by moving into a new multistory complex in a large downtown area. The executive vice president (VP) for planning and facilities has told the public relations (PR) and training and development (TD) departments that they are to be housed on the same floor because their departments report to the same vice president and have some functional overlap. She tells the departments together that the furnishings equipment budget is limited and they will have to compromise and work out an arrangement for spending the $2 million allocated for office space and computer support. She concludes by saying that the $2 million is theirs to spend as they wish as long as there is agreement between the departments. She gives the departments one month to reach their decision and report back to her.

The department members gather in their respective areas to formulate strategy for the upcoming bargaining sessions. Members of training and development are strongly in favor of fully enclosed, standard offices for private counseling sessions with clients and trainees. Equipment and computer support are important to them but not as important as private offices. The public relations people believe they must have a sophisticated computer network so that they can network with each other, enjoy graphics support, and print high-quality documents at high speed. Although the PR people really want standard offices, they are willing to live with cubicle offices if they can get the computer system. Both PR and TD plan to bargain for maximum benefits—that is, for both computers and offices.

Some other issues are likely to be discussed but are not directly relevant to the office/computer problem. Some members of the PR department are jealous of the attention focused on TD at this time. The previous vice president in charge of the departments was originally from PR and favored the PR department. The new vice president, however, is from TD and seems to favor it. Some members of PR used to be in TD and vice versa. There is considerable gossip between departments, and some personal feuds have developed between employees. The departments compete with each other for new positions, salaries, travel budgets, and operating expenses.

The following two scenarios are excerpts from the final bargaining session to decide on the new office setup. The first shows an effective use of information management, concessions, and positioning that leads to a mutually acceptable win-win outcome. Note where the negotiators use each strategy effectively.

Winning a Bargain at Treetop

TD: Now let's see. You want the computer system as well as fully enclosed offices, and you think we should make do with a less sophisticated system. Right?

PR: Well, in principle that may sound like an unfair exchange. But if you look at the last three annual budgets, you will notice that your operating expenses and travel budget have exceeded ours by 28 percent. Don't you think it is unfair for us to have to split the $2 million down the middle when we have been getting fewer funds all along?

Relational goals are not openly discussed as often as content goals because doing so draws attention to personal differences. They are, however, no less important than content goals. Indeed, conflict may not be managed until relational goals are managed. In the Strategic Skills box on pages 348–349, the relationship between the two bargainers emerges as a clear cause of additional conflict, despite the focus on content goals (new computers and offices) expressed by the communicators. Many people are willing to acknowledge only content goals when involved in a conflict, but it is rarely the case that relational goals do not also exist.

Now look back to the three examples of conflicting content goals. If you were to manage those conflict situations, it would help you to know that Jim and Joe have been competing for a promotion for the past few months, that Tanika and

TD: I thought we had already resolved that issue. In a paper company, training costs more money than public relations does. Besides, we must have private offices to do our job; it's a separate issue from computers that will make us more efficient.

PR: Now wait a minute! You can't be serious that you want more than 50 percent of the construction budget.

TD: Our department has increased productivity in every quarter over the last four years, whereas your department has only done so in three quarters. Your department has also expanded by three employees, while we have not been allowed to expand.

PR: Hold on now. You know that it is difficult to gauge the actual productivity of a public relations department. Nevertheless, those new positions are critical to maintaining our public awareness campaign.

TD: All I am saying is that from a bottom-line perspective, we are one of the most productive departments in the company, yet we receive little reward in return.

PR: What if we were to give up one position now and one new position in the next budget? In return you would allow us to get the new computer system.

TD: We still want the regular offices, but we might be willing to share some of our operating expenses with you.

PR: Would it be possible for you to give up some travel money so we can expand our public awareness campaign into the Southwest?

TD: Perhaps, if the positions that you are giving up are people with a training background.

PR: I think we have a deal.

TD: Fine.

Negotiations Breakdown

TD: Now let's see. You want the computer system as well as fully enclosed offices, and you think we should make do with a less sophisticated system. Right?

PR: Now hold on a minute! You people in TD always seem to be in a rush to get things settled. Let's clarify some issues first.

TD: What issues? You get either offices or computers. PR is always trying to distract us from the real issues. Our deadline for making the decision on the budget is approaching quickly, and we don't seem to be making much progress.

PR: Of course, wait until the last minute to make important decisions. I can't believe you people! What about travel budgets and operating expenses? Those are issues that ought to come into play here.

TD: Why? Those are fixed costs. If the CEO thought you needed more funds, he would give them to you. You have to prove yourself worthy first.

PR: Give me a break! When you were in PR, we were really unproductive but had a bigger budget. Now that you're in TD, you think you own the company.

TD: How dare you attack me personally! Why, I ought to . . .

PR: Forget it. You're no negotiator. Send someone in next time who can at least pretend to be objective.

TD: Right. And next time why don't you bring your babysitter with you?

Mary have different personalities and work styles that do not mesh, and that Roberto and Cicely formerly were dating but recently had a traumatic breakup. Relational goals are always present in conflict and have to be brought out for effective management to occur. Submerging or denying their existence can postpone a resolution.

Managing Conflicting Goals

To be manageable, goals must be clarified so that parties can accurately understand the respective positions of their counterparts. Both content and relational goals must be brought out into the open and honestly discussed to prevent confusion and misunderstanding. The only way that people in a conflict can share the perspective of their adversaries is by understanding their goals. The following steps can help you to clarify goals:

1. State your goals in clear, unambiguous language. Use language that the other party will understand.
2. Elicit clearly stated goals from the other party.
3. Openly discuss the difference between your content and relational goals.
4. Make sure that you and your opponent have a shared understanding of each other's goals.
5. Show that upholding your goals will not prevent productive management of the conflict.

The next step is to assemble collaborative goals. The key to managing any conflict is working toward an interdependent solution. If you consider only your own goals, without regard for the other party's interests, you will delay the productive resolution of differences. Adversaries probably will not want to work toward achieving your goals unless you show a willingness to do the same for them.

Collaboration begins by clarifying each party's goals. Then conflicting parties strive to promote collaboration by actively rejecting selfish or incompatible goals. Here are some ways to encourage goal collaboration:

1. Search for commonalities among the competing goals.
2. Recognize that some of your opponents' goals may not have long-term implications and you may be able to live with them.
3. Give some concessions while asking for some.
4. Develop new goals that incorporate and complement the competing goals of all parties.

Conflict Styles and Tactics

A useful tool for discussing conflict styles is the conflict grid (Figure 12.1). The conflict grid juxtaposes content and relational goals. Whether you are an employee, group leader, or manager, you will have both content and relational goals in a conflict situation. Because every conflict includes some level of concern for content goals and some level of concern for relational goals, we can characterize a particular conflict style by the relative importance it places on each of these goals.

The horizontal dimension of Figure 12.1 represents concern for content goals ("concern for production"). The vertical dimension depicts concern for relational goals ("concern for people"). By rating concern for production and concern for people each on a scale of 1 to 9, you can plot coordinates on the grid to represent particular conflict styles. Each strategy employs specific tactics, which you may recognize and with which you may be familiar.[19]

19. R. R. Blake and J. S. Mouton, *The Managerial Grid* (Houston: Gulf, 1964); K. W. Thomas and R. H. Kilmann, *Thomas-Kilmann Conflict MODE Instrument* (Tuxedo, N.Y.: Xicom, 1974); Womack, "Assessing the Thomas-Kilmann."

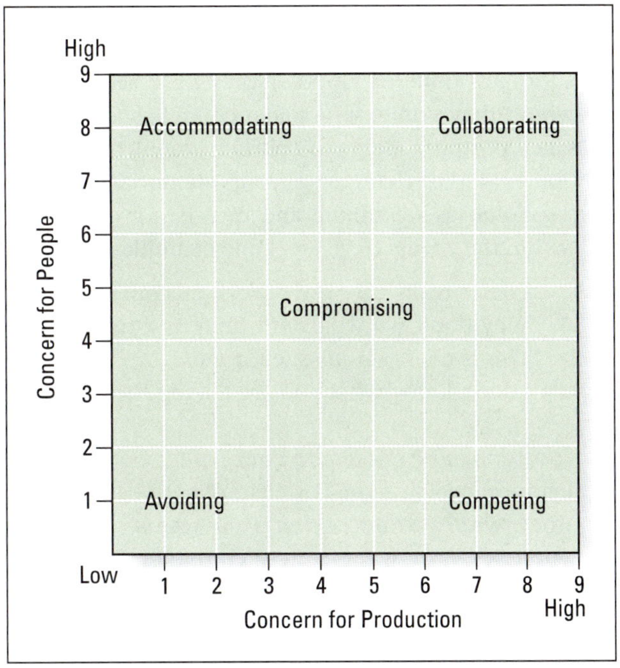

FIGURE 12.1

The Conflict Grid

Source: R. Blake and J. Mouton, "The Fifth Achievement," *Journal of Applied Behavioral Science* 6 (1970), 418. © 1970 by Sage Publications, Inc. Reprinted by permission of Sage Publications, Inc.

Competing A competing style represents a high concern for content goals and a low concern for the relationship. Tactics related to a competing strategy reflect more concern for content goal achievement than for relational stability. For example, a group member may be more concerned with wanting to get her solution accepted to win recognition from the boss rather than with listening open-mindedly to other possible solutions. Competitive messages include denial, hostility, confrontation, and verbal aggressiveness. Here are some examples:

- "That is simply not the case."
- "It's obvious that you do not pull your weight around here."
- "How can you argue for a position as groundless as this?"
- "If you ever bothered to look at the data, you might be able to see a trend in the direction I'm describing."

Accommodating At the opposite side of the grid is the accommodating style, which represents low concern for content goals and high concern for relational goals. The style is known as accommodating because the person using it places a high priority on the relationship with the conflict partner and in all likelihood will give in to his or her wishes to preserve it. Accommodating tactics reveal eagerness to satisfy the goals of the other party even if doing so means giving up content goals. Someone pursuing this strategy is unassertive, cooperative, yielding, and obliging. For example, an employee who believes that disagreeing with an idea expressed by another employee will create hostility or hurt feelings will accommodate her or him to prevent this situation. Here are some examples of accommodating messages:

- "If it's important to you, then let's do it."
- "I see your point of view."
- "Let's do it your way this time."

Avoiding The avoiding style represents low concern for both content goals and relationships. This is the preferred style of people who simply do not care whether a job gets done or whether they have satisfactory relationships with those with whom they compete. Avoidance tactics include passive and uncooperative messages, postponements of conflict, complete apathy, and denial that a conflict situation exists. For example, a group member may not care whether the group reaches a solution to a problem and thus is not concerned with any conflict that arises within the group. Here are some examples of avoidance messages:

- "I don't really care if we work this out."
- "Why don't we wait until there is a real problem before we argue over this?"
- "This is really a nonissue for me."
- "I don't know what you are talking about; I feel fine about our relationship."

Compromising Moderate concern for both content and relational goals results in a compromising style. For example, Paul and Wendy both want the newly vacated office with a window, but Paul wants to upgrade the furniture in his office, whereas Wendy wants a new computer. Even though they are not friends or colleagues, they respect each other. Their conflict over the vacated office is likely to be one of compromise. Compromising usually indicates only moderate concern for the goals and the relationship. Tactics of compromise include vagueness, conciliation, and concessions. Here are some examples of compromising messages:

- "I am not certain that we should be discussing this."
- "Perhaps I ought to reconsider my initial position."
- "Maybe we both ought to give a little."

Collaborating Extreme concern for both content and relationships promotes a collaborating style. Recall our explanation of how collaborative goals can help parties realize their goals in a conflict and at the same time maintain their relationship. An ideal strategy that promotes both content and relational goal attainment, collaborating emphasizes problem solving, qualified support, and integration. For example, employees assigned to a research and development department would examine all relevant evidence and data before reaching a decision. If conflict arose about the best possible solution, a reexamination of the data might occur. Here are some examples of collaborative messages:

- "Let's take a look at our respective positions and identify their strengths and weaknesses."
- "If the data are correct, I can back your plan."
- "If you combine our two requests, the end results will actually resemble our initial plans."

A STRATEGIC APPROACH TO CONFLICT

The conflict grid (Figure 12.1) is useful for demonstrating the various communication possibilities available for people engaging in conflict. But it does oversimplify, and it probably obscures what happens in real conflict. It is quite unlikely that there is one best style for any particular conflict situation.

When approaching conflict situations, communicators must remain flexible so that the strategy they select is suitable for the people concerned, the goals to be achieved, and the situational constraints involved. Multiple strategies may be

When workers like these go on strike, communication has broken down in negotiations between workers and management. Repairing broken relationships is a very difficult process so it is important to avoid negotiation breakdowns whenever possible. (Lisa Poole/© AP-Wide World Photos)

> **Where Do You Stand?**
>
> Consider the popular expression "In business, you don't get what you deserve; you get what you negotiate." Do you agree or disagree with this statement? Why?

necessary, especially when the conflict changes course and reveals new patterns of communication, goals, or motives for participants. Communicators must be able to respond to the changing conditions of a conflict situation. A number of factors can influence the selection of a conflict strategy.

Goal setting, situational knowledge, communication competence, and anxiety management are no less important to productive conflict management than to any other communication situation. Let us discuss each of these factors in turn to determine how it can lead to successful conflict resolution.

Goal Setting

An important consideration in any conflict situation is that the goals of communicators can change over the course of a conflict. Acknowledging valid arguments from opposition members, recognizing the importance of their goals to them, and understanding how they communicate can lead you to modify your initial content goals. If the goals of the conflict appear to be changing, you should be ready to respond with an alternative conflict style.

A second consideration for selecting a conflict style is the likelihood of multiple goals.[20] You choose a particular style (such as competing or accommodating) because of your main goal and your perception of your opponent's primary goal. But be flexible enough to shift to a more compromising position if it shows promise of promoting additional goals for both parties. If you boil down discussion to just one issue, there will be little room for negotiation.

20. Knapp, Putnam, and Davis, "Measuring Interpersonal Conflict in Organizations."

TECHNOLOGY TOOLS

Conflict and E-Mail

E-mail has a tendency to create a false sense of security in the minds of its users. Many employees have acknowledged that they have sent pointed, even aggressive, messages to colleagues that they would never have communicated in person—often with dire consequences. Because it is asynchronous and buffered by a computer screen, e-mail seems to encourage negative messages. Sometimes this is a good thing, allowing reticent or apprehensive people an opportunity to vent and speak their mind, which they would normally refrain from doing in public. In other instances, the vile and vicious barbs flying from the fingers of disgruntled or hurt employees are ill advised and have even led to reprimands and termination. There are three tactics you can use to help ensure that the "flaming" e-mail messages you send are appropriate and won't get you in trouble:

1. "Think before you type." Wait an hour, an afternoon, or even a weekend before typing the e-mail. Time has a way of tempering your emotions.
2. Type the e-mail but don't send it right away. Put it in your "drafts" folder and read it over after waiting a period of time. Sometimes just drafting the e-mail could be therapeutic and might even calm your emotions. However, after a waiting period you may find that the only audience it's appropriate for is you.
3. Send it to a trusted friend and ask for that person's honest advice. Hearing a different perspective may change your mind about sending that "e-mail from hell."

Relational goals also influence the choice of a conflict style. The degree of cohesiveness you feel with your conflict partner can affect your choice. If you feel connected to him or her in some personal way, you are less likely to use competing or avoiding strategies and more likely to use positive strategies.

Also consider the professional relationship you have with your conflict partner. Her or his status, influence, and organizational position will probably influence your choice of style. Research has shown, for example, that managers tend to be accommodating with superiors, collaborative with subordinates, and compromising with peers.[21]

When you decide on a conflict style, consider the long-term relational consequences of your actions. If your adversary is someone with whom you hope to carry on a long-term relationship, employing avoiding or competitive tactics throughout the conflict may destroy your relationship. The destruction of a long-term relationship may not be worth the short-term gains you make by using such tactics.

Situational Knowledge

Situational factors are elements in the conflict that affect the nature of conflict and the styles you select to deal with them. For example, the physical environment (where the conflict takes place, such as in a private office, in the cafeteria, or in a meeting) will affect how you communicate during a conflict. Aggressive tactics are particularly risky when the conflict occurs in public view.

21. M. A. Rahim, "A Measure of Styles of Handling Interpersonal Conflict," *Academy of Management Journal* 26 (1983), 368–376; M. A. Rahim, *Managing Conflict in Organizations* (New York: Praeger, 1986).

Time constraints can also affect how you use conflict tactics. For example, if you are expected to settle your differences with someone in a limited time period, you may feel unable to develop a successful, positive style and may resort to tactics such as avoiding or competing. If you have a lot of time in which to work out the conflict, more elaborate styles such as collaborating and compromising may be possible.

Communication Competence

In conflict situations be aware of your strengths and weaknesses—your **communication competence.** Competencies include argumentation skills, control of verbal aggressiveness, listening skills, and verbal and nonverbal skills. If you think back to the discussion of critical thinking skills in Chapter 11, you can easily understand how important the ability to analyze, evaluate, and communicate ideas is to the management of conflict. The better you understand the situation, the better chance you have of achieving your goals.

One of the challenges of effective conflict management is preventing the conflict from *escalating*. Conflicts escalate because of many factors, not the least of which is taking a competitive, rather than cooperative, posture during deliberations. **Conflict escalation** is particularly troublesome because, once it starts, it can perpetuate itself.[22] People in the conflict begin to feel trapped in a process of unproductive communication. For instance, Deutsch's research discovered that conflict escalation can result in the following:

- *Autistic hostility:* you break off contact with the conflict partner, thereby increasing chances of misunderstanding and misperceptions.
- *Self-fulfilling prophesies:* you make a false assumption about a partner that then leads to communication behavior that causes the very assumption you anticipated.
- *Unwitting commitments:* you overcommit to rigid positions and unwittingly commit to negative positions because of poor perceptions and unskillful communication.

One of the keys to reversing the escalation of conflict is to focus on issues and pursue cooperative and collaborative communication messages. If all else fails, parties may need to seek the help of a third party or a mediator to help them move back to positions of normalcy and objectivity.

Controlling verbal aggressiveness is important in conflict situations as well. Allowing (or encouraging) the discussion to drop to the level of personal attacks accomplishes nothing in the way of conflict management. It only escalates the conflict.

Listening skills are essential to the choice of a conflict style. Knowing what your opponents are saying and why they are saying it can tell you a lot about what style will work best in resolving conflict with them. Poor listening is a frequent cause of conflict and a large obstacle to conflict resolution.

A sincere effort to remain flexible also aids in resolving disputes. Flexibility allows you to adapt to the changing dynamics of a conflict. For example, you may decide that an accommodating strategy is effective in the initial stages of a conflict, but as the conflict progresses, the opponent's stubbornness or hostility may

22. H. Deutsch, "Cooperation and Competition," in M. Deutsch and P. Coleman (eds.), *The Handbook of Conflict Resolution* (San Francisco: Jossey-Bass, 2000), pp. 21–40.

ETHICAL ISSUES

To Tell, or Not to Tell?

Assume you work in a department with two other employees. One of them is an older person nearing retirement; the other is a new college graduate. Although you are friendly with both, they often use verbal aggressiveness toward each other. Your supervisor told them to work out their differences, but neither has made an effort to do so. A coworker in another department has confided to you that one of them is planning to delete an important message from the e-mail expected in this afternoon to create an impression of incompetence about the other. However, the coworker will not tell you which employee is planning this action and says that she will not get involved in their dispute. This rumor is the only evidence you have of potential foul play. Would you communicate your knowledge of the unethical behavior, and if so, to whom? Do you think it is ethical or unethical for you to become involved in a conflict between your coworkers?

make competitive tactics more useful. By remaining flexible, you will be able to make a change in your conflict style to counter the shift. In general, successful conflict managers are highly sensitive to shifts in conflict strategies by their opponents.

Anxiety Management

Conflict can be a major cause of anxiety in the workplace. You may dread or avoid particular situations, such as an argument with a superior, hostility in a group meeting, or even a sensitive bargaining session, if the possibility of conflict makes you uneasy. Conflict, however, can have productive outcomes, and on most occasions it is better to engage in conflict than to avoid it. The following example illustrates a common form of conflict in the workplace:

> Katrina and George have never liked one another, primarily because of contrasting personalities and competition for company resources. Their usual method of handling disagreement or competition has been to work behind the scenes to achieve their goals (gossip, grapevine, coalitions, and so on). One day their manager invited the two of them to a private meeting to discuss the problems that were arising from their conflict—tension, lowered morale and productivity, and less attention to their work, to name just a few. After controlling their anxiety at being confronted with the fact of their difficulties, both opened up and related why they did not appreciate the way the other operated. Each was surprised at how honest the other was and at how serious the conflict had grown simply because they had never faced it.

To lessen your anxiety in a conflict, focus on goals and outcomes. Consider the relief you will feel after working through a conflict situation rather than avoiding the conflict and allowing distrust, resentment, or other negative feelings to simmer. You can also manage conflict-related anxiety by viewing your conflict partner in positive, human terms rather than as an enemy who means to undermine you or your career.

Seeking the support of others who share your goals and position in a conflict can be reassuring. If you dread conflict because you feel isolated by it, discovering that others support your side can lessen your anxiety considerably.

Taking a break to collect your thoughts and clear your head is also an effective way to manage anxiety in conflict situations. Often the tension of a conflict continues to build as the conflict progresses, and you may find that you are becoming too anxious to use your communication skills effectively. If it is possible to call a time-out to take a deep breath and relax, doing so can help you to calm your nerves and regain your composure. All these tactics for managing anxiety can increase your chances of resolving the conflict in a successful and positive manner.

STRATEGIC SCENARIO WRAP-UP

Based on the material from this chapter, how would you advise Justin in the following areas?

- How can Justin avoid getting into a verbally aggressive shouting match with the local union officials?
- What types of goals would be most appropriate for Justin to set for his negotiations with the local union?
- Are there particular bargaining tactics that would work best in this situation?
- If Justin finds that interpersonal conflict is inevitable, what conflict management tactics would work best in this situation?

SUMMARY

- The nature of any conflict situation derives from how inclined the adversaries are to use argumentativeness and verbal aggressiveness. Argumentativeness is a willingness to stand up for and promote ideas despite opposition.
- Verbal aggressiveness is the tendency to attack the personal characteristics or self-concept of an opponent instead of the issues under discussion.
- Verbal aggressiveness is a negative trait that often results from poor critical thinking skills and that prevents conflict resolution.
- Most competitive communication situations can be addressed through negotiation, which can occur formally or informally.
- Three dimensions of negotiation are information management (being able to acquire, retrieve, and use information in a bargaining session), positioning (refocusing attention on issues of concern or advantage to you), and concessions (knowing when, where, and how much to give to opponents).
- Strategic bargaining consists of cooperative tactics (problem solving) and competitive tactics (maximizing one's own position at the expense of the other side's position).
- The selection of the most appropriate bargaining strategy depends on the situation, although general guidelines can be applied.
- Conflict, the struggle between interdependent parties who perceive incompatible goals, may exist in all levels, situations, and relationships in an organization.
- The primary cause of conflict is competing goals, which can be managed through clarification of opposing or conflicting goals so that collaborative goals can be worked out.
- Content as well as relational goals have to be specified so that a comprehensive resolution can be achieved.
- Conflict styles can be demonstrated through the use of a conflict grid. Five styles often used in conflicts are collaborating, competing, avoiding, compromising, and accommodating.
- Each style gives rise to particular tactics.
- Despite its usefulness, the conflict grid does not take into account the complexity and uniqueness of any particular conflict.
- Successfully resolving conflict requires strategic communication—goal setting, situational knowledge, communication competence, and anxiety management.

KEY TERMS

Argumentativeness: an inclination to argue or a fondness for arguing

Verbal aggressiveness: the tendency to attack other people instead of other points of view

Negotiation: a planned and structured process of communication in which two or more people with different goals exchange communication to produce a mutually desirable outcome

Formal bargaining: process that develops when recurring issues require deliberation and confrontation over time

Informal bargaining: process that involves spontaneous situations that are seldom repeated

Positioning: moving the focus of the negotiation to issues that are important to you

Concession: giving up some goals to obtain something in return

Cooperative strategies: open, honest, and upfront attempts at objective and productive problem solving

Competitive strategies: attempts to maximize one's own position at the expense of the adversary

Distributive: the bargainer's assumption that a gain for her or his side equals a loss to the other side

Conflict: "an expressed struggle between at least two interdependent parties who perceive incompatible goals, scarce rewards, and interference from the other party in achieving their goals"[23]

Content goals: the apparent issues or obvious reasons for a dispute

Relational goals: "define each party's importance to the other, the emotional distance they wish to maintain, the influence each is willing to grant the other, the degree to which the parties are seen as a unit, or the rights each party is willing to grant to the others"[24]

Situational factors: elements in the conflict that affect the nature of conflict and the styles you select to deal with them

Communication competence: the strengths and weaknesses you possess in any conflict situation

Conflict escalation: heightened tensions in conflict situations due to poor communication or misunderstandings

DISCUSSION

1. How do argumentativeness and verbal aggressiveness differ? What are the implications of each for organizational communication?
2. How do information management, concessions, and positioning affect the progress of negotiation and the agenda of issues to be discussed?
3. Describe the general guidelines for bargaining. When, if ever, might competitive tactics be used?
4. Discuss possible causes of and participants in conflict at work. Have you experienced work-related conflict? What were the causes and results?
5. How do content goals and relational goals differ? How can each contribute to conflict?
6. Discuss the conflict styles represented in Figure 12.1. What are some benefits and drawbacks of each style? Consider both short-term and long-term possibilities.
7. How are communication skills essential to managing conflict strategically? Discuss the role of setting goals and managing anxiety in successful conflict resolution.

ACTIVITIES

1. As a manager, you will be confronted with verbal aggressiveness by employees, peers, and superiors. What strategies can you employ to maintain high standards of communication effectiveness and professionalism in such circumstances?
2. Select two classmates as partners. The three of you round-robin the roles of manager, employee, and observer. The observer assesses how well each participant presents and then defends his or her position on these topics:
   a. Pay raise
   b. Time off to attend to personal activities without having to make up the time
   c. Business travel on personal instead of company time
3. What strategies do you believe are most effective in positioning? Your instructor will list these on the board until all positioning strategies in the class have been recorded. Then rank-order these as a class.
4. In an essay, discuss the consequences of competitive negotiating to a long-term relationship with the other party.

23. Hocker and Wilmot, *Interpersonal Conflict*, p. 14.
24. Ibid., p. 48.

PART FIVE

PUBLIC PRESENTATION STRATEGIES

CHAPTER 13

Uses the components of strategic communication to explain the principles of successful presentations.

CHAPTER 14

Focuses on the specific demands (on speakers and listeners) of a variety of informative presentation strategies, including the use of communication technology.

CHAPTER 15

Explores the process of persuasion and the goals that persuasive presentations can facilitate within an organization. Special speaking formats such as introductions and presentations of awards are also included.

Presentations play an important role in sharing information and guiding actions within organizations. Part V introduces the skills necessary to speak effectively and without apprehension during a presentation. Regardless of your position in a company, you can benefit from knowing and practicing these skills.

CHAPTER

13

Developing and Delivering Effective Presentations

After completing this chapter, you will be able to:

1. Manage speaking anxiety by understanding its causes and anticipating and rehearsing the delivery of your message
2. Identify goals, including topic and purpose, for your presentation
3. Assess the audience's needs and potential responses to your message by gathering situational knowledge
4. Identify the main points to be included in your presentation and research them thoroughly
5. Use supporting materials, an introduction, and a conclusion to enhance the credibility of your message
6. Put the pieces of the presentation together in the form of an outline
7. Demonstrate communication competence by choosing an appropriate and effective delivery style

STRATEGIC SCENARIO

Sangeeta Roy is an information technology major working as an intern in a graphic design studio. The head of the firm, Melinda Arroyave, has decided to explore the benefits/costs of replacing the current phone system with state-of-the-art VoIP (Voiceover/Internal Protocol) telephony units. She's asked Sangeeta to gather all the relevant data she can and, in two weeks, make a preliminary report to the firm's administrative committee.

As you read this chapter, you will learn the skills that Sangeeta must possess to prepare and deliver an effective presentation. At the end of the chapter, we will return to this scenario and solicit your advice.

OVERVIEW

Opportunities to speak publicly are multiplying rapidly in this age of information. Although many people think that information technologies such as electronic mail, videoconferencing, cellular phones, and fax machines have replaced some of the functions of business presentations, this assumption isn't true. Actually, increasing dependence on technology means that many business decisions are being made more quickly and that more diverse groups of people are participating in decision making than ever before. Face-to-face presentation is still the most effective way to reach these audiences.

Successful presentations demonstrate that the speaker is confident and sincerely believes in the message being delivered. In a successful presentation, the speaker and the audience establish a mutual understanding of or commitment to goals that is not possible through written or electronic channels. Given the large number of people who can usually be touched by the message, under the right circumstances an effective presentation can be even more powerful than small-group communication.

In general, presentational speaking shares some similarities with the other forms of oral communication we have already discussed. All depend on the components of strategic communication—goal setting, situational knowledge, communication competence, and anxiety management—which require adequate preparation and ensure effective performance. In addition, speaking to a group shares a common problem with all other forms of oral communication. Unlike visual or written communication, which can be reread or reviewed, any form of spoken communication must be clear and convincing the *first* time it is made.

Nevertheless, making a presentation is quite different from speaking with others in two-party or small-group contexts. Ensuring audience comprehension is more difficult because feedback is less direct and less spontaneous. During a presentation, the speaker must read the audience's nonverbal behavior to infer members' moods and reactions to the message being presented.

In the business world, public speaking takes the form of making presentations to fellow employees, managers, and supervisors or to an audience of people outside of the speaker's organization. The following scenarios illustrate two examples of such presentations.

> Nancy is a communication major working as an intern in the human resources division of a local computer software firm. The firm is experiencing strained management-employee relationships and a high turnover rate in its staff. Mark, the vice president of human resources, believes that the company will be severely hurt by the current situation. He assigns Nancy the job of researching the employees to determine how their needs can be better met. Two weeks into her research, Mark asks her to make a preliminary report of her findings to a group composed of Mark, the chief executive officer, the chief financial officer, and the three members of the company's communications department. Nancy realizes that she may not get another chance to speak directly to these people, and she wants to give them a clear and comprehensive understanding of her findings, their importance, and what each of her listeners can do about the situation. She knows this will be the most significant presentation she has ever been asked to make.

> Akbar is an entrepreneurial student who has been involved in a university-sponsored program to collect leftover or unused hotel food supplies and to distribute them to shelters. He would like to initiate a similar program in his hometown. To do this, he must persuade a group of hotel managers and

administrators that this project is an opportunity to benefit the community greatly and to reduce operating costs at the same time. He has already made contacts at a variety of hotels and has received replies from twelve interested managers. His final challenges are preparing the presentation (which includes targeting the hidden costs of wasted supplies), anticipating and overcoming legal or regulatory obstacles, and demonstrating how to get such a program started with minimum time and resources. He needs to have the managers agree with him and implement the program he believes in. He understands how crucial this presentation will be.

These scenarios show the potential range of presentations and audiences you will encounter in your career. For many people, speaking before a group is the most frightening activity imaginable. Yet some basic guidelines can help you understand the fundamentals of presentational speaking and make connections to skills we've discussed in earlier chapters, thus lessening your anxiety.

This chapter focuses on preparing for a presentation by using the model of strategic communication. We begin by explaining the phenomenon of public speaking apprehension and methods of handling it. Second, we discuss how to select and narrow a topic. Then we discuss the significance of situational knowledge and the importance of performing an audience analysis to understand the relationship between the topic and the audience. Finally, building on that preparation, we discuss communication competence as demonstrated in the creation, structure, and delivery of a message.

Our focus in this chapter is on basic principles; in Chapters 14 and 15, we will discuss special considerations for preparation and delivery of informative and persuasive presentations.

ANXIETY MANAGEMENT

Anxiety management is particularly important in presentational speaking. Consider the following example:

> A popular Washington hostess, entering a room in one of the capital's finest hotels, recognized a well-known government official. Hands clasped behind his back, head bowed, he was pacing up and down the length of the room.
>
> "I'm going to deliver a speech," he told her.
>
> "Do you usually get this nervous before addressing a large gathering?" asked the woman.
>
> "Why no," he answered. "I never get nervous."
>
> "In that case," demanded the woman, "what are you doing in the ladies' room?"[1]

The experience of this government official is one with which many people can identify. Although there are many symptoms besides disorientation, the sense of panic that frequently accompanies speaking before a group is quite unlike any other fear. When Americans are asked to answer the question "What are you most afraid of?" they report that one of their worst fears is having to speak before a group.[2] Fear of public speaking ranks highly, along with fear of the dentist, heights, insects or bugs, snakes, death, and flying, as a widespread phenomenon.

1. P. R. Evans, "'Tense' Is Good for You!" *This Week Magazine,* July 9, 1967, p. 4.
2. "The 14 Worst Human Fears," *Detroit Free Press,* June 7, 1977.

Given this fear's widespread nature, you are likely to encounter **communication apprehension**—which can appear as *reticence, shyness,* and *unwillingness to communicate*—sooner, rather than later, in your career as a speaker. Based on our discussion of apprehension in other contexts, you know that many conditions can cause communication anxiety, even in informal situations, and that anxiety may be a trait that some people are more likely to have than others. There are also some additional causes of anxiety about public speaking and some remedies to deal with them effectively.

Why Is Public Speaking Frightening?

To understand why public speaking frightens people, let us review the origins of anxiety about communicating in public and discuss specific suggestions for countering them. Experts have proposed three ways of explaining how apprehension develops, is maintained, and can be treated: skills deficit, conditioned anxiety, and negative cognitive appraisal.

Skills Deficit One explanation for anxiety is that the speaker lacks the adequate skills for making a successful presentation, and so he or she fears or even avoids doing it. A real lack of presentation skills results in the speaker's embarrassment, failure to reach the audience, and sense of frustration and helplessness. In a business setting, it may also result in loss of sales, fewer chances to participate in major projects that may lead to promotions, and a perception that the speaker is not a particularly talented or qualified employee. These are serious problems, so a speaker who feels she or he lacks adequate skills should do everything possible to bring them up to speed by targeting the points we will discuss in this chapter about choosing a topic, analyzing an audience, and so forth. Most important of all is *practice.* We cannot overemphasize the role of experience in calming anxiety—even if you are never completely comfortable speaking before a group, you can learn exactly what you are capable of and what to expect from yourself through experience. Once you have mastered the skills of public speaking, you no longer need to feel threatened by personal failure.

Conditioned Anxiety Conditioned anxiety results when neutral communication situations collect negative connotations, images, and memories over time. The speaker is informally "taught" to be anxious about speaking through a succession of negative events, such as a teacher punishing her or him for speaking up in class or a parent telling her or him to be quiet around adults. Being punished for early attempts to communicate can lead to fear of communication situations, especially public speaking, later in life.

One method for reducing conditioned anxiety is *systematic desensitization (SD).*[3] SD is based on the theory that a person cannot be relaxed and anxious at the same time, and so the process attempts to overlay pleasant, relaxing images and experiences on the anxiety-causing situation. SD also uses deep muscle relaxation techniques that can help the speaker maintain a real physical sense of

3. G. Friedrich and B. Goss, "Systematic Desensitization," in J. A. Daly and J. C. McCroskey (eds.), *Avoiding Communication: Shyness, Reticence, and Communication Apprehension* (Beverly Hills, Calif.: Sage, 1984), pp. 173–187.

relaxation while speaking. The following list illustrates a typical step-by-step process for using SD:

1. Before you begin, make a list of situations that cause you varying degrees of anxiety, from lowest to highest. For example, one list may include lying in bed just before going to sleep, discussing the upcoming speech a week before it is scheduled, getting dressed on the morning of the speech, entering the room on the day of the speech, walking up to the podium, and giving the speech.
2. Then assume a relaxed position, take several deep breaths, and become as relaxed as possible.
3. Moving from your hands through your feet, systematically tense muscle groups, hold the contraction for several seconds, relax the muscles, and then concentrate on the relaxed state you experience. For example, make a fist and tense the muscles of your right hand and forearm for five seconds; then relax and note how these muscles feel as relaxation flows through them.
4. After you relax all the muscle groups, envision a pleasant scene and associate the feeling of relaxation with the image.
5. Stay relaxed and think about the situation with the lowest anxiety level on your list.
6. Move down the list of progressively anxious situations. Stay relaxed and consciously link the physical feeling of relaxation with the scene you are thinking about.
7. If you feel a twinge of anxiety at any point, leave the list of situations and envision the original pleasant scene. Then take deep breaths and tense and relax muscle groups to bring back the sensation of relaxation.
8. When you have gone through every item on the list, return to the original relaxed state by breathing deeply and imagining pleasant scenes.

Although SD may not work for every person, it is one of the most successful techniques for reducing conditioned anxiety. For those who find it effective, SD's conscious efforts to promote relaxation inhibit anxiety, thus weakening the link between communication and nervousness.

Negative Cognitive Appraisal Negative cognitive appraisal is a process of unrealistic, negative self-evaluations in which communicators assume that they are going to fail and then worry about failure and its consequences. Negative cognitive appraisal is best handled by reducing negative self-statements (such as "I know I'm going to lose my train of thought") so that you are able to concentrate on your skills and the message and are able to speak more confidently and competently. This is done through the process of *cognitive restructuring (CR).*

CR attempts to change or modify the thought process by identifying the impact of negative statements you have made about the speaking situation. Once you see how the negative statements result in your discomfort and negative behavior during a presentation, you can then focus on reducing negative thoughts by substituting more positive, coping statements.

Keeping a log is important for using CR successfully. In the log, you note the negative self-statements that you use frequently. When writing these statements, you also become aware of what these statements really are: irrational. For example, if you find yourself thinking, "I'm going to sound stupid," consider your skill and experience and the preparation that you have put into the presentation. In reality, you will undoubtedly be among the people most knowledgeable about the topic in the room. Write down these positive coping statements in your log.

There are two types of coping statements. *Context statements* emphasize the nonstressful aspects of the situation. *Task statements* emphasize what you can do to ensure a successful presentation. To be most effective, confront negative self-statements that occur before, during, and after the presentation. The following is a sample entry in a CR log:

Situation: I have been asked to give a thirty-minute presentation at a monthly breakfast meeting.

Description: My presentation will deal with financial projections and strategic planning; my audience consists of colleagues as well as upper management.

Negative Self-Statement

Before: I will forget some of the data for my financial projections.

Coping Statements

Context: I have not forgotten important information in previous speeches.

Task: I will have all the important data on both my outline and my slides.

Negative Self-Statement

During: I'll sound amateur.

Coping Statements

Context: I know everyone in the audience, and we respect each other's knowledge.

Task: I am well prepared and have excellent visual aids.

Negative Self-Statement

After: Upper management won't find my projections credible.

Coping Statements

Context: I have an established track record with upper management.

Task: My charts are based on data provided by the company treasurer.

These techniques for managing anxiety are not independent—they work best together. If you wish to manage anxiety, you will find it useful to practice all three. Learn and practice the skills of public speaking, use relaxation and deep breathing to achieve physical comfort when speaking, and learn to identify irrational negative statements that increase your anxiety and replace them with positive task and context coping statements.

GOAL SETTING: IDENTIFYING THE TOPIC AND THE PURPOSE

The starting point for developing a message is selecting a topic. Making this decision in a work setting is usually quite easy; topics emerge naturally from the interplay of your job, your audience, and the organization's needs. For example, as a business manager, you may be asked to talk to new employees about the benefits package provided by your organization.

Nevertheless, you are also likely to encounter occasions when the topic is relatively unclear, when you must choose among several possible topics, or when you have been assigned an inappropriate topic and need to suggest an alternative.

In these situations, you can use several techniques to identify a topic. Although there are no fail-safe formulas, the following methods can assist you with the task:

1. Engage in personal brainstorming. Sit down and think about any special knowledge that you may already possess, things that you have done, experiences that you have had, or issues that are important to you.
2. Brainstorm with others. When you use this option, you not only gain additional ideas that result from group synergy, you also get a preview of how relevant a

These two photos capture settings for a public presentation. In the first, a professor of history at the College of New Jersey is speaking to students during a "teach-in" on the conflict in Iraq. In the second, a businessperson is addressing her colleagues at a luncheon meeting. What are the implications of these contrasting settings for the selection and narrowing of the topic for the presentation? Which speaker has the most challenging task?
(William Thomas Cain/Getty Images)
(© Royalty-Free/Corbis Images)

topic is to others. Thus, it can be helpful to use classmates, coworkers, friends, or colleagues to assist you in generating potential topics.

3. Use the reference room of your library. If necessary, ask the reference librarian for help in using general reference works. The following works may be particularly useful in preparing business presentations:

   The Reader's Guide to Periodical Literature
   Business Periodicals Index
   Business Information Sources
   Encyclopedia of Business Information Sources
   The Executive's Sourcebook to Marketing, Company, and Demographic Data
   Databasics: Guide to On-Line Business Information
   The BusinessWeek Almanac

4. Use World Wide Web search engines to surf the Net. Using Google (www.google.com), Yahoo! (www.yahoo.com), Lycos (www.lycos.com), and AltaVista (www.altavista.com) can be some of the best ways to locate information on the Internet. Each site has instructions for making your searches effective and efficient.

After you have generated several potential topics, you will select the actual topic for your presentation. As you do so, consider three criteria:

1. Are you knowledgeable and/or interested in this topic? Because you will speak most authoritatively on topics you know best, choose a familiar topic whenever possible. When circumstances prevent making such a choice, look for topics that you have always wanted to know more about. An active interest in the subject will make your research more exciting.
2. Is the topic relevant to your audience? Consider what you know about the audience. Will this group of people find your topic informative, useful, or interesting? While most, if not all, topics can be made interesting, starting with a topic that your listeners need and want to hear about will make your task much easier.
3. Is the topic a good one for this assignment or situation? Presentations are given for many reasons, and an effective topic may be inappropriate if it does not support or correspond to the reason for the presentation. For example, a company seminar on health-care benefits would appropriately include presentations on employees' health insurance choices, on how the company's wellness and nutrition program has improved work quality, or on changes in the workers' compensation policy. All these topics relate directly to health care as it is mediated by the company. Less appropriate would be a presentation detailing how an employee trained for and participated in a marathon, calling for a national health insurance program, or explaining a new treatment for diabetes. Although these topics are health related, they do not have a direct connection to the company's health-care policies. **Good speech topics,** then, are topics the speaker is knowledgeable about and/or interested in, are relevant for the audience, and meet the requirements of the assignment or situation.

When you are in doubt about either your assignment choice or the relevance of a particular topic, ask the person who is organizing the presentation (or the instructor supervising an in-class presentation). Be sure to have your questions answered far enough in advance so that you can change your topic if necessary.

IDENTIFYING THE GENERAL AND SPECIFIC PURPOSES OF THE PRESENTATION

General Purpose

Once you have selected a topic, the process of refining it begins. The first filter, or question to ask yourself, is about the **general purpose:** Why will you give a speech on this topic to this audience? This question identifies the basic goal of your presentation.

The goal is usually motivated by one of four general purposes: to *inform, persuade, motivate,* or *celebrate*. That is, you may want to enlighten your audience on a topic by providing new information or ideas (inform), change or reaffirm the audience's attitudes (persuade), urge audience action for your cause (motivate), or help your audience acknowledge an individual achievement or event (celebrate).

To Inform **Informative presentations** provide ideas, alternatives, data, or even opinions, but most important, they provide credible, reliable information to back up your major points. When giving an informative presentation, you function as your audience's teacher. It is not always easy, however, to know the audience's level of background knowledge on the topic, nor is it easy to narrow the topic so that you are working with a manageable and teachable amount of information.

Expanded sources of information, such as on-line databases and chat groups, make the selection of material for informative presentations more important and challenging than ever before. We discuss the issue of developing and structuring an informative presentation in greater detail in Chapter 14.

An informative presentation must be accurate, reliable, and credible. For example, if you are asked to give a report in your communication class on problems with financial aid disbursement at your school, check and double-check your statistical information, the conclusions you draw, and any other elements of the presentation that may contain inaccuracies. Cite your sources to increase both your credibility and the significance of the data. Remember that to teach your audience effectively, you are wise to be an expert, not simply a layperson with a few statistics to present.

To Persuade **Persuasive presentations** can work at three levels: they can change or reaffirm existing attitudes about important topics, strive to gain audience commitment, and motivate action. For example, if you are concerned about the environment, you may decide to attend a presentation on your company's recycling program. As you listen to a manager speak about recycling and conservation, you suddenly realize the importance of these issues. You leave the session determined to recycle cans and avoid Styrofoam coffee cups. If you actually follow through with these intentions, the manager's presentation was effective at all three levels.

In persuasive presentations, you are asking the audience to make a commitment to your viewpoint and to act in ways that you advocate. As with informative speaking, persuasive presentations require conscientious research to uncover the best available data on the topic. In addition, persuaders must present a course of action that can be accepted by a group of people who might choose otherwise. We discuss persuasive formats and techniques in detail in Chapter 15.

To Motivate Presentations designed to motivate audience members are a special type of persuasive speech. **Motivational presentations** employ persuasion but rely more extensively on stimulating the emotions and feelings of listeners as a method of

Where Do You Stand?

List several topics that you think might make good speeches for this class. For three or four of them, consider how you might convert that topic into a speech to inform, to persuade, to motivate, or to celebrate. Which of these general purposes would create the most difficulty for you? Why do you think so?

inducing action. Members of the clergy may use biblical images and the subconscious fears and hopes of their audiences to encourage spiritual action. Drill sergeants may use highly charged, emotional language to push "raw" recruits to new levels of physical exertion. Although drill sergeants and clerics employ different motivational strategies, the emotional intensity they can inspire is often very similar.

In the business world, managers are often called upon to motivate their employees. At a typical annual sales meeting, for example, during which sales representatives are brought together to learn about the latest company products and initiatives, sales managers and company executives are likely to take some time to "pump up" the sales force with tales of success in the past year and promises of good fortune to come.

To Celebrate **Ceremonial presentations** often share many of the elements found in informative, persuasive, and motivational speaking, as we will discuss in Chapter 15. Included among this group are the following presentations:

Introduction—introducing other speakers
Acceptance—welcoming an honor or reward
Tribute—making toasts
Goodwill—remembering and honoring the past
Inspiration—presenting a memorial or eulogy
Celebration—rejoicing in achievements

Ceremonial presentations demonstrate your commitment to organizational ideals or your organization's commitment to its valued ideals. For example, many organizations hold "roasts," or comic tributes, for retiring employees who have been vital members of the organization throughout the years. Ceremonial presentations require you to consider the common ties that bind participants together as a group.

While in this course you may be given a general purpose and asked to select a topic, in business you are frequently assigned a topic and must then choose the general purpose (approach) that will be most successful. As a result, general purpose normally takes a purer form within the classroom—an assignment for an informative presentation will largely avoid persuasive, motivational, or celebratory goals—whereas in the workplace it is not at all unusual for a manager to use one message to inform, persuade, motivate, and celebrate. In this book we focus on each of these goals separately, an approach that introduces beginning speakers to the unique characteristics and demands of each purpose and better prepares them to combine or adapt goals for presentations later in their speaking careers.

Specific Purpose

The second filter for refining your topic is determining the specific purpose. The **specific purpose** of a presentation is derived from the general purpose and identifies what you as the presenter want the audience to think, believe, feel, or do as a result of listening to your presentation. As we have discussed throughout this book, specific goals are far more effective for directing communication to achieve shared meaning and desired results. Public speaking requires deliberate and specific goals, just as interpersonal, group, and organizational communication do.

PRACTICING BUSINESS COMMUNICATION

American Red Cross

Entering its second century of existence, the American Red Cross continues its tradition of providing relief to victims of natural and man-made disasters. More than one hundred years have passed since founder Clara Barton carried in her purse the funds to conduct the tiny Red Cross operations. The organization has greatly expanded from the small association she had founded in 1881, but millions of relief workers, administrators, donors, and other volunteers are still motivated by that same concern for human life and well-being.

A recent national survey by Yankelovich Partners showed the American Red Cross to be the most highly regarded of major U.S. charities, and *Money* magazine has named the Red Cross one of the ten best-managed charities in the country. Proud as the Red Cross is of its achievements, the organization continuously tries to better prepare itself to respond to emergencies and to make both its communication efforts and its service efforts more efficient and more effective.

A GRASSROOTS CULTURE

The focal point of Red Cross activity in the United States is its headquarters in Washington, D.C. But its organizational culture reflects a grassroots, volunteer base of more than 2 million in more than two thousand Red Cross chapters nationwide. In fact, volunteers make up more than 97 percent of the Red Cross's total work force. Characterized by dedication, loyalty, a strong sense of the organization's mission, and commitment to social ideals, many Red Cross employees and volunteers view the organization as an integral part of their lives and as a way to give something of themselves back to their communities and to society.

An appreciation of the bottom-up nature and community focus of the Red Cross guides the national headquarters staff in supporting a complex organizational structure that employs, in addition to its volunteers, 30,500 paid staff and operates forty-four state offices, forty-five blood banks, and more than two hundred Red Cross stations on U.S. military installations.

Headquarters staff develop and guide the programs of service available through the Red Cross, help the federal government to abide by the Geneva Conventions, and participate, along with one hundred forty-nine other national Red Cross and Red Crescent organizations, in Red Cross International to provide humanitarian relief throughout the world.

Established by congressional charter in 1889, the American Red Cross shoulders two major national responsibilities: (1) providing assistance to disaster victims and (2) providing emergency communication between members of the U.S. armed forces and their families. Today, the Red Cross also operates the nation's largest blood service, collects and distributes donor tissue and organs for medical use, and educates more than 11 million Americans each year in first aid, health, and safety.

TARGETED COMMUNICATION

The information needs of individuals and local units of the Red Cross vary widely. The largest blood regions and urban chapters have hundreds of paid employees, while most chapters in smaller communities have only one or two staff members or are managed entirely by volunteers. Information needs run the gamut from general business

The specific purpose should contain a single idea. Some basic considerations for the specific purpose include the following: Is the idea manageable in the time allowed for the presentation? Is the idea challenging to the audience? Is the idea important to the organizational values and/or career goals of the audience? The specific purpose is then translated into a **thesis statement**—a single, declarative sentence that summarizes the main ideas to be presented to the audience.

The thesis statement may emerge as the speaker researches and develops the message. For example, a first specific purpose may be stated as "I want my audience to know about the role of personal computers in an advertising agency."

management and administration to highly technical subjects in the biomedical, health and safety, and disaster relief areas.

Internal publications range from general-interest newsletters to specialized information packages. Top Red Cross leaders receive a quarterly publication, *Talking Points,* to support their roles as spokespersons to internal and external audiences. A weekly one-page "Executive Bulletin" giving top-line corporate news is faxed from headquarters to executives and volunteer chairs of about one thousand Red Cross units.

New strategies are constantly introduced to permit a more rapid flow of information during emergencies and to support a more interactive relationship between chapters and headquarters. The Red Cross has used video extensively for over a quarter-century. Recorded information on 800 numbers gives chapters immediate access to the latest information on national and international disasters. One-page "Chapter Information Bulletins" provide critical information to the chapters that are linked into a broadcast fax system with headquarters.

EXPANDING INTERACTIVE COMMUNICATION

The Red Cross is committed to staying in the forefront in using state-of-the-art communications technology effectively to support its humanitarian work, from establishing an organization-wide intranet to its own direct-broadcast satellite (DBS) system, which enhances communication directly with individual volunteers and donors in their homes.

Within the Red Cross, business television, which has a two-way audio and one-way video capacity, has significantly strengthened the national-local link and improved interactive communication among blood regions, state offices, and local chapters. The advantages of business television are substantial. In one case, the directors of regional blood banks participated in a live ninety-minute symposium with the national blood services director at a fraction of the cost of bringing the audience to a central meeting place. In another, each of the forty-four state offices gathered statewide chapter reactions to a recommended new corporate fundraising strategy, then discussed the results directly with headquarters in a live television broadcast viewed by chapter staff across the country.

In all its communications, the American Red Cross looks for ways to expand its contact with those the organization is dedicated to serve: individual citizens and communities.

QUESTIONS FOR CRITICAL THINKING

1. What challenges does Red Cross headquarters face in communicating effectively within such a large, widespread organization?
2. How does Red Cross headquarters communicate its support for local units? Why is such support important?
3. What different communication strategies does the Red Cross incorporate? How does the Red Cross adapt these strategies to different audiences inside and outside the organization?
4. What are the advantages and disadvantages of business television?
5. What is the communication climate at the American Red Cross?

You can visit the American Red Cross on-line at http://www.redcross.org.

After the speaker researches the topic, he or she may devise a more specific (and useful) thesis statement: "Within an advertising agency, major uses for personal computers include word processing, business management, e-mail communication, and graphic design." A well-considered thesis statement is crucial for delivering an effective message.

The above speaker has identified a specific purpose and translated that purpose into a thesis statement for an informative presentation. The process is the same for all four general purposes (to inform, persuade, motivate, and celebrate). Say, for example, the speaker has been assigned the task of coordinating the company's participation in the United Way campaign (general purpose: to persuade). After reflection, the speaker decides that the specific purpose of the presentation is to convince coworkers to make a donation. This specific purpose is then translated into a thesis statement: "I want my audience to pledge to make a financial contribution to the United Way."

Successful communication results from the achievement of a series of interrelated goals, each flowing from the one before it. This element of continuity means that you must set goals at every stage of the presentation process, from selecting a topic and doing research to practicing your delivery. Goals prompt you to monitor your work continually, thereby ensuring that you attend carefully to each phase of your presentation's development.

SITUATIONAL KNOWLEDGE: ANALYZING THE AUDIENCE

In presentational speaking, the process of finding out about those to whom you will be speaking is termed **audience analysis,** and it corresponds to the second component of strategic communication: gathering situational knowledge. When preparing for a presentation, you can research individual members of the audience, organizational factors that affect the audience, and even location, time, or other physical influences. Audience analysis helps you to understand the speaking situation as it unfolds as well as how best to prepare for the audience's needs and likely responses to your message. In other words, effective speakers continue to gather information and monitor the situation throughout the presentation.[4]

Demographic information—the audience's size, age, social class, educational level, gender, cultural background, and occupational status—is fundamental to any audience analysis. Demography (the collection and study of such information) is a necessary first step toward establishing more specific and complex analyses of a target audience. The target audience—the key decision makers who are members of the general audience—is an important focus for your analysis. You are more likely to succeed by tailoring your ideas, information, and appeals to these audience members.[5]

Audience attitudes toward many social and economic issues can be predicted through careful demographic analysis. For example, if you learn that your audience will be composed of employees in the manufacturing division of your company—mostly blue-collar males ages forty to sixty who are union members—you can conclude that a presentation on why the company should deunionize to encourage new hiring policies will have to be approached with careful preparation and an understanding of possible negative audience response.

This is not to say that audience analysis encourages stereotyping or can be ignored if you think you already know, for example, what a typical clerical worker is like. It is vital to approach audience analysis with an open mind because you are likely to discover unexpected characteristics of audience members that may provide the key to connecting with them. By analyzing and understanding the implications of the audience analysis, you will have a good sense of how to aim your presentation and what language and imagery to employ.

Remember also that it is important to know whether you are speaking to accountants, engineers, marketers, janitors, or a combination of various employee

4. S. E. Berry and R. J. Garnston, "Become a State-of-the-Art Presenter," *Training and Development Journal* 41 (1987), 19–26.
5. G. A. Market, "Many Executives Must Learn How to Speak," *Marketing News* 22 (1988), 8–10.

groups. They may all work for your company, but each group has a different perspective on the organization, and it is also likely to differ from your own. Be sure to modify your presentation to accommodate each group because the most successful presentations are those that address every member of the audience and make each person feel involved and important.

Three categories of audience analysis can be considered when doing a profile. Each of the three categories provides a different starting point for thinking about your audience's needs.

Audience type—Why have these people decided to attend your presentation?

Audience characteristics—What are the religions, education levels, ages, ethnicities, and genders of typical audience members?

Environmental characteristics—How will the setting and surroundings affect the speaking situation?

Presentations made to familiar coworkers may require less investigative work than do presentations made to people you do not know; nevertheless, do not underestimate the importance of any category of demographic information just because it is easy to collect. For example, you will make presentations in this class, and you can simply look around the room to determine the gender ratio, ethnic makeup, approximate age bracket, and educational level of your audience members. Obtaining other demographic information may be more difficult, but not impossible. One excellent method is to ask questions of people who are knowledgeable about the audience—friends, supervisors, coworkers, or even people who have presented to the group before. Less obvious categories, such as sociopolitical status, religious affiliations, and economic status, can often be discovered through research, which can be done in the library with the assistance of a librarian. The environmental characteristics of the speaking situation, such as time limit, size of the audience, and location, can be learned by visiting the site ahead of time and by talking with the people who asked you to speak.

IDENTIFYING AND RESEARCHING MAIN IDEAS

Once you have narrowed a topic to a specific purpose and thesis statement and identified the outstanding characteristics of your audience, the next step is to identify and research your main points. Ask yourself, "What does the audience need to know and accept if I am to accomplish the specific purpose I have selected for the presentation?" If, for example, you are an account executive for an advertising agency and your goal is to persuade a local restaurant owner to select your agency to handle the restaurant's advertising campaign, what are the main ideas you need to stress to show her or him the benefits of selecting your agency?

Generating Potential Main Ideas

A good method for locating main ideas is to think systematically about the topic. Doing so reminds you of what you already know about the topic and suggests areas that require additional research.

Although there are many ways to generate main ideas, we recommend a *topical* system based on the methods of such famous writers on public speaking as Aristotle, Cicero, and Francis Bacon. The **topical system** uses a small set of headings or topics to identify standard ways of thinking and talking about any subject.

The basic premise of the approach is that the infinite number of possible topics contain a finite number of themes—a result of our shared ways of thinking about human affairs. The following sixteen topics can be used to describe any subject on which a presenter might choose to speak.[6]

A. Attributes
   1. Existence or nonexistence of things
   2. Degree or quantity of things or forces
   3. Spatial attributes, including location, distribution, and position of things, especially in relation to other things
   4. Time—when an event took place, how long it lasted, and so forth
   5. Motion or activity—type, degree
   6. Form—the physical or abstract shape of a thing
   7. Substance—the physical or abstract content of a thing
   8. Capacity to change—whether an event or situation is predictable or unpredictable
   9. Potency—power or energy, including the ability to further or hinder something else
   10. Desirability—whether the thing results in rewards or punishments
   11. Feasibility—how well the thing works or how practical it is

B. Basic relationships
   1. Causality—the relation of causes to effects, effects to causes, and so forth
   2. Correlation—correspondence between, coexistence of, or coordination of things or forces
   3. Genus-species relationships—common characteristics or distinguishing characteristics of a thing or group of things
   4. Similarity or dissimilarity in appearance, content, form, shape, and so forth
   5. Possibility or impossibility of an event happening

Let us return to our hypothetical account executive preparing to make a pitch to the restaurant owner and managers for an account. How can she or he stress any of the sixteen themes? After some thought, the account executive comes up with the following points:

1. The ad agency has been serving the community for more than thirty years (existence).
2. The agency handles more than twenty restaurant accounts and gains more every year (degree of experience/expertise).
3. The agency is conveniently located in the downtown business district (spatial attribute).
4. The agency can put together a trial campaign in two weeks (time).
5. Restaurants that have used the ad agency have reported substantial increases in customers (activity).

6. From J. F. Wilson, C. C. Arnold, and M. M. Wertheimer, *Public Speaking as a Liberal Art,* 6th ed. (Boston: Allyn & Bacon, 1990), pp. 112–113. Copyright © 1990 by Pearson Education. Reprinted with permission.

6. The agency can provide several choices for the look of the campaign and specializes in the latest design and graphics (form).
7. The agency will work with the restaurant owner to articulate a precise message for the campaign (substance).
8. The agency will modify the campaign if it is not bringing the desired results (capacity to change).
9. The agency projects a 32 percent increase in the restaurant's business based on campaigns done for similar restaurants in the past (potency).
10. The agency can promote increased business that will allow the restaurant owner to open another restaurant and enjoy greater profits (desirability).
11. The agency is a practical choice because of its expertise in the area of restaurant advertising and its competitive rates (feasibility).

Of course, it would be an overwhelming task to stress all these themes in the course of one presentation. Nevertheless, the account executive now has a wealth of main ideas and can select the two or three most suited to the needs of this restaurant owner.

Doing Research

The topical system, although useful for generating potential main points, must be supplemented by additional research to find information to support your ideas, especially if the topic is in an area in which you are not an expert. A good starting point for such research is consultation with experts and specialists on your topic through the process of informational interviewing described in Chapter 8. Questions to be asked in such an interview include "What books and articles do you recommend I read?"; "What resources have proven especially useful to you?"; and "Do you know other people who might provide additional help?"

Following up leads provided by experts and filling in missing details often mean visiting a library and/or using the Internet. The card catalog, reference room, and periodicals section are all good starting points for research, as are the reference works cited earlier in this chapter. If you don't know about the location of materials in the library, ask for help; reference librarians are trained to find relevant information quickly and efficiently. Not only will the reference librarian be familiar with special indexes and guides to materials; he or she will also be able to assist you with on-line computerized indexes, databases, and abstracts that provide the most up-to-date information. You can also use the general-purpose search engines identified earlier in this chapter to locate information on the World Wide Web.

One of the most useful tools for organizing your research and taking notes is the index card. You can use these cards to create a bibliography and to take comprehensive notes. A **bibliography** is a detailed list of all the books, articles, interviews, and abstracts you have reviewed in the course of your research. For each publication, write the complete title and reference information on the card in case you need to find it again later. On the back of the card, write a brief summary of the content.

Then take specific notes on each of the sources. You can code the sources by letter; write the letter of the source on one side of the card and the detailed information and the number of the page where you found it on the other. If you are writing a direct quote, be painstakingly careful to copy it exactly, including spelling and punctuation. Only include information related to one main idea per card—that way, you can easily organize your finished research into main ideas. These notes will be the basis for developing supporting materials for your presentation.

You are likely to generate dozens of viable main ideas. Although you may believe that the more ideas and research you include, the stronger the resulting presentation will be, using a large number of main ideas can test the audience's attention span and tolerance for fatigue and require you to exceed the normal time limit for a presentation (from five to thirty minutes). No strict definition exists for the "correct" number of main points, but for most messages it is wise to keep the number within the range of three to five.

PROVIDING SUPPORT FOR IDEAS

Regardless of the purpose of your presentation, you will use some form of **supporting materials** to give credibility to your main ideas and to make the message more informative, interesting, relevant, clear, and acceptable—all the better to reach the audience. Supporting materials facilitate learning. Although teaching the audience is a fundamental goal of most presentations, for some people learning something new or unexpected can be an uncomfortable or frightening experience and can therefore be resisted. Indeed, people tend to resist a speaker's attempts to change them or to provoke some action. Supporting materials can greatly help the speaker to overcome these barriers to complete a successful presentation. These materials include explanations, examples, statistics, testimony, and visual aids.

Explanations

Explanation is the act or process of making a subject plain or comprehensible. This is often accomplished through a simple statement of the relationship of a whole and its parts—for example, "The Southwestern Region is composed of the sales areas in Arizona, Utah, New Mexico, and Nevada." Other methods include the following:

Providing a definition: "The Southwestern Region contains sales representatives responsible for all product sales, new product leads, and recruitment in Arizona, Utah, New Mexico, and Nevada."

Using synonyms (words with approximately the same meanings) or antonyms (words with opposite meanings)

Using comparisons (showing listeners the similarities between something familiar and something unfamiliar): "Like the North Central Region, the Southwestern Region will have four sales representatives, with approximately seventy-five accounts totaling over $4 million."

Showing contrasts (supporting an idea by emphasizing differences between it and something else): "Unlike the California group, the Southwestern representatives will not be required to complete Spanish-language training."

Giving a brief history

Providing an operational definition (defining the term *logging off* by describing the steps involved in exiting a particular program on a computer): "Sales representatives will be account executives, responsible for all service aspects of their territories."

Explanations should be framed within the experiences of audience members. The presenter must also be careful not to make such explanations too long or too abstract.

Examples

Examples connect the main ideas of a presentation with a real or an ideal state envisioned by the speaker. Examples take a variety of forms, including extended, detailed illustrations and brief, specific instances. Illustrations can be either hypothetical (a story that could happen) or factual (a story that did happen). A presenter may involve the listeners in a hypothetical illustration by suggesting, "Imagine yourself in an employment interview. You want this job, and for the first ten minutes or so everything has been going smoothly. Then the interviewer starts to ask a series of personal and, in your view, illegal questions."

When using hypothetical or factual illustrations, the speaker is wise to consider whether the story is relevant and appropriate to the audience, whether it is typical rather than exceptional, and whether it is vivid and impressive in detail. If the illustration fails to fulfill any of these criteria, the speaker should find a more suitable alternative.

A specific instance is an undeveloped, very brief illustration—more a reference than an example. Using specific instances successfully requires that the audience recognize the names or events to which the speaker is referring. For example, a reference to "GATT" in a presentation on foreign trade will be ineffective if the audience is not familiar with the role of the General Agreement on Tariffs and Trade in the post–World War II international economy. Nevertheless, citing specific instances with which the audience is familiar can foster an audience's belief in and identification with the speaker as "one of us."

Statistics

As a form of supporting material, **statistics** describe the result of collecting, organizing, and interpreting numerical data. They are especially useful when you wish to accomplish the following objectives:

1. *Reduce* large masses of information to general categories ("The average score for college students on the Personal Report of Communication Apprehension is 75.")
2. *Emphasize* the size of something ("Business and industry currently spend more than $200 billion annually for training and development—more than is spent for education at primary, secondary, and college levels.")
3. *Indicate trends* ("From 1997 to 2000, state government expenditures on prisons increased by 30 percent while spending on higher education fell by 18 percent.")

When using statistics, you must concern yourself with their accuracy and bias as well as with their clarity and meaningfulness. Addressing the first issue involves answering such questions as these: Were correct data-collecting techniques used to obtain the statistics? Do the statistics cover sufficient cases and lengths of time? Are the statistics taken from competent sources? The second issue includes pragmatic considerations such as these: Can you translate these difficult-to-understand numbers into more immediately understandable terms? How can you provide adequate background for the data? Would a graph or visual aid clarify the data or statistical trends that you are presenting?

Testimony

Testimony is a statement by a credible person (source) that lends weight and authority to the speaker's presentation. Credibility is based on whether the source is an acknowledged expert on the specific subject and is free of bias and self-interest. The audience's perception of the source is important as well. Is the source well known to the audience? If not, the speaker must tell the audience why the source is a good authority. If the source is known, does the audience accept her or his opinion as knowledgeable and unbiased? To lend support to a message, the testimony of a source must *be credible* and *be perceived as credible* by the audience.

Visual Aids

Like all forms of supporting material, visual aids enhance the clarity and credibility of the message. And, by using multiple channels of communication, they appeal to multiple senses and so increase listeners' retention of significant points. They also help the presenter control his or her own apprehension by providing a point of familiarity in an uncertain situation.

These advantages are especially important for business and professional settings. As Tom Cothran points out:

> Numerous studies lend tangible support to the argument for using visuals. . . . At the University of Wisconsin, for example, researchers determined that learning improved up to 200 percent when visual aids were used in teaching vocabulary. Studies at Harvard and Columbia have found audiovisuals improve[d] retention by from 14 to 38 percent over presentations where no visuals were used. Research at both the University of Pennsylvania's Wharton School of Business and the University of Minnesota report[s] that the time required to present a concept can be reduced up to 40 percent when visuals complement a verbal presentation.
>
> Wharton's research considered presenters as well as their presentations. . . . Among its findings: Presenters who used visuals were perceived more favorably overall than those who did not use visuals. Specifically, presenters who used

TECHNOLOGY TOOLS

Finding Quotations on the Internet

One of the sites for finding quotations on the Internet (and links to other Internet quotation libraries) is Yahoo's reference section at http://www.yahoo.com/reference/quotations/. This site maintains a searchable database of quotations, broken down into convenient categories, as well as a quotation-of-the-day section. It also contains hotlinks to more than one hundred additional Web quotation sites. In addition to focusing on the utterances of certain famous individuals, these quotation libraries are organized by topics such as inspiration, wisdom, advertising, and labor. Bartlett's Familiar Quotations has a similarly useful and efficient counterpart on the Web at http://www.bartleby.com/100/.

Seen here is an artist's rendition of the aerial view of the World Trade Center memorial ("Reflecting Absence") as seen from the southeast looking north. Assuming that you are the speaker and want your audience to learn about this memorial, what are the advantages and disadvantages of using this visual as part of your presentation? What alternatives might you consider? What are some important criteria to remember when using this visual during your presentation? (© dbox for the Lower Manhattan Development Corporation/Corbis)

visuals were "perceived as significantly better prepared, more professional, more persuasive, and more interesting" than those using no visual support. In meetings where a decision was required, a larger percentage of decisions agreed with presentations made with visual support than without.

The Minnesota study's most startling finding was this: "Presentations using computer-generated graphics are 43 percent more persuasive than unaided presentations." In addition, "a typical presenter using presentation support has nothing to lose and can be as effective as a better presenter using no visuals," the researchers reported. "The better a presenter is, however, the more one needs to use high-quality visual support."[7]

Types of Visual Aids Obtaining these advantages requires skill in selecting appropriate aids and using them well. There are three basic categories of visual aids: the actual object or a model of it, pictorial reproductions, and pictorial symbols. In the first category, for example, an architectural model of a building may be used to present information about a new building design. Also consider logistics when using a visual aid from this category. Actual objects should be used only if they can be easily handled during the presentation. Likewise, a model built in painstaking detail may lose its impact if the audience is too far away to see it clearly.

Photographs, slides, sketches, videotapes, cartoons, and drawings are included in the category of pictorial reproductions. In keeping with the old saying "A picture

7. T. Cothran, "The Value of Visuals," *Presentation Technologies,* (July 1989), pp. 6-7.

is worth a thousand words," pictorial reproductions show the main ideas of a presentation in new, exciting, and interesting ways.

Abstract concepts and statistical data are often represented through pictorial symbols such as graphs, charts, and diagrams. These may be prepared on a variety of media, including flip charts, chalkboards, overhead projections, or handouts.

Selecting Visuals When considering using a visual aid for your presentation, keep several criteria in mind:

1. *Use aids that are large enough to be seen.* In addition to checking the size of the visual itself, you should ensure that all writing included on the visual is large enough to be easily readable. When possible, take the visual aid to the room where it will be used and test it for visibility from all sections of the room that the audience will occupy during the presentation. If doing so is not possible, ask advice from people who know the setting, and then make informed guesses about the potential number of listeners and the average viewing distances.
2. *Keep the content of visual aids simple and focused.* Pictures and words should be as uncrowded and simple as possible and should avoid unnecessary details that may distract the audience. Rather than trying to include too much information on one visual, use multiple visuals, each containing only those features and details essential to clarify and to highlight the specific point being made.
3. *Prepare visual materials carefully.* Audience members interpret the design and form of the visual aid as a reflection of your attitude toward them and toward the message. Thus, the form of the aid has great potential to enhance or detract from your credibility regardless of the visual's content. Professionals may be hired to prepare visuals for particularly important presentations, although for the most part, understanding the basic design and format rules described earlier can help you create visuals for your own presentations.

DEVELOPING AN INTRODUCTION AND A CONCLUSION

Up to this point, we have worked through basic principles for creating the body of a message—clarifying and focusing on the purpose, identifying and researching the main ideas, and using supporting materials. We now turn to the front and back sections of the message—the introduction and the conclusion.

The Introduction

As you think about how to begin a presentation, consider a similar situation: the first meeting of a class. When you took your seat on the first day of this class, for example, what was it that you wanted to know? If you are at all like other students we have asked, there were at least three categories of information you wanted to learn: course coverage (what will be the content and focus of the course?), course requirements (what is required to complete this course?), and course instructor (what kind of person will this teacher turn out to be?). These questions fall into three general categories: issues of *orientation* (what's happening?), *motivation* (what's in it for me?), and *rapport* (will I like and respect this instructor?). Although you may already have obtained partial answers to these questions before the first class session (from friends, former class members, and so forth), the questions

Where Do You Stand?

When you are listening to a speech, which of the forms of support (explanations, examples, statistics, testimony, visual aids) are most important to you? Why? Would your answer differ depending on general purpose (inform, persuade, motivate, celebrate)? Why?

most likely still remained, and you and the instructor probably spent at least a portion of the first meeting answering them.

The **introduction** to a presentation serves similar functions. It informs the listener what the message is about (orientation), why the listener should attend to it (motivation), and why the speaker is a credible source for the message (rapport). As the speaker thinks through the introduction, he or she should consider which of these issues requires attention and what kind.

Orientation One method of orienting the audience is to state the topic to be discussed, give the thesis statement, explain the presentation's title, or review the purpose of the presentation. A speaker at a business fundraiser for local arts groups may begin: "Some of you may wonder why this presentation is titled 'Give; Don't Give Up.' I'm here today to tell you why it's more important now, in the face of difficult economic times, than ever before to contribute to cultural organizations."

Another method of orienting the audience is to preview the structure of the message: "Cultural organizations provide three vital services to our community: they expand our view of the world and each other, they raise issues that we need to discuss, and they enrich our lives and our children's lives."

The speaker may also explain why the topic was narrowed as it was: "When I was asked to give a fundraising presentation to you, business leaders in the community, my first question was 'What can you do for us?' I soon realized that I needed to tell you what *we* are doing—and hope to continue to do—for *you.*"

Motivation Motivational strategies include linking the topic and thesis statement to listeners' lives: "How many of you have attended a cultural event in our community in the recent past? Think of how our city would be diminished if these events were no longer held."

Showing how the topic has affected or will affect the audience's past, present, or future is another motivational strategy. A speaker may begin a presentation by saying: "You may not have realized it, but tourism generated $34 million for our city last year. Surveys showed that many of these visitors came to participate in our numerous cultural events, and in the process they bolstered the profits of your businesses."

Demonstrating how the topic is linked to a basic need or goal of the audience is a third method of motivating an audience to listen. This can be done by saying: "Cultural events are an important part of making our community vital and prosperous, and I'm sure that all of us want to keep it that way."

Rapport Building rapport can take several forms. Language that demonstrates competence, such as citing important and respected people, noting relevant events, or describing your expertise on the topic, increases the audience's receptivity to your message.

Trustworthiness, another important factor in building rapport, can be demonstrated by showing that your present behavior is consistent with your past behavior on the topic under discussion, giving time to opposing points of view, and being consistent with verbal and nonverbal behavior. Nonverbal behavior that shows confidence and enthusiasm for the topic—such as a strong voice, direct eye contact with members of the audience, and a measured delivery—promotes an image of trustworthiness.

STRATEGIC SKILLS

Using Audiovisual Aids Competently

Overheads

Advantages: They are relatively inexpensive and easily available.

Disadvantages: The technology can fail (a defective light bulb, for example), and they require electricity and a screen.

Advice for their use:

1. Avoid blocking the screen.
2. Talk to the audience, not to the screen or the projector.
3. Before your presentation, learn how to use the projector, determine where to place the machine, and locate an electrical outlet.

Chalkboards and Flip Charts

Advantages: They are easily available and inexpensive.

Disadvantages: They are hard to "hide" from the audience and so can draw attention away from the speaker.

Advice for their use:

1. Face your audience as you write.
2. Before your presentation, practice using the writing surface.
3. Plan every written word, its placement, and its accuracy (content and grammar).
4. Collect and arrange materials ahead of time.

Audio and Audiovisual Equipment

Advantages: Either a tape recorder or a VCR can bring vivid examples to an audience.

Disadvantages: They require great effort to ensure that an audience can see and/or hear them. They also involve technologies that can fail.

Advice for their use:

1. Know where electrical outlets are and whether extension cords are needed.
2. Test the sound levels.
3. Test the quality of the recordings.
4. Check the sound volume and quality in all areas of the room.

Subject Objects

Advantages: They command attention and can enhance clarity.

Disadvantages: They can be overly complex and too large to easily manage.

Advice for their use:

1. Use only items that can be seen by everyone in the audience.
2. Use objects that are appropriate to the purpose and subject of your speech.
3. Plan the specific times in your presentation when you will use objects.

Complimenting the audience and using humor are additional techniques for developing rapport. Doing so shows that you identify with people in the audience, respect them, and can laugh with them.

In considering introductory strategies, you are wise to remember that many of the most effective strategies contribute to multiple functions. For example, a story can provide both orientation and motivation, and humor can enhance both motivation and rapport. Thus, when you are developing an introduction, make it as compact as possible and as effective as possible in fulfilling the audience's needs for orientation, motivation, and rapport.

The Conclusion

The **conclusion** seeks to provide a sense of completeness and closure. It is often signaled by the phrases "in conclusion" or "in summary" and is accomplished by reminding the audience of the highlights of the presentation and reemphasizing

Pictorial Reproductions or Symbols

Advantages: They can simplify complex ideas and objects.

Disadvantages: They require artistic skill to create.

Advice for their use:

1. Make sure that all pictorials are visible to everyone.
2. Label graphics and charts clearly with various colors.
3. Explain the source of, the significance of, and the context of any pictorials.
4. If posters are not glued, taped, or speared to a firm surface, they will flop or fall over. This will interrupt your audience's concentration and damage your credibility.

Handouts

Advantages: They are inexpensive and do not depend on technology for their use.

Disadvantages: The audience can too easily focus on them rather than on the speaker.

Advice for their use:

1. Use an assistant to pass out the materials.
2. Have more than enough handouts available.
3. Choose carefully when and how you plan to use handouts, because members of your audience will often read, make noise with, and doodle on your handout during your speech (thus ignoring you, the speaker).

Computer-Generated Presentations (including DVD-R)

Advantages: Programs such as PowerPoint* make them easy to generate. They allow connection to the Internet, making powerful resources available to the speaker.

Disadvantages: They can easily become gimmicky. Equipment and connection failures can create difficulties.

Advice for their use:

1. During the preparation process, always think in terms of how each slide will help achieve your purpose rather than in terms of what is technologically possible.
2. Always be prepared with a back-up strategy in the form of handouts or overheads in case a connection to the Internet fails or other technological glitches occur.
3. Talk to the audience rather than to the presentation screen.

*There are other presentation design programs besides PowerPoint, of course; and PowerPoint has detractors. Nevertheless, at the moment there is little on the horizon that threatens its dominance as a presentation design tool, so it is worth your time to master this versatile software. Some important resources for doing so are Microsoft's PowerPoint Site (www.microsoft.com/powerpoint); NetTech's Presentations Resources Page (www.nettechinc.com/present.htm); Presentations Magazine (www.presentations.com); and Effective Presentations (www.presentingsolutions.com/effectivepresentations.html.

their significance. The conclusion not only helps the audience remember what you have said (people often remember best what they heard last); it also allows you to reinforce the cohesion and importance of the message.

In addition to summarizing the main ideas of the message, you can use the conclusion to reestablish the connection of the topic to the larger context and to provide psychological closure by reminding audience members how the topic affects their lives. Both functions can be achieved by tying the conclusion of the speech to the introduction—bringing both together by reference to and elaboration of quotations, illustrations, or questions that were used in the beginning.

Because the conclusion serves as a summary and an ending, it should be brief and decisive; it should not trail off. When the audience hears a concluding phrase, it will—and is entitled to—believe that the presentation has reached an end. Thus, use your conclusion to reinforce the thesis for your audience, to place that thesis in the larger context known to your audience, and to provide, if possible, a "clincher" (a telling quotation, illustration, or question). Then sit down.

THE OUTLINE: BASIC CONSIDERATIONS

Now that we have identified all the pieces of the presentation—the main ideas, the supporting materials, the introduction, and the conclusion—the time has come to put them together. The **outline,** a visual, schematic summary of the message, shows the order of the ideas and the general relationships among them.

Types of Outlines

There are basically three types of outlines: **a complete-sentence outline,** which lists each head and subhead in complete-sentence form; a **topic outline,** which reduces the sentences to brief phrases or single words; and a **speaker's outline,** which includes only key words and important quotations or statistics written on index cards.

All three forms are useful for different purposes. The complete-sentence outline allows others to study the organizational structure and to give feedback on its strengths and weaknesses. For this reason, teachers who ask students to hand in outlines usually ask for this format. The topic outline allows the speaker to consider and reconsider organizational choices while working on the presentation. Once those choices have been made, the speaker creates a speaker's outline to aid or trigger her or his memory during the actual presentation. Since each method has different advantages, the speaker should work first with a complete-sentence outline and later reduce it to a speaker's outline for the actual presentation.

Basic Principles

For both complete-sentence and topic outlines, there are four major conventions for writing the outline.

Formal presentations may benefit from a variety of presentational aids such as flip charts, chalkboards, and computer-generated slide shows like the one pictured here. The key to success with such aids is a clear idea of purpose, an effective outline of main ideas, an interesting introduction, and a conclusion that pulls everything together.
(© R. W. Jones/Corbis)

Appropriate Numbering Systems The most widely used numbering system alternates letters and numbers, as shown in the following outline. The main heads are placed at the left margin and subheads are indented, forming a clearly identifiable column. Heads or subheads that run more than a single line are further indented so that the content portion of the entry aligns with the content above it.

Introduction (methods for establishing orientation, motivation, rapport)

I. First main point
A.
    1.
    2.
        a.
        b.
            (1)
            (2)
B.
    1.
    2.
        a.
        b.
II. Second main point
A.
    1.
    2.
B.
C.
    1.
    2.
III. Third main point
A.
B.

Conclusion (methods for summarizing, linking, and clinching)

Heads of Equal Importance The main points (Roman numerals I, II, and III) are the main divisions of the presentation and should be of equal importance to the topic. Similarly, the first subdivision of these heads (capital letters A and B) designates logical and equally important divisions of the first main point. This principle also applies to the other subdivisions represented by Arabic numerals and lowercase letters.

Consistency in Form A complete-sentence outline uses complete sentences throughout and does not lapse into topic heads; by contrast, a topic outline uses topic heads, not sentences. In the sentence outline, the punctuation follows written conventions (e.g., use of periods); by contrast, no punctuation is needed at the end of lines in a topic outline.

Balance in Form Because a topic is not "divided" unless there are at least two parts, an outline normally has at least two subheads under any main head. Even though exceptions are possible, normally for every heading marked I there is at least a II, and for every A there is at least a B.

Points and Subpoints In the outline on page 385, the "speech" contains three main **points** (I, II, and III). These are the major ideas that the speaker wishes the audience to understand and accept. Say, for example, the speaker using this outline is giving a speech suggesting that there are three behavioral commitments involved in being a leader in an organization: (I) confronting and changing the status quo, (II) inspiring a shared vision, and (III) enabling others to act.

In order to make these main points vivid, easily remembered, convincing, and so forth, the speaker needs to use a variety of forms of support (e.g., explanations, examples, statistics, testimony, and/or visual aids). These forms of support become **subpoints** in the outline, of which there can be multiple levels. In terms of the first main point, for example, our hypothetical speaker argues two subpoints in support of (I): (A) an effective leader searches out challenging opportunities to change, grow, innovate, and improve, and (B) and effective leader experiments, takes risks, and learns from the accompanying mistakes. To "support" the first subpoint (A), our speaker develops two additional subpoints (or sub-subpoints): (1) testimony from an acknowledged effective leader and (2) an example of a leader who has done so.

While, in principle, a speech (and the outline of it) can have points, subpoints, sub-subpoints, sub-sub-subpoints, and so forth, the speaker is advised to keep the attention span of the audience in mind and provide no more levels of support than are absolutely necessary to help an audience understand and accept the main points of the presentation.

Transitions

When an audience member listens to the presentation you have outlined, he or she lacks the advantages possessed by the reader of a book or the viewer of a videotape. That is, the audience member can neither reread a selection—using punctuation as a clue to meaning—nor rewind the tape to discover what was missed. If the listener misses your point, he or she has missed it completely. Thus, you must do what you can to guide your listeners through a presentation by providing clear transitions.

Transitions link the various elements of the outline, showing why and how each element relates to the other elements. Transitions help the audience understand the logical relationships among the main points and their subpoints, and they explain how the introduction, body, and conclusion fit together. In short, transitions serve as "signposts" that help listeners understand where you are going, where you are, and where you have been.

The speaker might, for example, forecast the purpose and structure of the message toward the end of the introduction ("Today, I will talk about five behaviors that characterize effective leaders. They are . . ."). As the speech proceeds, the speaker might use internal previews and summaries to review a main point and anticipate the next one ("Having described why leaders need to challenge the process, let's turn now to the need to inspire a shared vision"). The conclusion of the speech might include a final summary ("I've talked today about five behaviors that characterize effective leaders. Effective leaders . . ."). Transitions need not be elaborate, although they should be frequent and well spaced throughout the message. The transition from one point to the next should be smooth and obvious. When listeners find it difficult to follow your organizational structure, they rapidly lose interest and will neither remember nor accept the thesis of your message.

STRATEGIC SKILLS

Examples of Effective Language

State the relationship of a whole to its parts: "The executive committee is one of many. Committees are created to deal with specific problems in our organization."

Provide a definition: "The executive committee is a group of people responsible for maintaining up-to-date guidelines for the disposal of hazardous waste."

Use synonyms (words with approximately the same meaning) or antonyms (words with opposite meanings): "The word *executive* can mean *director* or *manager*. *Executive* does not mean *staff person*."

Use figures of speech:

Analogy: "Executives have much of the same power that generals of armies have."

Simile: "The CEO is *like* a general."

Metaphor: "The CEO *is* a general."

Make comparisons: "Household managers and CEOs share the need for similar communication and management skills; each needs to have both internal and external communication networks; each has to develop a wide variety of skills for motivation, conflict resolution, and participation in interpersonal, group, and organizational communication. The to-do lists of neither are ever completed."

Show contrasts: "Although executives can fire employees, unlike generals, they can't court-martial employees."

Give a brief history: "The growth of guilds in the Middle Ages, the emergence of a capitalistic system, the development of bureaucracies, and the expansion of national and transnational corporations have been instrumental in the development of the person called the *executive* in business organizations in the United States."

Provide an operational definition: "Executives often use *rifling* (reduction in force) as a method of reducing a work force. The executive might ask for a list of all people who are two years from retirement; he or she would then offer them an incentive to leave early; or the executive would dismiss all employees who had worked less than one year."

COMMUNICATION COMPETENCE: PRESENTING THE MESSAGE

Having generated a message and put it into a standard presentation format, a presenter is now in a position to think about effective methods for delivering the message to listeners. This stage of the presentation relates to the third component of strategic communication, communication competence. The speaker must be able to identify and employ a delivery that is both effective and appropriate for the message, audience, and occasion.

Support for a balanced emphasis on content and delivery is provided in the research literature on nonverbal communication. Judee Burgoon, David Buller, and Gill Woodall summarize approximately one hundred studies on channel reliance—which channels or codes most influence listeners as they assign meaning to communication events.[8] They conclude that adults place greater reliance on nonverbal cues (which include issues of delivery) than on verbal cues (issues of content) in determining meaning. They also conclude that 60 to 65 percent of the meaning in a communication exchange is conveyed nonverbally.

This general pattern, the authors suggest, has several qualifiers: (1) young children place greater reliance on verbal cues (the words) than adults do; (2) reliance on nonverbal cues is greatest when there is a conflict between the verbal and nonverbal channels; (3) "verbal content is more important for factual, cognitive, abstract, and persuasive interpretations, while nonverbal context is more important for judging emotional and attitudinal expressions, relational communication, and

8. J. Burgoon, D. Buller, and W. G. Woodall, *Nonverbal Communication: The Unspoken Dialogue* (New York: Harper & Row, 1989), pp. 154–161.

impression formation"; and (4) there are individual differences in channel dependence (some people rely on nonverbal channels, some typically rely on verbal content, and others adapt their channel choice to the situation).[9]

Types of Delivery

Given these findings on channel reliance, a presenter must carefully consider the choices available for the presentation of a message. She or he must choose an appropriate method of delivery early on. To do this, he or she must decide if the presentation will be developed on the spot (impromptu), given from brief notes (extemporaneous), written out and read (manuscript), or memorized word for word and recited (memorized).

Impromptu **Impromptu speaking** is best avoided when possible. If the presenter knows or anticipates being called on to make some remarks, the message should be prepared in advance. This preparation will increase the likelihood that the message is not weak in terms of organization, forms of support, quality of word choice, or effectiveness of delivery. Nevertheless, there will be times when the presenter is given little, if any, chance to prepare. For example, the presenter may be told to make a brief presentation to a committee at work, asked to say a few words on a topic about which she or he is knowledgeable, or asked on the spot to answer a question or describe a policy or procedure. (We discuss techniques for successfully handling impromptu presentations in Chapter 15.)

Extemporaneous **Extemporaneous speaking** encourages thorough preparation and adaptability to the particulars of the situation. The presenter starts with a full-sentence outline and then reduces it to a speaker's outline for rehearsal and actual presentation. Rehearsal helps the presenter to use a style similar to normal conversation. However, because she or he is working from ideas and key words rather than from complete sentences, the message is never delivered exactly the same way twice. The wording of the ideas remains flexible to let the presenter better adapt the message to the audience. With extemporaneous speaking, segments of the message can be expanded or reduced, depending on audience response.

Manuscript When the situation requires precise wording (e.g., a technical or research report where exact wording is crucial) or exact timing (e.g., a television presentation of exactly nine minutes), the appropriate mode of presentation may be **manuscript speaking.** In this mode, the speaker prepares an organized and easily readable manuscript that has an oral, conversational style. Starting with a full-sentence outline, the speaker writes out the whole message. To ensure that the final product is conversational, the speech is rehearsed orally (perhaps with a tape recorder) before it is written on paper. Once the message has been developed into its final form, the manuscript is prepared for reading (e.g., triple-spaced and marked for special emphases) and the speaker rehearses until she or he feels very comfortable with the delivery. In some situations, speakers will read their prepared speech from a teleprompter, which is a screen on which the speech is projected and scrolled as the speech is delivered. Teleprompters enable a speaker to avoid having to look down at the written speech. A successful speech delivery

9. Ibid., p. 158.

looks and sounds as if the speech were being given extemporaneously—that is, the delivery is conversational and unforced and includes eye contact with audience members.

Memorized Except for a lack of something to place on the lectern, podium, or teleprompter, **memorized speaking** is really no different from manuscript speaking. Thus, approaches to preparation and use overlap for these two modes of delivery.

The memorized speech is frequently used in situations in which reading a manuscript appears inappropriate. (In Chapter 15, for example, we describe forms of ceremonial speaking where a memorized speech is the appropriate choice.) In creating such a presentation, the speaker's goal is to make the speech sound as if it were being delivered extemporaneously.

Memorized presentations lack the security of a manuscript to which the speaker can refer, so the speaker anticipates and rehearses for the possibility of a memory block. If a block occurs, the speaker focuses on key words until he or she is able to click back into the memorized phrases of the presentation.

Characteristics of Effective Delivery

Regardless of the delivery method you choose, its function remains the same—to aid listeners in understanding, accepting, and retaining what you have said. Although there are multiple ways to achieve **effective delivery,** they all involve the application of four general criteria.[10]

Effective Delivery Is Intelligible Before audience members will accept a message, they must hear it. Thus, you have to practice speaking with adequate volume and appropriate rate. When you are using a microphone, this means keeping the proper distance away from it. With a standard podium mike, this is about six inches or a little closer. If you get too close to the mike, however, some sounds (e.g., the letter *P*) become overemphasized and create an annoying sound for audiences.

In addition to volume and rate, intelligibility also requires that you pay attention to articulation and pronunciation. Not only will mispronunciation inhibit clarity; it will also lead listeners to make negative judgments about your credibility. Thus, whenever you have the slightest doubt about proper pronunciation, it is worth the effort to consult a dictionary. Tape-recording a rehearsal version of the presentation or having a friend listen and comment is useful for evaluating how understandable your message is.

Effective Delivery Is Conversational In ordinary conversation participants use a great deal of variation in the pitch and volume of their voices. They also indicate their involvement in and commitment to the dialogue via body orientation and eye contact, and they reinforce the points they make with gestures and physical movement.

In short, variations in voice and physical action are used naturally and unconsciously to focus attention on and reinforce the content of a conversation. These variations provide an excellent model for a public presentation. The presenter

10. R. P. Hart, G. W. Friedrich, and B. Brummett, *Public Communication,* 2d ed. (New York: Harper & Row, 1983), pp. 183-185.

STRATEGIC SKILLS

What to Avoid in Public Speaking

Fillers: Habitually saying "uh" or "you know." Record your practice sessions on audio- or videotape, and consciously try to avoid these habits.

Nervous habits: Smoothing your hair, rubbing your ear nervously, rocking backward and forward, crossing your ankles, holding your arms behind your back, sticking your hands in your pockets (while rattling change). Videotape yourself, or give your speech in front of people who will honestly critique your behavior.

Lectern wars: Locking your hands on the podium, leaning on the lectern, looking at the lectern. Most professionals use a lectern because of the bank of microphones or cameras. If the acoustics will allow it or if a lapel microphone is available, don't hide behind a lectern.

Abuse of objects: Clicking a pen, using a pencil as a baton, hitting the lectern or overhead with a ring or fingers nervously. Except for audiovisuals and the one or two note cards on which you have a speaker's outline, do not hold anything while you are presenting.

Invisible syndrome: Speakers who behave dramatically differently before or after they have spoken lose credibility. You are "on stage" from the moment that any member of the audience sees you, and you do not "exit" until you leave the presentation site. Do not talk nervously about whether you will succeed or fail before you begin; don't laugh and "backslap" with friends just before your speech; don't give huge sighs of relief and discuss mistakes that you made during your delivery. Such behavior damages your credibility.

Inappropriate appearance: Your clothing, hair, odor, jewelry, shoes, style, neatness, degree of formality, and cosmetics are just some of the things that people consider as they evaluate you before, during, and after your presentation. Know the appropriate style of dress for the speech, yourself, the occasion, the audience, and the setting.

should attempt to talk with, rather than at, a group of listeners. Good delivery can be characterized as a conversation with an audience.

Effective Delivery Is Direct Good delivery signals to listeners that the speaker truly cares about communicating with them. In our culture, respect for and interest in an audience are communicated primarily with eye contact. Sustaining appropriate eye contact with listeners also helps the presenter discover how the message is being received.

Achieving these goals requires eye contact with all segments of the audience. A practical strategy for achieving this is to start the presentation by locating a small number of listeners in different parts of the room who are responding positively with smiles and head nods. Establishing eye contact with these people can help a speaker to gain confidence during the first moments of a speech. As the presentation proceeds, the speaker can then widen eye contact to include the total audience by moving her or his gaze randomly and smoothly, rather than systematically, throughout the room and looking directly into the eyes of individual listeners.

Effective Delivery Is Unobtrusive Good delivery focuses attention on the speaker's message, not on the speaker. The three principles we have just discussed—being intelligible, conversational, and direct—promote this goal. You can also try to eliminate distracting mannerisms such as playing with note cards, rocking back and forth while standing in one place, locking both hands on the lectern or in your pants pockets, or using pauses excessively (such as repeating "uh" or "you know").

You may not even be aware of your tendencies to exhibit these or similar mannerisms. One way to recognize them is to videotape yourself or to watch others.

Simply identifying distracting behaviors is often the greatest part of eliminating them. You can also engage in *negative practice*—consciously overemphasize the distracting mannerism while rehearsing the delivery of your presentation. This exercise allows you to become hyperaware of the behavior while you are speaking, thus making it easier to eliminate it from your presentation.

Other Considerations

In addition to the four general principles of effective delivery, there are several additional considerations worthy of comment.

TECHNOLOGY TOOLS

Computer-Mediated Presentations

Thanks to the Internet, you can see, hear, talk to, present in front of, and work with people in different locations around the world, without the expense of travel. One of the most compelling features of the Internet may well be the ability to communicate inexpensively in real time, via desktop computers.

Computer-mediated conferencing and presenting can take many forms, such as videoconferencing, audioconferencing, multimedia conferencing, screen sharing, and, to a lesser extent, what is referred to in Web parlance as *chat*. These types of systems can be relatively inexpensive to implement and are available on most computer platforms. This kind of conferencing can be done one-to-one, one-to-many (called multicast), and many-to-many (called multipoint).

Videoconferencing

Let's say you want to bring a geographically dispersed group of people together for a presentation followed by a brainstorming session. Conferencing programs, such as the popular CuseeMe (http://www.cuseeme.com/), allow work groups to use the Internet to see one another's faces in small windows on the computer screen and to hear their voices through computer speakers. You can use both video and audio simultaneously, use the audio alone, or use the screen-sharing capability without either audio or video.

Telephone Conferencing

The Internet can also be used to make telephone calls around the world for only the cost of a local connection. Audio conferencing allows you to communicate verbally, rather than typing messages via e-mail. It works by digitizing your voice, then sending the digital data to its final destination via the Internet. While the audio quality may leave something to be desired, you will save money on long-distance phone bills.

Speak Freely for Windows (http://fourmilab.ch/netfone/windows/speak_freely.html) offers audioconferencing as well as voice mail. If you have a MacIntosh, you can try DigiPhone (http://www.digiphone.co.uk/).

Other Forms of Conferencing

Conferencing without audio or video can be accomplished on the Web with various document management, multimedia conferencing, or screen-sharing packages. For example, Microsoft Internet Explorer (version 4.0 and higher) has a built-in conferencing program, called NetMeeting (http://www.microsoft.com/windows/netmeeting/).

Document conferencing software allows people in remote locations to work together on projects via the Web, without the need for high-bandwidth connections. Some programs allow participants of a presentation to make basic annotations to documents or proposals; others let participants jointly use a word processor or spreadsheet. Software programs for multimedia conferencing and screen sharing on the Internet provide basic tools for connecting work groups and in-depth collaboration tools that enable users to control and synchronize applications and presentation of text, graphics, images, sound, and video. Additionally, whiteboard applications feature real-time sketching, viewing, and annotation of documents.

Source: Article courtesy of Learn the Net (www.learnthenet.com).

Appearance As you recall from Chapters 7 and 8, first impressions of another person are to a large degree the result of physical appearance cues. In a presentation, this means that audiences use natural elements—such as the speaker's height, weight, and body shape—and planned cues—such as clothing, accessories, or cosmetics—as bases for making judgments about the speaker's credibility that affect the development of their subsequent impressions.

You are wise to analyze your appearance in terms of how you will be viewed by a particular audience. Ask yourself how the audience may react to your dress, accessories, neatness, or degree of formality in your clothing choice. What are audience members likely to conclude on the basis of this assessment? What judgments are they likely to form about you? An awareness of such issues increases your sensitivity to audience perceptions. Many speakers, for example, choose to dress slightly more formally when speaking than they normally do. This can boost your confidence and can also suggest to the audience that you care about the speech and the speaking situation.

Your appearance and delivery, however, must be comfortable for you. Efforts to completely change your natural style of speaking, dress, appearance, or even gesturing are likely to result in audience perceptions of incongruity and inconsistency. Although you can improve your style, an all-out attempt to "be someone else" during a presentation will likely decrease your rapport with the audience.

Use of Visual Aids Visual aids should be prepared early enough to allow you to practice with them until you can use them quickly and smoothly. Important points to remember during both practice and the actual presentation include the following.

1. *Visual aids must be easily seen by every member of the audience.* In many rooms, a projection screen may need to be set up, or a large, blank, light wall can be used. In addition, there are often hooks and clips at the front of the room where visual aids can be hung. When this is not the case, it is usually possible to place them on an easel. Wherever they are placed, the goal is to locate them high enough so that every member of the audience can see them quickly and easily. This situation requires both thinking about placement and rehearsing the actual placement of the visual aids ahead of time.
2. *Talk to the audience rather than to the visual aid.* Listeners want your attention, and you have to be able to see their reactions to your message. Neither is possible if you are talking to the visual aid. Thus, help listeners to understand your visual by telling them what you want them to see, hear, and understand. At the same time, maintain eye contact with them to determine whether this understanding is taking place.
3. *Display the visual aid only when it is being used.* Visual aids are intended to enhance understanding, not compete for the audience's attention. Keep aids from being seen until you are ready to use them, and remove them when you have finished with them. For this reason, avoid passing visual aids (such as handouts) through the audience while you are speaking. There is no surer way to lose the attention of portions of your audience!

Timing Your Presentation In many situations, particularly when there exists a program with multiple speakers, you may be asked to keep your remarks limited to a set time. Good speakers utilize several techniques to ensure they finish on time:

1. *Use a clock or watch.* Ideally, you will be able to see a wall clock in the back of the room. If you have a lectern, you can set a small clock on it (or set your wristwatch there) where it is easily visible. Avoid looking down at your wrist or showing obvious concern about time. As you begin to speak, take note not of the current time but of where the minute hand should be when you are to stop. If you are nervous, jot down the number where you can see it.
2. *Have a collaborator in the audience.* A well-placed collaborator in the audience can be very useful. A collaborator can tell you if your voice is projecting sufficiently to fill the room, for example, or can jumpstart a question-and-answer session with a prepared question. In situations where time is of the essence, the collaborator should have signs indicating "5 minutes left" and "1 minute left" to cue you when to wrap up.
3. *Practice your presentation aloud.* Rehearsal is essential to most successful presentations. Rehearsal strategies are discussed later in the chapter. Just remember that a speech—that is, a presentation that is not to be interrupted by questions—is likely to be a bit longer when it is delivered before an audience than when you practice it alone.

FIELDING AUDIENCE QUESTIONS

In most situations, questions are postponed until the end of the presentation. This doesn't have to be the case, however, and you should decide in advance whether questions will be handled during or after the speech. In either case, a small number of guidelines can contribute to a smooth and effective questioning period.

Anticipate Likely Questions As you think about your topic and audience, anticipate potential questions. Are there points that may be confusing? Are there points that may produce disagreement? Just as students must anticipate and prepare for teachers' questions at examination time, speakers can and should prepare responses to the questions they anticipate receiving from the audience.

Repeat Questions from the Audience In some situations—for example, with a large theater-seated group in which members don't have access to a microphone—audience members are unable to hear the questions asked by other members. In these cases, repeating questions from the audience helps everyone hear the questions. Repetition also allows you to buy time when hit with a surprise question for which there is no ready answer or to clarify confusing or unclear questions.

Use Answers to Reinforce the Goal of the Presentation Do not let questioners pull you away from the thesis of your message. Instead, use questions as an opportunity to frame responses that contribute to your goal. When questioners persist in asking irrelevant questions, say that you will talk with them individually after the meeting or will send them some additional information.

Treat All Questions with Respect Some questions—those that are difficult, rude, or hopelessly naïve—are a challenge to answer gracefully. Many speakers dread the possibility of a hostile question or critical remark during the question-and-answer session. This doesn't have to be the case. For example, a simple, yet effective,

ETHICAL ISSUES

Audience Challenge

Jim Cordoni has just finished his presentation. A member of the audience who has developed a reputation among his peers for such behavior belittles Jim's conclusions in a combative manner and, in doing so, misrepresents the data on which Jim has based his conclusions. Jim is tempted to make this person look foolish for asking the question. He even suspects the audience would approve. Should he do so? Why or why not?

method for coping with critical comments without getting into arguments or being locked into a defensive position is to compliment the questioner on her or his insight and respond to any points of truth or areas of agreement that you can find.[11] Difficult questions requiring complex answers—particularly if you are running long and are near the end of your presentation—may best be left for discussion with the audience member afterward. Lastly, no matter what the question, never try to be humorous at the expense of the questioner.

Give the Questioner a Genuine Compliment Say something positive about the ideas being expressed. People who attack speakers in an aggressive, critical way are frequently insecure and looking for recognition. They want to feel important, and they may be jealous of your central position in the situation. If somebody asks an intimidating, hostile question, you can simply say, "That's a very important question. Thank you for asking it." If you say this with sincerity, you can avoid an awkward debate that will make everyone tense. Complimenting people who ask questions encourages others in the audience to do the same because it creates a safe environment for them to share their ideas.

Finding a Point of Agreement or Truth Although looking for a point of agreement or truth may contradict your natural desire to argue and defend yourself, it is very effective to be flexible and open-minded. By doing so, you can better understand the issue and increase your credibility with the audience. Consider the following example:

AUDIENCE MEMBER: Your ideas about this new business proposal sound far-fetched to me. I think that we need to solidify our regional market before we try to expand abroad.

SPEAKER: You have a good point—our regional sales have traditionally been the backbone of this company. But we need to expand so that we can avoid slumps if the regional economy takes a downturn.

When you do not have an answer, punt.

Occasionally, you will receive a question for which you have no ready answer. When you are not able to answer, choose an alternative approach to the question so you don't lose control of the questioning period. There are several ways to do this:

11. Based on D. Burns, *The Feeling Good Handbook* (New York: William Morrow, 1989), pp. 311-312.

Rephrase the question into one that you can answer—for example, by narrowing it to an area of your expertise or relating it to the main idea of the presentation.

Redirect the question by saying, "That's a good point. What do *you* think we should do?" or "We just happen to have an expert on that topic in our audience. Dr. Stone, what do you think we should do?"

Acknowledge that you do not have an answer at this time and promise to get back to the questioner at a later date. Whatever the choice, implement it smoothly and confidently, just as you delivered the main body of your presentation.

Developing a Strategy for Rehearsal

You can make your presentation effective with self-analysis and rehearsal. Every speaker finds her or his own method of practicing. Some take advantage of the privacy of their bathroom, with its mirrors and great acoustics. Some record their practices on video- or audiotape. A few inflict their rehearsals on friends and family. Find what fits your needs, but you should practice. You need to time your speech, get used to the material, become accustomed to your audiovisual aids, and make the message your own so that your presentation sounds like you and is consistent with your personality.

Whatever your practice strategy, consider methods of collecting relevant data that provide answers to questions such as the following:

- Are the general purpose (inform, persuade, motivate, or celebrate) and specific purpose both clear to and relevant for your audience?
- Have you selected the three to five main points that will best lead your audience to understand and accept your specific purpose?
- Have you included a variety of supporting materials (explanations, examples, statistics, testimony, visual aids) that your audience will understand and find compelling?
- Does the introduction to your speech provide appropriate orientation, motivation, and rapport?
- Is the organizational structure of the body of your speech easy for your audience to follow? Have you used transitions well?
- Does your choice of language aid (rather than distract from) the accomplishment of your purpose?
- Does your conclusion provide a sense of completeness and closure?
- Is your choice of delivery mode (impromptu, extemporaneous, manuscript, or memorized) the best choice?
- Is the delivery of your speech intelligible, conversational, direct, and unobtrusive?

STRATEGIC SCENARIO WRAP-UP

At the beginning of this chapter we met Sangeeta Roy, a college student working as an intern for a graphic design studio. She has been asked to research the pluses and minuses of replacing the firm's phone system with VoIP telphony units. In two weeks she will make a presentation to the head of the firm, Melinda Arroyave, and her administrative committee on what she has discovered. What have you learned in this chapter that might help her prepare for this task?

- Do you have any advice for Sangeeta in terms of anxiety management?
- What should be the general purpose of her presentation? To inform? To persuade? To motivate? To celebrate? Some combination of these four?
- What advice do you have for Sangeeta in terms of audience analysis?
- How might Sangeeta best go about generating and selecting main ideas for her presentation?
- As Sangeeta thinks about ways of supporting her main ideas, what should be her concerns as she considers her alternatives?
- What should Sangeeta consider as she thinks about ways of introducing her presentation? What about the conclusion? Will there be any special requirements with regard to transitions?
- What mode of delivery should Sangeeta use? Will any of the characteristics of effective delivery be especially crucial?
- Do you have any additional advice for Sangeeta?

SUMMARY

- Presentations are vital to successful communication in business. If they are not assigned or determined by the context, their topic and purpose can be generated through brainstorming, mapping, or library research.
- Presentations can be less successful if the presenter is nervous about speaking in public.
- This apprehension can be caused by lack of skills, conditioned anxiety, and/or negative cognitive appraisal.
- Anxiety can be managed if the speaker practices public speaking, uses relaxation and deep-breathing techniques, and employs cognitive restructuring of irrational, negative self-statements.
- The topic and specific purpose correspond to the communication goals for the presentation.
- After these goals are set, a thorough audience analysis, which covers several categories, can provide the presenter with situational knowledge and insight into how to target the message to best achieve her or his goals.
- For the body of the presentation, main ideas can be identified by the topical system, which includes sixteen themes common to most subjects.
- The speaker should generally limit the presentation to three, four, or five of the themes that best suit the audience and the occasion.
- These main ideas can then be researched through a variety of resources, including informational interviews, reference books, databases, and queries to a reference librarian.
- Supporting materials can be drawn from research on the topic and can include explanations, examples, statistics, testimony, and visual aids.
- The purpose of supporting materials is to make the presentation varied and exciting for the audience and to increase the speaker's credibility.
- The introduction and the conclusion are prepared after the bulk of the presentation is complete.
- The introduction serves to orient, motivate, and build rapport between the audience and the speaker.
- The conclusion provides a summary and a sense of the significance of the presentation so that listeners will leave with a clear understanding and recollection of the main ideas discussed.
- An outline is the standard format for organizing the three parts (introduction, body, and conclusion) of a presentation.
- A full-sentence outline, topic outline, and speaker's outline serve different purposes but follow the same basic principles.
- These principles include using a correct numbering system for outline entries, choosing headings of equal importance, maintaining consistency in the form of outline entries, striving for balance in entries so that every heading has at least two subheadings, and appropriately supporting main points with subpoints.
- When it comes to delivering the presentation, the speaker can choose from several delivery styles—impromptu, extemporaneous, manuscript, and memorized—depending on the circumstances.
- The choice of a delivery style should be considered early in the process of preparing the presentation as each makes different demands on the

speaker's level of preparation, skill, and choice of material.

- Effective delivery focuses attention on the speaker's message rather than on the speaker and should be comfortable and natural rather than formal or forced.

KEY TERMS

Communication apprehension: the fear of speaking in public; also termed *reticence, shyness,* and *unwillingness to communicate*

Good speech topics: topics the speaker is knowledgeable about and/or interested in, are relevant for the audience, and meet the requirements of the assignment or situation

General purpose: the basic goal of a presentation, that is, to inform, to persuade, to motivate, or to celebrate

Informative presentations: presentations that provide ideas, alternatives, data, or even opinions and that provide credible, reliable information to back up major points

Persuasive presentations: presentations that change or reaffirm existing attitudes about important topics, strive to gain audience commitment, and motivate action

Motivational presentations: presentations that employ persuasion but rely extensively on stimulating the emotions and feelings of listeners as a method of inducing action

Ceremonial presentations: presentations that share many of the elements found in informative, persuasive, and motivational presentations; include introduction, acceptance, tribute, goodwill, inspiration, and celebration presentations

Specific purpose: purpose derived from the general purpose, identifying what the presenter wants the audience to think, believe, feel, or do as a result of listening to the presentation

Thesis statement: a single declarative sentence that summarizes the main ideas to be presented to the audience

Audience analysis: gathering information about an audience (i.e., audience type, audience characteristics, and environmental characteristics) so that the speaker can adapt the speech to the situation at hand

Topical system: method that uses a small set of headings or topics to identify standard ways of thinking and talking about any subject

Bibliography: a detailed list of all the books, articles, interviews, and abstracts you have reviewed in the course of your research

Supporting materials: explanations, examples, statistics, testimony, and visual aids used to give credibility to your main ideas and to make the message more informative, interesting, relevant, clear, and acceptable

Explanation: the act or process of making a subject plain or comprehensible

Examples: illustrations that connect the main ideas of a presentation with a real or an ideal state envisioned by the speaker

Statistics: descriptions of the result of collecting, organizing, and interpreting numerical data

Testimony: a statement by a credible person (source) that lends weight and authority to the speaker's presentation

Introduction: the beginning of a speech, which informs the listener about the topic of the speech (orientation), the reason for attending to the speech (motivation), and the credibility of the source delivering the message (rapport)

Conclusion: the ending of a speech, which provides a sense of completeness and closure

Outline: a visual, schematic summary of the message that shows the order of ideas and the general relationships among them

Complete-sentence outline: an outline that lists each head and subhead in complete-sentence form

Topic outline: an outline that reduces the sentences of a speech to brief phrases or single words

Speaker's outline: an outline that includes only key words and important quotations or statistics written on index cards

Point: the major ideas that a speaker wishes the audience to understand and accept

Subpoint: forms of support for the main ideas

Transitions: "signposts" that link the various elements of the outline, showing why and how each element relates to the other elements

Impromptu speaking: situation in which a presentation is developed and prepared "on the spot," with little or no time for preparation

Extemporaneous speaking: given from brief notes, this type of situation encourages thorough preparation and adaptability to the particulars of the situation at hand

Manuscript speaking: situation in which a speech is written out and read verbatim; used when a situation requires precise wording or exact timing

Memorized speaking: situation in which a speech is memorized word for word and then recited

Effective delivery: delivery that is intelligible, conversational, direct, and unobtrusive

DISCUSSION

1. What are some of the benefits of presentations in business and professional settings? What are some of the challenges to a successful presentation?
2. Describe the three techniques for managing communication apprehension discussed in the chapter. Why should all three be used to obtain the best results in decreasing anxiety? How have you handled your own anxiety in past speaking situations?
3. Discuss the methods for generating a topic covered in the chapter. Which have you used, and how effective were they?
4. What are the four general purposes for presentations? How does the speaker narrow the general purpose to a specific purpose and thesis statement?
5. Why is audience analysis important? How can it help the speaker in a business presentation? What are its limitations?
6. How can the topical system help a speaker to generate main ideas? According to this system, what are some of the themes common to all topics?
7. Describe the types of supporting materials that can be used during a presentation. What is their function? Give an example of when each would be appropriate.
8. What are the functions of an introduction? Of a conclusion? What are some techniques for accomplishing these functions?
9. What are the four types of delivery? When should each be used?
10. What role does delivery play in the overall success of a presentation?

ACTIVITIES

1. In business settings, the general purpose of a presentation does not usually represent a single goal. Think of situations in which you may have wanted to combine several goals in one presentation. What are some of the possibilities you worked out? Discuss your ideas with other class members and compare results.
2. How would you narrow and research the following topics: employment trends for college graduates, advertising budgets at major corporations, the "glass ceiling" and promotions for women and members of minority groups, and communication networks in multinational companies?
3. Describe the demographic characteristics that can be considered in an audience analysis. What adaptations can be made for the following audiences: college graduates versus high school graduates, senior citizens versus young adults, clerical workers versus manufacturing workers, and employees at a for-profit corporation versus volunteers at a nonprofit organization?
4. Make a list of visual aids that can enhance your presentation of the topics in question 2. Explain how each may be created and used.
5. Unscramble the following outline of a presentation describing a job description. Put the entries into standard outline form using the principles of outlining discussed in the chapter. Hint: the outline contains two main points.

   Benefits
   Analyze reports
   Collect completed reports
   Mid-range salary
   Health insurance
   Bonus possible
   One report from marketing
   Responsibilities
   Three weeks' vacation
   Group plan
   Summarize data
   File reports
   Prepare forecast
   One report from production
   Yearly raise
   Use file cabinets in main office
   Monthly premium
   Files should be alphabetized
6. Keep a CR log for your next in-class presentation. What were your most common negative self-statements? How did you respond to them?

CHAPTER

14 Informative Presentations

After working through this chapter, you will be able to:

1. Describe the importance and difficulty of making informative presentations in today's business world
2. Identify informative presentations in terms of function, type, and format
3. Utilize four basic principles for the successful creation and presentation of an informative message
4. Make technology-assisted presentations utilizing video, television, and multimedia components

STRATEGIC SCENARIO

Ching-Wen Lu is taking a course this semester on instructional technology. For her term project she is conducting survey research on the uses of instructional technology at her university. She intends to find out who is currently using technology (such as overheads, PowerPoint, videos, and LCD projectors) and who is not. And she is interested in discovering why this is the case. During the last week of the semester, students present the results of their term project to other members of the class.

In this chapter you will learn about the skills that Ching-Wen can use to make a successful presentation to her class. At the end of the chapter, we will return to this scenario and solicit your advice.

OVERVIEW

In the last chapter, our focus was on the key elements involved in developing effective presentations. In it we explored such components as (1) identifying the main points to be shared with an audience and researching them; (2) developing supporting materials to make those main points believable and credible; (3) organizing and outlining the total message, including introduction, body, transitions, and conclusion; and (4) selecting an appropriate type of delivery and developing a strategy for rehearsal that will make the delivery of the presentation both comfortable and effective. In this and the next chapter, we build on this analysis and elaborate it in terms of the two basic kinds of presentations: informative and persuasive.

Every time you give a presentation in a business or a professional context, you have a general purpose and a specific purpose. Whereas specific purposes vary widely, general purposes can usually be classified as either informative or persuasive. The dominant purpose of informative presentations is to share adequate, accurate information with an audience in ways that are interesting and understandable. The dominant purpose of persuasive presentations is to convince an audience to believe an idea or perform a task. In this chapter, we discuss the importance of the former presentations, along with guidelines and resources for you as a speaker. The next chapter takes up the latter presentations.

THE RANGE OF INFORMATIVE PRESENTATIONS

Organizational life is filled with informative presentations, and the range of possible uses for **informative presentations** in a corporate office is a wide one. Just consider the following situations:

Reviewing quarterly sales figures
Introducing a new policy for recruiting personnel
Explaining market research findings on the feasibility of introducing a new product line
Briefing executives on departmental performance goals
Training people to use new computer software
Reviewing a feasibility study for the purchase of new equipment
Demonstrating new machinery or equipment

What do all of these presentations have in common? They are informative! Their purpose is to tell listeners something they do not already know or to supplement or reinforce their existing knowledge.

That informative presentations are a regular part of organizational life in business and the professions alone justifies their study and importance. Nevertheless, there are many additional reasons that exhibiting skill in informative speaking is critical to your professional success.

ACCUMULATION OF INFORMATION

In today's modern organizations, more information and more sources of information are available than at any previous time. People have access to more information than they can possibly digest. There is no indication that this trend will do anything but continue to accelerate.

According to the *World List of Scientific Journals*, 59,961 journals are published throughout the world (in sixty-five languages), in which about 1 million articles

ETHICAL ISSUES

All Sides of the Issue

In deciding how much information to present, do you have an ethical responsibility to present all sides of an issue? For example, does a district attorney have a responsibility to tell a grand jury about all known facts of a case? Should a sales representative for a drug manufacturer tell doctors about the side effects of a drug? Should an army recruiter tell potential recruits about both the advantages and disadvantages of military life? What criteria did you use to arrive at answers to these questions?

appear yearly; in addition, some 300,000 scientific monographs are published each year, along with 15,000 conference proceedings. According to Louis Martin, associate editor of the Association of Research Libraries, "If an average reader tried to catch up with one year's output of learned publications in the sciences, it would take about 50 years of reading at 24 hours a day for seven days a week."[1]

People receive information through newspapers, televisions, radios, telephones, computer retrieval sources, satellite transmission sources, interactive video terminals, e-mail, and fax machines. Some of these now-common methods by which we send and receive information did not even exist twenty years ago.

These immense changes and developments all lead to the conclusion that the presentation of information is both important and challenging for people in modern organizations. To meet this challenge, a speaker must be knowledgeable about what informative presentations are and how best to give them.

FUNCTIONS OF INFORMATIVE PRESENTATIONS

The presentation's **function** is the answer to the question "What does this presentation do?" The function of a successful informative presentation is sharing information, shaping perceptions, and setting agendas.

Sharing Information and Ideas

One of the goals of many informative presentations is to share information and ideas. Speakers throughout organizations are called on to share with groups of coworkers ideas about new methods, new directions, and proposed changes. Other presentations share the latest information on status quo affairs within the organization, such as sales figures, employee absenteeism, results from market research studies, and budgeting procedures.

Shaping Perceptions

Most people who listen to informative presentations are not simply taking in what the speaker says at face value. As the speaker talks, they constantly react to the

1. J. Fiala, "Citation Analysis Controls the Information Flood," *Thermochimica Acta* 110 (1987), 11.

PRACTICING BUSINESS COMMUNICATION

Best Western International, Inc.

Best Western's Gold Crown logo is a familiar symbol along America's highways—a place for vacation lodging, meetings, and stopovers during long trips. What's surprising is that, unlike other franchises and corporate hoteliers, each of the more than five thousand Best Western hotels (that's more than 300,000 hotel rooms!) is independently owned and operated. That lends a unique feel to the company's culture—the feel of an extended family in which each member has an equal and experienced voice.

AN INFORMED CULTURE

Older family "members," as hotel owners are called, have a deep personal investment in Best Western. Many remember the company's earliest meetings and have built the traditions that form Best Western's organizational culture today. In preparation for its half-century celebration in 1996, members located and collected Best Western memorabilia such as old travel guides, correspondence, and postcards for display.

The fiftieth anniversary also marked a passing of generations and a continuing change in Best Western's corporate culture. The traditions established by the founding members are evolving as a younger generation of hoteliers replaces older members. While these new members include second- and third-generation Best Western families, more and more members are new to the organization. They see Best Western as an excellent marketing consortium that fits the needs of their hotels.

Perhaps the most visible symbol of the changes within Best Western was the introduction of its new corporate brand identity and logo in 1994. The new look, the result of more than two years of research and design, updated the familiar Best Western Gold Crown, which had seen only cosmetic changes since it was introduced in the 1960s. A previous attempt to update the logo in 1980 was rejected by the members.

In the fall of 1993, a new logo featuring a stylized crown denoting a more upscale image was approved by a two-thirds majority of the Best Western membership. Some fundamental shifts clearly were occurring within Best Western's corporate culture.

INFORMATIVE PRESENTATIONS

While membership and marketing changes are important, one foundation of Best Western's corporate culture—its democratic, nonprofit structure—remains basically unchanged. Monthly directors' meetings, an annual series of seven regional meetings, an annual international convention, and a variety of international meetings and conventions throughout Europe, Africa, South and Central America, Asia, and the Pacific Rim all serve to reinforce this structure.

material in their own minds. What the speaker says may produce questions, new thoughts, alternative ideas, and disagreement, among other responses. When a listener's perception is altered by a presentation, the speaker has been persuasive. Many informative presentations shape listeners' perceptions by narrowing down possibilities or by defining an issue in a particular way, even though standard persuasion techniques are not used.

Setting Agendas

In addition to sharing information and ideas and shaping perceptions, informative presentations often set agendas for the organization or for subdivisions of it. In order to accomplish this, an informative presentation gives listeners the knowledge they need to set priorities, order their goals, and put ideas in context.

At these events, members develop policies and informational programs that apply to all levels of management. Although an official written code of ethics is not in place, the strong sense of equality and interdependence within the organization fosters a clearly understood and upheld standard of values and expectations.

Communication plays a central role in the Best Western organization, a logical result of its corporate culture and service-industry orientation. Staff at the corporate headquarters and international operations center in Phoenix, Arizona, and at a major reservations center in Wichita, Kansas, have access to electronic bulletin boards, staff meetings, memos, and occasional informal meetings with the president and CEO.

Hotel owners get more communication support from Best Western's own tabloid-format newspaper, a twice-weekly fax newsletter, corporate intranet, regular face-to-face meetings with staff, and special publications (manuals and newsletters on specific topics, for example). Sales updates and "news of the day" messages appear when employees log on to their terminals. And an active and effective grapevine also links members, despite the geographic distance between hotels.

Finally, Best Western's education and training department sponsors seminars and classes both to hoteliers and their staff members, and to members of the corporate staff. These events often touch on communication issues.

Communication at Best Western is an interesting and challenging combination of the traditional and the innovative. While seeking to take full advantage of the ever-changing technology of communication, staff members strive to maintain the personal touch and feel of family that is the heart of Best Western. While technology will continue to assist in improving service, the goal of Best Western remains the person-to-person relationship—one person serving another.

QUESTIONS FOR CRITICAL THINKING

1. How does Best Western make independent hotel owners feel like a cohesive group?
2. How has Best Western's corporate culture changed since its founding in 1946?
3. How does Best Western maintain its values without a written code of ethics?
4. Why do you think informative presentations play such a big role at Best Western?
5. How will new communication technology likely change the communication climate of Best Western?

You can visit Best Western International, Inc., on-line at www.bestwestern.com.

ORGANIZING THE PRESENTATION

The pattern by which an informative presentation is organized can help the audience members grasp its content much more readily. The speaker's goal is to choose a method of organization that corresponds to the function of the presentation and the content of the material to be presented.

Informative speeches generally fall into one of three major categories: descriptive presentations, demonstrative presentations, or explanatory presentations. In the next sections, we provide suggestions and examples for preparing each type.

Description

Informative presentations that focus on **description** satisfy the audience members' needs for facts, figures, or other data. They answer "what" questions such as these:

What government regulations currently affect our operations?
What are the demographics of our membership?

What company library resources are checked out most frequently by our employees?
What types of company-sponsored programs do employees want to participate in?

When a speaker has researched the topic and collected the necessary data for the presentation, he or she must choose a pattern of organization that will enhance the audience members' comprehension and retention of the message. Although there are many ways that one might organize descriptive information, two structural patterns that work especially well for such presentations are the topical pattern and the chronological pattern.

Topical Pattern With a **topical pattern,** the main points of the message are organized as parallel elements of the topic itself. Perhaps the most common pattern for organizing presentations, it is useful when describing components of persons, places, things, or processes. Thus, for example, a speaker might use a topical pattern in a presentation on the various departments (such as sales, production, and human resources) that comprise a business organization, on the characteristics of an effective supervisor, or on reasons for giving a charitable contribution to the United Way.

When using a topical pattern, the sequence of topics is quite important. Presentations that begin with the most important topic and end with the least important topic may lose some audience members' interest along the way. On the other hand, a presentation that begins with the least important topic will have an exceedingly slow start and may fail to catch the audience's interest at all. The most successful topical arrangement is to choose the two most important topics and to begin and end with them—doing so creates immediate interest and provides a sense of closure and significance as well. While that is a good arrangement of topics under ideal circumstances, if time is a factor—as when you are the last speaker in a program that is running long—you should consider covering all your important points first to make sure they get covered.

To illustrate the application of the topical pattern to the task of presenting descriptive information, consider the following outline of a presentation responding to the question "What types of company-sponsored programs do our employees want to participate in?"

Thesis: My audience will know the five categories of programs that they want the company to sponsor, as indicated by their response to a survey.

Introduction: Briefly orient the audience by describing the employee survey, motivate their interest by noting that we plan to act on the information gathered, and achieve rapport by telling a story about various difficulties you encountered while conducting the survey.

I. First main point: The survey results showed that many of you would like programs on the history and current status of the organization.
   A. These topics were ranked highest by survey respondents:
      1. Visual aid: Use an overhead to display the survey results (see the Strategic Skills box on page 407).
      2. Your answers have alerted us to the need to keep all lines of communication open.

B. In response, we are planning exhibits, discussion groups, and more coverage of these issues in company publications.
   1. Our goal is to increase your understanding of where the organization has been and where it is going.
   2. We also hope to provide an open environment in which to discuss issues of importance to all of us.

II. Second main point: You also said you wanted programs on educational topics.
   A. One possibility is a symposium featuring the managers of various departments.
      1. Some topics for symposiums might include (a) conducting performance reviews, (b) determining when new employees should be hired, (c) improving quality control.
      2. Symposiums will allow you to compare how routine tasks are accomplished in other departments.
   B. Another suggestion is to have outside experts speak on such topics as health, safety, nutrition, and eldercare.

III. Third main point: Finally, many of you are interested in getting to know our CEO better.
   A. We would like George Smith to give more frequent presentations to the employees, especially in a small-group format.
   B. We are looking into other activities, such as a "Breakfast with the Boss," to promote this interaction.

Conclusion: Briefly summarize survey results and describe the next step in the process of implementing such programs. State the significance of the programs for the company as well as for individual employees.

Chronological Pattern A second organizational pattern that is well suited to providing description is known as a **chronological pattern.** When using this construction, the presenter organizes the main points of the message in a time-related sequence. The sequence could be highly generalized, for example:

Thesis: My audience will understand our company's past, present, and future approaches to conducting appraisal interviews.

I. Describe the organization's past use of management by objectives as an approach to conducting appraisal interviews.
II. Describe the present method of conducting appraisal interviews.
III. Describe the future plans for revising the organization's approach to appraisal interviews.

The sequence may also be highly specific:

I. On December 1, the reports came in.
II. The alterations detailed in the reports were completed and in place by December 4.
III. We sent out the replacement parts on December 5.

The chronological pattern is also useful when analyzing a process step by step. Thus, a presentation on how to use a new fax machine might be organized using a chronological pattern, as the following outline shows:

Thesis: My audience will be able to send a fax using our new fax machine.

I. First, place the papers face down onto the feeder.
II. Second, type in the fax number to which you are sending the material.
III. Third, press "start."
IV. Wait for the message "On Line—Receiving" to be displayed.
V. The pages should begin to move through the feeder.
VI. Check to be sure that all pages were transmitted.
VII. Call the receiver if you have doubts about the transmission.

To illustrate how the chronological pattern may be used for a descriptive informative presentation, consider the following outline of a presentation that compares company sales performance over the last five years.

Thesis: My audience will know the five-year sales trends for our company.

Introduction: Orient the audience by briefly summarizing the time period to be covered in the presentation, and build motivation and rapport by complimenting the audience members on their hard work and demonstrated success.

I. First main point: Five years ago, we held only 13 percent of the market for specialized testing equipment.
  A. Our major market entry was a portable unit to measure air quality.
  B. We sold an average of 23,000 units per year.
II. Second main point: Three years ago, we expanded our product line to include water-testing equipment and a new unit to test auto emissions.
  A. Our market share increased to 18 percent.
  B. We opened a regional office in the Northwest.
III. Third main point: Two years ago, we began to phase out all harmful chemicals used in our equipment and manufacturing processes as well as to search for environmentally safe alternatives.
  A. At the same time, we maintained our strong sales by benefiting from an increased interest in home water-testing.
  B. We sold more than 30,000 home testing units.
IV. Fourth main point: Last year, we had a record $56 million in sales.
  A. Our profit margin increased 8 percent.
  B. We were named one of the top ten small businesses in the region by a major business journal.
  C. We predict even better results for next year based on a new unit to test for chemicals in the groundwater supply that will be purchased by municipalities.

Conclusion: State the significance of the presentation by summarizing that the company has built its success on developing new products to meet emerging needs, and provide closure by reviewing the outlook for the next year.

In preparing a descriptive presentation, the speaker's purpose is not to persuade, motivate, or change the audience members' minds. The purpose of an informative presentation is to do just that: inform! The speaker should present the data at hand in as straightforward a manner as possible.

Demonstration

A **demonstration** answers "how" questions, such as "How does this work?" or "How does someone or something move from point A to point B?" Consider the

STRATEGIC SKILLS

Presenting Statistics Visually

When using visual aids to present statistics during informative presentations, ensure that percentages add to 100 and that numbers and categories are easily readable. The visual shown here supports the presentation on new employee programs.

Survey Results

Current status of the organization	30%
History of the organization	28%
Presentation by George A. Smith, CEO	24%
Symposium on health and safety featuring outside experts	10%
Symposium featuring department supervisors	8%

following example of a demonstrative presentation given by a member of the U.S. Postal Service to a group of business leaders who had made complaints about the quality of local mail delivery and handling.

In his presentation, the postal worker demonstrated the numerous checkpoints and distribution centers through which a piece of mail travels before it reaches its destination. He supplemented the demonstration with maps, flowcharts, and even photographs of the various locations. He followed the presentation with a question-and-answer session.

A demonstrative presentation has the potential to work in persuasive ways in the minds of listeners. You can probably see how this presentation, although technically informative, may have shaped the perspective of the audience. The speaker did not announce that he intended to vindicate the postal service, but by demonstrating the many quality checks, special distribution centers, and trained personnel staffing the post offices, he may well have changed some of the audience members' minds about their postal service.

When planning and organizing a demonstrative presentation, a **spatial** or **geographical pattern** of organizing ideas works well. A geographical pattern organizes main points in terms of their physical locations, especially in relation to each other. For example, the terms *north, south, east,* and *west* might be used in a presentation showing the physical layout of a business or the location of famous landmarks, such as the Mall in Washington, D.C.

A spatial pattern shows the physical layout of an object's parts, frequently through such directional cues as *top, bottom, outside, inside, left,* or *right*. When presenting a demonstration to an audience, the speaker is often involved in a range of communication from "tell" to "show," as he or she describes where the part is located and then shows the location through a visual aid. Successful spatial demonstrations are often "hands-on."

The following excerpt from a presentation given in a computer-training workshop uses a spatial pattern to describe how to create a comfortable environment for using a computer. The emphasis is on the relationships between and among the pieces of computer equipment and the user.

Thesis: I want my audience to understand basic principles for creating a comfortable computer workspace.

Introduction: Many factors go into creating a comfortable workspace, including proper placement and adjustment of furniture and equipment, good light, and other environmental considerations. Today I will share some suggestions that can make your work more comfortable. Comfort is very personal, though, and only you can judge what works best for you.

I. First point: Furniture and posture.
   A. Adjust the height of your chair and desk so that your body is comfortably aligned.
   B. Have your knees slightly lower than your hips, so that the angle of your torso and thighs is more than 90 degrees.
   C. Let your chair support you. Support your lower back with your chair's backrest.

II. Second point: Keyboard and input device.
   A. Place your keyboard and input device so that your forearms are parallel or almost parallel to the floor. Your wrist should not be extremely flexed or extended.
   B. Your hands and wrists should be in roughly the same neutral position as when your arms are loosely hanging by your sides. Your wrist should not be bent too much to one side or the other.
   C. You should not have to reach or stretch to use either the keyboard or the input device.

Although spatial and geographical patterns are most useful when showing how things or places relate to each other in physical space, the pattern of organization for a presentation should be chosen based on the goal of the speech. For example, if the speaker at the computer workshop wants to inform the audience of possible uses for computers, he or she might choose a topical pattern rather than a geographical pattern. If the goal of the presentation is to inform the audience of the technological advances in a particular component that have occurred over the last three years, he or she might choose a chronological pattern.

Explanation

The third type of informative presentation addresses "why" questions, such as these:

Why is our market share declining?
Why are we restructuring the department?
Why do we need to raise membership dues 15 percent by the end of the year?

Each of these topics challenges the speaker to inform the audience and to justify the actions or decisions in question. "Why" questions frequently address controversial issues, and the audience may be predisposed to hostility, anger, or skepticism. Thus, one benefit of an explanatory presentation is to calm the audience. Once the audience members know why a condition exists or why an action is being taken, they are more likely to consider it in a rational and calm manner. If an audience is informed, for example, of the specific factors that led to a 15 percent increase in membership dues, they are more likely to accept the increase.

Two patterns of organization are especially well suited to the goal of providing explanation: the cause/effect pattern and the comparison/contrast pattern. Once again, however, we emphasize that the pattern chosen should reflect the speaker's goal, the audience, and the occasion.

Cause/Effect Pattern With a **cause/effect pattern** of organization, the presenter organizes the message around the origins and the results of a series of events. For example, a presentation on the cost of air travel might employ a cause/effect pattern by first noting the rapid rise in the cost of fuel over the winter, resulting in higher operating costs for airlines and thus causing higher ticket prices.

The presenter might also choose to begin with a description of present conditions (the effects) and then identify and explore the possible causes of the effects. The choice between these approaches can be made based on which element (the cause or the effect) is most familiar to the audience. To illustrate how a cause/effect pattern might be used to explain an event, consider the following excerpt from an outline of a presentation on why membership dues for an organization must be raised 15 percent by the end of the year.

Thesis: My audience will both understand the rationale for and accept a membership dues increase of 15 percent.

Introduction: Orient the audience by giving a brief overview of the problem, and build rapport by explaining your long involvement with and belief in the organization.

I. First main point (cause): The costs of running the organization continue to rise, and we have had no dues increases for the past two years.
    A. The costs of producing our journal have risen dramatically.
    B. Administrative costs for operating the office have also increased.
    C. We estimate that our total costs have increased by more than 50 percent.

II. Second main point (additional cause): We have implemented as many cost-cutting measures as possible during the last two years, allowing us to have kept dues at the same amount.
    A. Budgets have been strictly monitored.
    B. We have also eliminated unnecessary spending.

STRATEGIC SKILLS

Comparative Statistics

Comparative statistics are most effective when presented graphically, as this bar graph illustrates. Graph headings should be simple and eye-catching.

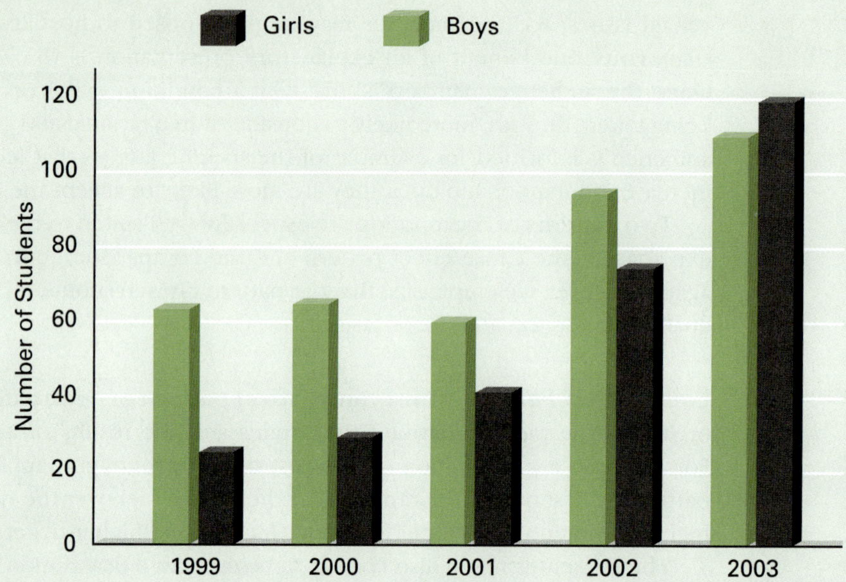

III. Third main point (effect): In light of our increased costs, and having reduced expenditures and eliminated unnecessary spending, it is now necessary to find other ways to keep the organization out of debt.
   A. A 15 percent increase in dues will cover our outstanding costs.
   B. We will begin a membership drive to increase our total dues revenue.
   C. We will look into fundraising ideas to increase the amount of money in our operating budget.

Comparison/Contrast Pattern A second way to organize an explanatory presentation is the **comparison/contrast pattern,** which identifies a familiar situation and then relates it to an unfamiliar situation that is either similar (for comparison) or different (for contrast). Consider the following outline of a presentation given to a group of management trainees in a large retail store.

Thesis: My audience will see their management training program as similar in function to the experience of their first few weeks of college.

Introduction: Orient the audience by briefly describing your role in the training process; provide rapport by noting that you went through the training program four years ago.

I. First main point (familiar situation): Many of you are recent college graduates. Think back to your first few weeks of school.
   A. You probably didn't know many other students.
   B. You probably got lost on campus more than a few times.
   C. Slowly you learned how to get around, study, organize your time, and set priorities.

II. Second main point (comparison): You will find many similarities to your initial college experiences as new employees here at Martingale Company.
   A. As the training program progresses, you will learn skills.
      1. Seminars on public speaking and interviewing are offered.
      2. Specialized training programs for the international department will be given.
   B. You will also get to know the other trainees and supervisors.
      1. Do not hesitate to ask questions.
      2. You can learn a lot through informal communication as well as through the training program.

Conclusion: Emphasize the significance of the training program and provide closure by thanking the audience for attending.

As you can see, the organization of an informative speech is an important tool to ensure that the audience members understand and remember your presentation. A logical and appropriate pattern boosts the impact of any informative presentation.

TYPICAL FORMATS

Formats are the structures or settings in which informative presentations are given. The format may reflect the setting, the audience's needs, the speaker's goal, or a combination of the three. Formats for informative presentations are meant to maximize the efficient transmission of information to audience members.

Briefings are relatively short presentations that inform an audience about a particular event. The White House press secretary provides frequent briefings for the press about the activities of the president.

Reports simply give an account of the status quo. Presentations that provide data such as the amount of money remaining in the budget and profit and loss figures are good examples of reports.

Training presentations educate listeners to help them to gain or improve on specific skills. Presentations that train as a format typically provide listeners with background information, introduce specific principles, and then follow through with skills practice, which the listeners perform.

Routine and regularly scheduled meetings: The weekly meeting is often a "telling format" wherein the supervisor, boss, or executive shares information that is to be transmitted down the chain of command or presents new goals for the week. The monthly meeting is often a formal meeting that attempts to present positive messages and summary reports by specific ad hoc or permanent committees or work groups. (*Ad hoc,* which translates literally as "to this," refers to a group set up for a specific purpose that is typically short-lived.)

For each of these formats, the presentation is only as good as the preparation that precedes it. A strong presentation depends on the "inside" (an appropriate pattern and effective supporting materials, introduction, and conclusion) as well as the "outside" (the format).

GUIDELINES FOR A SUCCESSFUL PRESENTATION

Now that you have an understanding of patterns and formats for informative presentations, it is important to attend to situational details.

Advance planning and preparation are the greatest defense against elements in the situation that can adversely affect your presentation. Put this book down for a moment and think about some of the *worst* possible things that could happen to you during a presentation. Next to each of these, jot down what you could do in advance to prevent them from ruining your presentation. You probably came up with as good a list as we can. Nevertheless, here are some guidelines for ensuring successful presentations that we think are particularly worth considering.

Analyze Potential Sources of Noise

Noise is anything that interferes with the communication process. Noise can occur at any time in the process. For purposes of illustration, let us look at three potential levels on which noise can occur: in the transmission of information from speaker to listener (e.g., does the listener even receive or hear the information?), in the comprehension of information (e.g., once the information is received and heard, does the listener understand the information the same way the speaker intended?), and in the pragmatics of information (e.g., once the information is heard and understood, does the listener do what the speaker wants?).

Note that these three levels of noise are hierarchical. Success on a lower level must be achieved before a higher level can even be an issue. A listener must hear information before he or she can understand it! Similarly, a listener must understand the information before acting on that information.

A speaking setting actually has three potential sources of noise—physical, physiological, and psychological. **Physical noise** refers to distractions in the environment of the presentation. Does the room in which you will speak require a microphone for you to be heard clearly? Are there windows that will invite listeners to daydream or not pay attention to you? These are just two possible sources of physical noise.

There is no reason to find out about these problems in the midst of your presentation. Scouting out the room before you start and making appropriate adjustments are well worth your time.

Physiological noise comes from competing personal needs the listener may have. For example, is the listener too hot or too cold? Thirsty? Tired? Think of times when you have been uncomfortable as an audience member. Did you really pay attention to the speaker? All you probably thought about was when the next break was scheduled.

By satisfying the listeners' physiological needs as much as possible, the speaker can increase the listeners' attention. Adjusting the temperature in the room the night before you are to present can be helpful. Arranging for pitchers of water and snacks such as fresh fruit or candy can alleviate thirst or hunger. Planning breaks at strategic times can enable listeners to digest what they have just heard and ready themselves for the information to come.

Psychological noise includes internal distractions within the mind of the listener. For example, if the listener is concerned about what he is wearing tonight, what she may say when she has to speak tomorrow, or whether the spouse picked up the kids from school on time, that person is not listening to you!

The best way to overcome psychological noise is to make sure that your presentation is more interesting and captivating than anything else the listener may prefer to think about. This is no easy task. But by using a range of voice inflections and pacing, providing a variety of supporting materials, and incorporating visual aids, you will have a much better chance of obtaining and maintaining the audience's attention.

The general point is that you as the presenter can and should control the circumstances in which you speak. Planning in advance and overcoming barriers that can create noise are crucial for your success as a speaker.

Adapt to Your Listeners

One common mistake made by beginning speakers is to assume that the *same speech* can be given to different audiences. Although the same *topic* can be presented to an infinite number of audiences, without adapting the material from group to group speakers can quite easily fail because the audience will not perceive their presentations as relevant.

Adaptation does not mean starting over. The same main points, basic premises, and even data or evidence may be quite applicable in every group with which you talk. But examples, illustrations, case studies, or incidents usually require adaptation to the particular group.

Consider these situations: An example that employees in an accounting department may find relevant and understandable may make no sense to employees in personnel. A brief reference to an incident (such as the Korean War) that is relevant to a group whose ages coincide with that conflict may be meaningless to an audience composed of younger people. Discussing the merits of investing in company stocks and bonds may be exciting to a group of executives but depressing to a group of hourly workers whose every dollar is spent even before it is made.

The successful speaker adapts the material of the presentation according to the audience's needs and requirements. There are actually three levels of adaptation: knowledge, interest, and acceptance. In terms of the **knowledge level,** the two basic extremes are audiences whose members are well informed versus those whose members are entirely uninformed. The differences in adaptation between these two audiences may be obvious to you. With an uninformed audience, you are obliged to provide more background material, define terms carefully, and link the material in the presentation to material already known. With an informed audience, you can assume more and de-emphasize the three preceding factors. Indeed, if you emphasize background material, term definition, and linkage of material with an informed audience, the participants may feel insulted or bored!

The **interest level** ranges from high initial interest to no interest at all. Some listeners, for example, may find any topic related to microcomputers fascinating but be completely uninterested in topics related to plant safety. Uninterested listeners will not meet any of your objectives for the presentation, whether they are to discover, learn, laugh, or review. If audience members are not interested, they will not listen; if they do not listen, they will not understand; and if they do not understand, your objective will not be met.

What are some ways that you can facilitate audience interest? Look at some of these lines from actual speeches given in businesses and organizations. Would they capture your interest? (If not, what are some that would?)

"Have you ever wondered how successful people choose which stocks and bonds to buy?"

"If I could tell you how to get a day's worth of work finished in half a day, would you be interested?"

"In the next ten minutes, I will outline a new program that will significantly increase almost all the benefits that you as an employee of this company can receive."

Successful informative presentations have one characteristic in common. They all give audience members a reason to listen. They connect with needs or values of audience members and motivate their curiosity.

The **acceptance level** comprises the audience members' preset attitudes toward the topic, which may range from favorable (they are likely to agree or react positively) to unfavorable (they are likely to disagree or react negatively). Audiences that you suspect will be unfavorably disposed toward your topic must be treated more carefully than those that are favorably disposed. For example, when the director of personnel for a large corporation called the division managers together and showed them the compensation levels that would be used to set raises for the next year, she realized she needed to prepare for a negative reaction from her audience. Although the presentation was informative, the topic was unlikely to be viewed favorably by the audience, as raises had been quite low over the last several years.

In this case, the personnel director began by giving an overview of the company's pay position for the previous five years, emphasizing that compared with others, the company had kept pace with similar firms. She then noted the company's loss in market share, profit, and volume for the previous year. Following the presentation of this background information, she showed the managers the new compensation levels. Even though the news was no different after the introductory material than it would have been without it, the background information set the stage and provided a rationale for the rates. To have simply dived in and said "Here are the rates for next year" would have produced a considerable amount of hostility.

Shared Perspectives

In every informative presentation, the data come from somewhere! Sharing with your listeners the origins of these data and providing a perspective on them are good ways to reduce unanswered questions in listeners' minds. Specific ways of doing this vary with topic and context, but they include sharing with your audience how certain numbers were figured, the source from which information was derived, how certain conclusions were drawn, where some possible problems are, and so forth.

A shared perspective benefits from including listeners' experiences and viewpoints as well. The more you link your message with what the audience already knows, the more successful you will be.

Shared perspective benefits from frequent use of analogies. **Analogies** compare two items and in essence argue that what is true in one case is also true in the other. You have heard speakers draw analogies between two time periods, two states, two presidential administrations, and even two families.

Analogies are quite useful in an informative presentation. If the audience is knowledgeable in one subject area and you are introducing new material, you can use an analogy from that area to explain how the new information is "just like what you have already heard before" or "very similar to the way we have discussed this in the past."

Shared perspective is also increased by avoiding jargon as much as possible. For example, communication specialists call a student who has a great deal of anxiety about giving a public presentation "high comm apps." To those who have not

What Would You Do?

Consider how you would cope with a variety of unusual events that can confront the public speaker. How would you address the following situations?

- Pillars in the room prevent some audience members from seeing the transparencies or slides you are projecting.
- You arrive to give your speech and are asked to speak for an hour instead of thirty minutes because a second speaker has canceled.
- You take out your speaking notes but, just as you are being introduced to the audience, discover that some of the notes are missing.
- The bulb in the projector suddenly burns out, preventing you from showing your transparencies or slides.
- Someone in the audience interrupts you to say that you are not speaking on the subject the audience has come to hear about.
- You are heckled.
- Someone in the audience begins laughing uncontrollably.
- The preceding speaker covers all of your material.
- Your introducer undermines your credibility with some caustic remarks.
- Nonverbal cues from your audience suggest that most members don't understand your supporting examples.
- An audience member challenges the statistics you have just cited.
- You can't tell whether the audience is accepting or rejecting your ideas.
- No one laughs at the joke you've just told to support a key idea.
- At the end of your speech the audience begins chanting, "Keep going!"
- Handouts are accidentally distributed ahead of schedule and the audience stops paying attention to your speech.
- The movements and facial expressions of the audience signal boredom, even though you've just begun to speak.
- A couple of audience questions can be interpreted as hints that your idea development is not sophisticated enough.

Source: Adapted from J. A. Jones, "Preparing Contingency Plans for Public Speaking Situations, *Communication Education* 30 (1981), 423–425. Copyright 1981 by Natl. Commun. Assn. Reproduced with permission of Natl. Commun. Assn. in the format Textbook via Copyright Clearance Center.

taken a communication course, communication specialists' use of this term—which means "high communication apprehensive"—may conjure up any number of confusing images. Confusion, misunderstanding, and resentment can result when jargon is introduced to listeners. If you must use jargon, define it so that you ensure audience understanding. A shared perspective facilitates the transfer and acceptance of information between speaker and listener.

SITUATIONAL KNOWLEDGE: TECHNOLOGY

Video

Many businesses and professions make extensive use of video. Medical schools videotape residents examining patients. Organizations such as Miles Laboratories provide videos of seminars in which physicians learn how to improve their credibility with patients and their public presentations. Professional organizations for attorneys and teachers use videos for in-service training, continuing education, and certification training. Manufacturing and service businesses and government agencies require employees to attend seminars and workshops at which instructional and informational videos are shown. The range of applications of video technology has expanded dramatically in the last ten years. Annual reports, product demonstrations, and training sessions are just three of the many uses of video in business and the professions.

Many of the skills and techniques of video production are similar to those required for live or taped television productions.

Television

Our discussion focuses on speeches given in one room and piped to different locations on multiple television monitors, speeches that are presented live to large audiences and that incorporate a big-screen monitor to aid the audience's view of the speaker, and speeches that are recorded on videocassette for playback on a monitor at a later time. Although we do not directly address interviews, debates, or panel discussions, these are televised on a regular basis, and many of the principles we refer to apply to them.

In business and the professions, speeches are often projected on a big screen. You may have attended conferences or conventions where this technique was used, especially for major or keynote presentations. You may also have attended concerts or sporting events where the audience's view of the star or the action was enhanced by big-screen technology. Television cameras project the speaker's image onto a big screen that is raised for all to see. These screens, which may be as tall as twenty-four feet, enable audiences to focus on the speaker's facial expressions, gestures, and other aspects of delivery that they otherwise would not see. There is no question that an audience is likely to respond more readily when it can see the speaker's face and expressions.

Of course, the big screen creates some difficulties for the speaker. Tiny variables are captured by the camera. Facial expressions such as raised eyebrows, smiles, frowns, or pauses with the mouth held slightly open are greatly emphasized. The screen reveals nervous tics as readily as it does friendly, conversational gestures such as upward palms to signal openness or downward pointing to indicate concreteness. Also, the speaker must restrict her or his body movement.

In the business world, one must give informal as well as formal presentations. Here, following her formal presentation, Hewlett-Packard chair and CEO Carly Fiorina is responding to media questions at a Special Meeting for Shareholders to vote on a proposed company merger with Compaq Computers. Both formal and informal informative presentations require analysis of audience needs, careful planning, and proper organization to be effective and successful. (Justin Sullivan/Getty Images)

Most speeches delivered through the big-screen medium are scripted and read from a prompter (a screen showing a large-type copy of the speech that can be seen by the speaker but not by the audience). It is difficult, if not impossible, for a speaker to read a presentation from a prompter if he or she is moving around the stage. In addition, the speaker's microphone is generally placed on the podium, and movement away from it causes her or his voice to fade. A lavaliere or lapel microphone (which is attached to the speaker's clothing and sometimes is wireless) can help to prevent fadeout.

The challenge for you as a speaker is to minimize the problems and take advantage of the benefits that the big screen offers. Television has the potential to reveal your confidence, forcefulness, and emotion much more readily than any other medium.

COMMUNICATION COMPETENCE: CAMERA SKILLS AND SPECIAL OCCASIONS

Communication competence for technology and special occasions depends on practice. Video and television presentations and special occasion speeches require the acquisition of skills through specific effort and situational knowledge.

Practice

Many people are frightened by the prospect of making a televised presentation because they have never done so before. If you were told that your presentation would be broadcast, would you have some of these concerns?

- "I'll look funny."
- "I won't sound like myself on television."

- "My lips will quiver, my voice will shake, and my tongue will stick to my teeth."
- "I don't want someone to be able to replay my speech."
- "Anything I wear will look unflattering on camera."

If you are prone to such negative self-assessments, you are not alone. These are natural feelings that cause apprehension. Remember that giving a speech in public is the behavior most feared by most adults. Having a presentation aired over television only heightens that apprehension, whether the speech is a live big-screen presentation, a live television appearance, or a taped presentation that will be distributed for viewing.

We cannot alleviate all your concerns. Nor do we believe that you should be completely calm when delivering your presentation. Some apprehension provides the adrenaline needed to keep you excited and energetic. Our goal is to help you to manage the additional apprehension caused by the televised medium. The following comments address some of the on-camera delivery skills that you will need.

The red light on one of the cameras signals that your presentation is being taped, broadcast, or both. Where should you look? Should you look directly at the camera? Should you look only at the camera whose red light indicates that it is operating? Should you ignore the camera and focus on the audience (even if you cannot see the audience because of the lights shining in your eyes)? If no audience is present, should you pretend that there is one and talk to it?

The answers to these questions are difficult to provide because many variables can affect individual televised performances. We offer the following general guidelines as a starting point for performing in some of the most common television setups.[2]

If you are speaking from a prompter that is located above or on the camera, you necessarily must look at that camera to read your manuscript. Getting the words right is your primary concern and should be emphasized over placement of eye contact.

If prompters are located to the left and right of the podium, you can alternate eye contact from one to the other (and to the audience seated in front of you) without losing focus on your manuscript. The camera operator will follow your gaze as you alternate between the TelePrompTers.

If you are not using a prompter, your notes or speaker's outline should be prepared on small blue or green note cards to avoid causing camera glare or distracting the audience. If a live audience is present, focus on the audience and let the cameras find you. Awkward changes in eye contact are likely to occur as you glance from one camera to another.

If a live audience is not present, decide to whom you want to direct the presentation. Looking directly at the camera gives those who watch the tape on a monitor the impression that you are speaking directly to them. If you want to convey the impression that you are actually speaking to an audience and that viewers are eavesdropping on the presentation, speak to the room and let the camera find you.

In many professional settings, the director will tell you where to look or not to look. Often, however, you may have to make your own judgments. For example, when guests on *Larry King Live* are being interviewed, some look at the camera

2. Some of this summary is taken from these sources: S. Hyde, *Television and Radio Announcing*, 6th ed. (Boston: Houghton Mifflin, 1990); S. Bension, *Producer's Masterguide, 1990: The International Production Manual for Motion Pictures, Broadcast Television, Commercials, Cable, and Videotape Industries*, 10th ed. (New York: NY Production Manual, 1990); Hyatt Research Corporation Staff, *The Executive's Guide to Network Media* (Fairfax, Va.: DataTrends Publications, 1990).

to answer callers' questions and others speak directly to Larry King, who is seated across a desk from them. Some critics say that looking at King reduces the guest's credibility; others say that looking at the camera and away from the interviewer seems artificial and awkward, especially when the camera pulls back for a long shot.

Appearance

What about your appearance? There are ways to optimize your appearance in a televised presentation.[3] While these are basics, we hope you take time to consider the particular needs of your own presentation.

Cosmetics A speaker's features often appear flat on television, and other distortions may occur as well. During the Nixon-Kennedy presidential debates of 1960, Richard Nixon refused to wear makeup. People who listened to the debate on radio thought Nixon beat John Kennedy. But viewers of the televised version saw Nixon's pallor and five-o'clock shadow and believed that Kennedy won the debate. Cosmetics, especially eyeliner and blush, restore the natural dimensions of the face. In professional settings, listen to the experts. If you lack access to professional guidance, try various types of cosmetics and make test videos. (Do not, however, expect to change your on-camera appearance radically through makeup!) Powder can reduce the glare and reflection produced by hot lights. If you are not skilled in applying powder, blush, or other cosmetics, have someone on hand to help you. Remember always to check yourself on a monitor to see how you look. The picture on the television monitor is the most accurate indicator of your appearance.

Both men and women should be aware of their hair. Neither should lapse into bad habits such as nervously brushing his or her hair. Because nonverbal behavior is clearly seen on screen, practice avoiding nervous habits.

Clothing On television and in formal settings in videos, men are generally requested to wear traditional suits for business and for most other professions. The context, of course, is the final determination. Both men and women should avoid white, although new lighting developments have made white less problematic. When men or women are seated during a presentation and they are wearing suit coats, they should sit on the bottom of their coats to avoid bunching at the back of the neck or shoulder area. Some suit jackets look better buttoned when the wearer is seated; others need to be unbuttoned. Experiment for the best results.

If men are to sit at a table without a curtain in front of it or in interview chairs like those the morning talk shows use, they should wear long dark socks to avoid a gap between the top of their socks and the beginning of their pants leg. U.S. culture determines that credible speakers do not expose that inch of bare skin!

Like men, women can have particular problems with clothing. Short skirts create difficulties for fashion-conscious female broadcasters. If you are an occasional video or television presenter, you might choose to wear a longer skirt to avoid the "struggle with the skirt" syndrome that causes female interviewers and interviewees to be uncomfortable on camera during long shots.

3. P. H. Lewis, "New Camera Simplifies Computer Processing of Images," *South Bend (Indiana) Tribune*, June 9, 1994, p. A11.

TECHNOLOGY TOOLS

Presentation Software

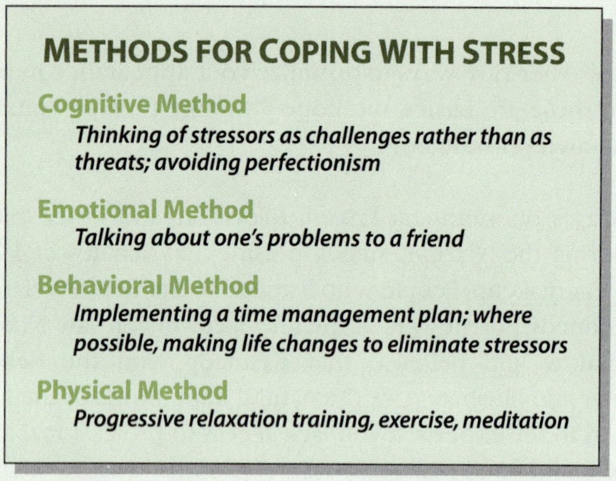

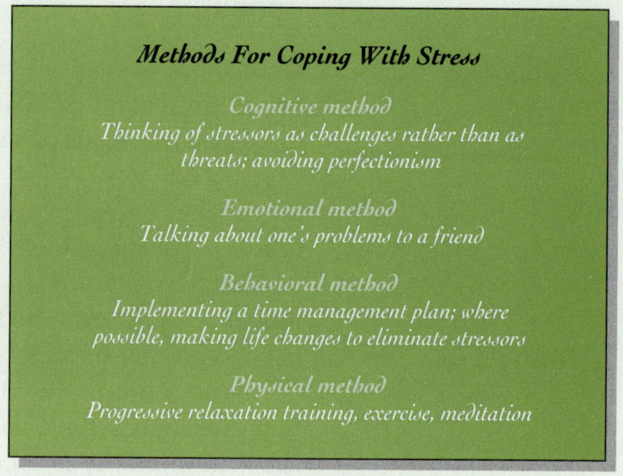

Presentation software, such as Microsoft's PowerPoint, is filled with wonderful features. Slides, electronic screen shows, overheads, handouts, and speaker notes can all be generated from a single file. Special effects, sound, photography, and animation are easily incorporated. Presenters have never had so many tools available that are so easy to use and so inexpensive. Once created, presentations can be converted into HTML, Java, Flash, autorun CDs, videotape, PDFs, or QuickTime movies for reuse. PowerPoint slides can also serve as the centerpiece of Web-conferencing presentations in which a facilitator and audience use the Web to engage in virtual collaborations.

This software is especially valuable for developing and delivering effective informative presentations. The last chapter identified several key sources for locating information that can help you begin to develop competency in using it. Two additional ones are www.indezine.com (an amazing repository of information on all things related to PowerPoint, including links, articles, templates, techniques, tutorials, books, product reviews, and a never-ending flow of new ideas) and www.powerpointers (a site that features a compilation of articles on communicating more effectively with PowerPoint in professional situations such as sales pitches, formal presentations, informal meetings, and media presentations).

When you are choosing clothing for a televised presentation, consider the background against which you will be speaking. Be sure to find out from the director what the background is before you begin the session. Dark clothing against a dark background or light clothing against a light background will cause problems for the studio engineers. In most cases, cool colors such as blue, gray, or pastels are preferable to black, and white should be avoided because it causes camera glare. The guiding principle is to avoid major color contrasts within your outfit or against the background. Avoid stripes, checks, and polka dots because they blur on camera. Minimize or avoid wearing jewelry; it can cause glare and distract the audience from your presentation.

By following these general principles, you can improve your appearance, self-confidence, and delivery on camera.

As you will discover, if you have not already, PowerPoint is easy to learn and use. With it, you can be building presentations in a very short amount of time. This ease of use, however, makes it equally easy to misuse it or not use it effectively. It is important to begin with general principles or guidelines that you can stretch or violate as you develop more experience with using the software. We suggest the following:

1. **Start simple.** Don't overuse special effects. While these can be powerful, you don't want your audience to focus on the "gee whiz" aspects of your presentation to the exclusion of your content. Think carefully before using animations, sound, video, and special effects. If used sparingly, they'll have greater impact.
2. **Be consistent.** Stick with the same backgrounds, styles, and transition effects throughout your presentation. As you choose them, think of the room where the presentation will be made. While light text on a dark background is a good choice for a dark or slightly darkened room, for example, in a brightly lit room the dark background may look so faded that the light text may not show up well.
3. **Avoid overcrowded slides.** You want your audience to focus on the content of your presentation and on you as the presenter of that content. Limit your points on a slide to three to five points. When you need more, break the points into separate slides. Crowded slides will turn off your audience and obscure your main points.
4. **Use a font size and style that is readable.** Put yourself in the audience and ask what they will be seeing. Do the font style and size make it easily readable?
5. **Find your own style.** PowerPoint gives you lots of style options. Use only those that you are comfortable with. Play with the "templates" and "wizards" that walk you through a set of choices for the format of your slides. Be observant when others use PowerPoint. If you like the colors or textures you see, find out what they are. If someone has a way of doing things you like, learn from it and use or modify it.
6. **Practice the delivery of your presentation.** Your success depends on how comfortable you are with using the program. To be comfortable, you need to practice giving the speech while running the laptop computer at the same time. If for some reason you can't do both, you should practice with the person who will run the computer for you and, if possible, in the room where you will make the presentation. When you know your presentation and are comfortable working with the computer, you are best able to focus on connecting with your audience and making an effective presentation.
7. **Prepare for the unexpected.** Anyone who has attended multiple presentations knows how easy it is for things to go wrong (incompatible cords, cables, or adaptors; burned-out bulbs; difficult seating arrangements). So ask if there is a technical person assigned to your presentation who can troubleshoot for you. Most important, if at all possible get to the room early and get everything set up and tested.

Multimedia Technology and Presentations

This rapidly expanding area of technology changes almost daily. Advances include the use of interactive computer programs in business and in education; videophones, which incorporate computer-generated hard-copy messages with real-time pictures and the voices of both sender and receiver; and video scanners, which through digitalization produce real-life pictures, an addition to the existing technology of simulation and graphics. Scanners that transform hard-copy documents and even photographs into computer files have been available for some time, but scanners for videotape and film are still relatively new to the market. These are just a few of the current advancements. As you enter the work force, be aware that technology is changing rapidly. It is to your advantage to keep current.

STRATEGIC SKILLS

The Informative Speech: A Checklist

- Do you have a clear purpose in mind?
- Is your speech best described as descriptive, demonstrative, or explanatory?
- Given a clear purpose, what are the three to five main points that the audience will need to understand and accept if you are to achieve it?
- What forms of support (e.g., explanations, examples, statistics, testimony, and visual aids) will make your main points most informative, interesting, relevant, clear, and acceptable?
- Would some form of information technology be most useful in making your presentation?
- What organizational pattern for your speech will best accommodate both your purpose and your forms of support: topical, chronological, spatial/geographical, cause/effect, or comparison/contrast?
- How can you best achieve the functions of the introduction (orientation, motivation, and rapport) and conclusion (completeness and closure) of your speech?
- Which type of delivery (impromptu, extemporaneous, manuscript, or memorized) is likely to be most effective in accomplishing your purpose?
- Independent of type of delivery, how can you make your delivery intelligible, conversational, direct, and unobtrusive?
- How will you prepare to field questions from the audience?
- How will you prepare to deal with the anxiety you are likely to experience?
- How will you rehearse your presentation?

ANXIETY MANAGEMENT: PRACTICE AND KNOWLEDGE

Practice is the key to reducing anxiety. When you become accustomed to cameras running, bright lights shining in your face, microphones clipped to your clothing, and eye contact with the camera, your level of apprehension will decrease. Only time and repetition of the experience will allow a televised presentation to seem like a natural behavior.

Nevertheless, there are ways to combat anxiety in your very first televised presentation. Watch yourself on tape with a critical but constructive eye. Do not say, "I look awful." Watch the tape and ask, "What actions can I take to improve my appearance during this presentation?" Are there some things you are wearing, ways you are standing, and so forth, that you could change?

Concentrate on the way you sound as well as on the way you look. If your microphone is on the podium, speak over the microphone rather than into it to avoid popping sounds. If you are using a lavaliere microphone, avoid excessive rustling and fidgeting, which will cause static or interference.

If possible, show your practice videotape to someone else for his or her comments. This person does not have to be an expert to offer you a constructive opinion. If you do not have access to video equipment before the presentation, practice in front of a mirror or with a friend. Doing so can go a long way toward reducing your anxiety when you actually have to perform on camera.

Translating ideas into clear and attractive forms is an increasingly important challenge for members of the business community. In addition to the techniques already presented, here are some other general hints for increasing your confidence and skill level as a speaker.[4]

4. R. P. Hart, G. W. Friedrich, and B. Brummett, *Public Communication*, 2d ed. (New York: Harper & Row, 1983), p. 141. Reprinted with permission of Barry Brummett and Rod Hart.

1. When you are speaking informatively, think of how you became interested in your topic and build your audience's motivation to listen by recapturing for them your own initial experience.
2. Oral rehearsal is especially important in an informative speech because you can never be really sure that you understand a concept until you hear yourself explain it.
3. Do not become overly specific too early in an informative speech because listeners forget foreign details easily; concentrate on explaining one central feature of your concept.
4. Try to recall the specific sequence of events that caused you suddenly to understand the topic you will be discussing; try leading listeners down the same path you took.
5. Dictionary definitions of key terms are rarely helpful in an informative speech because listeners need more fully amplified and more colorful explanations of a concept.
6. Long quotations from expert sources may be lacking in flair and clarity; oftentimes, you will have to supplement such remarks with your own better-adapted paraphrases.
7. Each major section of a speech outline should contain a minimum of one extended example and two or more brief examples if a concept is to be truly clarified for others.
8. We strongly advise preparing a sentence outline for every speech you make, although you may choose to use a shorter version of this outline when actually delivering your speech.
9. Put the burden of proof on the use of visual aids (that is, carefully assess their potential to enhance your presentation) because their distracting capacities can outweigh their helpfulness in clarifying ideas.
10. Remember this proposition above all others: if there is any chance that listeners can misunderstand you, they will.

STRATEGIC SCENARIO WRAP-UP

At the beginning of this chapter we encountered Ching-Wen Lu, a student in an instructional technology course. For her term project in this course, Ching-Wen Lu is conducting survey research on the uses of instructional technology at her university. She has found out who is currently using technology and who is not and why this is the case. It will soon be the last week of the semester, during which she will need to present her findings to other members of the class. What have you learned in this chapter that might help Ching-Wen to prepare for her presentation?

- Which of the three major categories of informative presentations (descriptive, demonstrative, or explanatory) best captures Ching-Wen's task?
- Which of the patterns of organization (e.g., topical, chronological, etc.) might work well for her presentation? Which should she rule out?
- Which of the formats for informative presentations (e.g., briefing, report, etc.) might she consider using?
- What are the major sources of noise that Ching-Wen should plan to cope with?
- What should Ching-Wen do to analyze and adapt to her audience?
- What advice would you give Ching-Wen for using technology in making her presentation?

- Are there any contingency plans that Ching-Wen ought to formulate?
- Do you have any advice for Ching-Wen in terms of anxiety management?

SUMMARY

- Informative speaking is an increasingly common form of presentation and one that most businesspeople will have to engage in at one time or another.
- The successful informative presentation shares traits with other kinds of presentations: it identifies the main points to be shared with an audience, it uses supporting materials to elaborate these points and increase their credibility, it presents a total message, and it is delivered in a style appropriate to the audience and its concerns.
- An informative presentation usually has one (or more) of three functions: to share information, shape perception, or set agendas.
- Likewise, the pattern of a presentation reflects its function: Is the presentation designed to describe, demonstrate, or explain?
- Possible patterns include topical, chronological, spatial/geographical, cause/effect, and comparison/contrast.
- Presentations also take different formats; among these are briefings, reports, and training sessions.
- Once a speaker has decided on the appropriate function, organization, and format of the presentation, the work of ensuring the success of the presentation begins.
- To do so, the speaker is wise to follow several principles. First, analyze and prepare for potential sources of noise (physical, physiological, and psychological). Second, adapt to the listeners. Successful adaptation requires discovery of each audience's knowledge, interest, and acceptance levels. Third, work toward a shared perspective with audience members by disclosing where information came from and using analogies to reach the listeners.
- A speaker can also increase his or her confidence and skill level by rehearsing the speech, avoiding simplistic dictionary definitions that are neither colorful nor broad enough, giving sufficient examples of major points, and using visual aids in ways that will minimize their capacity to distract the audience.
- Although these techniques do not guarantee that every speaker will finally come to public speaking with ease and self-assurance, they can help all potential public speakers realize the extent of their own resources and how to use them.
- Telephone, video, television, and multimedia presentations are parts of the ongoing and dramatic changes in presentations in business and in the professions.
- It is important to develop your audio-presentation skills as increasingly sophisticated technology becomes common in the workplace.
- Competent speakers can take advantage of technology to enhance their contact with and appeal to the audience.
- Understanding and practicing with broadcast technology can decrease anxiety and ensure a successful presentation.

KEY TERMS

Informative presentation: presentations that tell listeners something they do not already know, or that supplement or reinforce listeners' existing knowledge

Function: what the presentation accomplishes or aims to accomplish

Description: type of informative presentation that satisfies the audience members' needs for facts, figures, and other data

Topical pattern: structural pattern of organization in which the main points of the message are organized as parallel elements of the topic itself

Chronological pattern: structural pattern of organization in which the main points of the message are organized in a time-related sequence

Demonstration: type of informative presentation that aims to explain the *how* of an issue

Spatial or geographical pattern: structural pattern of organization in which main points are organized in terms of their physical locations, especially in relation to each other

Cause/effect pattern: structural pattern of organization in which the message is organized around the origins and the results of a series of events

Comparison/contrast pattern: structural pattern of organization that identifies a familiar situation and then relates it to an unfamiliar situation

Briefings: relatively short presentations that inform an audience about a particular event

Reports: informative accounts of the status quo

Training presentations: informative presentations that educate listeners to help them gain or improve on specific skills

Noise: anything that interferes with the communication process; can occur at any time in the process

Physical noise: distractions in the environment of the presentation

Physiological noise: competing personal needs of the listeners

Psychological noise: internal distractions within the mind of the listener

Adaptation: tailoring the message and material of the presentation to the audience's needs and requirements

Knowledge level: level of adaptation that is based on how much or little an audience knows about your message and material

Interest level: level of adaptation that is based on how much or little an audience is interested in your message and material

Acceptance level: level of adaptation that is based on audience members' preset attitudes toward the topic, ranging from favorable to unfavorable

Analogies: comparison of two items, with the argument that what is true in one case is also true in the other

DISCUSSION

1. Why are informative presentations useful? Describe and give examples of three major functions of informative presentations.
2. What is a topical pattern of organization? What types of messages would work well with this pattern?
3. How is a demonstrative presentation organized? What are its strengths and possible weaknesses?
4. What kinds of questions are addressed in an explanatory presentation? What additional demands are made on the speaker in an explanatory presentation?
5. What are the three categories of audience adaptation that the informative presentation should take into account? Describe how each might affect the success of the presentation.
6. How does shared perspective (including both the presenter's and the audience's perspective) contribute to increased audience understanding and acceptance of the message? What are some techniques to encourage a shared perspective?
7. What are some of the skills needed in videotaping or in television presentations?
8. How are televised presentations used in business? If you have been involved with producing or presenting a televised performance, how did you prepare?
9. How is television different from face-to-face presentations?

ACTIVITIES

1. Pick a topic and outline suitable main points for each of the following organizational patterns:
   a. chronological
   b. topical
   c. spatial/geographical
   d. cause/effect
   e. comparison/contrast
2. Use one of the outlines you prepared for question 1 and be prepared to share some appropriate transitions from one point to another.
3. Prepare an outline for a briefing (on a topic of your choice) to be presented to members of the press.
4. Analyze an informative presentation you have heard recently. How did the speaker organize the information, adapt to the audience, and share perspectives to make the speech a success?
5. Prepare a three-minute video on a topic that interests you and on which you already have information. As each class member is videotaped, note what works and what does not. Review all presentations with a monitor and then critique them again.
6. Speakers typically feel anxious about making a presentation that will be televised. What are your concerns? Write positive suggestions to allay these concerns.
7. In large businesses, informative presentations are rarely given without visual aids. This exercise is

designed to give you practice in constructing visual aids for an informative presentation.

The Situation: A company is relocating its headquarters to a new building in the city in about six months and will occupy five floors of the building. Planning committees have been assigned to each of the floors to decide how they should be organized. Each floor has two restrooms, two break rooms, fifteen cubicle offices and ten enclosed offices, two large conference rooms, four small conference rooms, two storerooms, and eight closets. Senior managers are willing to spend money on renovations if they understand that the changes will result in increased productivity, morale, and effective communication. The following departments have been assigned to each floor:

First floor—personnel (ten employees), information services (ten employees responsible for maintaining the computer network and for training employees on new computer applications), mailroom (five employees)

Second floor—office services (three employees responsible for purchasing supplies and supervising maintenance), senior management (seven employees), chief executive officer and staff (three employees), internal communication (five employees who produce the company newsletter and magazine and who plan events), planning and finance (seven employees responsible for developing long-term organizational goals)

Third floor—public relations (ten employees), marketing (ten employees)

Fourth floor—research and development (twenty-five employees)

Fifth floor—research and development (ten employees), accounting (five employees), payroll (three employees), legal services (four employees), inventory (five employees) (Production, manufacturing, and distribution are done at regional branches.)

The class can work on the project in groups of three to five people. Each group plays the role of a planning committee, which must decide "who goes where and why" and must present the information to management. In your presentation, you may need diagrams, drawings, tables, floor plans, and so on. Use your imagination. Each committee member delivers one portion of the presentation to senior management (the other class members). You must construct appropriate visual aids to back up all decisions. Do not limit yourself to only one type of visual aid; select the methods that best meet the objective of your presentation. The actual team presentation should take approximately twenty minutes. After each team's presentation, discuss these questions with the class:

A. Given the team's objective and specific proposals, were effective visual aids employed? If not, what are some other alternatives?

B. Did each visual aid support the point for which it was intended? Was it truly an "aid," or did it become the presentation itself?

C. Were the design and substance of each visual aid effective? What were some of the strengths and shortcomings of each?

D. How well did each team member follow the presentation techniques outlined in Chapter 12 for using visual aids? What suggestions can you make to help each participant to improve?

CHAPTER 15

Persuasive and Special Presentations

After working through this chapter, you will be able to:

1. Describe the importance of persuasive presentations in business
2. Identify the major functions of persuasive presentations
3. Select and organize supporting materials for persuasive presentations
4. Choose an appropriate format for the presentation
5. Understand the process by which persuasion occurs
6. Use a variety of resources to ensure a successful persuasive presentation
7. Know the various types of special presentation formats and develop situational knowledge that will increase your effectiveness in these various formats

STRATEGIC SCENARIO

Salendria Williams is a student in a communication class much like the course for which you're reading this book. A computer science major, she is very interested in information technology and how it can best be utilized in business and the professions. For a persuasive speech assignment, Salendria has decided to make a case that describes why all students need to do more to prepare themselves with skills in the use of information technology.

As you read this chapter, you will learn about the skills and competencies that Salendria needs in order to make a successful persuasive presentation. At the end of the chapter, we will return to this scenario and ask for your advice.

OVERVIEW

As important as informative presentations are in the business world, persuasive presentations are even more prevalent. Persuasive presentations identify and promote ideas and options to guide listeners toward the course of action desired by the speaker. One reason for their frequency is that many persuasive presentations occur informally. Employees further their views, ideas, or suggestions in meetings, in one-to-one discussions with a supervisor, or even in social groups, in addition to making formal presentations. Nevertheless, the basic resources for persuasion remain constant, although they must be adapted to the particular audience or setting.

Persuasive presentations incorporate the skills needed to prepare an informative presentation. Although the goal of a persuasive presentation may be to reinforce (or change) the audience members' beliefs or to act on the speaker's suggestions, informing the audience is one component of that process. Thus, this chapter builds on the skills introduced in Chapters 13 and 14.

Special presentations, which are made on special occasions or at ceremonial events, include introductions, the presentation of an award to an honored guest, the acceptance of an honor or award, and tributes and "roasts." Such presentations share many similarities. At the end of this chapter we compare and contrast the demands that are made on you as a speaker at such events. The model of strategic communication can guide your endeavors as you use technology and make presentations at special occasions.

FUNCTIONS OF PERSUASIVE PRESENTATIONS

Your goal for your persuasive speech should be related to the function, the audience, and the setting. This discussion is related to persuasion for U.S. audiences. Persuasion, like other communication processes, is closely tied to the culture in which it occurs. The function of a persuasive presentation should determine the pattern used to organize the information. The function and the pattern of organization become tools in achieving the presenter's goal and in meeting the audience's expectations.

Persuasive presentations perform one or more of the following functions: (1) to *reinforce* the listeners' beliefs, attitudes, or values; (2) to *refute,* or disprove, an idea or belief held by the listeners; (3) to *change* the listeners' beliefs, actions, or values; and (4) to *move* the listeners to action. As with informative presentations, the pattern used to organize the information in a persuasive presentation is itself a tool for achieving the presenter's goal.

The lines separating these four persuasive functions (as well, for that matter, as the line separating informing and persuading) are more permeable than solid. It is not uncommon for a speaker to discover that the audience considers the speaker's informative thesis to be a persuasive one (or vice versa). The audience, for example, may perceive a speaker's informative speech on a vegetarian lifestyle as an attempt to either reinforce or change their lifestyle (persuasive). While speakers should try to anticipate such problems, it is not always possible to avoid them, and the speaker needs to be prepared to adapt.

In the current case of the four functions of persuasive presentations, it is often the case that a presentation includes multiple functions—for example, the speaker may wish to refute some ideas or beliefs while reinforcing others; or the speaker may attempt to change the audience's beliefs or values before asking them to take a particular action. Thus, while in the next sections we pair function and pattern, the reality is seldom that simple. More frequently, the speaker will need to create a presentation by mixing and matching the options we present.

Reinforcement

Many persuasive presentations are designed to maintain the status quo by reinforcing audience members' decisions, actions, or opinions, especially if the presenter believes that they are under attack or are in danger of being changed or rendered obsolete. To make such a presentation persuasive, the speaker must show that existing favorable conditions are in danger of becoming nonexistent or unfavorable.

This approach can be used to achieve a variety of goals: alerting a sales force to the need to reverse a trend toward providing less personalized service to clients, recommending that a planning committee "get back to basics" and concentrate on core markets, or even petitioning a school board to back away from a proposed change in the process of textbook selection. When organizing the presentation, the speaker must first show the benefits of the present condition, then describe the threat to the status quo, and finally reemphasize the worth and viability of the present condition.

The following example shows how these steps are accomplished. It is an outline of a presentation made by a teacher to a school board that was considering legislation that would allow parents and community officials to participate in the process of selecting books for the school system. [*Note:* After each main point in the outline (and in other outlines in the chapter), we suggest options for locating and incorporating appropriate supporting materials.[1]]

Thesis: My audience will agree that the school system's current textbook selection process should be retained.

Introduction: Motivate the audience to listen by recounting a similar situation in Fargo, North Dakota; orient the audience by stating your opinion that book selection should be the responsibility of teachers and school officials; build rapport by describing your experience as a teacher in the school system.

I. First main point: Although selecting textbooks has always been the duty of school officials, parental and community intervention in book selection is gradually increasing.
   A. Testimony: A quotation from an urban history or history of education textbook can be used to describe the historical role of teachers and school officials in textbook selection.
   B. Statistics: Statistics from a contemporary newspaper or journal such as *USA Today* can provide evidence that intervention in the selection process is increasing.

II. Second main point: The problem with such intervention is that parents and community leaders often cannot agree (with one another or with the school board) on the proper curricula and objectives for students.
   A. Example: Use an illustration from a newsmagazine, newspaper, or education journal to highlight a similar situation in another city.
   B. Example: Provide a contrasting example of a city that has successfully avoided the problem.

1. This outline and others in this chapter are adapted from K. J. Krayer, *Basic Speech Communications Workbook* (Dallas: Bellwether Press, 1987).

FIGURE 15.1

Visual Impact

This visual enhances the impact of the speaker's words by using familiar images to represent the negative effect of a change in the status quo.

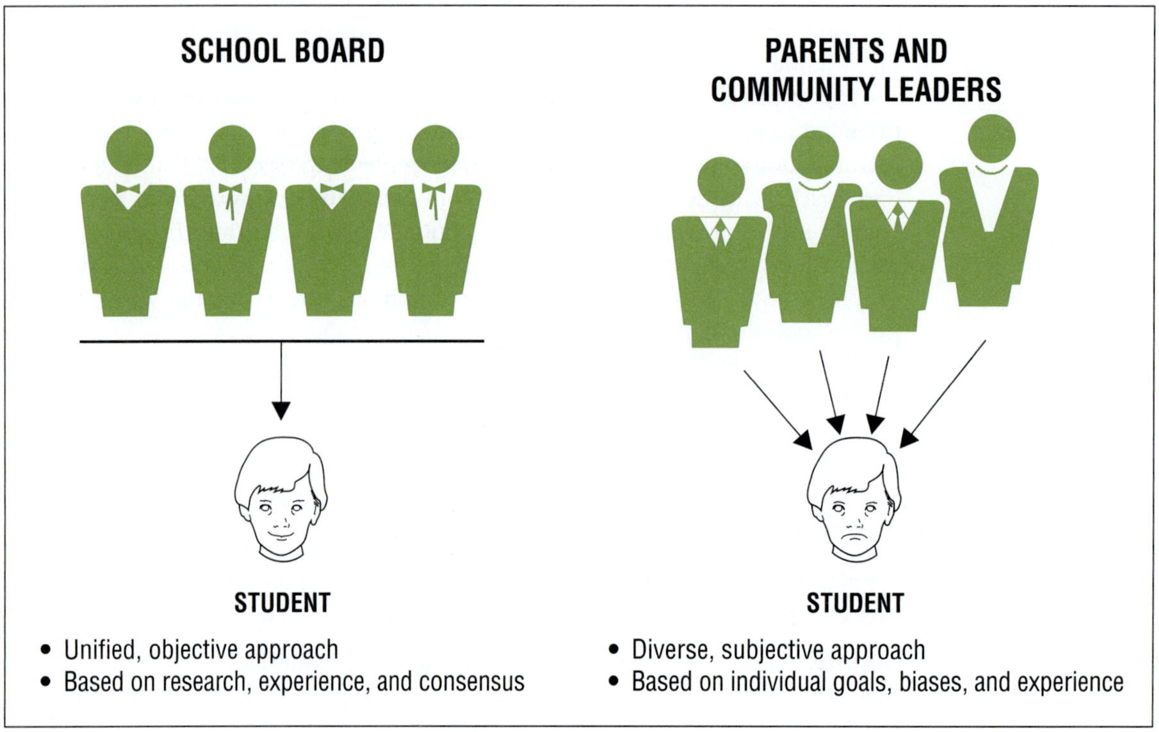

III. Third main point: Parental and community interference in the selection process may potentially limit learning.
   A. Statistics: Cite research done in this area, which may be found in an academic journal such as *Educational Psychologist* or *American Educational Research Journal.*
   B. Visual: Use an overhead or large chart to represent graphically the effect of interference on the student (Figure 15.1).

IV. Fourth main point: Parental input into textbook selection restricts student exposure to a variety of viewpoints.
   A. Explanation: Explain what "restriction" means in terms of a well-rounded education.
   B. Testimony: Quote a well-known and well-respected educational leader who disagrees with restrictions on learning.

Conclusion: Ask for the school board to reject legislation (maintain the status quo) based on these arguments. State the significance of doing so by noting that one role of education is to give students the means and information to decide among a variety of divergent perspectives. Close with testimony: quote students from your classes who are eager to learn and explore.

Refutation

A second type of persuasive presentation works to show listeners that a belief, event, or situation is misunderstood or misconceptualized so that the audience will accept a new or different interpretation of it. By effectively *refuting,* or arguing against, the existing perception, the speaker can correct or clarify the audience members' thinking on the subject and persuade them to accept her or his interpretation of it.

A refutative presentation generally begins by exposing the misunderstanding or incorrect assumption, then provides several points that disprove it or show that it is at best a partial truth. The following outline of a presentation given by a financial analyst to a consumer group shows how this can be achieved.

Thesis: My audience will understand that the causes of inflation are multiple and complex rather than singular and simple.

Introduction: Orient the audience members by welcoming them to the presentation; motivate the audience by reading a quote about inflation from a newsmagazine; build rapport by explaining that the purpose of the presentation is to help audience members understand that many interrelated factors cause inflation.

I. First main point: Many Americans blame the government for spiraling inflation.
   A. Statistics: Use statistics (which can be located through indexes such as the *Gallup Index*) to show that the public thinks the government is responsible for causing inflation.
   B. Example: Give an account of government spending on seemingly obscure or wasteful projects, such as studying methane production in cows.
II. Second main point: In reality, one of the major causes of inflation is consumers' erratic spending patterns.
   A. Testimony: Quote a respected economist on the subject.
   B. Visual: Use a graph or chart to show the relationship between consumer spending and inflation during the past ten years.
III. Third main point: Demands for higher wages without strong growth in the gross national product (GNP) may contribute to inflation as well.
   A. Statistics: Cite the recent slowdown in growth of the GNP. A newspaper such as the *Wall Street Journal* can provide statistics on the GNP.
   B. Example: Journals such as the *Journal of Human Resources* and the *Industrial and Labor Relations Review* may provide examples of wage negotiations in a range of industries.
IV. Fourth main point: Unwise investment, both by individuals and by banking institutions, is another problem.
   A. Testimony: Quote from noted financial analysts to show that many investments offering quick, high returns are deceptive and possibly fraudulent.
   B. Explanation: Provide a brief explanation of investment practices in the savings and loan industry and their results.

Conclusion: Summarize the complex nature of inflation; state the significance by noting that understanding is the first step toward tackling the problem; ask for questions.

Promoting Change

Persuasive presentations that call for a change in audience members' beliefs, attitudes, actions, or values go one step further than those that refute existing beliefs or values. The speaker attempts to *redirect* the course of the listeners' thoughts or behavior.

When organizing the presentation, the presenter first shows the prevalent belief or action. The successive main points provide reasons audience members should adopt a new belief or change their behavior. The presenter does this by citing the advantages of the new belief/behavior or the disadvantages that will occur by holding on to the old belief/behavior. The following example is excerpted from an outline of a presentation given to several groups of executives at a small department store.

Thesis: My audience will agree that our current policy of monthly promotional sales needs to be changed.

Introduction: Orient the audience to the reason for the presentation by citing declining sales revenues; motivate the audience to listen by telling the story of a customer who was surprised to find an item *not* included in a promotional sale; build rapport by noting your recent participation in a national promotional convention where alternative techniques for promotional sales were discussed.

I. First main point: We currently hold promotional sales in practically every department of our stores on a monthly basis.
    A. Explanation: Describe the practice of monthly promotional sales.
    B. Explanation: Use an article from the company newsletter to summarize why we have adhered to the policy.

II. Second main point: We need to change our policy for several reasons. One is that promotional sales do not necessarily increase customer traffic.
    A. Statistics: Specialized periodicals such as *Sales Promotion Monitor* and *Shopper Report* may contain research data in this area.
    B. Example: Describe an informal study you did over the last three months that showed nearly constant traffic, regardless of the promotional sales.

III. Third main point: Frequent promotional sales generally do not increase a store's sales revenues.
    A. Visual: Display a key quote from a professional journal such as *Ad Review* that supports this position (see the Strategic Skills box on page 433).
    B. Statistics: Note that statistics provided by our accounting department show that volume varies seasonally, but the pattern is not influenced by our promotional sales.

IV. Fourth main point: We should consider changes in our promotional sales policy that will help us achieve the goal of promotional sales—more customers making more purchases.
    A. We need to take advantage of natural trends in buying (such as seasonal trends).
    B. We need to hold less frequent, better advertised promotional sales at strategic points throughout the year.

Note that the fourth main point *restates the need for change* while *providing suggestions* to accomplish the change. Such an ending is more effective than simply giving the listeners several reasons why their current belief or practice is not the best one. By providing an alternate belief or plan of action, the speaker primes the audience to act on her or his suggestion, as we will discuss in the next section.

Call to Action

The main purpose of many persuasive presentations is to get listeners to act on the advice or direction of the speaker. This type of presentation differs slightly from one in which the speaker's goal is to bring about a change in the audience members' actions—an effective approach for *initiating* audience action differs from one meant to *modify* it.

STRATEGIC SKILLS

Using Expert Testimony

The testimony of a well-respected individual can persuade listeners to accept a change in their beliefs or actions. A visual that displays testimony as the presenter speaks it reinforces its effect by using multiple channels.

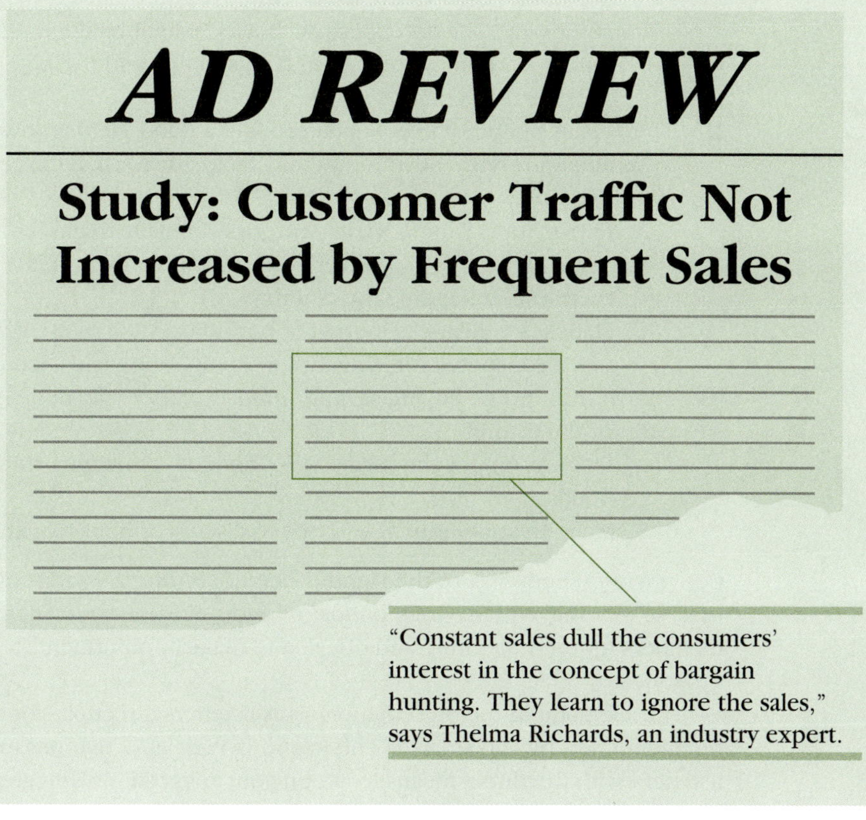

The first main point of a presentation that calls listeners to action identifies the problem or shortcoming that exists. The second main point, however, demonstrates that the problem will not or cannot be solved or that no attempt is being made to solve it at the current time. In the remaining points, the speaker presents her or his proposed solution and urges the audience to act on the suggestion.

The following example shows an outline of a presentation made by the payroll director at a large company to groups of employees who had enrolled in a series of seminars on investment. Because the employees had little previous experience with the various options for investment, this presentation, the first of the series, begins with the basics.

Thesis: My audience will accept savings bonds as a good investment and buy them.

Introduction: Orient the audience by giving a brief overview of what each lecture will contain and a specific preview of this first lecture; motivate and build rapport by giving some examples of how listeners will benefit from acting on what they learn during this presentation.

I. First main point: The number of savings bonds purchased has steadily declined, costing the country billions of dollars in liquid capital.
    A. Explanation: Describe what a savings bond is and how it works.
    B. Explanation: Give a definition of "liquid capital" in mainstream terms.

II. Second main point: Due to widespread misconceptions about the nature of savings bonds, they are often overlooked by beginning investors.
    A. Example: Illustrate the misconceptions held by our own work force by giving several brief examples of employees' attitudes toward savings bonds.
    B. Testimony: Cite an expert, such as a federal banking official, on reasons for the declining interest in savings bonds and the potential negative results for the economy.

III. Third main point: Savings bonds provide a good yield at low risk, contribute to national growth and stability, and have always been an excellent way to start investing.
    A. Explanation: Define "yield" and "risk" in mainstream terms.
    B. Visual: Show an old advertisement for savings bonds to demonstrate their role in building the country.
    C. Statistics: A financial journal or periodical such as the *Wall Street Journal* may be a source for statistics on comparing yields and calculating risks.

IV. Fourth main point: Buying savings bonds is very easily done—act now to prepare for the future!
    A. Pick up one of the forms I've provided explaining how to buy savings bonds.
    B. Make an appointment with me to discuss options for similar investments.

Conclusion: Reemphasize the significance of starting a savings plan now and the ease of starting with savings bonds; provide closure by thanking the audience members for their attention and offering to make appointments to answer specific questions.

The last point in the presentation gives listeners directions for taking the action recommended by the speaker. This tactic is very effective because by providing listeners with the direct means to act on your suggestions, you greatly increase the chances that they will do so.

PERSUASIVE FORMATS

Persuasive presentations in a business or organizational context can take a number of forms. Any of the purposes we have just discussed can be realized through these forms. Three of the most commonly used formats include sales, proposals, and motivational sessions.

Sales Presentations

Selling products, services, or ideas occupies a great deal of time in organizational life. In addition to one-on-one selling opportunities, in many cases sales presentations are formal events in which a speaker in the front of a room gives a presentation utilizing visual aids and the audience is seated in an organized fashion.

Note that in sales presentations the speaker may be required to reinforce a belief in his or her product if the organization is about to discontinue using it. The speaker may need to change the attitude of a group of buyers toward the product line. Or the speaker may attempt to close a sale at the time of the presentation by convincing the audience to purchase the product. Thus, a sales presentation frequently will incorporate several major functions of persuasion.

Proposals

Businesses and professional organizations are frequently inundated with proposals that must be acted upon. The choice of action often depends on the persuasiveness with which a proposal's backer presents it. Even when the speaker succeeds, proposals are often modified from their original form before they are accepted.

Here are a few examples of proposals that might be presented to business and professional audiences:

A plan to upgrade all personal computers in the corporate headquarters office
A budget for a ten-day "outward bound" training program for corporate executives at a remote site
A schedule for moving the home office of a company from one building to another
A method by which an employee's grievance may be settled without incurring costly court proceedings
A plan to employ a work force with greater multicultural diversity

Proposals can be designed to reinforce beliefs, change beliefs, or induce action. For example, a presentation by a marketing manager may be designed to reinforce a plan to print new brochures despite some disagreement or criticism of the plan. A presentation by a personnel administrator may attempt to persuade audience members to reverse their decision on allocating funding for professional travel. Or a presentation may call for the listeners to sign their benefits contracts or to return borrowed equipment.

Motivational Sessions

Persuasive presentations can certainly be motivational. You may be familiar with some of the great motivational speakers of our time, including Tom Peters, author of *In Search of Excellence;* Zig Ziglar, of *See You at the Top* fame; and Lou Holtz,

What Would You Do?

Your boss has asked you to chair a work group to recommend a vendor from which to purchase some new office furniture. Your group has met and reached a consensus, despite the objections you raised. How will you handle your reservations about the wisdom of the group's choice when your group meets with the boss and you are asked to make the report? Would your answer change if the issue were more significant (e.g., proposing the replacement of a product line for your organization)? Why or why not?

formerly of Notre Dame football.[2] Each of these speakers is enthusiastic and has a strong delivery, as demonstrated by the ways they vary inflection, emphasis, rate, volume, and gestures. Furthermore, their messages are typically upbeat and filled with inspiring words that instill confidence in the listener.

Many motivational speakers use persuasion to convince an audience to change its attitude so that each person becomes better, healthier, or happier. Some attempt to convince listeners to lose weight, invest money, perform a task better, manage employees differently, or be more enthusiastic communicators.

Crisis Situations

Times of crisis occur in all organizations. Corporate takeovers, consolidation of large industries, downsizing of companies, scandals in management, and erroneous administrative decisions in major U.S. companies are just a few examples of crises in business. In the medical, academic, government, and legal professions, societal changes and financial upswings and downturns have created controversial and unproductive climates. Within these organizations and professions, managers, employees, and outside consultants have used persuasive presentations to make transitions, facilitate change, and placate irate or displaced employees.

BASIC RESOURCES FOR PERSUASION

Persuasion is not just form and content; successful presentations in businesses and professional organizations take advantage of resources. We now turn our attention to some of the resources that are available to you as a persuasive speaker.

The Listeners' Perspective

As in informative presentations, audience analysis and adaptation are the key to success in a persuasive presentation. Nevertheless, the audience is considered from a slightly different angle. The power in a persuasive presentation resides in an analysis of what makes the listeners "tick"—knowing what triggers the listeners is crucial. Table 15.1 shows a variety of methods for connecting with listeners, as opposed to focusing on the speaker's needs and personal interests.

2. T. J. Peters and R. H. Waterman, Jr., *In Search of Excellence: Lessons from America's Best-Run Companies* (New York: Harper & Row, 1982); Z. Ziglar, *See You at the Top* (Gretna, La.: Pelican, 1975).

TABLE 15.1

Speaker Versus Listener Perspective

Speaker Perspective	Listener Perspective
Speaker uses arguments and appeals that are pleasing to him or her.	Speaker uses arguments and appeals that are pleasing to the audience.
Speaker uses style and delivery that are natural for him or her.	Speaker uses style and delivery that will be effective and liked by the audience.
Speaker says what makes him or her feel better.	Speaker says what will bring the desired response from the audience.
Speaker views the situation from his or her point of view.	Speaker views the situation from the audience's point of view.
Speaker selects sources and authorities that are his or her favorites.	Speaker selects sources and authorities that are likely to be acceptable to the listeners.
Speaker dresses to please himself or herself.	Speaker dresses in accordance with the tastes and preferences of the audience.
Speaker assumes others share his or her beliefs, attitudes, and values.	Speaker searches for the beliefs, attitudes, and values that are held by the audience.

More than just sharing a perspective, as in an informative presentation, a persuasive presenter must take the listeners' perspective because he or she (the presenter) is asking more of the audience, be it a change in beliefs or a call to action. Consider Martin Luther King Jr.'s famous address in 1963, in which he repeatedly chanted before each point, "I have a dream."

> I say to you today, my friends, so even though we face the difficulties of today and tomorrow, I still have a dream. It is a dream deeply rooted in the American dream.
>
> I have a dream that one day this nation will rise up and live out the true meaning of its creed: "We hold these truths to be self-evident; that all men are created equal."
>
> I have a dream that one day on the red hills of Georgia the sons of former slaves and the sons of former slaveowners will be able to sit down together at the table of brotherhood; I have a dream—
>
> That one day even the state of Mississippi, a state sweltering with the heat of injustice, sweltering with the heat of oppression, will be transformed into an oasis of freedom and justice; I have a dream—
>
> That my four little children will one day live in a nation where they will not be judged by the color of their skin but by the content of their character; I have a dream today.
>
> I have a dream that one day down in Alabama, with its vicious racists, with its governor having his lips dripping with the words of interposition and nullification, one day right there in Alabama little black boys and black girls will be able to join hands with little white boys and white girls as sisters and brothers; I have a dream today.

> I have a dream that one day every valley shall be exalted; every hill and mountain shall be made low, and rough places will be made plain and crooked places will be made straight, and the glory of the Lord shall be revealed, and all flesh shall see it together.[3]

When a speaker encounters an unsympathetic, or even hostile, audience, other adaptations are necessary. Some of the actions a speaker can take are (1) to appeal to the audience for a chance to explain his or her side of the story; (2) to begin the presentation with points that reflect shared values, attitudes, and beliefs on which to base later points of disagreement; (3) to minimize the differences and maximize the similarities in opinion between speaker and audience; and (4) to shorten the gap between points, thus rendering it more difficult for the audience to interrupt or to react in unfavorable ways. When Anson Mount, manager of public relations for *Playboy,* agreed to speak on the merits of the "*Playboy* philosophy" as part of a seminar sponsored by the Christian Life Commission of the Southern Baptist Convention at its meeting in Atlanta, Georgia, in 1970, he certainly needed to go further than merely sharing his perspective with the conventioneers. Note how Mount started his speech:

> I am sure we are all aware of the seeming incongruity of a representative of *Playboy* magazine speaking to an assemblage of representatives of the Southern Baptist Convention. I was intrigued by the invitation when it came last fall, though I was not surprised. I am grateful for your genuine and warm hospitality, and I am flattered (though again not surprised) by the implication that I would have something to say that could have meaning to you people. Both *Playboy* and the Baptists have indeed been considering many of the same issues and ethical problems; and even if we have not arrived at the same conclusions, I am impressed and gratified by your openness and willingness to listen to our views.[4]

Motivators

Motivators are a second valuable resource for persuasion. Discovering what motivates people is a topic that has been discussed since the beginning of time. The classic work on motivation and persuasion was written by Abraham Maslow, who established five levels of human needs.[5] He ranked the needs in order of their importance:

1. *Basic needs* include access to air, food, water, sex, sleep, and elimination of waste.
2. *Security needs* comprise freedom from threats to one's physical well-being.
3. *Love and belonging needs* include sympathy, friendship, and acceptance.
4. *Esteem needs* are needs for pride, honor, duty, reputation, recognition, loyalty, and competition.
5. *Self-actualization needs* include adventure and fulfillment of one's potential.

3. W. A. Linkugel, R. R. Allen, and R. L. Johannesen, *Contemporary American Speeches,* 5th ed. (Dubuque, Iowa: Kendall/Hunt, 1982), p. 369. Reprinted by arrangement with The Heirs to the Estate of Martin Luther King, Jr., c/o Writer's House, Inc. as agent for the proprietor. Copyright © 1963 by Martin Luther King, Jr., copyright renewed 1991 by Coretta Scott King.
4. Ibid., p. 178. Reprinted by permission of the Southern Baptist Convention, the Estate of Anson Mount, and the Christian Life Commission of the Southern Baptist Church.
5. A. H. Maslow, *Motivation and Personality* (New York: Harper & Row, 1954).

Without knowing the context in which this photo was taken, where on Maslow's hierarchy of needs would you place the three individuals? Why? (Riza Ozel/AFP/Getty Images)

Maslow's hierarchy of needs is based on the argument that lower-level needs must be satisfied before higher-level needs can be motivating factors. According to Maslow, once a lower-level need has been satisfied, it no longer serves as a motivating force. When this scheme is applied to persuasion, the speaker's task becomes to identify audience needs and then to phrase appeals that will fulfill those needs.

Let us look at an example of how this works in a presentation. A developer is planning a strategy to persuade members of a community group to invest funds to build a marina in their town. The appeal that the developer uses in her presentation is determined by her assessment of the listeners' needs.

The developer decides to appeal to the group's esteem needs by arguing that "this is the best contribution to the community your group can make; with this marina, your town will gain visibility and prestige and, of course, community members would have prime access to boat slips." The appeal could be successful if the community group members have all fulfilled their belonging and safety needs. But suppose that the group has an ongoing problem with vandalism and vagrancy in its neighborhood and that some residents do not feel safe on the streets at night. The esteem appeal will not be motivating for the group if lower-level needs are still wanting. To be persuasive, the developer will have to pitch an appeal to a need that is still unfulfilled.

The key to motivational resources is identifying the threshold level at which audience needs are fulfilled. Having identified that point, the speaker may then phrase an appeal that targets those needs that are still unfulfilled.

Opinion Leaders

Opinion leaders are people who are capable of influencing others' decisions, attitudes, and behavior. Their judgments, taste, and background are respected. They are credible sources for you on a wide range of topics. As such, they are a powerful resource for persuasive presentations.

Where Do You Stand?

Who are your opinion leaders? Compare your ideas with the ideas of others in your class, and discuss the reasons for your choices.

Practically every organized group has at least one opinion leader; some have several. Importantly, opinion leaders are not necessarily those who are high in rank within a business or organization; some very knowledgeable and respected individuals can be found within the "ranks." In the House of Representatives, for example, there are influential opinion leaders who will never be the Speaker of the House or even the chairperson of a committee. Yet their years of service and loyal constituent base make them influential. The same is true of business settings. Influence in an organization does not always follow the patterns outlined on an organizational chart. In many offices, for example, a key secretary may be the most influential opinion leader for many important issues.

Identifying opinion leaders in an audience can be an important resource for effective persuasion. Linking your message to a person whom the audience respects is a means of bringing about instant acceptance. Aligning your ideas to coincide with those of an individual whom the listeners already believe in or admire can be critical to persuasion as well.

If you want to use the influence of opinion leaders for your presentations, you cannot be shy about doing so. Remember that audience members rarely draw links for themselves. You must do this for them. Listeners will probably not think, "That sounds just like what Mr. Peters would say." If Mr. Peters is an opinion leader for this audience, overtly claim his support of the idea you wish your listeners to accept. To make effective use of opinion leaders, reference their names clearly and frequently, demonstrate ways in which your ideas are similar to their ideas, and give credit to their accomplishments through liberal use of examples, incidents, illustrations, or case studies.

Critical Thinking and Persuasion

The critical thinking skills—analysis, reasoning, interpretation, and evaluation—introduced in Chapter 10 play a vital role in persuasive presentations. Strong use of evidence (supporting materials) and reasoning enables the speaker to create a message that is logically sound and well argued and that can withstand questions or attacks. A presentation that incorporates logical reasoning, analysis, and interpretation works persuasively in the minds of listeners as they apply their own critical thinking skills to it. We strongly encourage you to review the section on critical thinking in Chapter 10 and to seek opportunities to apply these skills to your presentations.

Source Credibility

That a speaker can be persuasive because he or she is credible was recognized in ancient times by Greek and Roman scholars who labeled this concept **ethos.** In *Rhetoric,* Aristotle wrote:

> Persuasion is achieved by the speaker's personal character when the speech is so spoken as to make us think him credible. We believe good men more fully and more readily than others: this is true generally whatever the question is, and absolutely true where exact certainty is impossible and opinions are divided. . . . His character may almost be called the most effective means of persuasion he possesses.[6]

6. Aristotle, *Rhetoric* (New York: Modern Library, 1954).

As a persuasive speaker like the one pictured here, you will want your audience to care about your cause or want to move them to some action. To successfully do this, you will need to use appeals that touch their hearts as well as their minds. (© Ramin Talaie/ Corbis)

In essence, when we talk about credibility, we mean that an audience can be persuaded on the basis of who the speaker is or what he or she has to say. There are two sources that yield credibility in a presentational context and are thus important for persuasion: the speaker and his or her supporting materials. The audience perceives credibility in the speaker by what it knows about him or her before the presentation or learns about him or her during the presentation. The speaker, in turn, derives credibility from sources, whether they are quotations, testimonies, statistics from studies, or other evidence.

In American society, people are very influenced by source credibility. Why do people buy a name-brand can of green beans instead of a store-label version? What is so magical about a car with "Ltd." after its name? Is a professor with a Ph.D. more credible than one with an M.S. or an M.A.?

Put this book down for a moment. Who is the most credible source that you can think of? This person is instantly believable to you: if he or she says something, it must be right! We all have someone who is credible to us, whether it be our father or mother, a physician, a minister, an instructor whose courses we have taken several times, or a writer or broadcaster from the media. Indeed, the media also contain sources that have more or less credibility than others. Would you be more likely to believe something you read in the *New York Times* or something you read in *The Enquirer*?

Note, however, that credibility is based solely on the audience's perception; it does not exist in any absolute or tangible sense. As a speaker in a business or professional organization, you have control over the information you allow an audience to have, and you therefore can shape how the audience evaluates your character and grants you credibility.

Early studies on source credibility demonstrated its significance. In this research, investigators typically varied the credibility of the source while holding the message constant and using equivalent audiences. In one such study,[7] two audiences heard an audiotaped persuasive speech on zero population growth. The two audiences had been pretested for their attitudes about family planning, and they were roughly equivalent before the speech was given.

Both audiences heard the same presentation. One was told that the speaker was a "nationally famous expert on family planning." The other audience was told that the speaker was a "student at the University of Michigan." Posttesting revealed that the people who thought they were hearing a national expert changed their minds significantly more than the other audience did. Given that the speaker's background was the only variant, credibility obviously produced the difference.

There is no sensible reason not to enhance credibility during a presentation wherever possible. "If no other reason exists for seeking high credibility, being liked and respected is more pleasant than suffering the opposites."[8]

Where Do You Stand?

Describe your credibility with your family, your work colleagues (if you are employed), and your classmates. What are the implications of the similarities and differences in your descriptions of these three audiences for speaking in this class?

Components of Credibility Three primary components make up source credibility for presenters: trustworthiness, competence, and dynamism.[9] These factors are what audiences consider when they label a speaker or a source as either credible or not credible.

Trustworthiness refers to the way that a source is perceived as being honest, friendly, warm, agreeable, or safe, instead of dangerous or threatening. In his final White House days, Richard Nixon was no longer perceived as trustworthy by the American people and was forced to resign. In the world of business, Arthur Andersen (the accounting firm involved in the Enron scandal) lost the trust of its clients and of the American public—and went out of business as a result. Rudi Giuliani, through his masterful public speeches during the aftermath of the September 11 attacks in New York City, became one of the most trustworthy leaders in America.

The second dimension, **competence,** is based on the source's expertise, training, experience, skill, ability, authoritativeness, and intelligence. Many people believe that competence is the single most important factor in determining the degree to which a source has credibility. Thus, when a speaker's competence to speak on a topic is suspect, a major effort is required to remedy this perceived defect. Consider the case of James Michener, author of many best-selling novels, who addressed the U.S. Senate Subcommittee on Science, Technology, and Space in Washington, D.C., on February 1, 1975. Because an author, even a Pulitzer Prize-winning one, is not an expert on space, Michener began his speech by raising the question of his competence and offering a plausible defense of his right to testify:

> The only justification for allowing me to appear before your Committee is that for some years I have been studying the rise and fall of nations and in so doing have reached certain conclusions governing that process. There seem to be great tides which operate in the history of civilization, and nations are prudent if they estimate the force of those tides, their genesis, and the extent to which they can be utilized. A nation which guesses wrong on all its estimates is apt to be in serious trouble if not on the brink of decline. Toward the middle of the

7. E. P. Bettinghaus, *Persuasive Communication,* 2d ed. (New York: Holt, Rinehart & Winston, 1973).
8. W. N. Thompson, *The Process of Persuasion: Principles and Readings* (New York: Harper & Row, 1975), p. 72.
9. J. L. Whitehead, Jr., "Factors of Source Credibility," *Quarterly Journal of Speech* 54 (1968), 59–63.

fifteenth century the minds of sensible men were filled with speculations about the nature of their world and, although not much solid evidence was available, clever minds could piece together the fragments and achieve quite remarkable deductions.[10]

Finally, **dynamism** is composed of a speaker's energy, liveliness, boldness, activity, forcefulness, and frankness. Many competent speakers who would otherwise be perceived as quite credible damage this assessment because they fail to be dynamic. Some research has shown that speakers who demonstrate high levels of dynamism are likely to be perceived as more competent and believable than speakers who fail to do this.

Occurrences of Credibility You may ask, "Where does credibility come into play during a presentation?" The answer is that it comes into play at all stages of the process. Audiences are more likely to attend presentations by and pay attention to speakers they consider credible, making credibility an important pre-presentation concern. Credibility is also an important factor during the presentation, as audience members are more likely to accept what they hear from someone they consider credible. Finally, audience members are more willing to carry out a commitment urged by a credible speaker.

Audiences can learn about a speaker's credibility before he or she even utters a word. Because this learning occurs outside of the presentation the speaker gives, it is called extrinsic credibility. There are many ways that extrinsic credibility can be built. Some word about how "good" or "bad" a speaker is can float down from other people who have previously heard the speaker. A listener can also read about a speaker in the newspaper or company newsletter. And prior experience with the speaker lets audience members know what they can expect in the presentation to follow.

One of the most important ways that extrinsic credibility is communicated to an audience is through the introduction of the speaker immediately before the presentation. Items such as the speaker's qualifications, memberships in groups, past or present positions, and recent accomplishments can be given to bolster the speaker's credibility with the audience. Remember, however, that the audience decides whether credibility exists. If listeners do not understand a speaker's qualifications or do not have any admiration for the groups in which the speaker holds membership, her or his credibility will not be enhanced.

Credibility also plays an intrinsic role within the presentation itself. Here the audience learns about a speaker from listening, observing, and inferring. Factors such as the speaker's preparedness, seriousness, sincerity, poise, evenhandedness, firmness, dress, and appearance all give information to listeners that can affect their judgments of her or his credibility.

Extrinsic and intrinsic credibility can work well together. What a listener has heard about a speaker extrinsically can either be strengthened or weakened when assessments of intrinsic credibility are made. If a listener has heard that a speaker is "wonderful" (extrinsic), and he or she falls short on some of the factors just discussed (intrinsic), the listener's judgment of the speaker's credibility will be worsened. If, however, the listener has heard that a speaker is "not worth hearing" (ex-

10. Speech by James Michener as it appeared in Linkugel, Allen, and Johannesen, *Contemporary American Speeches,* 1982. Reprinted by permission of the William Morris Agency, Inc. on behalf of the author.

ETHICAL ISSUES

Vested Interests

Imagine that you are trying to persuade your employer to buy a particular Brand X portable computer for employees to use for business trips. You are to make a presentation to a management committee, and you want to give members convincing evidence for your recommendation. You also want to make the presentation in an ethical fashion.

You like the selected model for a variety of reasons, including the fact that your spouse works part-time for Brand X and has told you a lot of good things about it.

- As you think through the presentation, what, if any, ethical issues will you encounter? What are some possible ways of dealing with them? Which would you choose?
- Would your answer change if you or your family owned stock in Brand X? Why or why not?
- Can you imagine other situations that would make ethical issues more or less salient for your situation?

trinsic), but he or she does well in the speech (intrinsic), the listener's assessment will be favorably changed.

As a speaker, you can build your own credibility as well as the credibility of your sources by providing their qualifications, accomplishments, company or university affiliations, or academic degrees wherever necessary. If you are citing a research study as part of your evidence, build up the quality of the study by explaining the circumstances under which it was done and the methodology, the timeliness, or any other information that will lend credence to the findings.

THE PERSUASION PROCESS

We now turn to the process through which persuasion occurs and to some strategies you may be called on to use when speaking to, for, or within your business or professional organization.[11]

The **process of persuasion** has five distinct stages: awareness, interest, evaluation, trial, and adoption. If anywhere along the line the listener "withdraws" from the process, persuasion will not result. Listeners must first be aware that a proposal exists. They then have to be interested in hearing more. After learning more about the topic, they then evaluate the feelings or reactions that they have formed. In many cases, there is a trial period to assess the feasibility of the proposal. If the outcome of the trial is favorable, they then adopt the proposal and put it into practice or action.

Here is an example of how these five stages work, as applied to a presentation in which junior executives are proposing to senior management that they be allowed to travel on sales incentive trips. In this company, the trips are reserved only for top management.

Awareness: "Junior executives should be permitted to travel on sales incentive trips." (The management group may not have even known that competing companies offered trips to their junior executives!)

Interest: "The long-term results of sending junior executives on these trips are beneficial to the company." (The management group may want to know what these results are.)

Evaluation: "Think of the large return on such a small investment." (The management group may ponder this benefit.)

11. Bettinghaus, *Persuasive Communication,* pp. 248–272.

Trial: "Give this plan a chance for one year to see how it works." (The management group may consider a shorter period to assess results.)
Adoption: "If the trial period yields results that meet or exceed expectations, the activity will become permanent policy."

Of course, the process is not infallible. Think about how many times you have listened to a persuasive presentation and have "withdrawn" at some point in the process. It happens with great regularity. You may be made aware of an issue, become convinced of its logic, and even think it is a good idea, but you just do not want to implement it! As a result, you are not persuaded. The following strategies can help speakers prevent such persuasion "dropouts."

Ego Involvement

Ego involvement refers to how important a particular topic or issue is to a listener. For the most part, ego involvement is determined by the listener's commitment to the topic in terms of time, money, prestige, or even "ownership," or possession, of the topic.

Ego involvement is reflected by the *latitudes of acceptance and rejection* held by the listener. Latitudes of acceptance are determined by asking, "Given a person's commitment to an issue, how likely is the person to accept a particular persuasive message related to that issue?" Latitudes of rejection are determined by asking, "Given a person's commitment to an issue, how likely is the person to reject a particular persuasive message?" It follows that the higher the listener's ego involvement is, the smaller are the latitudes of acceptance and the greater are the latitudes of rejection. The lower the listener's ego involvement is, the greater are the latitudes of acceptance and the smaller are the latitudes of rejection.

Suppose you are speaking to three coauthors of a book who have worked diligently on it for several years. Their ego involvement in the project is quite high. Correspondingly, there are very few changes to the book that they will accept and many suggestions they will reject. The chance that you can convince them to restructure the book from start to finish is slight. But you may persuade them to modify the cover design or to add an extra chapter.

Order Effects

Every persuasive presentation has some arguments that are stronger than others. The question frequently facing a speaker is "In what order should I present my arguments?"[12] The speaker can usually choose from one of three options.

In a **climax order,** the weakest argument is presented first and the strongest last; this organization provides a recency effect, meaning that the audience will most likely remember the last (and strongest) argument. In an **anticlimax order,** the strongest argument is presented first, and weaker arguments follow; this plan gives a primacy effect (audience members are immediately struck by the strength of the argument). In a **pyramidal order,** the speaker places the strongest argument between two weaker ones.

The decision of which to employ is up to you. If you are planning to give the presentation more than once, you may wish to experiment until you are comfort-

12. H. Gulley and D. K. Berlo, "Effects of Intercellular and Intracellular Speech Structure on Attitude Change and Learning," *Speech Monographs* 23 (1956), 288–297.

STRATEGIC SKILLS

Additional Hints for Persuasive Presentations

Some of your most challenging presentations in the business world will be persuasive in nature. When you combine the resources specified in this chapter with the material in Chapters 13 and 14, you should be prepared to face persuasive challenges in a confident and effective way. When facing such a challenge, you can also consider the following hints:

1. In persuasion, try to give listeners the feeling that the proposal you are advocating is a natural extension of directions in which they are tending.
2. Because people agree more readily about abstract matters than about concrete matters, be especially selective about the specific examples you use early in your speech.
3. Even though all of us identify with certain reference groups, few of us like to admit such "dependence"; therefore, do not make careless attributions about your listeners in their presence.
4. Do not be glib when presenting large-scale statistical information; always try to show the "local consequences" of such data.
5. Even though it is good to have several reasons to support your thesis, using too many will cause your audience to be suspicious of your selectivity.
6. Never underestimate candor; looking at your audience directly and admitting that you disagree with them on some issue can be a prudent course of action.
7. When you speak to a hostile audience, never save your proposal until the conclusion lest you be viewed as a coward.
8. Do not underestimate the power of careful phrasing; language has great power to color ideas. Sometimes, the elimination of bothersome bits of jargon or hackneyed expressions can open up listeners' minds.
9. When you are dealing with a hostile audience, do not allow your voice to become shrill, even though your frustration at the audience's resistance may push you in that direction.

Source: R. P. Hart, G. W. Friedrich, and B. Brummett, *Public Communication,* 2d ed. (New York: Harper & Row, 1983), p. 286. Reprinted with permission of Barry Brummett and Rod Hart.

able with the ordering of your ideas. Research shows that arguments presented early and late are more effective than those presented in the middle. If you have high credibility in the mind of the audience, you will find it better to present strong arguments early in the speech.

One-Sided Versus Two-Sided Presentations

In what circumstances should you bring up the other side's position in your presentation? If you present only your position, the presentation is one-sided; if you bring up the other side's arguments and then refute them, the presentation is two-sided. Research shows the following:

Two-sided presentations are best if the weight of evidence is on your side.
Two-sided presentations are best for better-educated listeners.
Two-sided presentations are best when the listeners initially disagree with your position.
Two-sided presentations are preferable when you believe the listeners will be exposed to the other side following your own presentation.
One-sided presentations are best when the listeners already agree with you, provided that they are not likely to be influenced by later opposing arguments.

STRATEGIC SKILLS

The Persuasive Speech: A Checklist

- Do you have a clear purpose in mind?
- Is the purpose of your speech best described as reinforcing, refuting, promoting change, or calling to action?
- Does your presentation fit into one of the following formats: sales presentation, proposal, motivational session, or crisis situation?
- Given a clear purpose, what are the three to five main points that the audience will need to understand and accept if you are to achieve it?
- What forms of support (e.g., explanations, examples, statistics, testimony, and visual aids) will make your main points most informative, interesting, relevant, clear, and persuasive?
- Are any of the following resources for persuasion relevant to your speech: the listeners' perspective, motivators, opinion leaders, critical thinking, source credibility, ego involvement, order effects, or one-sided versus two-sided presentation?
- Would some form of information technology be most useful in making your presentation?
- How can you best achieve the functions of the introduction (orientation, motivation, and rapport) and conclusion (completeness and closure) of your speech?
- Which type of delivery (impromptu, extemporaneous, manuscript, or memorized) is likely to be most effective in accomplishing your purpose?
- Independent of type of delivery, how can you make your delivery intelligible, conversational, direct, and unobtrusive?
- How will you prepare to field questions from the audience?
- How will you prepare to deal with the anxiety you are likely to experience?
- How will you rehearse your presentation?

SPECIAL OCCASION PRESENTATIONS

Special occasions or ceremonial speeches play a variety of roles in business. Their function is to bring people together to recognize growth, celebrate achievement, support tradition, and reinforce organizational values. These occasions may also be used to boost employee morale or to strengthen commitment to the organization.

All cultures have special occasions. In the United States, special occasion speaking represents a broad spectrum of activities. Each of them has unspoken cultural rules that set boundaries for you as the speaker. These rules govern (1) length of speech, (2) purpose, (3) behavior, (4) appearance, (5) use of humor, (6) seriousness, and (7) language use.

Types of Presentations

Most special occasions are formal. If you are unsure of the appropriate standards, ask. It is better to overdress than to underdress; underdressing may offend some participants. Understanding such issues as dress codes should help you meet the cultural expectations of the people who are in your audience. We will briefly discuss nine types of special occasion presentations.

Introductions Guest speakers who address business and professional groups or are invited to make presentations on university campuses are formally introduced to their audience. The selection of the person who gives the introduction depends on the status of the speaker. For example, Wilma Mankiller, then chief of the Cherokee Nation, spoke in April 1994, in South Bend, Indiana, at a YWCA luncheon for twelve hundred people honoring women of achievement. The person deemed most appropriate to introduce Chief Mankiller was the highest-ranking woman tribal official in the local Potawatomie Nation. At other times the head of ceremonies or moderator, the person responsible for bringing the speaker to the group, or a close colleague may be selected to give the introduction.

Introductions should be brief (from three to five minutes) and should not be used to call attention to the introducer. The focus must be on the guest. The introduction should make the speaker feel welcome, indicate that the group feels privileged to have the person as the speaker, build credibility for the speaker by mentioning facts from his or her biography or résumé (usually supplied by the speaker or his or her public relations representative), announce the title or the subject of the presentation, and set an appropriate tone or mood.

Choose only pertinent facts from the biography or résumé to include in the introduction—information that will raise the credibility of the speaker. A few of your choices are the title of current or past positions held, academic degrees earned, honorary degrees earned, offices held in organizations, awards or honors received, places traveled to, books or other materials published, programs or panels participated in, outstanding career achievements, and personal achievements or interests (family, hobbies, skills). Obviously, not all of these should be included in the introduction, and other particulars may be more pertinent. Make your selection carefully.

Where Do You Stand?

Name someone you admire. Which of the categories listed in the last paragraph of the section describing speeches of introduction would you use to build credibility when introducing this person? Why?

Presentation of an Honor or Award Like an introduction, the presentation of an award should be brief. Inform the audience of the importance and perhaps give a brief history of the honor or award, demonstrate why the person is worthy of the award, and call the person to the front to accept the award.

Acceptance of an Honor or Award Because honors or awards are sometimes given without previous notice, you may be surprised to be named as the recipient. Naturally, your expressions of surprise and pleasure are to be expected and respected in your impromptu remarks. In such cases (and in instances when you *are* aware of the honor ahead of time), you should thank the people or organization responsible for giving the award, express appreciation to a very few individuals (be very selective), make a final expression of appreciation and gratitude, and leave the stage or podium with aplomb.

Tributes and "Roasts" A tribute is sometimes given to a person who has achieved greatness or success over a lifetime. Nobel Prizes, Pulitzer Prizes, and Academy Awards—as well as countless awards by corporations honoring long-term employees—are some examples of recognizing lifetime achievement. A tribute may also be for a single heroic act, a stellar performance, or a record-breaking sales month. The person giving the tribute should explain the purpose of the tribute, detail the achievement, and identify the recipient. These particulars can be arranged according to the context or to the speaker's preference.

"Roasts" are occasions at which a person is honored for her or his craft, career, or personal life through humorous and occasionally insulting speeches, skits, and entertainment performed by her or his peers and friends. The Friars Club in New York City has a long history of roasts that some consider to be a wonderful tradition and others view as controversial. In 1993, a popular actor was severely criticized for his appearance in "blackface" as part of a skit with an African American actress whom he was dating. In 1994, Barbara Walters was "roasted," but the humor was gentler and reflected the sincere respect of the participants.

Roasts can be good-natured and enjoyable or vicious and damaging. The tone and content of your contribution to a roast should reflect your sense of ethics and the context of the event.

Promotion of Goodwill Many organizations support or promote positive interaction among members and create positive rhetorical perspectives in public presentations. Not-for-profit service groups sometimes have luncheons or dinners designed to promote goodwill. Some companies promote activities that allow for presentations that encourage positive reactions. The division of education at a major southwestern university, for example, has a picnic on the first Friday afternoon after the beginning of the fall semester. All students, staff, faculty, and administrators are invited. The dean of the division gives a five-minute speech welcoming newcomers; honoring current students, staff, and faculty; and stating positive projections for the school year. Then everyone eats and socializes in the park.

Memorials Presentations that memorialize individuals sometimes occur in response to tragic events. Such presentations should be solemn and respectful and should present a positive perspective for the event. A eulogy is given at funerals or memorial services. The brevity of your presentation will be appreciated by the audience, but your presentation should include the following: identification of positive facts about the person, short anecdotes that reveal the personality of the person, gentle humor that can uplift spirits, and a conclusion that helps to heal the human spirit.

Celebrations When organizations experience success or an individual has a success that reflects on the group, appropriate celebrations encourage, enhance the status of, and support all members of the organization. A presentation at such an event should include the reasons for the celebration, the names of individuals or groups responsible for the success, and rhetoric that moves listeners to efforts that will result in more celebratory events.

TECHNOLOGY TOOLS

Great Speeches On-Line

One can learn a great deal about speech making by reading, watching, and listening to important speeches by well-known speakers. Two of the best resources that facilitate this are *Douglass: Archives of American Public Address* (www.douglassarchives.org) and the National Gallery of the Spoken Word. *Douglass* was created at Northwestern University as an electronic archive of American oratory and related documents. It includes links that include research libraries and government sites where current speeches are available on-line.

The National Gallery of the Spoken Word (www. ngsw. org) is a fully searchable digital library of spoken word collections spanning the twentieth century. The National Science Foundation funded this project under Digital Library Initiative II.

Entertainment Of all the speaking occasions, this one has the greatest potential for disaster for the speaker. We think of entertainment in public speaking as being comedy. Many presentations are comedic, but unfortunately very few public speakers can successfully present a sustained humorous presentation.

If you are called upon to give an entertaining speech—usually after a breakfast, lunch, or dinner meeting—examine the context carefully. Instead of relying on old jokes and anecdotes, use myths and stories about the organization that are interesting or entertaining, relate experiences that make you rather than other people the object of humor, keep your remarks ethical and appropriate for public gatherings (avoid slang, sexual innuendo, inflammatory remarks, and curses), and keep your speech brief.

Retirement If you are introducing or honoring a retiree, review the preceding material on presenting honors and on tributes and roasts. Additional suggestions are to avoid age-deprecating humor, derogatory jokes about retirement, and supposedly humorous slurs on the person's career.

If you are the retiree, review the section on accepting honors. Graciously accept the accolades, gifts, and comments of your supervisors, peers, and employees. This is not an occasion to right old wrongs or to criticize the organization. If your primary reaction to the company or organization has been negative, try to convince the organization not to have a retirement gathering for you.

These special occasions all require the following: brevity; appropriateness of purpose, behavior, appearance, humor, mood, and language use; and effective delivery skills. Each presentation will be affected by the local culture and by taken-for-granted styles. As in all public speaking situations, analyze the audience demographics, the reasons for the audience's presence, the organizational culture, and the environmental dynamics. Your behavior, your appearance, and the content of your presentation will determine your success.

STRATEGIC SCENARIO WRAP-UP

At the beginning of this chapter, we met Salendria Williams, a student in a communication class like yours who is thinking about giving a persuasive speech on why all students need to prepare themselves with skills in the use of information technology as part of their university experience. What have you learned in this chapter that might help Salendria prepare for her presentation?

- Is this a good topic for her speech? Why or why not?
- Which of the four functions for persuasive speeches (reinforce, refute, change, move) seems most appropriate to what Salendria wants to do?
- What basic resources of persuasion will be most salient for this speech? Why?
- Which dimensions of source credibility will be most relevant for Salendria? Do you have any suggestions for credibility-enhancing strategies?
- How important are ego involvement and order effects for Salendria's presentation?
- What additional advice do you have for Salendria?

SUMMARY

- Persuasive presentations, regardless of their setting and audience, usually have one of four functions: to reinforce listeners' beliefs or values, to refute these beliefs or values, to change these beliefs or values, or to move the listeners to action.

- Reinforcement and refutative presentations can be used to rebuild listeners' original beliefs or prove that these beliefs are untrue.
- From the latter use, it follows that change presentations seek to go one step further and to convince listeners to change a particular attitude, value, or belief.
- A call to action intends to get listeners to do something, such as sign a petition or donate money to a charitable cause, that they would not have done had they not heard the presentation.
- Persuasive presentations can take a variety of formats that reflect the speaker's approach and use of supporting materials.
- Sales presentations, proposals, and motivational sessions are three of the most common formats for persuasive presentations.
- To deliver a successful persuasive presentation, a speaker is wise to concentrate on the particular demands made on the audience.
- The effective presentation takes the listeners' perspective, discovering what makes listeners tick and whether they are likely to be favorably disposed toward a particular message.
- Presentational strategies differ, of course, depending on whether the audience is sympathetic or suspicious.
- A persuasive speaker benefits from addressing his or her appeals to the appropriate need level of the audience.
- An audience whose basic needs (for food, water, shelter) are not met is not likely to respond to a message geared toward higher-level needs.
- To work, persuasive messages have to be pitched to needs that are unfulfilled, not ones that are satisfied.
- The successful presentation also takes into account the opinion leaders in the audience and directs its appeals to or references them.
- The importance of opinion leaders also suggests the larger issue of credibility.
- A speaker who is not credible, or who uses sources that are not credible, is not likely to get very far in his or her persuasive efforts.
- Because credibility is in the eye of the beholder—it resides with the audience—the speaker is wise to present himself or herself in such a way as to signal trustworthiness, competence, and dynamism.
- The credibility gained in the process is called intrinsic credibility.
- Extrinsic credibility, however, is communicated through the introduction of the speaker and through other external sources of information about the speaker.
- Apart from the previously mentioned components, persuasion is also a process, and the effective speaker knows how to use each stage in the process to her or his advantage.
- In the first phase, listeners become aware that a message exists.
- In the second phase, they become interested in hearing more.
- In the third phase, they evaluate what they have heard and what they feel about what they have heard.
- In the fourth phase, they set aside a trial period to judge the feasibility of the message.
- In the fifth phase, they adopt the message and put it into practice.
- Not all persuasive presentations work out quite so neatly.
- A speaker may have to deal with highly ego-involved listeners, with the necessity of choosing among several options for ordering arguments (arguments presented early or late get audience attention more than do those presented in the middle), and with deciding whether to give both sides of the argument.
- But if the speaker employs candor, careful phrasing, respect for the audience, and equanimity, he or she is much more likely to achieve the objectives of the persuasive presentation.
- Nine types of special occasion or ceremonial speaking were discussed: introductions, the presentation of an award to an honored guest, the acceptance of an honor or award, tributes and roasts, the promotion of goodwill, memorials, celebrations, entertainment, and a retirement speech for or by a retiree.
- Each requires understanding of the cultural context, the audience, and the setting. And once again, your delivery skills and your content determine your success.

KEY TERMS

Persuasive presentations: presentations that perform one or more of the following functions: (1) *reinforce* the listeners' beliefs, attitudes, or values, (2) *refute,* or disprove, an idea or belief held by listeners, (3) *change* the listeners' beliefs, actions, or values, and (4) *move* the listeners to action

Maslow's hierarchy of needs: theory of motivation based on the argument that lower-level needs must be satisfied before higher-level needs can become motivating factors; includes basic needs, security needs, love and belonging needs, esteem needs, and self-actualization needs

Opinion leaders: people who are capable of influencing your decisions, attitudes, and behaviors

Ethos: the audience's perception of a speaker's character, intelligence, and goodwill

Trustworthiness: a component of credibility that refers to the way that a source is perceived as being honest, friendly, warm, agreeable, or safe, instead of dangerous or threatening

Competence: a component of credibility that is based on the source's expertise, training, experience, skill, ability, authoritativeness, and intelligence

Dynamism: a component of credibility that refers to a speaker's energy, liveliness, boldness, activity, forcefulness, and frankness

Process of persuasion: process characterized by five distinct stages: awareness, interest, evaluation, trial, and adoption

Ego involvement: how important a particular topic or issue is to a listener

Climax order: the weakest argument is presented first, and the strongest argument is presented last

Anticlimax order: the strongest argument is presented first, and the weaker arguments follow

Pyramidal order: the speaker places the strongest argument between two weaker ones

DISCUSSION

1. Why are many persuasive presentations made informally? What are the basic goals of a persuasive presentation?
2. What are the functions of persuasive presentations? Can you think of situations in which a presentation might perform several of these functions simultaneously?
3. Describe the typical formats for persuasive presentations. What are the strengths of each?
4. What is a listener's perspective? Why is it crucial to take a listener's perspective when making a persuasive presentation?
5. According to Maslow, what are the five levels of human need? How do they influence the preparation and delivery of a persuasive presentation?
6. How can opinion leaders be used to boost a persuasive presentation?
7. What are the components of source credibility? How does extrinsic credibility differ from intrinsic credibility?
8. Describe the process of persuasion. What strategies can you employ to prevent listeners from dropping out during the persuasion process?
9. What are the different types of special occasion speaking? Discuss preparation and delivery techniques for each.

ACTIVITIES

1. How do you use persuasion in informal presentations? Describe an informal occasion in which you persuaded (or did not persuade) others to choose an option or idea you favored.
2. Select a topic and construct main points for each of the presentation types discussed in this chapter: reinforcing the listeners' beliefs, attitudes, or values; changing the listeners' beliefs, attitudes, or values; and moving the listeners to action.
3. Apply the process of persuasion to outlining a presentation on the following topics: (a) persuading the company cafeteria to stop using Styrofoam plates and cups, (b) persuading a client to sample a higher-quality brand of office paper than he plans to buy, (c) persuading a personnel manager to hire several college interns for your department this summer.
4. Analyze a speaker you have heard recently according to the three components of credibility: trustworthiness, competence, and dynamism. Did all three aspects play an equal role in affecting your perception of the speaker's credibility?
5. Pretend that your college or university has just picked you to introduce the student representative to the board of regents for your university at the annual honors convocation. Present an introduction for this person. You will introduce him or her, and then the speaker will give the keynote address on "Responsibilities of Undergraduate Students as Political Partners with Their Universities."
6. Pick one of the special occasion presentation types. Develop it into a three- to five-minute presentation. After your speech, discuss with the class your difficulties and successes.

7. This chapter makes the case that source credibility is a major factor in audience acceptance of a persuasive message. We suggest that you attempt to enhance your credibility and that of your evidence whenever possible. Sources held in esteem by audiences are more likely to produce a positive, persuasive effect than are sources not viewed as credible.

   This exercise requires you to apply the principles of source credibility to an actual speech given to a business, professional, nonprofit, or service organization. You may attend the speech in person or view it on television or videotape. Simply reading the text of a speech will not provide the details that you need to complete this exercise.

   Take detailed notes during the presentation, and try to obtain other information by talking with audience members or participants after the event has concluded. If possible, interview the speaker, and, if appropriate, review any news coverage or press releases about the speech. Consider each of the following factors in your investigation:

   A. Who was the speaker? Where and when was the speech given?

   B. What do you believe the speaker's purpose was? What kind of audience was there? Could you discern the attitude of the audience toward the speaker, the purpose, or the event? Did any of the facility's physical features affect the speech?

   C. What was the speaker's reputation? Did the audience know the speaker? If another person introduced the speaker, what effect did the introduction play in establishing the speaker's credibility? Did the speaker's approach to the podium, physical appearance, or nonverbal behavior affect perceptions of credibility?

   D. How did the content and style of the speech's introduction affect credibility?

   E. Did the speaker seem well informed and competent? How did you assess these qualities? Did the speaker use credible sources? What were they? Did the speaker appear interested in the audience and the event? How did you evaluate the speaker's dynamism? Were there any direct and obvious qualities of delivery, style, or content that affected perceptions of credibility?

   F. What role did the speech's conclusion play in enhancing the credibility apparent in the speech up to that point?

   G. What was the overall effect of the speech? How well did the speaker achieve her or his purposes and move the audience to action? Assess the role that source credibility played in light of these results and effects.

Index